Mouse in a test of context fear conditioning.

Experimental chambers used in fear conditioning.

The chimpanzee Sherman working on an intradimensional discrimination task.

The chimpanzee Lana using a lexigram keyboard.

A pigeon in a test of comparative cognition.

A male quail showing a conditioned sexual fetish response.

FIGURE (ii)

Courtesy of Michael Fanselow

Courtesy of Michael Fanselow

Courtesy of Michael Beran

Courtesy of Michael Beran

Courtesy of Aaron Blaisdell

Courtesy of Michael Domjan

The Principles of Learning and Behavior

SEVENTH EDITION

MICHAEL DOMJAN
University of Texas at Austin

with neuroscience contributions by
James W. Grau
Texas A & M University

CENGAGE
Learning·

Australia · Brazil · Mexico · Singapore · United Kingdom · United States

CENGAGE
Learning

The Principles of Learning and Behavior, **Seventh Edition**
Michael Domjan

Product Director: Jon-David Hague

Content Developer: Wendy Langerud

Outsource Development Coordinator: Joshua Taylor

Product Assistant: Nicole Richards

Associate Media Developer: Jasmin Tokatlian

Marketing Director: Jennifer Levanduski

Art and Cover Direction, Production Management, and Composition: PreMediaGlobal

Manufacturing Planner: Karen Hunt

Rights Acquisitions Specialist: Don Schlotman

Cover Image: Peter Cade

For product information and technology assistance, contact us at
Cengage Learning Customer & Sales Support, 1-800-354-9706.

For permission to use material from this text or product, submit all requests online at **www.cengage.com/permissions**. Further permissions questions can be e-mailed to **permissionrequest@cengage.com**.

Library of Congress Control Number: 2013943623

ISBN-13: 978-1-285-08856-3

ISBN-10: 1-285-08856-5

Cengage Learning
200 First Stamford Place, 4th Floor
Stamford, CT 06902
USA

Cengage Learning is a leading provider of customized learning solutions with office locations around the globe, including Singapore, the United Kingdom, Australia, Mexico, Brazil, and Japan. Locate your local office at **www.cengage.com/global.**

Cengage Learning products are represented in Canada by Nelson Education, Ltd.

To learn more about Cengage Learning Solutions, visit **www.cengage.com.**

Purchase any of our products at your local college store or at our preferred online store **www.cengagebrain.com.**

Printed in the United States of America
3 4 5 6 7 17 16 15

Dedication

to Deborah

Brief Contents

Contents

Boxes on the Neuroscience of Learning

Preface

Originally, I had three basic goals in writing this book. First, I wanted to share with students the new ideas and findings that made me excited about conditioning and learning. Second, I wanted to emphasize that learning procedures do not operate in a vacuum but are built on behavior systems shaped by evolution. This belief provided the rationale for including *behavior* in the title of the book. Third, I wanted to provide an eclectic and balanced account of the field that was respectful of both the Pavlovian associationist tradition and the Skinnerian behavior-analytic tradition. I have remained faithful to these goals and sought to satisfy them in the seventh edition while being responsive to the ever-changing landscape of research on learning mechanisms.

Although the field of conditioning and learning dates back more than a century (during which some of our technical vocabulary has not changed much), the field continues to be enriched by numerous new phenomena and new interpretations. Recent national priorities for the pursuit of translational research have encouraged a great deal of new research on mechanisms of learning related to drug addiction, fear conditioning, and extinction. One of the interesting new developments is a greater respect for individual differences, which is now informing our understanding of some of the fundamental phenomena of Pavlovian conditioning, as well as punishment and choice behavior, among other topics. Incorporating new developments in the book required judgments about what was important enough to add and what material could be omitted to make room for the new information. Adding things is easy. Removing information that was previously deemed important is more painful but necessary to keep the book to a reasonable length.

A continuing challenge for the book has been how to represent the major advances that are being made in studies of the neuroscience of learning and memory. Unfortunately, a single course cannot do justice to both the basic behavioral mechanisms of learning and the neural mechanisms of these behavioral phenomena. I remain committed to the proposition that one cannot study the neural mechanisms of a behavioral phenomenon without first understanding that phenomenon at the behavioral level of analysis. Therefore, the book continues to be primarily concerned with behavioral phenomena. However, the seventh edition includes more information about the neuroscience of learning and memory than any previous edition.

As in the sixth edition, most of the neuroscience information is presented in boxes that can be omitted by instructors and students who do not wish to cover this material. I am grateful to James W. Grau, Professor of Psychology and Neuroscience at Texas A&M University, for writing the "neuroboxes." The seventh edition includes a neurobox in each chapter of the book. Furthermore, for the first time, Professor Grau organized these neuroboxes so that they tell a coherent and progressively unfolding story across the 12 chapters. For a bird's-eye view, a list of the neuroboxes is presented in a separate section of the table of contents.

In addition to advances in the neurosciences, new research on many aspects of basic learning phenomena dictated numerous changes from the sixth to the seventh edition. The changes are too numerous to list. Among other things, they include new findings related to habit formation and automatic processing, epigenetic influences on behavior, pathological fear and post-traumatic stress disorder, individual differences in sign tracking and goal tracking, the relation of the Rescorla–Wagner model to error-correction mechanisms in robotics, new work on voucher-based programs for the treatment of substance abuse, new research on self-control, S–O and R–O associations in drug addiction, expanded and updated discussion of response allocation and behavioral economics, new research on stimulus equivalence, new work on ways to enhance extinction, new theory and research on avoidance, and extensive new sections on memory mechanisms and various special topics in comparative cognition (Chapters 11 and 12).

One of the major developments in the field during the past decade is that the basic behavioral principles that are described in this book are being utilized by an increasingly broad range of scientists. I first noticed this trend when I was preparing the sixth edition. The trend has continued since then, with the consequence that the new references that have been added in the seventh edition were culled from about 85 different journals. New information on basic learning processes continues to be published in traditional psychology journals (such as the *Journal of the Experimental Analysis of Behavior* and the *Journal of Experimental Psychology: Animal Behavior Processes*). However, important new findings are also being published in journals dealing with behavior therapy, brain research and neuroscience, biological psychiatry, child development, drug and alcohol dependence, language and cognition, family violence, neuropsychology, pharmacology and therapeutics, and psychosomatic medicine.

The broadening range of disciplines that are finding basic behavioral principles to be relevant has also been evident in the range of students who have been signing up for my learning classes. During the past two years, my graduate course on learning has attracted students from integrative biology, communications, information science, marketing, music, special education, and neuroscience, in addition to psychology.

Identifying relevant sources that appear in a diverse range of journals is made possible by the search engines of the new information age. Early editions of the book provided extensive citations of research on various topics in conditioning and learning. Considering how easy it is to find sources using ever-improving search engines, the citations in the seventh edition are not as extensive and are intended to introduce students to new lines of research rather than provide a complete list of the relevant research. I apologize to investigators whose names may have been omitted because of this altered citation strategy.

I would like to thank the support of numerous instructors and students around the world who continue to look to this book for authoritative coverage of basic learning mechanisms. Without their support, successive editions (and translations) of the book would not be possible. Successive editions of the book also would not have been possible without the support of the good folks at Cengage Learning, especially Jon-David Hague, the product director of psychology. I am also grateful to Wendy Langerud (in Iowa) and Gunjan Chandola (in India) for all of their help in shepherding the seventh edition through the complexities of the production process. Finally, I would like to thank Professor Kevin Holloway of Vassar College for agreeing to prepare the Instructor's Manual and Test Bank for the book.

Michael Domjan
Austin, Texas

About the Authors

MICHAEL DOMJAN is a professor of Psychology at the University of Texas at Austin, where he has taught learning to undergraduate and graduate students since 1973. He also served as department chair from 1999 to 2005 and was the founding director of the Imaging Research Center from 2005 to 2008. Professor Domjan is noted for his functional approach to classical conditioning, which he has pursued in studies of sexual conditioning and taste aversion learning. His research was selected for a MERIT Award by the National Institutes of Mental Health as well as a Golden Fleece Award by U.S. Senator William Proxmire. He served as editor of the *Journal of Experimental Psychology: Animal Behavior Processes* for six years and continues to serve on editorial boards of various journals in the United States and other countries. He is a past president of the Pavlovian Society and also served as president of the Division of Behavioral Neuroscience and Comparative Psychology of the American Psychological Association. His former Ph.D. students hold faculty positions at various colleges and universities in the United States, Colombia, and Turkey. Domjan also enjoys playing the viola and teaches a course on Music and Psychology in which he talks about the role of habituation, sensitization, and Pavlovian and instrumental conditioning in musical experience and musical performance.

Neuroscience Contributor

JAMES GRAU is a professor at Texas A&M University, with appointments in Psychology and the Texas A&M Institute for Neuroscience (TAMIN). He received his Ph.D. under the direction of Dr. R. A. Rescorla and moved to Texas A&M University in 1987, where he is now the Mary Tucker Currier Professor of Liberal Arts. He is a fellow of both the Association for Psychological Science and the American Psychological Association (Divisions 3, 6, and 28), where he served as president of Division 6 (Behavioral Neuroscience and Comparative Psychology). His research has examined how learning and memory influence pain processing, the neurobiological mechanisms involved, and how physiological observations inform our understanding of learning. His current research focuses on neural plasticity within the spinal cord, with the aim of detailing its functional properties, how and when spinal neurons learn, and the implications of this work for recovery after a spinal cord injury. His work has been funded by the National Institutes of Mental Health (NIMH), Neurological Disorders and Stroke (NINDS), and Child Health and Development (NICHD). Since 1983, he has taught nearly 50 courses and seminars on learning.

CHAPTER **1**

Background and Rationale for the Study of Learning and Behavior

CHAPTER PREVIEW

The goal of Chapter 1 is to introduce the reader to contemporary studies of learning and behavior theory.
I begin by characterizing behavioral studies of learning and describing how these are related to cognition
and the conscious control of behavior. I then describe the historical antecedents of key concepts in modern
learning theory. This is followed by a discussion of the origins of contemporary experimental research in
studies of the evolution of intelligence, functional neurology, animal models of human behavior, and the
implications of contemporary research for the development of memory-enhancing drugs and the construction
of artificial intelligent systems or robots. I then provide a detailed definition of learning and discuss how
learning can be examined at different levels of analysis. Methodological features of studies of learning are
described in the next section. Because numerous experiments on learning have been performed with

nonhuman animals, I conclude the chapter by discussing the rationale for the use of nonhuman animals in research, with some comments on the public debate about animal research.

People have always been interested in understanding behavior, be it their own or the behavior of others. This interest is more than idle curiosity. Our quality of life depends on our actions and the actions of others. Any systematic effort to understand behavior must include consideration of what we learn and how we learn it. Numerous aspects of the behavior of both human and nonhuman animals are the results of learning. We learn to read, to write, and to count. We learn to walk downstairs without falling, to open doors, to ride a bicycle, and to swim. We also learn when to relax and when to become anxious. We learn what foods we are likely to enjoy and what foods will make us sick. We also learn the numerous subtle gestures that are involved in effective social interactions. Life is filled with activities and experiences that are shaped by what we have learned.

Learning is one of the biological processes that facilitates our survival and promotes our well-being. When we think of survival, we typically think of the importance of biological functions such as respiration, digestion, and resisting disease. Physiological systems have evolved to accomplish these tasks. However, for many species finely tuned physiological processes do not take care of all of the adaptive functions that are required for successful existence. Learning plays a critical role in improving how organisms adapt to their environment. Sometimes this takes the form of learning new responses. In other cases, learning serves to improve how physiological systems operate to accomplish important biological functions such as digestion and reproduction (Domjan, 2005).

Animals, including people, have to learn to find new food sources as old ones become unavailable or when they move to a new area. They also have to find new shelter when storms destroy their old homes, as happens in a hurricane or tornado. Accomplishing these tasks obviously requires motor responses, such as walking and manipulating objects. These tasks also require the ability to predict important events in the environment, such as when and where food will be available. All these things involve learning. Animals learn to go to a new water hole when their old one dries up and learn to anticipate new sources of danger. These learned adjustments to the environment are as important as physiological processes such as respiration and digestion.

It is common to think about learning as involving the acquisition of new behavior. Indeed, we learn new responses when we learn to read, ride a bicycle, or play a musical instrument. However, learning can also consist of the decrease or loss of a previously performed response. A child, for example, may learn to not cross the street when the traffic light is red, to not grab food from someone else's plate, and to not yell and shout when someone is trying to take a nap. Learning to withhold or *inhibit* responses is just as important as learning to *make* responses, if not more so.

When considering learning, we are likely to think about forms of learning that require special training—the learning that takes place in schools and colleges, for example. Solving calculus problems or making a triple somersault when diving requires special instruction and lots of practice. However, we also learn all kinds of things without an expert teacher or coach during the course of routine interactions with our social and physical environment. Children learn how to open doors and windows, what to do when the phone rings, when to avoid a hot stove, and when to duck so as not to get hit by a flying ball. College students learn how to find their way around campus, how to avoid heartburn from cafeteria food, and how to predict when a roommate will stay out late at night, all without special instruction.

In the coming chapters, I will describe research on the basic principles of learning and behavior. We will focus on basic types of learning and behavior that are fundamental to life but, like breathing, are often ignored. These pervasive and basic forms of learning are a normal (and often essential) part of daily life, even though they rarely command our attention. I will describe the learning of simple relationships between events in the environment, the learning of simple motor movements, and the learning of emotional reactions to stimuli. These forms of learning are investigated in experiments that involve conditioning or "training" procedures of various sorts. However, these forms of learning occur in the lives of human and nonhuman animals without explicit or organized instruction or schooling.

Much of the research that I will describe is in the behaviorist tradition of psychology that emphasizes analyzing behavior in terms of its antecedent stimuli and consequences. Conscious reflection and conscious reasoning are deliberately left out of this analysis. I will describe automatic procedural learning that does not require awareness (e.g., Lieberman, Sunnucks, & Kirk, 1998; Smith et al., 2005) rather than declarative learning that is more accessible to conscious report.

It is natural for someone to be interested in aspects of his or her behavior that are accessible to conscious reflection. However, both psychologists and neuroscientists have become increasingly convinced that most of what we do occurs without conscious awareness. The capacity of conscious thought is very limited. That is why people have difficulty driving and talking on the phone at the same time. However, people can walk and talk at the same time because walking is a much more automatic activity that does not require conscious control. Because of the limited capacity of conscious thought, we do and learn many things without awareness. In a recent discussion of neuroscience, Eagleman (2011) noted that "there is a looming chasm between what your brain knows and what your mind is capable of accessing" (p. 55). Based on his research on the experience of conscious intent, Wegner (2002) came to a similar conclusion, which is captured in the title of his book *The Illusion of Conscious Will*. The studies of automatic procedural learning that we will discuss serve to inform us about important aspects of our behavior that we rarely think about otherwise.

The following chapters will describe how features of the environment gain the capacity to trigger our behavior whether we like it or not. This line of research has its origins in what has been called behavioral psychology. During the last quarter of the twentieth century, behavioral psychology was overshadowed by "the cognitive revolution." However, the cognitive revolution did not eliminate the taste aversions that children learn when they get chemotherapy, it did not reduce the cravings that drug addicts experience when they see their friends getting high, and it did not stop the proverbial Pavlovian dog from salivating when it encountered a signal for food. Cognitive science did not grow by taking over the basic learning phenomena that are the focus of this book. Rather, it grew by extending psychology into new areas of research such as attention, problem solving, and knowledge representation. As important as these new topics of cognitive psychology have become, they have not solved the problems of how good or bad habits are learned or how debilitating fears or emotions may be effectively modified. Those topics remain at the core of studies of learning and behavior.

Basic behavioral processes remain important in the lives of organisms even as we learn more about other aspects of psychology. In fact, there is a major resurgence of interest in basic behavioral mechanisms. This is fueled by the growing appreciation of the limited role of consciousness in behavior and the recognition that much of what takes us through our daily lives involves habitual responses that we spend little time thinking about (Gasbarri & Tomaz, 2013; Wood & Neal, 2007). We don't think about how we brush our teeth, dry ourselves after a shower, put on our clothes, or chew our food. All of these are learned responses. Behavioral models of conditioning and learning are also fundamental to the understanding of recalcitrant clinical problems such as pathological fears and phobias and drug addiction. As Wiers and Stacy (2006) pointed out, "The problem, often, is not that substance abusers do not understand that the disadvantages of continued use outweigh the advantages; rather, they have difficulty resisting their automatically triggered impulses to use their substance of abuse" (p. 292). This book deals with how such behavioral impulses are learned.

Historical Antecedents

Theoretical approaches to the study of learning have their roots in the philosophy of René Descartes (Figure 1.1). Before Descartes, the prevailing view was that human behavior is entirely determined by conscious intent and free will. People's actions were not considered to be automatic or determined by mechanistic natural laws. What someone did was presumed to be the result of his or her will or deliberate intent. Descartes took exception to this view because he recognized that people do many things automatically in response to external stimuli. However, he was not prepared to abandon entirely the idea of free will and conscious control. He therefore formulated a dualistic view of human behavior known as Cartesian **dualism**.

According to Cartesian dualism, there are two classes of human behavior: involuntary and voluntary. Involuntary behavior consists of automatic reactions to external stimuli and is mediated by a special mechanism called a **reflex**. Voluntary behavior, by contrast, does not have to be triggered by external stimuli and occurs because of the person's conscious intent to act in that particular manner.

The details of Descartes's dualistic view of human behavior are diagrammed in Figure 1.2. Let us first consider the mechanisms of involuntary, or reflexive, behavior. Stimuli in the environment are detected by the person's sense organs. The sensory information is then relayed to the brain through nerves. From the brain, the impetus for action is sent through nerves to the muscles that create the involuntary response.

FIGURE 1.1 René Descartes (1596–1650)

Library of Congress Prints and Photographs Division [LC-USZ62-61365]

FIGURE 1.2 Diagram of Cartesian dualism. Events in the physical world are detected by sense organs. From here the information is transmitted to the brain. The brain is connected to the mind by way of the pineal gland. Involuntary action is produced by a reflex arc that involves messages sent from the sense organs to the brain and then from the brain to the muscles. Voluntary action is initiated by the mind, with messages sent to the brain and then the muscles.

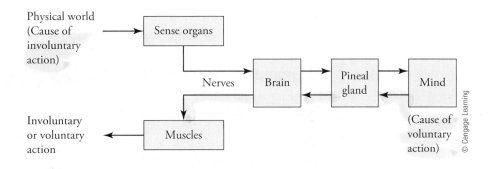

Thus, sensory input is *reflected* in the response output. Hence, Descartes called involuntary behavior *reflexive*.

Several aspects of this system are noteworthy. Stimuli in the external environment are assumed to be the cause of all involuntary behavior. These stimuli produce involuntary responses by way of a neural circuit that includes the brain. However, Descartes assumed that only one set of nerves was involved. According to Descartes, the same nerves transmitted information from the sense organs to the brain and from the brain down to the muscles. This circuit, he believed, permitted rapid reactions to external stimuli—for example, quick withdrawal of one's finger from a hot stove.

Descartes assumed that the involuntary mechanism of behavior was the only one available to animals other than humans. According to this view, all of nonhuman animal behavior occurs as reflexive behavior to external stimuli. Thus, Descartes believed that nonhuman animals lacked free will and were incapable of voluntary, conscious action. He considered free will and voluntary behavior to be uniquely human attributes. These unique human features existed because only human beings were thought to have a mind or a soul.

The mind was assumed to be a nonphysical entity. Descartes believed that the mind was connected to the physical body by way of the pineal gland, at the base of the brain. Because of this connection, the mind was aware of and could keep track of involuntary behavior. Through this mechanism, the mind could also initiate voluntary actions. Because voluntary behavior was initiated in the mind, its occurrence was not automatic and could occur independently of external stimulation.

The mind–body dualism introduced by Descartes stimulated two intellectual traditions, *mentalism* and *reflexology*. Mentalism was concerned with the contents and workings of the mind. In contrast, reflexology was concerned with the mechanisms of reflexive behavior. These two intellectual traditions form the foundations of the modern study of learning.

Historical Developments in the Study of the Mind

Philosophers concerned with the mind pondered questions about the contents of the mind and how the mind works. These considerations formed the historical foundations of present-day cognitive psychology. Because Descartes thought the mind was connected to the brain by way of the pineal gland, he believed that some of the contents of the mind came from sense experiences. However, he also believed that the mind contained ideas that were innate and existed in all human beings independent of personal experience. For example, he believed that all humans were born with the concept of God, the concept of self, and certain fundamental axioms of geometry (such as the fact that the shortest distance between two points is a straight line). The philosophical approach that assumes we are born with innate ideas about certain things is called **nativism**.

Some philosophers after Descartes took issue with the nativist position. In particular, the British philosopher John Locke (1632–1704) proposed that all of the ideas people had were acquired directly or indirectly through experiences after birth. He believed that human beings were born without any preconceptions about the world. According to Locke, the mind started out as a clean slate (*tabula rasa*, in Latin), to be gradually filled with ideas and information as the person encountered various sense experiences. This philosophical approach to the contents of the mind is called **empiricism**. Empiricism was accepted by a group of British philosophers who lived from the seventeenth to the nineteenth century and who came to be known as the *British empiricists*.

The nativist and empiricist philosophers disagreed not only about the contents of the mind at birth but also about how the mind worked. Descartes believed that the mind did not function in a predictable and orderly manner, according to strict rules or laws that one could identify. One of the first to propose an alternative to this position was the British philosopher Thomas Hobbes (1588–1679). Hobbes accepted the distinction between voluntary and involuntary behavior stated by Descartes and also accepted the notion that voluntary behavior was controlled by the mind. However, unlike Descartes, he believed that the mind operated just as predictably and lawfully as a reflex. More specifically, he proposed that voluntary behavior was governed by the principle of **hedonism**. According to this principle, people do things in the pursuit of pleasure and the avoidance of pain. Hobbes was not concerned with whether the pursuit of pleasure and the avoidance of pain are desirable or justified. For Hobbes, hedonism was simply a fact of life. As we will see, the notion that behavior is controlled by positive and negative consequences has remained with us in one form or another to the present day.

According to the British empiricists, another important aspect of how the mind works involved the concept of **association**. Recall that the empiricists assumed that all ideas originated from sense experiences. If that is true, how do our experiences of various colors, shapes, odors, and sounds allow us to arrive at more complex ideas? Consider, for example, the concept of a car. If someone says the word *car*, you have an idea of what the thing looks like, what it is used for, and how you might feel if you sat in it. Where do all these ideas come from given just the sound of the letters *c*, *a*, and *r*? The British empiricists proposed that simple sensations were combined into more complex ideas by associations. Because you have heard the word *car* when you saw a car, considered using one to get to work, or sat in one, connections or associations became established between the word *car* and these other attributes of cars. Once the associations became established, the word *car* would activate memories of the other aspects of cars that you have experienced. The British empiricists considered such associations to be the building blocks of mental activity. Therefore, they devoted considerable effort to discovering rules of associations.

Rules of Associations   The British empiricists accepted two sets of rules for the establishment of associations, one primary and the other secondary. The primary rules were originally set forth by the ancient Greek philosopher Aristotle. He proposed three principles for the establishment of associations: (1) contiguity, (2) similarity, and (3) contrast. Of these, the contiguity principle has been the most prominent in studies of associations and continues to play an important role in contemporary work. It states that if two events repeatedly occur together in space or time, they will become linked or associated. For example, if you encounter the smell of tomato sauce with spaghetti often enough, your memory of spaghetti will be activated by just the smell of tomato sauce. The similarity and contrast principles state that two things will become associated if they are similar in some respect (e.g., both are red) or have some contrasting characteristics (e.g., one might be strikingly tall and the other strikingly short). Similarity as a basis for the formation of associations has been confirmed by modern studies of learning (e.g., Cusato & Domjan, 2012; Rescorla & Furrow, 1977). However, there is no contemporary evidence that contrast (making one stimulus strikingly different from another) facilitates the formation of an association between them.

Secondary laws of associations were formulated by various empiricist philosophers. Prominent among these was Thomas Brown (1778–1820), who proposed that the association between two stimuli depended on the intensity of those stimuli and how frequently or recently the stimuli occurred together. In addition, the formation of an association between two events was considered to depend on the number of other associations in which each event was already involved and the similarity of these past associations to the current one being formed.

The British empiricists discussed rules of association as a part of their philosophical discourse. They did not perform experiments to determine whether or not the proposed rules were valid. Nor did they attempt to determine the circumstances in which one rule was more important than another. Empirical investigation of the mechanisms of associations did not begin until the pioneering work of the nineteenth-century German psychologist Hermann Ebbinghaus (1850–1909).

To study how associations are formed, Ebbinghaus invented **nonsense syllables**. Nonsense syllables were three-letter combinations (e.g., "bap") devoid of any meaning that might influence how someone might react to them. Ebbinghaus used himself as the experimental subject. He studied lists of nonsense syllables and measured his ability to remember them under various experimental conditions. This general method enabled him to answer such questions as how the strength of an association improved with increased training, whether nonsense syllables that were close together in a list were associated more strongly with one another than syllables that were farther apart, and whether a syllable became more strongly associated with the next one on the list (a forward association) rather than with the preceding one (a backward association). Many of the issues that were addressed by the British empiricists and Ebbinghaus have their counterparts in modern studies of learning and memory.

Historical Developments in the Study of Reflexes

Descartes made a very significant contribution to the understanding of behavior when he formulated the concept of the reflex. The basic idea that behavior can reflect a triggering stimulus remains an important building block of behavior theory. However, Descartes was mistaken in his beliefs about the details of reflex action. He believed that sensory messages going from sense organs to the brain and motor messages going from the brain to the muscles traveled along the same nerves. He thought that nerves were hollow tubes, and neural transmission involved the movement of gases called *animal spirits*. The animal spirits, released by the pineal gland, were assumed to flow through the neural tubes and enter the muscles, causing them to swell and create movement. Finally, Descartes considered all reflexive movements to be innate and to be fixed by the anatomy of the nervous system. Over the course of several hundred years since Descartes passed away, all of these ideas about reflexes have been proven wrong.

Charles Bell (1774–1842) in England and Francois Magendie (1783–1855) in France showed that separate nerves are involved in the transmission of sensory information from sense organs to the central nervous system and motor information from the central nervous system to muscles. If a sensory nerve is cut, the animal remains capable of muscle movements; if a motor nerve is cut, the animal remains capable of registering sensory information.

The idea that animal spirits are involved in neural transmission was also disproved. In 1669 John Swammerdam (1637–1680) showed that mechanical irritation of a nerve was sufficient to produce a muscle contraction. Thus, infusion of animal spirits from the pineal gland was not necessary. In other studies, Francis Glisson (1597–1677) tested whether muscle contractions were produced by the infusion of a gas into the muscle, as Descartes had postulated. Glisson showed that the volume of a muscle does not increase when it is contracted, demonstrating that a gas does not enter the muscle to produce motor movement.

Descartes and most philosophers after him assumed that reflexes were responsible only for simple reactions to stimuli. The energy in a stimulus was thought to be translated directly into the energy of the elicited response by the neural connections from sensory input to response output. The more intense the stimulus was, the more vigorous the resulting response would be. This simple view of reflexes is consistent with many casual observations. If you touch a stove, for example, the hotter the stove, the more quickly you withdraw your finger. However, some reflexes are much more complicated.

The physiological processes responsible for reflex behavior became better understood in the nineteenth century, and those experiments encouraged broader conceptions of reflex action. Two Russian physiologists, I. M. Sechenov (1829–1905) and Ivan Pavlov (1849–1936), were primarily responsible for these developments. Sechenov (Figure 1.3) proposed that stimuli did not elicit reflex responses directly in all cases. Rather, in some cases, a stimulus could release a response from inhibition. In instances where a stimulus released a response from inhibition, the vigor of the response would not depend on the intensity of the initiating stimulus. This simple idea opened up all sorts of new ways the concept of a reflex could be used to explain complex behavior.

If the vigor of an elicited response does not depend on the intensity of its triggering stimulus, a very faint stimulus could produce a large response. A small piece of dust in the nose, for example, can cause a vigorous sneeze. Sechenov took advantage of this type

FIGURE 1.3
I. M. Sechenov
(1829–1905)

RIA Novosti/Alamy

of mechanism to provide a reflex model of voluntary behavior. He suggested that actions or thoughts that occurred in the absence of an obvious eliciting stimulus were in fact reflexive responses. However, in these cases, the eliciting stimuli are too faint for us to notice. Thus, according to Sechenov, voluntary behavior and thoughts are actually elicited by inconspicuous, faint stimuli.

Sechenov's ideas about voluntary behavior greatly extended the use of reflex mechanisms to explain a variety of aspects of behavior. However, his ideas were philosophical extrapolations from the actual research results he obtained. In addition, Sechenov did not address the question of how reflex mechanisms can account for the fact that the behavior of organisms is not fixed and invariant throughout an organism's lifetime but can be altered by experience. From the time of Descartes, reflex responses were considered to be innate and fixed by the connections of the nervous system. Reflexes were assumed to depend on a prewired neural circuit connecting the sense organs to the relevant muscles. According to this view, a given stimulus could be expected to elicit the same response throughout an organism's life. Although this is true in some cases, there are also many examples in which responses to stimuli change as a result of experience. Explanation of such reflexive activity had to await the work of Ivan Pavlov.

Pavlov showed experimentally that not all reflexes are innate. New reflexes to stimuli can be established through mechanisms of association. Thus, Pavlov's role in the history of the study of reflexes is comparable to the role of Ebbinghaus in the study of the mind. Both were concerned with establishing laws of associations through empirical research. However, Pavlov did this in the physiological tradition of reflexology rather than in the mentalistic tradition.

Much of modern behavior theory has been built on the reflex concept of stimulus-response or S-R unit and the concept of associations. S-R units and associations continue to play prominent roles in contemporary behavior theory. However, these basic concepts have been elaborated and challenged over the years. As I will describe in later chapters, in addition to S-R units, modern studies of learning have also demonstrated the existence of stimulus-stimulus (S-S) connections and modulatory or hierarchical associative structures (for Bayesian approaches, see Fiser, 2009; Kruschke, 2008). Quantitative descriptions of learned behavior that do not employ associations have gained favor in some quarters (e.g., Gallistel & Matzel, 2013; Leslie, 2001) and have also been emphasized by contemporary scientists working in the Skinnerian tradition of behavioral analysis (e.g., Staddon, 2001; Lattal, 2013). However, associative analyses continue to dominate behavior theory and provide the conceptual foundation for much of the research on the neural mechanisms of learning.

The Dawn of the Modern Era

Experimental studies of basic principles of learning are often conducted with nonhuman animals and in the tradition of reflexology. Research in animal learning came to be pursued with great vigor starting a little more than a hundred years ago. Impetus for the research came from three primary sources (see Domjan, 1987). The first of these was interest in comparative cognition and the evolution of the mind. The second was interest in how the nervous system works (functional neurology), and the third was interest in developing animal models to study certain aspects of human behavior. As we will see in the ensuing chapters, comparative cognition, functional neurology, and animal models of human behavior continue to dominate contemporary research in learning.

Comparative Cognition and the Evolution of Intelligence

Interest in comparative cognition and the evolution of the mind was sparked by the writings of Charles Darwin (Figure 1.4). Darwin took Descartes's ideas about human nature one step further. Descartes started chipping away at the age-old notion that human

FIGURE 1.4 Charles
Darwin (1809–1882)

Philip Gendreau/Bettmann/CORBIS

beings have a unique and privileged position in the animal kingdom by proposing that
at least some aspects of human behavior (their reflexes) were animal-like. However,
Descartes preserved some privilege for human beings by assuming that humans (and
only humans) have a mind. Darwin attacked this last vestige of privilege.

In his second major work, *The Descent of Man and Selection in Relation to Sex*,
Darwin argued that "man is descended from some lower form, notwithstanding that
connecting links have not hitherto been discovered" (Darwin, 1897, p. 146). In claiming
continuity from nonhuman to human animals, Darwin sought to characterize not only
the evolution of physical traits but also the evolution of psychological or mental abilities.
He argued that the human mind is a product of evolution. In making this claim, Darwin
did not deny that human beings had mental abilities such as the capacity for wonder,
curiosity, imitation, attention, memory, reasoning, and aesthetic sensibility. Rather, he
suggested that nonhuman animals also had these abilities. For example, he maintained
that nonhuman animals were capable even of belief in spiritual agencies (Darwin,
1897, p. 95).

Darwin collected anecdotal evidence of various forms of intelligent behavior in animals in an effort to support his claims. Although the evidence was not compelling by
modern standards, the research question was. Ever since, investigators have been captivated by the possibility of tracing the evolution of cognition and behavior by studying
the abilities of various species of animals (Burghardt, 2009).

Before one can investigate the evolution of intelligence in a systematic fashion, one
must have a criterion for identifying intelligent behavior in animals. A highly influential
criterion was offered by George Romanes in his book *Animal Intelligence* (Romanes,
1882). Romanes proposed that intelligence be identified by whether an animal learns

"to make new adjustments, or to modify old ones, in accordance with the results of its own individual experience" (p. 4). Thus, Romanes defined intelligence in terms of the ability to learn. This definition was widely accepted by early comparative psychologists and served to make the study of animal learning the key to obtaining information about the evolution of intelligence.

As the upcoming chapters will show, much research on mechanisms of animal learning has not been concerned with trying to obtain evidence of the evolution of intelligence. Nevertheless, the cognitive abilities of nonhuman animals continue to fascinate both the lay public and the scientific community. In contemporary science, these issues are covered under the topic of "comparative cognition" or "comparative psychology" (e.g., Papini, 2008; Shettleworth, 2010). Studies of comparative cognition examine topics such as perception, attention, spatial representation, memory, problem solving, categorization, tool use, and counting in nonhuman animals (Zentall & Wasserman, 2012). We will discuss the results of contemporary research on comparative cognition in many chapters of this text, and especially in Chapters 11 and 12.

Functional Neurology

The modern era in the study of learning processes was also greatly stimulated by efforts to use studies of learning in nonhuman animals to gain insights into how the nervous system works. This line of research was initiated by the Russian physiologist Ivan Pavlov, quite independently of the work of Darwin, Romanes, and others interested in comparative cognition.

While still a medical student, Pavlov became committed to the principle of **nervism** according to which all key physiological functions are governed by the nervous system. Armed with this principle, Pavlov devoted his life to documenting how the nervous system controlled various aspects of physiology. Much of his work was devoted to identifying the neural mechanisms of digestion.

For many years, Pavlov's research progressed according to plan. But, in 1902, two British investigators (Bayliss and Starling) published results showing that the pancreas, an important digestive organ, was partially under hormonal, rather than neural, control. Writing some time later, Pavlov's friend and biographer noted that these novel findings produced a crisis in the laboratory because they "shook the very foundation of the teachings of the exclusive nervous regulation of the secretory activity of the digestive glands" (Babkin, 1949, p. 228).

The evidence of hormonal control of the pancreas presented Pavlov with a dilemma. If he continued his investigations of digestion, he would have to abandon his interest in the nervous system. On the other hand, if he maintained his commitment to nervism, he would have to stop studying digestive physiology. Nervism won out. In an effort to continue studying the nervous system, Pavlov changed from studying digestive physiology to studying the conditioning of new reflexes. Pavlov regarded his investigations of conditioned or learned reflexes to be studies of the functions of the nervous system—what the nervous system accomplishes. Pavlov's claim that studies of learning tell us about the functions of the nervous system is well accepted by contemporary neuroscientists. For example, in their comprehensive textbook, *Fundamental Neuroscience*, Lynch and colleagues (2003) noted that "neuroscience is a large field founded on the premise that all of behavior and all of mental life have their origins in the structure and function of the nervous system" (p. xvii).

The behavioral psychologist is like a driver who examines an experimental car by taking it out for a test drive instead of first looking under the hood. By driving the car, the scientist can learn a great deal about how it functions. She can discover its acceleration, its top speed, the quality of its ride, its turning radius, and how quickly it comes to a stop. Driving the car will not reveal how these various functions are accomplished, but one can get certain clues. For example, if the car accelerates sluggishly and never reaches high speeds, chances are it is not powered by a rocket engine. If the car only goes forward when facing downhill, it is probably propelled by gravity rather than by an engine. On the other hand, if the car cannot be made to come to a stop quickly, it may not have brakes.

In a similar manner, behavioral studies of learning provide clues about the machinery of the nervous system. Such studies tell us what kinds of plasticity the nervous system is capable of, the conditions under which learning can take place, how long learned responses persist, and the circumstances under which learned information becomes accessible or not. By detailing the functions of the nervous system, behavioral studies of learning provide the basic facts or behavioral endpoints that neuroscientists have to explain at more molecular and biological levels of analysis.

Animal Models of Human Behavior

The third major impetus for the modern era in the study of animal learning was the belief that research with nonhuman animals can provide information that may help us better understand human behavior. Animal models of human behavior are of more recent origin than comparative cognition or functional neurology. The approach was systematized by Dollard and Miller and their collaborators (Dollard et al., 1939; Miller & Dollard, 1941) and developed further by B. F. Skinner (1953).

Drawing inferences about human behavior on the basis of research with other animal species can be hazardous and controversial. The inferences are hazardous if they are unwarranted; they are controversial if the rationale for the model system approach is poorly understood. Model systems have been developed based on research with a variety of species, including several species of primates, pigeons, rats, and mice.

In generalizing from research with rats and pigeons to human behavior, one does not make the assumption that rats and pigeons are like people. Animal models are like other types of models. Architects, pharmacologists, medical scientists, and designers of automobiles all rely on models, which are often strikingly different from the real thing. Architects, for example, make models of buildings they are designing. Obviously, such models are not the same as a real building. They are much smaller, made of cardboard and small pieces of wood instead of bricks and mortar, and support little weight.

Models are commonly used because they permit investigation of certain aspects of what they represent under conditions that are simpler, more easily controlled, and less expensive. With the use of a model, an architect can study the design of the exterior of a planned building without the expense of actual construction. The model can be used to determine what the building will look like from various vantage points and how it will appear relative to other nearby buildings. Studying a model in a design studio is much simpler than studying an actual building on a busy street corner. Factors that may get in the way of getting a good view (e.g., other buildings, traffic, and power lines) can be controlled and minimized in a model.

In a comparable fashion, a car designer can study the wind resistance of various design features of a new automobile with the use of a model in the form of a computer program. The program can be used to determine how the addition of spoilers or changes in the shape of the car will change its wind resistance. The computer model bears little resemblance to a real car. It has no tires or engine and cannot be driven. However, the model permits testing the wind resistance of a car design under conditions that are much simpler, better controlled, and less expensive than if the actual car were built and driven down the highway under various conditions to measure wind resistance.

Considering all the differences between a model and the real thing, what makes a model valid for studying something? To decide whether a model is valid, one first has to identify what features or functions of the real object one is most interested in. These are called the *relevant features* or *relevant functions*. If the model of a building is used to study the building's exterior appearance, then all the exterior dimensions of the model must be proportional to the corresponding dimensions of the planned building. Other features of the model, such as its structural elements, are irrelevant. In contrast, if the model is used to study how well the building would withstand an earthquake, then its structural elements (beams and how the beams are connected) would be critical.

In a similar manner, the only thing relevant in a computer model of car wind resistance is that the computer program provides calculations for wind resistance that match the results obtained with real cars driven through real air. No other feature is relevant; therefore, the fact that the computer program lacks an engine or rubber tires is of no consequence.

Models of human behavior using other animal species are based on the same logic as the use of models in other domains. Animal models permit investigating problems that are difficult, if not impossible, to study directly with people. A model permits the research to be carried out under circumstances that are simpler, better controlled, and less expensive. The validity of animal models is based on the same criterion as the validity of other types of models. The key is similarity between the animal model and human behavior in features that are relevant to the problem at hand. The relevant feature is a behavioral trait or function, such as drug addiction in laboratory rats. The fact that the rats have long tails and walk on four legs instead of two is entirely irrelevant to the issue of drug addiction.

The critical task in constructing a successful animal model is to identify the relevant points of similarity between the animal model and the human behavior of interest. The relevant similarity concerns the causal factors that are responsible for particular forms of behavior. We can gain insights into human behavior based on the study of nonhuman animals if the causal relations in the two species are similar. Because animal models are often used to push back the frontiers of knowledge, the correspondence between the animal findings and human behavior has to be carefully verified by empirical data. This interaction between animal and human research continues to make important contributions to our understanding of human behavior (e.g., Haselgrove & Hogarth, 2012).

Applications of learning principles got a special boost in the 1960s with the accelerated development of behavior therapy during that period. As O'Donohue commented, "the model of moving from the learning laboratory to the clinic proved to be an extraordinarily rich paradigm. In the 1960s, numerous learning principles were shown to be relevant to clinical practice. Learning research quickly proved to be a productive source of ideas for developing treatments or etiological accounts of many problems" (1998, p. 4). This fervor was tempered during subsequent developments of cognitive behavior therapy. However, recent advances in learning theory have encouraged a return to learning-based treatments for important human problems such as anxiety disorders, autism spectrum disorders, and drug abuse and treatment (Schachtman & Reilly, 2011).

Animal Models and Drug Development

Whether we visit a doctor because we have a physical or psychiatric illness, we are likely to go away with a prescription to alleviate our symptoms. Pharmaceutical companies are eager to bring new drugs to market and to develop drugs for symptoms that were previously treated in other ways (e.g., erectile dysfunction). Drug development is not possible without animal models. The animal learning paradigms described in this text are especially important for developing new drugs to enhance learning and cognition. As people live longer, cognitive decline with aging is becoming more prevalent, and that is creating increased demand for drugs to slow the decline. Animal models of learning and memory are playing a central role in the development of these new drugs. Animal models are also important for the development of antianxiety medications and drugs that facilitate the progress of behavior and cognitive therapy (e.g., Otto et al., 2010; Gold, 2008). Another important area of research is the evaluation of the potential for drug abuse associated with new medications for pain relief and other medical problems (e.g., Ator & Griffiths, 2003). Many of these experiments employ methods described in this book.

Animal Models and Machine Learning

Animal models of learning and behavior are also of considerable relevance to robotics and intelligent artificial systems (machine learning). Robots are machines that are able to perform particular functions or tasks. The goal in robotics is to make the machines as "smart" as possible. Just as Romanes defined intelligence in terms of the ability to learn, contemporary roboticists view the ability to remember and learn from experience to be important features of smart artificial systems. Information about the characteristics and mechanisms of such learning may be gleaned from studies of learning in nonhuman animals. Learning mechanisms are frequently used in artificial intelligent systems to enable the response of those systems to be altered by experience or feedback. A prominent approach in this area is "reinforcement learning" (e.g., Busoniu, Babuska, De Schutter, & Ernst, 2010), which originated in behavioral studies of animal learning.

The Definition of Learning

Learning is such a common human experience that people rarely reflect on exactly what it means. A universally accepted definition of learning does not exist. However, many important aspects of learning are captured in the following statement:

> *Learning is an enduring change in the mechanisms of behavior involving specific stimuli and/or responses that results from prior experience with those or similar stimuli and responses.*

This definition may seem cumbersome, but each of its components serves to convey an important feature of learning.

The Learning–Performance Distinction

Whenever we see evidence of learning, we see the emergence of a change in behavior—the performance of a new response or the suppression of a response that occurred previously. A child becomes skilled in snapping the buckles of his or her sandals or becomes more patient in waiting for the popcorn to cook in the microwave oven. Such changes in behavior are the only way we can tell whether or not learning has occurred. However, notice that the preceding definition attributes learning to a change in the *mechanisms of behavior*, not to a change in behavior directly.

Why should we define learning in terms of a change in the mechanisms of behavior? The main reason is that behavior is determined by many factors in addition to learning. Consider, for example, eating. Whether you eat something depends on how hungry you are, how much effort is required to obtain the food, how much you like the food, and whether you know where to find food. Only some of these factors involve learning.

Performance refers to all of the actions of an organism at a particular time. Whether an animal does something or not (its performance) depends on many things, as in the above example of eating. Therefore, a change in performance cannot be automatically considered to reflect learning. Learning is defined in terms of a change in the mechanisms of behavior to emphasize the distinction between learning and performance. Because performance is determined by many factors in addition to learning, one must be very careful in deciding whether a particular aspect of performance does or does not reflect learning. Sometimes evidence of learning cannot be obtained until special test procedures are introduced. Children, for example, learn a great deal about driving a car just by watching others drive, but this learning is not apparent until they are permitted behind the steering wheel. In other cases (discussed in the next section), a change in behavior is readily observed but cannot be attributed to learning because it does not last long enough or does not result from experience with specific environmental events.

Learning and Other Sources of Behavior Change

Several mechanisms produce changes in behavior that are too short-lasting to be considered instances of learning. One such process is **fatigue**. Physical exertion may result in a gradual reduction in the vigor of a response because the individual becomes tired. This type of change is produced by experience. However, it is not considered an instance of learning because the decline in responding disappears if the individual is allowed to rest for a while.

Behavior also may be temporarily altered by a *change in stimulus conditions*. If the house lights in a movie theater suddenly come on in the middle of the show, the behavior of the audience is likely to change dramatically. However, this is not an instance of learning because the audience is likely to return to watching the movie when the house lights are turned off again.

Other short-term changes in behavior that are not considered learning involve alterations in the physiological or motivational state of the organism. Hunger and thirst induce responses that are not observed at other times. Changes in the level of sex hormones cause changes in responsiveness to sexual stimuli. Short-lasting behavioral effects also accompany the administration of psychoactive drugs.

In some cases, persistent changes in behavior occur, but without the type of experience with environmental events that satisfies the definition of learning. The most obvious example of this type is **maturation**. A child cannot get something from a high shelf until he or she grows tall enough. However, the change in behavior in this case is not an instance of learning because it occurs with the mere passage of time. The child does not have to be trained to reach high places as he or she becomes taller.

Generally, the distinction between learning and maturation is based on the importance of specific experiences in producing the behavior change of interest. Maturation occurs in the absence of specific training or practice. However, the distinction is blurred in cases where environmental stimulation is necessary for maturational development. Experiments with cats, for example, have shown that the visual system will not develop sufficiently to permit perception of horizontal lines unless the cats have been exposed to such stimuli early in life (e.g., Blakemore & Cooper, 1970). The appearance of sexual behavior at puberty also depends on developmental experience, in this case social play before puberty (e.g., Harlow, 1969).

Learning and Levels of Analysis

Because of its critical importance in everyday life, learning is being studied at many different levels of analysis (Byrne, 2008). Some of these are illustrated in Figure 1.5. Our emphasis will be on analyses of learning at the level of behavior. The behavioral level of analysis is rooted in the conviction that the function of learning is to facilitate an organism's interactions with its environment. We interact with our environment primarily through our actions. Therefore, the behavioral level of analysis occupies a cardinal position.

Much research on learning these days is also being conducted at the level of neural mechanisms (e.g., Gallistel & Matzel, 2013; Kesner & Martinez, 2007; Rudy, 2008). Interest in the neural mechanisms of learning has been stimulated by tremendous methodological

FIGURE 1.5 Levels of analysis of learning. Learning mechanisms may be investigated at the organismic level, at the level of neural circuits and transmitter systems, and at the level of nerve cells or neurons.

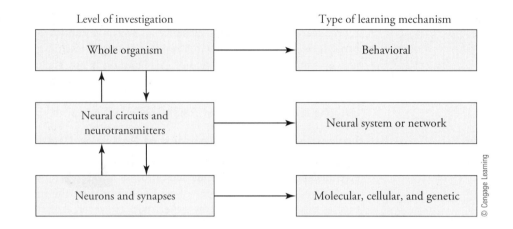

and technical advances that permit scientists to directly examine biological processes that previously were only hypothetical possibilities. The neural mechanisms involved in learning may be examined at the systems level. This level is concerned with how neural circuits and neurotransmitter systems are organized to produce learned responses. Neural mechanisms may also be examined at the level of individual neurons and synapses, with an emphasis on molecular and cellular mechanisms, including genetic and epigenetic mechanisms. (Contemporary research on the neurobiology of learning will be presented in "neuroboxes" in each chapter of the book.)

Periodically, we will describe changes in learning that occur as a function of age. These are referred to as *developmental* changes. We will also consider how learning helps animals adapt to their environment and increase their success in reproducing and passing along their genes to future generations. These issues involve the *adaptive significance of learning*. Most scientists agree that learning mechanisms evolved because they increase reproductive fitness. The contribution of learning to reproductive fitness is often indirect. By learning to find food more efficiently, for example, an organism may live longer and have more offspring. However, learning can also have a direct effect on reproductive fitness. Studies of sexual conditioning have shown that learning can increase how many eggs are fertilized and how many offspring are produced as a result of a sexual encounter (Domjan et al., 2012).

Methodological Aspects of the Study of Learning

There are two prominent methodological issues that are important to keep in mind when considering behavioral studies of learning. The first of these is a direct consequence of the definition of learning and involves the exclusive use of experimental research methods. The second methodological feature of studies of learning is reliance on a general-process approach. Reliance on a general-process approach is a matter of intellectual preference rather than a matter of necessity.

Learning as an Experimental Science

Studies of learning focus on identifying how prior experience causes long-term changes in behavior. At the behavioral level, this boils down to identifying the critical components of training or conditioning protocols that are required to produce learning. The emphasis on identifying causal variables necessitates an experimental approach.

BOX 1.1

The Material Mind

During the last 30 years, a new era has emerged in the study of learning, detailing the neurobiological mechanisms that underlie key learning phenomena. Some of these discoveries will be highlighted in boxes that appear in each chapter. These boxes will introduce you to new research that has revealed how and where learning occurs within the nervous system. We begin by discussing the relation between behavioral and biological studies and by reviewing some key terms and concepts needed to understand the material presented in subsequent boxes dealing with neural mechanisms (for additional details, see Kalat, 2009, and Prus, 2014).

Our aim in this book is to understand learning, to elucidate what it is, when and why it occurs, and how it is produced. In short, we want to know its cause, and this, in turn, requires that we look at learning from multiple perspectives. As in any field of enquiry, the first task involves describing the phenomenon and the circumstances under which it is observed, what Aristotle called the *efficient cause* (Killeen, 2001). As we gain insight into the phenomenon, we gain the knowledge needed to develop formal models (the *formal cause*) of the process that allow us to predict, for example, when learning will occur. At the same time, we seek a context in which to understand our observations, a form of explanation that focuses on why a phenomenon is observed (the *final cause*). Finally, we hope to detail the underlying biological mechanisms of learning (the *material cause*).

The foundation of learning rests on the elucidation of its efficient cause, work that has allowed us to understand how experience can engage distinct forms of learning, the

types of processes involved, and their long-term behavioral consequences. We now understand that learning does not depend on contiguity alone, and we have developed formal models of this process. As we will see, researchers have also discovered that whether learning occurs is wedded to the "why"—the evolutionary benefit gained from preparing the organism to learn in particular ways. A century of work has provided detailed answers to the efficient, formal, and final causes of learning. This has provided the basis for much of the content of this book and has prepared us to begin to investigate the material cause of learning—its neurobiological basis.

Our discussion of the material cause assumes little background in neurobiology and will introduce biological terms as needed. There are, however, some overarching concepts that are essential, and, for that reason, I begin by providing a brief overview of how the underlying machinery (the neurons) operates and is organized.

Your nervous system entails both a central component (the brain and spinal cord) and a peripheral component. Both of these are composed of **neurons** that transmit signals that relay sensory information, process it, and execute motor commands. Key components of a neuron are illustrated in Figure (i) on the inside front cover. Neural communication begins at the **dendrites**, which contain specialized receptors that transform input from another cell (a sensory receptor or neuron) into an electrical impulse. This is accomplished by allowing sodium ions (Na^+) to enter the cell. Under normal circumstances, neurons are impermeable to Na^+, and if any leaks in, it is actively pumped out of the cell (into the extracellular space). Because Na^+ has a positive charge, the excess of Na^+ outside the cell sets up an electrical

charge across the cell membrane (Figure 1.6A). Think of this as a miniature battery, with the positive side oriented toward the extracellular space. This battery-like effect establishes a small difference in voltage, with the inside of the cell lying approximately -70 mV below the outside.

Channels positioned in the dendritic cell membrane are designed to allow Na^+ into the cell. The circumstances that open these channels depend on the cell's function. For example, the Na^+ channels on a sensory neuron may be engaged by a mechanoreceptor, whereas a cell that receives input from another neuron could have receptors that are activated by a neurotransmitter. In either case, opening the channel allows Na^+ to rush into the cell (Figure 1.6B). This movement of positive charge depolarizes the interior of the cell, causing the voltage to move from -70 mV toward zero (a process known as **depolarization**). Other Na^+ channels are voltage sensitive and swing open once the cell is sufficiently depolarized, allowing even more Na^+ to rush into the cell. Indeed, so much Na^+ rushes into the cell (pushed by an osmotic force that acts to equate the concentration gradient) that the interior actually becomes positive (Figure 1.6C). At this point, the Na^+ channels close and channels that regulate the ion potassium (K^+) open. At rest, the interior of a cell contains an excess of K^+, which is repelled by the positively charged Na^+ outside the cell. But when Na^+ rushes in, the game is switched and now it is the inside of the cell that has a positive charge. This allows K^+ to flow down its concentration gradient and exit the cell. As it does so, the inside of the cell becomes negative again. These ionic changes set off a chain reaction that

Continued

BOX 1.1 (continued)

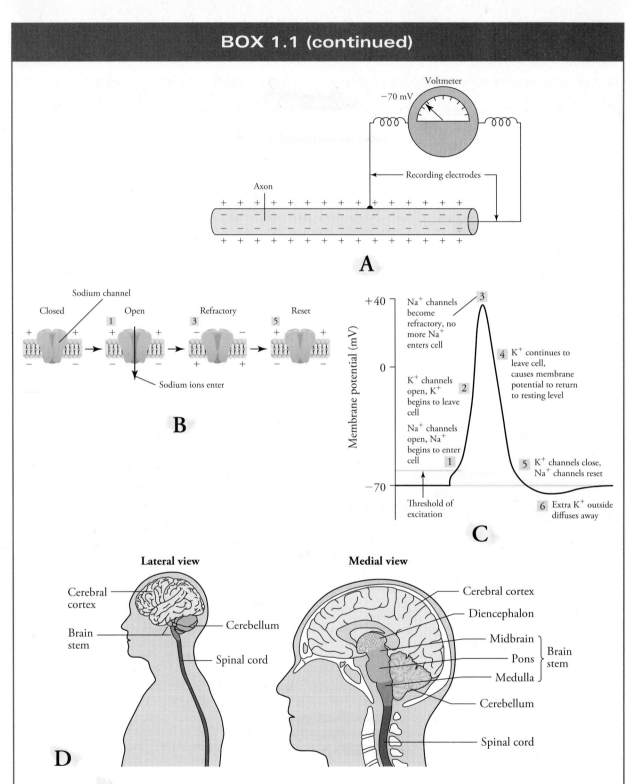

FIGURE 1.6 (A) At rest, the distribution of electrically charged particles across the cell membrane establishes a charge of approximately −70 mV. (Adapted from Gleitman, 2010.) (B) A sodium channel regulates the flow of Na⁺. (© Cengage Learning 2015) (C). Allowing Na⁺ to flow into a neuron reduces (depolarizes) the internal voltage of the cell, which engages electrically sensitive Na⁺ channels. Na⁺ rushing into the cell produces a rapid rise in voltage (1). K⁺ flowing out of the cell acts to reestablish the resting potential (4). (Adapted from Carlson, 2012.) (D) The major structures of the central nervous system from a side (lateral) and middle (medial) perspective. The brainstem lies above the spinal cord and includes the medulla, pons, and midbrain. The forebrain lies directly above and includes the diencephalon (thalamus and hypothalamus) and cerebral cortex. The cerebellum lies under the cerebral cortex, behind the pons. (Adapted from Kandel et al., 2013.)

Continued

BOX 1.1 (continued)

travels across the cell membrane to the *cell body* (a region that contains the genes and much of the biological machinery needed to maintain the cell). From there, the electrical impulse (the **action potential**) travels down the **axon** to its end, where the cell forms a chemical connection (a **synapse**) with another cell (Figure (ii) on the inside front cover).

When an action potential arrives at a synapse, it causes channels that are permeable to the ion Ca^{++} to open, allowing Ca^{++} to flow into the cell. The increase in intracellular Ca^{++} causes the vesicles that contain the **neurotransmitter** to migrate over to the *presynaptic* neural membrane and dump their contents into the space (the *synaptic cleft*) between the cells. The transmitter than engages receptors on the *postsynaptic* cell, which could be another neuron or an effector organ (e.g., a muscle).

Experience can modify how a neuron operates, providing a kind of adaptability (plasticity) that allows learning. As we will see, there are multiple forms of *neural plasticity*. For example, a neural input to the presynaptic side of a terminal can augment transmitter release (Box 2.2). In addition, cellular processes can augment (potentiate) or depress the postsynaptic response to transmitter release (Box 8.2). In addition, there are many different kinds of transmitters, some of which (e.g., *glutamate*) are excitatory and elicit an action potential while others (e.g., *GABA*) inhibit neural activity.

Another important neurobiological principle concerns the structure of the nervous system: how neurons are organized to form units and pathways to perform particular functions (Figure 1.6D). In creatures without a spinal cord (invertebrates), neurons are organized into bundles known as *ganglia*. In vertebrates, ganglia are found in the *peripheral nervous system* (the portion that lies outside the bony covering of the spine and skull). The *central nervous system* (the spinal cord and brain) lies within the bony covering. As we will see, the brain is organized into structures and *nuclei* (a set of neurons within a structure) that mediate particular functions (e.g., fear conditioning [Box 4.3], reward learning [Boxes 6.3 and 7.1], and timing [Box 12.1]).

A wide variety of methods have been used to explore the neurobiological mechanisms that underlie learning, including genetic techniques that target particular genes, electrophysiological and imaging procedures that map neural activity, treatments that engage (stimulate) or disrupt (lesion) neurons in specific regions, and pharmacological procedures that target specific receptors and intracellular processes. Together, the research has revealed some surprising commonalities regarding the material causes of learning. For example, as we will see, a specialized postsynaptic receptor (the *N*-methyl-D-aspartate [NMDA] receptor) contributes to nearly every instance of learning we will discuss. At the same time, we will also learn that the

organization of behavior is derived from a neural system that has partitioned the task of learning across multiple components, each tuned to perform a particular function. The research we will describe in the book provides the map needed to link these neural mechanisms to behavioral systems.

J. W. Grau

---

action potential An electrical impulse caused by the rapid flow of charged particles (ions) across the neural membrane. The nerve impulse conducts an electrical signal along the axon of a neuron and initiates the release of neurotransmitter at the synapse.

axon A slender projection of a neuron that allows electrical impulses to be conducted from the cell body to the terminal ending.

dendrites The branched projections of a neuron that receive electrochemical input from other cells (e.g., sensory receptors or neurons).

depolarization A reduction in the electrical charge across the neural membrane, typically caused by the inward flow of the ion Na^+. Depolarization causes the inside of the neuron to be less negative, which can initiate an action potential.

neuron A specialized cell that functions to transmit, and process, information within the nervous system by means of electrical and chemical signals.

neurotransmitter A chemical released by a neuron at a synapse. Neurotransmitters allow communication across cells and can have either an excitatory or inhibitory effect.

synapse A structure that allows a neuron to pass a chemical signal (neurotransmitter) to another cell.

Consider the following example. Mary goes into a dark room. She quickly turns on a switch near the door and the lights in the room go on. Can you conclude that turning on the switch "caused" the lights to go on? Not from the information provided. Perhaps the lights were on an automatic timer and would have come on without Mary's actions. Alternatively, the door may have had a built-in switch that turned on the lights after a slight delay. Another possibility is that there was a motion detector in the room that activated the lights when Mary entered.

FIGURE 1.7 Two versions of the fundamental learning experiment. In the left panel, two groups of individuals are compared. The training procedure is provided for participants in the experimental group but not for those in the control group. In the right panel, a single individual is observed before and during training. The individual's behavior during training is compared to what we assume its behavior would have been without training.

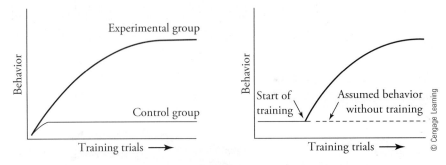

How could you determine that manipulation of the wall switch caused the lights to go on? You would have to evaluate various scenarios to test the causal model. For example, you might ask Mary to enter the room again but ask her not to turn on the wall switch. If the lights do not go on under those circumstances, you could conclude that the lights were not turned on by a motion detector or by a switch built into the door. As this simple example illustrates, to identify a cause, an experiment has to be conducted in which the presumed cause is removed. The results obtained with and without the presumed cause are then compared.

In the study of learning, the behavior of living organisms is of interest, not the behavior of lights. However, scientists have to proceed in a similar fashion. They have to conduct experiments in which behavior is observed with and without the presumed causal factor. The most basic question is to identify whether a training procedure produces a particular behavior change. To answer this question, individuals who receive the training procedure have to be compared with individuals who do not receive that training. This requires experimentally varying the presence versus absence of the training experience. Because of this, *learning can be investigated only with experimental methods.* This makes the study of learning primarily a laboratory science.

The necessity of using experimental techniques to investigate learning is not adequately appreciated by allied scientists. Many aspects of behavior can be studied with observational techniques that do not involve experimental manipulations. For example, observational studies can provide a great deal of information about when and how animals set up territories, what they do to defend those territories, how they engage in courtship and sexual behaviors, how they raise their offspring, and how the activities of the offspring change as they mature.

Much fascinating information about animals has been obtained with observational techniques that involve minimal intrusion into their ongoing activities. Unfortunately, learning cannot be studied that way. To be sure that a change in behavior is due to learning rather than changes in motivation, sensory development, hormonal fluctuations, or other possible nonlearning mechanisms, it is necessary to conduct experiments in which the presumed training experiences are systematically manipulated. The basic learning experiment compares two groups of participants (Figure 1.7). The experimental group receives the training procedure of interest, and how this procedure changes behavior is measured. The performance of the experimental group is compared with a control group that does not receive the training procedure but is otherwise treated in a similar fashion. Learning is presumed to have taken place if the experimental group responds differently from the control group. A similar rationale can be used to study learning in a single individual provided that one can be certain that the behavior is stable in the absence of a training intervention.

The General-Process Approach to the Study of Learning

The second prominent methodological feature of studies of learning is the use of a general-process approach. This is more a matter of preference than of necessity.

However, in adopting a general-process approach, investigators of animal learning are following a long-standing tradition in science.

Elements of the General-Process Approach   The most obvious feature of nature is its diversity. Consider, for example, the splendid variety of minerals that exist in the world. Some are soft, some are hard, some are brilliant in appearance, others are dull, and so on. Plants and animals also occur in many different shapes and sizes. Dynamic properties of objects are also diverse. Some things float, whereas others rapidly drop to the ground; some remain still; others remain in motion.

In studying nature, one can either focus on differences or try to ignore the differences and search for commonalities. Scientists ranging from physicists to chemists, biologists, and psychologists have all elected to search for commonalities. Rather than being overwhelmed by the tremendous variety of things in nature, scientists have opted to look for uniformities. They have attempted to formulate general laws with which to organize and explain the diversity of the universe. Investigators of animal learning have followed this well-established tradition.

Whether or not general laws are discovered often depends on the level of analysis that is pursued. The diversity of the phenomena scientists try to understand and organize makes it difficult to formulate general laws at the level of the observed phenomena. It is difficult, for example, to discover the general laws that govern chemical reactions by simply documenting the nature of the chemicals involved in various reactions. Similarly, it is difficult to explain the diversity of species in the world by cataloging the features of various animals. Major progress in science comes from analyzing phenomena at a more elemental or molecular level. For example, by the nineteenth century, chemists knew many specific facts about what would happen when various chemicals were combined. However, a general account of chemical reactions had to await the development of the periodic table of the elements, which organized chemical elements in terms of their constituent atomic components.

Investigators of conditioning and learning have been committed to the general-process approach from the inception of this field of psychology. They have focused on the commonalities of various instances of learning and have assumed that learning phenomena are products of elemental processes that operate in much the same way in different learning situations.

The commitment to a general-process approach guided Pavlov's work on functional neurology and conditioning. Commitment to a general-process approach to the study of learning is also evident in the writings of early comparative psychologists. For example, Darwin (1897) emphasized commonalities among species in cognitive functions: "My object ... is to show that there is no fundamental difference between man and the higher mammals in their mental faculties" (p. 66). At the start of the twentieth century, Jacques Loeb (1900) pointed out that commonalities occur at the level of elemental processes: "Psychic phenomena ... appear, invariably, as a function of an elemental process, namely the activity of associative memory" (p. 213). Another prominent comparative psychologist of the time, C. Lloyd Morgan, stated that elementary laws of association "are, we believe, universal laws" (Morgan, 1903, p. 219).

The assumption that "universal" elemental laws of association are responsible for learning phenomena does not deny the diversity of stimuli different animals may learn about, the diversity of responses they may learn to perform, and the fact that one species may learn something more slowly than another. The generality is assumed to exist in the rules or processes of learning—not in the contents or speed of learning. This idea was clearly expressed nearly a century ago by Edward Thorndike, one of the first prominent American psychologists who studied learning:

Formally, the crab, fish, turtle, dog, cat, monkey, and baby have very similar intellects and characters. All are systems of connections subject to change by the laws of exercise and effect. The differences are: first, in the concrete particular connections, in what stimulates the animal to response, what responses it makes, which stimulus connects with what response, and second, in the degree of ability to learn. (Thorndike, 1911, p. 280)

What an animal can learn about (the stimuli, responses, and stimulus-response connections it learns) varies from one species to another. Animals also differ in how fast they learn ("in the degree of ability to learn"). However, Thorndike assumed that the rules of learning were universal. We no longer share Thorndike's view that these universal rules of learning are the "laws of exercise and effect." However, contemporary scientists continue to embrace the idea that universal rules of learning exist. The job of the learning psychologist is to discover those universal laws.

Methodological Implications of the General-Process Approach   If we assume that universal rules of learning exist, then we should be able to discover those rules in any situation in which learning occurs. Thus, an important methodological implication of the general-process approach is that general rules of learning may be discovered by studying any species or response system that exhibits learning. This implication has encouraged scientists to study learning in a small number of experimental situations. Investigators have converged on a few "standard" or conventional experimental paradigms. Figure 1.8, for example, shows an example of a pigeon in a standard Skinner box. I will describe other examples of standard experimental paradigms as I introduce various learning phenomena in future chapters.

Conventional experimental paradigms have been fine-tuned over the years to fit well with the behavioral predispositions of the research animals. Because of these improvements, conventional experimental preparations permit laboratory study of reasonably naturalistic responses (Timberlake, 1990).

FIGURE 1.8 A pigeon in a standard Skinner box. Three circular disks, arranged at eye level, are available for the bird to peck. Access to food is provided in the hopper below.

Proof of the Generality of Learning Phenomena   The generality of learning processes is not proven by adopting a general-process approach. Assuming the existence of common elemental learning processes is not the same as empirically demonstrating those commonalities. Direct empirical verification of the existence of common learning processes in a variety of situations remains necessary in efforts to build a truly general account of how learning occurs. The generality of learning processes has to be proven by studying learning in many different species and situations.

The available evidence suggests that elementary principles of learning of the sort that will be described in this text have considerable generality (Papini, 2008). Most research on animal learning has been conducted with pigeons, rats, and (to a much lesser extent) rabbits. Similar forms of learning have been found with fish, hamsters, cats, dogs, human beings, dolphins, and sea lions. In addition, some of the principles of learning observed with these vertebrate species also have been demonstrated in newts, fruit flies, honeybees, terrestrial mollusks, wasps, and various marine mollusks.

Use of Nonhuman Animals in Research on Learning

Although the principles described in this book apply to people, many of the experiments we will be considering have been conducted with nonhuman animals. The experiments involved laboratory animals for both theoretical and methodological reasons.

Rationale for the Use of Nonhuman Animals in Research on Learning

As I noted earlier, experimental methods have to be used to study learning phenomena so that the acquisition of new behaviors can be attributed to particular previous training experiences. Experimental control of past experience cannot always be achieved with the same degree of precision in studies with human participants as in studies with laboratory animals. In addition, with laboratory animals, scientists can study how strong emotional reactions are learned and how learning is involved in acquiring food, avoiding pain or distress, or finding potential sexual partners. With human participants, investigators can study how maladaptive emotional responses (e.g., fears and phobias) may be reduced, but they cannot experimentally manipulate how these emotions are learned in the first place.

Knowledge of the evolution and biological bases of learning also cannot be obtained without the use of nonhuman animals in research. How cognition and intelligence evolved is one of the fundamental questions about human nature. The answer to this question will shape our view of what it means to be human, just as knowledge of the solar system shaped our view of the place of the Earth in the universe. As I have discussed, investigation of the evolution of cognition and intelligence rests heavily on studies of learning in nonhuman animals.

Knowledge of the neurobiological bases of learning may not change our views of human nature, but it is apt to yield important dividends in the treatment of learning and memory disorders. Many of the detailed investigations that are necessary to unravel how the nervous system learns and remembers simply cannot be conducted with people. Studying the neurobiological bases of learning first requires documenting the nature of learning processes at the behavioral level. Therefore, behavioral studies of learning in animals are a necessary prerequisite to any animal research on the biological bases of learning.

Laboratory animals also provide important conceptual advantages over people for studying learning processes. The processes of learning may be simpler in animals reared under controlled laboratory conditions than in people, whose backgrounds are more varied and often poorly documented. The behavior of nonhuman animals is not complicated by linguistic processes that have a prominent role in certain kinds of human behavior. In research with people, one has to make sure that the actions of the participants are not governed by their efforts to please (or displease) the experimenter. Such factors are not likely to complicate what rats and pigeons do in an experiment.

Laboratory Animals and Normal Behavior

Some have suggested that domesticated strains of laboratory animals may not provide useful information because such animals have degenerated as a result of many generations of inbreeding and long periods of captivity (e.g., Lockard, 1968). However, this notion is probably mistaken. In an interesting test, Boice (1977) took five male and five female albino rats of a highly inbred laboratory stock and housed them in an outdoor pen in Missouri without artificial shelter. All 10 rats survived the first winter with temperatures as low as −22°F. The animals reproduced normally and reached a stable population of about 50 members. Only three of the rats died before showing signs of old age during the two-year study period. Given the extreme climatic conditions, this level of survival is remarkable. Furthermore, the behavior of these domesticated rats in the outdoors was very similar to the behavior of wild rats observed in similar circumstances.

Domesticated rats act similar to wild rats in other tests as well, and there is some indication that they perform better than wild rats in learning experiments (see, e.g., Boice, 1973, 1981; Kaufman & Collier, 1983). Therefore, the results I will describe in this text should not be discounted because many of the experiments were conducted with domesticated animals. In fact, it may be suggested that laboratory animals are preferable in research to their wild counterparts. Human beings live in what are largely artificial environments. Therefore, research may prove most relevant to the human behavior if the research is carried out with domesticated animals that live in artificial laboratory situations. As Boice (1973) commented, "The domesticated rat may be a good model for domestic man" (p. 227).

Public Debate about Research With Nonhuman Animals

There has been much public debate about the pros and cons of research with nonhuman animals (see Perry & Dess, 2012, for a recent review). Part of the debate has centered on the humane treatment of animals. Other aspects of the debate have centered on what constitutes ethical treatment of animals, whether human beings have the right to benefit at the expense of animals, and possible alternatives to research with nonhuman animals.

The Humane Treatment of Laboratory Animals   Concern for the welfare of laboratory animals has resulted in the adoption of strict federal standards for animal housing and for the supervision of animal research. Some argue that these rules are needed because without them scientists would disregard the welfare of the animals in their zeal to obtain research data. However, this argument ignores the fact that good science requires good animal care. Scientists, especially those studying behavior, must be concerned about the welfare of their research subjects. Information about normal learning and behavior cannot be obtained from diseased or disturbed animals. Investigators of animal learning must ensure the welfare of their subjects if they are to obtain useful scientific data.

Learning experiments sometimes involve discomfort. Discomfort is an inevitable aspect of life for all species, including people. Scientists make every effort to minimize the degree of discomfort for their research participants. In studies of food reinforcement, for example, animals are food deprived before each experimental session to ensure their interest in food. However, the hunger imposed in the laboratory is no more severe than the hunger animals encounter in the wild, and often it is less severe (Poling, Nickel, & Alling, 1990).

The investigation of certain forms of learning and behavior require the administration of aversive stimulation. Important topics, such as punishment or the learning of fear and anxiety, cannot be studied without some discomfort to the participants. However, even in such cases, efforts are made to keep the discomfort to a minimum for the research question at hand.

What Constitutes the Ethical Treatment of Animals?

Although making sure that animals serving in experiments are comfortable is in the best interests of the animals as well as the research, formulating general ethical principles is difficult. Animal "rights" cannot be identified in the way we identify human rights (Lansdell, 1988), and animals seem to have different "rights" under different circumstances.

Currently, substantial efforts are made to house laboratory animals in conditions that promote their health and comfort. However, a laboratory mouse or rat loses the protection afforded by federal regulations when it escapes from the laboratory and takes up residence in the walls of the laboratory building (Herzog, 1988). The trapping and extermination of rodents in buildings is a common practice that has not been the subject of either public debate or restrictive federal regulation. Mites, fleas, and ticks are also animals, but we do not tolerate them in our hair or our homes. Which species have the right to life, and under what circumstances do they have that right? Such questions defy simple answers.

Assuming that a species deserves treatment that meets government-mandated standards, what should those standards be? Appropriate treatment of laboratory animals is sometimes described as "humane treatment." However, we have to be careful not to take this term literally. "Humane treatment" means treating someone as we would treat a human being. It is important to keep in mind that rats (and other laboratory animals) are not human beings. Rats prefer to live in dark burrows made of dirt that they never clean. People in contrast prefer to live in well-illuminated and frequently cleaned rooms. Laboratories typically have rats in well-lit rooms that are frequently cleaned. One cannot help but wonder whether these housing standards were dictated more by considerations of human comfort rather than rat comfort.

Should Human Beings Benefit From the Use of Animals?

Part of the public debate about animal rights has been fueled by the argument that human beings have no right to benefit at the expense of animals, that humans have no right to "exploit" animals. This argument goes far beyond issues concerning the use of animals in research. Therefore, I will not discuss the argument in detail here, except to point out that far fewer animals are used in research than are used in the food industry, for clothing, and in recreational hunting and fishing. In addition, a comprehensive count of human exploitation of animals has to include disruptions of habitats that occur whenever we build roads, housing developments, and office buildings. We should also add the millions of animals that are killed by insecticides and other pest-control efforts in agriculture and elsewhere.

Alternatives to Research With Animals

Increased awareness of ethical issues involved in the use of nonhuman animals in research has encouraged a search for alternative techniques. Some years ago, Russell and Burch (1959) formulated the "three Rs" for animal research: *replacement* of animals with other testing techniques, *reducing* the number of animals used with statistical techniques, and *refining* the experimental procedures to cause less suffering. Replacement strategies have been successful in the cosmetic industry and in the manufacture of certain vaccines and hormones (e.g., Murkerjee,

1997). Motivated by this strategy, a recent task force of the National Institutes of Health on the use of chimpanzees in research (Altevogt et al., 2011) recommended that most forms of medical research with chimpanzees be terminated because alternative methodologies and species have been developed in recent years. Interestingly, however, the task force identified comparative cognition and behavior as one of only three research areas that should be continued because no good alternatives to chimpanzees are available for those investigations. Indeed, many common alternatives to the use of animals in research are not suitable to study learning processes (Gallup & Suarez, 1985). Some of these alternatives are the following.

1. *Observational techniques.* As I discussed earlier, learning processes cannot be investigated with unobtrusive observational techniques. Experimental manipulation of past experience is necessary in studies of learning. Therefore, field observations of undisturbed animals cannot yield information about the mechanisms of learning.

2. *Plants.* Learning cannot be investigated in plants because plants lack a nervous system, which is required for learning.

3. *Tissue cultures.* Although tissue cultures may reveal the operation of cellular processes, how these cellular processes work in an intact organism can be discovered only by studying the intact organism. Furthermore, the relevance of a cellular process for learning has to be demonstrated by showing how that cellular process operates to generate learned behavior at the organismic level.

4. *Computer simulations.* Writing a computer program to simulate a natural phenomenon requires a great deal of knowledge about that phenomenon. To simulate a particular form of learning, programmers would first have to obtain detailed knowledge of the circumstances under which that type of learning occurs and the factors that influence the rate of that learning. The absence of such knowledge necessitates experimental research with live organisms. Thus, experimental research with live organisms is a prerequisite for effective computer simulations. For that reason, computer simulations cannot be used in place of experimental research.

Computer simulations can serve many useful functions in science. Simulations are effective in showing us the implications of the experimental observations that were previously obtained or in showing the implications of various theoretical assumptions. They can be used to identify gaps in knowledge, and they can be used to suggest important future lines of research. However, they cannot be used to generate new, previously unknown facts about behavior. As Conn and Parker (1998) pointed out, "Scientists depend on computers for processing data that we already possess, but can't use them to explore the unknown in the quest for new information."

Sample Questions

1. Describe how historical developments in the study of the mind contributed to the contemporary study of learning.

2. Describe Descartes's conception of the reflex and how the concept of the reflex has changed since his time.

3. Describe the rationale for using animal models to study human behavior.

4. Describe the definition of learning and how learning is distinguished from other forms of behavior change.

5. Describe the different levels of analysis that can be employed in studies of learning and how they are related.

6. Describe why learning requires the use of experimental methods of inquiry.

7. Describe alternatives to the use of animals in research and their advantages and disadvantages.

Key Terms

association   A connection between the representations of two events (two stimuli or a stimulus and a response) such that the occurrence of one of the events activates the representation of the other.

dualism   The view of behavior according to which actions can be separated into two categories: voluntary behavior controlled by the mind and involuntary behavior controlled by reflex mechanisms.

empiricism   A philosophy according to which all ideas in the mind arise from experience.

fatigue   A temporary decrease in behavior caused by repeated or excessive use of the muscles involved in the behavior.

hedonism   The philosophy proposed by Hobbes according to which the actions of organisms are determined by the pursuit of pleasure and the avoidance of pain.

learning   An enduring change in the mechanisms of behavior involving specific stimuli and/or responses that results from prior experience with similar stimuli and responses.

maturation   A change in behavior caused by physical or physiological development of the organism in the absence of experience with particular environmental events.

nativism   A philosophy according to which human beings are born with innate ideas.

nervism   The philosophical position adopted by Pavlov that all behavioral and physiological processes are regulated by the nervous system.

nonsense syllable   A three-letter combination (two consonants separated by a vowel) that has no meaning.

performance   An organism's activities at a particular time.

reflex   A mechanism that enables a specific environmental event to elicit a specific response.

Elicited Behavior, Habituation, and Sensitization

CHAPTER PREVIEW

Chapter 2 begins the discussion of contemporary principles of learning and behavior with a description of modern research on elicited behavior, behavior that occurs in reaction to specific environmental stimuli. Many of the things we do are elicited by discrete stimuli, including some of the most extensively investigated forms of behavior. Elicited responses range from simple reflexes (an eyeblink in response to a puff of air) to more complex behavior sequences (courtship and sexual behavior) and complex emotional responses and goal-directed behavior (drug seeking and drug abuse). Interestingly, simple reflexive responses can be involved in the coordination of elaborate social interactions. Elicited responses are also involved in two of the most basic and widespread forms of behavioral change: habituation and sensitization. Habituation and sensitization are important because they are potentially involved in all learning procedures. They modulate simple elicited responses like the startle response and are also involved in the regulation of complex emotions and motivated behavior like drug seeking.

We typically think about learning as the result of deliberate instruction and practice. We spend relatively little time trying to train our pet goldfish or cat. However, we devote considerable effort to training our children and ourselves to do all sorts of things, such as driving a car, playing tennis, or operating a new smartphone. On the face of it, people seem capable of learning a much wider range of skills than goldfish or cats. What is rarely appreciated, however, is that in all species what and how learning takes place depends on the preexisting behavioral organization of the organism.

Behavior is not infinitely flexible, easily moved in any direction. Rather, organisms are born with preexisting behavior systems and tendencies that constrain how learning occurs and what changes one may expect from a training procedure. These limitations were described elegantly in an analogy by Rachlin (1976), who compared learning to sculpting a wooden statue. The sculptor begins with a piece of wood that has little resemblance to a statue. As the carving proceeds, the piece of wood comes to look more and more like the final product. But the process is not without limitation since the sculptor has to take into account the direction and density of the wood grain and any knots the wood may have. Wood carving is most successful if it is in harmony with the pre-existing grain and knots of the wood. In a similar fashion, learning is most successful if it takes into account the preexisting behavior structures of the organism. In this chapter, I describe the most prominent of these behavioral starting points for learning as I describe the fundamentals of elicited behavior. I will then describe how elicited behavior can be modified by experience through the processes of habituation and sensitization. These processes are important to understand before we consider more complex forms of learning because they are potentially involved in all learning procedures.

The Nature of Elicited Behavior

All animals, whether they are single-celled paramecia or complex human beings, react to events in their environment. If something moves in the periphery of your vision, you are likely to turn your head in that direction. A particle of food in the mouth elicits salivation. Exposure to a bright light causes the pupils of the eyes to constrict. Touching a hot stove elicits a quick withdrawal response. Irritation of the respiratory passages causes sneezing and coughing. These and similar examples illustrate that much behavior occurs in response to stimuli. Much of behavior is elicited. In considering the nature of elicited behavior, we begin by describing its simplest form: reflexive behavior.

The Concept of the Reflex

A light puff of air directed at the cornea makes the eye blink. A tap just below the knee causes the leg to kick. A loud noise causes a startle reaction. These are all examples of reflexes. A **reflex** involves two closely related events: an *eliciting stimulus* and a *corresponding response*. Furthermore, the stimulus and response are linked. Presentation of the stimulus is followed by the response, and the response rarely occurs in the absence of the stimulus. For example, dust in the nasal passages elicits sneezing, which does not occur in the absence of nasal irritation.

The specificity of the relation between a stimulus and its accompanying reflex response is a consequence of the organization of the nervous system. In vertebrates (including humans), simple reflexes are typically mediated by three neurons, as illustrated in Figure 2.1. The environmental stimulus for a reflex activates a **sensory neuron** (also called **afferent neuron**), which transmits the sensory message to the spinal cord. Here, the neural impulses are relayed to the **motor neuron** (also called **efferent neuron**), which activates the muscles involved in the reflex response.

FIGURE 2.1 Neural organization of simple reflexes. The environmental stimulus for a reflex activates a sensory neuron, which transmits the sensory message to the spinal cord. Here, the neural impulses are relayed to an interneuron, which in turn relays the impulses to the motor neuron. The motor neuron activates muscles involved in movement.

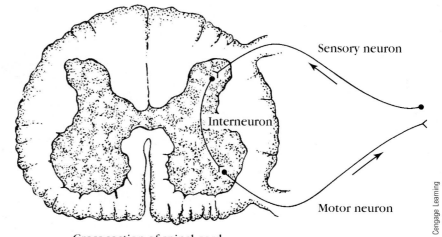

Sensory neuron

Interneuron

Motor neuron

Cross-section of spinal cord

© Cengage Learning

However, sensory and motor neurons rarely communicate directly. Rather, the impulses from one to the other are relayed through at least one **interneuron**. The neural circuitry ensures that particular sensory neurons are connected to a corresponding set of motor neurons. Because of this restricted "wiring," a particular reflex response is elicited only by a restricted set of stimuli. The afferent neuron, interneuron, and efferent neuron together constitute the *reflex arc*.

The reflex arc in vertebrates represents the fewest neural connections necessary for reflex action. However, additional neural structures also may be involved in the elicitation of reflexes. For example, sensory messages may be relayed to the brain, which in turn may modify the reflex reaction in various ways. I will discuss such effects later in the chapter. For now, it is sufficient to keep in mind that the occurrence of even simple reflexes can be influenced by higher nervous system activity.

Reflexes rarely command much attention in psychology, but they are very important because they contribute to the well-being of the organism in many ways. Reflexes keep us alive. In newborn infants, for example, reflexes are essential for feeding. If you touch an infant's cheek with your finger, the baby will reflexively turn his or her head in that direction, with the result that your finger will fall in the baby's mouth. This head-turning reflex no doubt evolved to facilitate finding the nipple. Once your finger has fallen in the newborn's mouth, the baby will begin to suckle. The sensation of an object in the mouth causes reflexive sucking (Figure 2.2). The more closely the object resembles a nipple, the more vigorous will be the suckling response.

Interestingly, successful nursing involves reflex responses not only on the part of the infant but also on the part of the mother. The availability of milk in the breast is determined by the milk-letdown reflex. During early stages of nursing, the milk-letdown reflex is triggered by the infant's suckling behavior. However, after extensive nursing experience, the milk-letdown reflex can be also stimulated by cues that reliably predict the infant's suckling, such as the time of day or the infant's crying when he or she is hungry. Thus, successful nursing involves an exquisite coordination of reflex activity on the part of both the infant and the mother.

Another important reflex, the *respiratory occlusion reflex*, is stimulated by a reduction of air flow to the baby, which can be caused by a cloth covering the baby's face or by the accumulation of mucus in the nasal passages. In response to the reduced air flow,

FIGURE 2.2 Suckling in infants. Suckling is one of the most prominent reflexes in infants.

the baby's first reaction is to pull his or her head back. If this does not remove the eliciting stimulus, the baby will move his or her hands in a face-wiping motion. If this also fails to remove the eliciting stimulus, the baby will begin to cry. Crying involves vigorous expulsion of air, which may be sufficient to remove whatever was obstructing the air passages.

Modal Action Patterns

Simple reflex responses, such as pupillary constriction to a bright light and startle reactions to a brief loud noise, are evident in many species. By contrast, other forms of elicited behavior occur in just one species or in a small group of related species. Sucking in response to an object placed in the mouth is a characteristic of mammalian infants. Herring gull chicks are just as dependent on parental feeding as newborn mammals, but their feeding behavior is very different. When a parent gull returns to the nest from a foraging trip, the chicks peck at the tip of the parent's bill (Figure 2.3). This causes the parent to regurgitate. As the chicks continue to peck, they manage to get the parent's regurgitated food, and this provides their nourishment.

Response sequences, such as those involved in infant feeding, that are typical of a particular species are referred to as **modal action patterns (MAPs)** (Baerends, 1988). Species-typical MAPs have been identified in many aspects of animal behavior, including sexual behavior, territorial defense, aggression, and prey capture. Ring doves, for example, begin their sexual behavior with a courtship interaction that culminates in the selection of a nest site and the cooperative construction of the nest by the male and female. By contrast, in the three-spined stickleback, a small fish, the male first establishes a territory and constructs a nest. Females that enter the territory after the nest has been built are then courted and induced to lay their eggs in the nest. Once a female has deposited her eggs, she is chased away, leaving the male stickleback to care for and defend the eggs until the offspring hatch.

G. P. Baerends

FIGURE 2.3 Feeding of herring gull chicks. The chicks peck a red patch near the tip of the parent's bill, causing the parent to regurgitate food for them.

An important feature of MAPs is that the threshold for eliciting such activities varies (Camhi, 1984; Baerends, 1988). The same stimulus can have widely different effects depending on the physiological state of the animal and its recent actions. A male stickleback, for example, will not court a female who is ready to lay eggs until he has completed building his nest. And, after the female has deposited her eggs, the male will chase her away rather than court her as he did earlier. Furthermore, these sexual and territorial responses will only occur when environmental cues induce physiological changes that are characteristic of the breeding season in both males and females.

Eliciting Stimuli for Modal Action Patterns

The eliciting stimulus is fairly easy to identify in the case of a simple reflex, such as infant suckling. The stimulus responsible for an MAP can be more difficult to isolate if the response occurs in the course of complex social interactions. For example, let us consider again the feeding of a herring gull chick. To get fed, the chick has to peck the parent's beak to stimulate the parent to regurgitate food. But exactly what stimulates the chick's pecking response?

Pecking by the chicks may be elicited by the color, shape, or length of the parent's bill, the noises the parent makes, the head movements of the parent, or all of these in combination. To isolate which of these stimuli elicits pecking, Tinbergen and Perdeck (1950) tested chicks with various artificial models instead of live adult gulls. From this research, they concluded that the eliciting stimulus had to be a long, thin, moving object that was pointed downward and had a contrasting red patch near the tip. The yellow color of the parent's bill, the shape and coloration of the parent's head, and the noises the parent made were all not required for eliciting pecking in the gull chicks. The few essential features are called, collectively, the **sign stimulus**, or **releasing stimulus**, for pecking on the part of the chicks. Once a sign stimulus has been identified, it can be exaggerated to elicit an especially vigorous response. Such an exaggerated sign stimulus is called a **supernormal stimulus**. Eating behavior, for example, is elicited by the taste of the food in the mouth. Something that tastes sweet and is high in fat content is especially effective in encouraging eating. Thus, one can create a supernormal stimulus for eating by adding sugar and fat. This is well known in the fast-food industry. Although sign stimuli were originally identified in studies with nonhuman subjects, sign stimuli also play a major role in the control of human behavior (Barrett, 2010).

With troops returning from Iraq, post-traumatic stress disorder (PTSD) and fear and anxiety attendant to trauma are frequently in the news. Better understanding of PTSD requires knowledge about how people react to danger and how they learn from those experiences (Kirmayer, Lemelson, & Barad, 2007). Responding effectively to danger has been critical in the evolutionary history of all animals, including human beings. Individuals who did not respond effectively to danger succumbed to the assault and did not pass their genes on to future generations. Therefore, traumatic events have come to elicit strong defensive MAPs. Vestiges of this evolutionary history are evident in laboratory studies showing that both children and adults detect snakes faster than flowers, frogs, or other nonthreatening stimuli (e.g., LoBue & DeLoache, 2010, 2011). Early components of the defensive action pattern include the eyeblink reflex and the startle response. Because of their importance in defensive behavior, we will discuss these reflexes later in this chapter and subsequent chapters.

Sign stimuli and supernormal stimuli also have a major role in social and sexual behavior. Copulatory behavior involves a complex sequence of motor responses that have to be elaborately coordinated with the behavior of one's sexual partner. The MAPs involved in sexual arousal and copulation are elicited by visual, olfactory, tactile, and other types of sign stimuli that are specific to each species. Visual, tactile, and olfactory stimuli are important in human social and sexual interactions as well. The cosmetic and perfume industries are successful because they take advantage of the sign stimuli that elicit human social attraction and affiliation and enhance these stimuli. Women put rouge on their lips rather than on their ears because only rouge on the lips enhances the natural sign stimulus for human social attraction. Plastic surgery to enhance the breasts and lips are also effective because they enhance naturally occurring sign stimuli for human social behavior.

The studies of learning that we will be describing in this book are based primarily on MAPs involved in eating, drinking, sexual behavior, and defensive behavior.

BOX 2.1

Learning versus Instinct

Because MAPs occur in a similar fashion among members of a given species, they include activities that are informally characterized as *instinctive*. Historically, instinctive behaviors were assumed to be determined primarily by the genetic and evolutionary history of a species, whereas learned behaviors were assumed to be acquired during the lifetime of the organism through its interactions with its environment. This distinction is similar to the distinction between nativism and empiricism pursued by Descartes and the British empiricists. The innate versus learned distinction also remains in current folk biology (Bateson & Mameli, 2007), but it is no longer tenable scientifically.

Scientists no longer categorize behavior as instinctive versus learned for two major reasons (Domjan, 2012). First, the fact that all members of a species exhibit the same sexual or feeding behaviors does not mean that these behaviors are inherited rather than learned. Similar behaviors among all members of a species may reflect similar learning experiences. As the ethologist G. P. Baerends (1988) wrote, "Learning processes in many variations are tools, so to speak, that can be used in the building of some segments in the species-specific behavior organization" (p. 801).

Second, the historical distinction between learning and instinct was based on an antiquated conception of how genes determine behavior. Genes do not produce behavioral end points directly in the absence of environmental or experiential input. Rather, recent research has unveiled numerous epigenetic processes that determine the circumstances under which DNA is transcribed and expressed. It is only through these epigenetic processes, which often involve experiential and environmental inputs, that DNA can produce particular behavioral traits (e.g., Champagne, 2010).

The Sequential Organization of Behavior

Responses do not occur in isolation of one another. Rather, individual actions are organized into functionally effective behavior sequences. To obtain food, for example, a squirrel first has to look around for potential food sources, such as a pecan tree with nuts. It then has to climb the tree and reach one of the nuts. After obtaining the nut, it has to crack the shell, extract the meat, and chew and swallow it. All motivated behavior, whether it is foraging for food, finding a potential mate, defending a territory, or feeding one's young, involves systematically organized sequences of actions. Ethologists called early components of a behavior sequence **appetitive behavior** and the end components **consummatory behavior** (Craig, 1918). The term *consummatory* was meant to convey the idea of *consummation* or *completion* of a species' typical response sequence. In contrast, appetitive responses occur early in a behavior sequence and serve to bring the organism into contact with the stimuli that will release the consummatory behavior.

Photoshot

Nikolaas Tinbergen

Chewing and swallowing are responses that complete activities involved in foraging for food. Hitting and biting an opponent are actions that consummate defensive behavior. Copulatory responses serve to complete the courtship and sexual behavior sequence. In general, consummatory responses are highly stereotyped species-typical behaviors that have specific eliciting or releasing stimuli. In contrast, appetitive behaviors are more variable and can take a variety of different forms depending on the situation (Tinbergen, 1951). In getting to a pecan tree, for example, a squirrel can run up one side or the other or jump from a neighboring tree. These are all possible appetitive responses leading up to actually eating the pecan nut. However, once the squirrel is ready to put the pecan meat in its mouth, the chewing and swallowing responses that it makes are fairly stereotyped.

As is evident from the varieties of ethnic cuisine, people of different cultures have many different ways of preparing food (appetitive behavior), but they all pretty much chew and swallow the same way (consummatory behavior). Actions that are considered to be rude and threatening (appetitive defensive responses) also differ from one culture to another. But people hit and hurt one another (consummatory defensive behavior) in much the same way regardless of culture. Consummatory responses tend to be species-typical MAPs. In contrast, appetitive behaviors are more variable and more apt to be shaped by learning.

The sequential organization of naturally occurring behavior is of considerable importance to scientists interested in learning because learning effects often depend on which component of the behavior sequence is being modified. As I will describe in later chapters, the outcomes of Pavlovian and instrumental conditioning depend on how these learning procedures modify the natural sequence of an organism's behavior. Learning theorists are becoming increasingly aware of the importance of considering natural behavior sequences and have expanded on the appetitive/consummatory distinction made by early ethologists.

In considering how animals obtain food, for example, it is now common to characterize the foraging response sequence as starting with a ***general search mode***, followed by a ***focal search mode***, and ending with a ***food handling and ingestion mode***. Thus, in modern learning theory, the appetitive response category has been subdivided into general search and focal search categories (e.g., Timberlake, 2001). General search responses occur when the animal does not yet know where to look for food. Before a squirrel has identified a pecan tree with ripe nuts, it will move around looking for potential sources of food. General search responses are not spatially localized. Once the squirrel has found a pecan tree, however, it will switch to the focal search mode and begin to search for ripe nuts only in that tree. Thus, focal search behavior is characterized by greater spatial specificity than general search. Once focal search behavior has led to a pecan ripe for picking, the squirrel's behavior changes to the food handling and ingestion mode (consummatory behavior).

Effects of Repeated Stimulation

A common assumption is that an elicited response, particularly a simple reflex response, will automatically occur the same way each time the eliciting stimulus is presented. This is exactly what Descartes thought. In his view, reflexive behavior was unintelligent in the sense that it was automatic and invariant. According to Descartes, each occurrence of the eliciting stimulus will produce the same reflex reaction because in his conception the energy of the eliciting stimulus was transferred to the motor response through a direct physical connection. If the eliciting stimulus remained the same, the elicited response would also be the same.

Contrary to Descartes, elicited behavior is not invariant. In fact, one of the most impressive features of elicited behavior (and one reason we are spending so much time discussing it) is that elicited behavior is readily subject to modification through experience. Elicited behavior can either decrease or increase through the activation of habituation and sensitization mechanisms. Because these are some of the simplest and most basic forms of learning, we will consider them next.

Salivation and Hedonic Ratings of Taste in People

Habituation plays a major role in how we respond to the foods we eat (Epstein et al., 2009). The taste of food elicits salivation as a reflex response. This occurs as readily in people as in Pavlov's dogs. In one study, salivation was measured in eight women in response to the taste of either lemon juice or lime juice (Epstein et al., 1992). A small amount of one of the flavors (.03 ml) was placed on the participant's tongue on each of 10 trials. The participant was asked to rate how much she liked the taste on each trial, and salivation to each taste presentation was also measured. The results are summarized in Figure 2.4.

FIGURE 2.4 Salivation and ratings of pleasantness in response to a taste stimulus (lime or lemon) repeatedly presented to women on Trials 1 through 10. The alternate taste was presented on Trial 11, causing a substantial recovery in responding (Based on Epstein, Rodefer, Wisniewski & Caggiula, 1992).

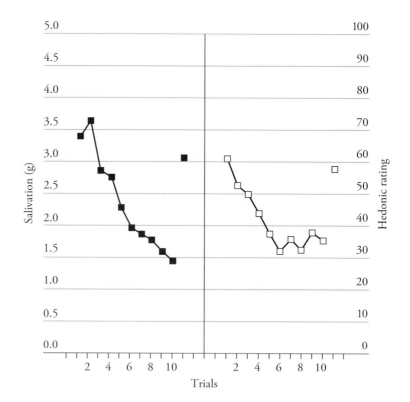

Salivation in response to the taste increased slightly from Trial 1 to Trial 2, but from Trial 2 to Trial 10, responding systematically decreased. Interestingly, a similar decrease was observed in hedonic ratings of the taste. The flavor became less pleasant as it was repeatedly encountered. On Trial 11, the taste was changed (to lime for participants who had been exposed to lemon, and to lemon for participants who had been previously exposed to lime). This produced a dramatic recovery in both the salivary reflex and the hedonic rating. (For similar results in a study with children, see Epstein et al., 2003.)

The results presented in Figure 2.4 are relatively simple but tell us a number of important things about the plasticity of elicited behavior. First, and most obviously, they tell us that elicited behavior is not invariant across repetitions of the eliciting stimulus. Both salivation and hedonic ratings decreased with repeated trials. In the case of salivation, the ultimate decline in responding was preceded by a brief increase from Trial 1 to Trial 2. The decline in responding that occurs with repeated presentation of a stimulus is called a **habituation effect**. Habituation is a prominent feature of elicited behavior that is evident in virtually all species and situations (Rankin et al., 2009).

Another prominent feature of the results presented in Figure 2.4 is that the decrease in responding was specific to the habituated stimulus. Individuals habituated to the taste of lemon showed invigorated responding when tested with the taste of lime at the end of the experiment (and vice versa). This recovery occurred in both the salivary response to the taste as well as the hedonic response and illustrates one of the cardinal properties of habituation, namely, that habituation is *stimulus specific*.

The stimulus specificity feature means that habituation can be easily reversed by changing the stimulus. Consider what this means for eating. As you take repeated bites of the same food, your interest in the food declines, and at some point this will cause you to stop eating. However, if the flavor of the food is changed, the habituation effect will be gone and your interest in eating will return. Thus, you are likely to eat more if you are eating food with varied flavors than if your meal consists of one flavor. It is hard to resist going back to a buffet table given the variety of flavors that are offered, but rejecting a second helping of mashed potatoes is easy if the second helping tastes the same as the first.

Another major variable that influences the rate of taste habituation is attention to the taste stimulus. In a fascinating study, children were tested for habituation to a taste stimulus while they were working on a problem that required their close attention. In another condition, either no distracting task was given or the task was so easy that it did not require much attention. Interestingly, if the children's attention was diverted from the taste presentations, they showed much less habituation to the flavor (Epstein et al., 2005). This is a very important finding because it helps us understand why food tastes better and why people eat more if they are having dinner with friends or are eating while watching TV. Having one's attention directed to nonfood cues keeps the food from becoming uninteresting through habituation.

The above examples illustrate some of the ways in which habituation can influence food intake and weight gain. As it turns out, obesity itself may influence taste habituation. In an interesting study, habituation to the taste of lemon yogurt was examined in women who were either obese or of normal weight (Epstein, Paluch, & Coleman, 1996). Salivary responding showed the usual habituation effect in women of normal weight. In contrast, overweight women did not show the standard habituation effect but continued their vigorous response to the yogurt across all taste trials (Figure 2.5). This is a remarkable finding and suggests that obesity may be at least in part a disorder of habituation. (For similar findings with children, see Epstein et al., 2008.)

FIGURE 2.5 Change in salivation from baseline levels in response to the taste of lemon yogurt in obese and normal weight women in blocks of 2 trials.

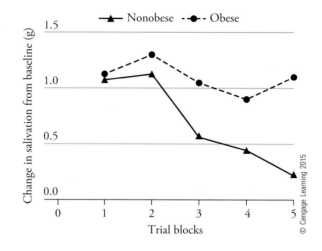

Visual Attention in Human Infants

Human infants have a lot to learn about the world. One way they obtain information is by looking at things. Visual cues elicit a looking response, which can be measured by how long the infant keeps his or her eyes on an object before shifting gaze elsewhere (Figure 2.6).

In one study of visual attention (Bashinski, Werner, & Rudy, 1985), four-month-old infants were assigned to one of two groups, and each group was tested with a different visual stimulus. The stimuli are shown in the right panel of Figure 2.7. Both were checkerboard patterns, but one had 4 squares on each side (the 4 × 4 stimulus), whereas the other had 12 squares on each side (the 12 × 12 stimulus). Each stimulus presentation lasted 10 seconds, and the stimuli were presented eight times with a 10-second interval between trials.

Both stimuli elicited visual attention initially, with the babies spending an average of about 5.5 seconds looking at the stimuli. With repeated presentations of the 4 × 4 stimulus, visual attention progressively decreased, showing a *habituation effect*. By contrast, the 12 × 12 stimulus produced an initial *sensitization effect*, evident in increased looking during the second trial as compared to the first. But, after that, visual attention to the 12 × 12 stimulus also habituated.

FIGURE 2.6 Experimental setup for the study of visual attention in infants. The infant is seated in front of a screen that is used to present various visual stimuli. How long the infant looks at the display before diverting his or her gaze elsewhere is measured in each trial.

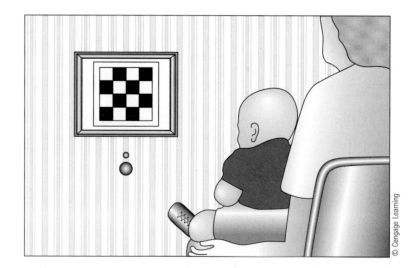

FIGURE 2.7 How long infants spent looking at a visual stimulus during successive trials. For one group, the stimulus consisted of a 4 × 4 checkerboard pattern. For a second group, the stimulus consisted of a 12 × 12 checkerboard pattern. The stimuli are illustrated to the right of the results. (Based on "Determinants of Infant Visual Attention: Evidence for a Two-Process Theory," by H. Bashinski, J. Werner, and J. Rudy, *Journal of Experimental Child Psychology*, 39, pp. 580–598.)

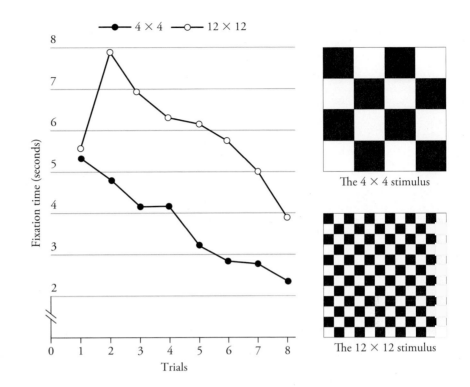

The 4 × 4 stimulus

The 12 × 12 stimulus

This relatively simple experiment tells us a great deal both about visual attention and about habituation and sensitization. The results show that visual attention elicited by a novel stimulus changes as babies gain familiarity with the stimulus. The nature of the change is determined by the nature of the stimulus. With a relatively simple 4 × 4 pattern, only a progressive habituation effect occurs. With a more complex 12 × 12 pattern, a transient sensitization occurs, followed by habituation. Thus, whether or not sensitization is observed depends on the complexity of the stimulus. With both stimuli, the infants eventually showed less interest as they became more familiar with the stimulus. Other studies have shown that interest in what appeared on the screen would have recovered if a new or different stimulus had been presented after the familiarization phase, just as we saw in the taste habituation study described earlier.

Infants cannot tell us in words how they view or think about things. Scientists are therefore forced to use behavioral techniques to study infant perception and cognition. The visual attention task can provide information about visual acuity. For example, from the data in Figure 2.7, we may conclude that these infants were able to distinguish the two different checkerboard patterns. This type of habituation procedure has also been used to study a wide range of other, more complicated questions about infant cognition and perception (see Colombo & Mitchell, 2009, for a review). One recent study, for example, examined how newborn infants perceive human faces.

Faces provide a great deal of information that is critical in interpersonal interactions. People are experts at recognizing and remembering faces. How about newborn infants 1–3 days of age? Recognizing a face requires not only remembering its features but also recognizing the face when it is turned a bit to one side or the other. Do newborns know a face is the same even if it is turned a bit to one side? How could we answer this question considering that newborn infants cannot speak or do much?

Turati, Bulf, and Simion (2008) adapted the visual attention task to study face perception. Newborn infants less than 3 days of age were first familiarized with a photograph of a face presented either in a full-face pose or turned slightly to one side (Figure 2.8). To avoid having the infants use cues related to the model's hair, the model's hair was blocked out with Photoshop. After the infants became habituated to looking at the training stimulus, they were tested with two different photos. Both the test faces were in a different orientation from the training stimulus. One of the test faces was of the same person as the infant saw during the habituation phase; the second face was of a different person. If the infant recognized the original face, the baby was expected to spend less time looking at that than the new face. When presented with the two test faces, the infant spent less time looking at the face of the familiar person than the face of the novel person. This shows that the newborns could tell that the two faces were different. In addition, the results show that the newborns could tell which face they had seen before, even though the face appeared in a new orientation during the test trial. This is a truly remarkable feat of learning and memory considering that faces are complex stimuli and the infants were less than 3 days old. This is just one example of how the behavioral techniques described in this book can be used to study cognition in nonverbal organisms.

The visual attention paradigm has become a prominent tool in the study of infant perception as well as more complex forms of cognition. For example, it has been used to study whether infants are capable of rudimentary mathematical operations, reasoning about the laws of the physical world, discriminating between drawings of objects that are physically possible versus ones that are physically not possible, and discriminating between the properties of liquids and solids (Baillargeon, 2008; Hespos, Ferry, & Rips, 2009; McCrink & Wynn, 2007; Shuwairi, Albert, & Johnson, 2007). Some of this type of research has stimulated spirited debate about the extent to which the perceptual properties of the stimuli rather than their meaning within the knowledge structure of the infant controls visual attention (Schöner & Thelen, 2006). Regardless of how this debate is resolved, there is no doubt that the visual attention paradigm has provided a wealth of information about infant cognition at ages that long precede the acquisition of language.

FIGURE 2.8 Photographs of faces used by Turati and colleagues (2008) in tests of visual attention in newborn infants. Infants were habituated to photos of a face in one of two orientations. They were then tested with photos of faces in a different orientation, but one of the test faces was of the same person as the photo used during habituation. The novel face reliably elicited greater visual attention during the test.

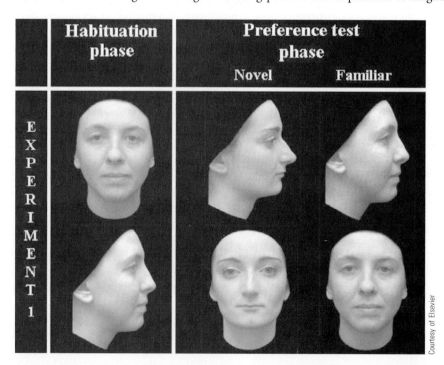

Courtesy of Elsevier

The Startle Response

As I mentioned earlier, the startle response is part of an organism's defensive reaction to potential or actual attack. If someone unexpectedly blows a whistle behind your back, you are likely to jump. This is the startle response. It consists of a sudden jump and tensing of the muscles of the upper part of the body, usually involving the raising of the shoulders and pulling the head into the shoulders. It also includes blinking of the eyes. The startle reaction can be measured by placing the organism on a surface with a pressure sensor. The startle reaction briefly increases pressure against the floor.

The startle response has been investigated extensively because of its role in fear and defensive behavior. Scientists interested in the neurobiology of fear and in the development of drugs that help alleviate fear have found the startle response to be a highly effective measure. Many of the original studies of the startle response were done with laboratory rats and mice (e.g., Halberstandt & Geyer, 2009). However, in recent years the technique has also been developed for use with rhesus monkeys (Davis et al., 2008).

Figure 2.9 shows a diagram of a *stabilimeter chamber* used to measure the startle response in rats. When startled, the rat jumps, and when it comes down, it puts extra pressure on the floor of the chamber. This activates the pressure sensor under the chamber. Changes in pressure are used as indicators of the vigor of the startle reaction.

The startle reaction is usually elicited in experiments with laboratory rats by a brief loud sound. In one experiment (Leaton, 1976), the startle stimulus was a loud, high-pitched tone presented for 2 seconds. The animals were first allowed to get used to the experimental chamber without any tone presentations. Each rat then received a single tone presentation once a day for 11 days. In the next phase of the experiment, the tones were presented much more frequently (every 3 seconds) for a total of 300 trials. Finally, the animals were given a single tone presentation on each of the next three days, as in the beginning of the experiment.

Figure 2.10 shows the results. The most intense startle reaction was observed the first time the tone was presented. Progressively less intense reactions occurred during the next 10 days. Because the animals received only one tone presentation every 24 hours in this phase, the progressive decrements in responding indicated that the habituating effects of the stimulus presentations persisted throughout the 11-day period.

M. Davis

FIGURE 2.9 Stabilimeter apparatus to measure the startle response of rats. A small chamber rests on a pressure sensor. Sudden movements of the rat are detected by the pressure sensor and recorded on a computer.

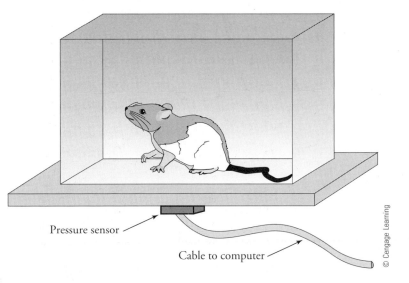

Pressure sensor

Cable to computer

FIGURE 2.10 Startle response of rats to a tone presented once a day in Phase 1, every 3 seconds in Phase 2, and once a day in Phase 3. (Based on "Long-Term Retention of the Habituation of Lick Suppression and Startle Response Produced by a Single Auditory Stiumuls," by R.N. Leaton, 1976, *Journal of Experimental Psychology: Animal Behavior Processes*, 2, pp. 248–259.)

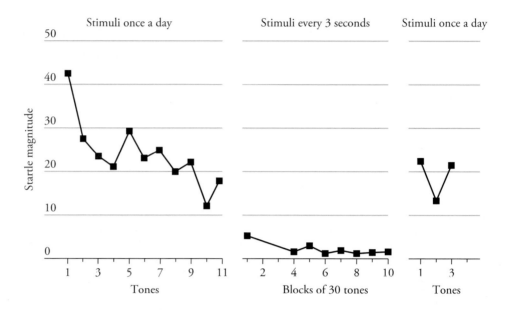

It is worth noting, though, that this long-term habituation did not result in complete loss of the startle reflex. Even on the 11th day, the animals still reacted a little.

By contrast, startle reactions quickly ceased when the tone presentations occurred every 3 seconds in Phase 2 of the experiment. However, this dramatic loss of responsiveness was only temporary. In Phase 3 of the experiment, when trials were again administered just once each day, the startle response recovered to the level of the 11th day of the experiment. This recovery, known as **spontaneous recovery**, occurred simply because the tone had not been presented for a long time (24 hours).

This experiment illustrates that two different forms of habituation occur depending on the timing of the stimulus presentations. If the stimuli are presented widely spaced in time, a long-term habituation effect occurs, which persists for 24 hours or longer. In contrast, if the stimuli are presented very closely in time together (every 3 seconds in this experiment), a short-term habituation effect occurs. The short-term habituation effect is identified by spontaneous recovery of responding following a period without stimulation. Spontaneous recovery is one of the defining features of habituation (Rankin et al., 2009).

Repeated presentations of a stimulus do not always result in both long-term and short-term habituation effects. With the spinal leg-flexion reflex in cats, for example, only the short-term habituation effect is observed (Thompson & Spencer, 1966). In such cases, spontaneous recovery completely restores the animal's reaction to the eliciting stimulus if a long enough period of rest is provided after habituation. By contrast, spontaneous recovery is never complete in situations that involve long-term habituation, as in Leaton's experiment. As Figure 2.10 indicates, the startle response was restored to some extent in the last phase of the experiment, but even then the rats did not react as vigorously to the tone as they had the first time it was presented.

Sensitization and the Modulation of Elicited Behavior

Consider your reaction when someone walks up behind you and taps you on the shoulder. If you are in a supermarket, you will be mildly startled and will turn toward the side where you were tapped. Orienting toward a tactile stimulus is a common elicited response. Being tapped on the shoulder is not a big deal if you are in a supermarket. However, if you are walking in a dark alley at night in a dangerous part of town, being tapped on the shoulder could be a very scary experience and will no doubt elicit a much more vigorous reaction. In a scary place, being touched could mean that you are about to be attacked. Generally speaking, if you are already aroused, the same eliciting stimulus will trigger a much stronger reaction. This is called a **sensitization effect**.

It is easier to study sensitization of the startle response in the laboratory than in a dark alley. In a classic study, Davis (1974), examined sensitization of the startle response of laboratory rats to a brief (90 millisecond) loud tone (110 decibels [dB], 4,000 cycles per second [cps]). Two groups of rats were tested. Each group received 100 trials presented at 30-second intervals. In addition, a noise generator provided background noise that sounded something like a water fall. For one group, the background noise was relatively quiet (60 dB); for the other, the background noise was rather loud (80 dB) but of lower intensity than the brief, startle-eliciting tone.

The results of the experiment are shown in Figure 2.11. Repeated presentations of the eliciting stimulus (the 4,000 cps tone) did not always produce the same response. For rats tested with soft background noise (60 dB), repetitions of the tone resulted in habituation of the startle reaction. By contrast, when the background noise was loud (80 dB), repetitions of the tone elicited progressively more vigorous startle responses. This reflects a gradual buildup of sensitization created by the loud background.

Reflex responses are sensitized when the organism becomes aroused for some reason. Arousal intensifies our experiences, whether those experiences are pleasant or unpleasant. As is well known in the entertainment industry, introducing loud noise is a relatively simple way to create arousal. Live performances of rock bands are so loud that band members suffer hearing loss if they don't wear earplugs. The music does not have to be so loud for everyone to hear it. The main purpose of the high volume is to create arousal and excitement. Turning a knob on an amplifier is a simple way to increase excitement. Making something loud is also a common device for increasing the enjoyment of movies, circus acts, car races, and football games and is effective because of the phenomenon of sensitization.

Sensitization also plays a major role in sexual behavior. A major component of sexual behavior involves reacting to tactile cues. Consider the tactile cues of a caress or a kiss. The reaction to the same physical caress or kiss is totally different if you are touching

FIGURE 2.11

Magnitude of the startle response of rats to successive presentations of a tone with a background noise of 60 or 80 dB. (Based on "Sensitization of the Rat Startle Response by Noise," by M. Davis, 1974, *Journal of Comparative and Physiological Psychology,* 87, pp. 571–581.)

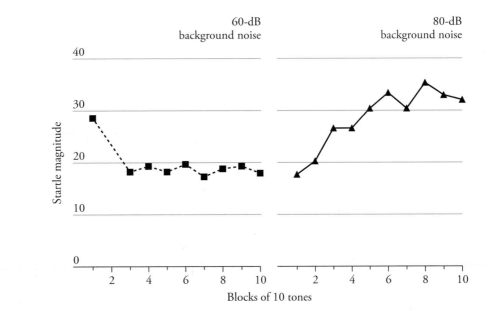

your grandmother than if you are touching your romantic partner. The difference reflects sensitization and arousal. In a recent study of this issue, heterosexual males were tested for their sensitivity to a tactile stimulus presented to the right index finger (Jiao, Knight, Weerakoon, & Turman, 2007) before and after watching an erotic movie that was intended to increase their sexual arousal. Tactile sensitivity was significantly increased by the erotic movie. Watching a nonerotic movie did not produce the same effect.

Sensitization has been examined most extensively in the defensive behavior system. Numerous studies have shown that fear potentiates the startle response (Davis et al., 2008). Startle can be measured using a stabilimeter similar to that shown in Figure 2.9, which measures the reaction of the entire body. A simpler procedure, particularly with human participants, is to measure the eyeblink response. The eyeblink is an early component of the startle response and can be elicited in people by directing a brief puff of air toward the eye.

In one study, using the eyeblink startle measure (Bradley, Moulder, & Lang, 2005), college students served as participants and were shown examples of pleasant and unpleasant pictures. To induce fear, one group of students was told that they could get shocked at some point when they saw the pleasant pictures but not when they saw the unpleasant pictures. The second group of participants received a shock threat associated with the unpleasant pictures but not the pleasant pictures. Shock was never delivered to any of the participants, but to make the threat credible, they were fitted with shock electrodes. To measure fear-potentiated startle, the magnitude of the eyeblink response to a puff of air was measured during presentation of the pictures.

The results are shown in Figure 2.12. Let us first consider the startle reaction during presentations of the pleasant pictures. If the pleasant pictures were associated with shock threat, the eyeblink response was substantially greater than if the pictures were safe. This represents the fear-potentiated startle effect. The results with the unpleasant pictures were a bit different. With the unpleasant pictures, the startle response was elevated whether or not the pictures were associated with the threat of shock. This suggests that

FIGURE 2.12 Magnitude of the eyeblink response of college students to pleasant and unpleasant pictures that signaled shock or were safe. (Based on Bradley, Moulder, & Lang, 2005.)

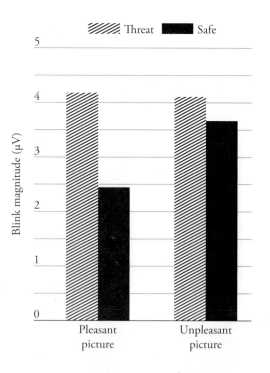

the unpleasant pictures were sufficiently discomforting to sensitize the defensive blink response independent of any shock threat.

Fear-potentiated startle is just one example of a broader category of findings showing that the magnitude of the startle reaction can be altered by emotional states. Because of this, the startle response is a useful technique for studying psychological disorders that have a strong emotional component, such as panic and anxiety disorders and depression (Vaidyanathan, Patrick, & Cuthbert, 2009). In fact, fear-potentiated startle is a better measure of fear in individuals with PTSD than the more familiar galvanic skin response (GSR) measure (Glover et al., 2011).

Adaptiveness and Pervasiveness of Habituation and Sensitization

Organisms are constantly experiencing a host of stimuli. Consider the act of sitting at your desk. Even such a simple situation involves a myriad of sensations. You are exposed to the color, texture, and brightness of the paint on the walls; the sounds of the air-conditioning system; noises from other rooms; odors in the air; the color and texture of the desk; the tactile sensations of the chair against your legs, seat, and back; and so on. If you were to respond to all of these stimuli, your behavior would be disorganized and chaotic. Habituation and sensitization effects help sort out what stimuli to ignore and what to respond to. Habituation and sensitization effects are the end products of processes that help prioritize and focus behavior in the buzzing and booming world of stimuli that organisms live in.

There are numerous instances of habituation and sensitization in common human experience (Simons, 1996). Consider a grandfather clock. Most people who own such a clock do not notice each time it chimes. They have completely habituated to the clock's sounds. In fact, they are more likely to notice when the clock misses a scheduled chime. This is unfortunate because they may have purchased the clock because they liked its sound. People who live on a busy street or near a railroad track often become entirely habituated to the noises that frequently intrude into their homes. Visitors who have not heard the sounds as often are much more likely to be bothered by them.

Driving a car involves exposure to a large array of complex visual and auditory stimuli. In becoming an experienced driver, a person habituates to the numerous stimuli that are irrelevant to driving, such as details of the color and texture of the road, the kind of telephone poles that line the sides of the highway, tactile sensations of the steering wheel, and routine noises from the engine. Habituation to irrelevant cues is particularly prominent during long driving trips. On a long drive, you are likely to become oblivious to all kinds of stimuli on the road, which may make you drowsy and inattentive. If you come across an accident or arrive in a new town, you are likely to "wake up" and again pay attention to various things that you had been ignoring. Passing a bad accident or coming to a new town is arousing and sensitizes orienting responses that were previously habituated.

Habituation also determines how much we enjoy something. In his popular book, *Stumbling on Happiness*, Daniel Gilbert (2006) noted that "Among life's cruelest truths is this one: Wonderful things are especially wonderful the first time they happen, but their wonderfulness wanes with repetition" (p. 130). He went on to write, "When we have an experience—hearing a particular sonata, making love with a particular person, watching the sun set from a particular window with a particular person—on successive occasions, we quickly begin to adapt to it, and the experience yields less pleasure each time" (p. 130).

Habituation and sensitization effects can occur in any situation that involves repeated exposures to a stimulus. Therefore, an appreciation of habituation and sensitization effects is critical for studies of learning. As I will describe in Chapter 3, habituation and sensitization are of primary concern in the design of control procedures for Pavlovian conditioning. Habituation and sensitization also play a role in operant conditioning (McSweeney & Murphy, 2009).

Habituation Versus Sensory Adaptation and Response Fatigue

The key characteristic of habituation effects is a decline in the response that was initially elicited by a stimulus. However, not all instances in which repetitions of a stimulus result in a response decline represent habituation. To understand alternative sources of response decrement, we need to return to the concept of a reflex. A reflex consists of three components. First, a stimulus activates one of the sense organs, such as the eyes or ears. This generates sensory neural impulses that are relayed to the central nervous system (spinal cord and brain). The second component involves relay of the sensory messages through interneurons to motor nerves. Finally, the neural impulses in motor nerves, in turn, activate the muscles that create the observed response.

Given the three components of a reflex, there are several reasons why an elicited response may fail to occur (Figure 2.13). The response will not be observed if, for some reason, the sense organs become disabled. A person may be temporarily blinded by a bright light, for example, or suffer a temporary hearing loss because of exposure to loud noise. Such decreases in sensitivity are called **sensory adaptation** and are different from habituation. The response also will not occur if the muscles involved become incapacitated by **fatigue**. Sensory adaptation and response fatigue are impediments to responding that are produced outside the nervous system in sense organs and muscles. Therefore, they do not represent habituation.

The terms *habituation* and *sensitization* are limited to neurophysiological changes that hinder or facilitate the transmission of neural impulses from sensory to motor neurons. In habituation, the organism ceases to respond, even though it remains fully capable of sensing the eliciting stimulus and making the muscle movements required for the response. The response fails because of changes that disrupt neurotransmission involving the interneurons.

In studies of habituation, sensory adaptation is ruled out by evidence that *habituation is response specific*. An organism may stop responding to a stimulus in one aspect of its behavior while continuing to respond to the stimulus in other ways. When a teacher makes an announcement while you are concentrating on taking a test, you may look up from your test at first, but only briefly. However, you will continue to listen to the announcement until it is over. Thus, your orienting response habituates quickly, but other attentional responses to the stimulus persist.

FIGURE 2.13 Diagram of a simple reflex. Sensory adaptation occurs in the sense organs, and response fatigue occurs in effector muscles. In contrast, habituation and sensitization occur in the nervous system.

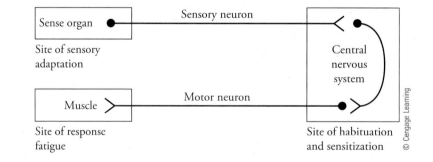

Response fatigue as a cause of habituation is ruled out by evidence that *habituation is stimulus specific*. A habituated response will quickly recover when a new stimulus is introduced. This was illustrated in the taste habituation study summarized in Figure 2.5. After the salivary and hedonic responses habituated during the first 10 trials, presentation of the alternate taste in Trial 11 resulted in a recovery of both response measures. The stimulus specificity of habituation is also key to using the visual attention task to study perception and cognition in preverbal infants. By examining how a stimulus has to be altered to produce recovery of the visual attention response, investigators can figure out what aspects of the habituated stimulus the infants learned about (Figure 2.8).

The Dual-Process Theory of Habituation and Sensitization

Habituation and sensitization effects are changes in behavior or performance. These are outward behavioral manifestations of stimulus presentations. What factors are responsible for such changes? To answer this question, we have to shift our level of analysis from behavior to presumed underlying process or theory. Habituation effects can be satisfactorily explained by a single-factor theory that characterizes how repetitions of a stimulus change the efficacy of that stimulus (e.g., Schöner & Thelen, 2006). However, a second factor has to be introduced to explain why responding is enhanced under conditions of arousal. The dominant explanation of habituation and sensitization remains the dual-process theory of Groves and Thompson (1970; Thompson, 2009).

The dual-process theory assumes that different types of underlying neural processes are responsible for increases and decreases in responsiveness to stimulation. One neural process produces decreases in responsiveness. This is called the **habituation process**. Another produces increases in responsiveness. This is called the **sensitization process**. The habituation and sensitization processes are not mutually exclusive. In fact, often both are activated at the same time. The behavioral outcome or end result that is observed reflects the net effect of the two processes. It is unfortunate that the underlying processes that suppress and facilitate responding have the same names (habituation and sensitization) as the resulting behavioral changes that are observed. One may be tempted to think, for example, that decreased responding, or a habituation effect, is a direct reflection of the habituation process. However, decreased responding may occur under conditions that also involve increased arousal or sensitization, but the arousal may only slow the rate of response decline. In fact, all habituation and sensitization effects are the sum, or net, result of both habituation and sensitization processes. Whether the net result is an increase or a decrease in behavior depends on which underlying process is stronger in a particular situation. The distinction between *effects* and *processes* in habituation and sensitization is analogous to the distinction between *performance* and *learning* discussed in Chapter 1. Effects refer to observable behavior and processes refer to underlying mechanisms.

On the basis of neurophysiological research, Groves and Thompson (1970) suggested that habituation and sensitization processes occur in different parts of the nervous system (see also Thompson, 2009). Habituation processes are assumed to occur in what is called the **S-R system**. This system consists of the shortest neural path that connects the sense organs activated by the eliciting stimulus and the muscles involved in making the elicited response. The S-R system may be viewed as the reflex arc. Each presentation of an eliciting stimulus activates the S-R system and causes some buildup of habituation.

Sensitization processes are assumed to occur in what is called the **state system**. This system consists of parts of the nervous system that determine the organism's general level of responsiveness or readiness to respond. In contrast to the S-R system, which is activated every time an eliciting stimulus occurs, only arousing events activate the state system. The state system is relatively quiescent during sleep, for example. Drugs, such as stimulants or depressants, may alter the functioning of the state system and thereby change responsiveness. The state system is also altered by emotional experiences. For example, the heightened reactivity that accompanies fear is caused by activation of the state system and is the basis for the fear-potentiated startle response (Davis et al., 2008).

Applications of the Dual-Process Theory

The examples of habituation and sensitization (illustrated in the experimental evidence I previously reviewed) can be easily interpreted in terms of the dual-process theory. Repeated exposure to the 4 × 4 checkerboard pattern produced a decrement in visual orientation in infants (Figure 2.7). This presumably occurred because the 4 × 4 stimulus did not create much arousal. Rather, the 4 × 4 stimulus activated primarily the S-R system and, hence, activated primarily the habituation process. The more complex 12 × 12 checkerboard pattern produced a greater level of arousal, activating the state system, and this resulted in the increment in visual attention that occurred after the first presentation of the 12 × 12 pattern. However, the arousal or sensitization process was not strong enough to entirely counteract the effects of habituation. As a result, after a few trials, visual attention also declined in response to the 12 × 12 stimulus.

A different type of application of the dual-process theory is required for the habituation and sensitization effects we noted in the startle reaction of rats (Figure 2.11). When the rats were tested with a relatively quiet background noise (60 dB), there was little to arouse them. Therefore, we can assume that the experimental procedures did not activate the state system. Repeated presentations of the startle-eliciting tone merely activated the S-R system, which resulted in habituation of the startle response.

The opposite outcome occurred when the animals were tested in the presence of a loud background noise (80 dB). In this case, stronger startle reactions occurred to successive presentations of the tone. Because the identical tone was used for both groups, the difference in the results cannot be attributed to the tone. Rather, one must assume that the loud background noise increased arousal or readiness to respond in the second group. This sensitization of the state system was presumably responsible for increasing the startle reaction to the tone in the second group. Activation of the state system was no doubt also responsible for the increased startle responding that occurred when participants were tested under conditions of threat and in the presence of an unpleasant picture (Figure 2.12).

Implications of the Dual-Process Theory

The preceding interpretations of habituation and sensitization effects illustrate several important features of the dual-process theory. Because the habituation process resides in the S-R system, which is activated every time a stimulus elicits a response, habituation is a universal feature of elicited behavior. By contrast, the state system becomes involved only in special circumstances. Some extraneous event, such as intense background noise, may increase the individual's alertness and sensitize the state system. Alternatively, the state system may be sensitized by the repeated presentations of the test stimulus itself if that stimulus is sufficiently intense or excitatory (as occurred with the 12 × 12 checkerboard pattern, as compared with the 4 × 4 pattern). If the arousing stimulus is repeated soon enough so that the second presentation occurs while the organism remains sensitized from the preceding trial, an increase in responding will be observed.

Both the habituation process and the sensitization process are assumed to decay with the passage of time without stimulation. Thus, *spontaneous recovery* occurs with both processes. Spontaneous recovery from both habituation and sensitization serves to return responding to baseline levels (hence the term *recovery*).

Because habituation resides in the S-R circuit, the dual-process theory predicts that *habituation will be stimulus specific*. If after habituation training the eliciting stimulus is changed, the new stimulus will elicit a nonhabituated response because it activates a different S-R circuit. We saw this outcome in the experiment on habituation of salivation and hedonic ratings to a taste (Figure 2.5). After the salivary and affective responses to one taste stimulus (e.g., lime) had substantially habituated (Trials 1–10), the responses showed total recovery when a different taste (lemon) was presented (Trial 11). The stimulus specificity of habituation was also evident in the study of face perception in newborn infants (Figure 2.8). Similar effects occur in common experience. For example, after you have become completely habituated to the sounds of your car engine, your attention to the engine is likely to return if it malfunctions and begins to make new noises.

Unlike habituation, sensitization is not highly stimulus specific. As the fear-potentiated startle phenomenon illustrates, if you become aroused by fear, this will increase your startle response to a puff of air (Figure 2.12) or a burst of noise (Davis et al., 2008). In laboratory rats, pain induced by foot-shock increases the reactivity of the rats to both auditory and visual cues. In contrast, feelings of illness or malaise make rats more reactive or suspicious of eating novel foods. Interestingly, however, shock-induced sensitization appears to be limited to exteroceptive cues, and illness-induced sensitization is limited to gustatory stimuli (Miller & Domjan, 1981). Thus, cutaneous pain and internal malaise seem to activate separate sensitization systems.

BOX 2.2

Learning in an Invertebrate

How does the brain acquire, store, and retrieve information? To answer this question, we need to know how neurons operate and how neural circuits are modified by experience. Studying these issues requires that we delve into the neural machinery to record and manipulate its operations. Naturally, people are not keen on volunteering for such experiments. Therefore, such research has to be conducted using other species.

Much can be learned from the vertebrates (rats, mice) that are typically used in behavioral studies of learning. Yet, at a neural level, even a rat poses technical challenges for a neurobiologist. Therefore, neurobiologists have focused on creatures with simpler nervous systems. Invertebrates are attractive because some of their neurons are very large, and they have far simpler nervous systems. Using this approach, Eric Kandel and

his colleagues have uncovered the mechanisms that mediate some basic learning processes in the marine snail, **Aplysia**. Here, I provide an overview of the mechanisms that underlie habituation and sensitization (for recent reviews, see Hawkins, Kandel, & Bailey, 2006; Kandel et al., 2013).

Aplysia have two wing-like flaps (the parapodium) on their back (dorsal) surface. These flaps cover the gill and other components of the respiratory apparatus (Figure 2.14A). The gill lies under a mantle shelf, and a siphon helps to circulate water across the gill. In the relaxed state, the gill is extended, maximizing chemical exchange across its surface. It is a fragile organ that must be protected. For this reason, nature has given Aplysia a protective gill-withdrawal reflex. This reflex can be elicited by a light touch applied to either the siphon or mantle. In the laboratory, the reflex is often elicited by

a jet of water produced from a Water Pik. While the mechanisms that underlie this reflex can be studied in the intact Aplysia, it is often easier to study the underlying system after the essential components have been removed and placed in a nutrient bath that sustains the tissue (an *in vitro* preparation, Latin from "in glass").

With this simple preparation, it is an easy matter to demonstrate both *habituation* and *sensitization*. Habituation can be produced by repeatedly applying the tactile stimulus to the siphon. With continued exposure, the magnitude of the gill-withdrawal reflex becomes smaller (habituates). Interestingly, this experience has no effect on the magnitude of the gill-withdrawal elicited by touching the mantle shelf. Conversely, if we repeatedly touch the mantle, the withdrawal response observed habituates without affecting the response elicited by touching the siphon.

Continued

BOX 2.2 (continued)

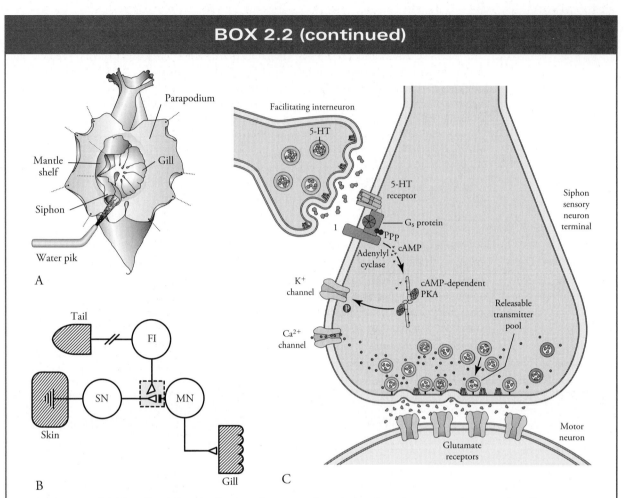

FIGURE 2.14 (A) The gill-withdrawal reflex in *Aplysia*. A touch applied to the siphon or mantle causes the gill to retract (adapted from Kandel et al., 2013). (B) The neural circuit that mediates habituation and sensitization. A touch engages a sensory neuron (SN), which synapses onto a motor neuron (MN) that contributes to gill withdrawal. A shock to the tail activates a facilitatory interneuron (FI) that presynaptically innervates the sensory neuron. The shaded box indicates the region depicted in Panel C (adapted from Dudai, 1989). (C) A neurochemical pathway that contributes to neural sensitization. The release of serotonin from the facilitating interneuron engages serotonin receptors on the sensory neuron. This activates a G-protein and adenylyl cyclase, leading to the production of cAMP and engaging a cAMP-dependent kinase (protein kinase A [PKA]). PKA alters a subset of the K^+ channels by adding a phosphate group (phosphorylation), which reduces the outward flow of K^+. This prolongs the action potential, augmenting the flow of Ca^{++} into the cell and transmitter release (adapted from Kandel et al., 2013).

A modification in one stimulus-response (S-R) pathway has no effect on the response vigor in the other.

In vertebrates, a painful shock engages a mechanism that generally sensitizes behavior, augmenting a variety of response systems including those that generate a startle response (Davis, 1997). A similar effect can be demonstrated in Aplysia. If a shock stimulus is applied to the tail, it sensitizes the gill-withdrawal

response elicited by touching the mantle or siphon (Walters, 1994). This is a general effect that augments behavioral reactivity in both the mantle and siphon circuits.

The essential neural components that underlie gill-withdrawal in response to a siphon touch are illustrated in Figure 2.14B. A similar diagram could be drawn for the neurons that underlie the gill-withdrawal elicited by touching the mantle.

Touching the siphon skin engages a mechanical receptor that is coupled to a sensory neuron. Just one receptor is illustrated here, but additional receptors and neurons innervate adjoining regions of the siphon skin. The degree to which a particular receptor is engaged will depend on its proximity to the locus of stimulation, being greatest at the center of stimulation and weakening as distance increases. This yields the neural

Continued

BOX 2.2 (continued)

equivalent to a generalization gradient, with the maximum activity being produced by the neuron that provides the primary innervation for the receptive field stimulated.

The mechanical receptors that detect a touch engage a response within the dendrites of the sensory neuron. This neural response is conveyed to the cell body (soma) and down a neural projection, the *axon*, to the motor neuron. The sensory neuron is the *presynaptic cell*. The motor neuron is the postsynaptic cell. The motor neuron is engaged by the release of a chemical (*neurotransmitter*) from the sensory neuron. The motor neuron, in turn, carries the signal to the muscles that produce the gill-withdrawal response. Here, the release of the neurotransmitter activates muscle fibers that cause the gill to retract.

A sensitizing tail-shock engages neurons that activate a type of neuron known as the *facilitatory interneuron*. As shown in the figure, the facilitatory interneuron impinges upon the end of the presynaptic sensory neuron. In more technical terms, the facilitatory interneuron presynaptically innervates the sensory neuron. Because of this, the facilitatory interneuron can alter the operation of the sensory neuron.

The magnitude of the gill-withdrawal response depends on the amount of neurotransmitter released from the motor neurons. The more that is released, the stronger is the response. Similarly, the probability that a response will be engaged in the motor neuron, and the number of motor neurons that are engaged, depends on the amount of

neurotransmitter released from the sensory neuron. Increasing the amount released will usually enhance the motor neuron response and the gill-withdrawal response.

Research has shown that with repeated stimulations of the sensory neuron there is no change in the action potential generated within the sensory neuron, but less transmitter is released, producing the behavioral phenomenon of habituation (Kandel et al., 2013). When an action potential arrives at the synapse, it causes calcium channels on the membrane surface to open, which allows the positively charged ion calcium (Ca^{++}) to flow into the cell (Figure 1.6C). This in turn triggers intracellular events that initiate transmitter release. Habituation inactivates some of the Ca^{++} channels, which reduces the amount of Ca^{++} that enters the cell. As a result, less transmitter is released and a less vigorous motor response occurs.

Sensitization engages the facilitatory interneuron, which produces a change within the sensory neuron that causes it to release more neurotransmitter. Because more transmitter is released, the motor neurons are engaged to a greater extent, and the gill-withdrawal response is more vigorous. The facilitatory interneuron releases a neurotransmitter (*serotonin*) that activates receptors on the surface of the sensory neuron. These receptors engage a biochemical cascade that inactivates potassium (K^+) channels. The duration of an action potential is determined by the rate at which K^+ is allowed to flow out of the cell. Inactivating some of the K^+ channels slows

this process, and, as a result, the action potential lasts a little longer. This is important because the duration of the action potential determines how long the Ca^{++} channels remain open. Reducing the flow of K^+ out of the sensory neuron causes an increase in the duration of the action potential, which in turn increases the amount of Ca^{++} that enters the cell. Allowing more Ca^{++} to enter the cell increases transmitter release and increases the vigor of the motor response, producing behavioral sensitization. Additional processes also contribute, including a form of *long-term potentiation* (see Box 8.2; Glanzman, 2008).

Preexisting proteins underlie the synaptic modifications that produce short-term habituation and sensitization. If stimulation is continued, intracellular signals initiate the expression of genes that yield protein products that bring about structural modifications (Box 9.1; Bailey & Kandel, 2008). For example, long-term habituation is associated with a reduction in the number of synaptic connections. Conversely, repeated exposure to a sensitizing stimulus produces an increase in synaptic connections, which promotes the initiation of a response in the post-synaptic cell.

J. W. Grau

Aplysia An invertebrate sea slug, about the size of a rat, that lives in the tidal zones of tropical waters. *Aplysia* have been used to study the neurobiology of learning because they have a simple, and relatively invariant, nervous system with large neurons.

Habituation and Sensitization of Emotions and Motivated Behavior

To this point, our discussion of changes produced by repetitions of an eliciting stimulus has been limited to relatively simple responses. However, stimuli may also evoke complex emotions such as love, fear, euphoria, terror, or satisfaction. I have already described habituation of an emotional response to repeated presentations of a taste (Figure 2.5).

R. L. Solomon

The concepts of habituation and sensitization also have been extended to changes in more complex emotions (Solomon & Corbit, 1974) and various forms of motivated behavior, including feeding, drinking, exploration, aggression, courtship, and sexual behavior (McSweeney & Swindell, 1999). An area of special interest is drug addiction (e.g., Baker et al., 2004; Koob, 2009; Koob & Le Moal, 2008).

Emotional Reactions and Their Aftereffects

In their landmark review of examples of emotional responses to various stimuli, including drugs, Solomon and Corbit (1974) noticed a couple of striking features. First, intense emotional reactions are often biphasic. One emotion occurs during the eliciting stimulus, and the opposite emotion is observed when the stimulus is terminated. Consider, for example, the psychoactive effects of alcohol. Someone who is sipping vodka becomes mellow and relaxed as they are drinking. These feelings, which are generally pleasant, reflect the primary sedative effects of alcohol. In contrast, something quite different occurs after a night of drinking. Once the sedative effects of alcohol have dissipated, the person is likely to become irritable and may experience headaches and nausea. The pleasant sedative effects of alcohol give way to the unpleasant sensations of a hangover. Both effects depend on dosage. The more you drink, the more sedated or drunk you become, and the more intense will be the hangover afterward. Other drugs produce similar biphasic responses. With amphetamine, for example, the presence of the drug makes you feel alert, energetic, and self-confident. After the drug has worn off, the person is likely to feel tired, depressed, and drowsy.

Another common characteristic of emotional reactions is that they change with experience. The primary reaction becomes weaker and the after-reaction becomes stronger. Habitual drinkers are not as debilitated by a few beers as someone drinking for the first time. However, habitual drinkers experience more severe withdrawal symptoms if they quit drinking.

Habituation of a primary drug reaction is called **drug tolerance**. Drug tolerance refers to a decline in the effectiveness of a drug with repeated exposures. Habitual users of all psychoactive drugs (e.g., alcohol, nicotine, heroin, caffeine, sleeping pills, antianxiety drugs) are not as greatly affected when taking the drug as first-time users. A strong vodka tonic that would make a casual drinker a bit tipsy is not likely to have any effect on a frequent drinker. (We will revisit the role of opponent processes in drug tolerance in Chapter 4.)

Because of the development of tolerance, habitual drug users sometimes do not enjoy taking the drug as much as naive users. People who smoke frequently, for example, do not derive much enjoyment from doing so (e.g., Hogarth, Dickinson, & Duka, 2010). Accompanying this decline in the primary drug reaction is a growth in the opponent after-reaction. Accordingly, habitual drug users experience much more severe hangovers when the drug wears off than do naive users. A habitual smoker who has gone a long time without a cigarette will experience headaches, irritability, anxiety, tension, and general dissatisfaction. A heavy drinker who stops consuming alcohol is likely to experience hallucinations, memory loss, psychomotor agitation, delirium tremens, and other physiological disturbances. For a habitual user of amphetamine, the fatigue and depression that characterize the opponent aftereffect may be severe enough to produce suicidal thoughts.

Solomon and Corbit (1974) noted that similar patterns of emotional reaction occur with all emotion-arousing stimuli. Consider, for example, love and attachment. Newly-weds are usually very excited about each other and are very affectionate whenever they are together. This primary emotional reaction habituates as the years go by. Gradually, the couple settles into a comfortable mode of interaction that lacks the excitement of the honeymoon. However, this habituation of the primary emotional reaction is accompanied by a strengthening of the affective after-reaction. Couples who have been together for many years become more intensely unhappy if they are separated by death or disease. After partners have been together for several decades, the death of one will cause an intense grief reaction in the survivor. This strong affective after-reaction is remarkable, considering that by this stage in their relationship the couple may have entirely ceased to show any overt signs of affection.

The Opponent Process Theory of Motivation

The above examples illustrate three common characteristics of emotional reactions: (1) Emotional reactions are biphasic; a primary reaction is followed by an opposite after-reaction. (2) The primary reaction becomes weaker or habituates with repeated stimulations. (3) The weakening of the primary reaction with repetition is accompanied by a strengthening of the after-reaction. These characteristics are at the core of the *opponent process theory of motivation* (Solomon & Corbit, 1974). More recently, investigators have made significant progress in delineating the neural mechanisms of opponent processes (e.g., Koob, 2009; Radke, Rothwell, & Gewirtz, 2011).

The opponent process theory assumes that neurophysiological mechanisms involved in emotional behavior serve to maintain emotional stability. Thus, the opponent process theory is a *homeostatic* theory. It is built on the premise that an important function of mechanisms that control emotions is to keep us on an even keel and minimize the highs and the lows. The concept of homeostasis was originally introduced to explain the stability of our internal physiology, such as body temperature. Since then, the concept has also become important in the analysis of behavior. (I will discuss other types of homeostatic theories in later chapters.)

How might physiological mechanisms maintain emotional stability and keep us from getting too excited? Maintaining any system in a stable state requires that a disturbance that moves the system in one direction is met by an opposing force that counteracts the disturbance. Consider, for example, trying to keep a seesaw level. If something pushes one end of the seesaw down, the other end will go up. To keep the seesaw level, a force pushing one end down has to be met by an opposing force on the other side.

The idea of opponent forces serving to maintain a stable state is central to the opponent process theory of motivation. The theory assumes that an emotion-arousing stimulus pushes a person's emotional state away from neutrality. This shift away from emotional neutrality triggers an opponent process that counteracts the shift. The patterns of emotional behavior observed initially and after extensive experience with a stimulus are the net result of the direct effects of an emotion-arousing stimulus and the opponent process that is activated to counteract this direct effect.

The presentation of an emotion-arousing stimulus initially elicits what is called the **primary process**, or *a* **process**, which is responsible for the quality of the emotional state (e.g., happiness) that occurs in the presence of the stimulus. The primary, or *a* process, is assumed to elicit, in turn, an **opponent process**, or *b* **process**, that generates the opposite emotional reaction (e.g., irritability and melancholia). Because the opponent process is activated by the primary reaction, it lags behind the primary emotional disturbance.

Opponent Mechanisms During Initial Stimulus Exposure   Figure 2.15 shows how the primary and opponent processes determine the initial responses of an organism to an emotion-arousing stimulus. The underlying primary and opponent processes are represented in the bottom of the figure. The net effects of these processes (the observed emotional reactions) are represented in the top panel. When the stimulus is first presented, the *a* process occurs unopposed by the *b* process. This permits the primary emotional reaction to reach its peak quickly. The *b* process then becomes activated and begins to

FIGURE 2.15 Opponent process mechanism during the initial presentation of an emotion arousing stimulus. The observed emotional reactions are represented in the top panel. The underlying opponent processes are represented in the bottom panel. Notice that the *b* process starts a bit after the onset of the *a* process. In addition, the *b* process ends much later than the *a* process. This last feature allows the opponent emotions to dominate after the end of the stimulus. (From "An Opponent Process Theory of Motivation: I. The Temporal Dynamics of Affect," by R. L. Solomon and J. D. Corbit, 1974, *Psychological Review, 81,* pp. 119–145.)

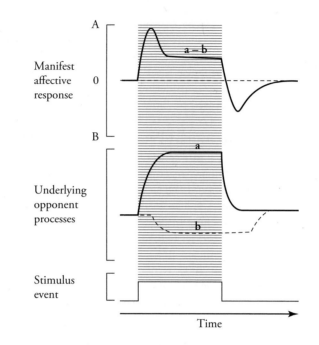

oppose the *a* process. However, the *b* process is not strong enough to entirely counteract the primary emotional response, and the primary emotional response persists during the eliciting stimulus. When the stimulus is withdrawn, the *a* process quickly returns to baseline, but the *b* process lingers for awhile. At this point, the *b* process has nothing to oppose. Therefore, emotional responses characteristic of the opponent process become evident for the first time at this point.

Opponent Mechanisms After Extensive Stimulus Exposure Figure 2.16 shows how the primary and opponent processes operate after numerous previous exposures to a stimulus. As I noted earlier, a highly familiar stimulus does not elicit strong emotional reactions when it is presented, but the affective after-reaction tends to be much stronger. The opponent process theory explains this outcome by assuming that the *b* process becomes strengthened with repeated use. As a result of this strengthening, the *b* process becomes activated sooner after the onset of the stimulus, its maximum intensity becomes greater, and it becomes slower to decay when the stimulus ceases. Because of these changes, the primary emotional responses are more effectively counteracted by the opponent process. An associated consequence of the growth of the opponent process is that the affective after-reaction become stronger when the stimulus is withdrawn (Figure 2.16).

Opponent Aftereffects and Motivation If the primary pleasurable effects of a psychoactive drug are gone for habitual users, why do they continue taking the drug? Why are they addicted? The opponent process theory suggests that drug addiction is mainly an attempt to reduce the aversiveness of the affective after-reaction to the drugs such as the bad hangovers, the amphetamine "crashes," and the irritability that comes from not having the usual cigarette. Based on their extensive review of research on emotion and cognition, Baker and colleagues (2004) proposed an affective processing model of drug addiction that is built on opponent process concepts and concludes that "addicted drug users sustain their drug use largely to manage their misery" (p. 34) (see also Ettenberg, 2004).

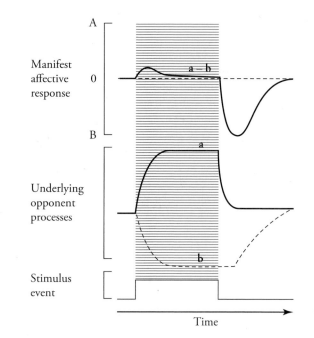

FIGURE 2.16 Oppo-
nent process mechanism
that produces the affec-
tive changes to a habit-
uated stimulus. The
observed emotional re-
actions are represented
in the top panel. The
underlying opponent
processes are represented
in the bottom panel.
Notice that the *b* process
starts promptly after the
onset of the *a* process and
is much stronger than in
Figure 2.15. In addition,
the *b* process ends much
later than the *a* process.
Because of these changes
in the *b* process, the primary emotional response
is nearly invisible during
the stimulus, but the af-
fective after-reaction is
very strong. (From "An
Opponent Process
Theory of Motivation: I.
The Temporal Dynamics
of Affect," by R. L.
Solomon and J. D. Corbit,
1974, *Psychological
Review, 81,* pp. 119–145.)

The opponent process interpretation of drug addiction as escape from the misery of withdrawal is also supported by a large body of neuroscience evidence. In their review of this evidence, Koob and Le Moal (2008) concluded that extensive drug use results in reduced activity in brain circuits associated with reward and strengthening of opponent neural mechanisms referred to as the *antireward* circuit. Drug-seeking behavior is rein-forced in part by the fact that drug intake reduces activity in the antireward circuit. As Koob and Le Moal pointed out, "The combination of decreases in reward neurotransmit-ter function and recruitment of antireward systems provides a powerful source of nega-tive reinforcement that contributes to compulsive drug-seeking behavior and addiction" (p. 38). Thus, drug addicts are not "trapped" by the pleasure they derive from the drug. Rather, they take the drug to reduce withdrawal pains. (Other factors involved in drug addiction will be considered in subsequent chapters.)

Concluding Comments

The quality of life and survival itself depends on how behavior is coordinated with the complexities of the environment. Elicited behavior represents one of the fundamental ways in which the behavior of all animals, from single-celled organisms to people, is adjusted to environmental events.

Elicited behavior takes many forms, ranging from simple reflexes mediated by just three neurons to complex emotional reactions. Although elicited behavior occurs as a reaction to a stimulus, it is not rigid and invariant. In fact, one of its hallmark features is that elicited behavior is altered by experience. If an eliciting stimulus does not arouse the organism, repeated presentations of the stimulus will evoke progressively weaker responses (a habituation effect). If the organism is in a state of arousal, the elicited response will be enhanced (a sensitization effect).

Repeated presentations of an eliciting stimulus produce changes in simple responses as well as in more complex emotional reactions. Organisms tend to minimize changes in emotional state caused by external stimuli. According to the opponent process theory of motivation, emotional responses elicited by an environmental event are counteracted by an opposing process in the organism. If the original elicited emotion is rewarding, the opponent process will activate antireward circuits and create an aversive state. The compensatory, or opponent, process is assumed to become stronger each time it is activated. Drug addiction involves efforts to minimize the aversive nature of the opponent or antireward processes attendant to repeated drug intake.

Habituation, sensitization, and changes in the strength of opponent processes are the simplest mechanisms, whereby organisms adjust their reactions to environmental events on the basis of past experience.

Sample Questions

1. Describe how elicited behavior can be involved in complex social interactions, like breast feeding.
2. Describe sign stimuli involved in the control of human behavior.
3. Compare and contrast appetitive and consummatory behavior and describe how these are related to general search, focal search, and food handling.
4. Describe components of the startle response and how the startle response may undergo sensitization.
5. Describe the distinction between habituation, sensory adaptation, and response fatigue.
6. Describe the two processes of the dual-process theory of habituation and sensitization and the differences between these processes.
7. Describe how habituation and sensitization are involved in emotion regulation and drug addiction.

Key Terms

a **process**   Same as *primary process* in the opponent process theory of motivation.

afferent neuron   A neuron that transmits messages from sense organs to the central nervous system. Also called *sensory neuron*.

appetitive behavior   Behavior that occurs early in a natural behavior sequence and serves to bring the organism in contact with a releasing stimulus. (See also *general search mode* and *focal search mode*.)

b **process**   Same as *opponent process* in the opponent process theory of motivation.

consummatory behavior   Behavior that serves to bring a natural sequence of behavior to consummation or completion. Consummatory responses are usually species-typical modal action patterns. (See also *food handling mode*.)

drug tolerance   Reduction in the effectiveness of a drug as a result of repeated use of the drug.

efferent neuron   A neuron that transmits impulses to muscles. Also called a *motor neuron*.

fatigue   A temporary decrease in behavior caused by repeated or excessive use of the muscles involved in the behavior.

focal search mode   The second component of the feeding behavior sequence following general search, in which the organism engages in behavior focused on a particular location or stimulus that is indicative of the presence of food. Focal search is a form of appetitive behavior that is more closely related to food than general search.

food handling and ingestion mode   The last component of the feeding behavior sequence, in which the organism handles and consumes the food. This is similar to what ethologists referred to as *consummatory behavior*.

general search mode   The earliest component of the feeding behavior sequence, in which the organism engages in nondirected locomotor behavior. General search is a form of appetitive behavior.

habituation effect   A progressive decrease in the vigor of elicited behavior that may occur with repeated presentations of the eliciting stimulus.

habituation process   A neural mechanism activated by repetitions of a stimulus that reduces the magnitude of responses elicited by that stimulus.

interneuron   A neuron in the spinal cord that transmits impulses from afferent (or sensory) to efferent (or motor) neurons.

modal action pattern (MAP)   A response pattern exhibited by most, if not all, members of a species in much the same way. Modal action patterns are used as basic units of behavior in ethological investigations of behavior.

motor neuron   Same as *efferent neuron*.

opponent process   A compensatory mechanism that occurs in response to the primary process elicited by biologically significant events. The opponent process causes physiological and behavioral changes that are the opposite of those caused by the primary process. Also called the *b* process.

primary process   The first process in the opponent process theory of motivation that is elicited by a biologically significant stimulus. Also called the *a* process.

reflex   A close relation between an eliciting stimulus and a resulting response that is mediated by a neural circuit (the reflex arc) that links afferent neurons activated by the stimulus with efferent neurons that trigger response output. As a consequence, the eliciting stimulus usually produces the reflex response, which rarely occurs otherwise.

releasing stimulus   Same as *sign stimulus*.

sensitization effect   An increase in the vigor of elicited behavior that may result from repeated presentations of the eliciting stimulus or from exposure to a strong extraneous stimulus.

sensitization process   A neural mech, increases the magnitude of responses eli stimulus.

sensory adaptation   A temporary reduction in the sensitivity of sense organs caused by repeated or excessive stimulation.

sensory neuron   Same as *afferent neuron*.

sign stimulus   A specific feature of an object or animal that elicits a modal action pattern. Also called *releasing stimulus*.

spontaneous recovery   Return of responding to baseline levels produced by a period of rest after habituation or sensitization.

S-R system   The shortest neural pathway that connects the sense organs stimulated by an eliciting stimulus and the muscles involved in making the elicited response.

state system   Neural structures that determine the general level of responsiveness, or arousal of the organism.

Supernormal stimulus   A sign stimulus whose features have been artificially enhanced or exaggerated to produce an abnormally large modal action pattern.

Classical Conditioning: Foundations

CHAPTER PREVIEW

Chapter 3 provides an introduction to another basic form of learning, namely classical conditioning. Investigations of classical conditioning began with the work of Pavlov, who studied how dogs learn to anticipate food. Since then, the research has been extended to a variety of other organisms and response systems. Some classical conditioning procedures establish an excitatory association between two stimuli and serve to activate behavior. Other procedures promote learning to inhibit the operation of excitatory associations. I will describe both excitatory and inhibitory conditioning procedures and discuss how these are involved in various important life experiences.

In Chapter 2, I described how environmental events can elicit behavior and how such elicited behavior can be modified by sensitization and habituation. These relatively simple processes help to bring the behavior of organisms in tune with their environment. However, if human and nonhuman animals only had the behavioral mechanisms described in Chapter 2, they would remain rather limited in the kinds of things they could do. For the most part, habituation and sensitization involve learning about just one stimulus. However, events in the world do not occur in isolation. Rather, much of our experience consists of predictable and organized sequences of stimuli. Every significant event (e.g., a hug from a friend) is preceded by other events (your friend approaching with extended arms) that are part of what leads to the target outcome.

Cause-and-effect relationships in the world ensure that certain things occur in combination with others. Your car's engine does not run unless the ignition has been turned on; you cannot walk through a doorway unless the door was first opened; it does not rain unless there are clouds in the sky. Social institutions and customs also ensure that events occur in a predictable order. Classes are scheduled at predictable times; people are better dressed at church than at a picnic; a person who smiles is more likely to act in a friendly manner than one who frowns. Learning to predict events in the environment and learning what stimuli tend to occur together help us interact more effectively with our environment. Imagine how much trouble you would have if you could not predict how long it takes to make coffee, when stores are likely to be open, or whether your key will work to unlock your apartment.

The simplest mechanism whereby organisms learn about relations between one event and another is classical conditioning. Classical conditioning enables human and nonhuman animals to take advantage of the orderly sequence of events in their world to take appropriate action in anticipation of what is about to happen. Classical conditioning is the process whereby we learn to predict when and what we might eat, when we are likely to face danger, and when we are likely to be safe. It is also integrally involved in the learning of new emotional reactions (e.g., fear or pleasure) to stimuli that have become associated with a significant event.

The Early Years of Classical Conditioning

Systematic studies of classical conditioning began with the work of the great Russian physiologist Pavlov (Box 3.1). Classical conditioning was also independently discovered by Edwin Twitmyer in a Ph.D. dissertation submitted to the University of Pennsylvania in 1902 (see Twitmyer, 1974). Twitmyer repeatedly tested the knee-jerk reflex of college students by sounding a bell .5 seconds before hitting the patellar tendon just below the knee cap. After several trials of this sort, the bell was sufficient to elicit the knee-jerk reflex in some of the students. However, Twitmyer did not explore the broader implications of his discoveries, and his findings did not attract much attention initially.

Pavlov's studies of classical conditioning were an extension of his research on the processes of digestion. Pavlov made major advances in the study of digestion by developing surgical techniques that enabled dogs to survive for many years with artificial fistulae that permitted the collection of various digestive juices. With the use of a stomach fistula, for example, Pavlov was able to collect stomach secretions in dogs that otherwise lived normally. Technicians in the laboratory soon discovered that the dogs secreted stomach juices in response to the sight of food, or even just upon seeing the person who usually fed them. The laboratory produced considerable quantities of stomach juice in this manner and sold the excess to the general public. The popularity of this juice as a remedy for various stomach ailments helped to supplement the income of the laboratory.

Assistants in the laboratory referred to stomach secretions elicited by food-related stimuli as *psychic secretions* because they seemed to be a response to the expectation or thought of food. However, the phenomenon of psychic secretions generated little scientific interest until Pavlov recognized that it could be used to study the mechanisms of association learning and could inform us about the functions of the nervous system (Pavlov, 1927). Thus, as many great scientists, Pavlov's contributions were important not just because he discovered something new but because he figured out how to place the discovery into a compelling conceptual framework.

The Discoveries of Vul'fson and Snarskii

The first systematic studies of classical conditioning were performed by S. G. Vul'fson and A. T. Snarskii in Pavlov's laboratory (Boakes, 1984; Todes, 1997). Both these students focused on the salivary glands, which are the first digestive glands involved in the breakdown of food. Some of the salivary glands are rather large and have ducts that are accessible and can be easily externalized with a fistula (Figure 3.1). Vul'fson studied salivary responses to various substances placed in the mouth: dry food, wet food, sour water, and sand. After the dogs had experienced these things placed in the mouth, the mere sight of the substances was enough to make the dogs salivate.

Whereas Vul'fson used naturally occurring materials in his studies, Snarskii extended these observations to artificial substances. In one experiment, Snarskii gave his dogs sour water (such as strong lemon juice) that was artificially colored black. After several encounters with the black sour water, the dogs also salivated to plain black water or to the sight of a bottle containing a black liquid.

The substances tested by Vul'fson and Snarskii could be identified at a distance by sight. They also produced distinctive texture and taste sensations in the mouth. Such sensations are called *orosensory stimuli*. The first time that sand was placed in a dog's mouth, only the feeling of the sand in the mouth elicited salivation. However, after sand had been placed in the mouth several times, the sight of sand (its visual features) also came to elicit salivation. The dog learned to associate the visual features of the sand with its orosensory features. The association of one feature of an object with another is called **object learning**.

To study the mechanisms of associative learning, the stimuli to be associated have to be manipulated independently of one another. This is difficult to do when the two stimuli are properties of the same object. Therefore, in later studies of conditioning, Pavlov used procedures in which the stimuli to be associated came from different sources. This led to the experimental methods that continue to dominate studies of classical conditioning to the present day. However, contemporary studies are no longer conducted with dogs.

The Classical Conditioning Paradigm

Pavlov's basic procedure for the study of conditioned salivation is familiar to many. The procedure involves two stimuli. One of these is a tone or a light that does not elicit salivation at the outset of the experiment. The other stimulus is food or the taste of a sour solution placed in the mouth. In contrast to the light or tone, the food or sour taste elicits vigorous salivation even the first time it is presented.

FIGURE 3.1 Diagram of the Pavlovian salivary conditioning preparation. A cannula attached to the animal's salivary duct sends drops of saliva to a data-recording device. (From "The Method of Pavlov in Animal Psychology," by R. M. Yerkes and S. Morgulis, 1909, *Psychological Bulletin, 6,* pp. 257–273.)

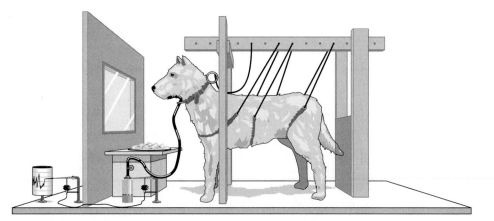

BOX 3.1

Ivan P. Pavlov: Biographical Sketch

Born in 1849 into the family of a priest in Russia, Pavlov dedicated his life to scholarship and discovery. He received his early education in a local theological seminary and planned a career of religious service. However, his interests soon changed, and when he was 21, he entered the University of St. Petersburg, where his studies focused on chemistry and animal physiology. After obtaining the equivalent of a bachelor's degree, he went to the Imperial Medico-Surgical Academy in 1875 to further

his education in physiology. Eight years later, he received his doctoral degree for his research on the efferent nerves of the heart and then began investigating various aspects of digestive physiology. In 1888 he discovered the nerves that stimulate the digestive secretions of the pancreas—a finding that initiated a series of experiments for which Pavlov was awarded the Nobel Prize in Physiology in 1904.

Pavlov did a great deal of original research while a graduate student, as

well as after obtaining his doctoral degree. However, he did not have a faculty position or his own laboratory until 1890, when, at the age of 41, he was appointed professor of pharmacology at the St. Petersburg Military Medical Academy. Five years later, he became professor of physiology at the same institution. Pavlov remained active in the laboratory until close to his death in 1936. In fact, much of the research for which he is famous today was performed after he received the Nobel Prize.

Pavlov referred to the tone or light as the **conditional stimulus** because the effectiveness of this stimulus in eliciting salivation depended on (or was *conditional* on) pairing it several times with the presentation of food. By contrast, the food or sour taste was called the **unconditional stimulus** because its effectiveness in eliciting salivation did not depend on any prior training. The salivation that eventually came to be elicited by the tone or light was called the **conditional response**, and the salivation that was always elicited by the food or sour taste was called the **unconditional response**. Thus, stimuli and responses whose properties did not depend on prior training were called *unconditional*, and stimuli and responses whose properties emerged only after training were called *conditional*.

In the first English translation of Pavlov's writings, the term unconditio*nal* was erroneously translated as unconditio*ned*, and the term conditio*nal* was translated as conditio*ned*. The -ed suffix was used exclusively in English writings for many years, and our usage will follow that tradition. However, we should not forget that the term conditio*ned* does not capture Pavlov's original meaning of "dependent on" as accurately as the term conditio*nal* (Gantt, 1966).

Because the terms *conditioned* and *unconditioned stimulus* and *conditioned* and *unconditioned response* are used frequently in discussions of classical conditioning, they are often abbreviated. Conditioned stimulus and conditioned response are abbreviated **CS** and **CR**, respectively. Unconditioned stimulus and unconditioned response are abbreviated **US** and **UR**, respectively.

Experimental Situations

Classical conditioning has been investigated in a variety of situations and species (e.g., Domjan, 2005; Turkkan, 1989). Pavlov did his experiments with dogs, often using the salivary fistula technique. Contemporary experiments on Pavlovian conditioning are carried out with many different species (rats, mice, rabbits, pigeons, quail, and human participants) using procedures developed primarily by North American scientists during the second half of the twentieth century.

Fear Conditioning

Following the early work of Watson and Rayner (1920/2000), a major focus of investigators of Pavlovian conditioning has been the conditioning of emotional reactions. Watson and Rayner believed that infants are at first limited in their emotional reactivity. They assumed that "there must be some simple method by means of which the range of stimuli which can call out these emotions and their compounds is greatly increased." That simple method was Pavlovian conditioning. In a famous demonstration, Watson and Rayner conditioned a fear response to the presence of a docile white laboratory rat in a nine-month-old infant named Albert.

There was hardly anything that Albert was afraid of. However, after testing a variety of stimuli, Watson and Rayner found that little Albert reacted with alarm when he heard the loud noise of a steel bar being hit by a hammer behind his head. Watson and Rayner used this unconditioned alarming noise to condition fear to a white rat. Each conditioning trial consisted of presenting the rat to Albert and then striking the steel bar. At first Albert reached out to the rat when it was presented to him. But, after just two conditioning trials, he became reluctant to touch the rat. After five additional conditioning trials, Albert showed strong fear responses. He whimpered or cried, leaned as far away from the rat as he could, and sometimes fell over and moved away on all fours. Significantly, these fear responses were not evident when Albert was presented with his toy blocks. However, the conditioned fear did generalize to other furry things (a rabbit, a fur coat, cotton wool, a dog, and a Santa Claus mask).

Fear and anxiety are sources of considerable human discomfort, and if sufficiently severe, they can lead to serious psychological and behavioral problems. To better understand and treat these disorders, scientists are working to figure out how fear and anxiety are acquired, what are the neural mechanisms of fear, and how fear may be attenuated with behavioral and pharmacological techniques (e.g., Craske, Hermans, & Vansteenwegen, 2006; Oehlberg & Mineka, 2011). Many of these questions cannot be addressed experimentally using human subjects. Therefore, much of the research on fear conditioning has been conducted with laboratory rats and mice. The aversive US in these studies is a brief electric shock delivered through a metal grid floor. Shock is used because it can be regulated with great precision and its intensity can be adjusted to avoid any physical harm. It is aversive primarily because it is startling, unlike anything the animal has encountered before. The CS may be a discrete stimulus (like a tone or a light) or the contextual cues of the place where the aversive stimulus is encountered.

Unlike little Albert, who showed signs of fear by whimpering and crying, rats show their fear by freezing. Freezing is a common defense response that occurs in a variety of species in anticipation of aversive stimulation (see Chapter 10). Freezing probably evolved as a defensive behavior because animals that are motionless are not easily seen by their predators. For example, a deer standing still in the woods is difficult to see because its coloration blends well with the colors of bark and leaves. However, as soon as the deer starts moving, you can tell where it is.

Freezing is defined as immobility of the body (except for breathing) and the absence of movement of the whiskers associated with sniffing (Bouton & Bolles, 1980). Measurement of freezing as an index of conditioned fear has become popular in recent years, especially in neurobiological studies of fear (e.g., Jacobs, Cushman, & Fanselow, 2010). Automated systems are now available to quantify the degree of freezing exhibited by rats and mice. These systems identify freezing by how much movement is detected across successive frames of a video recording.

Figure 3.2 shows an example of the acquisition of freezing in response to an auditory CS (white noise) in laboratory rats. The rats received 10 conditioning trials. On each

FIGURE 3.2 Acquisition of conditioned freezing to an auditory CS (white noise) in laboratory rats during noise-shock conditioning trials. Each data point shows the percentage of time the rats were observed freezing during each CS presentation (based on Reger et al., 2012).

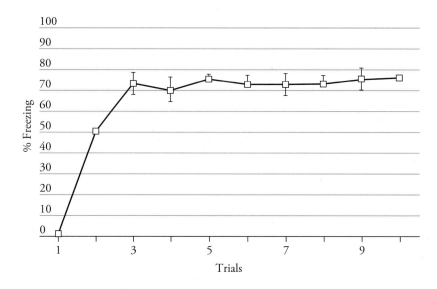

trial, the CS was presented for 46 seconds, ending in a 2-second mild (.5 milliamp) foot shock. The conditioning trials were separated by an intertrial interval of 210 seconds. Notice that there was little freezing during the first presentation of the noise CS, before the rats received their first shock. The percentage of time the rats spent freezing during subsequent conditioning trials increased fairly rapidly. By the third conditioning trial, the rats were freezing about 70% of the time, which was the asymptote or limit of learning evident in this experiment.

In addition to freezing, two other indirect measures of fear-induced immobility are also used in investigations of fear conditioning. Both involve the suppression of ongoing behavior and are therefore referred to as **conditioned suppression** procedures. In one case, the ongoing behavior is licking a drinking spout that contains water. The rats and mice in these experiments are slightly water deprived and therefore lick readily when placed in an experimental chamber. If a fear CS (e.g., tone) is presented, their licking behavior is suppressed, and they take longer to make a specified number of licks. Hence, this technique is called the **lick-suppression procedure**.

In another variation of the conditioned suppression technique, rats are first trained to press a response lever for food reward in a small experimental chamber. This lever-press activity provides the behavioral baseline for the measurement of fear. Once the rats are lever pressing at a steady rate, fear conditioning is conducted by pairing a tone or light with a brief shock. As the participants acquire the conditioned fear, they come to suppress their lever pressing during the CS (Ayres, 2012).

The conditioned suppression procedure has also been adapted for experiments with human participants. In that case, the behavioral baseline is provided by an ongoing activity such as playing a video game (e.g., Nelson & del Camen Sanjuan, 2006).

Eyeblink Conditioning

As I mentioned in Chapter 2, the eyeblink reflex is an early component of the startle response and occurs in a variety of species. To get someone to blink, all you have to do is clap your hands close to the person's head or blow a puff of air toward the eyes. If each air puff is preceded by a brief tone, the blink response will become conditioned and the person will blink in response to the tone.

Because of its simplicity, eyeblink conditioning was extensively investigated in studies with human participants early in the development of learning theory (see Kimble, 1961).

Eyeblink conditioning continues to be a very active area of research because it provides a powerful tool for the study of problems in development, aging, Alzheimer's disease, fetal alcohol syndrome, and other disorders (Brown & Woodruff-Pak, 2011; Freeman & Nicholson, 2004; Steinmetz, Tracey, & Green, 2001). Thus, eyeblink conditioning is a prominent technique for translational research involving classical conditioning. Eyeblink conditioning also continues to attract a great deal of interest because it has been used extensively in studies of the neurobiology of learning (Freeman & Steinmetz, 2011).

A study of eyeblink conditioning in five-month-old infants (Ivkovich et al., 1999) illustrates the technique. Each infant sat on a parent's lap facing a platform with brightly colored objects that maintained the infant's attention during the experimental sessions. Eyeblinks were recorded by a video camera. The CS was a 1,000 cps tone presented for 750 milliseconds, and the US was a gentle puff of air delivered to the right eye through a plastic tube. For one group of infants, the CS always ended with the puff of air, and these conditioning trials occurred an average of 12 seconds apart. The second group received the same number and distribution of CS and US presentations, but for them, the CSs and USs were spaced 4–8 seconds apart in an explicitly unpaired fashion. Thus, the second group served as a control. Each participant received two training sessions, one week apart.

The results of the experiment are presented in Figure 3.3 in terms of the percentage of trials on which the infants blinked during the CS. The rate of eyeblinks for the two groups did not differ statistically during the first experimental session. However, the paired group responded to the CS at a significantly higher rate from the beginning of the second session. This experiment illustrates a number of important points about learning. First, it shows that classical conditioning requires the pairing of a CS and US. Responding to the CS did not develop in the unpaired control group. Second, the learning was not observable at first. The infants in the paired group did not respond much in the first session but showed a dramatic increase when they were returned to the experimental situation for the second session. This provides an example of the

FIGURE 3.3 Eyeblink conditioning in five-month-old infants. For the infants in the paired group, a tone CS ended in a gentle puff of air to the eye. For the infants in the unpaired group, the tone and air puff never occurred together. (Based on D. Ivlovich, K. L. Collins, C. O. Eckerman, N. A. Krasnegor, and M. E. Stanton (1999). Classical delay eyeblink conditioning in four and five month old human infants. *Psychological Science*, 10, Figure 1, p. 6.)

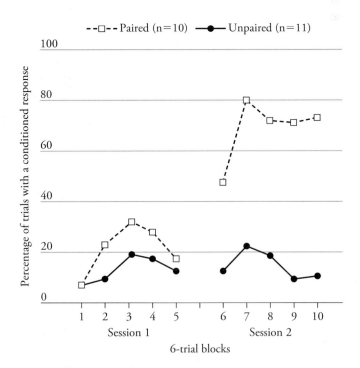

I. Gormezano

learning/performance distinction we discussed in Chapter 1. The babies started to learn that the CS was related to the US during the first session, but their learning was not evident until the beginning of the second session.

Contemporary interest in eyeblink conditioning in humans stems from the fact that substantial progress has been made in understanding the neurobiological substrates of this type of learning (Box 3.2). Neurobiological investigations of eyeblink conditioning have been conducted primarily in studies with domesticated rabbits. The rabbit eyeblink preparation was developed by Gormezano (see Gormezano, Kehoe, & Marshall, 1983). Domesticated rabbits are ideal for this type of research as they are sedentary and rarely blink in the absence of an air puff or irritation of the eye. Therefore, conditioned increases in responding can be readily detected.

BOX 3.2

Eyeblink Conditioning and the Search for the Engram

When an organism learns something, the results of this learning must be stored in the brain. Somehow, the network of neurons that make up your central nervous system is able to encode the relationship between biologically significant events and use this information to guide the selection of CRs. This biological memory is known as an **engram**. The traditional view is that the engram for a discrete CR is stored in a localized region of the brain. This raises a basic question in neurobiology: How and where is the engram stored?

As a student, your task would be easier if nature provided just one answer. This, however, is not the case; how an experience is encoded and stored by the nervous system varies across learning tasks. As a rule, more difficult problems require the most advanced portions of your brain and, not surprisingly, unraveling how these problems are solved at a neural level has proven to be a challenging task. Given this, neurobiologists have gravitated toward simpler learning tasks, where both the conditions that generate learning and its behavioral effect are well defined.

Richard Thompson and his colleagues recognized that the Pavlovian conditioning of an eyeblink response provides an attractive paradigm for unraveling how and where an engram is stored (Fanselow & Poulos, 2005; Steinmetz, Gluck, & Solomon, 2001; Thompson, 2005). Prior work had shown that a CS (e.g., a tone) that is repeatedly paired with an air puff to the eye (the US) acquires the ability to elicit a defensive eyeblink response. Decades of work has defined the circumstances under which this learning occurs, and the motor output has been precisely specified.

The search for the engram began with the **hippocampus**. Studies of humans with damage to this region revealed that the ability to consciously remember a recent event depends on the hippocampus (Box 8.2). Small electrodes were lowered into the hippocampus of laboratory animals, and neural activity was recorded during eyeblink conditioning. These studies revealed that cells in this region reflect the learning of a CS–US association. However, to the surprise of many investigators, removing the hippocampus did not eliminate the animal's ability to acquire and retain a conditioned eyeblink response. In fact, removing all of the brain structures above the *midbrain*

(Figure 1.6D) had little effect on eyeblink conditioning with a delayed conditioning procedure. This suggests that the essential circuitry for eyeblink conditioning lies within the lower neural structures of the *brainstem* and **cerebellum**. Subsequent experiments clearly showed that the acquisition of a well-timed conditioned eyeblink response depends on a neural circuit that lies within the cerebellum (Ohyama et al., 2003; Mauk & Buonomano, 2004).

The UR elicited by an air puff to the eye is mediated by neurons that project to a region of the brainstem known as the *trigeminal nucleus* (Figure 3.4A). From there, neurons travel along two routes, either directly or through the *reticular formation* to the *cranial motor nucleus*, where the behavioral output is organized. Three basic techniques were used to define this pathway. The first involved **electrophysiological** recordings to verify that neurons in this neural circuit are engaged in response to the US. The second technique involved inactivating nuclei within the circuit, either permanently (by killing the cells) or temporarily (by means of a drug or cooling), to show that the

Continued

BOX 3.2 (continued)

FIGURE 3.4 (A) A block diagram of the brain circuitry required for eyelid conditioning (adapted from Thompson, 1993 and 2005). (B) Structural plasticity within the cerebellar cortex. Mossy fiber input from the CS synapses on to parallel fibers that project across the cortical surface. Each Purkinje cell receives input from many parallel fibers (CSs), but just one climbing fiber (the US). The US input provides a form of instruction that selects the appropriate pattern of parallel fiber (CS) activity to drive the CR (adapted from Dudai, 1989).

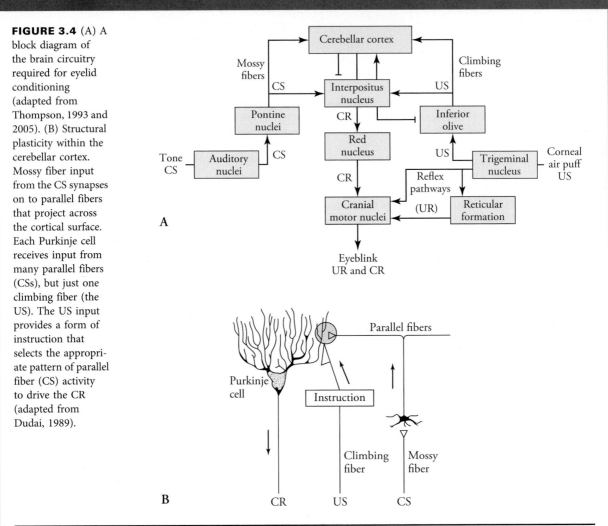

region plays an essential (*necessary*) role in the eyeblink UR. Finally, specific nuclei were artificially stimulated to show that activity in these areas is *sufficient* to produce the behavioral response.

The same techniques (electrical recording, inactivation, and stimulation) have been used to define the neural pathway that mediates the acquisition and performance of the CR. As illustrated in Figure 3.4A, the CS input travels to a region of the brainstem known as the *pontine nucleus*. From there, it is carried by *mossy fibers* that convey the signal to the cerebellum. The US signal is relayed to the cerebellum through the *climbing fibers*. These two signals meet in the *cerebellar cortex* where coincident activity brings about a synaptic modification that alters the neural output from the cerebellum. In essence, the climbing fibers act as teachers, selecting a subset of connections to be modified (Figure 3.4B). This change defines the stimulus properties (the characteristics of the CS) that engage a discrete motor output. The output is mediated by neurons that project from the *interpositus nucleus* to the *red nucleus* and finally to the *cranial motor nucleus*.

As an eyeblink CR is acquired, conditioned activity develops within the interpositus nucleus. Neurons from this nucleus project back to the US pathway and inhibit the US signal within the *inferior olive*. This provides a form of negative feedback that decreases the effectiveness of the US.

Continued

BOX 3.2 (continued)

Many researchers believe that phenomena such as blocking and overshadowing occur because a predicted CS is less effective. In the eyeblink paradigm, this might occur because the US input is inhibited within the inferior olive. Consistent with that prediction, Kim and colleagues (1998) showed that eliminating this source of inhibition eliminated the blocking effect.

Earlier I noted that the hippocampus is not needed for simple delayed conditioning. It is, however, required for more complex forms of learning. An example is provided by trace conditioning, in which a temporal delay is inserted between the end of the CS and the start of the US. A normal animal can readily acquire a conditioned eyeblink to a

CS that ends .5 seconds before the US. However, it cannot span this gap if the hippocampus is removed. A similar pattern of results is observed in amnesic patients who have damage to the hippocampus (Clark & Squire, 1998). These patients cannot consciously remember the CS–US relation. In the absence of this explicit memory, they fail to learn with a trace-conditioning procedure. Learning in the delayed procedure is not affected, even though the patient cannot consciously remember the CS–US relation from one session to the next. Interestingly, disrupting conscious awareness in a normal person undermines the appreciation of the CS–US relation with the trace procedure. Again, individuals who

cannot explicitly report the relation fail to learn.

J. W. Grau

cerebellum   A neural structure that lies at the bottom of the brain, behind the brainstem and under the cerebral hemispheres. The cerebellum plays a role in motor coordination and motor learning (e.g., eyeblink conditioning).

electrophysiology   An experimental technique that uses probes (electrodes) to monitor the electrical properties of neurons.

engram   The neurobiological representation and storage of learned information in the brain.

hippocampus   A subcortical region of the limbic system that plays an important role in spatial learning, trace conditioning, and episodic memory. Degeneration of this area contributes to Alzheimer's disease.

Sign Tracking and Goal Tracking

Pavlov's research concentrated on salivation and other highly reflexive responses. This encouraged the belief that classical conditioning occurs only in reflex response systems. In recent years, however, such a restrictive view of Pavlovian conditioning has been abandoned. One experimental paradigm that has contributed significantly to this change in thinking is the **sign tracking**, or **autoshaping**, paradigm.

Animals often approach and contact stimuli that signal the availability of food. In the natural environment, food can be predicted on the basis of cues that originate from the food source but are detectable at a distance. For a hawk, for example, the sight and noises of a mouse some distance away are cues indicating the possibility of a meal. By approaching and contacting these stimuli, the hawk is likely to end up catching the mouse. Similarly, a squirrel can predict the availability of acorns on the basis of the leaves and shape of the oak trees that grow acorns.

Sign tracking is often investigated in the laboratory by presenting a discrete, localized visual stimulus just before each delivery of a small amount of food. The first experiment of this sort was performed by Brown and Jenkins (1968) with pigeons. The pigeons were placed in an experimental chamber that had a small circular key that could be illuminated and that the pigeons could peck (similar to what is shown in Figure 1.8). Periodically, the birds were given access to food for a short period (4 seconds). The key light was illuminated for 8 seconds immediately before each food delivery.

The birds did not have to do anything for the food to be delivered. Because they were hungry, one might predict that when they saw the key light, they would go to the food dish and wait for the food that was coming. Interestingly, that is not what happened. Instead of using the key light to tell them when they should go to the food dish, the pigeons started pecking the key itself. This behavior was remarkable because it was not required to gain access to the food. Presenting the key light at random times or

unpaired with food did not lead to pecking (e.g., Gamzu & Williams, 1973), indicating that for the conditioned pecking to occur the key light had to be paired with food.

The tracking of signals for food is dramatically illustrated by instances in which the signal is located far away from the food cup. In the first such experiment (see Hearst & Jenkins, 1974), the food cup was located about 3 feet (90 cm) from the key light. Nevertheless, the pigeons went to the key light rather than the food cup when the CS was presented. Burns and Domjan (2000) extended this "long-box" procedure in studies of sexual conditioning. Male domesticated quail, which copulate readily in captivity, were served in the experiment. The CS was a wood block lowered from the ceiling 30 seconds before a female copulation partner was introduced. The unusual feature of the experiment was that the CS and the female were presented at opposite ends of an 8-foot long chamber (Figure 3.5). Despite this long distance, when the CS was presented the birds approached the CS rather than the door where the female was to be released. Pairing the CS with sexual reinforcement made the CS such an attractive stimulus that the birds were drawn to it nearly 8 feet away from the female door.

Although sign tracking is a frequent outcome in Pavlovian conditioning, it is not always observed. Under certain experimental conditions, there can be considerable variation in which animals develop sign tracking and the degree of sign tracking they exhibit. Historically, individual differences in conditioned responding were ignored in studies of conditioning because they were attributed to poor experimental control. However, that is no longer the case because individual differences in sign tracking are correlated with individual differences in impulsivity and vulnerability to drug abuse (Tomie, Grimes, & Pohorecky, 2008). This has made sign tracking a valuable model system for studying learning processes and neural mechanisms that contribute to the development of drug addiction.

Individual differences in sign tracking are typically examined using laboratory rats. A common experimental situation is illustrated in Figure 3.6. Rats are placed in a small experimental chamber that has a food cup in the middle of one of the walls. There is a slot on either side of the food cup through which a response lever can be inserted. The presentation of the lever serves as the CS, and a pellet of food delivered to the food cup serves as the US. Each conditioning trial consists of inserting one of the levers for a brief duration (e.g., 8 seconds). The lever is then withdrawn and the pellet of food is delivered.

Conditioning trials in which a response lever is paired with food do not produce the same result in all rats (see bottom of Figure 3.6). About one third of the rats become

M. Burns

FIGURE 3.5 Test of sign tracking in sexual conditioning of male domesticated quail. The CS was presented at one end of an 8-foot long chamber before the release of a female from the other end. In spite of this distance, the male birds went to the CS when it appeared (based on Burns & Domjan, 2000).

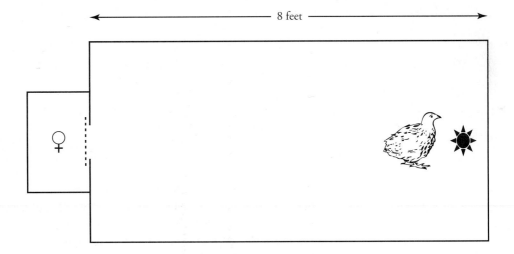

FIGURE 3.6 Rats in an experimental chamber with a recessed food cup in the middle and a slot on either side of the food cup through which a response lever can be inserted. Presentation of the left or right lever was the CS. A pellet of food in the food cup was the US. Sign tracking was measured by contacts with the CS lever (Panel A). Goal tracking was measured by contacts with the food cup (Panel B). About one third of the rats (Panel C) developed sign tracking as the CR (black circles) and one third of the rats (Panel D) developed goal tracking as the CR (white circles). The remaining rats showed some of each behavior (grey circles). Results are shown in blocks of 50 conditioning trials (based on Flagel, Akil, & Robinson, 2009).

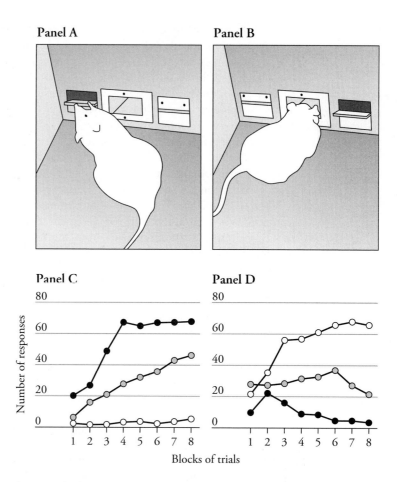

conditioned to track the CS. Sign trackers approach, touch, and sometimes gnaw the response lever that serves as the CS. Another third of the rats ignore the lever but approach and poke their heads into the food cup when the CS is presented. This type of conditioned behavior is called **goal tracking** because it tracks the goal object, which is food. The remaining rats show a combination of sign tracking and goal tracking responses.

These individual differences in sign tracking and goal tracking are of considerable interest because the two subsets of rats also differ in other respects that are associated with susceptibility to drug abuse (Flagel, Akil, & Robinson, 2009). Sign trackers show greater psychomotor sensitization to cocaine, greater activation of the dopamine reward circuit, and elevated plasma corticosterone levels. These individual differences are genetically based. Rats selectively bred for high locomotor responsivity in a novel environment show sign tracking, whereas those bred for low locomotor responsivity show goal tracking. Furthermore, these genetic differences are accompanied by differences in dopamine release in the reward circuit of the brain in response to the CS that signals food (Flagel et al., 2011). Studies of individual differences in sign tracking and goal tracking are exciting because they may some day tell us how learning and experience regulate gene expression to produce impulsive behavior and drug abuse.

Learning Taste Preferences and Aversions

The normal course of eating provides numerous opportunities for the learning of associations. Essentially, each eating episode is a conditioning trial. Whenever we eat, the sight, taste, and smell of the food are experienced before the food is swallowed and

Shelly Flagel

digested. The sensory aspects of the food serve as CSs that become associated with the postingestional consequences of eating, which are USs. Through this process, food cues come to signal what, when, and how much we eat (Polivy, Herman, & Girz, 2011).

Pavlovian conditioning can lead to the learning of food preferences and aversions. A taste preference is learned if a flavor is paired with nutritional repletion or other positive consequences (e.g., Capaldi, Hunter, & Lyn, 1997). In contrast, a conditioned taste aversion is learned if ingestion of a novel flavor is followed by an aversive consequence such as indigestion or food poisoning (Reilly & Schachtman, 2009). The learning of taste aversions and taste preferences has been investigated extensively in various animal species. A growing body of evidence indicates that many human taste aversions are also the result of Pavlovian conditioning (Scalera, 2002). Much of this evidence has been provided by questionnaire studies (e.g., Logue, 1985, 1988). People report having acquired at least one food aversion during their life time. The typical aversion learning experience involves eating a distinctively flavored food and then getting sick. Such a flavor–illness experience can produce a conditioned food aversion in just one trial, and the learning can occur even if the illness is delayed several hours after ingestion of the food. Another interesting finding is that in about 20% of the cases, the individuals were certain that their illness was not caused by the food they ate. Nevertheless, they learned an aversion to the food. This indicates that food aversion learning can be independent of rational thought processes and can go against a person's own conclusions about the causes of the illness.

Questionnaire studies can provide thought-provoking data, but systematic experimental research is required to isolate the mechanism of food-aversion learning. Experimental studies have been conducted with people in situations where they encounter illness during the course of medical treatment. Chemotherapy for cancer is one such situation. Chemotherapy often causes nausea as a side effect. Both child and adult cancer patients have been shown to acquire aversions to foods eaten before a chemotherapy session (Bernstein & Webster, 1980; Scalera & Bavieri, 2009). Such conditioned aversions may contribute to the lack of appetite that is a common side effect of chemotherapy.

Conditioned food aversions also may contribute to anorexia nervosa, a disorder characterized by severe and chronic weight loss (Bernstein & Borson, 1986). Suggestive evidence indicates that people suffering from anorexia nervosa experience digestive disorders that may increase their likelihood of learning food aversions. Increased susceptibility to food-aversion learning may also contribute to loss of appetite seen in people suffering from severe depression.

Many of our ideas about food-aversion learning in people have their roots in research with laboratory animals. In the typical procedure, the participants receive a distinctively flavored food or drink and are then made to feel sick by the injection of a drug or exposure to radiation. As a result of the taste–illness pairing, the animals acquire an aversion to the taste and suppress their subsequent intake of that flavor. Although taste-aversion learning is similar to other forms of classical conditioning in many respects (e.g., Domjan, 1983), it also has some special features. First, strong taste aversions can be learned with just one pairing of the flavor and illness. Although one-trial learning also occurs in fear conditioning, such rapid learning is rarely observed in eyeblink conditioning, salivary conditioning, or sign tracking.

The second unique feature of taste-aversion learning is that it occurs even if the illness does not occur until several hours after exposure to the novel taste (Garcia, Ervin, & Koelling, 1966; Revusky & Garcia, 1970). Dangerous substances in food often do not produce illness effects until the food has been digested, absorbed in the blood stream, and distributed to various body tissues. This process takes time. *Long-delay*

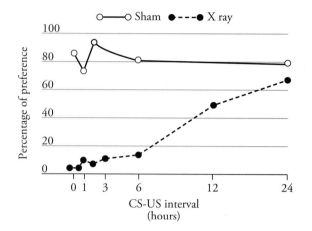

FIGURE 3.7 Mean percent preference for the saccharin CS flavor during a test session conducted after the CS flavor was paired with X irradiation (the US) or sham exposure. Percent preference is the percentage of the participant's total fluid intake (saccharin solution plus water) that consisted of the saccharin solution. During conditioning, the interval between exposure to the CS and the US ranged from 0 to 24 hours for different groups of rats. (Based on "Trace Conditioning with X-rays as an Aversive Stimulus," by J. C. Smith and D. L. Roll, *Psychonomic Science*, 1967, 9, pp. 11–12.)

J. Garcia

learning of taste aversions probably evolved to enable human and other animals to avoid poisonous foods that have delayed ill effects.

Long-delay taste-aversion learning was reported in an early study by Smith and Roll (1967). Laboratory rats were first adapted to a water deprivation schedule so that they would readily drink when a water bottle was placed on their cage. On the conditioning day, the water was flavored with the artificial sweetener saccharin (to make a .1% saccharin solution). At various times after the saccharin presentation ranging from 0 to 24 hours, different groups of rats were exposed to radiation from an X-ray machine to induce illness. Control groups of rats were also taken to the X-ray machine but were not irradiated. They were called the sham-irradiated groups. Starting a day after the radiation or sham treatment, each rat was given a choice of the saccharin solution or plain water to drink for 2 days.

The preference of each group of rats for the saccharin solution is shown in Figure 3.7. Animals exposed to radiation within 6 hours after tasting the saccharin solution showed a profound aversion to the saccharin flavor in the postconditioning test. They drank less than 20% of their total fluid intake from the saccharin drinking tube. Much less of an aversion was evident in animals irradiated 12 hours after the saccharin exposure, and hardly any aversion was observed in rats irradiated 24 hours after the taste exposure. In contrast to this gradient of saccharin avoidance in the irradiated rats, all the sham-irradiated groups strongly preferred the saccharin solution. They drank more than 70% of their total fluid intake from the saccharin drinking tube.

A flavor can also be made unpalatable by pairing it with another taste that is already disliked. In an analogous fashion, the pairing of a neutral flavor with a taste that is already liked will increase preference for that flavor. For example, in a study with undergraduate students, Dickinson and Brown (2007) used banana and vanilla as neutral flavors. To induce a flavor aversion or preference, the students received these flavors mixed with a bitter substance (to condition an aversion) or sugar (to condition a preference). In subsequent tests with the CS flavors, the undergraduates reported increased liking of the flavor that had been paired with sugar and decreased liking of the flavor that had been paired with the bitter taste.

These examples of how people learn to like or dislike initially neutral flavors is part of the general phenomenon of **evaluative conditioning** (De Houwer, 2011; Hoffmann et al., 2010). In evaluative conditioning, our evaluation or liking of a stimulus is changed by having that stimulus associated with something we already like or dislike. Evaluative conditioning is responsible for many of our likes and dislikes. It is the basis of much of what is done in the advertising industry. The product the advertiser is promoting is paired with things people already like in an effort to induce a preference for the product (Schachtman, Walker, & Fowler, 2011). Evaluative conditioning may also be involved in how we come to like somebody. If we participate in activities we enjoy with a particular person, we will come to like that person through association of features of the person with the enjoyable activities.

Excitatory Pavlovian Conditioning Methods

What we have been discussing so far are instances of excitatory Pavlovian conditioning. In excitatory conditioning, organisms learn a relation between a CS and US. As a result of this learning, presentation of the CS activates behavioral and neural activity related to the US in the absence of the actual presentation of that US. Thus, pigeons learn to approach and peck a key light that had been paired with food, rats learn to freeze to a sound that previously preceded foot shock, babies learn to blink in response to a tone that preceded a puff of air, and people learn to avoid a flavor that was followed by illness on an earlier occasion.

Common Pavlovian Conditioning Procedures

One of the major factors that determines the course of classical conditioning is the relative timing of the CS and the US. Often small and seemingly trivial variations in how a CS is paired with a US can have profound effects on how vigorously the participant exhibits a conditioned response and when the CR occurs.

Five common classical conditioning procedures are illustrated in Figure 3.8. The horizontal distance in each diagram represents the passage of time; vertical displacements represent when a stimulus begins and ends. Each configuration of CS and US represents a single **conditioning trial**.

FIGURE 3.8 Five common classical conditioning procedures.

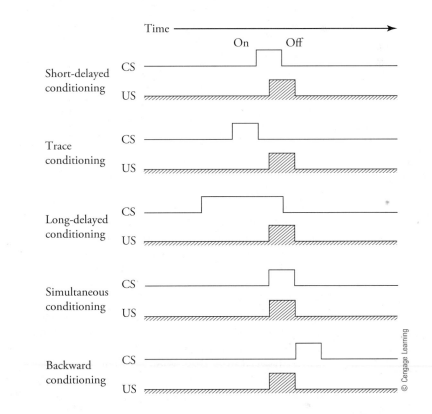

In a typical classical conditioning experiment, CS–US episodes are repeated a number of times during an experimental session. The time from the end of one conditioning trial to the start of the next trial is called the **intertrial interval**. By contrast, the time from the start of the CS to the start of the US within a conditioning trial is called the **interstimulus interval** or **CS-US interval**. For conditioned responding to develop, it is advisable to make the interstimulus interval much shorter than the intertrial interval (e.g., Sunsay & Bouton, 2008). In many experiments, the interstimulus interval is a few seconds, whereas the intertrial interval may be 2–3 minutes or more.

1. *Short-delayed conditioning.* The most frequently used procedure for Pavlovian conditioning involves delaying the start of the US slightly after the start of the CS on each trial. This procedure is called **short-delayed conditioning**. The critical feature of short-delayed conditioning is that the CS starts each trial, and the US is presented after a brief (less than 1 minute) delay. The CS may continue during the US or end when the US begins.

2. *Trace conditioning.* The **trace-conditioning** procedure is similar to the short-delayed procedure in that the CS is presented first and is followed by the US. However, in trace conditioning, the US is not presented until some time after the CS has ended. This leaves a gap between the CS and US. The gap is called the **trace interval**.

3. *Long-delayed conditioning.* The **long-delayed conditioning** procedure is also similar to the short-delayed conditioning in that the CS starts before the US. However, in this case the US is delayed much longer (510 minutes or more) than in the short-delayed procedure. Importantly, the long-delayed procedure does not include a trace interval. The CS lasts until the US begins.

4. *Simultaneous conditioning.* Perhaps the most obvious way to expose subjects to a CS and a US is to present the two stimuli at the same time. This procedure is called **simultaneous conditioning**. The critical feature of simultaneous conditioning is that the CS and US are presented concurrently.

5. *Backward conditioning.* The last procedure depicted in Figure 3.8 differs from the others in that the US occurs shortly *before*, rather than after, the CS. This technique is called **backward conditioning** because the CS and US are presented in a "backward" order compared to the other procedures.

Measuring Conditioned Responses

Pavlov and others after him have conducted systematic investigations of procedures such as those depicted in Figure 3.8 to find out how the conditioning of a CS depends on the temporal relation between CS and US presentations. To make comparisons among the various procedures, one has to use a method for measuring conditioning that is equally applicable to all procedures. This is typically done with the use of a **test trial**. A test trial consists of presenting the CS by itself (without the US). Responses elicited by the CS can then be observed without contamination from responses elicited by the US. Such CS-alone test trials can be introduced periodically during the course of training to track the progress of learning.

Behavior during the CS can be quantified in several ways. One aspect of conditioned behavior is how much of it occurs. This is called the **magnitude** of the CR. Pavlov, for example, measured the number of drops of saliva that were elicited by a CS. Other examples of the magnitude of CRs are the amount of freezing or response suppression that occurs in fear conditioning (Figure 3.2) and the degree of depressed flavor preference that is observed in taste-aversion learning (Figure 3.7).

The vigor of responding can also be measured by how often the CS elicits a CR. For example, we can measure the percentage of trials on which a CR is elicited by the CS. This measure is frequently used in studies of eyeblink conditioning (Figure 3.3) and reflects the likelihood, or **probability**, of responding. Sometimes investigators also measure how soon the CR occurs after the onset of the CS. This is called the **latency** of the CR.

In the delayed and trace-conditioning procedures, the CS occurs by itself at the start of each trial (Figure 3.8). Any conditioned behavior that occurs during this initial CS-alone period is uncontaminated by behavior elicited by the US and therefore can be used as a measure of learning. In contrast, responding during the CS in simultaneous and backward conditioning procedures is bound to be contaminated by responding to the US or the recent presentation of the US. Therefore, test trials are critical for assessing learning in simultaneous and backward conditioning.

Control Procedures for Classical Conditioning

Devising an effective test trial is not enough to obtain conclusive evidence of classical conditioning. As I noted in Chapter 1, learning is an inference about the causes of behavior based on a comparison of at least two conditions. Participants who receive a conditioning procedure have to be compared with participants in a control group who do not receive training. If the control group does not receive the conditioning procedure, what treatment should it receive? In studies of habituation and sensitization, we were interested only in the effects of prior exposure to a stimulus. Therefore, the comparison or control procedure was rather simple: it consisted of no prior stimulus exposures. In studies of classical conditioning, our interest is in how the CS and US become associated. Concluding that an association has been established requires more carefully designed control procedures.

An association between a CS and a US implies that the two events have become connected in some way. An association requires more than just familiarity with the CS and US. It presumably depends on having the two stimuli presented in a special way that leads to a connection between them. Therefore, to conclude that an association has been established, one has to make sure that the observed change in behavior could not have been produced by prior separate presentations of the CS or the US.

As I described in Chapter 2, increased responding to a stimulus can be a result of sensitization, which is not an associative process. Presentations of an arousing stimulus, such as food to a hungry animal, can increase the behavior elicited by a more innocuous stimulus, such as a visual cue, without an association having been established between the two stimuli. Increases in responding observed with repeated CS-US pairings can sometimes result from exposure to just the US. If exposure to just the US produces increased responding to a previously ineffective stimulus, this is called **pseudo-conditioning**. Control procedures are required to determine whether responses that develop to a CS represent a genuine CS–US association rather than just pseudo-conditioning.

Investigators have debated at length about what is the proper control procedure for classical conditioning. Ideally, a control procedure should involve the same number and distribution of CS and US presentations as the experimental procedure, but with the CSs and USs arranged so that they do not become associated. One possibility is to present the US at random times during both the CS and the intertrial interval, making sure that the probability of the US is the same during the intertrial interval as it is during the CS. Such a procedure is called a **random control procedure**. The random control procedure was promising when it was first proposed (Rescorla, 1967). However, it has not turned out to be a useful method because it does not prevent the development of conditioned responding (e.g., Kirkpatrick & Church, 2004; Williams et al., 2008).

A more successful control procedure involves presenting the CS and US on separate trials. Such a procedure is called the **explicitly unpaired control**. In the explicitly unpaired control, the CS and US are presented far enough apart to prevent their association, but the

Doug Williams

total number of CS and US presentations is the same as in the conditioned or paired group. How much time separates CS and US presentations depends on the response system. In taste-aversion learning, much longer separation is necessary between the CS and US than in other forms of conditioning. In one variation of the explicitly unpaired control, only CSs are presented during one session and only USs are presented during a second session.

Effectiveness of Common Conditioning Procedures

There has been considerable interest in determining which of the procedures depicted in Figure 3.8 produces the strongest evidence of learning. This interest was motivated by a search to find the "best" procedure for producing Pavlovian conditioning. However, that has turned out to be the wrong question to ask. Research has shown that delayed, simultaneous, trace, and backward conditioning can all produce strong learning and vigorous conditioned responding (e.g., Albert & Ayres, 1997; Akins & Domjan, 1996; Marchand & Kamper, 2000; Romaniuk & Williams, 2000; Schreurs, 1998; Williams & Hurlburt, 2000). However, different behavioral and neural mechanisms are engaged by these different procedures. For example, in fear conditioning the CS elicits conditioned freezing if a short-delayed procedure is used, but with a simultaneous conditioning procedure, the CR is movement away from the CS, or escape (Esmorís-Arranz, Pardo-Vázquez, & Vázquez-Garcia, 2003). (We will revisit these issues in Chapter 4).

Trace-conditioning procedures have been of special interest because they can have the same CS–US interval as delayed conditioning procedures. However, in trace procedures the CS is turned off a short time before the US occurs, resulting in a *trace interval.* This temporal gap between the CS and the US activates different behavioral and neural mechanisms. The trace interval makes termination of the CS a better predictor of the US than the onset of the CS. As a consequence, CRs that reflect anticipation of the US are more likely to occur during the trace interval than during the CS. In addition, trace conditioning involves medial forebrain cortical neurons that are not involved in delayed conditioning (Kalmbach et al., 2009; Woodruff-Pak & Disterhoft, 2008). Because of this difference, lesions of the prefrontal cortex that disrupt trace conditioning do not disrupt delayed conditioning. Interestingly, whereas both delayed and trace conditioning show a decline with aging, the decline is less severe with delayed conditioning (Woodruff-Pak et al., 2007).

Another procedure that has attracted special interest is backward conditioning. Backward conditioning produces mixed results. Some investigators observed excitatory responding with backward pairings of a CS and US (e.g., Spetch, Wilkie, & Pinel, 1981). Others reported inhibition of conditioned responding with backward conditioning (e.g., Maier, Rapaport, & Wheatley, 1976; Siegel & Domjan, 1971). To make matters even more confusing, in a rather remarkable experiment, Tait and Saladin (1986) found both excitatory and inhibitory conditioning effects resulting from the same backward conditioning procedure (see also, McNish et al., 1997).

One reason why there is no "best" procedure for Pavlovian conditioning is that instead of learning just a CS–US association, participants also learn *when* the US occurs in relation to the CS (Balsam, Drew, & Yang, 2001; Ohyama & Mauk, 2001). In fact, some have suggested that learning *when* the US occurs may be more important than learning that a CS is paired with a US (Balsam & Gallistel, 2009; Balsam, Drew, & Gallistel, 2010). The view that classical conditioning involves not only learning what to expect but when to expect it is called the **temporal coding hypothesis** (Amundson & Miller, 2008).

A particularly elegant demonstration of learning when the US occurs is provided by a study in which the CS was a 1-second tone in conditioning the nictitating membrane

FIGURE 3.9 Timing of the conditioned response during test trials with a 1000 millisecond conditioned tone stimulus in nictitating membrane conditioning. During conditioning trials, the US could occur 150 or 500 milliseconds after CS onset. (Based on Dudeney, Olsen, & Kehoe, 2007.)

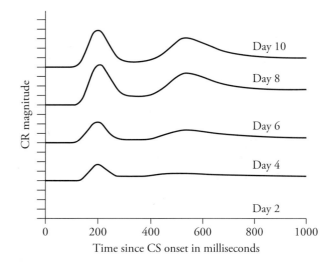

response of rabbits (Dudeney, Olsen, & Kehoe, 2007). (The nictitating membrane is an "extra" eyelid in rabbits.) During each session, the rabbits got 20 trials in which the US occurred 150 milliseconds after the onset of the CS and 20 trials in which the US occurred 500 milliseconds after the onset of the CS. Additional trials without the US were also included to measure responding to the CS by itself. The investigators were interested in whether the timing of the CR on the test trials would match the two possible time points when the US occurred during the CS.

Measures of the magnitude of the CR at different points during the CS are presented in Figure 3.9. No conditioned responding was observed early in training, but responding developed after that. Notice that when the CR emerged, it occurred at the points during the CS when the US had been delivered. Responding around 150 milliseconds developed first. By day 6, responding was also evident around 500 milliseconds. The end result was that there were two peaks in the CR, corresponding to the two times when the US could occur during the 1,000-millisecond tone CS. This clearly shows that the rabbits learned not just that the US would occur but also exactly when the US would happen. Furthermore, these two forms of learning developed at the same rate.

Inhibitory Pavlovian Conditioning

So far I have been discussing Pavlovian conditioning in terms of learning to predict when a significant event or US will occur. But there is another type of Pavlovian conditioning, **inhibitory conditioning**, in which you learn to predict the *absence* of the US. Why would you want to predict the absence of something?

Consider being in an environment where bad things happen to you without warning. Civilians in war can encounter roadside bombs or suicide bombers without much warning. A child in an abusive home experiences unpredictable bouts of yelling, slamming doors, and getting hit for no particular reason. Getting pushed and shoved in a crowd also involves danger that arises without much warning and independent of what you might be doing. Research with laboratory animals has shown that exposure to unpredictable aversive stimulation is highly aversive and results in stomach ulcers and other physiological symptoms of stress. If one has to be exposed to aversive stimulation, predictable or signaled aversive stimuli are much preferred to unpredictable aversive

Michelle Craske

stimulation (Mineka & Henderson, 1985), especially among anxiety-prone individuals (Lejuez et al., 2000).

The benefit of predictability is evident even in the case of a panic attack. A panic attack is a sudden sense of fear or discomfort, accompanied by physical symptoms (e.g., heart palpitations) and a sense of impending doom. If such attacks are fairly frequent and become the source of considerable anxiety, the individual is said to suffer from panic disorder. Sometimes, individuals with panic disorder are able to predict the onset of a panic attack. At other times, they may experience an attack without warning. In a study of individuals who experienced both predictable and unpredictable panic attacks, Craske, Glover, and DeCola (1995) measured the general anxiety of the participants before and after each type of attack. The results are summarized in Figure 3.10. Before the attack, anxiety ratings were similar whether the attack was predictable or not. Interestingly, however, anxiety significantly increased after an unpredicted panic attack and decreased after a predicted attack. Such results indicate that the distress generated by the experience of a panic attack occurs primarily because of the unpredictability of the attack.

The ability to predict bad things is very helpful because it also enables you to predict when bad things will not happen. Consistent with this reasoning, many effective stress-reduction techniques, such as relaxation training or meditation, involve creating a predictable period of safety or a time when you can be certain that nothing bad will happen. Stress management consultants recognize that it is impossible to eliminate aversive events from one's life altogether. For example, a teacher supervising a playground with preschool children is bound to encounter the unexpected stress of a child falling or hitting another child. One cannot prevent accidents or make sure that children won't hit each other. However, introducing even short periods of predictable safety (e.g., by allowing the teacher to take a break) can substantially reduce stress. That is where conditioned inhibition comes in. A conditioned inhibitor is a signal for the absence of the US.

Although Pavlov discovered inhibitory conditioning early in the twentieth century, this type of learning did not command the serious attention of psychologists until decades later (Rescorla, 1969b; Williams, Overmier, & LoLordo, 1992). I will describe two major procedures used to produce conditioned inhibition and the special tests that are necessary to detect and measure conditioned inhibition.

FIGURE 3.10 Ratings of general anxiety in individuals with panic disorder before and after predicted and unpredicted panic attacks. (From M. G. Craske, D. Glover, and J. DeCola (1995). Predicted versus unpredicted panic attacks: Acute versus general distress. *Journal of Abnormal Psychology, 104*, Figure 1, p. 219.)

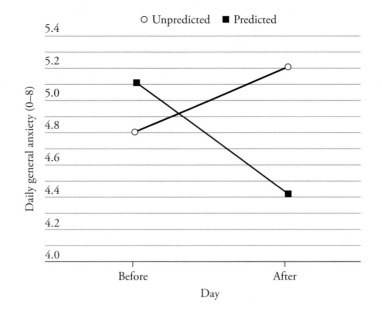

Procedures for Inhibitory Conditioning

Unlike excitatory conditioning, which can proceed without special preconditions, conditioned inhibition has an important prerequisite. For the absence of a US to be a significant event, the US has to occur periodically in the situation. There are many signals for the absence of events in our daily lives. Signs such as "Closed," "Out of Order," and "No Entry" are all of this type. However, these signs provide meaningful information and influence what we do only if they indicate the absence of something we otherwise expect to see. For example, if we encounter the sign "Out of Gas" at a service station, we may become frustrated and disappointed. The sign "Out of Gas" provides important information here because we expect service stations to have fuel. The same sign does not tell us anything of interest if it is in the window of a lumberyard, and it is not likely to discourage us from going to buy lumber. This illustrates the general rule that inhibitory conditioning and inhibitory control of behavior occur only if there is an excitatory context for the US in question (e.g., LoLordo & Fairless, 1985). This principle makes inhibitory conditioning very different from excitatory conditioning, which has no such prerequisites.

Pavlov's Procedure for Conditioned Inhibition Pavlov recognized the importance of an excitatory context for the conditioning of inhibition and was careful to provide such a context in his standard inhibitory training procedure (Pavlov, 1927). The procedure he used, diagrammed in Figure 3.11, involves two CSs and two kinds of conditioning trials, one for excitatory conditioning and the other for inhibitory conditioning. The US is presented on excitatory conditioning trials (Trial Type A in Figure 3.11), and whenever the US occurs, it is announced by a stimulus labeled CS+ (e.g., a tone). Because of its pairings with the US, the CS+ becomes a signal for the US and can then provide the excitatory context for the development of conditioned inhibition.

During inhibitory conditioning trials (Trial Type B in Figure 3.11), the CS+ is presented together with the second stimulus called the CS− (e.g., a light), and the US does not occur. Thus, the CS− is presented in the excitatory context provided by the CS+, but the CS− is not paired with the US. This makes the CS− a conditioned inhibitor or signal for the absence of the US. During the course of training, A-type and B-type trials are alternated randomly. As the participant receives repeated trials of CS+ followed by the US and CS+/CS− followed by no US, the CS− gradually acquires inhibitory properties (e.g., Campolattaro, Schnitker, & Freeman, 2008).

Pavlov's conditioned inhibition procedure is analogous to a situation in which something is introduced that prevents an outcome that would occur otherwise. A red traffic light at a busy intersection is a signal for potential danger because running the light could get you into an accident. However, if a police officer indicates that you should

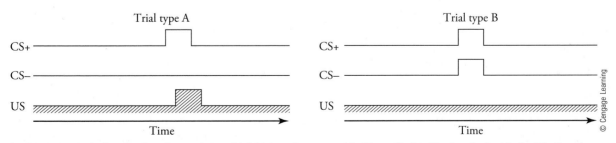

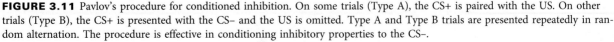

FIGURE 3.11 Pavlov's procedure for conditioned inhibition. On some trials (Type A), the CS+ is paired with the US. On other trials (Type B), the CS+ is presented with the CS− and the US is omitted. Type A and Type B trials are presented repeatedly in random alternation. The procedure is effective in conditioning inhibitory properties to the CS−.

cross the intersection despite the red light (perhaps because the traffic light is malfunctioning), you will probably not have an accident. Here the red light is the CS+ and the gestures of the officer constitute the CS–. The gestures inhibit, or block, your hesitation to cross the intersection because of the red light.

A CS– acts as a safety signal in the context of danger. Children who are afraid will take refuge in the arms of a parent because the parent serves as a safety signal. Adults who are anxious also use safety signals to reduce or inhibit their fear or anxiety. People rely on prayer, a friend, a therapist, or a comforting food at times of stress (Barlow, 1988). These work in part because we have learned that bad things don't happen in their presence.

Negative CS-US Contingency or Correlation Another common procedure for producing conditioned inhibition does not involve an explicit excitatory stimulus or CS+. Rather, it involves just a CS– that is negatively correlated with the US. A negative correlation or contingency means that the US is less likely to occur after the CS than at other times. Thus, the CS signals a reduction in the probability that the US will occur. A sample arrangement that meets this requirement is diagrammed in Figure 3.12. The US is periodically presented by itself. However, each occurrence of the CS is followed by the predictable absence of the US for a while.

Consider a child who periodically gets picked on or bullied by his or her classmates when the teacher is out of the room. This is like periodically receiving an aversive stimulus or US. When the teacher returns, the child can be sure he or she will not be bothered. Thus, the teacher serves as a CS– that signals a period free from harassment, or the absence of the US.

Conditioned inhibition is reliably observed in procedures in which the only explicit CS is negatively correlated with the US (Rescorla, 1969a). What provides the excitatory context for this inhibition? In this case, the environmental cues of the experimental chamber provide the excitatory context (Dweck & Wagner, 1970). Because the US occurs periodically in the experimental situation, the contextual cues of the experimental chamber acquire excitatory properties. This in turn permits the acquisition of inhibitory properties by the CS. (For a study of the role of context in inhibitory conditioning, see Chang, Blaisdell, & Miller, 2003.)

In a negative CS–US contingency procedure, the aversive US may occur shortly after the CS occasionally but it is much more likely to occur in the absence of the CS; that is what defines the negative CS–US contingency. However, even in the absence of the CS, the exact timing of the US cannot be predicted exactly because the US occurs at various times probabilistically. This is in contrast to Pavlov's procedure for conditioned inhibition. In Pavlov's procedure, the US always occurs at the end of the CS+ but never occurs when the CS– is presented together with the CS+. Because Pavlov's procedure permits predicting the exact timing of the US, it also permits predicting exactly when the US will *not* occur. The US will not occur at the end of CS+ if the CS+ is presented with the CS–. Tests of temporal learning have shown that in Pavlov's procedure for conditioned inhibition participants learn exactly when the US will be omitted (Denniston, Blaisdell, & Miller, 2004; Williams, Johns, & Brindas, 2008).

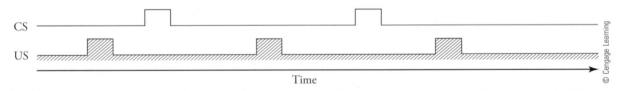

Time

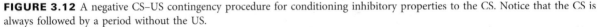

© Cengage Learning

FIGURE 3.12 A negative CS–US contingency procedure for conditioning inhibitory properties to the CS. Notice that the CS is always followed by a period without the US.

Measuring Conditioned Inhibition

How are conditioned inhibitory processes manifested in behavior? For conditioned excitation, the answer to this type of question is straightforward. Excitatory stimuli elicit new CRs such as salivation, approach, or eye blinking. One might expect that conditioned inhibitory stimuli would elicit the opposites of these reactions—namely, suppression of salivation, approach, or eye blinking—but how are we to measure such response opposites?

Bidirectional Response Systems   Identification of an opposing response tendency is easy with response systems that can change in opposite directions from baseline or normal performance. Heart rate, respiration, and temperature can all increase or decrease from a baseline level. Certain behavioral responses are also bidirectional. For example, animals can either approach or withdraw from a stimulus or drink more or less of a flavored solution. In these cases, conditioned excitation results in a change in behavior in one direction, and conditioned inhibition results in a change in behavior in the opposite direction.

Unfortunately, many responses are not bidirectional. Consider freezing or response suppression as a measure of conditioned fear. A conditioned excitatory stimulus will elicit freezing, but a conditioned inhibitor will not produce activity above normal levels. A similar problem arises in eyeblink conditioning. A CS+ will elicit increased blinking, but the inhibitory effects of a CS– are difficult to detect because the baseline rate of blinking is low to begin with. It is hard to see inhibition of blinking below an already low baseline. Because of these limitations, conditioned inhibition is typically measured indirectly using the compound-stimulus test and the retardation of acquisition test.

The Compound-Stimulus, or Summation, Test   The **compound-stimulus test** (or **summation test**) was particularly popular with Pavlov and remains one of the most widely accepted procedures for the measurement of conditioned inhibition. The test is based on the simple idea that conditioned inhibition counteracts or inhibits conditioned excitation. Therefore, to observe conditioned inhibition, one has to measure how the presentation of a CS– disrupts or suppresses responding that would normally be elicited by a CS+.

A particularly well-controlled demonstration of conditioned inhibition using the compound-stimulus or summation test was reported by Cole, Barnet, and Miller (1997). The experiment was conducted using the lick-suppression procedure with laboratory rats. The rats received inhibitory conditioning in which the presentation of a flashing light by itself always ended in a brief shock (A+), and the presentation of an auditory cue (X) together with the light ended without shock (AX–). Thus, Pavlov's procedure for conditioned inhibition was used, and X was expected to become an inhibitor of fear. A total of 28 A+ trials and 56 AX– trials were conducted over seven sessions. The rats also received training with another auditory stimulus (B) in a different experimental chamber, and this stimulus always ended in the brief shock (B+). The intent of these procedures was to establish conditioned excitation to A and B and conditioned inhibition to X.

Cole and colleagues then asked whether the presumed inhibitor X would suppress responding to the excitatory stimuli A and B. The results of those tests are summarized in Figure 3.13. How long the rats took to accumulate 5 seconds of uninterrupted drinking was measured. Conditioned fear was expected to slow the rate of drinking. Notice that when the excitatory stimuli, A and B, were presented by themselves, the rats required substantial amounts of time to complete the 5-second drinking criterion. In contrast, when the excitatory stimuli were presented together with the conditioned inhibitor (AX and BX tests), the drinking requirement was completed much faster. Thus,

FIGURE 3.13

Compound-stimulus test of inhibition in a lick-suppression experiment. Stimuli A and B were conditioned as excitatory stimuli by being presented alone with shock (A+ and B+). Stimulus X was conditioned as an inhibitor by being presented with stimulus A without shock (AX–). Stimulus Y was a control stimulus that had not participated in either excitatory or inhibitory conditioning. A was a flashing light; B, X, and Y were auditory cues (a clicker, white noise, and a buzzer, counterbalanced across participants.) A and AX were tested in the original training context. B, BX, and BY were tested in a different context. (Based on Cole, R. P., Barner, R. C., & Miller, R. R. (1997). An evaluation of conditioned inhibition as defined by Rescorla's two-testing strategy in *Learning and Motivation*, Volume 28, 333, copyright 1997, Elsevier Science (USA).)

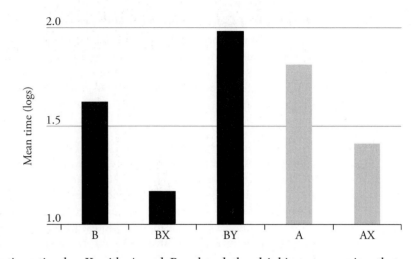

presenting stimulus X with A and B reduced the drinking suppression that occurred when A and B were presented alone. X inhibited conditioned fear elicited by A and B.

Figure 3.13 includes another test condition: stimulus B tested with another auditory cue, Y. Stimulus Y was not previously conditioned as an inhibitor and was presented to be sure that introducing a new stimulus with stimulus B would not cause disruption of the conditioned fear response just because of novelty. As Figure 3.13 illustrates, no such disruption occurred with stimulus Y. Thus, the inhibition of conditioned fear was limited to the stimulus (X) that received conditioned inhibition training. Another important aspect of these results is that X was able to inhibit conditioned fear not only to the exciter with which it was trained (A) but also to another exciter (B) that had never been presented with X during training. Thus, X became a general safety signal.

The compound-stimulus test for conditioned inhibition indicates that the presentation of a conditioned inhibitor or safety signal can reduce the stressful effects of an aversive experience. This prediction has been tested with patients who were prone to experience panic attacks (Carter et al., 1995). Panic attack patients were invited to the laboratory and accompanied by someone with whom they felt safe. Panic was experimentally induced by having the participants inhale a mixture of gas containing elevated levels of carbon dioxide. The participants were then asked to report on their perceived levels of anxiety and catastrophic ideation triggered by the carbon dioxide exposure. The experimental manipulation was the presence of another person with whom the participants felt safe (the conditioned inhibitor). The presence of a safe acquaintance reduced the anxiety and catastrophic ideation associated with the panic attack. These results explain why children are less fearful during a medical examination if they are accompanied by a trusted parent or allowed to carry a favorite toy or blanket.

The Retardation of Acquisition Test   Another frequently used indirect test of conditioned inhibition is the **retardation of acquisition test** (Rescorla, 1969b). The rationale for this test is straightforward. If a stimulus actively inhibits a particular response, then it should be especially difficult to turn that stimulus into a conditioned excitatory CS. In other words, the rate of excitatory conditioning should be retarded if the CS was previously established as a conditioned inhibitor. This prediction was tested by Cole and colleagues (1997) in an experiment very similar to their summation test study described earlier.

After the same kind of inhibitory conditioning that produced the results summarized in Figure 3.13, Cole and colleagues took stimulus X (which had been conditioned as an inhibitor) and stimulus Y (which had not been used in a conditioning procedure

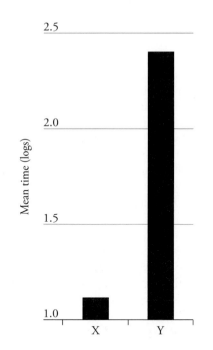

FIGURE 3.14 Effects of a retardation of acquisition test of inhibition in a lick-suppression experiment after the same kind of inhibitory conditioning as was conducted to produce the results presented in Figure 3.13. Stimulus X was previously conditioned as an inhibitory stimulus, and stimulus Y previously received no training. (Based on Cole, R. P., Barner, R. C., & Miller, R. R. (1997). An evaluation of conditioned inhibition as defined by Rescorla's two-testing strategy in *Learning and Motivation*, Volume 28, 333, copyright 1997, Elsevier Science (USA).)

before) and conducted a retardation of acquisition test by pairing each stimulus with shock on three occasions. (Three acquisition trials were sufficient because conditioned fear is learned faster than the inhibition of fear.) Stimuli X and Y were then tested to see which would cause greater suppression of drinking. The results are presented in Figure 3.14. The time to complete 5 seconds of drinking took much longer in the presence of the control stimulus Y than in the presence of stimulus X, which had previously been trained as a conditioned inhibitor. This indicates that Y elicited greater conditioned fear than stimulus X. Evidently, the initial inhibitory training of X retarded its acquisition of excitatory conditioned fear.

Conditioned inhibition can be difficult to distinguish from other behavioral processes. Therefore, the best strategy is to use more than one test and be sure that all of the results point to the same conclusion. Rescorla (1969b) advocated using both the compound-stimulus test and the retardation of acquisition test. This dual-test strategy has remained popular ever since.

Prevalence of Classical Conditioning

Classical conditioning is typically investigated in laboratory situations. However, we do not have to know much about classical conditioning to realize that it also occurs in a wide range of situations outside the laboratory. Classical conditioning is most likely to develop when one event reliably precedes another in a short-delayed CS-US pairing. This occurs in many aspects of life. As I mentioned at the beginning of the chapter, stimuli in the environment occur in an orderly temporal sequence, largely because of the physical constraints of causation. Some events simply cannot happen before other things have occurred. Eggs won't be hard boiled until they have been put in boiling water. Social institutions and customs also ensure that things happen in a predictable order. Whenever one stimulus reliably precedes another, classical conditioning may occur.

One area of research that has been of particular interest is how people come to judge one event as the cause of another. In studies of human causal judgment, participants are exposed to repeated occurrences of two events (pictures of a blooming flower and a watering can are briefly presented on a computer screen) in various temporal arrangements. In one condition, for example, the watering can may always occur before the flower; in another it may occur at random times relative to the flower. After observing numerous appearances of both objects, the participants are asked to indicate their judgment about the strength of causal relation between them. Studies of human causal judgment are analogous to studies of Pavlovian conditioning in that both involve repeated experiences with two events and responses based on the extent to which those two events become linked to each other. Given this correspondence, one might suspect that there is considerable commonality in the outcomes of causal judgment and Pavlovian conditioning experiments. That prediction has been supported in numerous studies, suggesting that Pavlovian associative mechanisms are not limited to Pavlov's dogs but may play a role in the numerous judgments of causality we all make during the course of our daily lives (see Allan, 2005).

As I described earlier in the chapter, Pavlovian conditioning can result in the conditioning of food preferences and aversions. It can also result in the acquisition of fear. Conditioned fear responses have been of special interest because they may contribute significantly to anxiety disorders, phobias, and panic disorder (Craske, Hermans, & Vansteenwegen, 2006; Oehlberg & Mineka, 2011). As I will discuss further in Chapter 4, Pavlovian conditioning is also involved in drug tolerance and addiction. Cues that reliably accompany drug administration can elicit drug-related responses through conditioning. In discussing this type of learning among crack addicts, Dr. Scott Lukas of McLean Hospital in Massachusetts described the effects of drug-conditioned stimuli by saying that "these cues turn on crack-related memories, and addicts respond like Pavlov's dogs" (*Newsweek*, February 12, 2001, p. 40).

Pavlovian conditioning is also involved in infant and maternal responses in nursing. Suckling involves mutual stimulation for the infant and the mother. To successfully nurse, the mother has to hold the baby in a particular position that provides special tactile and olfactory cues for both the infant and the mother. The tactile stimuli experienced by the infant may become conditioned to elicit orientation and suckling responses on the part of the baby (Blass, Ganchrow, & Steiner, 1984). Olfactory cues experienced by the infant during suckling can also become conditioned. In one study (Allam et al., 2010), infants preferred to play with objects that had the odor of camomile if their mother previously used a camomile-scented lotion on her breast. Interestingly, this preference was evident more than a year after the mothers had stopped using the lotion.

Tactile stimuli provided by the infant to the mother may also become conditioned, in this case to elicit the milk let-down response in anticipation of having the infant suckle. Mothers who nurse their babies experience the milk let-down reflex when the baby cries or when the usual time for breast-feeding arrives. All these stimuli (special tactile cues, the baby's crying, and the time of normal feedings) reliably precede suckling by the infant. Therefore, they can become conditioned by the suckling stimulation to elicit milk let-down as a CR. The anticipatory conditioned orientation and suckling responses and the anticipatory conditioned milk let-down response make the nursing experience more successful for both the baby and the mother.

Pavlovian conditioning is also important in sexual situations. Studies have shown that sexual behavior can be shaped by learning experiences in both people and in various animal species (Hoffmann, 2011; Woodson, 2002). In these studies, males typically serve as the research participants, and the US is provided either by the sight of a sexually receptive female or by physical access to a female. Conditioned males approach stimuli that signal the availability of a sexual partner (Burns & Domjan, 1996; Hollis, Cadieux, & Colbert, 1989). As we will describe in Chapter 4, a sexually

K. L. Hollis

CS also facilitates various aspects of reproductive behavior. Most importantly, the presentation of a Pavlovian CS+ before a sexual encounter greatly increases the number of offspring that result from the reproductive behavior. This Pavlovian conditioned fertility effect was originally demonstrated in a fish species (Hollis, 1997) but has since been also found in studies with domesticated quail (Domjan, Mahometa, & Matthews, 2012). In one of the more dramatic experiments, Pavlovian conditioning determined the outcome of sperm competition in domesticated quail (Matthews et al., 2007). To observe sperm competition, two male quail were permitted to copulate with the same female. A copulatory interaction in quail can fertilize as many as 10 of the eggs the female produces after the sexual encounter. If two males copulate with the same female in succession, the male whose copulation is signaled by a Pavlovian CS+ sires significantly more of the resulting offspring. By influencing which male's genes are represented in the next generation, Pavlovian conditioning can bias the evolutionary changes that result from sexual competition.

Concluding Comments

This chapter continued our discussion of elicited behavior by turning attention from habituation and sensitization to classical conditioning. Classical conditioning is a bit more complex in that it involves associatively mediated elicited behavior. In fact, classical conditioning is one of the major techniques for investigating how associations are learned. As we have seen, classical conditioning may be involved in many important aspects of behavior. Depending on the procedure used, the learning may occur quickly or slowly. With some procedures, excitatory responses are learned; with other procedures, the organism learns to inhibit an excitatory response tendency. Excitatory and inhibitory conditioning occur in many aspects of common experience and serve to help us interact more effectively with significant biological events (USs).

Sample Questions

1. Describe the similarities and differences among habituation, sensitization, and classical conditioning.
2. What is object learning, and how is it similar to or different from conventional classical conditioning?
3. Why is it difficult to identify the type of conditioning procedure that produces the best conditioning?
4. What is a control procedure for excitatory conditioning, and what processes is the control procedure intended to rule out?
5. Are conditioned excitation and conditioned inhibition related? If so, how?
6. Describe procedures for conditioning and measuring conditioned inhibition.
7. Describe four reasons why classical conditioning is of interest to psychologists.

Key Terms

autoshaping   Same as *sign tracking.*

backward conditioning   A procedure in which the CS is presented shortly after the US on each trial.

compound-stimulus test   A test procedure that identifies a stimulus as a conditioned inhibitor if that stimulus reduces the responding elicited by a conditioned excitatory stimulus. Also called *summation test.*

conditional or **conditioned response (CR)**   The response that comes to be made to the CS as a result of classical conditioning.

conditional or **conditioned stimulus (CS)**   A stimulus that does not elicit a particular response initially, but comes to do so as a result of becoming associated with an US.

conditioned suppression Suppression of ongoing behavior (e.g., drinking or lever pressing for food) produced by the presentation of a CS that has been conditioned to elicit fear through association with an aversive US.

conditioning trial A training episode involving presentation of a CS with (or without) a US.

CS-US interval Same as *interstimulus interval*.

evaluative conditioning Changing the hedonic value or liking of an initially neutral stimulus by having that stimulus associated with something that is already liked or disliked.

explicitly unpaired control A procedure in which both CS and US are presented, but with sufficient time between them so that they do not become associated with each other.

goal tracking Conditioned behavior elicited by a CS that consists of approaching the location where the US is usually presented.

inhibitory conditioning A type of classical conditioning in which the CS becomes a signal for the absence of the US.

interstimulus interval The amount of time that elapses between the start of the CS and the start of the US during a classical conditioning trial. Also called the *CS-US interval*.

intertrial interval The amount of time that elapses between two successive trials.

latency The time elapsed between a stimulus (or the start of a trial) and the response that is made to the stimulus.

lick-suppression procedure A procedure for testing fear conditioning in which presentation of a fear-conditioned CS slows down the rate of drinking.

long-delayed conditioning A conditioning procedure in which the US occurs more than several minutes after the start of the CS, as in taste-aversion learning.

magnitude of a response A measure of the size, vigor, or extent of a response.

object learning Learning associations between different stimulus features of an object, such as what it looks like and how it tastes.

probability of a response The likelihood of making the response, usually represented in terms of the percentage of trials on which the response occurs.

pseudo-conditioning Increased responding that may occur to a stimulus whose presentations are intermixed with presentations of a US in the absence of the establishment of an association between the stimulus and the US.

random control procedure A procedure in which the CS and US are presented at random times with respect to each other.

retardation of acquisition test A test procedure that identifies a stimulus as a conditioned inhibitor if that stimulus is slower to acquire excitatory properties than a comparison stimulus.

short-delayed conditioning A classical conditioning procedure in which the CS is initiated shortly before the US on each conditioning trial.

sign tracking Movement toward and possibly contact with a stimulus that signals the availability of a positive reinforcer, such as food. Also called *autoshaping*.

simultaneous conditioning A classical conditioning procedure in which the CS and the US are presented at the same time on each conditioning trial.

summation test Same as *compound-stimulus test*.

temporal coding hypothesis The idea that Pavlovian conditioning procedures lead not only to learning that the US happens but exactly when it occurs in relation to the CS. The CS represents (or codes) the timing of the US.

test trial A trial in which the CS is presented without the US. This allows measurement of the CR in the absence of the UR.

trace conditioning A classical conditioning procedure in which the US is presented after the CS has been terminated for a short period.

trace interval The interval between the end of the CS and the start of the US in trace-conditioning trials.

unconditional or **unconditioned response (UR)** A response that occurs to a stimulus without the necessity of prior training.

unconditional or **unconditioned stimulus (US)** A stimulus that elicits a particular response without the necessity of prior training.

Classical Conditioning: Mechanisms

CHAPTER PREVIEW

Chapter 4 continues the discussion of classical conditioning, focusing on the mechanisms and outcomes of this type of learning. The discussion is organized around three key issues. First, I will describe features of stimuli that determine their effectiveness as conditioned and unconditioned stimuli. Then, I will discuss factors that determine the types of responses that come to be made to conditioned stimuli and how conditioning alters how organisms respond to the unconditioned stimulus. In the third and final section of the chapter, I will discuss the mechanisms of learning involved in the development of conditioned responding. Much of the discussion will deal with how associations are established and expressed in behavior. However, I will also describe a nonassociate model of learning based on information theory.

What Makes Effective Conditioned and Unconditioned Stimuli?

This is perhaps the most basic question one can ask about classical conditioning. The question was first posed by Pavlov but continues to attract the attention of contemporary researchers.

Initial Responses to the Stimuli

Pavlov's answer to what makes effective conditioned and unconditioned stimuli was implied by his definitions of the terms *conditioned* and *unconditioned.* According to these definitions, the CS does not elicit the conditioned response initially but comes to do so as a result of becoming associated with the US. By contrast, the US is effective in eliciting the target response from the outset (unconditionally) without any special training.

Pavlov's definitions were stated in terms of the elicitation of the response to be conditioned. Because of this, identifying potential CSs and USs requires comparing the responses elicited by each stimulus before conditioning. Such a comparison makes the identification of CSs and USs *relative.* A particular event may serve as a CS relative to one stimulus and as a US relative to another.

Consider, for example, food pellets flavored with sucrose. The taste of the sucrose pellets may serve as a CS in a taste-aversion conditioning procedure, in which conditioning trials consist of pairing the sucrose pellets with illness. As a result of such pairings, the participants will acquire an aversion to eating the sucrose pellets.

In a different experiment, Franklin and Hall (2011) used sucrose pellets as a US in a sign-tracking experiment with rats. The conditioning trials in this case involved inserting a response lever (the CS) before each delivery of the sucrose pellet (the US). After a number of trials of this sort, the rats began to approach and press the response lever. Thus, sucrose pellets could be either a US or a CS depending on how presentations of the pellets are related to other stimuli in the situation.

Novelty of Conditioned and Unconditioned Stimuli

As we saw in studies of habituation, the behavioral impact of a stimulus depends on its novelty. Highly familiar stimuli elicit less vigorous reactions than do novel stimuli. Novelty is also important in classical conditioning. If either the conditioned or the unconditioned stimulus is highly familiar, learning occurs more slowly than if the CS and US are novel.

The Latent-Inhibition or CS-Preexposure Effect Numerous studies have shown that if a stimulus is highly familiar, it will not be as effective as a CS than if it were novel. This phenomenon is called the **latent-inhibition effect** or **CS-preexposure effect** (Hall, 1991; Lubow & Weiner, 2010). Experiments on the latent-inhibition effect involve two phases. Participants are first given repeated presentations of the CS by itself. This is called the preexposure phase because it comes before the Pavlovian conditioning trials. CS preexposure makes the CS highly familiar and of no particular significance because at this point the CS is presented alone. After the preexposure phase, the CS is paired with a US using conventional classical conditioning procedures. The common result is that participants are slower to acquire responding because of the CS preexposure. Thus, CS preexposure disrupts or retards learning (e.g., De la Casa, Marquez, & Lubow, 2009). The effect is called *latent inhibition* to distinguish it from the phenomenon of conditioned inhibition I described in Chapter 3.

Latent inhibition is similar to habituation. Both phenomena serve to limit processing and attention to stimuli that are presented without a US and are therefore inconsequential.

FIGURE 4.3 Diagram of Garcia and Koelling's (1966) experiment. A compound taste–audiovisual stimulus was first paired with either shock or sickness for separate groups of laboratory rats. The subjects were then tested with the taste and audiovisual stimuli separately.

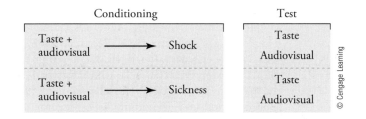

activated a brief audiovisual stimulus (a click and a flash of light). Thus, the rats encountered the taste and audiovisual stimuli at the same time. After exposure to these CSs, the animals either received a brief shock through the grid floor or were made sick.

Because both USs were aversive, the rats were expected to learn an aversion of some kind. To observe these aversions, the taste and audiovisual CSs were presented individually after conditioning. During tests of the taste CS, the water was flavored as before, but now licks did not activate the audiovisual cue. During tests of the audiovisual CS, the water was unflavored, but the audiovisual cue was briefly turned on each time the animal licked the spout. Conditioned aversions were inferred from the suppression of drinking.

The results of the experiment are summarized in Figure 4.4. Animals conditioned with shock subsequently suppressed their drinking much more when tested with the audiovisual stimulus than when tested with the taste CS. The opposite result occurred for animals that had been conditioned with sickness. These rats suppressed their drinking much more when the taste CS was presented than when drinking produced the audiovisual stimulus.

Garcia and Koelling's experiment demonstrates the principle of CS–US *relevance*, or *belongingness*. Learning depended on the relevance of the CS to the US. Taste became readily associated with illness, and audiovisual cues became readily associated with peripheral pain. Rapid learning occurred only if the CS was combined with the appropriate US. The audiovisual CS was not generally more effective than the taste CS. Rather, the audiovisual CS was more effective only when shock served as the US. Correspondingly, the shock US was not generally more effective than the sickness US. Rather, shock conditioned stronger aversions than sickness only when the audiovisual cue served as the CS.

FIGURE 4.4 Results from Garcia and Koelling's experiment. Rats conditioned with sickness learned a stronger aversion to taste than to audiovisual cues. By contrast, rats conditioned with shock learned a stronger aversion to audiovisual than to taste cues (adapted from Garcia and Koelling, 1966).

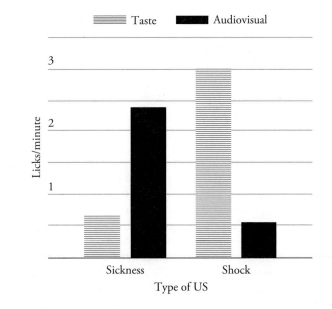

The CS–US relevance effect obtained by Garcia and Koelling was not readily accepted at first. However, numerous subsequent studies have confirmed the original findings (e.g., Domjan, 1983; Rescorla, 2008). The selective-association effect occurs even in rats one day after birth (Gemberling & Domjan, 1982). This observation indicates that extensive experience with tastes and sickness (or audiovisual cues and peripheral pain) is not necessary for the stimulus-relevance effect. Rather, the phenomenon appears to reflect a genetic predisposition for the selective learning of certain combinations of conditioned and unconditioned stimuli. (For evidence of stimulus relevance in human food-aversion learning, see Logue et al., 1981; Pelchat & Rozin, 1982.)

Stimulus-relevance effects have been documented in other situations as well. In Chapter 8 we will visit a prominent example of stimulus relevance contrasting learning about appetitive events versus aversive events. Stimulus-relevance effects are also prominent in the acquisition of fear in primates (Öhman & Mineka, 2001; Mineka & Öhman, 2002). Experiments with both rhesus monkeys and people have shown that fear conditioning progresses more rapidly with fear-relevant cues (the sight of a snake) than with fear-irrelevant cues (the sight of a flower or mushroom). However, this difference is not observed if an appetitive US is used. This selective advantage of snake stimuli in fear conditioning does not require conscious awareness (e.g., Öhman et al., 2007) and seems to reflect an evolutionary adaptation to rapidly detect biologically dangerous stimuli and acquire fear to such cues. Consistent with this conclusion, infants as young as 8–14 months orient more quickly to pictures of snakes than to pictures of flowers (LoBue & DeLoache, 2010). As Mineka and Öhman (2002) pointed out, "Fear conditioning occurs most readily in situations that provide recurrent survival threats in mammalian evolution" (p. 928).

Learning Without an Unconditioned Stimulus

So far, we have been discussing classical conditioning in situations that include a US: a stimulus that has a large behavioral impact unconditionally, without prior training. If Pavlovian conditioning were only applicable to situations that involve a US, it would be somewhat limited. It would occur only if you received food, shock, or had sex. How about the rest of time, when you are not eating or having sex? As it turns out, Pavlovian conditioning can also take place in situations where you do not encounter a US. There are two different forms of classical conditioning without a US. One is *higher-order conditioning* and the other is *sensory preconditioning*.

Higher-Order Conditioning   Irrational fears are often learned through **higher-order conditioning**. For example, Wolpe (1990) described the case of a lady who developed a fear of crowds. Thus, for her being in a crowd was a CS that elicited conditioned fear. How this fear was originally learned is unknown. Perhaps she was pushed and shoved in a crowd (CS) and suffered an injury (US). To avoid arousing her fear, the lady would go to the movies only in the daytime when few people were in the theater. On one such visit, the theater suddenly became crowded with students. The lady became extremely upset by this and came to associate cues of the movie theater with crowds. Thus, one CS (crowds) had conditioned fear to another (the movie theater) that previously elicited no fear. The remarkable aspect of this transfer of fear is that the lady never experienced bodily injury or an aversive US in the movie theater. In that sense, her new fear of movie theaters was irrational.

As this case study illustrates, higher-order conditioning occurs in two phases. During the first phase, a cue (call it CS_1) is paired with a US often enough to condition a strong response to CS_1. In the above case study, the stimuli of crowds constituted CS_1. Once CS_1 elicited the conditioned response, pairing CS_1 with a new stimulus CS_2

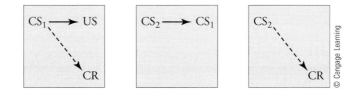

FIGURE 4.5 Procedure for higher-order conditioning. CS_1 is first paired with the US and comes to elicit the conditioned response. A new stimulus (CS_2) is then paired with CS_1. Subsequent tests show that CS_2 also comes to elicit the conditioned response.

(cues of the movie theater) was able to condition CS_2 to also elicit the conditioned response. The conditioning of CS_2 occurred in the absence of the US. Figure 4.5 summarizes these stages of learning that result in higher-order conditioning.

As the term "higher order" implies, conditioning may be considered to operate at different levels. In the preceding example, the experience of crowds (CS_1) paired with injury (US) is *first-order conditioning*. Pairing of CS_2 (movie theaters) with CS_1 (crowds) is *second-order conditioning*. If after becoming conditioned, CS_2 were used to condition yet another stimulus, CS_3, that would be *third-order conditioning*.

The procedure for second-order conditioning shown in Figure 4.5 is similar to the standard procedure for inhibitory conditioning that was described in Chapter 3 (Figure 3.11). In both cases, one conditioned stimulus (CS_1 or CS^+) is paired with the US ($CS_1 \rightarrow$ US or $CS^+ \rightarrow$ US), and a second CS (CS_2 or CS^-) is paired with the first one without the unconditioned stimulus ($CS_1/CS_2 \rightarrow$ noUS or $CS^+/CS^- \rightarrow$ noUS). Why does such a procedure produce conditioned inhibition in some cases and excitatory second-order conditioning under other circumstances? One important factor appears to be the number of noUS or nonreinforced trials. With relatively few noUS trials, second-order excitatory conditioning occurs. With extensive training, conditioned inhibition develops (Yin, Barnet, & Miller, 1994). Another important variable is whether the first- and second-order stimuli are presented simultaneously or sequentially (one after the other). Simultaneous presentations of CS_1 and CS_2 on nonreinforced trials favor the development of conditioned inhibition to CS_2 (Stout, Escobar, & Miller, 2004; see also Wheeler, Sherwood, & Holland, 2008).

Although there is no doubt that second-order conditioning is a robust phenomenon (e.g., Rescorla, 1980; Witnauer & Miller, 2011), little research has been done to evaluate the mechanisms of third and higher orders of conditioning. However, even the existence of second-order conditioning is of considerable significance because it greatly increases the range of situations in which classical conditioning can take place. With second-order conditioning, classical conditioning can occur without a primary US. The only requirement is the availability of a previously conditioned stimulus.

Many instances of conditioning in human experience involve higher-order conditioning. For example, money is a powerful conditioned stimulus (CS_1) for human behavior because of its association with candy, toys, movies, and other things money can buy (USs). A child may become fond of his or her uncle (CS_2) if the uncle gives the child some money on each visit. The positive conditioned emotional response to the uncle develops because the child comes to associate the uncle with money, in a case of second-order conditioning.

Advertising campaigns also make use of higher-order conditioning. A new product (CS_2) is paired with something we have already learned to like (CS_1) to create a preference for the new product (Schachtman, Walker, & Fowler, 2011).

Sensory Preconditioning   Associations can also be learned between two stimuli, each of which elicits only a mild orienting response before conditioning. Consider, for example, two flavors (i.e., vanilla and cinnamon) that you often encounter together in pastries without ill effects. Because of these pairings, the vanilla and cinnamon flavors may become

FIGURE 4.6 Procedure for sensory preconditioning. First, CS_2 is paired with CS_1 without a US in the situation. Then, CS_1 is paired with a US and comes to elicit a conditioned response (CR). In a later test session, CS_2 is also found to elicit the CR, even though CS_2 was never paired with the US. Notice that the procedure for sensory preconditioning is similar to the procedure for second-order conditioning, but the first two phases are presented in the opposite order.

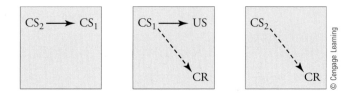

associated with one another. What would happen if you then acquired an aversion to cinnamon through food poisoning or illness? Chances are your acquired aversion to cinnamon would lead you to also reject things with the taste of vanilla because of the prior association of vanilla with cinnamon. This is an example of **sensory preconditioning**.

As with higher-order conditioning, sensory preconditioning involves a two-stage process (Figure 4.6). The cinnamon and vanilla flavors become associated with one another in the first phase when there is no illness or US. Let's call these stimuli CS_1 and CS_2. The association between CS_1 and CS_2 that is established during the sensory preconditioning phase is usually not evident in any behavioral responses because neither CS has been paired with a US yet, and, therefore, there is no reason to respond.

During the second phase, the cinnamon flavor (CS_1) is paired with illness (US), and a conditioned aversion (CR) develops to CS_1. Once this first-order conditioning has been completed, the participants are tested with CS_2 and now show an aversion to CS_2 for the first time. The response to CS_2 is noteworthy because CS_2 was never directly paired with a US. (For recent examples of sensory preconditioning, see Dunsmoor, White, & LaBar, 2011; Leising, Sawa, & Blaisdell, 2007; Rovee-Collier & Giles, 2010.)

Sensory preconditioning and higher-order conditioning help us make sense of things we seem to like or dislike for no apparent reason. What we mean by "no apparent reason" is that these stimuli were not directly associated with a positive or negative US. In such cases, the conditioned preference or aversion probably developed through sensory preconditioning or higher-order conditioning.

What Determines the Nature of the Conditioned Response?

Classical conditioning is usually identified by the development of a new response to the conditioned stimulus. As we have seen, a large variety of responses can become conditioned, including salivation, eye blinking, fear, locomotor approach and withdrawal, and aversion responses. Why does one set of responses become conditioned in one situation but other responses develop to the CS in other circumstances?

The US as a Determining Factor for the CR

The most obvious factor that determines the nature of the conditioned response is the unconditioned stimulus that is used. Animals learn to salivate when conditioned with food and to blink when conditioned with a puff of air to the eye. Salivation is not conditioned in eyeblink experiments, and eyeblink responses are not conditioned in salivary-conditioning experiments.

Interestingly, even small variations in the nature of the US can produce changes in the nature of the CR. In a famous experiment, Jenkins and Moore (1973) compared Pavlovian conditioning in pigeons with food versus water as the US. When presented with grain, pigeons make rapid and hard pecking movements directed at the grain with their beak open. By contrast, when presented with water, pigeons lower their beak into the water with their beak mostly closed. Once the beak is under water, it opens

FIGURE 4.7 Diagram of Pavlov's stimulus substitution model. The solid arrow indicates preexisting neural connections. The dashed arrow indicates neural connections established by conditioning. Because of these new functional connections, the CS comes to elicit responses previously elicited by the US.

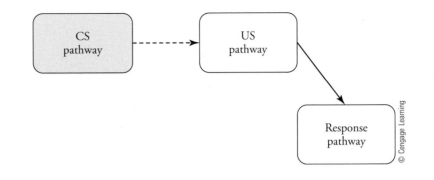

periodically to permit the bird to suck up the water (Klein, LaMon, & Zeigler, 1983). Thus, the unconditioned responses of eating and drinking differ in both speed and form.

Jenkins and Moore found that responses conditioned to a key light CS paired with food and water differ in a similar fashion. When grain was the US, the pigeons pecked the key light as if eating: The pecks were rapid with the beak open at the moment of contact. When water was the US, the conditioned pecking movements were slower, made with the beak closed, and were often accompanied by swallowing. Thus, the form of the conditioned responses resembled the form of the unconditioned responses to food and water (see also Allan & Zeigler, 1994; Ploog & Zeigler, 1996; Spetch, Wilkie, & Skelton, 1981). Similar findings have been obtained with food pellets and milk as unconditioned stimuli with laboratory rats (Davey & Cleland, 1982; Davey, Phillips, & Cleland, 1981).

The fact that the form of the conditioned response is determined by the US encouraged Pavlov to propose the **stimulus substitution** model. According to this model, the association of a CS with a US turns the conditioned stimulus into a surrogate US. The conditioned stimulus comes to function much like the US did previously. Thus, the CS is assumed to activate neural circuits previously activated only by the US and elicit responses similar to those elicited by the US (Figure 4.7).

The stimulus substitution model correctly emphasizes that the nature of the CR depends a great deal on the US that is used in a conditioning procedure. However, in many situations the CR does not resemble the UR. For example, foot shock causes rats to leap into the air, but the conditioned response to a tone paired with foot shock is freezing and immobility. In addition, as we will see, in many situations the biologically important consequence of Pavlovian conditioning is not a change in responding to the CS but a change in how the organism responds to the US.

The CS as a Determining Factor for the CR

Another important factor that determines the form of the CR is the nature of the conditioned stimulus. This was first demonstrated in a striking experiment by Timberlake and Grant (1975), who investigated classical conditioning in laboratory rats with food as the US. However, instead of a conventional light or tone, Timberlake and Grant presented another rat just before food delivery as the CS. One side of the experimental chamber was equipped with a sliding platform that could be moved in and out of the chamber through a flap door (Figure 4.8). A live rat was gently restrained on the platform. Ten seconds before each delivery of food, the platform was moved into the experimental chamber, thereby transporting the stimulus rat through the flap door.

The stimulus-substitution model predicts that CS–US pairings will generate responses to the CS that are similar to responses elicited by the food US. Because food elicits gnawing and biting, these responses were also expected to be elicited by the CS.

FIGURE 4.8 Diagram of the experiment by Timberlake and Grant (1975). The CS for food was presentation of a stimulus rat on a movable platform through a flap door on one side of the experimental chamber.

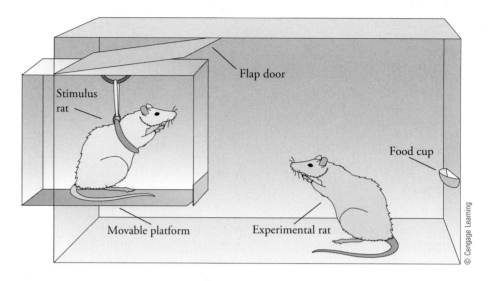

Contrary to this prediction, as the CS rat was repeatedly paired with food, it came to elicit social affiliative responses (orientation, approach, sniffing, and social contacts). Such responses did not develop if the CS rat was presented at times unrelated to food.

The outcome of this experiment does not support any model that explains the form of the conditioned response solely in terms of the US that is used. The conditioned social responses that were elicited by the CS rat were no doubt determined by having another rat serve as the CS. As we saw in Chapter 3, if the extension of a response lever into the experimental chamber serves as the CS for food, rats either contact and gnaw the lever (showing sign tracking) or go to the food cup (showing goal tracking). They do not respond to the CS lever with social affiliative responses. The nature of the CS is also important in sexual conditioning with quail. A CS object that male quail can mount and copulate with is more likely to elicit conditioned copulatory responses than a light or wood block CS (see photo of a male quail showing a conditioned sexual fetish in the inside front cover). (For other investigations of how the CS determines the nature of the conditioned response, see Holland, 1984; Kim et al., 1996; Sigmundi & Bolles, 1983).

The CS–US Interval as a Determining Factor for the CR

Another variable that is a major factor in what kinds of responses become conditioned is the interval between the conditioned stimulus and the unconditioned stimulus. Seeing a car coming toward you is a CS for potential injury. How you react to this danger will depend on how quickly the car will reach you (the CS–US interval). If the car is within 1–2 seconds of reaching you, you will panic and jump out of the way. In contrast, if the car is within 15–20 seconds of reaching you, you will be concerned and take evasive action, but you will not panic and jump. Generally, conditioning with a short CS–US interval activates responses that are appropriate for immediately dealing with the US. In contrast, conditioning with a long CS–US interval activates responses that prepare the organism for the US over a longer time horizon. Consistent with this view, laboratory studies with rats have shown that conditioned fear or panic is more likely with a short CS–US interval, whereas conditioned anxiety is more likely with a long CS–US interval (Waddell, Morris, & Bouton, 2006; see also Esmorís-Arranz, Pardo-Vázquez, & Vázquez-Garcia, 2003).

Analogous results have been obtained in appetitive conditioning situations. In the sexual conditioning of male quail, for example, access to a female copulation partner is the US. Most studies of sexual conditioning employ a rather short CS–US interval

C. K. Akins

(1 minute or less) and measure approach to the CS or sign tracking as the conditioned response (Chapter 3). In a study of the effects of the CS–US interval on sexual conditioning, Chana Akins (2000) conditioned different groups of quail with either a 1-minute or a 20-minute CS–US interval and measured not only CS approach responses but also general locomotor behavior (pacing between one half of the experimental chamber and the other). Control groups were exposed to the CS and US in an unpaired fashion.

The results of the experiment are presented in Figure 4.9. With a 1-minute CS–US interval, the conditioning procedure resulted in CS approach behavior but not increased locomotion. In contrast, with the 20-minute CS–US interval, the predominant conditioned response was increased locomotor behavior rather than CS approach.

Conditioned Responding and Behavior Systems

How are we to make sense of the fact that conditioned responding depends not only on the US but also on the CS and the CS–US interval? Pavlov's stimulus substitution model clearly cannot handle such a rich pattern of findings. To understand these types of results, we have to step out of the restricted physiological framework in which Pavlov worked and consider how Pavlovian conditioning might function in the natural history of organisms. The most successful framework for addressing these issues so far has been behavior systems theory (Domjan, 1997; Timberlake, 2001; Rau & Fanselow, 2007).

Different systems of behavior have evolved to enable animals to accomplish various critical tasks such as procuring and eating food, defending their territory, avoiding predation, producing and raising offspring, and so on. As I discussed in Chapter 2, a behavior system consists of a series of response modes, each with its own controlling stimuli and responses, arranged spatially and/or temporally. Consider, for example, the sexual behavior of male quail. When sexually motivated, the male will engage in a general search response that brings it into an area where a female may be located. Once he is in the female's territory, the male will engage in a more focal search response to actually locate the female. Finally, once he finds her, the male will engage in courtship and copulatory responses. This sequence is illustrated in Figure 4.10.

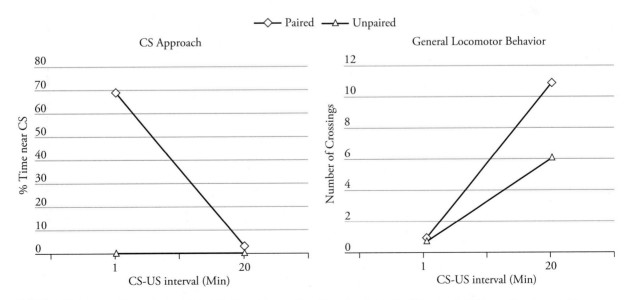

FIGURE 4.9 Effects of the CS–US interval in the sexual conditioning of male quail. CS approach (left panel) and general locomotor behavior (right panel) were measured in response to the CS in groups that received paired or unpaired CS–US presentations (based on Akins, 2000).

FIGURE 4.10 Sequence of responses, starting with general search and ending with copulatory behavior, that characterize the sexual behavior system. A conditioning procedure is superimposed on the behavior system. The CS–US interval determines where the CS becomes incorporated into the behavioral sequence.

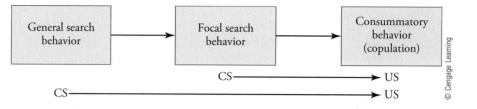

Behavior systems theory assumes that the presentation of a US in a Pavlovian conditioning procedure activates the behavior system relevant to that US. Food unconditioned stimuli activate the foraging and feeding system. A sexual US, by contrast, activates the sexual behavior system. Classical conditioning procedures involve superimposing a CS–US relationship on the behavioral system activated by the US. As a CS becomes associated with the US, it becomes integrated into the behavioral system and elicits components of that system. Thus, food-conditioned stimuli elicit components of the feeding system, and sexual-conditioned stimuli elicit components of the sexual behavior system.

Behavior systems theory readily explains why the US is an important determinant of the CR. The theory is also consistent with the fact that the nature of the CR depends on the type of CS that is employed. As we saw in our discussion of CS-US relevance (see pages 90–92), different CSs vary in terms of how readily they can become incorporated into a behavior system. In addition, the nature of the CS will determine what kinds of conditioned responses can develop. CS approach responses, for example, will only occur if the CS is highly localized. A diffuse stimulus (change in overall noise level) cannot generate CS approach as a conditioned response.

The most innovative prediction of behavior systems theory is that the form of the CR will also depend on the CS–US interval that is used. The CS–US interval is assumed to determine where the CS becomes incorporated into the sequence of responses that makes up the behavior system. Consider, for example, the sexual conditioning experiment by Akins (2000) in which different groups were training with a CS–US interval that was either short (1 minute) or long (20 minute). As illustrated in Figure 4.10, with a short CS–US interval, the CS occurs just before the female is available and is therefore incorporated into the behavior system at the focal search stage. Therefore, the CS is predicted to elicit focal search behavior: The male should approach and remain near the CS. In contrast, with a long CS–US interval, the CS becomes incorporated into an earlier portion of the behavior system and elicits general search behavior. General search behavior is manifest in increased nondirected locomotion.

The results obtained by Akins (Figure 4.9) confirm these predictions. The 1-minute CS–US interval conditioned CS approach but not general locomotor behavior, whereas the 20-minute CS–US interval conditioned locomotor behavior but not CS approach. Similar evidence in support of behavior system theory has been obtained in appetitive conditioning with food (Silva & Timberlake, 1997) and aversive conditioning with shock (Esморís-Arranz, Pardo-Vázquez, & Vázquez-Garcia, 2003; Waddell, Morris, & Bouton, 2006). In all of these cases, the conditioned response that reflects anticipation of the US depends on how long one has to wait before the US is presented. Therefore, as Balsam and colleagues (2009) put it, "No single response represents a pure measure of anticipation" (p. 1755).

S–R Versus S–S Learning

So far we have been discussing various accounts of the nature of conditioned behavior without saying much about how a CS produces responding. Let's turn to that question next.

Historically, conditioned behavior was viewed as a response elicited directly by the CS. According to this idea, conditioning establishes a new *stimulus–response*, or the S–R connection between the CS and the CR. An important alternative view is that subjects learn a new *stimulus–stimulus* (S–S) connection between the CS and the US. According to this interpretation, participants respond to the CS not because it elicits a CR directly but because the CS activates a representation or memory of the US. Conditioned responding is assumed to reflect the status of the activated US representation.

How might we decide between **S–R learning** and **S–S learning** mechanisms? A popular research method that has been used to decide between these alternatives involves the technique of **US devaluation**. This technique has been used to answer many important questions in behavior theory. (I will describe applications of it in instrumental conditioning in Chapter 7.) Therefore, it is important to understand its rationale.

The basic strategy of a US devaluation experiment is illustrated in Figure 4.11. The strategy was employed in a classic experiment by Holland and Rescorla (1975). Two groups of mildly food-deprived rats received conditioning in which a tone was repeatedly paired with pellets of food. This initial phase of the experiment was assumed to establish an association between the tone CS and the food US, as well as to get the rats to form a representation of the food that was used. Conditioned responding was evident in increased activity elicited by the tone.

In the next phase, the experimental group received a treatment designed to make the US less valuable to them. This US devaluation was accomplished by giving the rats sufficient free food to completely satisfy their hunger. Presumably satiation reduced the value of food and thus devalued the US representation. The deprivation state of the control group was not changed in Phase 2, and, therefore, the US representation remained intact for those rats (Figure 4.11). Both groups then received a series of test trials with the tone CS. During these tests, the experimental group showed significantly less conditioned responding than the control group.

If conditioning had established a new S–R connection between the CS and CR, the CR would have been elicited whenever the CS occurred, regardless of the value of the food. That did not happen. Rather, US devaluation reduced responding to the CS. This outcome suggests that conditioning resulted in an association between the CS and a representation of the US (S–S learning). Presentation of the CS activated the US representation, and the CR was determined by the current status of that US representation.

R. A. Rescorla

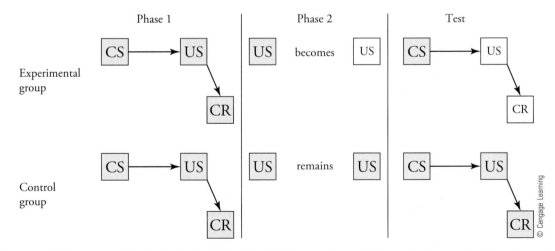

FIGURE 4.11 Basic strategy and rationale involved in US-devaluation experiments. In Phase 1, the experimental and control groups receive conventional conditioning to establish an association between the CS and the US and to lead the participants to form a representation of the US. In Phase 2, the US representation is devalued for the experimental group but remains unchanged for the control group. If the CR is elicited by way of the US representation, devaluation of the US representation should reduce responding to the CS.

US devaluation experiments have provided evidence of S–S learning in a wide range of classical conditioning situations (e.g., Colwill & Motzkin, 1994; Delamater et al., 2006; Hilliard et al., 1998; Storsve, McNally, & Richardson, 2012). However, not all instances of classical conditioning involve S–S learning. In some cases, the participants appear to learn a direct S–R association between the CS and the CR. I will have more to say about S–R learning in Chapter 7.

Pavlovian Conditioning as Modification of Responses to the Unconditioned Stimulus

So far we have followed the convention of focusing on how new responses come to be elicited by a Pavlovian conditioned stimulus. Indeed, standard definitions of Pavlovian conditioning emphasize that the CS comes to elicit a new response as a result of being paired with a US. However, learning to respond to a CS is useful to an organism only if the CR helps it cope with the US. Be it food, a predator, or a sexual partner, the US is the biologically significant event that the organism has to deal with effectively. To be of biological benefit, Pavlovian conditioning should enable the organism to interact with the US more effectively. The conditioned salivation that Pavlov observed helped his dogs prepare for the food that was coming and enabled them to digest the food more efficiently. Indeed, if the food was not delivered, the conditioned salivation was a useless false start.

Two different experimental designs that are used to demonstrate conditioned modification of the UR are outlined in Figure 4.12. In the *common testing design,* two groups are compared. During training, one group receives a conditioned stimulus (A) paired with the US while the other group gets stimulus A and the US unpaired. Following these contrasting histories, both groups receive stimulus A followed by the US during a test trial. However, instead of focusing on how the organism responds to A, investigators measure responding during the US. In the *common training design,* all of the participants receive a procedure in which stimulus A is paired with the US and stimulus B is presented unpaired. Following this common training, responding to the US is evaluated following presentations of stimuli A and B.

Research has shown that Pavlovian conditioning modifies responding to the US in a wide range of situations (Domjan, 2005). The effect was reported in an early eyeblink conditioning experiment by Kimble and Ost (1961) with human participants. Conditioning trials consisted of the presentation of the CS light just before the delivery of a gentle puff of air to the eyes. Once the CS became conditioned, presentation of the CS reduced how vigorously the participants blinked when they received the air puff. This phenomenon has come to be called **conditioned diminution of the UR**. (For a study of the brain mechanisms of the conditioned diminution effect, see Box 3.2 and Knight et al., 2010.)

FIGURE 4.12 Experimental designs used to demonstrate conditioned modification of the unconditioned response.

Conditioning phase	Test phase
Common testing design	
Experimental Group	
A → US (Paired)	A → US
Control group	
A/US (Unpaired)	
Common training design	
A → US (Paired)	A → US
B/US (Unpaired)	B → US

© Cengage Learning, 2015

Conditioned Analgesia   Conditioned diminution of the UR is a prominent phenomenon in aversive conditioning and in conditioning experiments where pharmacological agents serve as unconditioned stimuli. In both these cases, a conditioned stimulus elicits physiological processes that serve to counteract the effects of the US.

We previously discussed how an aversive stimulus activates the defensive behavior system. Defensive responses like fleeing or striking back at a predator can be effective in coping with an attack. However, to engage in active defensive responses, the organism cannot be debilitated by pain. Interestingly, exposure to an aversive stimulus or physical injury results in the release of endogenous opiates that counteract the pain induced by the injury. Endogenous opiates are produced internally by the body and function like morphine or heroin to reduce pain sensitivity and provide analgesia.

The release of endogenous opiates can become conditioned to cues associated with an aversive stimulus or injury. That is, a CS that has been paired with foot-shock will stimulate the release of endogenous opiates, resulting in *conditioned analgesia*. Through this process, foot-shock becomes less and less painful with successive conditioning trials (Zelikowsky & Fanselow, 2011). This is a prominent example of conditioned diminution of the UR.

Conditioned Drug Tolerance   Another prominent example of conditioned diminution of the UR comes from studies of conditioned **drug tolerance**. Tolerance to a drug is said to develop when repeated administrations of the drug have progressively less effect. Because of this, increasing doses become necessary to produce the same results. Tolerance develops with nearly all psychoactive drugs. A beer or two can have a substantial effect on first-time drinkers but not on habitual drinkers, who may require four to six beers to feel the same level of intoxication. People who take pain pills or sleeping pills have similar experiences. The pills are highly effective at first, but with repeated use higher doses are required to produce the same effects.

There is now substantial evidence that drug tolerance can result from Pavlovian conditioning. Pavlovian conditioning is involved because each administration of a drug constitutes a conditioning trial in which cues that accompany administration of the drug are paired with the pharmacological effects of the drug. Thus, drug administration cues constitute the CS and the pharmacological effects are the US. Caffeine, for example, is a commonly used drug whose pharmacological effects are typically preceded by the smell and taste of coffee. Thus, the taste and smell of coffee can serve as a conditioned stimulus that is predictive of the physiological effects of caffeine (e.g., Flaten & Blumenthal, 1999).

A Pavlovian perspective views the development of drug tolerance as another example of conditioned diminution of the UR (Siegel, 1999). Given that each drug-taking episode is a conditioning trial, the conditioned stimuli that precede each drug administration become associated with the physiological effects of the drug. One consequence of this learning is that the CS elicits physiological processes that counteract the drug effect. The process is illustrated in Figure 4.13 and is related to the opponent-process theory of motivation we discussed in Chapter 2.

As we noted in Chapter 2, emotion-arousing events (including drugs that induce emotions) trigger a sequence of two processes. The first of these is the primary *a process*, which represents the initial effects of the drug. For alcohol, these are the symptoms of intoxication and sedation. The *a process* is followed by the opponent *b process*, which is opposite to and counteracts the *a process*. For alcohol, the *b process* causes the irritability and malaise of a hangover. According to the mechanisms of conditioned drug tolerance, the opponent or compensatory process comes to be elicited by a drug-conditioned stimulus, and that is why the drug effect is substantially reduced if the drug is administered following the CS.

S. Siegel

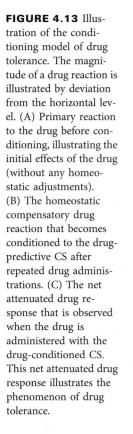

FIGURE 4.13 Illustration of the conditioning model of drug tolerance. The magnitude of a drug reaction is illustrated by deviation from the horizontal level. (A) Primary reaction to the drug before conditioning, illustrating the initial effects of the drug (without any homeostatic adjustments). (B) The homeostatic compensatory drug reaction that becomes conditioned to the drug-predictive CS after repeated drug administrations. (C) The net attenuated drug response that is observed when the drug is administered with the drug-conditioned CS. This net attenuated drug response illustrates the phenomenon of drug tolerance.

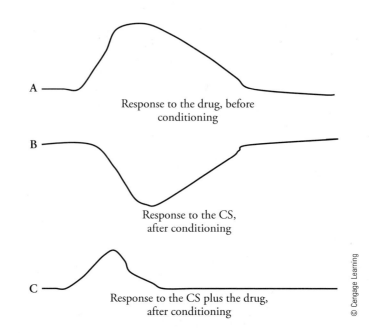

A —— Response to the drug, before conditioning

B —— Response to the CS, after conditioning

C —— Response to the CS plus the drug, after conditioning

© Cengage Learning

A key prediction of these mechanisms is that drug tolerance will be reduced if participants receive the drug under novel circumstances or in the absence of the usual drug-predictive cues. The model also suggests that various factors (such as CS preexposure and Pavlovian extinction) that attenuate the development of conditioned responding will also attenuate the development of drug tolerance. A large body of research has confirmed these and other predictions of the conditioning model in laboratory studies with numerous drugs including opiates (i.e., morphine and heroin), alcohol, scopolamine, benzodiazepines, and amphetamine (see reviews by Siegel, 2005, 2008). Conditioned drug tolerance is one of the ways in which learning processes are involved in drug addiction (McCarthy et al., 2011).

BOX 4.1

Drug "Overdose" Caused by the Absence of Drug-Conditioned Stimuli

According to the conditioning model of drug tolerance, the impact of a drug will be reduced if the drug is consumed in the presence of cues that were previously conditioned to elicit **conditioned compensatory responses**. Consider a heroin addict who usually shoots up in the same place, perhaps with the same friends. That place and company will become conditioned to elicit physiological reactions that reduce the effects of the heroin, forcing the addict to inject higher doses to get the same

effect. As long as the addict shoots up in the usual place and with the usual friends, he or she is protected from the full impact of the increased heroin dosage by the conditioned compensatory responses. But what if the addict visits a new part of town and shoots up with new acquaintances? In that case, the familiar CSs will be absent, as will the protective conditioned compensatory responses. Therefore, the addict will get the full impact of the heroin he or she is using, and may suffer an

"overdose." The word "overdose" is in quotation marks because the problem is not that too high a dose of heroin was consumed but that the drug was taken in the absence of the usual CS. Without the CS, a dose of heroin that the addict never had trouble with might kill him on this occasion. Evidence for this interpretation has been obtained both in experimental research with laboratory animals and in human cases of drug overdose (Siegel, Baptista, Kim, McDonald, & Weise-Kelly, 2000).

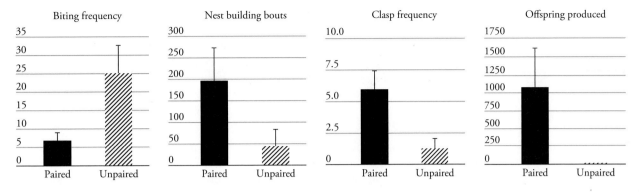

FIGURE 4.14 Interactions between male and female gourami following exposure to a Pavlovian CS for males that previously had the CS paired or unpaired with visual access to a female (based on Hollis et al., 1997).

Conditioned Reproduction and Fertility   Pavlovian conditioning also results in changes in responding to the US in appetitive conditioning situations. These effects have been examined most extensively in studies of sexual conditioning. In a landmark experiment with a fish species, the blue gourami, Hollis and colleagues (1997) conducted conditioning trials in which a CS light was presented for 10 seconds to male gourami, followed by visual exposure to a female for 5 minutes behind a barrier as the unconditioned stimulus. For a control group, the CS and US were presented unpaired. After 18 conditioning trials, all of the fish received a test trial in which exposure to the CS for 10 seconds was followed by removal of the barrier separating the male from the female so that the two could interact. Notice that this was the first time the barrier between the male and female compartments was removed. The fish were permitted to interact for six days during which they courted, built a nest, and copulated.

How the males interacted with the female (the US in this experiment) during the test trial is summarized in Figure 4.14. Basically, males that received access to a female after exposure to the Pavlovian CS showed far more effective courtship and copulatory interactions with the female than males in the unpaired control group. Pavlovian males showed less aggression toward the female, they spent more time building a nest, they clasped the female more often, and most importantly, they produced far more offspring. Keep in mind that none of these were responses to the CS, which lasted just 10 seconds before the barrier between the male and female was removed. Rather, all these changes in behavior were altered response to the US or female gourami.

Results similar to those obtained by Hollis and colleagues (1997) have been observed in numerous experiments on sexual conditioning with domesticated quail. As in the gourami, exposure to a sexually conditioned CS produces widespread changes in the sexual behavior of quail. These changes include increased receptivity of females to being mounted by a male, more rapid and more efficient copulation, increased sperm release during copulation, increased fertilization of eggs, and the production of greater numbers of offspring (e.g., Domjan & Akins, 2011; Domjan, Mahometa, & Matthews, 2012).

How Do Conditioned and Unconditioned Stimuli Become Associated?

I have described numerous situations in which classical conditioning occurs, and I have discussed various factors that determine how behavior (to both the CS and the US) changes as a result of this learning. However, I have yet to address in detail the critical issue of how conditioned and unconditioned stimuli become associated. What are the mechanisms of learning, or the underlying processes that are activated by conditioning procedures to produce learning? This question has been the subject of intense scholarly work. The evolution of theories of classical conditioning continues today, as investigators strive to formulate comprehensive theories that can embrace all of the diverse findings of research in Pavlovian conditioning. (For reviews, see Pearce & Bouton, 2001; Mowrer & Klein, 2001; Vogel, Castro, & Saavedra, 2004.)

The Blocking Effect

The modern era in theories of Pavlovian conditioning got underway about 45 years ago with the discovery of several provocative phenomena that stimulated the application of information processing ideas to the analysis of classical conditioning (e.g., Rescorla, 1967b, 1969a; Wagner, Logan, Haberlandt, & Price, 1968). One of the most prominent of these was the **blocking effect**.

To get an intuitive sense of the blocking effect, consider the following scenario. Each Sunday afternoon, you visit your grandmother who always serves bread pudding that slightly disagrees with you. Not wanting to upset her, you politely eat the pudding during each visit and, consequently, acquire an aversion to bread pudding. One of the visits falls on a holiday, and to make the occasion a bit more festive, your grandmother makes a special sauce to serve with the bread pudding. You politely eat the bread pudding with the sauce, and as usual you get a bit sick to your stomach. Will you now develop an aversion to the sauce? Probably not. Knowing that bread pudding disagrees with you, you probably will attribute your illness to the proven culprit and not learn to dislike the newly added sauce.

The above example illustrates the basic sequence of events that produces the blocking effect (Figure 4.15). Two conditioned stimuli are employed (in the above example these were the taste of the bread pudding and the taste of the special sauce). In Phase 1, the experimental group receives repeated pairings of one of the stimuli (A) with the US. This phase of training is continued until a strong CR develops to stimulus A. In the next phase of the experiment, stimulus B is presented together with stimulus A and paired with the US. After several such conditioning trials, stimulus B is presented alone in a test trial to see if it also elicits the CR. Interestingly, very little responding occurs to stimulus B even though B was repeatedly paired with the US during Phase 2.

In Phase 2 of the blocking design, the control group receives the same kind of conditioning trials (A+B paired with the US) as the experimental group (Figure 4.15). However, for the control group, stimulus A is not conditioned prior to these compound-stimulus trials. Rather, during Phase 1, the control group receives presentations of stimulus A and the US in an unpaired fashion. In many replications of this design, stimulus B invariably produces less conditioned responding in the experimental group than in the control group. (For a more detailed discussion of controls for blocking, see Taylor et al., 2008.)

The blocking effect was initially investigated in fear conditioning using the conditioned suppression technique with rats (Kamin, 1968, 1969). Subsequently, the phenomenon has been demonstrated in various other conditioning preparations with both human participants and laboratory animals (e.g., Bradfield & McNally, 2008; Holland & Kenmuir, 2005; Mitchell et al., 2006). One area of considerable contemporary interest is blocking in learning about geometric cues (Miller & Shettleworth, 2007). In one recent study with college students, the conditioned stimuli were geometric cues provided by two different triangles that I will refer to as A and B. The cover story was that the triangles depicted the floor plan of a room that had food in one of the corners that the participants had to find.

Courtesy of L. J. Kamin

L. J. Kamin

FIGURE 4.15 Diagram of the blocking procedure. During Phase 1, stimulus A is conditioned with the US in the experimental group, while the control group receives stimulus A presented unpaired with the US. During Phase 2, both experimental and control groups receive conditioning trials in which stimulus A is presented simultaneously with stimulus B and paired with the US. A later test of stimulus B alone shows less conditioned responding to stimulus B in the experimental group than in the control group.

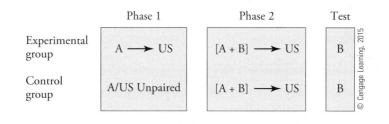

The experiment is outlined in Figure 4.16. In Phase I, the blocking group received training with triangle A (an isosceles triangle). One of the internal angles of this triangle (indicated by + in Figure 4.16) was designated as "correct." Clicking on this angle produced a clapping sound. Clicking on either of the other corners produced the sound of an explosion, indicating that the response was incorrect. The triangle was presented in different orientations so that a particular location on the screen was not correlated with the correct response. During Phase II, the blocking group received the previously conditioned stimulus (A) in combination with a new triangle B, with the correct corner as indicated in Figure 4.16. The blocking procedure was compared to two control procedures. Control group 1 received training only with the combination of triangles A and B, without any prior training with triangle A. Control group 2 received training only with triangle B in Phase 2. As in Phase 1, the orientation of the triangles used in Phase 2 varied across trials.

At the end of the experiment, all three groups were tested to see if they learned which was the correct corner for finding food in triangle B. As expected, control group 2, which was trained only with triangle B, responded very well (92% correct) when tested with triangle B. Control group 1 responded nearly as well (79% correct). The high performance of control group 1 indicates that learning the correct location in triangle B was not disrupted much by presenting triangle B in combination with triangle A during training. However, a major disruption in performance occurred if triangle A was pretrained before being presented with B. Participants in the blocking group responded correctly during the test trials with triangle B only 20% of the time. This illustrates the blocking effect.

Since the time of Aristotle, temporal contiguity has been considered the primary means by which stimuli become associated. The blocking effect is a landmark phenomenon in classical conditioning because it calls into question the assumption that temporal

FIGURE 4.16 Blocking in human learning about geometric cues. Human participants had to move a cursor to the correct geometric location (indicated by + in each triangle) on conditioning trials in Phase 1 (for the blocking group) and Phase 2 (for all groups). Percent correct during the test trials is indicated in the third column (based on Prados, 2011).

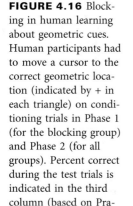

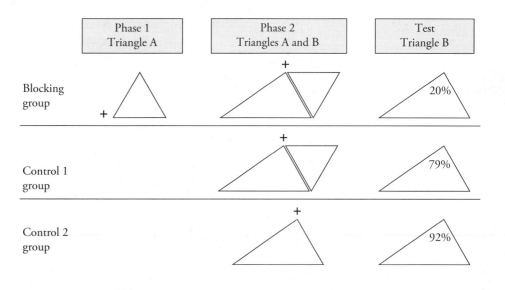

BOX 4.2

The Picture–Word Problem in Teaching Reading: A Form of Blocking

Early instruction in reading often involves showing children a written word, along with a picture of what that word represents. Thus, two stimuli are presented together. The children have already learned what the picture is called (e.g., a horse). Therefore, the two stimuli in the picture–word compound include one that is already learned (the picture) and one that is not (the word). This makes the picture–word compound much like the compound stimulus in a blocking experiment: A previously trained stimulus is presented along with a new one the child does not know yet. Research on the blocking effect predicts that the presence of the previ-ously trained picture should disrupt learning about the word. Singh and Solman (1990) found that this is indeed the case in a study of reading with students who had mild intellec-tual disabilities.

The children were taught to read words such as *knife, lemon, radio, stamp,* and *chalk.* Some of the words were taught using a variation of the blocking design in which the picture of the object was presented first and the child was asked to name it. The picture was then presented together with its written word, and the child was asked, "What is that word?" In other condi-tions, the words were presented with-out their corresponding pictures. All eight participants showed the slowest learning for the words that were taught with the corresponding pictures present. By contrast, six of the eight children showed the fastest learning of the words that were taught without their corresponding pictures. (The remaining two participants learned most rapidly with a modified procedure.) These results suggest that processes akin to blocking may occur in learning to read. The results also suggest that pictorial prompts should be used with caution in reading instruction because they may disrupt rather than facilitate learning (see also Didden, Prinsen, & Sigafoos, 2000; Dittlinger & Lerman, 2011).

contiguity is sufficient for learning. The blocking effect clearly shows that pairings of a CS with a US are not enough for conditioned responding to develop. During Phase 2 of the blocking experiment, CS_B is paired with the US in an identical fashion for the exper-imental and the control group. Nevertheless, CS_B comes to elicit vigorous conditioned responding only in the control group.

Why does the presence of the previously conditioned stimulus A block the acquisi-tion of responding to the added cue B? Kamin, who discovered the blocking effect, explained the phenomenon by proposing that a US has to be surprising to be effective in producing learning. If the US is signaled by a previously conditioned stimulus (A), it will not be surprising. Kamin reasoned that if the US is not surprising, it will not activate the "mental effort" required for learning.

If something is not surprising, we already know a lot about it and therefore have little to learn. Learning is necessary with unexpected events because what makes some-thing unexpected is that we don't know enough to make good predictions about it. The basic idea that learning occurs when something is surprising is a fundamental concept in learning theory. For example, in their discussion of a Bayesian approach to learning, Courville and colleagues noted that "change increases uncertainty, and speeds subse-quent learning, by making old evidence less relevant to the present circumstances" (Courville, Daw, & Touretzky, 2006).

The Rescorla–Wagner Model

The idea that the effectiveness of a US is determined by how surprising it is forms the basis of a formal mathematical model of conditioning proposed by Robert Rescorla and Allan Wagner (Rescorla & Wagner, 1972; Wagner & Rescorla, 1972). With the use of this model, investigators have extended the implications of the concept of US surprise to a wide variety of conditioning phenomena. The Rescorla–Wagner model has become a reference point for all subsequent learning theories (Siegel & Allen, 1996), and its basic

A. R. Wagner

assumptions are being identified in studies of the neural mechanisms of learning (e.g., Spoormaker et al., 2011; Zelikowsky & Fanselow, 2011).

What does it mean to say that something is surprising? How might we measure the level of surprise of a US? By definition, *an event is surprising if it is different from what is expected.* If you expect a small gift for your birthday and get a car, you will be very surprised. This is analogous to an unexpectedly large US. Correspondingly, if you expect a car and receive a box of candy, you will also be surprised. This is analogous to an unexpectedly small US. According to the Rescorla–Wagner model, an unexpectedly large US is the basis for excitatory conditioning and an unexpectedly small US (or the absence of the US) is the basis for inhibitory conditioning.

Rescorla and Wagner assumed that the level of surprise, and hence the effectiveness of a US, depends on how different the US is from what the individual expects. Furthermore, they assumed that expectation of the US is related to the conditioned or associative properties of the stimuli that precede the US. Strong conditioned responding indicates strong expectation of the US; weak conditioned responding indicates a low expectation of the US.

These ideas can be expressed mathematically by using λ to represent the US that is delivered on a given trial and V to represent the associative value of the stimuli that precede the US. The level of US surprise will then be $(\lambda - V)$, or the difference between what occurs (λ) and what is expected (V). On the first conditioning trial, what occurs (λ) is much larger than what is expected (V), and the surprise factor $(\lambda - V)$ will be large (Figure 4.17). As learning proceeds, expectations (V) will come in line with what occurs (λ), and the surprise term $(\lambda - V)$ will get smaller and smaller. Eventually, V will grow to match λ. At the limit or asymptote of learning, $V = \lambda$ and the surprise term $(\lambda - V)$ is equal to zero.

Learning on a given conditioning trial is the change in the associative value of a stimulus. That change can be represented as ΔV. The idea that learning depends on the level of surprise of the US can be expressed as follows:

$$\Delta V = k(\lambda - V), \tag{4.1}$$

where k is a constant related to the salience of the CS and US. This is the fundamental equation of the Rescorla–Wagner model. It is also known as the *delta rule*, in reference

FIGURE 4.17 Growth of associative value (V) during the course of conditioning until the asymptote of learning (λ) is reached. Note that the measure of surprise ($\lambda - V$) is much larger early in training than late in training.

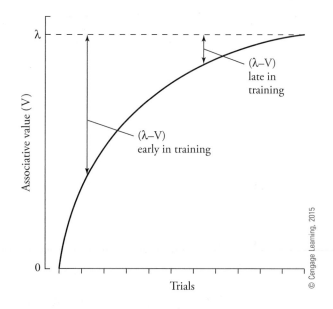

to the Greek symbol delta (Δ) to refer to *change* in the associative value of a stimulus as a result of a conditioning trial.

The delta rule indicates that the amount of learning (ΔV) is proportional to how far predictions of the US (V) differ from what actually occurs (λ), or how big the error is in predicting the US. The prediction error ($\lambda - V$) is large at first but is gradually eliminated as learning proceeds. Thus, the Rescorla–Wagner equation is an *error-correction* mechanism. Some form of the delta rule is common in theories of learning and is also used extensively in robotics where error corrections are required to bring a system (V) in line with a target (λ).

Application of the Rescorla–Wagner Equation to the Blocking Effect The Rescorla–Wagner model clearly predicts the blocking effect. In applying the model, it is important to keep in mind that expectations of the US are based on all of the cues available during the conditioning trial. As was presented in Figure 4.15, the experimental group in the blocking design first receives extensive conditioning of stimulus A so that it acquires a perfect expectation that the US will occur whenever it encounters stimulus A. Therefore, by the end of Phase 1, V_A will be equal to the asymptote of learning, or $V_A = \lambda$.

In Phase 2, Stimulus B is presented together with stimulus A, and the two CSs are followed by the US. To predict what will be learned about stimulus B, the basic Rescorla–Wagner equation has to be applied to stimulus B: $\Delta V_B = k(\lambda - V)$. In carrying out this calculation, keep in mind that V is based on all of the stimuli present on a trial. In Phase 2, there are two cues: A and B. Therefore, $V = V_A + V_B$. Because of its Phase 1 training, $V_A = \lambda$ at the start of Phase 2. In contrast, V_B starts out at zero. Therefore, at the start of Phase 2, $V_A + V_B$ is equal to $\lambda + 0$, or λ. Substituting this value into the equation for ΔV_B gives a value for ΔV_B of $k(\lambda - \lambda)$, or $k(0)$, which is equal to zero. This indicates that stimulus B will not acquire associative value in Phase 2. Thus, the conditioning of stimulus B will be blocked.

Loss of Associative Value Despite Pairings with the US The Rescorla–Wagner model has become a prominent theory of learning because it makes some unusual predictions. One unusual prediction is that the associative value of a CS can decrease despite continued pairings with the US. How might this happen? Stimuli are predicted to lose associative value if they are presented together on a conditioning trial after having been trained separately. Such an experiment is outlined in Figure 4.18.

Figure 4.18 shows a three-phase experiment. In Phase 1, stimuli A and B are paired with the same US (e.g., one pellet of food) on separate trials. This continues until both A and B predict the one food pellet US perfectly. Thus, at the end of Phase 1, both V_A and V_B will equal λ. In Phase 2, stimuli A and B are presented simultaneously for the first time, and this stimulus compound is followed by the usual single food pellet. What happens to the conditioned properties of A and B as a result of the Phase 2 training?

Note that the same US that was used in Phase 1 continues to be presented in Phase 2. Given that there is no change in the US, informal reflection suggests that the conditioned properties of A and B should also remain unchanged. In contrast to this common-sense prediction, the Rescorla–Wagner model predicts that the conditioned properties of the individual cues A and B will decrease in Phase 2.

As a result of training in Phase 1, A and B both predict the one food pellet US ($V_A = \lambda$; $V_B = \lambda$). When A and B are presented simultaneously for the first time in Phase 2, the expectations based on the individual stimuli are added together, with the result that two food pellets are predicted rather than one ($V_{A+B} = V_A + V_B = 2\lambda$). This is an over-expectation because the US remains only one food pellet. The US in Phase 2 is surprisingly

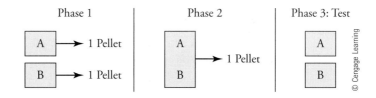

Phase 1 | Phase 2 | Phase 3: Test

A → 1 Pellet
B → 1 Pellet

A
B → 1 Pellet

A
B

© Cengage Learning

FIGURE 4.18 Diagram of the overexpectation experiment. In Phase 1, stimuli A and B are separately conditioned to asymptote with a one-pellet US. In Phase 2, an overexpectation is created by presenting A and B simultaneously and pairing the compound stimulus with a one-pellet US. In Phase 3, A and B are tested individually and found to have lost associative value because of the overexpectation in Phase 2.

small. To bring US expectancy in line with what actually occurs in Phase 2, the participants have to decrease their expectancy of the US based on stimuli A and B. Thus, A and B are predicted to lose associative value despite continued presentations of the same US. The loss in associative value will continue until the sum of the expectancies based on A and B equals one food pellet. The predicted loss of the CR to the individual cues in this type of procedure is highly counterintuitive but has been verified in a number of experiments (e.g., Kehoe & White, 2004; Lattal & Nakajima, 1998; see also Sissons & Miller, 2009).

Conditioned Inhibition   How does the Rescorla–Wagner model explain the development of conditioned inhibition? Consider, for example, Pavlov's procedure for inhibitory conditioning (Figure 3.11). This procedure involves two kinds of trials: one in which the US is presented (reinforced trials), and one in which the US is omitted (nonreinforced trials). On reinforced trials, a conditioned excitatory stimulus (CS+) is presented and paired with the US. On nonreinforced trials, the CS+ is presented together with the conditioned inhibitory stimulus CS–, and the compound is followed by the absence of the US.

Application of the Rescorla–Wagner model to such a procedure requires considering reinforced and nonreinforced trials separately. To accurately anticipate the US on reinforced trials, the CS+ has to gain excitatory properties. The development of such conditioned excitation is illustrated in the panel on the left of Figure 4.19. Excitatory conditioning involves the acquisition of positive associative value and ceases once the organism predicts the US perfectly on each reinforced trial.

On nonreinforced trials, the CS+ and CS– are presented together. Once the CS+ has acquired some degree of conditioned excitation (because of its presentation on reinforced

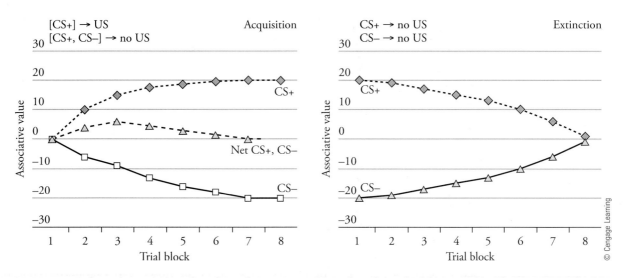

FIGURE 4.19 Left panel: Acquisition of conditioned excitation to CS+ and conditioned inhibition to CS–. The *Net* curve is the associative value of the CS+ and CS– presented simultaneously. Right panel: Predicted extinction of excitation to CS+ and inhibition to CS– when these cues are presented repeatedly without the US, according to the Rescorla–Wagner model.

trials), the organism will expect the US whenever the CS+ occurs, including on nonreinforced trials. However, the US does not happen on nonreinforced trials. Therefore, this is a case of overexpectation, similar to the example in Figure 4.18. To accurately predict the absence of the US on nonreinforced trials, the associative value of the CS+ and the value of the CS− have to sum to zero (the value represented by noUS). How can this be achieved? Given the positive associative value of the CS+, the only way to achieve a net zero expectation of the US on nonreinforced trials is to make the associative value of the CS− negative. Hence, the Rescorla–Wagner model explains conditioned inhibition by assuming that the CS− acquires negative associative value (see the panel on the left of Figure 4.19).

Extinction of Excitation and Inhibition   In an extinction procedure, the CS is presented repeatedly without the US (Chapter 9). Predictions of the Rescorla–Wagner model for extinction are illustrated in the panel on the right of Figure 4.19. If a CS has acquired excitatory properties, there will be an overexpectation of the US the first time the CS+ is presented without the US in extinction. Repeated nonreinforced presentations of the CS+ will result in a progressive reduction of the associative value of the CS+ until V_{CS+} reaches zero.

The Rescorla–Wagner model predicts an analogous scenario for extinction of conditioned inhibition (panel on the right of Figure 4.19). At the start of extinction, the CS− has negative associative value. This may be thought of as creating an underprediction of the US: The organism predicts less than the zero US that occurs on extinction trials. To align expectations with the absence of the US, the negative associative value of the CS− is gradually reduced and the CS− ends up with zero associative strength.

Problems with the Rescorla–Wagner Model   The Rescorla–Wagner model stimulated a great deal of research and led to the discovery of many new and important phenomena in classical conditioning (Siegel & Allen, 1996). Not unexpectedly, however, the model has also encountered a number of difficulties (see Miller, Barnet, & Grahame, 1995).

One of the difficulties with the model is that its analysis of the extinction of conditioned inhibition is not correct. As indicated in Figure 4.19, the model predicts that repeated presentations of a conditioned inhibitor (CS−) by itself will lead to loss of conditioned inhibition. However, this does not happen (Zimmer-Hart & Rescorla, 1974; Witcher & Ayres, 1984). In fact, some investigators have found that repeated nonreinforcement of a CS− can enhance its conditioned inhibitory properties (e.g., DeVito & Fowler, 1987; Hallam et al., 1992). Curiously, an effective procedure for reducing the conditioned inhibitory properties of a CS− does not involve presenting the CS− at all. Rather, it involves extinguishing the excitatory properties of the CS+ with which the CS− was presented during inhibitory training (Best et al., 1985; Lysle & Fowler, 1985).

Another difficulty is that the Rescorla–Wagner model views extinction as the reverse of acquisition, or the return of the associative value of a CS to zero. However, as we will see in Chapter 9, a growing body of evidence indicates that extinction should not be viewed as simply the reverse of acquisition. Rather extinction appears to involve the learning of a new relationship between the CS and the US (namely, that the US no longer follows the CS).

Devising a comprehensive theory of classical conditioning is a formidable challenge. Given that classical conditioning has been studied for more than a century, a comprehensive theory must account for many diverse findings. No theory available today has been entirely successful in accomplishing that. Nevertheless, interesting new ideas about classical conditioning continue to be proposed and examined. Some of these proposals supplement the Rescorla–Wagner model. Others are incompatible with the Rescorla–Wagner model and move the theoretical debate in new directions.

BOX 4.3

Conditioning and the Amygdala

Our emotional reaction to stimuli is modulated by a group of structures known as the **limbic system**, which lies under the cerebral cortex and encircles the upper brain stem (Figure (iii) on the inside back cover.). Two components of this system are especially important for learning and memory: the amygdala and the hippocampus. The *hippocampus* is involved in learning about complex relations, the stimulus configurations that encode particular locations and episodes in time (Wang & Morris, 2010). The nature of this learning, and the underlying neurobiological mechanisms, will be discussed in Box 8.2. Here I focus on the **amygdala** (Latin for *almond*), a structure that plays a key role in linking new affective responses to previously neutral stimuli (Fanselow & Poulos, 2005; Johansen, Cain, Ostroff, & LeDoux, 2011).

Interest in the amygdala stemmed from early observations implicating this structure in the regulation of fear. Although rare, people who have experienced damage to this neural structure exhibit a peculiar lack of fear to stimuli that signal danger. Brain scans have revealed that processing fear-related stimuli (e.g., pictures of a fearful faces) activates the amygdala, and electrically stimulating this region produces feelings of fear and apprehension.

What makes the amygdala especially interesting is that it does more than organize our behavioral response to stimuli that innately elicit fear; it also mediates the conditioning of fear to signals of danger. How this occurs has been tuned through our biological history, predisposing us to exhibit heightened fear to particular kinds of stimuli (e.g., snakes, heights). Ordinarily, this type of learning provides an adaptive function, motivat-

ing the organism to avoid dangerous situations. Sometimes, however, the level of fear elicited can grow out of proportion to the true level of danger, producing a phobic response that can interfere with everyday function.

Laboratory studies have shown that discrete regions of the amygdala serve distinct functions. For our purposes, three regions are of particular interest: the lateral (side), basal (lower), and central nuclei. As in the cerebellum, these nuclei can be distinguished on both anatomical and functional criteria. Further, their role in learning has been studied using similar methods (stimulation, inactivation or lesioning, and recording). For example, electrical stimulation of the central nucleus produces a range of behavioral and physiological responses indicative of fear, including freezing, enhanced startle to a loud acoustic stimulus, and a change in heart rate (Figure 4.20A). Conversely, lesioning the amygdala produces a fearless creature that no longer avoids dangerous situations. Rats normally show signs of fear in the presence of a predator (e.g., a cat). After having the amygdala lesioned, a rat will approach a cat as if the cat were a long lost friend.

Lesioning the amygdala also disrupts learning about cues (CSs) that have been paired with an aversive event (e.g., a shock US) in a Pavlovian paradigm. As you have learned, animals can associate many different types of stimuli with shock. In some cases, the cue may be relatively simple, such as a discrete light or tone. In other cases, a constellation of cues, such as the environmental context in which shock occurs, may be associated with shock. In both cases, pairing the stimulus with shock produces conditioned fear, as indicated by a CS-induced increase in freezing and startling.

In fear conditioning, the neural signals elicited by the CS and US converge within the lateral amygdala (Figure 4.20A). Information about the US is provided by a number of distinct neural circuits, each of which is sufficient to support conditioning (Lanuza, Nader, & LeDoux, 2004). Likewise, multiple pathways can transmit information about the CS. A relatively direct path from the sensory *thalamus* provides a coarse input that sacrifices stimulus detail for speed. Additional CS inputs arrive from the *cortex* and likely provide a slower, but more precise, representation of the features of the CS. Even further downstream, the hippocampus can provide a cue based on the current configuration of sensory stimuli, allowing the organism to learn that a particular environmental context or spatial location signals danger (Box 8.2).

Evidence suggests that neurons within the lateral and basal region of the amygdala (collectively known as the *basolateral amygdala*) provide a biological link that endows a CS with the capacity to elicit fear. Throughout the nervous system, many forms of learning depend on a kind of gated channel known as the *NMDA receptor*. As I will discuss in a subsequent section (Box 8.2), engaging this receptor can initiate a cellular process that enhances synaptic connectivity, allowing a previously neutral cue (the CS) to elicit a new response. Unlocking the NMDA gate requires a strong input, such as that provided by a shock US. Under these conditions, the cue-elicited input to the basolateral amygdala (the CS) may gain the capacity to drive the neural machinery that generates fear (the CR). Evidence for this comes from studies demonstrating that conditioning endows a CS with the capacity to

Continued

BOX 4.3 (continued)

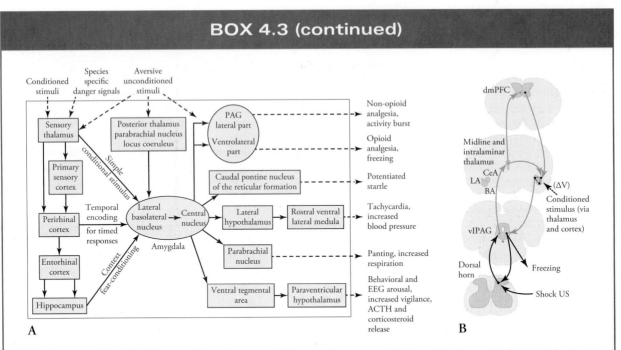

FIGURE 4.20 (A) A block diagram illustrating some of the neural components that mediate fear and defensive behavior. An aversive US engages parallel pathways that project to the lateral/basolateral amygdala. Information about the CS is conveyed from the sensory thalamus, the cortex, or by means of a hippocampal-dependent process. Output is channeled through the central nucleus of the amygdala, which organizes the expression of fear-mediated behavior. Distinct behavioral outcomes are produced by projections to various brain structures (adapted from Fendt & Fanselow, 1999). (B) A hypothetical model for computing an error signal in fear conditioning. The vlPAG receives sensory input from the US through ascending fibers from the spinal cord. It also receives input regarding the expectation of the US from the central amygdala (CeA) through descending fibers. Conditioned expectation of the US drives both freezing behavior and a conditioned analgesia that can reduce the incoming pain signal. Ascending output from the vlPAG is proposed to reflect the difference between the US input (lamda) and what was expected (Vt), providing an error signal (delta V) that is sent to portions of the forebrain (dmPFC and BLA) through the thalamus (adapted from McNally, Johansen, & Blair, 2011).

engage cellular activity within the basolateral amygdala. Further, chemically inactivating this region, or microinjecting a drug that disrupts NMDA receptor function, blocks fear conditioning.

The output of the fear circuit is channeled through the *central nucleus* of the amygdala, which organizes the expression of fear. Fear can be manifested in a variety of ways, depending upon factors such as US intensity, relative expectation, and the environmental context. The diversity of outputs from the central nucleus allows the fear response to be tuned to the context and level of danger.

One output pathway projects to a region of the midbrain known as the **periaqueductal gray (PAG)**. Here too, different regions have been linked to distinct functions. The portion that lies along the upper sides (the dorsolateral PAG) organizes active defensive behaviors needed for fight and flight. These circa-strike behaviors are engaged by direct contact with a noxious, or life-threatening, stimulus. The lower (ventral) portion of the PAG mediates CS-elicited freezing behavior. Rats that have lesions limited to the ventral PAG exhibit other fear-elicited behaviors but do not freeze.

A key premise of the Rescorla–Wagner model (Rescorla & Wagner, 1972) is that unexpected (surprising) events engender more processing than those that are expected. Human imaging and animal studies have shown that unexpected events induce greater neural activity within the amygdala (McNally et al., 2011). This suggests that the input to the amygdala is regulated by a form of prediction error that determines whether learning occurs. This instructive input may be provided by the PAG, which receives both sensory input regarding the magnitude of the US and a CS-dependent signal from the amygdala

Continued

BOX 4.3 (continued)

that is proportional to the current expectation of the US (Figure 4.20B). The CS signal to the ventral PAG may dampen the US input by engaging a conditioned analgesia that reduces pain through the release of an internally manufactured (endogenous) opioid. This conditioned opioid release reduces the painfulness of the shock and thereby its effectiveness in generating new learning within the amygdala. Supporting this, microinjecting an opioid into the PAG interferes with learning. Conversely, administration of a drug that prevents an opioid from acting (an opioid antagonist) can reinstate learning about an expected US in a blocking paradigm (McNally et al., 2011).

The amygdala is also involved in learning about appetitive events, but its role in appetitive conditioning differs in some fundamental ways. For example, lesioning the basolateral amygdala eliminates the CR elicited by a CS that has been paired with an aversive US but does not affect the response elicited by a cue that predicts an appetitive US (Holland & Gallagher, 1999). The lesion does, however, prevent an appetitive CS from acting as a reinforcer in both second-order conditioning and secondary reinforcement with a food or drug reward (Box 7.1). The function of the central nucleus also differs. Rather than organizing the behavioral output, for appetitive CSs, the region appears to modulate behaviors related to attentional processing. For example, rats tend to orient toward a cue that predicts food. Also, an unexpected event can increase attention to a CS, yielding an enhancement in associability that augments learning (Pearce & Hall, 1980). Lesioning the central nucleus eliminates both these effects.

J. W. Grau

---

amygdala An almond-shaped structure that is part of the limbic system. Nuclei (clusters of neurons) within the amygdala play a role in emotional conditioning, regulating fear-related behaviors and attention.

limbic system A set of forebrain structures, which includes the amygdala and hippocampus, involved in the regulation of emotion and motivated behavior.

periaqueductal gray (PAG) A region of the midbrain that plays a role in regulating fear-related behavior (e.g., freezing) and pain.

Attentional Models of Conditioning

In the Rescorla–Wagner model, how much is learned on a conditioning trial depends on the effectiveness of the US on that trial. North American psychologists have favored theories of learning that focus on changes in the impact of the US. In contrast, British psychologists have approached phenomena such as the blocking effect by postulating changes in how well the CS commands attention. The assumption is that increased attention facilitates learning about a stimulus, and procedures that disrupt attention to a CS disrupt learning (Mitchell & Pelley, 2010).

Attentional theories differ in their assumptions about what determines how much attention a CS commands on a conditioning trial. Early theories postulated a single attentional mechanism. For example, Pearce and Hall (1980) proposed that the amount of attention an animal devotes to a CS is determined by how surprising the US was on the preceding trial (see also Hall, Kaye, & Pearce, 1985; McLaren & Mackintosh, 2000). Animals have a lot to learn if the US was surprising, and that increases attention to the CS on the next trial. In contrast, if a CS was followed by an expected US, not much learning is necessary and the CS commands less attention on the next trial. (For related neural mechanisms, see Roesch et al., 2012.)

In contrast to classic single-category theories, more recent attention theories assume that there are several different forms of attention relevant to learning and conditioned behavior. For example, Hogarth, Dickinson, and Duka (2011) suggested that there are three types of attention. The first category, "looking for action," is the attention a stimulus commands after it has become a good predictor of the US and can generate a CR with minimal cognitive effort. *Looking for action* is similar to the attentional mechanism of Mackintosh (1975) and reflects the behavioral control by well-trained cues. The second category, called "looking for learning," is the type of

N. J. Mackintosh

attention that is involved in processing cues that are not yet good predictors of the US and therefore have much to be learned about. Thus, *looking for learning* is similar to the Pearce and Hall (1980) attentional mechanism I described earlier. The third category, "looking for liking," refers to the attention that stimuli command because of their emotional value (how much they are liked or disliked). In addition to specifying different categories of attention, investigators are starting to identify the neural circuits responsible for these differences (e.g., Holland & Maddux, 2010).

An important feature of attention theories is that they assume that the outcome of a given trial alters the degree of attention commanded by the CS on future trials. For example, if Trial 10 ends in a surprising US, it will increase the *looking for learning* form of attention on Trial 11. Thus, US surprise is assumed to have a *prospective*, or *proactive*, influence on attention and conditioning. This is an important contrast to US-reduction models such as the Rescorla–Wagner model, in which the "surprisingness" of the US on a given trial determines what is learned on that same trial.

The assumption that the outcome of a given trial influences what is learned on the next trial has made attention models unique in explaining a number of interesting findings (e.g., Mackintosh, Bygrave, & Picton, 1977). However, attention models cannot explain one-trial blocking. The presence of the previously conditioned CS_A in Phase 2 of the blocking design makes the US fully expected. Any reduction in attention to CS_B that results from this would only be manifest on subsequent trials of Phase 2. CS_B should command full attention on the first trial of Phase 2, and learning about CS_B should proceed normally. However, that does not occur. The conditioning of CS_B can be blocked by CS_A even on the first trial of Phase 2 (e.g., Azorlosa & Cicala, 1986; Dickinson, Nicholas, & Mackintosh, 1983; Gillan & Domjan, 1977).

Timing and Information Theory Models

Neither the Rescorla–Wagner model nor attentional models were designed to explain the effects of time in conditioning. However, time is obviously a critical factor. One important temporal variable is the CS–US interval. As illustrated in Figure 4.9, focal search responses become conditioned with a relatively short CS–US interval, whereas general search responses become conditioned with a long CS–US interval. Most studies of classical conditioning measure responses closely related to the US. Therefore, less conditioned behavior is evident with increases in the CS–US interval.

The generally accepted view now is that in a Pavlovian procedure, participants learn not only that a CS is paired with a US, but when that US will occur (e.g., Balsam, Drew, & Yang, 2001; Balsam, Drew, & Gallistel, 2010). Based on their findings, Williams and colleagues (2008) went even further to claim that learning *when* the US occurs trumps learning *whether* it occurs.

The idea that participants learn about the point in time when the US occurs is called *temporal coding*. The *temporal coding hypothesis* states that participants learn when the US occurs in relation to a CS and use this information in blocking, second-order conditioning, and other paradigms in which what is learned in one phase of training influences what is learned in a subsequent phase. Numerous studies have upheld interesting predictions of the temporal coding hypothesis (e.g., Amundson & Miller, 2008; Cole, Barnet, & Miller, 1997; Savastano & Miller, 1998).

Another important temporal variable is the interval between successive trials. Generally, more conditioned responding is observed with longer intertrial intervals (e.g., Sunsay & Bouton, 2008). In addition, the intertrial interval and the CS duration (or CS–US interval) act in combination to determine responding. Numerous studies have shown that the critical factor is the relative duration of these two temporal intervals rather than the absolute value of either one by itself (Gallistel & Gibbon, 2000; Balsam & Gallistel, 2009). A particularly

P. D. Balsam

J. Gibbon

FIGURE 4.21 Percentage of time rats spent nosing the food cup during an auditory CS in conditioning with either a 10-second or a 20-second trial duration (*T*) and various intertrial intervals (*I*) that created *I/T* ratios ranging from 1.5 to 48.0. Data are shown in relation to responding during baseline periods when the CS was absent. (Based on "Trial and Intertribal Durations in Appetitive Conditioning in Rats," by P. C. Holland, 2000, *Animal Learning & Behavior*, Vol. 28, Figure 2, p. 125.)

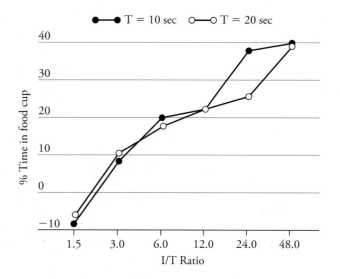

clear example of this relationship was reported by Holland (2000) based on an experiment with laboratory rats.

Conditioning trials consisted of an auditory cue (white noise) presented just before delivery of food into a cup. The conditioned response that developed to the CS was nosing of the food cup (goal tracking). Each group was conditioned with one of two CS durations, either 10 seconds or 20 seconds, and one of six intertrial intervals (ranging from 15 seconds to 960 seconds). (Intertrial intervals were measured from one US delivery to the next.) Each procedure could be characterized in terms of the ratio of the intertrial interval (*I*) and the CS duration, which Holland called the trial duration (*T*). The results of the experiment are summarized in Figure 4.21. Time spent nosing the food cup during the CS is shown as a function of the relative value of the intertrial interval (*I*) and the trial duration (*T*) for each group. Notice that conditioned responding was directly related to the *I/T* ratio. At each *I/T* ratio, the groups that received the 10-second CS responded similarly to those that received the 20-second CS. (For other types of results involving the *I/T* ratio, see Burns & Domjan, 2001; Kirkpatrick & Church, 2000; Lattal, 1999.)

Why is conditioned responding determined by the *I/T* ratio? A ratio suggests a comparison, in this case between events during the intertrial interval (*I*) and the conditioning trial (*T*). What is being compared has been expressed in various ways over the years (Gibbon & Balsam, 1981; Gallistel & Gibbon, 2000). According to the **relative-waiting-time hypothesis** (Jenkins, Barnes, & Barrera, 1981), the comparison is between how long one has to wait for the US during the CS versus how long one has to wait for the US during the intertrial interval (the interval from one US presentation to the next). When the US waiting time during the CS is much shorter than during the intertrial interval, the *I/T* ratio is high. Under these circumstances, the CS is highly informative about the next occurrence of the US and high levels of responding occur. In contrast, with a low *I/T* ratio the US waiting time during the intertrial interval is similar to the US waiting time during the CS. In this case, the CS provides little new information about the next US, and not much conditioned responding develops.

The idea that conditioned responding depends on the information value of the CS has been developed in greater mathematical detail by Balsam and Gallistel (2009). Based on these calculations, Balsam and Gallistel concluded that "the CS is associable with a US … only to the extent that it reduces the expected time to the next US" (p. 77).

Although this conclusion helps us understand effects of the *I/T* ratio on conditioned responding, it is primarily applicable to situations that involve multiple conditioning trials (where there is a "next US"). These and related ideas (e.g., Gallistel & Gibbon, 2000) are difficult to apply to situations in which learning occurs in a single trial (e.g., taste-aversion learning or fear conditioning) and there is no "next US" (see also Domjan, 2003).

The Comparator Hypothesis

R. R. Miller

The relative-waiting-time hypothesis and related theories were developed to explain the effects of temporal factors in excitatory conditioning. One of their important contributions was to emphasize that conditioned responding depends not only on what happens during the CS but also on what happens in other aspects of the experimental situation. The idea that both these factors influence learned performance is also central to the **comparator hypothesis** and its successors developed by Ralph Miller and his collaborators (Denniston, Savastano, & Miller, 2001; Miller & Matzel, 1988; Stout & Miller, 2007).

The comparator hypothesis was motivated by an interesting set of findings known as *revaluation effects.* Consider, for example, the blocking phenomenon (Figure 4.15). Participants first receive a phase of training in which CS_A is paired with the US. CS_A is then presented simultaneously with CS_B, and this stimulus compound is paired with the US. Subsequent tests of CS_B by itself show little responding to CS_B. As we discussed, the Rescorla–Wagner model interprets the blocking effect as a failure of learning to CS_B. The presence of CS_A blocks the conditioning of CS_B.

The comparator hypothesis takes a different approach. It assumes that what is blocked is responding to CS_B, not learning about CS_B. If that is true, then responding to CS_B should become evident if the block is removed somehow. How might that be accomplished? As it turns out, one way to remove the block to CS_B is to eliminate responding to CS_A after compound conditioning by presenting CS_A repeatedly without the US. A number of studies have shown that such extinction of CS_A following the blocking procedure unmasks conditioned responding to CS_B (e.g., Blaisdell, Gunther, & Miller, 1999; Boddez et al., 2011). This is called a *revaluation effect* because it involves changing the conditioned value of a stimulus (CS_A) that was present during the training of the target stimulus CS_B. The unmasking of responding to CS_B shows that blocking did not prevent the conditioning of CS_B but disrupted performance of the response to CS_B.

Inspired by revaluation effects, the comparator hypothesis is a theory of performance rather than learning. It assumes that conditioned responding depends not only on associations between a target CS and the US but also on associations that may be learned between the US and other stimuli that were present when the target CS was being conditioned. These other stimuli are called the *comparator* cues and include the experimental context and other discrete CSs. In the blocking experiment, the target stimulus is CS_B and the primary comparator cue is the previously trained CS_A that is present during the conditioning of CS_B.

Another key assumption of the comparator hypothesis is that it only allows for the formation of excitatory associations with the US. Whether conditioned responding reflects excitation or inhibition is assumed to be determined by the relative strengths of excitation conditioned to the target CS as compared to the excitatory value of the comparator stimuli that were present with the target CS during training.

The comparator process is represented by the balance in Figure 4.22. As Figure 4.22 illustrates, a comparison is made between the excitatory value of the target CS and the excitatory value of the comparator cues that are present during the training of the target

FIGURE 4.22 Illustration of the comparator hypothesis. Whether the target CS elicits inhibitory or excitatory responding depends on whether the balance tips to the left or the right. If the excitatory value of the target CS is greater than the excitatory value of the comparator cues present during training of the target, the balance tips to the right, in favor of excitatory responding. As the associative value of the comparator stimuli increases, the balance becomes less favorable for excitatory responding and may tip to the left, in favor of inhibitory responding.

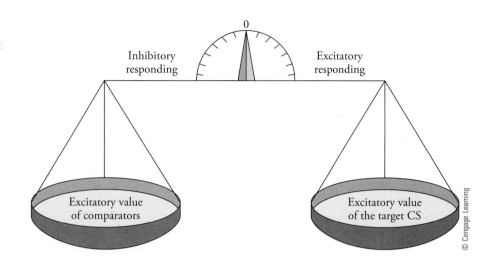

CS. If the excitatory value of the target CS exceeds the excitatory value of the comparator cues, the balance of the comparison will be tipped in favor of excitatory responding. In contrast, if the excitatory value of the comparator cues exceeds the excitatory value of the target CS, the balance will be tipped in favor of inhibitory responding to the target CS.

Unlike the relative-waiting-time hypothesis, the comparator hypothesis emphasizes associations rather than time. In its simpler form, the theory assumes that organisms learn three associations during the course of conditioning. These are illustrated in Figure 4.23. The first association (Link 1 in Figure 4.23) is between the target CS (X) and the US. The second association (Link 2) is between the target CS (X) and the comparator cues. Finally, there is an association between the comparator stimuli and the US (Link 3). With all three of these links in place, once the CS is presented, it activates the US representation directly (through Link 1) and indirectly (through Links 2 and 3). A comparison of the direct and indirect activations determines the degree of excitatory or inhibitory responding that occurs (for further elaboration, see Stout & Miller, 2007).

FIGURE 4.23 The associative structure of the comparator hypothesis. The target CS is represented as X. Excitatory associations result in activation of the US representation, either directly by the target (Link 1) or indirectly (through Links 2 and 3). (Based on Friedman, et al. (1998). *Journal of Experimental Psychology: Animal Behavior Processes, 2,* p. 454.)

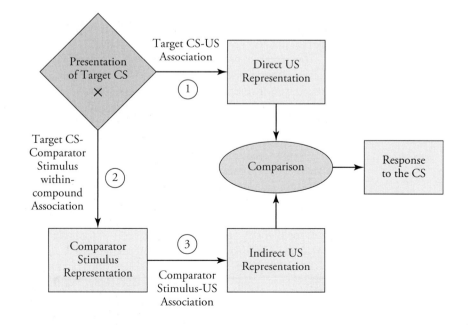

An important corollary to the theory is that the comparison that determines responding is made when participants are tested for their conditioned behavior. Because of this assumption, the comparator hypothesis makes the unusual prediction that extinction of comparator–US associations following training of a target CS will enhance responding to that target CS. It is through this mechanism that the comparator hypothesis is able to predict that the blocking effect can be reversed by extinguishing the blocking stimulus (CS_A). (For additional examples of such revaluation effects, see McConnell, Urushihara, & Miller, 2010; Miguez, Witnauer, & Miller, 2012.)

The comparator hypothesis has also been tested in studies of conditioned inhibition. In a conditioned inhibition procedure (e.g., see Figure 3.11), the target is the CS–. During conditioned inhibition training, the CS– is presented together with a CS+ that provides the excitatory context for the learning of inhibition. Thus, the comparator stimulus is the CS+. Consider the comparator balance presented in Figure 4.21. According to this balance, inhibitory responding will occur to the target (CS–) because it has less excitatory power than its comparator (the CS+). Thus, the comparator hypothesis predicts inhibitory responding in situations where the association of the target CS with the US is weaker than the association of the comparator cues with the US. Conditioned inhibition is not viewed as the result of negative associative value but as the result of the balance of the comparison tipping away from the target and in favor of the comparator stimulus. An interesting implication of the theory is that extinction of the comparator CS+ following inhibitory conditioning will reduce inhibitory responding. As I noted earlier in the discussion of the extinction of conditioned inhibition, this unusual prediction has been confirmed (e.g., Best et al., 1985; Lysle & Fowler, 1985).

Concluding Comments

Initially, some psychologists regarded classical conditioning as a relatively simple and primitive type of learning that is involved in the regulation only of glandular and visceral responses, such as salivation. The establishment of CS–US associations was assumed to occur fairly automatically with the pairing of a CS and a US. Given the simple and automatic nature of the conditioning, it was not viewed as important in explaining the complexity and richness of human experience. Clearly, this view of classical conditioning is no longer tenable.

The research reviewed in Chapters 3 and 4 has shown that classical conditioning involves numerous complex processes and is involved in the control of a wide variety of responses, including not only responses to the CS but also modifications in how the organism responds to the unconditioned stimulus. Classical conditioning does not occur automatically with the pairing of a CS with a US. Rather, it depends on the organism's prior experience with each of these stimuli, the presence of other stimuli during the conditioning trial, and the extent to which the CS and US are relevant to each other. Furthermore, the processes of classical conditioning are not limited to CS–US pairings. Learned associations can occur between two biologically weak stimuli (sensory preconditioning) or in the absence of a US (higher-order conditioning).

These and other complexities of classical conditioning have created significant challenges for theories of learning. The last 40 years have yielded a rich variety of theoretical approaches. No theory provides a comprehensive account of all of the data, but each has served to highlight the importance of various factors in how conditioning alters the properties of conditioned and unconditioned stimuli. These factors include error-correction mechanisms, attentional mechanisms, temporal and informational variables, and memories of the US activated by the target CS and its comparators. The richness of classical conditioning mechanisms makes them highly relevant to understanding the richness and complexity of human experience.

Sample Questions

1. What, if any, limits are there on the kinds of stimuli that can serve as conditioned and unconditioned stimuli in Pavlovian conditioning?
2. Describe several examples of how Pavlovian conditioning can modify how one responds to the unconditioned stimulus. What is the adaptive significance of this type of learning?
3. Describe an experimental design that allows investigators to distinguish between S–R and S–S learning.
4. Describe the basic idea of the Rescorla–Wagner model. What aspect of the model allows it to explain the blocking effect and make some unusual predictions?
5. Describe three different types of attention that are relevant to learned behavior.
6. In what respects are attentional theories of learning different from other theories?
7. How does the intertrial interval influence learning?
8. How does the comparator hypothesis explain the blocking effect?

Key Terms

blocking effect   Interference with the conditioning of a novel stimulus because of the presence of a previously conditioned stimulus.

comparator hypothesis   The idea that conditioned responding depends on a comparison between the associative strength of the conditioned stimulus (CS) and the associative strength of other cues present during training of the target CS.

conditioned compensatory-response   A conditioned response opposite in form to the reaction elicited by the US and that therefore compensates for this reaction.

conditioned diminution of the UR   A reduction in the magnitude of the response to an unconditioned stimulus caused by presentation of a CS that had been conditioned with that US.

CS-preexposure effect   Interference with conditioning produced by repeated exposures to the CS before the conditioning trials. Also called *latent-inhibition effect.*

drug tolerance   Reduction in the effectiveness of a drug as a result of repeated use of the drug.

higher-order conditioning   A procedure in which a previously conditioned stimulus (CS_1) is used to condition a new stimulus (CS_2).

latent-inhibition effect   Same as *CS-preexposure effect.*

relative-waiting-time hypothesis   The idea that conditioned responding depends on how long the organism has to wait for the US in the presence of the CS, as compared to how long the organism has to wait for the US in the experimental situation irrespective of the CS.

stimulus–response (S–R) learning   The learning of an association between a stimulus and a response, with the result that the stimulus comes to elicit the response directly.

stimulus–stimulus (S–S) learning   The learning of an association between two stimuli, with the result that exposure to one of the stimuli comes to activate a representation, or "mental image," of the other stimulus.

sensory preconditioning   A procedure in which one biologically weak stimulus (CS_2) is repeatedly paired with another biologically weak stimulus (CS_1). Then, CS_1 is conditioned with an unconditioned stimulus. In a later test trial, CS_2 also will elicit the conditioned response, even though CS_2 was never directly paired with the US.

stimulus salience   The significance or noticeability of a stimulus. Generally, conditioning proceeds more rapidly with more salient conditioned and unconditioned stimuli.

stimulus substitution   The theoretical idea that as a result of classical conditioning participants come to respond to the CS in much the same way that they respond to the US.

US-preexposure effect   Interference with conditioning produced by repeated exposures to the unconditioned stimulus before the conditioning trials.

US devaluation   Reduction in the attractiveness of an unconditioned stimulus, usually achieved by aversion conditioning or satiation.

CHAPTER 5

Instrumental Conditioning: Foundations

CHAPTER PREVIEW

This chapter begins our discussion of instrumental conditioning and goal-directed behavior. This is the type of conditioning that is involved in training a quarterback to throw a touchdown or a child to skip rope. In this type of conditioning, obtaining a goal or reinforcer depends on the prior occurrence of a designated response. I will first describe the origins of research on instrumental conditioning and the investigative methods used in contemporary research. This discussion lays the groundwork for the following section in which the four basic types of instrumental conditioning procedures are described. I will conclude the chapter with discussions of three fundamental elements of the instrumental conditioning paradigm: the instrumental response, the reinforcer or goal event, and the relation between the instrumental response and the goal event.

In the preceding chapters, I discussed various aspects of how responses are elicited by discrete stimuli. Studies of habituation, sensitization, and classical conditioning are all concerned with the mechanisms of elicited behavior. Because of this emphasis, the procedures used in experiments on habituation, sensitization, and classical conditioning do not require the participant to make a particular response to obtain food or other unconditioned or conditioned stimuli. Classical conditioning reflects how organisms adjust to events in their environment that they do not directly control. In this chapter, we turn to the analysis of learning situations in which the stimuli an organism encounters are a result or consequence of its behavior. Such behavior is commonly referred to as *goal-directed* or *instrumental* because responding is necessary to produce a desired environmental outcome.

By studying hard, a student can earn a better grade; by turning the car key in the ignition, a driver can start the engine; by putting a coin in a vending machine, a child can obtain a piece of candy. In all these cases, some aspect of the individual's behavior is instrumental in producing a significant stimulus or outcome. Furthermore, the behavior occurs because similar actions produced the same type of outcome in the past. Students would not study if doing so did not yield better grades; drivers would not turn the ignition key if this did not start the engine; and children would not put coins in a vending machine if they did not get a candy in return. Behavior that occurs because it was previously effective in producing certain consequences is called **instrumental behavior**.

The fact that the consequences of an action can determine whether you make that response again is obvious to everyone. If you happen to find a dollar bill when you glance down, you will keep looking at the ground as you walk. How such a consequence influences future behavior is not so readily apparent. Many of the upcoming chapters of this book are devoted to the mechanisms responsible for the control of behavior by its consequences. In this chapter, I will describe some of the history, basic techniques, procedures, and issues in the experimental analysis of instrumental, or goal-directed, behavior.

How might one investigate instrumental behavior? One way would be to go to the natural environment and look for examples. However, this approach is not likely to lead to definitive results because factors responsible for goal-directed behavior are difficult to isolate without experimental manipulation. Consider, for example, a dog sitting comfortably in its yard. When an intruder approaches, the dog starts to bark vigorously, and the intruder goes away. Because the dog's barking is followed by the departure of the intruder, we may conclude that the dog barked to produce this outcome—that barking was goal-directed. However, an equally likely possibility is that barking was elicited by the novelty of the intruder and persisted as long as this eliciting stimulus was present. The departure of the intruder may have been incidental to the dog's barking. Deciding between such alternatives is difficult without experimental manipulations of the relation between barking and its consequences. (For an experimental analysis of a similar situation in a fish species, see Losey & Sevenster, 1995.)

Early Investigations of Instrumental Conditioning

Laboratory and theoretical analyses of instrumental conditioning began in earnest with the work of the American psychologist E. L. Thorndike. Thorndike's original intent was to study animal intelligence (Thorndike, 1898, 1911; for a more recent commentary, see Lattal, 1998). As I noted in Chapter 1, the publication of Darwin's theory of evolution encouraged scientists to think about the extent to which human intellectual capacities were present in animals. Thorndike pursued this question through empirical research.

E. L. Thorndike

He devised a series of puzzle boxes for his experiments. His training procedure consisted of placing a hungry animal (often a young cat) in the puzzle box with some food left outside in plain view of the animal. The task for the animal was to learn how to get out of the box and get the food.

Different puzzle boxes required different responses to get out. Some were easier than others. Figure 5.1 illustrates two of the easier puzzle boxes. In Box A, the required response was to pull a ring to release a latch that blocked the door on the outside. In Box I, the required response was to push down a lever, which released a latch. Initially, the cats were slow to make the correct response, but with continued practice on the task, their latencies became shorter and shorter. Figure 5.2 shows the latencies of a cat to get out of Box A on successive trials. The cat took 160 seconds to get out of Box A on the first trial. Its shortest latency later on was 6 seconds (Chance, 1999).

Thorndike's careful empirical approach was a significant advance in the study of animal intelligence. Another important contribution was Thorndike's strict avoidance of anthropomorphic interpretations of the behavior he observed. Although he titled his treatise *Animal Intelligence*, to Thorndike many aspects of behavior seemed rather unintelligent. He did not think that his animals got faster in escaping from a puzzle box because they gained insight into the task or figured out how the release mechanism was

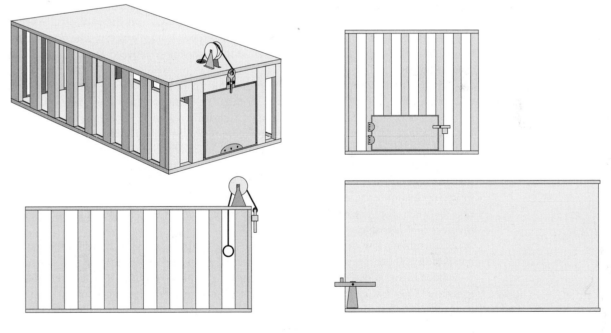

Box A   Box I

FIGURE 5.1 Two of Thorndike's puzzle boxes, A and I. In Box A, the participant had to pull a loop to release the door. In Box I, pressing down on a lever released a latch on the other side. (*Left:* Based on "Thorndike's Puzzle Boxes and the Origins of the Experimental Analysis of Behavior," by P. Chance, 1999, *Journal of the Experimental Analysis of Behaviour, 72*, pp. 433–440. *Right:* Based on Thorndike, *Animal Intelligence Experimental Studies*, 1898.)

FIGURE 5.2 Latencies to escape from Box A during successive trials. The longest latency was 160 seconds; the shortest was 6 seconds. (Notice that the axes are not labeled, as in Thorndike's original report.)

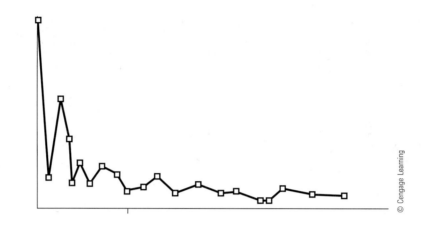

© Cengage Learning

designed. Rather, he interpreted the results of his studies as reflecting the learning of a new S–R association.

When a cat was initially placed in a box, it displayed a variety of responses typical of a confined animal. Eventually, some of these responses resulted in opening the door. Thorndike believed that such successful escapes led to the learning of an association between the stimuli of being in the puzzle box (S) and the effective escape response (R). As the association, or connection, between the box cues and the successful response became stronger, the animal came to make that response more quickly. The consequence of a successful escape response strengthened the association between the box stimuli and that response.

On the basis of his research, Thorndike formulated the **law of effect**. The law of effect states that if a response R in the presence of a stimulus S is followed by a *satisfying event*, the association between the stimulus S and the response R becomes strengthened. If the response is followed by an *annoying event*, the S–R association is weakened. It is important to stress here that, according to the law of effect, what is learned is an association between the response and the stimuli present at the time of the response. Notice that the consequence of the response is not one of the elements in the association. The satisfying or annoying consequence simply serves to strengthen or weaken the association between the preceding stimulus and response. Thus, Thorndike's law of effect involves *S–R learning*.

Thorndike's law of effect and S–R learning continue to be of considerable interest more than 100 years since these ideas were first proposed. A key feature of Thorndike's S–R mechanism is that it compels the organism to make response R whenever stimulus S occurs. This feature has made the law of effect an attractive mechanism to explain compulsive habits that are difficult to break, such as biting one's nails, snacking, or smoking cigarettes. Once you start on a bucket of popcorn while watching a movie, you cannot stop eating because the sight and smell of the popcorn (S) compels you to grab some more popcorn and eat it (R). The compulsive nature of eating popcorn is such that you continue to eat beyond the point of enjoying the taste. Once learned, habitual responses occur because they are triggered by an antecedent stimulus and not because they result in a desired consequence (Everitt & Robbins, 2005; Wood & Neal, 2007). A habitual smoker who knows that smoking is harmful will continue to smoke because S–R mechanisms compel lighting a cigarette independent of the consequences of the response.

BOX 5.1

E. L. Thorndike: Biographical Sketch

Edward Lee Thorndike was born in1874 and died in 1949. As an undergraduate at Wesleyan University, he became interested in the work of William James, who was then at Harvard. Thorndike himself entered Harvard as a graduate student in 1895. During his stay, he began his research on instrumental behavior, at first using chicks. Because there was no laboratory space in the psychology department at the university, he set up his project in William James's cellar. Soon after that, he was offered a fellowship at Columbia University. This time, his laboratory was located

in the attic of psychologist James Cattell.

Thorndike received his Ph.D. from Columbia in 1898, for his work entitled *Animal Intelligence: An Experimental Analysis of Associative Processes in Animals*. This included the famous puzzle-box experiments. Thorndike's dissertation has turned out to be one of the most famous dissertations in more than a century of modern psychology. After obtaining his Ph.D., Thorndike spent a short stint at Western Reserve University in Cleveland and then returned to Columbia, where he served as professor of educational

psychology in the Teachers College for many years. Among other things, he worked to apply to children the principles of trial-and-error learning he had uncovered with animals. He also became interested in psychological testing and became a leader in that newly formed field. By his retirement, he had written 507 scholarly works (without a computer or word processor), including about 50 books (Cumming, 1999). Several years before his death, Thorndike returned to Harvard as the William James Lecturer, a fitting honor considering the origins of his interests in psychology.

Modern Approaches to the Study of Instrumental Conditioning

Thorndike used 15 different puzzle boxes in his investigations. Each box required different manipulations for the cat to get out. As more scientists became involved in studying instrumental learning, the range of tasks they used became smaller. A few of these became "standard" and have been used repeatedly to facilitate comparison of results obtained in different experiments and laboratories.

Discrete-Trial Procedures

Discrete-trial procedures are similar to the method Thorndike used in that each training trial begins with putting the animal in the apparatus and ends with removal of the animal after the instrumental response has been performed. Discrete-trial procedures these days usually involve the use of some type of maze. The use of mazes in investigations of learning was introduced at the turn of the twentieth century by the American psychologist W. S. Small (1899, 1900). Small was interested in studying rats and was encouraged to use a maze by an article he read in *Scientific American* describing the complex system of underground burrows that kangaroo rats build in their natural habitat. Small reasoned that a maze would take advantage of the rats' "propensity for small winding passages."

Figure 5.3 shows two mazes frequently used in contemporary research. The runway, or straight-alley, maze contains a start box at one end and a goal box at the other. The rat is placed in the start box at the beginning of each trial. The barrier separating the start box from the main section of the runway is then raised. The rat is allowed to make its way down the runway until it reaches the goal box, which usually contains a reinforcer, such as food or water.

Behavior in a runway can be quantified by measuring how fast the animal gets from the start box to the goal box. This is called the **running speed**. The running speed

FIGURE 5.3 Top view of a runway and a T-maze. S is the start box; G is the goal box.

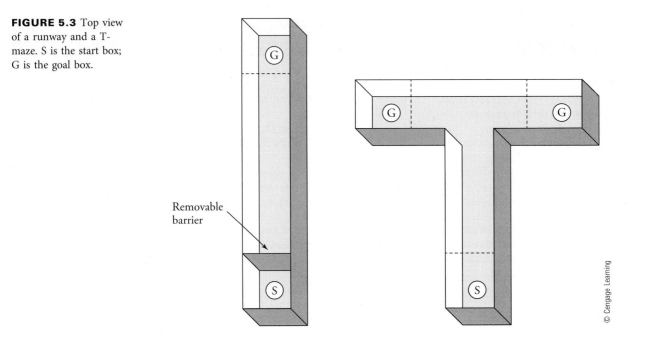

typically increases with repeated training trials. Another common measure of behavior in runways is response **latency**. The latency is the time it takes the animal to leave the start box and begin running down the alley. Typically, latencies become shorter as training progresses.

Another maze that has been used in many experiments is the T maze, shown on the right in Figure 5.3. The T maze consists of a start box and alleys arranged in the shape of a T. A goal box is located at the end of each arm of the T. Because the T maze has two choice arms, it can be used to study more complex questions. For example, Panagiotaropoulos and colleagues (2009) were interested in whether rats that are less than two weeks old (and still nursing) could learn where their mother is located in contrast with another female. To answer this question, they placed the mother rat in the goal box on the right arm of a T maze and a virgin female rat in the goal box on the left arm of the T. The rat pups learned to turn to the right rather than the left arm of the maze with successive trials. Furthermore, this conditioned preference persisted when the pups were tested at the end of training without a female in either goal box. The results show that nursing rat pups can distinguish their mother from a virgin female and can learn to go where their mother is located.

Free-Operant Procedures

In a runway or a T maze, after reaching the goal box, the animal is removed from the apparatus for a while before being returned to the start box for its next trial. Thus, the animal has limited opportunities to respond, and those opportunities are scheduled by the experimenter. By contrast, **free-operant procedures** allow the animal to repeat the instrumental response without constraint over and over again without being taken out of the apparatus until the end of an experimental session. The free-operant method was invented by B. F. Skinner (1938) to study behavior in a more continuous manner than is possible with mazes.

Skinner (Figure 5.4) was interested in analyzing in the laboratory a form of behavior that would be representative of all naturally occurring ongoing activity. However, he

FIGURE 5.4 B. F. Skinner (1904–1990)

Bettmann/CORBIS

recognized that before behavior can be experimentally analyzed, a measurable unit of behavior must be defined. Casual observation suggests that ongoing behavior is continuous; one activity leads to another. Behavior does not fall neatly into units, as do molecules of a chemical solution or bricks on a sidewalk. Skinner proposed the concept of the operant as a way of dividing behavior into meaningful measurable units.

Figure 5.5 shows a typical Skinner box used to study free-operant behavior in rats. (A Skinner box used to study pecking in pigeons was presented in Figure 1.8). The box is a small chamber that contains a lever that the rat can push down repeatedly. The

FIGURE 5.5 A Skinner box equipped with a response lever and food-delivery device. Electronic equipment is used to program procedures and record responses automatically.

Photo Researchers, Inc.

chamber also has a mechanism that can deliver a reinforcer, such as food or water, into a cup. The lever is electronically connected to the food-delivery system so that when the rat presses the lever, a pellet of food automatically falls into the food cup.

An **operant response**, such as the lever press, is defined in terms of the effect that the behavior has on the environment. Activities that have the same environmental effect are considered to be instances of the same operant response. Behavior is not defined in terms of particular muscle movements but in terms of how the behavior *operates* on the environment. The lever-press operant is typically defined as sufficient depression of the lever to activate a recording sensor. The rat may press the lever with its right paw, its left paw, or its tail. These different muscle movements constitute the same operant if they all depress the lever sufficiently to trigger the sensor and produce a food pellet. Various ways of pressing the lever are assumed to be functionally equivalent because they all have the same effect on the environment.

We perform numerous operants during the course of our daily lives. In opening a door, it does not matter whether we use our right hand or left hand to turn the door knob. The operational outcome (opening the door) is the critical measure of success. Similarly, in basketball or baseball, it's the operational outcome that counts—getting the ball in the basket or hitting the ball into the outfield—rather than the way the task is accomplished. With an operational definition of behavioral success, one does not need a sophisticated judge to determine whether the behavior has been successfully accomplished. The environmental outcome keeps the score. This contrasts with behaviors such as figure skating or gymnastics. In those cases, the way something is performed is just as important as is the environmental impact of the behavior. Getting a ball into the basket is an operant behavior. Performing a graceful dismount from the parallel bars is not. However, any response that is required to produce a desired consequence is an *instrumental response* because it is "instrumental" in producing a particular outcome.

Magazine Training and Shaping　When children first attempt to toss a basketball in the basket, they are not very successful. Many attempts end with the ball bouncing off the backboard or not even landing near the basket. Similarly, a rat placed in a Skinner box will not press the lever that produces a pellet of food right away. Successful training of an operant or instrumental response often requires carefully designed training steps that move the student from the status of a novice to that of an expert. This is clearly the case with something like championship figure skating that requires hours of daily practice under the careful supervision of an expert coach. Most parents do not spend money hiring an expert coach to teach a child basketball. However, even there, the child moves through a series of training steps that may start with a small ball and a Fisher Price basketball set that is much lower than the standard one and is easier to reach. The training basket is also adjustable so that it can be gradually raised as the child becomes more proficient.

There are also preliminary steps for establishing lever-press responding in a laboratory rat. First, the rat has to learn when food is available in the food cup. This involves classical conditioning: The sound of the food-delivery device is repeatedly paired with the release of a food pellet into the cup. The food-delivery device is called the *food magazine*. After enough pairings of the sound of the food magazine with food delivery, the sound elicits a classically conditioned approach response: The animal goes to the food cup and picks up the pellet. This preliminary phase of conditioning is called **magazine training**.

After magazine training, the rat is ready to learn the required operant response. At this point, food is given if the rat does anything remotely related to pressing the lever. For example, at first the rat may be given a food pellet each time it gets up on its hind legs anywhere in the experimental chamber. Once the rearing response has been established, the food pellet may be given only if the rat makes the rearing response over the response lever. Rearing in other parts of the chamber would no longer be reinforced. Once rearing over the lever has been established, the food pellet may be given only if the rat touches and depresses the lever. Such a sequence of training steps is called **response shaping**.

As the preceding examples show, the shaping of a new operant response requires training components or approximations to the final behavior. Whether you are trying to teach a child to throw a ball into a basket, or a rat to press a response lever, at first any response that remotely approximates the final performance can be reinforced. Once the child becomes proficient at throwing the ball into a basket placed at shoulder height, the height of the basket can be gradually raised. As the shaping process continues, more and more is required, until the reinforcer is given only if the final target response is made.

Successful shaping of behavior involves three components. First, you have to clearly define the final response you want the trainee to perform. Second, you have to clearly assess the starting level of performance, no matter how far it is from the final response you are interested in. Third, you have to divide the progression from the starting point to the final target behavior into appropriate training steps or successive approximations. The successive approximations make up your training plan. The execution of the training plan involves two complementary tactics: *reinforcement of successive approximations to the final behavior* and *withholding reinforcement for earlier response forms.*

Although the principles involved in shaping behavior are not difficult to understand, their application can be tricky. If the shaping steps are too far apart, or you spend too much time on one particular shaping step, progress may not be satisfactory. Sports coaches, piano teachers, and driver education instructors are all aware of how tricky it can be to design the most effective training steps or successive approximations. The same principles of shaping are involved in training a child to put on his or her socks or to drink from a cup without spilling, but the training in those cases is less formally organized. (For a study of shaping drug-abstinence behavior in cocaine users, see Preston, Umbricht, Wong, & Epstein, 2001.)

Shaping and New Behavior   Shaping procedures are often used to generate new behavior, but exactly how new are those responses? Consider, for example, a rat's lever-press response. To press the bar, the rat has to approach the bar, stop in front of it, raise its front paws, and then bring the paws down on the bar with sufficient force to push it down. All of these response components are things the rat is likely to have done at one time or another in other situations (while exploring its cage, interacting with another rat, or handling materials to build a nest). In teaching the rat to press the bar, we are not teaching new response components. Rather, we are teaching the rat how to combine familiar responses into a new activity. Instrumental conditioning often involves the construction, or synthesis, of a new behavioral unit from preexisting response components that already occur in the organism's repertoire (Balsam et al., 1998).

Instrumental conditioning can also be used to produce responses unlike anything the trainee ever did before. Consider, for example, throwing a football 60 yards down the field. It takes more than putting familiar behavioral components together to achieve such a feat. The force, speed, and coordination involved in throwing a football 60 yards is unlike anything an untrained individual might do. It is an entirely new response. Expert performances in sports, in playing a musical instrument, or in ballet all involve such novel response forms. Such novel responses are also created by shaping (Figure 5.6).

The creation of new responses by shaping depends on the inherent variability of behavior. If a new shaping step requires a trainee to throw a football 30 yards, each

FIGURE 5.6 Shaping is required to learn special skills, such as the pole vault.

Ryan Remiorz/AP Photo

throw is likely to be somewhat different. The trainee may throw the ball 25, 32, 29, or 34 yards on successive attempts. This variability permits the coach to set the next successive approximation at 33 yards. With that new target, the trainee will start to make longer throws. Each throw will again be different, but more of the throws will now be 33 yards and longer. The shift of the distribution to longer throws will permit the coach to again raise the response criterion, perhaps to 36 yards this time. With gradual iterations of this process, the trainee will make longer and longer throws, achieving distances that he or she would have never performed otherwise. The shaping process takes advantage of the variability of behavior to gradually move the distribution of responses away from the trainee's starting point and toward responses that are entirely new in the trainee's repertoire. Through this process, spectacular new feats of performance are learned in sports, dancing, or the visual arts. (For laboratory studies of shaping, see Deich, Allan, & Zeigler, 1988; and Stokes, Mechner, & Balsam, 1999.)

Response Rate as a Measure of Operant Behavior   In contrast to discrete-trial techniques for studying instrumental behavior, free-operant methods permit continuous observation of behavior over long periods. With continuous opportunity to respond, the organism, rather than the experimenter, determines the frequency of its instrumental response. Hence, free-operant techniques provide a special opportunity to observe changes in the likelihood of behavior over time.

How might we take advantage of this opportunity and measure the probability of an operant response? Measures of response latency and speed that are commonly used in discrete-trial procedures do not characterize the likelihood of repetitions of a response. Skinner proposed that the *rate of occurrence* of operant behavior (e.g., frequency of the response per minute) be used as a measure of response probability. Highly likely responses occur often and have a high rate. In contrast, unlikely responses occur seldom and have a low rate. Response rate has become the primary measure in studies that employ free-operant procedures.

Instrumental Conditioning Procedures

In all instrumental conditioning situations, the participant makes a response and thereby produces an outcome or consequence. Paying the boy next door for mowing the lawn, yelling at a cat for getting on the kitchen counter, closing a window to prevent the rain from coming in, and revoking a teenager's driving privileges for staying out late are all forms of instrumental conditioning. Two of these examples involve pleasant events (getting paid, driving a car), whereas the other two involve unpleasant stimuli (the sound of yelling and rain coming in the window). A pleasant event is technically called an **appetitive stimulus**. An unpleasant stimulus is technically called an **aversive stimulus**. The instrumental response may produce the stimulus, as when mowing the lawn results in getting paid. Alternatively, the instrumental response may turn off or eliminate a stimulus, as in closing a window to stop the incoming rain. Whether the result of a conditioning procedure is an increase or a decrease in the rate of responding depends on whether an appetitive or aversive stimulus is involved and whether the response produces or eliminates the stimulus. Four basic instrumental conditioning procedures are described in Table 5.1.

Positive Reinforcement

A father gives his daughter a cookie when she puts her toys away; a teacher praises a student for handing in a good report; an employee receives a bonus check for performing well on the job. These are all examples of **positive reinforcement**. Positive reinforcement is a procedure in which the instrumental response produces an appetitive stimulus. If the response occurs, the appetitive stimulus is presented; if the response does not occur, the appetitive stimulus is not presented. Thus, there is a positive contingency between the instrumental response and the appetitive stimulus. Positive reinforcement procedures produce an increase in the rate of responding. Requiring a hungry rat to press a response lever to obtain a food pellet is a common laboratory example of positive reinforcement.

Punishment

A mother reprimands her child for running into the street; your boss criticizes you for being late to a meeting; a teacher gives you a failing grade for answering too many test questions incorrectly. These are examples of **punishment** (also called **positive punishment**). In a punishment procedure, the instrumental response produces an unpleasant, or aversive, stimulus. There is a positive contingency between the instrumental response and the stimulus outcome (the response produces the outcome), but the outcome is aversive. Effective punishment procedures produce a decrease in the rate of instrumental responding.

TABLE 5.1	**TYPES OF INSTRUMENTAL CONDITIONING PROCEDURES**	
NAME OF PROCEDURE	**RESPONSE-OUTCOME CONTINGENCY**	**RESULT OF PROCEDURE**
Positive Reinforcement	*Positive:* Response produces an appetitive stimulus	*Reinforcement* or increase in response rate
Punishment (Positive Punishment)	*Positive:* Response produces an aversive stimulus	*Punishment* or decrease in response rate
Negative Reinforcement (Escape or Avoidance)	*Negative:* Response eliminates or prevents the occurrence of an aversive stimulus	*Reinforcement* or increase in response rate
Omission Training (DRO) or Negative Punishment	*Negative:* Response eliminates or prevents the occurrence of an appetitive stimulus	*Punishment* or decrease in response rate

© Cengage Learning

Negative Reinforcement

Opening an umbrella to stop the rain from getting you wet, putting on a seatbelt to silence the chimes in your car, and putting on your sunglasses to shield you from bright sunlight are examples of **negative reinforcement**. In all of these cases, the instrumental response turns off an aversive stimulus. Hence, there is a *negative contingency* between the instrumental response and the aversive stimulus. Negative reinforcement procedures increase instrumental responding. You are more likely to open an umbrella because it stops you from getting wet when it is raining.

People tend to confuse negative reinforcement and punishment. An aversive stimulus is used in both procedures. However, the relation of the instrumental response to the aversive stimulus is drastically different. In punishment procedures, the instrumental response produces the aversive event, whereas in negative reinforcement, the response terminates the aversive event. This difference in the response–outcome contingency produces very different results. Instrumental behavior is decreased by punishment and increased by negative reinforcement.

Omission Training or Negative Punishment

In omission training or negative punishment, the instrumental response results in the removal of a pleasant or appetitive stimulus (Sanabria, Sitomer, & Killeen, 2006). Omission training is being used when a child is given a time-out (e.g., Donaldson & Vollmer, 2011) or told to go to his or her room after doing something bad. There is nothing aversive about the child's room. Rather, by sending the child to the room, the parent is withdrawing sources of positive reinforcement, such as playing with friends or watching television. Suspending someone's driver's license for drunken driving also constitutes **omission training or negative punishment** (withdrawal of the pleasure and privilege of driving). Omission training or negative punishment involves a negative contingency between the response and an environmental event (hence the term "negative") and results in a decrease in instrumental responding (hence the term "punishment"). Negative punishment is often preferred over positive punishment as a method of discouraging human behavior because it does not involve delivering an aversive stimulus.

BOX 5.2

DRO as Treatment for Self-Injurious Behavior and Other Behavior Problems

Self-injurious behavior is a problematic habit that is evident in some individuals with developmental disabilities. Bridget was a 50-year-old woman with profound mental retardation whose self-injurious behavior was hitting her body and head and banging her head against furniture, walls, and floors. Preliminary assessments indicated that her head banging was maintained by the attention she received from others when she banged her head against a hard surface. To discourage the self-injurious behavior, an omission training procedure, or DRO, was put into place (Lindberg, Iwata, Kahng, & DeLeon, 1999). The training procedure was implemented in 15-minute sessions. During the omission training phase, Bridget was ignored when she banged her head against a hard surface but received attention periodically if she was not head banging. The attention consisted of the therapist talking to Bridget for 3–5 seconds and occasionally stroking her arm or back.

The results of the study are presented in Figure 5.7. During the first 19 sessions, when Bridget received attention for her self-injurious behavior, the rate of head banging fluctuated around six responses per minute. The first phase of DRO training (sessions 20–24) resulted in a rapid decline in head banging. The self-injurious behavior returned during sessions 25–31, when the baseline condition was reintroduced. DRO training was resumed in session 32 and remained in effect for the

Continued

BOX 5.2 (continued)

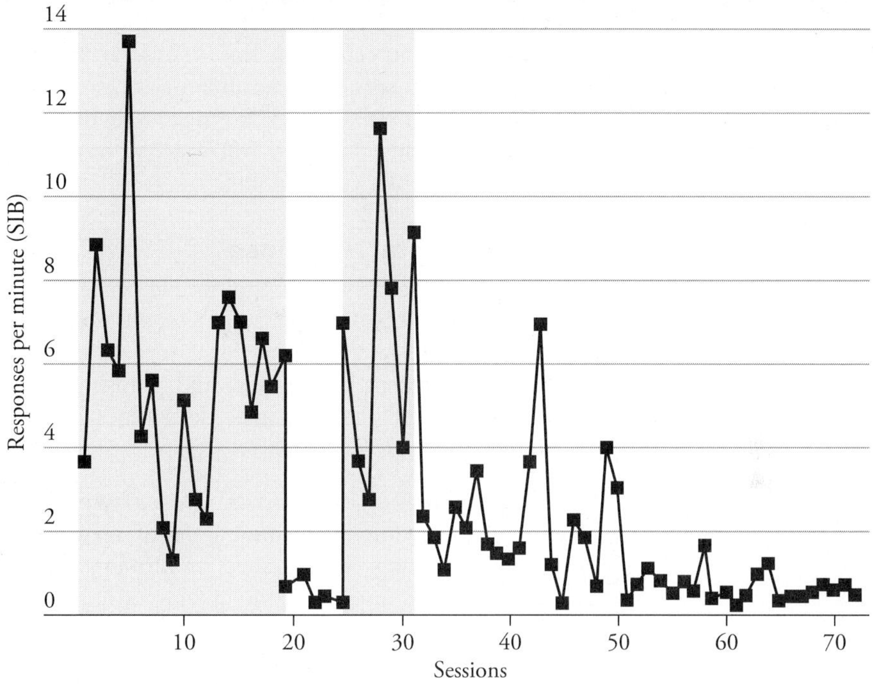

FIGURE 5.7 Rate of Bridget's self-injurious behavior during baseline sessions (1–19 and 25–31) and during sessions in which a DRO contingency was in effect (20–24 and 32–72) (based on Lindberg et al., 1999).

remainder of the study. These results show that self-injurious behavior was decreased by the DRO procedure.

The study with Bridget illustrates several general principles. One is that attention is a very powerful reinforcer for human behavior. People do all sorts of things for attention. As with Bridget, even responses that are injurious to the individual can develop if these responses result in attention. Unfortunately, some responses are difficult to ignore, but in attending to them, one may be actually encouraging them. A child misbehaving in a store or restaurant is difficult to ignore, but paying attention to the child will serve to encourage the misbehavior. As with Bridget, the best approach is to ignore the disruptive behavior and pay attention when the child is doing something else. Deliberately reinforcing other behavior is not easy and requires conscious effort on the part of the parent.

No one questions the need for such conscious effort in training complex responses in animals. As Amy Sutherland (2008) pointed out, animal "trainers did not get a sea lion to salute by nagging. Nor did they teach a baboon to flip by carping, nor an elephant to paint by pointing out everything the elephant did wrong.… Progressive animal trainers reward the behavior they want and, equally importantly, ignore the behavior they don't" (p. 59). In her engaging book, *What Shamu Taught Me About Life, Love, and Marriage,* Amy Sutherland argues that one can profitably use the same principles to achieve better results with one's spouse by not nagging them about leaving their dirty socks on the floor but by providing attention and social reinforcement for responses other than the offending habits.

Omission-training procedures are also called **differential reinforcement of other behavior (DRO)**. This term highlights the fact that in omission training, the individual periodically receives the appetitive stimulus provided he or she is engaged in behavior other than the response specified by the procedure. Making the target response results in omission of the reinforcer that would have been delivered had the individual performed some *other* behavior. Thus, omission training involves the reinforcement of *other* behavior.

Fundamental Elements of Instrumental Conditioning

As we will see in the following chapters, analysis of instrumental conditioning involves numerous factors and variables. However, the essence of instrumental behavior is that it is controlled by its consequences. Thus, instrumental conditioning fundamentally involves three elements: the instrumental response, the outcome of the response (the reinforcer), and the relation or contingency between the response and the outcome. In the remainder of this chapter, I will describe how each of these elements influences the course of instrumental conditioning.

The Instrumental Response

The outcome of instrumental conditioning procedures depends in part on the nature of the response being conditioned. Some responses are more easily modified than others. In Chapter 10, I will describe how the nature of the response influences the outcome of negative reinforcement (**avoidance**) and punishment procedures. This section describes how the nature of the response determines the results of positive reinforcement procedures.

Behavioral Variability Versus Stereotypy   Thorndike described instrumental behavior as involving the *stamping in* of an S–R association, while Skinner wrote about behavior being strengthened or *reinforced*. Both of these pioneers emphasized that reinforcement increases the likelihood that the instrumental response will be repeated in the future. This emphasis encouraged the belief that instrumental conditioning produces repetitions of the same response—that it produces uniformity or stereotypy in behavior. Stereotypy in responding does develop if that is allowed or required by the instrumental conditioning procedure (e.g., Schwartz, 1988). However, that does not mean that instrumental conditioning cannot be used to produce creative or variable responses.

We are accustomed to thinking about the requirement for reinforcement being an observable action, such as pressing a lever or hitting a baseball. Interestingly, however, the criteria for reinforcement can also be defined in terms of more abstract dimensions of behavior, such as its novelty. The behavior required for reinforcement can be defined as doing something unlike what the participant did on the preceding four or five trials. To satisfy this requirement, the participant has to perform differently on each trial. In such a procedure, *response variability* is the basis for instrumental reinforcement.

Numerous experiments with laboratory rats, pigeons, and human participants have shown that response variability increases if variability is the response dimension required to earn reinforcement (Neuringer, 2004; Neuringer & Jensen, 2010). In one study, college students were asked to draw rectangles on a computer screen (Ross & Neuringer, 2002). They were told they had to draw rectangles to obtain points but were not told what kind of rectangles they should draw. For one group of participants, a point was dispensed if the rectangle drawn on a given trial differed from other rectangles the student previously drew. The new rectangle had to be novel in size, shape, and location on the screen. This group was designated VAR for the variability requirement. Students in another group were paired up or yoked to students in group VAR and received a point on each trial that their partners in group VAR were reinforced. However, the YOKED participants had no requirements about the size, shape, or location of their rectangles.

The results of the experiment are shown in Figure 5.8. Students in group VAR showed considerably greater variability in the rectangles they drew than participants

Courtesy of A. Neuringer

A. Neuringer

FIGURE 5.8 Degree response variability along three dimensions of drawing a rectangle (size, shape, and location) for human participants who were reinforced for varying the type of rectangles they drew (VARY) or received reinforcement on the same trials but without any requirement to vary the nature of their drawings (YOKED). Higher values of U indicate greater variability in responding (based on Ross & Neuringer, 2002).

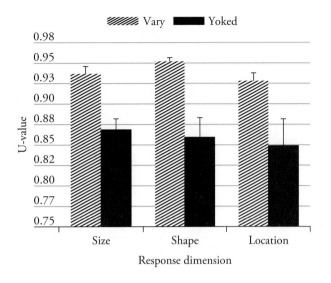

in group YOKED. This shows response variability can be increased if the instrumental reinforcement procedure requires variable behavior. Another experiment by Ross and Neuringer (2002) demonstrated that different aspects of drawing a rectangle (the size, shape, and location of the rectangle) can be controlled independently of one another by contingencies of reinforcement. For example, participants who are required to draw rectangles of the same size will learn to do that but will vary the location and shape of the rectangles they draw. In contrast, participants required to draw the same shape rectangle will learn to do that while they vary the size and location of their rectangles.

These experiments show that response variability can be increased with instrumental conditioning. Such experiments have also shown that in the absence of explicit reinforcement of variability, responding becomes more stereotyped with continued instrumental conditioning (e.g., Page & Neuringer, 1985). Thus, Thorndike and Skinner were partially correct in saying that responding becomes more stereotyped with continued instrumental conditioning. However, they were wrong to suggest that this is an inevitable outcome.

BOX 5.3

Detrimental Effects of Reward: More Myth Than Reality

Reinforcement procedures have become commonplace in educational settings as a way to encourage students to read and do their assignments. However, some have been concerned that reinforcement may actually undermine a child's intrinsic interest and willingness to perform a task once the reinforcement procedure is removed. Similar concerns have been expressed about possible detrimental effects of reinforcement on creativity and originality. Extensive research on

these questions has produced inconsistent results. However, more recent metaanalyses of the results of numerous studies indicate that under most circumstances reinforcement increases creative responses without reducing intrinsic motivation (Akin-Little et al., 2004; Byron & Khazanchi, 2012; Cameron, Banko, & Pierce, 2001). Research with children also indicates that reinforcement makes children respond with less originality only under limited circumstances

(e.g., Eisenberger & Shanock, 2003). As in experiments with pigeons and laboratory rats, reinforcement can increase or decrease response variability, depending on the criterion for reinforcement. If highly original responding is required to obtain reinforcement, originality increases, provided that the reinforcer is not so salient as to distract the participant from the task. (For a more general discussion of creativity, see Stokes, 2006.)

Novel response forms can be readily produced by instrumental conditioning if response variation is a requirement for reinforcement.

Relevance or Belongingness in Instrumental Conditioning

As the preceding section showed, instrumental conditioning can act on abstract dimensions of behavior, such as its variability. How far do these principles extend? Are there any limitations on the types of new behavioral units or response dimensions that may be modified by instrumental conditioning? A growing body of evidence indicates that there are important limitations.

In Chapter 4, I described how classical conditioning occurs at different rates depending on the combination of conditioned and unconditioned stimuli used. For example, rats readily learn to associate tastes with sickness, but associations between tastes and shock are not so easily learned. For conditioning to occur rapidly, the CS has to belong with the US or be relevant to the US. Analogous belongingness and relevance relations occur in instrumental conditioning. As Jozefowiez and Staddon (2008) commented, "A behavior cannot be reinforced by a reinforcer if it is not naturally linked to that reinforcer in the repertoire of the animal" (p. 78).

This type of natural linkage was first observed by Thorndike. In many of his puzzle-box experiments, the cat had to manipulate a latch or string to escape from the box. However, Thorndike also tried to get cats to scratch or yawn to be let out of a puzzle box. The cats could learn to make these responses. However, the form of the responses changed as training proceeded. At first, the cat would scratch itself vigorously to be let out of the box. On later trials, it would only make aborted scratching movements. It might put its hind leg to its body but would not make a true scratch response. Similar results were obtained in attempts to condition yawning. As training progressed, the animal would open its mouth, but it would not give a *bona fide* yawn.

Thorndike used the term **belongingness** to explain his failures to train scratching and yawning as instrumental responses. According to this concept, certain responses naturally *belong with* the reinforcer because of the animal's evolutionary history. Operating a latch and pulling a string are manipulatory responses that are naturally related to release from confinement. By contrast, scratching and yawning characteristically do not help animals escape from confinement and therefore do not *belong with* release from a puzzle box.

The concept of belongingness in instrumental conditioning is nicely illustrated by a more recent study involving a small fish species, the three-spined stickleback (*Gasterosteus aculeatus*). During the mating season each spring, male sticklebacks establish territories in which they court females but chase away and fight other males. Sevenster (1973) used the presentation of another male or a female as a reinforcer in instrumental conditioning of male sticklebacks. One group of fish was required to bite a rod to obtain access to the reinforcer. When the reinforcer was another male, biting behavior increased; access to another male was an effective reinforcer for the biting response. By contrast, biting did not increase when it was reinforced with the presentation of a female fish. However, the presentation of a female was an effective reinforcer for other responses, such as swimming through a ring. Biting "belongs with" territorial defense and can be reinforced by the presentation of a potentially rival male. By contrast, biting does not belong with the presentation of a female, which typically elicits courtship rather than aggression.

Thorndike's difficulties in conditioning scratching and yawning did not have much impact on behavior theory until additional examples of misbehavior were documented by Breland and Breland (1961). The Brelands set up a business to train animals to perform entertaining response chains for displays in amusement parks and zoos. During the

M. Breland-Bailey

course of this work, they observed dramatic behavior changes that were not consistent with the reinforcement procedures they were using. For example, they described a raccoon that was reinforced for picking up a coin and depositing it in a coin bank:

> We started out by reinforcing him for picking up a single coin. Then the metal container was introduced, with the requirement that he drop the coin into the container. Here we ran into the first bit of difficulty: he seemed to have a great deal of trouble letting go of the coin. He would rub it up against the inside of the container, pull it back out, and clutch it firmly for several seconds. However, he would finally turn it loose and receive his food reinforcement. Then the final contingency: we [required] that he pick up [two] coins and put them in the container.
>
> Now the raccoon really had problems (and so did we). Not only could he not let go of the coins, but he spent seconds, even minutes, rubbing them together (in a most miserly fashion), and dipping them into the container. He carried on this behavior to such an extent that the practical application we had in mind—a display featuring a raccoon putting money in a piggy bank—simply was not feasible. The rubbing behavior became worse and worse as time went on, in spite of nonreinforcement (p. 682).

From "The Misbehavior of Organisms," by K. Breland and M Breland, 1961. In *American Psychologist, 16*, 682.

The Brelands had similar difficulties with other species. Pigs, for example, also could not learn to put coins in a piggy bank. After initial training, they began rooting the coins along the ground. The Brelands called the development of such responses **instinctive drift**. As the term implies, the extra responses that developed in these food reinforcement situations were activities the animals instinctively perform when obtaining food. Pigs root along the ground in connection with feeding, and raccoons rub and dunk food-related objects. These natural food-related responses were apparently very strong and competed with the responses required by the training procedures. The Brelands emphasized that such instinctive response tendencies have to be taken into account in the analysis of behavior.

Behavior Systems and Constraints on Instrumental Conditioning The response limitations on instrumental conditioning described above are consistent with behavior systems theory. I previously described this theory in Chapter 4, in discussions about the nature of the conditioned response (see Timberlake, 2001; Timberlake & Lucas, 1989). According to behavior systems theory, when an animal is food deprived and is in a situation where it might encounter food, its feeding system becomes activated, and it begins to engage in foraging and other food-related activities. An instrumental conditioning

It is difficult to condition raccoons with food reinforcement to drop a coin into a slot.

procedure is superimposed on this behavior system. The effectiveness of the procedure in increasing an instrumental response will depend on the compatibility of that response with the preexisting organization of the feeding system. Furthermore, the nature of other responses that emerge during the course of training (or instinctive drift) will depend on the behavioral components of the feeding system that become activated by the instrumental conditioning procedure.

According to the behavior systems approach, we should be able to predict which responses will increase with food reinforcement by studying what animals do when their feeding system is activated in the absence of instrumental conditioning. This prediction has been confirmed in several ways. For example, in a study of the effects of food deprivation in hamsters, Shettleworth (1975) found that responses that become more likely when the animal is hungry are readily reinforced with food, whereas responses that become less likely when the animal is hungry are difficult to train as instrumental responses.

Another way to diagnose whether a response is a part of a behavior system is to perform a classical conditioning experiment. Through classical conditioning, a CS elicits components of the behavior system activated by the US. If *instinctive drift* reflects responses of the behavior system, responses akin to instinctive drift should be evident in a classical conditioning experiment. Timberlake and his associates (see Timberlake, 1983; Timberlake, Wahl, & King, 1982) confirmed this prediction in studies with rats.

Courtesy of Donald A. Dewsbury

S. J. Shettleworth

The Instrumental Reinforcer

Several aspects of a reinforcer determine its effects on the learning and performance of instrumental behavior. I will first consider the direct effects of the quantity and quality of a reinforcer on instrumental behavior. I will then discuss how responding to a particular reward amount and type depends on the organism's past experience with other reinforcers.

Quantity and Quality of the Reinforcer   The quantity and quality of a reinforcer are obvious variables that would be expected to determine the effectiveness of positive reinforcement. This is certainly true at the extreme. If a reinforcer is very small and of poor quality, it will not increase instrumental responding. Indeed, studies conducted in straight alley runways generally show faster running with larger and more palatable reinforcers (see Mackintosh, 1974, for a review).

The magnitude of the reinforcer also influences the rate of free-operant responding. Chad, a 5-year-old boy diagnosed with autism, was a participant in a study of the effects of amount of reinforcement on free-operant responding (Trosclair-Lasserre et al., 2008). Preliminary assessment indicated that social attention was an effective reinforcer for Chad. Attention consisted of praise, tickles, hugs, songs, stories, and interactive games. If Chad pressed a button long enough to produce an audible click, he received social attention for 10, 105, or 120 seconds. Chad preferred reinforcers of 120 seconds over reinforcers of just 10 seconds.

A progressive ratio schedule of reinforcement was used to evaluate the effects of reinforcer magnitude. I will describe schedules of reinforcement in greater detail in Chapter 6. For now, it is sufficient to note that in a progressive ratio schedule the participant has to make increasing numbers of responses to obtain the reinforcer. At the start of each session, Chad had to make just one button press to get reinforced, but as the session went on, the number of button presses required for each reinforcer progressively increased (hence the name *progressive ratio* schedule). The response requirement was raised from 1 press to 2, 5, 10, 20, 30, and finally 40 presses per reinforcer.

The results of the experiment are presented in Figure 5.9 in terms of the number of times Chad obtained each reinforcer as a function of how many times he had to press

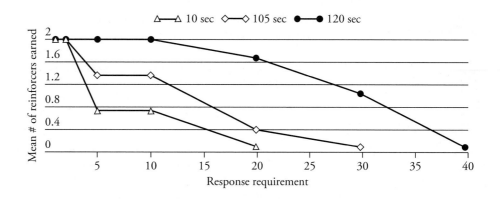

FIGURE 5.9 Average number of reinforcers earned by Chad per session as the response requirement was increased from 1 to 40. (The maximum possible was two reinforcers per session at each response requirement.) Notice that responding was maintained much more effectively in the face of increasing response requirements when the reinforcer was 120 seconds long [from Trosclair-Lasserre et al. (2008), Figure 3, p. 215].

the button. As expected, increasing the number of required presses resulted in fewer reinforcers earned for all three reinforcer magnitudes. Increasing the response requirement from 1 to 20 responses produced a rapid drop in the number of reinforcers earned if the reinforcer was 10 seconds. Less of a drop was evident if the reinforcer was 105 seconds. When the reinforcer was 120 seconds, not much of a decrease was evident until the response requirement was raised to 30 or 40 button presses for each reinforcer. Thus, the longer reinforcer was much more effective in maintaining instrumental responding.

The magnitude of the reinforcer has also been found to be a major factor in voucher programs for the reinforcement of abstinence in the treatment of substance-use disorder. Individuals who are addicted to cocaine, methamphetamine, opiates, or other drugs have been treated successfully in programs based on the principles of instrumental conditioning (Higgins, Heil, & Sigmon, 2012). The target response in these programs is absence from drug use as verified by drug tests conducted two or three times per week. Reinforcement is provided in the form of vouchers that can be exchanged for money. A metaanalysis of studies of the success of voucher reinforcement programs indicated that the magnitude of the reinforcer contributed significantly to abstinence (Lussier et al., 2006). Studies in which individuals could earn upwards of $10 per day for remaining drug free showed greater success in encouraging abstinence than those in which smaller payments were earned. Providing reinforcement soon after the evidence of abstinence was also important. Getting paid right after the drug test was more effective than getting paid one or two days later. I will have more to say about the importance of immediate reinforcement later in this chapter.

Shifts in Reinforcer Quality or Quantity The effectiveness of a reinforcer depends not only on its quality and quantity but also on what the subject received previously. If a teenager receives an allowance of $25 per week, a decrease to $10 may be a great disappointment. But if he or she never got used to receiving $25 per week, an allowance of $10 might seem OK. As this example suggests, the effectiveness of a reinforcer depends not only on its own properties but also on how that reinforcer compares with others the individual received in the recent past.

We saw in Chapter 4 that the effectiveness of a US in classical conditioning depends on how the US compares with the individual's expectations based on prior experience. This idea served as the foundation of the Rescorla–Wagner model. If the US is larger (or more intense) than expected, it will support excitatory conditioning. By contrast, if it is smaller (or weaker) than expected, the US will support inhibitory conditioning. Analogous effects occur in instrumental conditioning. Numerous studies have shown that the effects of a particular amount and type of reinforcer depend on the quantity

C. F. Flaherty

and quality of the reinforcers the individual experienced previously. Speaking loosely, a large reward is treated as especially good after reinforcement with a small reward, and a small reward is treated as especially poor after reinforcement with a large reward (for a comprehensive review, see Flaherty, 1996). These phenomena are called positive and negative **behavioral contrast** effects.

Behavioral contrast effects were first described by Crespi (1942) and have been documented in a variety of situations since then. A clear example of negative behavioral contrast was recently reported by Ortega and colleagues (2011). Laboratory rats were given a sucrose solution to drink for 5 minutes each day. For one group of rats, the sucrose solution was always 4% throughout the experiment. For a second group, the sucrose solution was much more tasty (32%) on the first 10 trials and was then decreased to 4% for the remaining four trials.

How long the rats spent licking the sucrose solution on each trial is summarized in Figure 5.10. Notice that during the first 10 trials, the rats spent a bit more time licking the more tasty 32% sucrose solution than the 4% solution. However, when the 32% solution was changed to 4%, these rats showed a dramatic decrease in licking time. In fact, the shifted group licked significantly less of the 4% sucrose on trials 11 and 12 than the nonshifted group that received 4% sucrose all along. This illustrates the phenomenon of *negative behavioral contrast.*

Behavioral-contrast effects can occur either because of a shift from a prior reward magnitude (as in Figure 5.10) or because of an anticipated reward. Behavioral contrast due to an anticipated large reward may explain a long-standing paradox in the drug-abuse literature. The paradox arises from two seemingly conflicting findings. The first is that drugs of abuse, such as cocaine, will support the conditioning of a place preference in laboratory animals. Rats given cocaine in a distinctive chamber will choose that area over a place where they did not get cocaine. This suggests that cocaine is reinforcing. The conflicting finding is that rats given a saccharin solution to drink before receiving cocaine suppress their saccharin intake. Thus, cocaine can condition a taste aversion even though it appears to be reinforcing in place preference conditioning. Grigson and her colleagues have conducted a series of studies that suggest that the saccharin aversion conditioned by cocaine reflects an anticipatory contrast effect (Grigson et al., 2008). Because cocaine is so highly reinforcing and occurs after exposure to saccharin, the saccharin flavor loses its hedonic value in anticipation of the much greater hedonic value of cocaine. This type of *anticipatory negative contrast* may explain why individuals addicted to cocaine derive little satisfaction from conventional reinforcers (a tasty meal) that others enjoy on a daily basis.

FIGURE 5.10 Time rats spent drinking when the solution was either 32% sucrose or 4% sucrose. Rats in the 32–4 group were shifted to 4% sucrose after trial 10 (based on Ortega et al., 2011).

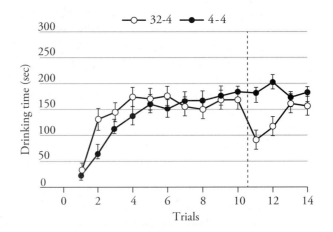

The Response–Reinforcer Relation

The hallmark of instrumental behavior is that it produces and is controlled by its consequences. In some cases, there is a strong relation between what a person does and the consequences of that action. If you put a dollar into a soda machine, you will get a can of soda. As long as the machine is working, you will get your can of soda every time you put in the required money. In other cases, there is no relation between behavior and an outcome. You may wear your lucky hat to a test and get a good grade, but the grade would not be caused by the hat you were wearing. The relation between behavior and its consequences can also be probabilistic. For example, you might have to call several times before you get to talk to your friend on the phone.

Human and other animals perform a continual stream of responses and encounter all kinds of environmental events. You are always doing something, even if it is just sitting around, and things are continually happening in your environment. Some of the things you do have consequences; others don't. It makes no sense to work hard to make the sun rise each morning because that will happen anyway. Instead, you should devote your energy to fixing breakfast or working for a paycheck: things that do not happen without your effort. To be efficient, you have to know when you have to do something to obtain a reinforcer and when the reinforcer is likely to be delivered independent of your actions. Efficient instrumental behavior requires sensitivity to the response–reinforcer relation.

There are actually two types of relationships between a response and a reinforcer (Williams, 2001). One is the **temporal relation**. The temporal relation refers to the time between the response and the reinforcer. A special case of the temporal relation is **temporal contiguity**. Temporal contiguity refers to the delivery of the reinforcer immediately after the response. The second type of relation between a response and the reinforcer is the *causal relation* or **response–reinforcer contingency**. The response–reinforcer contingency refers to the extent to which the instrumental response is necessary and sufficient to produce the reinforcer.

Temporal and causal factors are independent of each other. A strong temporal relation does not require a strong causal relation, and vice versa. For example, there is strong causal relation between taking your clothes to the cleaners and getting clean clothes back. However, the temporal delay may be a day or two.

Effects of the Temporal Relation   Since the early work of Grice (1948), learning psychologists have correctly emphasized that instrumental conditioning requires providing the reinforcer immediately after the occurrence of the instrumental response. Grice reported that instrumental learning can be disrupted by delays as short as .5 seconds. More recent research has indicated that instrumental conditioning is possible with delays as long as 30 seconds (Critchfield & Lattal, 1993; Okouchi, 2009). However, the fact remains that immediate reinforcement is much more effective.

The effects of delayed reinforcement on learning to press a response lever in laboratory rats is shown in Figure 5.11 (Dickinson, Watt, & Griffiths, 1992). Each time the rats pressed the lever, a food pellet was set up to be delivered after a fixed delay. For some rats, the delay was short (2–4 seconds). For others, the delay was considerable (64 seconds). If the rat pressed the lever again during the delay interval, the new response resulted in another food pellet after the specified delay. (In other studies, such *extra* responses were programmed to reset the delay interval.) Figure 5.11 shows response rates as a function of the mean delay of reinforcement experienced by each group. Responding decreased fairly rapidly with increases in the delay of reinforcement. No learning was evident with a 64-second delay of reinforcement in this experiment.

FIGURE 5.11 Effects of delay of reinforcement on acquisition of lever pressing in rats. (Based on "Free-Operant Acquisition with Delayed Reinforcement," by A. Dickinson, A. Watt, and W. J. H. Griffiths, 1992, *The Quarterly Journal of Experimental Psychology, 45B,* pp. 241–258.)

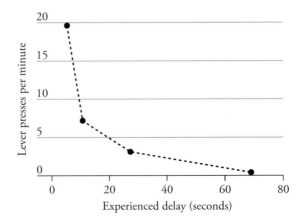

D. A. Lieberman

Why is instrumental conditioning so sensitive to a delay of reinforcement? A major culprit is the credit-assignment problem. With delayed reinforcement, it is difficult to figure out which response deserves the credit for the delivery of the reinforcer. As I pointed out earlier, behavior is an ongoing, continual stream of activities. When reinforcement is delayed after performance of a specified response, R1, the participant does not stop doing things. After performing R1, the participant may perform R2, R3, R4, and so on. If the reinforcer is set up by R1 but not delivered until sometime later, the reinforcer may occur immediately after some other response, let's say R6. To associate R1 with the reinforcer, the participant has to have some way to distinguish R1 from the other responses it performs during the delay interval.

There are a couple of ways to overcome the credit-assignment problem. The first technique, used by animal trainers and coaches for centuries, is to provide a secondary or conditioned reinforcer immediately after the instrumental response, even if the primary reinforcer cannot occur until sometime later (Cronin, 1980; Winter & Perkins, 1982). A **secondary**, or **conditioned**, **reinforcer** is a conditioned stimulus that was previously associated with the reinforcer. Verbal prompts in coaching, such as "good," "keep going," and "that's the way" are conditioned reinforcers that can provide immediate reinforcement for appropriate behavior. In the clicker-training methodology for animal training, the sound of a clicker is first paired with the delivery of food to make the clicker an effective conditioned reinforcer. The clicker then can be delivered immediately after a desired response even if the primary food reinforcer is delayed. Effective coaches and animal trainers are constantly providing immediate verbal feedback as conditioned reinforcers.

Another technique that facilitates learning with delayed reinforcement is to *mark* the target instrumental response in some way to make it distinguishable from the other activities of the organism. Marking can be accomplished by introducing a brief light or noise after the target response or by picking up the animal and moving it to a holding box for the delay interval. The effectiveness of a **marking procedure** was first demonstrated by David Lieberman and his colleagues (Lieberman, McIntosh, & Thomas, 1979) and has since been replicated in various other studies (e.g., Thomas & Lieberman, 1990; Urcuioli & Kasprow, 1988).

In an interesting variation of the marking procedure, Williams (1999) compared the learning of a lever-press response in three groups of rats. For each group, the food reinforcer was delayed 30 seconds after a press of the response lever. (Any additional lever presses during the delay interval were ignored.) The no-signal group received this procedure without a marking stimulus. For the marking group, a light was presented for

5 seconds right after each lever press. For a third group of subjects (called the *blocking* group), the 5-second light was presented at the end of the delay interval, just before food delivery.

Results of the experiment are shown in Figure 5.12. Rats in the no-signal group showed little responding during the first three blocks of two trials and only achieved modest levels of lever pressing after that. In contrast, the marking group showed much more robust learning. Clearly, introducing a brief light to mark each lever-press response substantially facilitated learning with the 30-second delay of reinforcement. However, placing the light at the end of the delay interval, just before food, had the opposite effect. Rats in the blocking group never learned the lever-press response. For those animals, the light became associated with the food, and this blocked the conditioning of the instrumental response. (For a further discussion delay of reinforcement, see Lattal, 2010.)

The Response–Reinforcer Contingency   As I noted earlier, the response–reinforcer contingency refers to the extent to which the delivery of the reinforcer depends on the prior occurrence of the instrumental response. In studies of delayed reinforcement, there is a perfect causal relation between the response and the reinforcer, but learning is disrupted. This shows that a perfect causal relation between the response and the reinforcer is not sufficient to produce vigorous instrumental responding. Even with a perfect causal relation, conditioning does not occur if reinforcement is delayed too long. Such data encouraged early investigators to conclude that response–reinforcer contiguity, rather than contingency, was the critical factor producing instrumental learning. However, this

B. A. Williams

FIGURE 5.12 Acquisition of lever pressing in rats with a 30-second delay of reinforcement. For the marking group, a light was presented for 5 seconds at the beginning of the delay interval, right after the instrumental response. For the blocking group, the light was introduced at the end of the delay interval, just before the delivery of food (based on Williams, 1999).

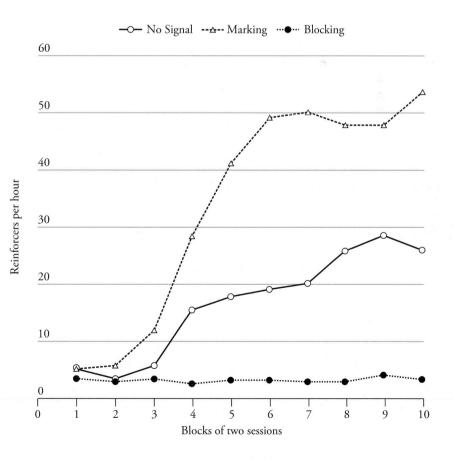

view has turned out to be incorrect. The response–reinforcer contingency is also important.

Skinner's Superstition Experiment   The role of **contiguity** versus contingency in instrumental learning became a major issue with Skinner's superstition experiment (Skinner, 1948). Skinner placed pigeons in separate experimental chambers and set the equipment to deliver a bit of food every 15 seconds irrespective of what the pigeons were doing. The birds were not required to peck a key or perform any other response to get the food. After some time, Skinner returned to see what his birds were doing. He described some of what he saw as follows:

> *In six out of eight cases the resulting responses were so clearly defined that two observers could agree perfectly in counting instances. One bird was conditioned to turn counterclockwise about the cage, making two or three turns between reinforcements. Another repeatedly thrust its head into one of the upper corners of the cage. A third developed a "tossing" response, as if placing its head beneath an invisible bar and lifting it repeatedly. (p. 168)*

The pigeons appeared to be responding as if their behavior controlled the delivery of the reinforcer when, in fact, the food was provided irrespective of what the pigeons were doing. Accordingly, Skinner called this **superstitious behavior**.

Skinner's explanation of superstitious behavior rests on the idea of **accidental**, or **adventitious**, **reinforcement**. Adventitious reinforcement refers to the accidental pairing of a response with delivery of the reinforcer. Animals are always doing something, even if no particular responses are required to obtain food. Skinner suggested that whatever response a pigeon happened to make just before it got free food became strengthened and subsequently increased in frequency because of adventitious reinforcement. One accidental pairing of a response with food increased the chance that the same response would occur just before the next delivery of the food. As this process was repeated, the response came to be performed often enough to be identified as superstitious behavior.

Skinner's interpretation was appealing and consistent with views of reinforcement that were widely held at the time. Impressed by studies of delay of reinforcement, behaviorists thought that temporal contiguity was the main factor responsible for learning. Skinner's experiment appeared to support this view and suggested that a positive response–reinforcer contingency is not necessary for instrumental conditioning.

Reinterpretation of the Superstition Experiment   Skinner's bold claim that temporal contiguity, rather than response-reinforcer contingency, is most important for instrumental conditioning was challenged by subsequent empirical evidence. In a landmark study, Staddon and Simmelhag (1971) repeated Skinner's experiment. However, Staddon and Simmelhag made more extensive and systematic observations. They defined a variety of responses, such as orienting to the food hopper, pecking the response key, wing flapping, turning in quarter circles, and preening. They then recorded the frequency of each response according to when it occurred during the interval between successive free deliveries of food.

Figure 5.13 shows the data obtained by Staddon and Simmelhag for several responses for one pigeon. Clearly, some of the responses occurred predominantly toward the end of the interval between successive reinforcers. For example, R1 and R7 (orienting to the food magazine and pecking at something on the magazine wall) occurred more often at the end of the food–food interval than at other times. Staddon and Simmelhag called these **terminal responses**. Other activities increased in frequency after the delivery of food and then decreased as the time for the next food delivery drew closer. The

J. E. R. Staddon

FIGURE 5.13

Probability of several responses as a function of time between successive deliveries of a food reinforcer. R1 (orienting toward the food magazine wall) and R7 (pecking at something on the magazine wall) are terminal responses, having their highest probabilities at the end of the interval between food deliveries. R3 (pecking at something on the floor), R4 (a quarter turn), and R8 (moving along the magazine wall) are interim responses, having their highest probabilities somewhere near the middle of the interval between food deliveries. (From "The 'Superstition' Experiment: A Reexamination of Its Implications for the Principles of Adaptive Behavior," by J. E. R. Staddon and V. L. Simmelhag, 1971, *Psychological Review, 78,* pp. 3–43.

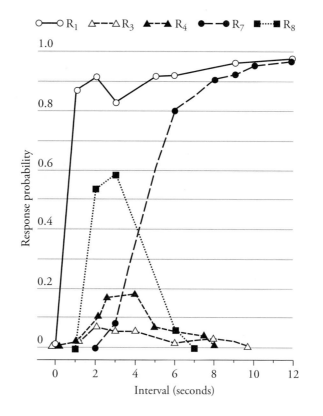

pigeons were most likely to engage in R8 and R4 (moving along the magazine wall and making a quarter turn) somewhere near the middle of the interval between food deliveries. These activities were called **interim responses**.

Which actions were terminal responses and which were interim responses did not vary much from one pigeon to another. Furthermore, Staddon and Simmelhag failed to find evidence for accidental reinforcement effects. Responses did not always increase in frequency merely because they occurred coincidentally with food delivery. Food delivery appeared to influence only the strength of terminal responses, even in the initial phases of training.

Subsequent research has provided much additional evidence that presentations of a reinforcer at fixed intervals produce behavioral regularities, with certain responses predominating late in the interval between successive food presentations and other responses predominating earlier in the food–food interval (Anderson & Shettleworth, 1977; Innis, Simmelhag-Grant, & Staddon, 1983; Silva & Timberlake, 1998). It is not clear why Skinner failed to observe such regularities in his experiment. One possibility is that he focused on different aspects of the behavior of different birds in an effort to document that each bird responded in a unique fashion. For example, he may have focused on the terminal response of one bird and interim responses in other birds. Subsequent investigators have also noted some variations in behavior between individuals but have emphasized the more striking similarities among individuals in their interim and terminal responses.

Explanation of the Periodicity of Interim and Terminal Responses What is responsible for the development of similar terminal and interim responses in animals exposed to the same schedule of response-independent food presentations? Staddon and

Simmelhag (1971) suggested that terminal responses are species-typical responses that reflect the anticipation of food as time draws closer to the next food presentation. By contrast, they viewed interim responses as reflecting other sources of motivation that are prominent early in the interfood interval, when food presentation is unlikely.

Subsequent investigators have expanded on Staddon and Simmelhag's ideas in the more comprehensive framework of behavior systems theory (Timberlake & Lucas, 1985; Silva & Timberlake, 1998). The critical idea is that periodic deliveries of food activate the feeding system and its preorganized species-typical foraging and feeding responses. Different behaviors occur depending on when food was last delivered and when food is going to occur again. Just after the delivery of food, the organism is assumed to display *post-food focal search* responses that involve activities near the food cup. In the middle of the interval between food deliveries (when the subjects are least likely to get food), *general search* responses are evident that take the animal away from the food cup. As the time for the next food delivery approaches, the subject exhibits *focal search* responses that are again concentrated near the food cup. In Figure 5.13, the terminal responses, R1 and R7 were distributed in time in the manner expected of focal search behavior, and R4 and R8 were distributed in the manner expected of general search responses.

Effects of the Controllability of Reinforcers

Effects of the Controllability of Reinforcers   A strong contingency between an instrumental response and a reinforcer essentially means that the response controls the reinforcer. With a strong contingency, whether the reinforcer occurs depends on whether the instrumental response has occurred. Studies of the effects of control over reinforcers have provided the most extensive body of evidence on the sensitivity of behavior to response–reinforcer contingencies. Some of these studies have involved positive reinforcement (e.g., Job, 2002). However, most of the research has focused on the effects of control over aversive stimulation.

Contemporary research on this problem originated with the pioneering studies of Overmier and Seligman (1967) and Seligman and Maier (1967), who investigated the effects of exposure to uncontrollable shock on subsequent escape-avoidance learning in dogs. The major finding was that exposure to uncontrollable shock disrupted subsequent learning. This phenomenon has been called the **learned-helplessness effect**.

The learned-helplessness effect continues to be the focus of a great deal of research (LoLordo & Overmier, 2011), but dogs are no longer used in the experiments. Instead, most of the research is conducted with laboratory rats and mice and human participants. The research requires exposing animals to stressful events, and some may find the research objectionable because of that. However, this line of work has turned out to be highly informative about the mechanisms of stress and coping at the behavioral, hormonal, and neurophysiological levels.

The Triadic Design   Learned-helplessness experiments are usually conducted using the *triadic design* presented in Table 5.2. The design involves two phases: an exposure phase and a conditioning phase. During the exposure phase, one group of rats (E, for

Courtesy of Donald A. Dewsbury

S. F. Maier

TABLE 5.2   THE TRIADIC DESIGN USED IN STUDIES OF THE LEARNED-HELPLESSNESS EFFECT

GROUP	EXPOSURE PHASE	CONDITIONING PHASE	RESULT
Group E	Escapable shock	Escape-avoidance training	Rapid-avoidance learning
Group Y	Yoked inescapable shock	Escape-avoidance training	Slow-avoidance learning
Group R	Restricted to apparatus	Escape-avoidance training	Rapid-avoidance learning

© Cengage Learning

escape) is exposed to periodic shocks that can be terminated by performing an escape response (e.g., rotating a small wheel or tumbler). Each subject in the second group (Y, for yoked) is assigned a partner in Group E and receives the same duration and distribution of shocks as its Group E partner. However, animals in Group Y cannot turn off the shocks. For them, the shocks are inescapable. The third group (R, for restricted) receives no shocks during the exposure phase but is restricted to the apparatus for as long as groups E and Y. During the conditioning phase, all three groups receive escape-avoidance training. This is usually conducted in a shuttle apparatus that has two adjacent compartments (see Figure 10.3). The animals have to go back and forth between the two compartments to avoid shock (or escape any shocks that they failed to avoid).

The remarkable finding in experiments on the learned-helplessness effect is that the impact of aversive stimulation during the exposure phase depends on whether or not the shock is escapable. Exposure to uncontrollable shock (Group Y) produces a severe disruption in subsequent escape-avoidance learning. In the conditioning phase of the experiment, Group Y typically shows much poorer escape-avoidance performance than both Group E and Group R. By contrast, little or no deleterious effects are observed after exposure to escapable shock. Group E often learns the subsequent escape-avoidance task as rapidly as Group R, which received no shock during the exposure phase. Similar detrimental effects of exposure to yoked inescapable shock have been reported on subsequent responding for food reinforcement (e.g., Rosellini & DeCola, 1981).

The fact that Group Y shows a deficit in subsequent learning in comparison to Group E indicates that the animals are sensitive to the procedural differences between escapable and yoked inescapable shocks. The primary difference between Groups E and Y is the presence of a response–reinforcer contingency for Group E but not for Group Y during the exposure phase. Therefore, the difference in the rate of learning between these two groups shows that the animals are sensitive to the response–reinforcer contingency.

Courtesy of M. E. P. Seligman

M. E. P. Seligman

The Learned-Helplessness Hypothesis

The **learned-helplessness hypothesis** was the first major explanation of the results of studies employing the triadic design (Maier & Seligman, 1976; Maier, Seligman, & Solomon, 1969). The learned-helplessness hypothesis assumes that during exposure to uncontrollable shocks, animals learn that the shocks are independent of their behavior—that there is nothing they can do to control the shocks. Furthermore, they come to expect that reinforcers will continue to be independent of their behavior in the future. This expectation of future lack of control undermines their ability to learn a new instrumental response. The learning deficit occurs for two reasons. First, the expectation of lack of control reduces the motivation to perform an instrumental response. Second, even if they make the response and get reinforced in the conditioning phase, the previously learned expectation of lack of control makes it more difficult for the subjects to learn that their behavior is now effective in producing reinforcement.

It is important to distinguish the learned-helplessness *hypothesis* from the learned-helplessness *effect*. The effect is the pattern of results obtained with the triadic design (disruption of instrumental conditioning caused by prior exposure to inescapable shock). The learned-helplessness effect has been replicated in numerous studies and is a firmly established finding. By contrast, the learned-helplessness hypothesis is an explanation or interpretation of the effect, which has been provocative and controversial since its introduction (LoLordo & Overmier, 2011).

Alternatives to the Helplessness Hypothesis

The activity deficit hypothesis. According to the *activity deficit hypothesis*, animals in Group Y show a learning deficit following exposure to inescapable shock because inescapable shocks encourage animals to become inactive or freeze. As we discussed in Chapter 3, freezing is a common response to fear.

The activity deficit hypothesis received some empirical support early in the history of research on the learned helplessness effect. However, it cannot explain instances in which exposure to inescapable shock disrupts choice learning. For example, Jackson, Alexander, and Maier (1980) found that following exposure to inescapable shock, rats were deficient in learning an escape response that consisted of selecting the correct arm of a Y maze. Failure to learn this choice response was not due to lack of activity but to choice of the incorrect arm of the maze.

The attention deficit hypothesis. According to the *attention deficit hypothesis*, exposure to inescapable shock reduces the extent to which animals pay attention to their own behavior, and that is why these animals show a learning deficit. The attention deficit hypothesis has been considerably more successful as an alternative to the learned helplessness hypothesis than the activity deficit hypothesis. For example, manipulations that increase attention to response-generated cues have been found to reduce the deleterious effects of prior exposure to inescapable shock (Maier, Jackson, & Tomie, 1987).

Stimulus relations in escape conditioning. In another line of research that has challenged the helplessness hypothesis, investigators reframed the basic issue addressed by the triadic design. Instead of focusing on why inescapable shock disrupts subsequent learning, they asked why exposure to *escapable* shock is not nearly as bad (Minor, Dess, & Overmier, 1991). What is it about the ability to make an escape response that makes exposure to shock less debilitating? This question has stimulated a closer look at stimulus relations in escape conditioning.

The defining feature of escape behavior is that the instrumental response results in the termination of an aversive stimulus. Termination of shock is an external stimulus event. However, the act of performing any skeletal response also provides internal sensory feedback cues. For example, you can feel that you are raising your hand even if your eyes are closed. Because of these response-produced internal cues, you don't have to see your arm go up to know that you are raising your arm.

Courtesy of N. K. Dess

N. K. Dess

BOX 5.4

Helplessness, Depression, and Post-traumatic Stress Disorder

The fact that a history of lack of control over reinforcers can severely disrupt subsequent instrumental performance has important implications for human behavior. The concept of helplessness has been extended and elaborated to a variety of areas of human concern, including aging, athletic performance, chronic pain, academic achievement, susceptibility to heart attacks, and victimization and bereavement (e.g., Overmier, 2002; Peterson, Maier, & Seligman, 1993). Perhaps the most prominent area to which the concept of

helplessness has been applied is depression (Abramson, Metalsky, & Alloy, 1989; Pryce et al., 2011).

Animal research on uncontrollability and unpredictability of aversive stimuli is also becoming important for the understanding of human post-traumatic stress disorder or PTSD (Foa, Zinbarg, & Rothbaum, 1992). Victims of assault or combat stress have symptoms that correspond to the effects of chronic uncontrollable and unpredictable shock in animals. For example, exposure to inescapable shock greatly facilitates

the subsequent acquisition of fear and makes it more difficult to extinguish the conditioned fear (e.g., Baratta et al., 2007). Enhanced fear reactivity is one of the major symptoms of PTSD. Recognition of these similarities between animal models and human symptoms of PTSD promises to provide new insights into the origin and treatment of PTSD. Animal models of helplessness have also contributed to the understanding of the long-term effects of sexual abuse and revictimization (Bargai, Ben-Shakhar, & Shalev, 2007; Marx, Heidt, & Gold, 2005).

Making an escape response such as pressing a lever similarly results in internal sensations or response feedback cues. These are illustrated in Figure 5.14. Some of the response-produced stimuli are experienced at the start of the escape response, just before the shock is turned off. These are called *shock-cessation feedback cues.* Other response-produced stimuli are experienced as the animal completes the response, just after the shock has been turned off at the start of the intertrial interval. These are called *safety-signal feedback cues.*

At first, investigations of stimulus factors involved with escapable shock centered on the possible significance of safety-signal feedback cues. Safety-signal feedback cues are reliably followed by the intertrial interval and hence by the absence of shock. Therefore, such feedback cues can become conditioned inhibitors of fear and limit or inhibit fear elicited by contextual cues of the experimental chamber. (For a discussion of conditioned inhibition, see Chapter 3.) No such safety signals exist for animals given yoked, inescapable shock because for them, shocks and shock-free periods are not predictable. Therefore, contextual cues of the chamber in which shocks are delivered are more likely to become conditioned to elicit fear with inescapable shock.

These considerations have encouraged analyzing the triadic design in terms of group differences in signals for safety rather than in terms of differences in whether shock is escapable or not. In an experiment conducted by Jackson and Minor (1988), for example, one group of rats received the usual inescapable shocks in the exposure phase of the triadic design. However, at the end of each shock presentation, the houselights were turned off for 5 seconds as a safety signal. The introduction of this safety signal entirely eliminated the disruptive effects of shock exposure on subsequent shuttle-escape learning. Another study (Minor, Trauner, Lee, & Dess, 1990) also employed inescapable shocks, but this time an audiovisual cue was introduced during the last 3 seconds of each shock presentation. This was intended to mimic shock cessation cues. The introduction of these shock cessation cues also largely eliminated the helplessness effect (see also Christianson et al., 2008).

The aforementioned studies indicate that significant differences in how animals cope with aversive stimulation can result from differences in the ability to predict when shocks will end and when a safe intertrial interval without shocks will begin. Learning to predict shock termination and shock absence can be just as important as being able to escape from shock. This is good news. We encounter many aversive events in life that we cannot control (e.g., the rising price of gas or a new demanding boss). Fortunately, controlling a stressful event need not be our only coping strategy. Learning to

Courtesy of T. R. Minor

T. R. Minor

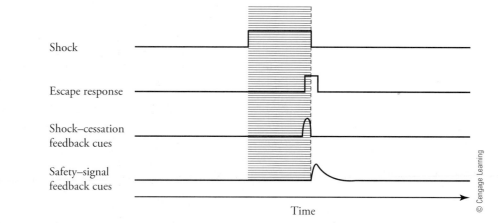

FIGURE 5.14 Stimulus relations in an escape-conditioning trial. Shock-cessation feedback cues are experienced at the start of the escape response, just before the termination of shock. Safety-signal feedback cues are experienced just after the termination of shock, at the start of the intertrial interval.

Shock

Escape response

Shock–cessation feedback cues

Safety–signal feedback cues

Time

© Cengage Learning

predict when we will encounter the stressful event (and when we will not encounter it) can be just as effective in reducing the harmful effects of stress.

Contiguity and Contingency: Concluding Comments As we have seen, organisms are sensitive to the contiguity as well as the contingency between an instrumental response and a reinforcer. Typically, these two aspects of the relation between response and reinforcer act jointly to produce learning (Williams, 2001). Both factors serve to focus the effects of reinforcement on the instrumental response. The causal relation, or contingency, ensures that the reinforcer is delivered only after occurrence of the specified instrumental response. The contiguity relation ensures that other activities do not intrude between the specified response and the reinforcer to interfere with conditioning of the target response.

BOX 5.5

Learned Helplessness: Role of the Prefrontal Cortex and Dorsal Raphe

We have seen that aversive stimulation can impact the organism in different ways, depending upon whether the stimulation is given in a controllable or uncontrollable manner. In general, exposure to uncontrollable stimulation induces a constellation of behavioral effects that undermine the subject's ability to cope, a behavioral phenomenon known as *learned helplessness* (Maier & Seligman, 1976). Importantly, these adverse effects are not observed in individuals who can control (e.g., terminate) the aversive stimulus. Moreover, exposure to controllable stimulation has a lasting protective effect that blocks the induction of helplessness if the organism later encounters uncontrollable stimulation. Behavioral control and helplessness are of clinical interest because these phenomena can contribute to conditions such as PTSD and depression (Forgeard et al., 2011; Hammack, Cooper, & Lezak, 2012).

At a neural level, research suggests that the long-term consequences of uncontrollable stimulation depend on a region of the midbrain known as the **dorsal raphe nucleus** (DRN). The DRN lies just ventral to another key region, the periaqueductal gray

(PAG), discussed in Box 4.3. Like the PAG, the DRN can regulate neural activity in other regions of the central nervous system (Figure 5.15). It does so through neurons that release the neurotransmitter *serotonin* (5-HT). Because these 5-HT neurons project to regions implicated in stress and fear (Graeff, Viana, & Mora, 1997), Maier and his colleagues hypothesized that the DRN is involved in helplessness (Maier & Watkins, 1998, 2005). Supporting this, they showed that exposure to uncontrollable shock activates 5-HT neurons within the DRN and has a sensitizing effect, enhancing the amount of 5-HT released at distant sites. Importantly, these effects are not observed after an equivalent exposure to controllable stimulation. They further showed that pharmacologically inhibiting the DRN during uncontrollable stimulation blocked the induction of learned helplessness. Conversely, pharmacologically activating the DRN had a behavioral effect similar to that observed after uncontrollable stimulation. Together, these observations suggest that the activation of the DRN is both necessary and sufficient to produce learned helplessness.

Maier and Watkins (2010) hypothesized that behavioral control

regulates DRN activity through neurons that project from the *prelimbic* and *infralimbic* regions of the ventral medial **prefrontal cortex** (vmPFC) (Figure 5.15). These excitatory neurons engage GABAergic interneurons within the DRN that have an inhibitory effect. As a result, pharmacological activation of the vmPFC inhibits 5-HT neural activity within the DNR and blocks the development of learned helplessness. If behavioral control inhibits the DNR through the vmPFC, then pharmacologically disrupting the vmPFC function should eliminate the protective effect of instrumental control. Minus the dampening action of the vmPFC input, controllable aversive stimulation should engage 5-HT neurons within the DNR and paradoxically produce a helplessness-like effect. Research has shown that disrupting vmPFC function has exactly this effect.

One of the most interesting and clinically relevant features of behavioral control is that it has a lasting effect that behaviorally immunizes the organism from becoming helpless when later exposed to uncontrollable stimulation. Here too, the vmPFC plays a key role. This was shown by first exposing animals to controllable

Continued

BOX 5.5 (continued)

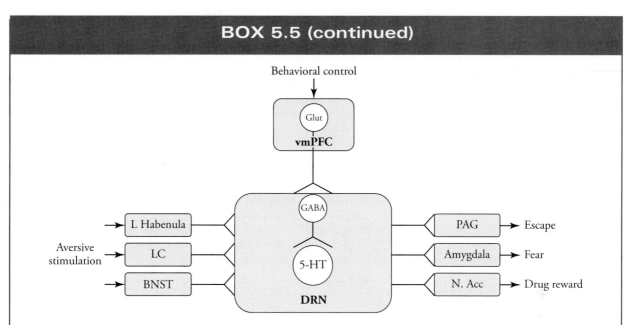

FIGURE 5.15 A model of how aversive stimulation and behavioral control regulate physiological responses to stress. Aversive stimulation engages structures such as the lateral habenula (L Habenula), locus coeruleus (LC), and bed nucleus of the stria terminalis (BNST), which project to the dorsal raphe nuclei (DRN). This engages serotonergic (5-HT) fibers that activate neural regions implicated in defensive responding (periaqueductal gray [PAG] and amygdala) and reward (nucleus accumbens [N Acc]). Behavioral control activates excitatory glutamatergic (Glut) neurons within the ventral medial prefrontal cortex (vmPFC) that project to the DRN, where they engage inhibitory (GABA) neurons that reduce 5-HT activity (adapted from Maier and Watkins, 2010).

shock. A week later, the animals were exposed to uncontrollable shock, which alone induced helplessness. As expected, prior exposure to controllable stimulation blocked the induction of helplessness. Most importantly, this protective effect was not observed when the vmPFC was inhibited during uncontrollable stimulation. Minus the vmPFC, uncontrollable shock induced helplessness in rats that had previously received controllable stimulation.

If the vmPFC is critical, then pharmacologically activating it should substitute for behavioral control and transform how an uncontrollable aversive input affects the nervous system. We already know that activating the vmPFC will prevent uncontrollable shock from inducing helplessness. The stronger claim is that activating the vmPFC will induce a long-term effect analogous to that produced by instrumental control. As predicted, combining vmPFC activation with uncontrollable shock yielded an effect equivalent to controllable stimulation, engaging a protective effect that blocked the subsequent induction of helplessness.

Controllable and uncontrollable stimulation also have divergent effects on Pavlovian fear conditioning. Uncontrollable stimulation generally enhances conditioning, whereas controllable stimulation has an inhibitory effect. As we saw in Box 4.3, fear conditioning depends on neurons within the amygdala. Input from the CS and US appear to be associated within the basolateral region of the amygdala, while the performance of the CR is orchestrated by the central nucleus. Evidence suggests that uncontrollable stimulation enhances fear-related CRs through 5-HT neurons that project to the basolateral amygdala

(Amat, Matus-Amat, Watkins, & Maier, 1998). The calming effect of controllable stimulation has been linked again to the vmPFC and, more specifically, to the infralimbic region which sends a projection to the intercalated cell region of the amygdala (Maier & Watkins, 2010). This portion of the amygdala is composed of inhibitory (GABAergic) cells that project to the central nucleus. Consequently, engaging the infralimbic region inhibits the output from the central nucleus and fear behaviors.

Given the above observations, Maier and his colleagues hypothesized that output from the infralimbic area of the vmPFC acts to inhibit the performance of fear-elicited CRs (within the central nucleus) rather than learning (within the basolateral nucleus). To explore this idea, rats were given controllable or uncontrollable shock. A third group

Continued

BOX 5.5 (continued)

remained untreated. Rats were conditioned a week later by administering shock in a novel context. The next day, they were tested to see if the context elicited conditioned fear (freezing). To explore the role of the infralimbic area, the investigators inactivated this region in half the subjects by administering the GABA agonist muscimol, either before conditioning or before testing. In rats that received the drug vehicle alone, the usual pattern of results was obtained: controllable shock reduced

behavioral signs of fear, whereas prior exposure to uncontrollable shock enhanced conditioned freezing. Inhibiting the infralimbic region prior to conditioning had no effect, which suggests that behavioral control does not affect learning. Turning off the infralimbic region prior to testing had little effect on rats that had received uncontrollable shock, but eliminated the calming (antifear) effect of controllable shock. As hypothesized, it appears that a history of behavioral control reduces

the expression of fear, but not its acquisition.

J. W. Grau

dorsal raphe nucleus (DRN)   A region of the midbrain that regulates neural activity in structures (e.g., the periaqueductal gray, amygdala) related to stress and emotion.

prefrontal cortex (PFC)   The most anterior (forward) region of the frontal lobes. The PFC has been implicated in executive control, working memory, and planning.

Sample Questions

1. Compare and contrast free-operant and discrete-trial methods for the study of instrumental behavior.
2. What are the similarities and differences between positive and negative reinforcement?
3. What is the current thinking about instrumental reinforcement and creativity, and what is the relevant experimental evidence?
4. How does the current status of a reinforcer depend on prior experience with that or other reinforcers?
5. What are the effects of a delay of reinforcement on instrumental learning, and what causes these effects?
6. What was the purpose of Skinner's superstition experiment? What were the results, and how have those results been reinterpreted?
7. Describe alternative explanations of the learned-helplessness effect.

Key Terms

accidental reinforcement   An instance in which the delivery of a reinforcer happens to coincide with a particular response, even though that response was not responsible for the reinforcer presentation. Also called *adventitious reinforcement.* This type of reinforcement was considered to be responsible for "superstitious" behavior.

adventitious reinforcement   Same as accidental reinforcement.

appetitive stimulus   A pleasant or satisfying stimulus that can be used to positively reinforce an instrumental response.

aversive stimulus   An unpleasant or annoying stimulus that can be used to punish an instrumental response.

avoidance   An instrumental conditioning procedure in which the instrumental response prevents the delivery of an aversive stimulus.

behavioral contrast   Change in the value of a reinforcer produced by prior experience with a reinforcer of a higher or lower value. Prior experience with a lower valued reinforcer increases reinforcer value (positive behavioral contrast), and prior experience with a higher valued reinforcer reduces reinforcer value (negative behavioral contrast).

belongingness   The idea, originally proposed by Thorndike, that an organism's evolutionary history makes certain responses fit or belong with certain reinforcers. Belongingness facilitates learning.

conditioned reinforcer   A stimulus that becomes an effective reinforcer because of its association with a primary or unconditioned reinforcer. Also called *secondary reinforcer.*

contiguity   The occurrence of two events, such as a response and a reinforcer, at the same time or very close together in time. Also called *temporal contiguity.*

differential reinforcement of other behavior (DRO) An instrumental conditioning procedure in which a positive reinforcer is periodically delivered only if the participant does something other than the target response.

discrete-trial procedure A method of instrumental conditioning in which the participant can perform the instrumental response only during specified periods, usually determined either by placement of the participant in an experimental chamber or by the presentation of a stimulus.

escape An instrumental conditioning procedure in which the instrumental response terminates an aversive stimulus. (See also *negative reinforcement.*)

free-operant procedure A method of instrumental conditioning that permits repeated performance of the instrumental response without intervention by the experimenter. (Compare with *discrete-trial procedure.*)

instinctive drift A gradual drift of instrumental behavior away from the responses required for reinforcement to species-typical, or instinctive, responses related to the reinforcer and to other stimuli in the experimental situation.

instrumental behavior An activity that occurs because it is effective in producing a particular consequence or reinforcer.

interim response A response that has its highest probability in the middle of the interval between successive presentations of a reinforcer, when the reinforcer is not likely to occur.

latency The time between the start of a trial (or the start of a stimulus) and the instrumental response.

law of effect A mechanism of instrumental behavior, proposed by Thorndike, which states that if a response (R) is followed by a satisfying event in the presence of a stimulus (S), the association between the stimulus and the response (S-R) will be strengthened; if the response is followed by an annoying event, the S-R association will be weakened.

learned-helplessness effect Interference with the learning of new instrumental responses as a result of exposure to inescapable and unavoidable aversive stimulation.

learned-helplessness hypothesis The proposal that exposure to inescapable and unavoidable aversive stimulation reduces motivation to respond and disrupts subsequent instrumental conditioning because participants learn that their behavior does not control outcomes.

magazine training A preliminary stage of instrumental conditioning in which a stimulus is repeatedly paired with the reinforcer to enable the participant to learn to go and get the reinforcer when it is presented. The sound of the food-delivery device, for example, may be repeatedly paired with food so that the animal will learn to go to the food cup when food is delivered.

marking procedure A procedure in which the instrumental response is immediately followed by a distinctive event (the participant is picked up or a flash of light is presented) that makes the instrumental response more memorable and helps overcome the deleterious effects of delayed reinforcement.

negative punishment Same as *omission training* or *differential reinforcement of other behavior.*

negative reinforcement An instrumental conditioning procedure in which there is a negative contingency between the instrumental response and an aversive stimulus. If the instrumental response is performed, the aversive stimulus is terminated or canceled; if the instrumental response is not performed, the aversive stimulus is presented.

omission training An instrumental conditioning procedure in which the instrumental response prevents the delivery of a reinforcing stimulus. (See also *differential reinforcement of other behavior.*)

operant response A response that is defined by the effect it produces in the environment. Examples include pressing a lever and opening a door. Any sequence of movements that depresses the lever or opens the door constitutes an instance of that particular operant.

positive reinforcement An instrumental conditioning procedure in which there is a positive contingency between the instrumental response and an appetitive stimulus or reinforcer. If the participant performs the response, it receives the reinforcer if the participant does not perform the response, it does not receive the reinforcer.

positive punishment Same as *punishment.*

punishment An instrumental conditioning procedure in which there is a positive contingency between the instrumental response and an aversive stimulus. If the participant performs the instrumental response, it receives the aversive stimulus; if the participant does not perform the instrumental response, it does not receive the aversive stimulus.

response–reinforcer contingency   The relation of a response to a reinforcer defined in terms of the probability of getting reinforced for making the response as compared to the probability of getting reinforced in the absence of the response.

response shaping   Reinforcement of successive approximations to a desired instrumental response.

running speed   How fast (e.g., in feet per second) an animal moves down a runway.

secondary reinforcer   Same as *conditioned reinforcer.*

superstitious behavior   Behavior that increases in frequency because of accidental pairings of the delivery of a reinforcer with occurrences of the behavior.

temporal contiguity   Same as *contiguity.*

temporal relation   The time interval between an instrumental response and the reinforcer.

terminal response   A response that is most likely at the end of the interval between successive reinforcements that are presented at fixed intervals.

CHAPTER **6**

Schedules of Reinforcement and Choice Behavior

CHAPTER PREVIEW

Instrumental responses rarely get reinforced each time they occur. This chapter continues our discussion of the importance of the response–reinforcer relation in instrumental behavior by describing the effects of intermittent schedules of reinforcement. A schedule of reinforcement is a program or rule that determines which occurrence of the instrumental response is followed by delivery of the reinforcer. Schedules of reinforcement are important because they determine the rate, pattern, and persistence of instrumental behavior. To begin, I will describe simple fixed-ratio, variable-ratio, fixed interval, and variable-interval schedules and the patterns of instrumental responding that are produced by these schedules. Then, I will describe how schedules of reinforcement determine the choices organisms make between different response alternatives. Concurrent and concurrent-chain schedules of reinforcement are techniques that have been widely used to examine the mechanisms of choice in laboratory experiments. A particularly interesting form of choice is between modest short-term gains versus larger long-term gains because these alternatives represent the dilemma of self-control.

In describing various instrumental conditioning procedures in Chapter 5, I may have given the impression that every occurrence of the instrumental response invariably results in delivery of the reinforcer. Casual reflection suggests that such a perfect contingency between response and reinforcement is rare in the real world. You do not get a

155

high grade on a test each time you study. You don't get an immediate response from a friend every time you send a text message, and going on a date with someone does not always result in a good time. In fact, in most cases the relation between instrumental responses and consequent reinforcement is rather complex. Laboratory investigations have been examining how these complex relations determine the rate and pattern of instrumental behavior.

A **schedule of reinforcement** is a program or rule that determines which occurrence of a response is followed by the reinforcer. There are an infinite number of ways that such a program could be set up. The delivery of a reinforcer could depend on the occurrence of a certain number of responses, the passage of time, the presence of certain stimuli, the occurrence of other responses, or any number or combination of other factors. One might expect that cataloging the behavioral effects produced by various possible schedules of reinforcement would be difficult. However, research so far has shown that the job is quite manageable. Reinforcement schedules that involve similar relations between responses and reinforcers usually produce similar patterns of behavior. The exact rate of responding may differ from one situation to another, but the pattern of behavior is highly predictable. This regularity has made the study of reinforcement schedules both interesting and very useful.

Schedules of reinforcement influence both how an instrumental response is learned and how it is then maintained by reinforcement. Traditionally, however, investigators of schedule effects have been concerned primarily with the maintenance of behavior. Thus, schedule effects are highly relevant to the motivation of behavior. Whether someone works hard or is lazy depends less on their personality than on the schedule of reinforcement that is in effect.

Schedules of reinforcement are important for managers who have to make sure their employees continue to perform a job after having learned it. Even public school teachers are often concerned with encouraging the occurrence of already learned responses rather than teaching new ones. Many students who do poorly in school know how to do their homework and how to study but simply choose not to. Schedules of reinforcement can be used to motivate more frequent studying behavior.

Studies that focus on schedules of reinforcement have provided important information about the reinforcement process and have also provided "useful baselines for the analysis of other behavioral phenomena" (Lattal, 2013). The behavioral effects of drugs, brain lesions, or manipulation of neurotransmitter systems often depend on the schedule of reinforcement that is in effect during the behavioral testing. This makes the understanding of schedule performance critical to the study of a variety of other issues in behavior theory and behavioral neuroscience.

Laboratory studies of schedules of reinforcement are typically conducted using a Skinner box that has a clearly defined response that can occur repeatedly, so that changes in the rate of responding can be readily observed and analyzed (Ferster & Skinner, 1957). The manner in which a rat's lever-press or pigeon's key-peck response is initially shaped and conditioned is usually of little interest. Rather, the focus is on schedule factors that control the timing and repetition of the operant response (see Morgan, 2010, for a recent review).

Simple Schedules of Intermittent Reinforcement

In simple schedules, a single factor determines which occurrence of the instrumental response is reinforced. The single factor can be how many responses have occurred or how much time has passed before the target response can be reinforced.

Ratio Schedules

The defining characteristic of a **ratio schedule** is that reinforcement depends only on the number of responses the organism has to perform. A ratio schedule requires merely counting the number of responses that have occurred and delivering the reinforcer each time the required number is reached. If the required number is one, every response results in delivery of the reinforcer. Such a schedule is technically called **continuous reinforcement (CRF)**.

Contingency management programs used in the treatment of drug abuse often employ a continuous reinforcement schedule. The clients are required to come to the clinic several times a week to be tested for drug use. If the test indicates that they have not used drugs since the last visit, they receive a voucher, which can be exchanged for money. In an effective variation of this procedure, the amount of money paid is increased with successive drug-free tests and is reset to zero if the participant relapses (Roll & Newton, 2008).

Continuous reinforcement occurs outside the laboratory where there is a direct causal link between the instrumental response and the outcome. Unlocking your car door enables you to get in the car, entering the correct code using your ATM card enables you to withdraw money from the ATM machine, and turning on the hot water in the shower enables you to take a comfortable shower. Barring any malfunctions, all of these are examples of continuous reinforcement. However, if the lock on your car door malfunctions, or if you don't have enough money in your ATM account, your instrumental behavior will not be reinforced every time. Situations in which responding is reinforced only some of the time are said to involve **partial reinforcement** or **intermittent reinforcement**. The following are simple schedules of intermittent reinforcement.

Fixed-Ratio Schedule Consider, for example, delivering the reinforcer after every 10th lever-press response in a study with laboratory rats. In such a schedule, there would be a fixed ratio between the number of responses the rat made and the number of reinforcers it got (10 responses per reinforcer). This makes the procedure a **fixed-ratio schedule (FR)**. More specifically, the procedure would be called a *fixed-ratio 10* or *FR 10*.

FR schedules are found in daily life wherever a fixed number of responses or a fixed amount of effort is required for reinforcement. People who distribute flyers are typically paid a certain amount for every batch of 50 flyers that they place on apartment doors. This is an FR 50 schedule of reinforcement. Checking class attendance by reading the roll is on an FR schedule, set by the number of students on the class roster. Making a phone call also involves an FR schedule, as each phone number includes a predetermined number of digits.

A continuous reinforcement schedule is also an FR schedule. Continuous reinforcement involves a fixed ratio of one response per reinforcer. On a continuous reinforcement schedule, organisms typically respond at a steady and moderate rate. Only brief and unpredictable pauses occur. A very different pattern of responding occurs when an FR schedule is in effect that requires a larger number of responses. You are not likely to pause in the middle of dialing a phone number. However, you may take a while to start making the call. This is the typical pattern for FR schedules. There is a steady and high rate of responding once the behavior gets under way. But there may be a pause before the start of the required number of responses. These features of responding are clearly evident in a **cumulative record** of the behavior.

A *cumulative record* is a special way of representing how a response is repeated over time. It shows the total (or cumulative) number of responses that have occurred up to a particular point in time. When Ferster and Skinner (1957) did their research on schedules of reinforcement, cumulative records were obtained with the use of a chart recorder (Figure 6.1). The recorder consisted of a rotating drum that pulled paper out

FIGURE 6.1 The plotting of a cumulative record by a cumulative recorder for the continuous recording of behavior. The paper moves out of the machine toward the left at a constant speed. Each response causes the pen to move up the paper one step. No responses occurred between Points A and B. A moderate rate of responding occurred between Points B and C, and a rapid rate occurred between Points C and D. At Point E, the pen reset to the bottom of the page.

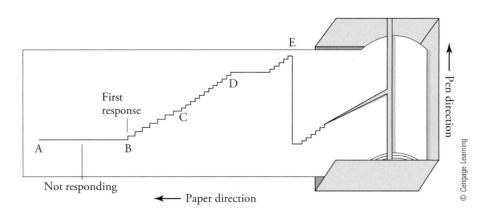

of the recorder at a constant speed. A pen rested on the surface of the paper. If no responses occurred, the pen remained at the same level and made a horizontal line as the paper came out of the machine. If the pigeon performed a key-peck response, the pen moved one step vertically on the paper. Because each key-peck response caused the pen to move one step up the paper, the total vertical distance traveled by the pen represented the cumulative (or total) number of responses the participant made. Because the paper came out of the recorder at a constant speed, the horizontal distance on the cumulative record provided a measure of how much time had elapsed in the session. The slope of the line made by the cumulative recorder represents the participant's *rate of responding* (number of responses per unit of time).

The cumulative record provides a complete visual representation of when and how frequently the participant responds during a session. In the record of Figure 6.1, for example, the participant did not perform the response between Points A and B, and a slow rate of responding occurred between Points B and C. Responses occurred more frequently between Points C and D, but the participant paused at D. After responding resumed, the pen reached the top of the page (at Point E) and reset to the bottom for additional responses.

Figure 6.2 shows the cumulative record of a pigeon whose responding had stabilized on a reinforcement schedule that required 120 pecks for each delivery of the reinforcer (an FR 120 schedule). Each food delivery is indicated by the small downward deflections of the recorder pen. The bird stopped responding after each food delivery, as would be expected. However, when it resumed pecking, it responded at a high and steady rate. The zero rate of responding that typically occurs just after reinforcement on a fixed ratio schedule is called the **post-reinforcement pause**. The high and steady rate of responding that completes each ratio requirement is called the **ratio run**.

If the ratio requirement is increased a little (e.g., from FR 120 to FR 150), the rate of responding during the ratio run may remain the same. However, with higher ratio requirements, longer post-reinforcement pauses occur (e.g., Felton & Lyon, 1966; Williams, Saunders, & Perone, 2008). If the ratio requirement is suddenly increased a great deal (e.g., from FR 120 to FR 500), the animal is likely to pause periodically before the completion of the ratio requirement (e.g., Stafford & Branch, 1998). This effect is called **ratio strain**. In extreme cases, ratio strain may be so great that the animal stops responding altogether. To avoid ratio strain during training, one must be careful not to raise the ratio requirement too quickly in approaching the desired FR response requirement.

Although the pause that occurs before a ratio run in FR schedules is historically called the *post-reinforcement pause*, research has shown that the length of the pause is

FIGURE 6.2 Sample cumulative records of different pigeons pecking a response key on four simple schedules of food reinforcement: fixed ratio 120, variable ratio 360, fixed interval 4 minutes, and variable interval 2 minutes. (Based on *Schedules of Reinforcement*, by C. B. Ferster and B. F. Skinner, 1957, Appleton-Century-Crofts.)

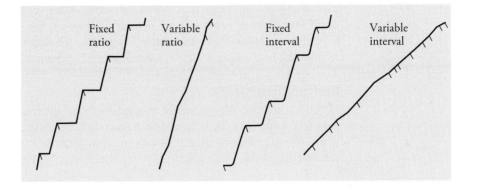

controlled by the upcoming ratio requirement (e.g., Baron & Herpolsheimer, 1999; see also Wade-Galuska, Perone, & Wirth, 2005). Consider, for example, washing your car by hand rather than driving through a car wash. Washing a car by hand is an FR task since it requires a set number of responses and a set amount of effort each time, as determined by the size of your car. If you procrastinate before starting to wash your car, it is because you are not quite ready to tackle the job, not because you are resting from the previous time you did the work. Thus, the *post-reinforcement pause* would be more correctly labeled the *pre-ratio pause*.

Variable-Ratio Schedule   In an FR schedule, a predictable number of responses or amount of effort is required for each reinforcer. This predictability can be disrupted by varying the number of responses required for reinforcement from one occasion to the next, which would be the case if you worked at a car wash where you had to work on cars of different sizes. Such a situation is still a ratio schedule because washing each car still depends on a set number of responses or effort. However, now a different number of responses is required to obtain successive reinforcers. Such a procedure is called a **variable-ratio schedule (VR)**. We may, for example, require a pigeon to make 10 responses to earn the first reinforcer, 13 to earn the second, 7 for the next one, and so on. Such a schedule requires on average 10 responses per reinforcer and would be a variable-ratio 10 schedule (VR 10).

VR schedules are found in daily life whenever an unpredictable amount of effort is required to obtain a reinforcer. For example, each time a custodian goes into a room on his or her rounds, he or she knows that some amount of cleaning will be necessary but does not know exactly how dirty the room will be. Gamblers playing a slot machine are also responding on a VR schedule. They have to play the machine to win. However, they never know how many plays will produce the winning combination. VR schedules are also common in sports. A certain number of strokes are always required to finish a hole in golf. But, most players cannot be sure how many strokes they will need when they begin a hole.

Because the number of responses required for reinforcement is not predictable, predictable pauses in the rate of responding are less likely with VR schedules than with FR schedules. Rather, organisms respond at a fairly steady rate on VR schedules. Figure 6.2 shows a cumulative record for a pigeon whose pecking behavior was maintained on a VR 360 schedule of reinforcement. Notice that even though on average the VR 360 schedule required many more pecks for each reinforcer than the FR 120 schedule shown in Figure 6.2, the VR 360 schedule maintained a much steadier pattern of responding.

Although post-reinforcement pauses can occur on VR schedules (e.g., Schlinger, Blakely, & Kaczor, 1990), such pauses are longer and more prominent with FR schedules.

The overall response rate on FR and VR schedules is similar provided that, on average, similar numbers of responses are required. However, the overall response rate tends to be distributed in a pause–run pattern with FR schedules, whereas a steady pattern of responding is observed with VR schedules (e.g., Crossman, Bonem, & Phelps, 1987).

Interval Schedules

In ratio schedules, reinforcement depends only on the number of responses the participant has performed. Time is irrelevant. In other situations, a response is reinforced only if the response occurs after a certain amount of time has passed. This is the case for **interval schedules**.

Fixed-Interval Schedule   In a simple interval schedule, a response is reinforced only if it occurs more than a set amount of time after a reference point, the last delivery of the reinforcer or the start of the trial. In a **fixed-interval schedule (FI)**, the amount of time that has to pass before a response is reinforced is constant from one trial to the next. A washing machine, for example, operates on a fixed interval schedule. A fixed amount of time is required to complete the wash cycle. No matter how many times you open the washing machine before the required time has passed, you will not be reinforced with clean clothes. Once the cycle is finished, the clothes are clean, and you can take them out any time after that.

Similar contingencies can be set up in the laboratory. Consider, for example, a fixed-interval 4-minute schedule (FI 4 min) for pecking in pigeons. In this case, 4 minutes would be required to set up the reinforcer. A pigeon would get reinforced for the first peck it made after completion of the 4-minute setup time. Because pecks made less than 4 minutes into the trial are never reinforced, the pigeons would learn to wait to respond until the end of the fixed interval (Figure 6.2). As the time for the availability of the next reinforcer draws closer, the response rate increases. This increase in response rate is evident as an acceleration in the cumulative record toward the end of each fixed interval and is called the **fixed-interval scallop**.

BOX 6.1

The Post-Reinforcement Pause and Procrastination

The post-reinforcement pause that occurs in FR schedules in the laboratory is also evident in common human experience. As I noted earlier, the pause occurs because a predictably large number of responses are required to produce the next reward. Such procrastination is legendary in human behavior. Consider, for example, a semester in which you have several term papers to write. You are likely to work on one term paper at a time. However, when you have completed one paper, you probably will not start working on the next one right away. Rather, there will be a post-reinforcement pause. After completing a large project, people find it difficult to jump right into the next one. In fact, procrastination between tasks or before the start of a new job is the rule rather than the exception.

FR-schedule performance in the laboratory indicates that once animals begin to respond on a ratio run, they respond at a high and steady rate until they complete the ratio requirement. This suggests that if somehow you got yourself to start on a task, chances are you will not find it difficult to keep going. Only the beginning is hard. One technique that works pretty well is to tell yourself that you will start by just doing a little bit of the job. If you are trying to write a paper, tell yourself that you will write only one paragraph to start with. You may find that once you have completed the first paragraph, it will be easier to write the second one, then the one after that, and so on. If you are procrastinating about spring cleaning, instead of thinking about doing the entire job, start with a small part of it, such as washing the kitchen floor. The rest will then come more easily. (For a broader discussion of procrastination, see Steel, 2007.)

Performance on an FI schedule reflects the participant's accuracy in telling time. (I will have more to say about the psychology of timing in Chapter 12.) If the participant were entirely incapable of telling time, it would be equally likely to respond at any point in the FI cycle. The post-reinforcement pause and the subsequent acceleration toward the end of the interval reflect a rudimentary ability to tell time. How could this ability be improved? Common experience suggests that having a watch or clock of some sort makes it much easier to judge time intervals. The same thing happens with pigeons on an FI schedule. In one study, the clock consisted of a spot of light that grew as time passed during the FI cycle. Introduction of this clock stimulus increased the duration of the post-reinforcement pause and caused responding to shift closer to the end of the FI cycle (Ferster & Skinner, 1957).

It is important to realize that an FI schedule does not guarantee that the reinforcer will be provided at a certain point in time. Pigeons on an FI 4-min schedule do not automatically receive access to grain every four minutes. The interval determines only when the reinforcer *becomes available*, not when it is delivered. To receive the reinforcer after it has become available, the participant still has to make the instrumental response. (For reviews of FI timing and operant behavior, see Staddon & Cerutti, 2003; Jozefowiez & Staddon, 2008.)

The scheduling of tests in college courses has major similarities to the basic FI schedule. Usually there are only two or three tests, and the tests are evenly distributed during the term. The pattern of studying that such a schedule encourages is very similar to what is observed with an FI schedule in the laboratory. Students spend little effort studying at the beginning of the semester or just after the midterm exam. Rather, they begin to study a week or two before each exam, and the rate of studying rapidly increases as the day of the exam approaches. Interestingly, members of the U.S. Congress behave the same way, writing bills at much higher rates as the end of the congressional session approaches (Critchfield et al., 2003).

Variable-Interval Schedule   In FI schedules, responses are reinforced if they occur after a fixed amount of time has passed after the start of the trial or schedule cycle. Interval schedules also can be unpredictable. With a **variable-interval schedule (VI)**, the time required to set up the reinforcer varies from one trial to the next. The subject has to respond to obtain the reinforcer that has been set up, but now the set-up time is not as predictable.

VI schedules are found in situations where an unpredictable amount of time is required to prepare the reinforcer. A mechanic who cannot tell you how long it will take to fix your car has imposed a VI schedule on you. The car will not be ready for some time, during which attempts to get it will not be reinforced. How much time has to pass before the car will be ready is unpredictable. A sales clerk at a bakery is also on a VI schedule of reinforcement. Some time has to pass after waiting on a customer before another will enter the store to buy something. However, the interval between customers is unpredictable.

In a laboratory study, a VI schedule could be set up in which the first food pellet will be available when at least 1 minute has passed since the beginning of the session, the second food pellet will be available when at least 3 minutes have passed since the previous pellet, and the third reinforcer will be available when at least 2 minutes have passed since the previous pellet. In this procedure, the average set-up time for the reinforcer is 2 minutes. Therefore, the procedure would be called a VI two-minute schedule, or VI 2 min.

As in FI schedules, the participant has to perform the instrumental response to obtain the reinforcer. Reinforcers are not given just because a certain amount of time has passed. Rather, they are given if the individual responds after the variable interval has timed out. Like VR schedules, VI schedules maintain steady and stable rates of responding without regular pauses (Figure 6.2).

Interval Schedules and Limited Hold   In simple interval schedules, once the reinforcer becomes available, it remains available until the required response is made, no matter how long that may take. For example, on an FI 2-min schedule, the reinforcer becomes available 2 minutes after the start of the schedule cycle. If the animal responds at exactly this time, it will be reinforced. If it waits and responds 90 minutes later, it will still get reinforced. Once the reinforcer has been set up, it remains available until the response occurs.

With interval schedules outside the laboratory, it is more common for reinforcers to become available for only limited periods. Consider, for example, a dormitory cafeteria. Meals are served at fixed times of day. Therefore, going to the cafeteria is reinforced only after a certain amount of time has passed since the last meal (the set-up time). However, once a meal becomes available, you have a limited amount of time in which to get it. This kind of restriction on how long a reinforcer remains available is called a **limited hold**. Limited-hold restrictions can be added to either FI or VI schedules.

Comparison of Ratio and Interval Schedules

There are striking similarities between the patterns of responding maintained by simple ratio and interval schedules. As we have seen, with both FR and FI schedules, there is a post-reinforcement pause after each delivery of the reinforcer. In addition, both FR and FI schedules produce high rates of responding just before the delivery of the next reinforcer. By contrast, VR and VI schedules both maintain steady rates of responding without predictable pauses. Does this mean that interval and ratio schedules motivate behavior in the same way? Not at all! The surface similarities hide fundamental differences in the underlying motivational mechanisms of interval and ratio schedules.

Early evidence of fundamental differences between ratio and interval schedules was provided in an important experiment by Reynolds (1975). Reynolds compared the rate of key pecking in pigeons reinforced on VR and VI schedules. Two pigeons were trained to peck the response key for food reinforcement. One of the birds was reinforced on a VR schedule. Therefore, for this bird the frequency of reinforcement was entirely determined by how many responses it made. The other bird was reinforced on a VI schedule. To make sure that the opportunities for reinforcement would be identical for the two birds, the VI schedule was controlled by the behavior of the bird reinforced on the VR schedule. Each time the VR pigeon was just one response short of the requirement for reinforcement on that trial, the experimenter set up the reinforcer for the VI bird. With this arrangement, the next response made by each bird was reinforced. Thus, the frequency of reinforcement was virtually identical for the two animals.

Figure 6.3 shows the cumulative record of pecking exhibited by each bird. Even though the two pigeons received the same frequency and distribution of reinforcers, they behaved very differently. The pigeon reinforced on the VR schedule responded at a much higher rate than the pigeon reinforced on the VI schedule. The VR schedule motivated much more vigorous instrumental behavior. This basic finding has since been replicated in numerous studies and has stimulated lively theoretical analysis.

Results similar to those Reynolds observed with pigeons also have been found with undergraduate students (e.g., Raia et al., 2000). The task was akin to a video game. A target appeared on a computer screen and the students had to maneuver a spaceship and "fire" at the target with a joystick as the instrumental response. Following a direct hit of the target, the participants received 5¢. However, not every "hit" was reinforced.

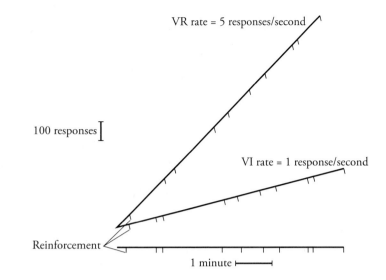

FIGURE 6.3 Cumulative records for two pigeons, one reinforced on a VR schedule and the other yoked to it on a VI schedule. Although the two pigeons received the same rate of reinforcement, the VR bird responded five times as fast as the VI bird. (Based on *A Primer of Operant Conditioning*, 2nd ed., by G. S. Reynolds.)

Which occurrence of the instrumental response was reinforced depended on the schedule of reinforcement programmed into the software. The students were assigned to pairs but each worked in a separate cubicle and didn't know that he or she had a partner. One member of each pair received reinforcement on a VR schedule. The other member of the pair was reinforced on a VI schedule that was yoked to the VR schedule. Thus, as in the pigeon experiment, reinforcers became available to both participants at the same time, but one controlled access to the reinforcer through a VR schedule and the other did not.

Raia and colleagues (2000) studied the effects of response shaping, instructions, and the presence of a consummatory response on performance on the VR–VI yoking procedure. (The consummatory response was picking up the 5¢ reinforcer each time it was delivered and putting it into a piggy bank.) One set of conditions was quite similar to the pigeon studies: The students were shaped to make the instrumental response, they received minimal instructions, and they were required to make the consummatory response. Interestingly, under these conditions, the college students performed just like the pigeons. Higher rates of responding occurred for the student of each pair who was reinforced on the VR schedule.

The higher response rates that occur on ratio as compared to interval schedules powerfully illustrate how schedules can alter the motivation for instrumental behavior. A simplistic theory might assume that the rate of responding is just a function of how many reinforcers the participant earns. But, in these experiments , the rates of reinforcement were identical with the ratio and interval schedules. Nevertheless, the ratio schedules produced much more behavior. This is important news if you are a manager trying to get the most effort from your employees. The reinforcer in an employment situation is provided by the wages individuals earn. The Reynolds experiment tells you that you can get employees to work harder for the same pay if the wages are provided on a ratio rather than an interval schedule.

Reinforcement of Inter-Response Times   Why might ratio schedules produce higher rates of responding than interval schedules? According to one explanation, the critical factor is the reinforcement of short inter-response times. The **inter-response time (IRT)** is the interval between successive responses. I noted in Chapter 5 that various features of behavior can be increased by reinforcement. The IRT is one such behavioral feature. If the participant is reinforced for a response that occurs shortly after the preceding one, then a short IRT is reinforced and short IRTs become more likely in the future. On the other hand, if the participant is reinforced for a response that ends a long IRT, then a long IRT is reinforced and long IRTs become more likely in the future. A participant who has mostly short IRTs is responding at a high rate. By contrast, a participant who has mostly long IRTs is responding at a low rate.

How do ratio and interval schedules determine the reinforcement of IRTs? Consider a ratio schedule. With a ratio schedule there are no time constraints, and the faster the participant completes the ratio requirement, the faster he or she will receive the reinforcer. Thus, a ratio schedule favors not waiting long between responses. It favors short IRTs. In fact, ratio schedules differentially reinforce short IRTs.

In contrast, interval schedules provide little advantage for short IRTs. Rather, interval schedules favor waiting longer between responses. Consider, for example, an FI 2-min schedule of food reinforcement. Each food pellet becomes available 2 minutes after the last one was delivered. If the participant responds frequently before the food pellet is set up, those responses and short IRTs will not be reinforced. On the other hand, if the participant waits a long time between responses (emitting long IRTs), those responses are more likely to occur after the 2 minutes has timed out and are more likely to be reinforced. Thus, interval schedules differentially reinforce long IRTs and, thus, result in lower rates of responding than ratio schedules (Baum, 1993; Cole, 1994, 1999; Tanno & Sakagami, 2008).

Feedback Functions   The second major explanation of the higher response rates on ratio schedules focuses on the relationship between response rates and reinforcement rates calculated over an entire experimental session or an extended period of time (e.g., Reed, 2007a, b). This relationship is called the *feedback function* because reinforcement is considered to be the feedback or consequence of responding.

In the long run, what is the relationship between response rate and reinforcement rate on ratio schedules? The answer is pretty straightforward. Because the only requirement for reinforcement on a ratio schedule is making a certain number of responses, the faster the participant completes the ratio requirement, the faster it obtains the next reinforcer. Thus, response rate is directly related to reinforcement rate. The higher the response rate, the more reinforcers the participant will earn and the higher will be its reinforcement rate. Furthermore, there is no limit to this increasing function. No matter how rapidly the participant responds, if it can increase its response rate even further, it will enjoy a corresponding increase in the rate of reinforcement. Thus, the feedback function for a ratio schedule is an increasing linear function with no limit.

How about the feedback function for an interval schedule? Interval schedules have an upper limit on the number of reinforcers a participant can earn. On a VI 2-min schedule, for example, if the participant obtains each reinforcer as soon as it becomes available, it can earn a maximum of 30 reinforcers per hour. Because each reinforcer requires a certain amount of time to be set up, there is an upper limit on the number of reinforcers a participant can earn. A participant cannot increase its reinforcement rate above this limit no matter how much he or she increases the rate of responding.

Doctors, lawyers, and hair dressers in private practice are all paid on a ratio schedule with a linearly increasing feedback function. Their earnings depend on the number of clients they see or procedures they perform each day. The more clients they see, the more money they make, and there is no limit to this function. No matter how much money they are making, if they can squeeze in another client, they can earn another fee. This is in contrast to salaried employees in a supermarket or the post office, who cannot increase their income as readily by increasing their efforts. Their only hope is that their diligence is recognized when employees are considered for a raise or promotion. The wage scale for salaried employees has strong interval-schedule components.

Choice Behavior: Concurrent Schedules

The reinforcement schedules I described thus far were focused on a single response and reinforcement of that response. The simplicity of single-response situations facilitates scientific discovery, but experiments in which only one response is being measured ignore some of the richness and complexity of the real world. Even in a simple situation like a Skinner box, organisms engage in a variety of activities and are continually choosing among possible alternatives. A pigeon can peck the only response key in the box, or preen, or move about the chamber. People are also constantly having to make choices about what to do. Should you go to the movies or stay at home and watch TV? If you stay at home, which show should you watch and should you watch it to the end or change the channel before the end of a show? Understanding the mechanisms of choice is fundamental to understanding behavior because much of what we do is the result of choosing one activity over another.

Choice situations can be rather complicated. For example, a person may have a choice of 12 different activities (playing a video game, watching television, texting a friend, playing with the dog, and the like), each of which produces a different type of reinforcer according to a different reinforcement schedule. Analyzing all the factors that control someone's choices can be a formidable task, if not an impossible one. Therefore, psychologists have begun experimental investigations of the mechanisms of choice by studying simpler situations. The simplest choice situation is one which has two response alternatives, and each response is followed by a reinforcer according to its own schedule of reinforcement.

Numerous studies of choice have been conducted in Skinner boxes equipped with two pecking keys a pigeon can peck. In the typical experiment, responding on each key is reinforced on some schedule of reinforcement. The two schedules are in effect at the same time (or concurrently), and the pigeon is free to switch from one key to the other. This type of procedure is called a **concurrent schedule**. Concurrent schedules allow for continuous measurement of choice because the organism is free to change back and forth between the response alternatives at any time.

Playing slot machines in a casino is on a concurrent schedule, with lots of response options. Each type of slot machine operates on a different schedule of reinforcement, and you can play any of the machines. Furthermore, you are at liberty to switch from one machine to another at any time. Closer to home, operating the remote control for your TV is also on a concurrent schedule. You can select any one of a number of channels to watch. Some channels are more interesting than others, which indicates that your watching behavior is reinforced on different schedules of reinforcement. As with slot machines, you can change your selection at any time. Talking to various people at a party involves similar contingencies. You can talk to whomever you want and move to someone else if a conversation gets boring, indicating a reduced rate of reinforcement.

Figure 6.4 shows a laboratory example of a concurrent schedule. If the pigeon pecks the key on the left, it receives food according to a VI 60-second schedule. Pecks on the right key produce food according to an FR 10 schedule. The pigeon is free to peck either side at any time. The point of the experiment is to see how the pigeon distributes its pecks on the two keys and how the schedule of reinforcement on each key influences its choices.

FIGURE 6.4 Diagram of a concurrent schedule for pigeons. Pecks at the left key are reinforced according to a VI 60-second schedule of reinforcement. Pecks on the right key are reinforced according to an FR 10 schedule of reinforcement.

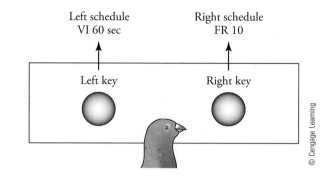

Left schedule
VI 60 sec

Right schedule
FR 10

Left key

Right key

© Cengage Learning

Measures of Choice Behavior

The individual's choice in a concurrent schedule is reflected in the distribution of its behavior between the two response alternatives. This can be measured in several ways. One common technique is to calculate the *relative rate of responding* on each alternative. The relative rate of responding on the left key, for example, is calculated by dividing the rate of responding on the left by the total rate of responding (left key plus right key). To express this mathematically, let's designate B_L as pecking or behavior on the left, and B_R as behavior on the right. Then, the relative rate of responding on the left is

$$\frac{B_L}{(B_L + B_R)} \tag{6.1}$$

If the pigeon pecks equally as often on the two response keys, this ratio will be .5. If the rate of responding on the left is greater than the rate of responding on the right, the ratio will be greater than .5. On the other hand, if the rate of responding on the left is less than the rate of responding on the right, the ratio will be less than .5. The relative rate of responding on the right (B_R) can be calculated in a comparable manner.

As you might suspect, how an organism distributes its behavior between the two response alternatives is greatly influenced by the reinforcement schedule in effect for each response. For example, if the same VI reinforcement schedule is available for each response alternative, as in a concurrent VI 60-second, VI 60-second procedure, the pigeon will peck the two keys equally often. The relative rate of responding for pecks on each side will be .5. This result is intuitively reasonable. Because the VI schedule available on each side is the same, there is no advantage in responding more on one side than on the other.

By responding equally often on each side of a concurrent VI 60-second, VI-60 second schedule, the pigeon will also earn reinforcers equally often on each side. The relative rate of reinforcement earned for each response alternative can be calculated in a manner comparable to the relative rate of response. Let's designate r_L as the rate of reinforcement on the left and r_R as the rate of reinforcement on the right. Then, the relative rate of reinforcement on the left will be r_L divided by the total rate of reinforcement (the sum of the rate of reward earned on the left and the rate of reward earned on the right). This is expressed in the formula

$$\frac{r_L}{(r_L + r_R)} \tag{6.2}$$

On a concurrent VI 60-second, VI 60-second schedule, the relative rate of reinforcement for each response alternative will be .5 because the participant earns reinforcers equally often on each side.

The Matching Law

As we have seen, with a concurrent VI 60-second, VI 60-second schedule, both the relative rate of responding and the relative rate of reinforcement for each response alternative are .5. Thus, the relative rate of responding is equal to the relative rate of reinforcement. Will this equality also occur if the two response alternatives are not reinforced according to the same schedule? This important question was asked by Herrnstein (1961).

Herrnstein studied the distribution of responses on various concurrent VI–VI schedules in which the maximum total rate of reinforcement the pigeons could earn was fixed at 40 per hour. Depending on the exact value of each VI schedule, different proportions of the 40 reinforcers could be obtained by pecking the left and right keys. Consider, for example, a concurrent VI 6–min, VI 2–min schedule. With such a schedule, a maximum of 10 reinforcers per hour could be obtained by responding on the VI 6–min alternative, and a maximum of 30 reinforcers per hour could be obtained by responding on the VI 2–min alternative.

There was no constraint on which side the pigeons could peck on the various concurrent VI–VI schedules Herrnstein tested. The pigeons could respond exclusively on one side or the other, or they could split their pecks between the two sides in various proportions. As it turned out, the pigeons distributed their responses in a highly predictable fashion. The results, summarized in Figure 6.5, indicate that the relative rate of responding on a given alternative was always close to the relative rate of reinforcement earned on that alternative. If the pigeons earned a greater proportion of their reinforcers on the left, they made a correspondingly greater proportion of their responses on that side. The relative rate of responding on an alternative *matched* the relative rate of reinforcement on that alternative. Similar findings have been obtained in numerous other experiments, which encouraged Herrnstein to call the relation the **matching law**. (For recent reviews, see Dallery & Soto, 2013; Grace & Hucks, 2013.)

There are two common mathematical expressions of the matching law. In one formulation, rate of responding or behavior (B) and rate of reinforcement (r) on one

R. J. Herrnstein

FIGURE 6.5 Results of various concurrent VI–VI schedules were tested with pigeons. Note that throughout the range of schedules, the relative rate of responding nearly equals (matches) the relative rate of reinforcement. (Based on "Relative and Absolute Strength of Response as a Function of Frequency of Reinforcement," by R. J. Herrnstein, 1961, *Journal of the Experimental Analysis of Behavior, 4,* pp. 267–272.)

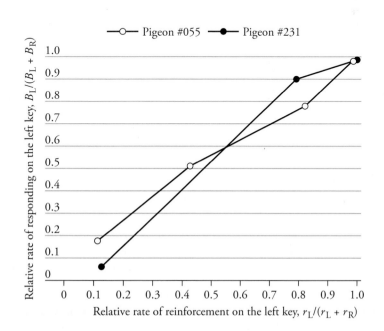

choice alternative are expressed as a proportion of total response and reinforcement rates, as follows:

$$\frac{B_\mathrm{L}}{(B_\mathrm{L} + B_\mathrm{R})} = \frac{r_\mathrm{L}}{(r_\mathrm{L} + r_\mathrm{R})} \tag{6.3}$$

The second form of the matching law is simpler but mathematically equivalent to Equation 6.3. In the second version, the rates of responding and reinforcement on one alternative are expressed as a proportion of the rates of responding and reinforcement on the other alternative, as follows:

$$\frac{B_\mathrm{L}}{B_\mathrm{R}} = \frac{r_\mathrm{L}}{r_\mathrm{R}} \tag{6.4}$$

Both mathematical expressions of the matching law represent the same basic principle, namely that *relative rates of responding match relative rates of reinforcement.*

The matching law has had a profound impact on the way in which scientists think about instrumental behavior. The major insight provided by the matching law is that the rate of a particular response does not depend on the rate of reinforcement of that response alone. Whether a behavior occurs frequently or infrequently depends not only on its own schedule of reinforcement but also on the rates of reinforcement of other activities the individual may perform. A given simple reinforcement schedule that is highly effective in a reward-impoverished environment may have little impact if there are numerous alternative sources of reinforcement. Therefore, how we go about training and motivating a particular response (e.g., studying among high school students) has to take into account other activities and sources of reinforcement the individuals have at their disposal.

The importance of alternative sources of reinforcement has provided useful insights into problematic behaviors such as unprotected sex among teenagers, which results in unwanted pregnancies, abortions, and sexually transmitted diseases. Based on the concepts of the matching law, Bulow and Meller (1998) predicted that "adolescent girls who live in a reinforcement-barren environment are more likely to engage in sexual behaviors than those girls whose environments offer them a fuller array of reinforcement opportunities" (p. 586). To test this prediction, they administered a survey to adolescent girls that asked them about the things they found reinforcing. From these data, the investigators estimated the rates of sexual activity and contraceptive use and the rates of reinforcement derived from sexual and other activities. These data were then entered into the equations of the matching law. The results were impressive. The matching law predicted the frequency of sexual activity with an accuracy of 60% and predicted contraceptive use with 67% accuracy. These findings suggest that efforts to reduce unprotected sex among teenagers have to consider not only their sexual activities but other things they may learn to enjoy (such as playing a sport or musical instrument). (For a review translational research involving the matching law, see Jacobs, Borrero, & Vollmer, 2013.)

Undermatching, Overmatching, and Response Bias   The matching law clearly indicates that choices are not made capriciously. Rather, choice is an orderly function of rates of reinforcement. Although the matching law has enjoyed considerable success and has guided much research over the past 50 years, relative rates of responding do not always match relative rates of reinforcement exactly.

Most instances in which choice behavior does not correspond perfectly to the matching relation can be accommodated by the generalized form of the matching law

W. M. Baum

(Baum, 1974). The generalized matching law has two parameters, b and s, added to Equation 6.4 and is expressed as follows:

$$B_\text{L}/B_\text{R} = b\left(\frac{r_\text{L}}{r_\text{R}}\right)^s \qquad (6.5)$$

The exponent s represents *sensitivity* of the choice behavior to the relative rates of reinforcement for the response alternatives or the discriminability of the alternatives. When perfect matching occurs, s is equal to 1. The most common deviation from perfect matching involves reduced sensitivity of the choice behavior to the relative rates of reinforcement. Such results are referred to as **undermatching** and can be accommodated by Equation 6.5 by making the exponent s less than one. Notice that if the exponent s is less than 1, the value of the term representing relative reinforcer rates, (r_A/r_B), becomes smaller, indicating reduced sensitivity to the relative rate of reinforcement.

Numerous variables have been found to influence the sensitivity parameter, including the species tested, the effort or difficulty involved in switching from one alternative to the other, and the details of how the schedule alternatives are constructed.

The parameter b in Equation 6.5 represents *response bias*. In Herrnstein's original experiment (and in most others that have followed), animals chose between two responses of the same type (pecking one or another response key), and each response was reinforced by the same type of reinforcer (brief access to food). Response bias occurs when the response alternatives require different amounts of effort or if the reinforcer provided for one response is much more attractive than the reinforcer for the other response. A preference (or bias) for one response or one reinforcer over the other results in more responding on the preferred side and is represented by higher values of the bias parameter b.

Mechanisms of the Matching Law

The matching law describes how organisms distribute their responses in a choice situation, but it does not explain what mechanisms are responsible for these choices. It is a descriptive law of nature rather than a mechanistic law. Factors that may be responsible for matching in choice situations have been the subject of continuing experimentation and theoretical debate (see Davison & McCarthy, 1988; Grace & Hucks, 2013).

The matching law is stated in terms of rates of responding and reinforcement averaged over the entire duration of experimental sessions. It ignores when individual responses are made. Some theories of matching are similar in that they ignore what might occur at the level of individual responses. Such explanations are called *molar theories*. Molar theories explain aggregates of responses. They deal with the distribution of responses and reinforcers in choice situations during an entire experimental session.

In contrast to molar theories, other explanations of the matching relation operate on a shorter time frame and focus on what happens at the level of individual responses. Such explanations are called *molecular theories* and view the matching relation as the net result of these individual choices. I previously described molecular and molar explanations of why ratio schedules produce higher response rates than interval schedules. The explanation that emphasized the reinforcement of inter-response times was a molecular or local account. In contrast, the explanation that emphasized feedback functions of ratio and interval schedules was a molar theory. (For a detailed discussion of molecular versus molar approaches to the analysis of behavior, see Baum, 2002.)

Maximizing Rates of Reinforcement The most extensively investigated explanations of choice behavior are based on the intuitively reasonable idea that organisms distribute their actions among response alternatives so as to receive the maximum amount

---

BOX 6.2

The Matching Law and Complex Human Behavior

The matching law and its implications have been found to apply to a wide range of human behaviors, including social conversation (Borrero et al., 2007), courtship and mate selection (Takeuchi, 2006), and the choices that lead to substance abuse (e.g., Frisher & Beckett, 2006; Vuchinich & Tucker, 2006). In an interesting recent study, Vollmer and Bourret (2000) examined the choices that college basketball players made during the course of intercollegiate games. A basketball player can elect to shoot at the basket from an area close to the basket and thereby get two points or shoot from an area farther away and thereby get three points. Teams compile statistics on the number of two- and three-point shots attempted by individual players. These data provide information about the relative rates of selecting each

response alternative. The team statistics also include information about the success of each attempt, and these data can be used to calculate the rate of reinforcement for each response alternative. Vollmer and Bourret examined the data for 13 players on the men's team and 13 players on the women's team of a large university and found that the relative choice of the different types of shots was proportional to the relative rates of reinforcement for those shots. Thus, the choice behavior of these athletes during regular games followed the matching law.

The matching law has also been used to analyze the choice of plays in professional football games of the American National Football League (Reed, Critchfield, & Martins, 2006). Data on running plays versus passing plays were analyzed in terms of the

number of yards that were gained as a consequence of each play. This way of looking at the game provided response rates (frequency of one or the other type of play) and reinforcement rates (yards gained). The generalized matching law accounted for 75% of the choice of plays. The sensitivity parameter showed that the relative frequency of passing versus running plays undermatched the relative yardage gained by these plays. Thus, the choice of plays did not take full advantage of the yardage gains that could have been obtained. The response bias parameter in the generalized matching law indicated that there was a significant bias in favor of running plays. Interestingly, teams whose play calling followed the matching law more closely had better win records than teams that significantly deviated from matching.

---

of reinforcement possible. According to this idea, animals switch back and forth between response alternatives so as to receive as many reinforcers as they possibly can. The idea that organisms maximize reinforcement has been used to explain choice behavior at both molecular and molar levels of analysis.

Molecular Maximizing   According to molecular theories of maximizing, organisms always choose whichever response alternative is most likely to be reinforced at a given moment in time. An early version of molecular matching (e.g., Shimp, 1969) stated that when two schedules (A and B) are in effect simultaneously, the participant will switch from Schedule A to Schedule B when the probability of reinforcement on Schedule B becomes greater than on Schedule A. The participant will switch back to A when the probability of reinforcement on A becomes greater than on B. Thus, this model claims that the matching relation is a byproduct of prudent switching behavior that tracks momentary changes in the probability of reinforcement. Detailed studies of the patterns of switching from one response to another have not always supported this type of molecular maximizing mechanism. However, scientists have remained interested in molecular explanations of matching.

According to a more recent molecular account, a situation involving two response Alternatives A and B actually involves four different behavioral options: staying with Alternative A, switching from A to B, staying with Alternative B, and switching from B to A. Each of these four behavioral options gets reinforced at various times. The relative distribution of responses on A and B is presumed to depend on the relative rate of reinforcement for staying on each side versus switching from one side to the other (MacDonall, 2000, 2005). (For other analyses of local reinforcement effects in choice, see Davison & Baum, 2003; Krägeloh, Davison, & Elliffee, 2005.)

Molar Maximizing Molar theories of maximizing assume that organisms distribute their responses among various alternatives so as to maximize the amount of reinforcement they earn over the long run. What is long enough to be considered a *long run* is not clearly specified. However, in contrast to molecular theories, molar theories focus on aggregates of behavior over some period of time, usually the total duration of an experimental session, rather than on individual choice responses.

Molar maximizing theory was originally formulated to explain choice on concurrent schedules made up of ratio components. In concurrent ratio schedules, animals rarely switch back and forth between response alternatives. Rather, they respond exclusively on the ratio component that requires the fewest responses. On a concurrent FR 20, FR 10 schedule, for example, the pigeon is likely to respond only on the FR 10 alternative. In this way, it maximizes its rate of reinforcement with the least effort.

In many situations, molar maximizing accurately predicts the results of choice procedures. However, certain findings present difficulties. One difficulty arises from the results of concurrent VI–VI schedules. On a concurrent VI–VI schedule, participants can obtain close to all of the available reinforcers on both VI options provided they occasionally sample each alternative. Therefore, the total amount of reinforcement obtained on a concurrent VI–VI schedule can be close to the same despite wide variations in how responding is distributed between the two alternatives. The matching relation is only one of the many different possibilities that yield close to maximal rates of reinforcement on concurrent VI–VI schedules.

Another challenge for molar matching is provided by studies involving a choice between a VR and a VI schedule. On a VR schedule, the participant can obtain reinforcement at any time by making the required number of responses. By contrast, on a VI schedule, the participant only has to respond occasionally to obtain close to the maximum number of reinforcers possible. For maximum return on a concurrent VR–VI schedule, participants should concentrate their responses on the VR alternative and respond only occasionally on the VI component. Evidence shows that both pigeons and college students favor the VR component but not always as strongly as predicted by molar maximizing (e.g., Heyman & Herrnstein, 1986; Savastano & Fantino, 1994).

Melioration The third major mechanism of choice, **melioration**, operates on a time scale between molar and molecular mechanisms. Instead of aggregating data over an entire session or focusing on individual responses, melioration theory focuses on local rates of responding and reinforcement.

Local rates are calculated only over the time period that a participant devotes to a particular choice alternative. With two options (A and B), for example, the local rate of responding on A is calculated by dividing the frequency of responses on A by the time the participant spends on side A. This contrasts with the *overall rate*, which is calculated over the entire duration of an experimental session.

Local rates are always higher than overall rates. For example, if you obtain 10 reinforcers in a 60-minute session by responding on the left response key, the overall rate of reinforcement on the left will be 10 per hour. However, if you only spend 15 minutes on the left side, the local rate of reinforcement on the left will be 10 per 15 minutes or 40 per hour.

The term *melioration* means making something better. Melioration theory predicts that participants will shift their behavior toward whichever choice alternative provides the higher (or better) local rate of reinforcement. However, any change in time spent on a

E. Fantino

choice alternative will probably change the local rate of reinforcement for that alternative. Melioration assumes that adjustments in the distribution of behavior between choice alternatives will continue until the participant is obtaining the same local rate of reinforcement on each alternative (Herrnstein, 1997; Vaughan, 1981). Once this is achieved, there is no incentive for any further changes in response allocation. It can be shown mathematically that when participants distribute their responses so as to obtain the same local rate of reinforcement on each alternative, they are behaving in accordance with the matching law. Therefore, the mechanism of melioration results in matching. (For a human study of choice consistent with melioration, see Madden, Peden, & Yamaguchi, 2002.)

Complex Choice and Self-Control

In a standard concurrent schedule of reinforcement, two (or more) response alternatives are available at the same time, and switching from one to the other can occur at any time. At a potluck dinner, for example, if you don't like what you are eating, you can switch at any time to something else. Similarly, you can visit one or another booth at a county fair and make a new selection at any time. That is not the case when you choose a movie at a multiplex. Once you have paid your ticket and started watching the movie, you cannot change your mind and go see another one at any time. Choosing one movie makes the others unavailable until you buy another ticket.

Many complex human decisions limit your options once you have made a choice. When you are finishing high school and contemplating where to go to college, you may have a number of options available. However, after you have selected and enrolled in a particular college, the other schools are no longer available until the next semester or next year. Choosing where to go on vacation or which car to buy similarly involves choice with commitment. Once the selection is made, the other alternatives are no longer available for a while.

Concurrent-Chain Schedules

To study how organisms make choices that involve commitment to one alternative or the other, investigators developed the **concurrent-chain schedule of reinforcement** (Kyonka & Grace, 2010; Mazur, 2006).

A concurrent-chain schedule of reinforcement involves two stages or links (Figure 6.6). The first is called the *choice link*. In this link, the participant is allowed to choose between two schedule alternatives by making one of two responses. In the example diagrammed in Figure 6.6, the pigeon makes its choice by pecking either the left or the right response key. Pecking the left key produces Alternative A, the opportunity to

R. C. Grace

FIGURE 6.6
Diagram of a concurrent-chain schedule. Pecking the left key in the choice link activates reinforcement Schedule A in the terminal link. Pecking the right key in the choice activates reinforcement Schedule B in the terminal link.

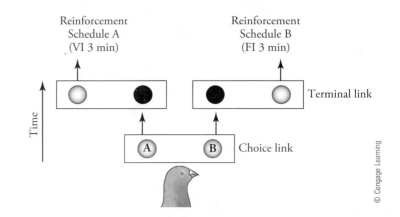

peck the left key on a VI 3-min schedule of reinforcement. If the pigeon pecks the right key in the choice link, it produces Alternative B, which is the opportunity to peck the right key on an FI 3-min schedule.

Responding on either key during the choice link does not yield food. The opportunity for reinforcement occurs only after the initial choice has been made and the pigeon has entered the *terminal link*. Another important feature of the concurrent-chain schedule is that once the participant has made a choice, it is stuck with that alternative until the end of the terminal link of the schedule or the end of the trial. Thus, concurrent-chain schedules involve *choice with commitment*.

The pattern of responding that occurs in the terminal component of a concurrent-chain schedule is characteristic of whatever schedule of reinforcement is in effect during that component. In our example, if the pigeon selected Alternative A, its pattern of pecking during the terminal component will be similar to the usual response pattern for a VI 3-min schedule. If the pigeon selected Alternative B, its pattern of pecking during the terminal component will be characteristic of an FI 3-min schedule.

We have all heard that *variety is the spice of life*. Studies of concurrent-chain schedules can tell us whether such a claim is supported by empirical evidence. If variety is the spice of life, then participants should prefer a variable schedule over a fixed schedule that yields the same overall rate of reinforcement. Studies of concurrent-chain schedules with VI and FI terminal components have shown that participants prefer the variable-schedule alternative. In fact, pigeons favor the VI alternative even if the VI schedule requires more time on average for the reinforcer to become available than the FI alternative (e.g., Andrzejewski et al., 2005). This indicates that variety is indeed the spice of life in concurrent-chain schedules.

As I noted, the consequence of responding during the choice link of a concurrent schedule is not the primary reinforcer (food). Rather, it is entry into one of the terminal links, each of which is typically designated by a particular color on the pecking key. Thus, the immediate consequence of an initial-link response is a stimulus that is associated with the terminal link that was chosen. Because that stimulus is present when the primary reinforcer is provided, the terminal link stimulus becomes a *conditioned reinforcer*. Thus, one may regard a concurrent schedule as one in which the initial-link responses are reinforced by the presentation of a conditioned reinforcer. Differences in the value of the conditioned reinforcer will then determine the relative rate of each choice response in the initial link. Because of this, concurrent-chain schedules provide an important tool for the study of conditioned reinforcement (Jimenez-Gomez & Shahan, 2012; Savastano & Fantino, 1996).

Although many studies of concurrent-chain schedules represent efforts to determine how organisms select between different situations represented by the terminal links, the consensus of opinion is that choice behavior is governed by both the terminal link schedules and whatever schedule is in effect in the initial link. Several different models have been proposed to explain how variables related to the initial and terminal links act in concert to determine concurrent-choice performance (e.g., Christensen & Grace, 2010).

Self-Control Choice and Delay Discounting

Self-control is an especially important form of complex choice. Self-control is a matter of choosing a large delayed reward over an immediate small reward. Should you get out of bed when your alarm rings and go to class, or turn off the alarm and sleep an extra hour? Going to class will help your grade point average and help you obtain a college degree. Those are very significant benefits, but you cannot enjoy them until some time in the future. Staying in bed for an extra hour provides a much smaller benefit but one that you can enjoy immediately. Similarly, self-control in eating involves selecting the large delayed reward of maintaining a healthy weight over the immediate small reward of eating a piece of cake. Many choices involved in a healthy lifestyle require selecting a larger delayed reward (being healthy) over a smaller, more immediate reward (getting a cup of coffee with friends instead of going to the gym).

Why is it so difficult to be motivated to work for large but delayed rewards? That is the crux of the problem of self-control. The answer, which originated in early studies of concurrent-chain schedules (Rachlin & Green, 1972), is based on the concept of **delay discounting**. Delay discounting is one of the major contemporary advances in our thinking about reinforcement and refers to the idea that the value of a reinforcer declines as a function of how long you have to wait to obtain it.

If I ask you whether you would prefer $25 today or $25 next week, there is no doubt that you will choose to get the money today. This shows that the value of $25 is less if you have to wait a week to get it. How much less? We can determine that by posing a series of choices that pit $25 next week against various smaller amounts today. Given such a series of choices, we might determine that for you getting $10 today is equivalent to getting $25 next week. Such a result would show that for you one week's delay results in the value of $25 being reduced to $10.

Delay discounting functions have been examined in numerous studies with human participants as well as various animal species (e.g., Calvert, Green, & Myerson, 2011; Madden & Bickel, 2010). One cannot ask laboratory animals hypothetical questions about their choice between monetary reinforcers that differ in amount and delay. Rather, ingestible reinforcers have to be used. When ingestible reinforcers are also tested with human participants, similar discounting functions are obtained.

Figure 6.7 shows the results of a study with undergraduate students given choices between different amounts and delays of their preferred juice (Jimura et al., 2011). Notice that the subjective value of both 16 ml and 8 ml of juice declined with increasing delays. This illustrates the basic phenomenon of delay discounting. Figure 6.7 also shows that the smaller (8 ml) reward lost its value faster than the larger (16 ml) reward.

Delay discounting is a well-established phenomenon. There is no longer any doubt that reinforcers lose their value the longer one has to wait for them. However, the exact mathematical form of the *value discounting function* has taken a bit of empirical effort to

L. Green

FIGURE 6.7 The subjective value of 16 ml and 8 ml of juice as a function of delay in college students. Curves represent best-fitting hyperboloid functions (based on Jimura et al., 2009).

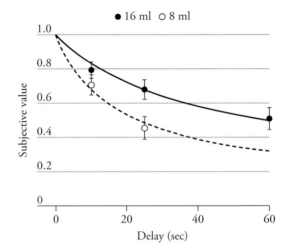

James E. Mazur

pin down. The current consensus is that the value of a reinforcer (V) is directly related to reward magnitude (M) and inversely related to reward delay (D), according to the formula

$$V = \frac{M}{(1 + kD)} \tag{6.6}$$

where k is the discounting rate parameter (Mazur, 1987). Equation 6.6 is called the *hyperbolic decay function.* (For a generalized version of the hyperbolic decay function, see Grace, 1999.) According to this equation, if the reinforcer is delivered with no delay ($D = 0$), the value of the reinforcer is directly related to its magnitude (larger reinforcers have larger values). The longer the reinforcer is delayed, the smaller is its value.

I noted earlier that the concept of delay discounting provides the key to understanding the problem of self-control, which involves choice between a small reward available soon versus a much larger reward available after a long delay. But, how can that be? Given that reinforcers rapidly lose their value with longer delays, won't participants always select the small, more immediate reward? Not necessarily. Different results occur depending on the size of the reinforcer and how rapidly its value is discounted.

In analyzing the problem of self-control, it is useful to plot delay discounting functions backwards, as shown in Figure 6.8. In this figure, the vertical axis again shows the perceived value of the reinforcer, and time is represented by the horizontal axis. The figure represents the value of a large and a small reward as a function of how long you have to wait to receive the reward. The bar for the large reward is to the right of the bar for the small reward because you have to wait longer to receive the large reward. T_1 and T_2 identify different points in time when you might make your choice response.

The usual self-control dilemma occurs if your choice is made at T_1. At T_1 there is a very short wait for the small reward and a longer wait for the large reward. Waiting for each reward reduces its value. Because reward value decreases rapidly at first, given the delays involved at T_1, the value of the large reward is smaller than the value of the small reward. Hence, the model predicts that if the choice occurs at T_1, you will select the small reward (the impulsive option). However, the discounting functions cross over with further delays. The value of both rewards is less at T_2 than at T_1 because T_2 involves longer delays. However, notice that at T_2 the value of the large reward is now greater than that of the small reward. Therefore, a choice at T_2 would have you select the large reward (the self-control option).

The delay discounting functions illustrated in Figure 6.8 predict the results of numerous studies of self-control. Most importantly, the functions show that increasing

FIGURE 6.8 Hypothetical relations between reward value and waiting time to reward delivery for a small reward and a large reward presented sometime later.

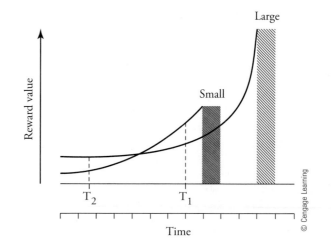

A. W. Logue

the delay to both the small and large reward (by moving from T_1 to T_2) makes it easier to exhibit self-control. Because the delay discounting functions cross over with longer delays, the larger delayed reward becomes more attractive with longer delays. (For a broader discussion of these issues, see Logue, 1995; Rachlin, 2000.)

Delay Discounting in Human Affairs   As I noted above, the parameter k in Equation 6.6 indicates how rapidly reward value declines as function of delay. The steeper a person's delay discounting function is, the more difficulty that person will have in exhibiting self-control because the larger more remote reward will seem much less valuable. Lack of self-control is potentially associated with a wide range of human problems. Engaging in unprotected sex, drinking too much at a party, driving while intoxicated, and throwing a punch instead of walking away from an argument are all examples of lack of self-control. Are people who engage in such problematic behaviors more apt to discount delayed rewards? This question has stimulated a great deal of research on human delay discounting (e.g., Madden & Bickel, 2010).

A critical issue in this area is the stability of delay discounting functions. Only if such functions are highly stable could they be used to better understand repeated patterns of risky behavior. Kirby (2009) tested delay discounting for hypothetical monetary reinforcers in college students on two occasions. For one group, the two assessments were separated by 5 weeks. For another group, the two assessments were more than a year apart (57 weeks). Test–retest reliability dropped a bit from 5 to 57 weeks. However, the test–retest reliability of delay discounting rates was about the same as the test–retest reliability of standard personality traits (Kirby, 2009). Thus, individual differences in reward discounting can be treated as a personality variable.

Other studies have examined changes in delay discounting across different ages. In one study, for example, the discounting of hypothetical monetary rewards was measured in college students and older adults (mean 71 years of age). The results are presented in Figure 6.9. Notice that the rate of discounting of monetary rewards decreases as a function of months. This contrasts with the much faster discounting that we encountered for ingestible rewards (Figure 6.7). Figure 6.9 also shows that the rate of discounting is substantially slower among older adults than among young adults. Interestingly, no differences were found in the rate of discounting of a consumable reinforcer (juice) at these ages.

In addition to age, investigators have examined numerous variables to see how they may be related to the rate of reward discounting (see Odum & Baumann, 2010, for a review). These studies have shown that individuals with higher IQ, higher educational level, and higher income tend to show slower reward discounting. Interestingly, grade point average and grades in specific courses are also negatively correlated with the rate

FIGURE 6.9 Delay discounting for hypothetical monetary rewards among college students and senior adults (mean age 71). Notice that the rate of discounting is significantly slower among the older participants (based on Jimura et al., 2011).

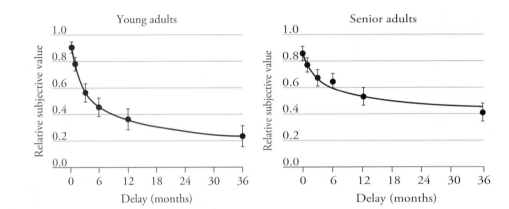

Courtesy of T. S. Critchfield

T. S. Critchfield

of reward discounting (e.g., Kirby, Winston, & Santiesteban, 2005). Students who are less apt to discount delayed rewards do better in their course work. In another study, college students who engaged in unprotected sex were found to have steeper discounting functions than those who used condoms. These and related studies show that reward-discounting reflects an important feature of behavior that is relevant to self-control in a broad range of situations (Critichfield & Kollins, 2001).

Perhaps the most widely investigated aspect of human behavior that has been examined from the perspective of delay discounting is drug addiction and drug abuse (Yi, Mitchell, & Bickel, 2010). For example, a recent metaanalysis of drug users concluded that individuals with addictive behaviors involving alcohol, tobacco, stimulants, and opiates all showed significantly steeper discounting functions than control participants who were not using these drugs (MacKillop et al., 2011). Although provocative, such evidence does not reveal the direction of causation. It may be that individuals who steeply discount delayed rewards are more apt to consume drugs of abuse. Alternatively, drug addiction may cause more rapid discounting of rewards.

Whether delay discounting contributes to the development of drug abuse or is a symptom of it may be determined by longitudinal studies or experiments with laboratory animals. Both strategies have implicated rapid discounting as causal to drug abuse. For example, Audrain-McGovern and colleagues (2009) studied a sample of 947 teenagers from the age of 15–20 and found that those who showed steeper delayed discounting functions at the age of 15 were more likely to take up smoking. In another recent study, students and their parents and teachers were interviewed each year from the 6th to the 11th grade to obtain information about self-control, attentional difficulties, and drug use. Greater difficulties with self-control in grade 6 were predictive of alcohol, marijuana, and cigarette use in high school (King et al., 2011). Interestingly, in this study attentional difficulties were also predictive of later drug use.

In what is probably the most ambitious and comprehensive study of the relationship between self-control early in life and subsequent behavior, nearly 1,000 children were tracked from birth to the age of 32 in New Zealand (Moffitt et al., 2011). A number of different measures of self-control were obtained during the first 10 years of life and related to various life outcomes during the ensuing 22 years. Higher levels of self-control in childhood were predictive of better health, lower rates of drug use, higher income levels, lower rates of single parenting, and lower rates of criminal behavior. A sample of these results is presented in Figure 6.10.

Experiments with laboratory animals have confirmed that rate of reward discounting is related to drug intake and possible drug abuse (see Carroll et al., 2010, for a review). Typically rats serve as participants in these experiments, although other species have been also studied. Delay discounting is first assessed using food as the reinforcer. Based on these tests, the rats are categorized as showing a steep or shallow discounting rate. The two groups are then tested using various drug self-administration procedures. Rats that show steep delay discounting have been found to subsequently take in more alcohol or cocaine, show greater escalation of drug intake when given the opportunity, and are more likely to relapse in their drug consumption following extinction. Thus, delay discounting is predictive of many aspects of drug abuse in these laboratory models.

Courtesy of M. E. Carroll

M. E. Carroll

Can Self-Control be Trained?   As we have seen, lack of self-control is associated with serious negative life outcomes. How might these be avoided? One possibility is to establish self-control through training. In fact, some have suggested that self-control is a critical component of socialization and emotional adjustment.

Evidence suggests that self-control can be trained. In one study (Eisenberger & Adornetto, 1986), for example, second- and third-grade students in a public elementary

FIGURE 6.10 Relationship between childhood self-control and physical health and substance dependence in early adulthood (based on Moffitt et al., 2011).

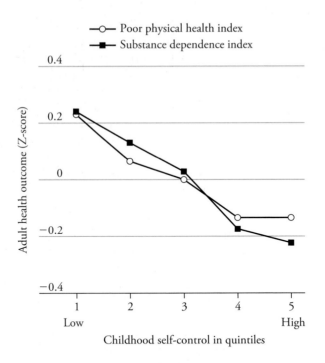

school were first tested for self-control by being asked whether they wanted to get 2¢ immediately or 3¢ at the end of the day. Children who elected the immediate reward were given 2¢. For those who elected the delayed reward, 3¢ was placed in a cup to be given to the child later. The procedure was repeated eight times to complete the pretest. The children then received three sessions of training with either immediate or delayed reward.

During each training session, various problems were presented (counting objects on a card, memorizing pictures, and matching shapes). For half the students, correct responding was reinforced immediately with 2¢. For the remaining students, correct responses resulted in 3¢ being placed in a cup that was given to the child at the end of the day. After the third training session, preference for a small immediate reward versus a larger delayed reward was measured as in the pretest. Provided that the training tasks involved low effort, training with delayed reward increased the subsequent preference of the children for the larger delayed reward.

Another strategy for training self-control involves a shaping procedure in which the large reward is initially presented without a delay, and the delay is then gradually increased across trials (e.g., Schweitzer & Sulzer-Azaroff, 1988). When there is no delay in a choice between a small and a large reward, the participant invariably selects the larger reward. This choice can be sustained if the delay to the large reward is increased in small steps.

Another technique that facilitates self-control is to introduce a distracting task during the delay to the large reward or distract attention from the large reward during the delay period (e.g., Mischel, Ebbesen, & Zeiss, 1972). In some examples of successful training, providing an intervening response is combined with gradually increasing the delay to the large reward (e.g., Dixon et al., 1998; Dixon & Holcomb, 2000).

Although investigators have identified some effective procedures for training self-control, much work remains to be done in this area. Future research needs to identify what factors are critical for the learning of self-control and how to maximize the effectiveness of those variables. In addition, we need to better understand what factors are responsible for the generalization of self-control skills and how to promote generalization of self-control from one situation to another.

BOX 6.3

Neuroeconomics: Imaging Habit and Executive Control

In its simplest form, instrumental behavior is shaped by rewards and stimuli that signal reward. This requires a mechanism to represent reward (its magnitude and valence) and a system for encoding reward signals. By monitoring how these events are related to behavior, these neural mechanisms can shape what we do, fostering adaptive responses (go) and inhibiting maladaptive behavior (no-go). These processes alone seem sufficient to guide the development of simple habits, where reward is immediate and response options are constrained.

Natural situations, though, are typically far more complex than this, allowing for a range of possible responses and outcomes, both immediate and delayed. To organize behavior in such complex situations, the organism must represent not just reward (the immediate advantage accrued by the outcome of a behavior) but also its value (an estimate of how much reward, or punishment, will be gained from the choice, both now and in the future) (Montaque, King-Casas, & Cohen, 2006). To weigh these alternatives requires a form of *working memory* to select among choice options and update expectancies in the face of new information. Such a view extends instrumental behavior to problems related to goal setting and planning, to help us understand how humans make choices that balance long-term gains with short-term costs. Here I consider these issues within the framework of **neuroeconomics**, a discipline that draws from neuroscience, economics, and psychology, to explore the brain mechanisms that underlie decision-making and choice (Bickel et al., 2007).

The field of neuroeconomics builds upon animal research to

explain choice behavior in humans. The aim is to couple behavioral data with neurobiological observations. In nonhuman species, these issues can be explored using techniques that disrupt function in a particular region or involve recording from neurons using electrodes that have been lowered into the animal's brain. Unless warranted by medical concerns, such procedures cannot be used with humans and, as a result, progress in this area has been slow. A major turning point was the development of a noninvasive method to image the brain using **functional magnetic resonance imaging (fMRI)**. fMRI takes advantage of the fact that brain activity requires oxygen, which is transported in the blood by hemoglobin. When hemoglobin binds oxygen to form *oxyhemoglobin*, it alters the magnetic properties of the molecule. It is this change that is detected by an MRI scanner, allowing researchers to monitor the flow of oxyhemoglobin within the brain. As neural activity increases, more oxyhemoglobin is directed to the region, producing a *blood oxygenation level dependent (BOLD)* signal (Bickel et al., 2007).

Using fMRI, researches have shown that the presentation of reward consistently engages neural activity within a common set of neural structures that includes the *orbitofrontal cortex (OFC)*, the *amygdala*, the *striatum*, and the *nucleus accumbens* (McClure, York, & Montaque, 2004). The striatum and nucleus accumbens are part of the **basal ganglia**, a subcortical cluster of structures that also includes the *globus pallidus*, adjoining components of the thalamus (the *subthalamic nuclei*), and a region of the midbrain (the *substantia nigra*) (EP-7 at the back of

the book). The orbitofrontal cortex lies directly above the eye sockets (orbits) and represents the ventral (lower) portion of the *prefrontal cortex (PFC)* (EP-6 at the front of the book). Here, I will focus on just three components: the amygdala, striatum, and the OFC.

Earlier, I discussed how the amygdala plays an important role in processing biologically significant stimuli, both appetitive and aversive (Box 4.3). We also saw that the *basolateral amygdala (BLA)* contributes to learning about Pavlovian relations. With regard to instrumental learning, the amygdala appears to play two important roles. First, neural activity within this region provides an index of reward magnitude and valence. Second, processing within the amygdala can endow neutral cues with an affective code that can motivate behavior and reinforce new learning. We will see later that drug-paired cues can facilitate drug-taking behavior, and this secondary reinforcement is eliminated by lesioning the BLA. Likewise, lesioning the BLA disrupts instrumental behavior motivated by escape from a fear-eliciting cue. In an appetitive task, devaluing a food reward (e.g., by pairing it with an illness-inducing agent) normally reduces instrumental responding. Devaluation has no effect on performance in BLA-lesioned participants.

The striatum and its associated nuclei provide a system for integrating positive and negative outcomes over multiple trials to modify behavioral habits. Research suggests that it does so through two pathways that project to the thalamus (Figure 6.11), a direct path that sends a "go" signal to facilitate the execution of a response and an indirect path that sends a "no-go" signal to suppress

Continued

BOX 6.3 (continued)

FIGURE 6.11 A model of basal ganglia function. A direct output pathway is proposed to generate a "go" signal that facilitates behavioral responses. An indirect pathway sends a "no-go" signal that suppresses competing responses (adapted from Kolb and Wishaw, 2008).

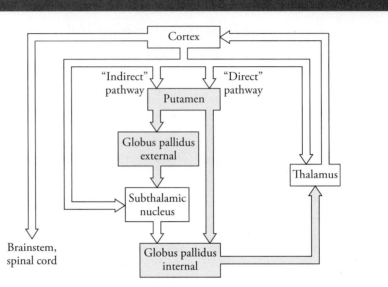

competing responses (Frank & Claus, 2006). These differential effects are mediated, in part, by the action of the neurotransmitter *dopamine* (*DA*), which can engage either the excitatory D1 receptor (go) or the inhibitory D2 receptor (no-go). As we will see later (Box 7.1), DA activity is modulated by predictability, providing an error signal that shapes behaviors. Evidence that the striatum is involved in reward comes from studies demonstrating that rats find highly rewarding both electrical stimulation and DA microinjection within this region. Conversely, striatal lesions undermine habitual responding and increase sensitivity to reinforcer devaluation (McClure et al., 2004). In humans, a loss of DA input from the substantia nigra (an outcome of Parkinson's disease) causes a disruption in motor behavior.

The OFC lies within the PFC, an evolutionarily younger brain region found in humans and higher mammals (Bickel et al., 2007). Research suggests that the PFC plays a role in higher brain functions, such as planning and decision making. The OFC corresponds to the ventral region of

the PFC and is anatomically connected with structures implicated in reward, such as the amygdala and striatum. The OFC appears to provide a form of executive control that allows the organism to weigh the relative value of alternative choices. Interestingly, there is some evidence for a subdivision of labor within the OFC, with rewarded actions (approach) eliciting greater neural activity within the medial regions and punished actions (response inhibition) engaging more lateral areas (McClure et al., 2004). Damage to the OFC interferes with learning when reward contingencies no longer apply (e.g., when reinforcer contingencies are reversed). Likewise, humans with damage to the OFC cannot use the value of a predicted outcome to guide their behavior in a gambling task (Saddoris, Gallagher, & Schoenbaum, 2005).

The work reviewed above suggests that instrumental learning is guided by two competing systems. One reflects a kind of habit learning. It relies on lower-level structures, such as the amygdala and striatum, and learns in an incremental fashion,

guided by predictability and signal error. The other relies on the OFC and provides a form of executive control that can rapidly bias behavior in the face of new information. It is the executive system that evaluates potential outcomes, weighs the benefit of delayed reward, and sets goals (Bickel et al., 2007). Individuals who have disrupted executive function (from damage to the OFC) have trouble incorporating negative feedback from previous behavior to guide future behavior. As a result, their behavior is governed by the impulsive amygdala.

I have characterized the functioning of these systems using the kinds of reinforcers typically used in laboratory studies. The system is not, however, limited in this way. A wide range of stimuli, including smells and sexual cues, engage the reward system. So too does money and social reward (e.g., from positive feedback). Likewise, arbitrary stimuli (CSs) that predict reward engage a similar pattern of neural activity (McClure et al., 2004). Even the administration of punishment to a deserving defector can elicit reward-related neural

Continued

BOX 6.3 (continued)

activity (Montaque et al., 2006). As McClure and colleagues (2004) suggested, representing reward in terms of a common pattern of neural activity may facilitate the comparison of alternative outcomes that differ on multiple dimensions (quality, immediacy, magnitude, and valence).

The competition between the impulsive habit-based system and executive oversight can help us understand how organisms weigh the relative value of a delayed reward. As discussed in the text, organisms will often choose a smaller immediate reward over a delayed larger reward, a phenomenon known as *delayed discounting* (Rachlin, 2006). Researchers have suggested that it is the OFC that allows us to delay gratification—to select a delayed larger reward. Supporting this, lesioning the OFC biases behavior toward immediate reward (Roesch, Calu, Burke, & Schoenbaum, 2007). Conversely, damage to the nucleus accumbens increases delayed discounting (Peters & Büchel, 2011). Imaging studies have revealed that the choice of an immediate reward elicits greater activity in limbic areas,

whereas delayed reward engenders more activity in the frontal cortex.

In addictive behavior, individuals repeatedly choose an immediate outcome in the face of knowledge that doing so will likely entail long-term negative consequences. Such a pattern suggests a deficiency in weighing the value of outcomes over time to mentally project that choosing the delayed alternative will yield greater reward. Supporting this, research has shown that opioid addicts discount more (that is, undervalue a delayed reward) than nonaddicted individuals. Moreover, if the outcome is heroin, addicts (surprisingly) discount even more. It has been proposed that addiction arises because the hyperreactive impulsive system overcomes the influence of the executive system, with a corresponding emphasis on immediate reward (Bickel et al., 2007). As we will learn in Chapter 7 (Box 7.1), drugs of abuse artificially engage reward systems and, with experience, sensitize the reward circuit, further biasing it toward an impulsive choice. This view suggests that treatment for addiction will require

a multifaceted approach to both dampen drug reactivity and strengthen executive control.

Research has revealed a striking similarity in how the brain processes a diverse set of rewards, from food to social rewards. Across these domains, instrumental learning is reinforced by common neurochemical systems and regulated by an error signal, the occurrence of which is well predicted by formal models (e.g., Rescorla & Wagner, 1972). These observations suggest a remarkable degree of conservation in structure and function with regard to reinforcement learning (Montaque et al., 2006).

J. W. Grau

basal ganglia   A subcortical cluster of structures implicated in instrumental behavior and the assessment of time. Degeneration of this area contributes Parkinson's disorder.

functional magnetic resonance imaging (fMRI)   A noninvasive procedure that can be used to measure brain activity based on changes in blood flow.

neuroeconomics   An interdisciplinary approach to the study of choice and decision making that relies on both behavioral and neurobiological observations.

Concluding Comments

The basic principle of instrumental conditioning is very simple: reinforcement increases (and punishment decreases) the future probability of an instrumental response. However, as we have seen, the experimental analysis of instrumental behavior can be rather intricate. Many important aspects of instrumental behavior are determined by the schedule of reinforcement. There are numerous schedules that can be used to reinforce behavior. Reinforcement can depend on how many responses have occurred, how much time has passed, or a combination of these factors. Furthermore, more than one reinforcement schedule may be available to the organism at the same time. The pattern of instrumental behavior, as well as choices between various response alternatives, are strongly determined by the schedules of reinforcement that are in effect. These various findings have told us a great deal about how reinforcement controls behavior in a variety of circumstances and have encouraged numerous powerful applications of reinforcement principles to important aspects of human behavior such as self-control.

Sample Questions

1. Compare and contrast ratio and interval schedules in terms of how the contingencies of reinforcement are set up and the effects they have on the instrumental response.
2. Describe how concurrent schedules of reinforcement are designed and what are typical findings with concurrent schedules.
3. Describe the generalized matching law equation and explain each of its parameters.
4. Describe various theoretical explanations of the matching law.
5. How are concurrent-chain schedules different from concurrent schedules, and what kinds of research questions require the use of concurrent-chain schedules?
6. What is a reward discounting function, and how is it related to the problem of self-control?
7. How have studies of self-control informed us about other important aspects of human behavior?

Key Terms

concurrent-chain schedule of reinforcement A complex reinforcement procedure in which the participant is permitted to choose during the first link which of several simple reinforcement schedules will be in effect in the second link. Once a choice has been made, the rejected alternatives become unavailable until the start of the next trial. Concurrent-chain schedules allow for the study of choice with commitment.

concurrent schedule A complex reinforcement procedure in which the participant can choose any one of two or more simple reinforcement schedules that are available simultaneously. Concurrent schedules allow for the measurement of direct choice between simple schedule alternatives.

continuous reinforcement (CRF) A schedule of reinforcement in which every occurrence of the instrumental response produces the reinforcer.

cumulative record A graphical representation of how a response is repeated over time, with the passage of time represented by the horizontal distance (or x axis), and the total or cumulative number of responses that have occurred up to a particular point in time represented by the vertical distance (or y axis).

delay discounting Decrease in the value of a reinforcer as a function of how long one has to wait to obtain it.

fixed-interval scallop The gradually increasing rate of responding that occurs between successive reinforcements on a fixed-interval schedule.

fixed-interval schedule (FI) A reinforcement schedule in which the reinforcer is delivered for the first response that occurs after a fixed amount of time following the last reinforcer or the beginning of the trial.

fixed-ratio schedule (FR) A reinforcement schedule in which a fixed number of responses must occur in order for the next response to be reinforced.

intermittent reinforcement A schedule of reinforcement in which only some of the occurrences of the instrumental response are reinforced. The instrumental response is reinforced occasionally, or intermittently. Also called *partial reinforcement*.

inter-response time (IRT) The interval between one response and the next. IRTs can be differentially reinforced in the same fashion as other aspects of behavior, such as response force or response variability.

interval schedule A reinforcement schedule in which a certain amount of time is required to set up the reinforcer. A response is reinforced only if it occurs after the reinforcer has been set up.

limited hold A restriction on how long a reinforcer remains available. In order for a response to be reinforced, it must occur before the end of the limited-hold period.

matching law A rule for instrumental behavior, proposed by R. J. Herrnstein, which states that the relative rate of responding on a particular response alternative equals the relative rate of reinforcement for that response alternative.

melioration A mechanism for achieving matching by responding so as to improve the local rates of reinforcement for response alternatives.

partial reinforcement Same as *intermittent reinforcement.*

post-reinforcement pause A pause in responding that typically occurs after the delivery of the reinforcer on FR and FI schedules of reinforcement.

ratio run The high and invariant rate of responding observed after the post-reinforcement pause on FR schedules. The ratio run ends when the ratio requirement has been completed and the participant is reinforced.

ratio schedule A schedule in which reinforcement depends only on the number of responses the participant performs, irrespective of when those responses occur.

ratio strain Disruption of responding that occurs on ratio schedules when the response requirement is increased too rapidly.

schedule of reinforcement A program, or rule, that determines how and when the occurrence of a response will be followed by the delivery of the reinforcer.

undermatching Less sensitivity to the relative rate of reinforcement than predicted by the matching law.

variable-interval schedule (VI) A reinforcement schedule in which reinforcement is provided for the first response that occurs after a variable amount of time from the last reinforcer or the start of the trial.

variable-ratio schedule (VR) A reinforcement schedule in which the number of responses necessary to produce reinforcement varies from trial to trial. The value of the schedule refers to the average number of responses required for reinforcement.

CHAPTER 7

Instrumental Conditioning: Motivational Mechanisms

CHAPTER PREVIEW

This chapter is devoted to a discussion of the processes that motivate and direct instrumental behavior. Two distinctively different approaches have been pursued in efforts to understand why instrumental behavior occurs. The first of these is in the tradition of Thorndike and Pavlov and focuses on identifying the associative structure of instrumental conditioning. The associative approach considers molecular mechanisms rather than the long-range goal or function of instrumental behavior. The second strategy is in the Skinnerian tradition and considers instrumental behavior in the broader context of how organisms distribute or allocate their behavior among various response options. The response-allocation approach considers reinforcement effects to be a consequence of constraints on response options imposed by an instrumental conditioning procedure. How behavior is reallocated in the face of these constraints is analyzed using concepts from behavioral ecology and behavioral economics. The associative and response-allocation approaches provide an exciting illustration of the sometimes turbulent course of scientific inquiry. Investigators studying the motivational substrates of instrumental behavior have moved boldly to explore radical new conceptions when older ideas did not meet the challenges posed by new empirical findings.

In Chapters 5 and 6, I defined instrumental behavior, pointed out how this type of learning is investigated, and described how instrumental behavior is influenced by various experimental manipulations, including schedules of reinforcement. Along the way, I did not say much about what motivates instrumental responding, perhaps because the answer seemed obvious. Casual reflection suggests that individuals perform instrumental responses because they are motivated to obtain the goal or reinforcer that results from the behavior. Is this true, and what does it mean to be motivated to obtain the reinforcer? Furthermore, what is the full impact of setting up a situation in which the reinforcer can be obtained only by making the required instrumental response? Answers to these questions have occupied scientists for more than a century and have encompassed some of the most important and interesting research in the analysis of behavior.

The motivation of instrumental behavior has been considered from two radically different perspectives. The first originated with Thorndike and involves analysis of the *associative structure of instrumental conditioning.* As this label implies, this approach relies heavily on the concept of associations and hence is compatible with the theoretical tradition of Pavlovian conditioning. In fact, much of the research relevant to the associative structure of instrumental conditioning was stimulated by efforts to identify the role of Pavlovian mechanisms in instrumental learning. In addition, experiments on the associative structure of instrumental conditioning have often employed methods that were developed to study Pavlovian conditioning.

The associative approach takes a molecular perspective. It focuses on individual responses and the specific stimulus antecedents and outcomes of those responses. To achieve this level of detail, the associative approach examines instrumental learning in isolated behavioral preparations, not unlike studying something in a test tube or a Petri dish. Because associations can be substantiated in the nervous system, the associative approach also provides a convenient framework for studying the neural mechanisms of instrumental conditioning (e.g., Balleine & Ostlund, 2007).

The second strategy for analyzing motivational processes in instrumental learning is *the response-allocation approach.* This approach was developed in the Skinnerian tradition and involves considering instrumental conditioning within the broader context of the numerous activities that organisms are constantly doing. In particular, the response-allocation approach is concerned with how an instrumental conditioning procedure limits an organism's free flow of activities and the consequences of this limitation. Unlike the associative approach, response allocation considers the motivation of instrumental behavior from a more molar perspective. It considers long-term goals and how organisms manage to achieve those goals within the context of all of their behavioral options. Thus, the response allocation approach views instrumental behavior from a more functional perspective.

To date, the associative and response-allocation approaches have proceeded pretty much independently of one another. Each approach has identified important issues, but it has become clear that neither can stand alone. The hope is that at some point, the molecular analyses of the associative approach will make sufficient contact with the more molar functional analyses of response allocation to provide a comprehensive integrated account of the motivation of instrumental behavior.

The Associative Structure of Instrumental Conditioning

Edward Thorndike was the first to recognize that instrumental conditioning involves more than just a response and a reinforcer. The instrumental response occurs in the context of specific environmental stimuli. The instrumental behavior of sending a text message occurs

FIGURE 7.1 Diagram of instrumental conditioning. The instrumental response (R) occurs in the presence of distinctive stimuli (S) and results in delivery of the reinforcer outcome (O). This allows for the establishment of several different types of associations.

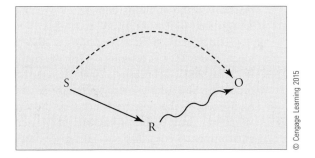

in the context of tactile stimuli provided by holding your cell phone and visual cues provided by looking at the keyboard. Turning the key in the ignition of your car occurs in the context of your sitting in the driver's seat and holding the key between your fingers. One can identify such environmental stimuli in any instrumental situation. Hence, there are three events to consider in an analysis of instrumental learning: the stimulus context (S), the instrumental response (R), and the response outcome (O), or reinforcer. Skinner also subscribed to the idea that there are three events to consider in an analysis of instrumental or operant conditioning. He described instrumental conditioning in terms of a *three-term contingency* involving S, R, and O (Davison & Nevin, 1999). The relation among these three terms is presented in Figure 7.1.

The S–R Association and the Law of Effect

The basic structure of an instrumental conditioning procedure permits the development of several different types of associations. The first of these was postulated by Thorndike and is an association between the contextual stimuli (S) and the instrumental response (R): the *S–R association*. Thorndike considered the S–R association to be the key to instrumental learning and central to his *law of effect*. According to the law of effect, instrumental conditioning involves the establishment of an S–R association between the instrumental response (R) and the contextual stimuli (S) that are present when the response is reinforced. The role of the reinforcer is to "stamp in" or strengthen this S–R association. Thorndike thought that, once established, this S–R association was solely responsible for the occurrence of the instrumental behavior. Thus, the basic impetus, or motivation, for the instrumental behavior was the activation of the S–R association by exposing the participant to the contextual stimuli (S), in the presence of which the response was previously reinforced.

An important implication of the law of effect is that instrumental conditioning does not involve learning about the reinforcer or response outcome (O) or the relation between the response and the reinforcing outcome (the R–O association). The law of effect assumes that the only role of the reinforcer is to strengthen the S–R association. The reinforcer itself is not a party or participant in this association.

The S–R mechanism of the law of effect played a dominant role in behavior theory for many years but fell into disfavor during the cognitive revolution that swept over psychology during the latter part of the twentieth century. Interestingly, however, there has been a resurgence of interest in S–R mechanisms in recent efforts to characterize habitual behavior in people. Habits are things we do automatically and in the same way each time without thinking. Estimates are that habits constitute about 45% of human behavior. Wood and Neal (2007) proposed a comprehensive model of human habits, which assumes that habits "arise when people repeatedly use a particular behavioral means in particular contexts to pursue their goals. However, once acquired, habits are performed without mediation of a goal" (p. 844). Rather, the habitual response is an automatic reaction to the stimulus context in which the goal was previously obtained, similar to Thorndike's S–R association.

Thorndike's S–R association is also being seriously entertained as one of the mechanisms that is responsible for the habitual nature of drug addiction (e.g., Everitt & Robbins, 2005; Belin et al., 2009; Zapata, Minney, & Shippenberg, 2010). In this model, procuring and taking a drug of abuse is viewed as instrumental behavior that is initially reinforced by the positive aspects of the drug experience. However, with repetitive use, taking the drug becomes habitual in the sense that it becomes an automatic reaction to environmental cues that elicit drug seeking and drug consumption without regard to its consequences. Compulsive eating, gambling, or sexual behavior can be thought of in the same way. What makes these behaviors compulsive is that the person "cannot help" doing them given the triggering contextual cues, even though the activities can have serious negative consequences. According to the S–R mechanism, those consequences are not relevant. To borrow terminology from Wood and Neal (2007), the S–R association "stipulates an outsourcing of behavioral control to contextual cues that were, in the past, contiguous with performance" (p. 844).

Expectancy of Reward and the S–O Association

The idea that reward expectancy might motivate instrumental behavior was not considered seriously until about 40 years after the formulation of the law of effect. How might we capture the notion that individuals learn to expect the reinforcer during the course of instrumental conditioning? You come to expect that something important will happen when you encounter a stimulus that activates the memory of the significant event or allows you to predict that the event will occur. Pavlovian conditioning is the basic process of signal learning. Hence, one way to look for reward expectancy is to consider how Pavlovian processes may be involved in instrumental learning.

As Figure 7.1 illustrates, specification of an instrumental response ensures that the participant will always experience certain distinctive stimuli (S) in connection with making the response. These stimuli may involve the place where the response is performed, the texture of the object the participant manipulates, or distinctive olfactory or visual cues. Whatever the stimuli may be, reinforcement of the instrumental response will inevitably result in pairing these stimuli (S) with the reinforcer or response outcome (O). Such pairings provide the potential for classical conditioning and the establishment of an association between S and O. This S–O association is represented by the dashed line in Figure 7.1 and is one of the mechanisms of reward expectancy in instrumental conditioning.

One of the earliest and most influential accounts of the role of classical conditioning in instrumental behavior was offered by Clark Hull (1930, 1931) and later elaborated by Kenneth Spence (1956). Their proposal was that the instrumental response increases during the course of instrumental conditioning for two reasons. First, the presence of S comes to evoke the instrumental response directly through Thorndike's S–R association. Second, the instrumental response also comes to be made in response to an S–O association that creates the expectancy of reward. Exactly how the S–O association comes to motivate instrumental behavior has been the subject of considerable debate and experimental investigation. A particularly influential formulation was the *two-process theory* of Rescorla and Solomon (1967).

Two-Process Theory　　Two-process theory assumes that there are two distinct types of learning: Pavlovian and instrumental conditioning—nothing too radical there. The theory further assumes that these two learning processes are related in a special way. In particular, during the course of instrumental conditioning, the stimuli (S) in the presence

TABLE 7.1   EXPERIMENTAL DESIGN TO TEST PAVLOVIAN INSTRUMENTAL TRANSFER

PHASE 1	PHASE 2	TRANSFER TEST
Instrumental conditioning	Pavlovian conditioning	Present Pavlovian CS during performance of the instrumental response
Lever press → Food	Tone → Food	Lever press → Food tone versus no tone

© Cengage Learning

of which the instrumental response is reinforced become associated with the response outcome (O) through Pavlovian conditioning, and this results in an S–O association. Rescorla and Solomon assumed that the S–O association activates an emotional state that motivates the instrumental behavior. The emotional state was assumed to be either positive or negative, depending on whether the reinforcer was an appetitive or an aversive stimulus (e.g., food or shock). Thus, various appetitive reinforcers (e.g., food and water) were assumed to lead to a common positive emotional state and various aversive stimuli were assumed to lead to a common negative emotion.

How could we test the idea that an S–O association (and the expectancies or emotions that such an association activates) can motivate instrumental behavior? The basic experimental design for evaluating this hypothesis has come to be called the *Pavlovian instrumental transfer experiment*. The experiment involves three separate phases (Table 7.1). In one phase, participants receive standard instrumental conditioning (e.g., lever pressing is reinforced with food). In the next phase, they receive a pure Pavlovian conditioning procedure (the response lever is removed from the experimental chamber and a tone is paired with food). The critical transfer phase occurs in Phase 3, where the participants are again permitted to perform the instrumental lever-press response, but now the Pavlovian CS is presented periodically. If a Pavlovian S–O association motivates instrumental behavior, then the rate of lever pressing should increase when the tone CS is presented. The experiment is called the Pavlovian instrumental transfer test because it determines how an independently established Pavlovian CS transfers to influence or motivate instrumental responding.

Phase 1 can precede or follow Phase 2 in a Pavlovian instrumental transfer experiment. The two phases of training can also be conducted in different experimental chambers. In fact, that is often the case. The basic requirement is to establish a Pavlovian CS to activate an S–O association and then see how this CS influences the performance of an instrumental response during the transfer test.

The two-process theory has stimulated a great deal of research using the Pavlovian instrumental transfer design. As predicted, the presentation of a Pavlovian CS for food increases the rate of instrumental responding for food (e.g., Estes, 1948; Lovibond, 1983). This presumably occurs because the positive emotion elicited by the CS+ for food summates with the appetitive motivation that is involved in lever pressing for food. The opposite outcome (a suppression of responding) is predicted if the Pavlovian CS elicits a negative emotion. I described such a result in Chapter 3 where I described the conditioned suppression procedure. In that case, the Pavlovian CS was paired with shock (and came to elicit conditioned fear). Presentation of the CS+ for shock was then tested when the subjects were lever pressing for food. The result was that the Pavlovian CS suppressed the instrumental lever-press behavior (Ayres, 2012; Blackman, 1977). According to the two-process theory, conditioned suppression occurs because the CS+ for shock elicits an emotional state (fear) that is contrary to the positive emotion or expectancy (hope) that is established in instrumental conditioning with food. (For a more detailed discussion of other predictions of the two-process theory, see Domjan, 1993.)

Marvin Krank

Response Interactions in Pavlovian Instrumental Transfer Classically conditioned stimuli elicit not only emotional states but also overt responses such as sign tracking (Chapter 3). Consequently, the overt responses elicited by a Pavlovian CS may influence the results in a Pavlovian instrumental transfer experiment. This is nicely illustrated by a recent study of the effects of a Pavlovian CS for alcohol on instrumental responding reinforced by alcohol (Krank et al., 2008). The experiment was done with laboratory rats in a chamber that had two response levers, one on either side of a water well. The rats were first trained to press either response lever reinforced by a drop of artificially sweetened water. Once the rats were pressing both response levers, the sweetener was gradually replaced by ethanol, which then served as the reinforcer. A concurrent VI 20-second, VI 20-second schedule established stable responding for ethanol on each response lever.

Pavlovian conditioning was conducted during the next eight sessions. The CS was a light presented above each of the response levers. However, during the Pavlovian conditioning sessions the response levers were removed from the chambers. On a given trial, the CS appeared for 10 seconds either on the right or the left side and was paired with presentation of .2 ml of ethanol. For the unpaired control group, the CS and ethanol presentations were separated by 10 seconds. As is common with this type of Pavlovian conditioning, the CS light came to elicit a sign-tracking response if it was paired with the reinforcer. The rats approached and sniffed the light, whether it was on the right or the left.

Following the Pavlovian conditioning phase, the response levers were placed back into the chambers and the rats were again permitted to lever press for ethanol reinforcement. For the Pavlovian instrumental transfer tests, the CS light was periodically presented while the rats were responding for ethanol. On some test trials, the CS was presented above the right lever; on other trials, the CS appeared above the left lever.

The results of the transfer tests are presented in Figure 7.2. The rats pressed each response lever about twice per minute before the CS was presented. For the unpaired group, lever pressing did not change much when the CS was presented either on the right or the left. In contrast, the paired group showed a significant increase in lever pressing during the CS period if the CS was presented on the same side as the lever the rat was pressing. These results show that a Pavlovian CS for ethanol will increase instrumental responding reinforced by ethanol. The increased lever pressing during the CS shows that an independently established S–O association can facilitate instrumental responding reinforced by that outcome. Because the response levers were removed from the chambers during the Pavlovian phase, no S–R associations could have been learned during that phase.

FIGURE 7.2 Rate of lever pressing for ethanol in a Pavlovian instrumental transfer test. Responding is shown during the pre-CS period and during the CS when the CS was on the same side as the lever being pressed or on the alternate or different side. (Based on Krank et al., 2008).

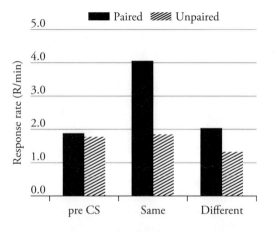

Another important aspect of the results was that the facilitation of instrumental responding occurred only if the Pavlovian CS was presented on the same side as the lever the rat was pressing. If the rat was pressing the lever on the right and the CS appeared on the left, the rat approached and sniffed the light on the left, and this prevented it from increasing its lever pressing on the right side. Thus, the results of the transfer test depended on the compatibility of the Pavlovian CR and the instrumental response. (For a more detailed discussion of these issues and their relevance to studying the neural basis of Pavlovian instrumental transfer effects, see Holmes, Marchand, & Coutureau, 2010.)

BOX 7.1

The Role of Dopamine in Addiction and Reward

Drug addiction is a long-standing societal problem. What underlies compulsive drug use, and why is it that individuals with a history of drug use are so prone to relapse? Answers to these questions require an understanding of how learning influences drug-taking behavior. It is now widely recognized that drugs of abuse usurp control over the neural circuitry that mediates learning about natural rewards, producing an artificial high that tricks the brain into following a path that leads to maladaptive consequences (for reviews, see Berridge & Krinelbach, 2008; Hyman, Malenka, & Nestler, 2006; Koob & Le Moal, 2008; Lee, Seo, & Jung, 2012). Understanding how drugs exert their effects at a neurobiological level should help address the problem of drug addiction and shed light on the mechanisms that underlie learning about natural rewards.

Understanding addiction requires some background in **psychopharmacology**, the study of how drugs impact the nervous system to influence psychological and behavioral states. There are many ways that this can occur, but for present purposes we can focus on how drugs influence neural communication at the *synapse* (EP-2 at the front of the book). Drugs can influence synaptic communication at multiple sites. For example, an agonist can substitute for the endogenous (internally manufactured) chemical, binding to the receptor on the postsynaptic cell and producing a similar cellular effect. Conversely, *drug antagonists* bind to the receptor but do not engage the same cellular consequences. Instead, the antagonist acts as a kind of roadblock that effectively prevents an agonist from having its usual effect on the postsynaptic cell. Drugs can also influence function in a less direct manner. For example, some drugs increase neurotransmitter availability by enhancing release or by blocking their reabsorption or (*reuptake*) into the presynaptic neuron.

In general, drugs of abuse impact the nervous system by promoting the release of a particular neurotransmitter or by emulating its action. For example, *psychostimulants* influence the neurotransmitter *dopamine* (DA) by blocking its reuptake (e.g., cocaine) or promoting its release (e.g., amphetamine). Opiates, such as morphine and heroin, have their effect by emulating endogenous opioids (*endorphins*) that engage the μ-opioid receptor. Another common addictive substance, nicotine, engages acetylcholine receptors while sedatives (alcohol, valium) act, in part, through their impact on GABAergic neurons.

Drugs of abuse appear to promote addiction by influencing neurons within particular brain regions, such as the **nucleus accumbens (NA)** (Figure 7.3A). Many of the neurons within this region have spiny dendritic fields that allow for multiple synaptic contacts (Hyman et al., 2006). These *medium spiny neurons* receive input from neurons that release an endogenous opioid that engages the μ-receptor. In addition, dopaminergic neurons project from a region of the midbrain (the *ventral tegmental area* [VTA]) and innervate the spiny neurons as they pass en route to other regions (e.g., the prefrontal cortex). Other psychoactive drugs influence the activity of neurons within the nucleus accumbens (NA) by modulating opioid or dopamine release, or by influencing the inhibitory action of GABAergic neurons that regulate neural activity (Figure 7.3B).

Neurons within the nucleus accumbens also receive input from other regions, such as the cortex. These neurons release the excitatory neurotransmitter *glutamate*. As discussed in Box 8.2, changes in how a postsynaptic cell responds to glutamate can produce a lasting change (e.g., a long-term potentiation) in how a neural circuit operates, a physiological alteration that has been

Continued

BOX 7.1 (continued)

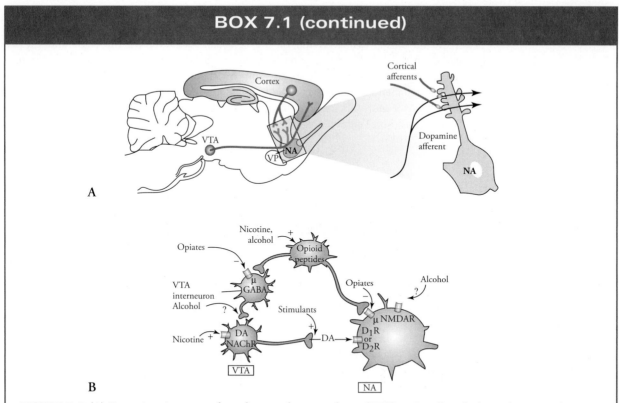

FIGURE 7.3 (A) Dopaminergic neurons from the ventral tegmental area (VTA) project through the nucleus accumbens (NA) and synapse onto the dendrites of medium spiny neurons. These neurons also receive input from cortical neurons. Neurons from the nucleus accumbens project to the ventral pallidum (VP) (adapted from Hyman et al., 2006). (B) Neurons that release an opioid or dopamine directly impact neurons within the nucleus accumbens. The release of these neurochemicals is influenced by other psychoactive drugs, such as alcohol and nicotine (adapted from Hyman et al., 2006).

linked to learning and memory. Within the nucleus accumbens, cortical neurons that release glutamate provide a rich input to the nucleus accumbens, an input that is thought to carry information about the specific details of the sensory systems engaged. At the same time, dopaminergic input on to these neurons provides a diffuse input that can signal the motivational state of the organism. When paired, this dopaminergic input may help select the relevant pattern of glutamatergic input, acting as a kind of teacher that binds sensory attributes with reward value, thereby enhancing the motivational significance of these cues (Hyman et al., 2006).

When does the dopaminergic teacher instruct the nucleus accumbens to learn? To answer this question, researchers have examined neural activity in monkeys while they work for reward (e.g., a sip of fruit juice). Electrodes were lowered into the source of the dopaminergic input, neurons within the ventral tegmental area (Schultz, 2007). These neurons exhibit a low level of tonic activity. When the animal received an unexpected reward, the neurons showed a burst of firing. If the animal was then trained with signaled reward, the signal began to elicit a burst of activity. The expected reward itself produced no effect. If, however, the expected reward was omitted, there

was an inhibition of neural activity at the time of reward. What these observations suggest is that dopamine activity does not simply report whether or not a reward has occurred. Instead, dopamine activity seems to code the "reward prediction error"— the deviation between what the animal received and what it expected (Schultz, 2006):

Dopamine response = Reward occurred − Reward predicted

The notion that learning is a function of the discrepancy between what the animal received and what it expected parallels the learning rule proposed by Rescorla and Wagner (1972). As discussed in Chapter 4,

Continued

BOX 7.1 (continued)

K. C. Berridge

T. E. Robinson

learning appears to occur when an event is unexpected. The best example of this is observed in the blocking paradigm, where prior learning that one cue (e.g., a tone) predicts the US blocks learning about an added cue (e.g., a light). Interestingly, dopaminergic neurons within the ventral tegmentum exhibit this phenomenon, producing a burst of activity to the originally paired cue but not the added one. Notice too that this represents another instance in which a portion of the midbrain (the ventral tegmental area) acts as an informed instructor to promote learning within the forebrain. An analogous function was ascribed earlier to the periaqueductal gray (Box 4.3) and dorsal raphe nucleus (Box 5.5).

Abused drugs may encourage a cycle of dependency because they have a pharmacological advantage. For example, psychostimulants artificially drive dopaminergic activity, and in this way act as a kind of Trojan horse that fools the nervous system, producing a spike in dopamine activity that the brain interprets as a

positive prediction error (Hyman et al., 2006). This reinforces new learning and links the sensory cues associated with drug administration to reward, giving them a motivational value that fuels the acquired drug craving and predisposes an addict to relapse. Anyone who has quit smoking can tell you that they are weakest, and most prone to relapse, when they are reexposed to the cues associated with smoking. Individuals who have not smoked for months may experience an irresistible urge to smoke again if they enter a bar where other people are smoking. These observations suggest that cues associated with drug consumption acquire an incentive value that can fuel drug craving.

Interestingly, the craving that fuels drug taking appears to be physiologically and psychologically distinct from the process that underlies how much we consciously "like" an addictive substance (Berridge, Robinson, & Aldridge, 2009; Robinson & Berridge, 2003). Liking is related to the hedonic state elicited by reward and can be inferred behaviorally from facial expressions. For example, both humans and rats exhibit a stereotyped pattern of oral activity (a "yum" response) when a sweet substance is placed on the tongue. Interestingly, microinjecting an opioid into small regions (*hedonic hot spots*) of the nucleus accumbens enhances signs of liking. A second hedonic hot spot has been identified within an adjoining region, the *ventral pallidum* (*VP*). Here too, local infusion of an opioid agonist enhances the liking response to a sweet solution. Observations such as these have led researchers to suggest that the pleasurable component of reward is linked to opioid activity within the nucleus accumbens and ventral pallidum (Berridge & Krinelbach, 2008).

For many years, researchers have assumed that dopamine release plays a key role in mediating pleasure. Given this, it was surprising that the complete destruction of dopaminergic neurons innervating the nucleus accumbens had no effect on opioid-induced liking (Robinson & Berridge, 2003). Conversely, liking reactions to sweet tastes are not elicited by manipulations that engage dopaminergic neurons. These observations suggest that dopamine activity is neither required (necessary) nor sufficient to generate liking. Yet it was well known that manipulations that impact dopaminergic neurons can dramatically affect drug-taking behavior (Koob, 1999; Hyman et al., 2006). For example, self-administration of a psychostimulant is blocked by pretreatment with a dopamine antagonist or a physiological manipulation that destroys dopaminergic neurons in this region. Across a range of tasks, in the absence of dopamine, rats cannot use information about rewards to motivate goal-directed behavior; they cannot act on their preferences.

Robinson and Berridge have suggested that manipulations of the dopamine system affect motivation because they impact a distinct quality of reward (Berridge, Robinson, & Aldridge, 2009; Robinson & Berridge, 2003). Rather than influencing how much the animal consciously likes the reward, they propose that dopamine activity is coupled to an unconscious process that they call wanting. They see wanting as related to the underlying motivational value of the reward, encoding the degree to which the organism is driven to obtain and consume the reward independent of whether consumption engenders pleasure. From this perspective, cues paired with reward gain an incentive salience that drives a form of wanting, transforming

Continued

BOX 7.1 (continued)

sensory signals of reward into attractive, desired goals. These cues act as motivational magnets that unconsciously pull the animal to approach the reward. More formally, a positive prediction error engages dopamine activity and acts as a teacher, fostering the association of sensory cues with reward. From this view, dopamine activity within the nucleus accumbens binds the hedonic properties of a goal to motivation, driving the wanting that can fuel drug craving. Supporting this, research has shown that drug-paired cues acquire conditioned value and will support new instrumental learning in a Pavolian-to-instrumental transfer test. This effect depends on dopamine activity and learning within the basolateral amygdala (Box 4.3).

J. W. Grau

nucleus accumbens   A portion of the basal ganglia involved in reward, addiction, and reinforcement learning.

psychopharmacology   The study of how drugs affect psychological processes and behavior.

Conditioned Emotional States or Reward-Specific Expectancies?   The two-process theory assumes that classical conditioning mediates instrumental behavior through the conditioning of positive or negative emotions depending on the emotional valence of the reinforcer. However, organisms also acquire specific reward expectancies instead of just categorical positive or negative emotions during instrumental and classical conditioning (Peterson & Trapold, 1980). Furthermore, in some cases reward-specific expectancies appear to determine the outcome of Pavlovian instrumental transfer experiments (e.g., Urcuioli, 2005).

In one study, for example, solid food pellets and a sugar solution were used as USs in a Pavlovian instrumental transfer test with rats (Kruse et al., 1983). During the transfer phase, the CS+ for food pellets facilitated instrumental responding reinforced with pellets much more than instrumental behavior reinforced with the sugar solution. Correspondingly, a CS+ for sugar increased instrumental behavior reinforced with sugar more than instrumental behavior reinforced with food pellets. Thus, expectancies for specific rewards rather than a general positive emotional state determined the results in the transfer test. (For reward-specific expectancies in human drug-seeking behavior, see Hogarth et al., 2007.)

R–O and S(R–O) Relations in Instrumental Conditioning

So far we have considered two different associations that can motivate instrumental behavior, Thorndike's S–R association and the S–O association, which activates a reward-specific expectancy or emotional state. However, the instigation of instrumental behavior involves more than just these two associations. Notice that neither the S–R nor the S–O association involves a direct link between the response (R) and the reinforcer or outcome (O). This is counterintuitive. If you asked your roommate why she was combing her hair, she would reply that she expected that combing her hair (R) would improve her appearance (O). Similarly, you turn on a movie because you expect that watching the movie will be entertaining, and you open the refrigerator because you anticipate that doing so will enable you to get something to eat. All of these accounts are descriptions of R–O associations between the instrumental response and the reinforcing outcome. Although our informal explanations of instrumental behavior emphasize R–O associations, such associations do not exist in two-process models.

Evidence of R–O Associations   The most common technique used to demonstrate the existence of R–O associations involves devaluing the reinforcer after conditioning. Reinforcer devaluation involves making the reinforcer less attractive. If the reinforcer

B. Balleine

is food, for example, one can make the food less attractive by conditioning a taste aversion to the food. If the instrumental response occurs because of an R–O association, devaluation of the reinforcer should reduce the rate of the instrumental response.

The reinforcer devaluation procedure used in instrumental conditioning is similar to the US devaluation procedure I previously described in studies of Pavlovian conditioning (Chapter 4). There, US devaluation was used to determine whether the conditioned response is mediated by the memory of the US. If US devaluation disrupts the ability of the CS to elicit a CR, one may conclude that the CS activated the memory of the US and responding declined because the US memory was no longer as attractive. Following a similar rationale, if reinforcer devaluation disrupts instrumental behavior, this shows that the memory of the outcome (O) was involved in motivating the instrumental behavior.

For many years, studies of the role of R–O associations in instrumental conditioning were conducted primarily with laboratory rats (for reviews, see Colwill & Rescorla, 1986; Ostlund, Winterbauer, & Balleine, 2008). More recently, however, R–O associations have also been examined in experiments with human participants. Many of these experiments have been conducted as a part of efforts to better understand the learning mechanisms that contribute to drug-seeking behavior.

One recent study, for example, was conducted with students at the University of Nottingham who smoked at least several times a week (Hogarth & Chase, 2011). A two-choice concurrent schedule of reinforcement was used. The two responses were pressing two different keys on a computer keyboard. Pressing one of the keys was reinforced with the picture of one-fourth of a cigarette on the screen, whereas pressing the other key was reinforced with the picture of one-fourth of a chocolate bar. Each response had a 50% chance of being reinforced on any given trial. The cigarettes and chocolate bars earned were summed across trials, and the corresponding number of each item was placed in a basket on the participant's desk.

After 60 acquisition trials, the participants were assigned to one of two outcome devaluation groups. For one group, the value of the cigarette outcome was reduced. For the other, the value of the chocolate bar outcome was devalued. Devaluation was accomplished by satiating the participants with the corresponding reinforcer. Participants in the chocolate devaluation group were allowed to eat up to eight chocolate bars in 10 minutes. Participants in the cigarette devaluation group were allowed to smoke an entire cigarette.

Right after the devaluation procedure, the participants were again tested on the concurrent schedule but this time they were told that although they would continue to earn cigarettes and chocolate bars, they would not find out how many of each they obtained until the end of the session. This was intended to maintain responding on the basis of the current status of the memory of each reinforcer.

Figure 7.4 shows how often the participants elected to press the response that was reinforced with cigarettes during the training phase and after the devaluation procedure. During training, about 50% of the responses were made on the cigarette key, with the remaining responses performed for chocolate bars. This indicates that the two outcomes were equally preferred before devaluation. When the tobacco outcome was devalued, responding on the cigarette key significantly declined. In contrast, when the chocolate outcome was devalued, responding on the cigarette key increased, indicating a decline in the chocolate response. Thus, devaluation produced a decline in behavior specific to the response whose reinforcer had been devalued.

The result of the devaluation tests indicate that training established an R–O association linking each response with its specific reinforcer. The results cannot be explained by S–R associations because S–R associations are not influenced by reinforcer devaluation.

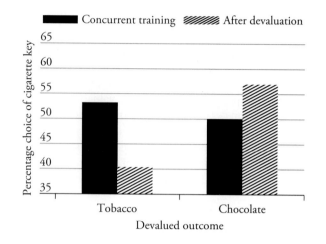

FIGURE 7.4 Percentage of responses on the cigarette key during original training and following devaluation of either the tobacco or chocolate response outcome. (Based on Hogarth & Chase, 2011.)

The results also cannot be explained by S–O associations because S–O associations could not explain the response specificity of the devaluation effects that were observed.

The present results indicate that R–O associations are involved in instrumental drug-seeking behavior. This claim appears to be at odds with my previous description of drug addiction as driven by S–R mechanisms. As it turns out, both views are correct and have been incorporated into a theory that suggests that R–O mechanisms predominate in free-operant situations, whereas S–R mechanisms are activated when drug taking is a response to drug-related cues (Hogarth & Chase, 2011; Hogarth, Dickinson, & Duka, 2010).

Hierarchical S(R–O) Relations   The evidence cited above clearly shows that organisms learn to associate an instrumental response with its outcome. However, R–O associations cannot act alone to produce instrumental behavior. As Mackintosh and Dickinson (1979) pointed out, the fact that the instrumental response activates an expectancy of the reinforcer is not sufficient to tell us what caused the response in the first place. An additional factor is required to activate the R–O association. One possibility is that the R–O association is activated by the stimuli (S) that are present when the response is reinforced. According to this view, in addition to activating R directly, S also activates the R–O association. Stated informally, the subject comes to think of the R–O association when it encounters S and that motivates it to make the instrumental response.

Skinner (1938) proposed many years ago that S, R, and O in instrumental conditioning are connected through a conditional S(R–O) relation, which he called the *three-term contingency*. The idea that instrumental behavior is mediated by the S(R–O) relation was vigorously pursued at the end of the twentieth century by investigators working in the associationist tradition. The accumulated body of evidence, with both laboratory animals and human participants, has firmly established that S(R–O) associations are learned during the course of instrumental conditioning (e.g., Colwill & Rescorla, 1990; Gámez & Rosas, 2007). Experiments on S(R–O) associations typically use complicated discrimination training procedures that are beyond the scope of the present discussion. I will describe discrimination training procedures in Chapter 8.

Response Allocation and Behavioral Economics

Although contemporary associative analyses of instrumental motivation go far beyond Thorndike's law of effect, they are a part of the Thorndikeian and Pavlovian tradition that views the world of behavior in terms of stimuli, responses, and associations. The response-allocation approach is based on a radically different worldview. Instead of considering instrumental conditioning in terms of the reinforcement of a response in the presence of certain stimuli, response allocation is a molar approach that focuses on how instrumental conditioning procedures put limitations on an organism's activities and cause redistributions of behavior among available response options.

Antecedents of the Response-Allocation Approach

Reinforcers were initially considered to be special kinds of stimuli. Thorndike, for example, characterized a reinforcer as a stimulus that produces a *satisfying state of affairs*. Various proposals were made about the special characteristics a stimulus must have to serve as a reinforcer. Although there were differences of opinion, for about a half a century after Thorndike's law of effect, theoreticians agreed that reinforcers were special stimuli that strengthened instrumental behavior.

Consummatory-Response Theory   The first challenge to the idea that reinforcers are stimuli came from Fred Sheffield and his colleagues, who formulated the **consummatory-response theory**. Many reinforcers, such as food and water, elicit species-typical unconditioned responses, such as chewing, licking, and swallowing. The consummatory-response theory attributes reinforcement to these species-typical behaviors. It asserts that species-typical consummatory responses (eating, drinking, and the like) are themselves the critical feature of reinforcers. In support of this idea, Sheffield, Roby, and Campbell (1954) showed that saccharin, an artificial sweetener, can serve as an effective reinforcer, even though it has no nutritive value and hence cannot satisfy a biological need. The reinforcing properties of artificial sweeteners now provide the foundations of a flourishing diet food industry. Apart from their commercial value, however, artificial sweeteners were important in advancing our thinking about instrumental motivation.

The consummatory-response theory was a radical innovation because it moved the search for reinforcers from special kinds of stimuli to special types of responses. Reinforcer responses were assumed to be special because they involved the consummation, or completion, of an instinctive behavior sequence. (See discussion of consummatory behavior in Chapter 2.) The theory assumed that consummatory responses (e.g., chewing and swallowing) are fundamentally different from various potential instrumental responses, such as running, opening a latch, or pressing a lever. David Premack took issue with this and suggested that reinforcer responses are special only because they are more likely to occur than the instrumental responses they follow.

The Premack Principle   Premack pointed out that responses that accompany commonly used reinforcers involve activities that individuals are highly likely to perform. In a food reinforcement experiment, participants are typically food-deprived and therefore are highly likely to eat. By contrast, instrumental responses are typically low-probability activities. An experimentally naive rat, for example, is much less likely to press a response lever than it is to eat. Premack (1965) proposed that this difference in response probabilities is critical for reinforcement. Formally, the **Premack principle** can be stated as follows:

> *Given two responses of different likelihood, H and L, the opportunity to perform the higher probability response (H) after the lower probability response (L) will result in reinforcement of response L. (L → H reinforces L.) The opportunity to perform the lower probability response (L) after the higher probability response (H) will not result in reinforcement of response H. (H → L does not reinforce H.)*

The Premack principle focuses on the difference in the likelihood of the instrumental and reinforcer responses. Therefore, it is also called the **differential probability principle**. Eating will reinforce bar pressing because eating is typically more likely than bar pressing. Beyond that, Premack's theory denied that there is anything special about food or eating behavior.

The Premack principle has been repeatedly demonstrated in studies with both human participants and laboratory animals. The power of the Premack principle is that potentially any high-probability activity can be an effective reinforcer for a response that the individual is not inclined to perform. In laboratory rats, for example, drinking a drop of sucrose is a high-probability response, and as one might predict, sucrose is effective in reinforcing lever pressing. Running in a running wheel is also a high-probability response in rats. Thus, one might predict that running would also effectively reinforce lever pressing. Numerous studies have confirmed this prediction. Belke and Hancock (2003), for example, compared lever pressing on a fixed-interval 30-second schedule, reinforced by either sucrose or the opportunity to run in a wheel for 15 seconds. In different phases of the experiment, the rats were tested with different concentrations of the sucrose reinforcer.

Lever pressing on the FI 30-second schedule is summarized in Figure 7.5 for the wheel-running reinforcer and for sucrose concentrations ranging from 0 to 10%. The data are presented in terms of the rate of lever pressing in successive 5-second periods of the FI 30-second schedule. As expected with a fixed-interval schedule, response rates increased closer to the end of the 30-second period. Wheel running as the reinforcer was just as effective as 2.5% sucrose. Wheel running was more effective than 0% sucrose, but at a sucrose concentration of 10%, responding for sucrose exceeded responding for running.

Applications of the Premack Principle The Premack principle had an enduring impact in the design of reinforcement procedures used to help various clinical populations and remains the basis for various point systems and voucher systems used in residential treatment settings. In an early application, Mitchell and Stoffelmayr (1973) studied two hospitalized patients with chronic schizophrenia who refused all tangible reinforcers that were offered (candy, cigarettes, fruit, and biscuits). The other patients on the ward participated in a work project that involved removing tightly wound copper

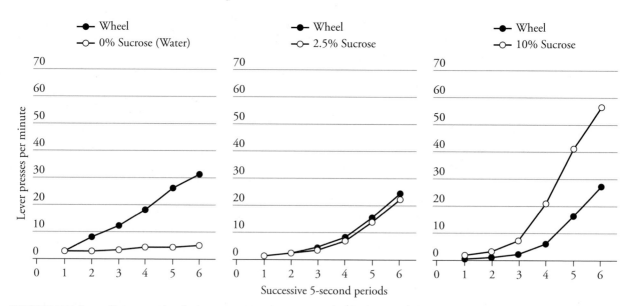

FIGURE 7.5 Rate of lever pressing during successive 5-minute periods of a fixed interval 30-second schedule reinforced with access to a running wheel or access to various concentrations of sucrose. (Based on Belke & Hancock, 2003.)

wire from coils. The two participants in this study did not take part in the coil-stripping project and spent most of their time just sitting. Given this limited behavioral repertoire, what could be an effective reinforcer? The Premack principle suggests that the opportunity to sit should be a good reinforcer for these patients considering how much time they spent sitting. To test this idea, the investigators gave the patients a chance to sit down only if they worked a bit on the coil-stripping task.

Each participant was trained separately. At the start of each trial, they were asked or coaxed into standing. A piece of cable was then handed to them. If they made the required coil-stripping responses, they were permitted to sit for about 90 seconds, and then the next trial started. This procedure was highly successful. As long as the instrumental contingency was in effect, the two patients worked at a much higher rate than when they were simply told to participate in the coil-stripping project. Normal instructions and admonitions to participate in coil stripping were entirely ineffective, but taking advantage of the high-probability sitting response worked very well.

Other interesting studies have been conducted with children with autism who engaged in unusual repetitive or stereotyped behaviors. One such behavior, called *delayed echolalia*, involves repeating words. For example, one autistic child was heard to say over and over again, "Ding! ding! ding! You win again," and "Match Game 83." Another form stereotyped behavior, *perseverative behavior*, involves persistent manipulation of an object. For example, the child may repeatedly handle only certain plastic toys.

The high probability of echolalia and perseverative behavior in children with autism suggests that these responses may be effectively used as reinforcers in treatment procedures. Charlop, Kurtz, and Casey (1990) compared the effectiveness of different forms of reinforcement in training various academic-related skills in several children with autism (see also Hanley et al., 2000). The tasks included identifying which of several objects was the same or different from the one held up by the teacher, adding up coins, and correctly responding to sentences designed to teach receptive pronouns or prepositions. In one experimental condition, a preferred food (e.g., a small piece of chocolate, cereal, or a cookie) served as the reinforcer, in the absence of programmed food deprivation. In another condition, the opportunity to perform a stereotyped response for 3–5 seconds served as the reinforcer.

Some of the results of the study are illustrated in Figure 7.6. Each panel represents the data for a different student. Notice that in each case, the opportunity to engage in a prevalent stereotyped response resulted in better performance on the training tasks than food reinforcement. Delayed echolalia and perseverative behavior both served to increase task performance above what was observed with food reinforcement. These results indicate that high-probability responses can serve to reinforce lower probability responses, even if the reinforcer responses are not characteristic of normal behavior.

The Premack principle advanced our thinking about reinforcement in significant ways. It encouraged thinking about reinforcers as responses rather than as stimuli, and it greatly expanded the range of activities investigators started to use as reinforcers. With the Premack principle, any behavior could serve as a reinforcer provided that it was more likely than the instrumental response. Differential probability as the key to reinforcement paved the way for applications of reinforcement procedures to all sorts of human problems. However, problems with the measurement of response probability and a closer look at instrumental conditioning procedures moved subsequent theoretical developments past the Premack principle.

The Response-Deprivation Hypothesis

In most instrumental conditioning procedures, the probability of the reinforcer activity is kept at a high level by restricting access to the reinforcer. Laboratory rats reinforced with food are typically not given food before

FIGURE 7.6 Task performance for two children with autism. One student's behavior was reinforced with food or the opportunity to engage in delayed echolalia. Another student's behavior was reinforced with food or the opportunity to engage in perseverative responding. (Responding during baseline periods was also reinforced with food.) (Based on "Using Aberrant Behaviors as Reinforcers for Autistic Children," by M. H. Charlop, P. F. Kurtz, and F. G. Casey, *Journal of Applied Behavior Analysis, 23,* pp. 163–181.)

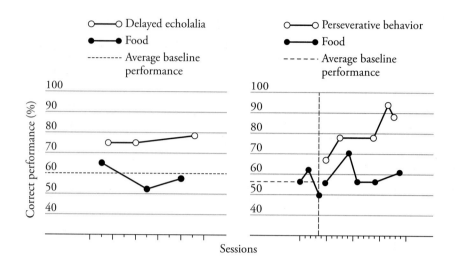

Courtesy of W. Timberlake

W. Timberlake

the experimental session and receive a small pellet of food for each lever-press response. These limitations on access to food (and eating) are very important. If we were to give the rat a full meal for one lever press, chances are it would not respond more than once or twice a day. Generally, restrictions on the opportunity to engage in the reinforcing response increase its effectiveness as a reinforcer.

Premack (1965) recognized the importance of restricting access to the reinforcer, but that was not the main idea behind his theory. By contrast, Timberlake and Allison (1974; see also Allison, 1993) abandoned the differential probability principle altogether and argued that restriction of the reinforcer activity was the critical factor for instrumental reinforcement. This proposal is called the **response-deprivation hypothesis**.

In particularly decisive tests of the response-deprivation hypothesis, several investigators found that even a low-probability response can serve as a reinforcer provided that participants are restricted from making this response (Timberlake & Allison, 1974; Eisenberger et al., 1967). Johnson and colleagues (2003) tested this prediction in a classroom setting with students who had moderate-to-severe mental retardation. For each student, teachers identified things the students were not likely to do. For example, filing cards and tracing letters were both low-probability responses for Edgar, but tracing was the less likely of the two responses. Nevertheless, the opportunity to trace became an effective reinforcer for filing behavior if access to tracing was restricted below baseline levels. This result is contrary to the Premack principle and shows that response deprivation is more basic to reinforcement effects than differential response probability.

The response-deprivation hypothesis provided a simple new strategy for creating reinforcers, namely restricting access to the reinforcer activity. It is interesting to note that some restriction is inherent to all instrumental conditioning procedures. All instrumental conditioning procedures require withholding the reinforcer until the specified instrumental response has been performed. The response-deprivation hypothesis points out that this defining feature of instrumental conditioning is critical for producing a reinforcement effect.

Traditional views of reinforcement assume that a reinforcer is something that exists independent of an instrumental conditioning procedure. Food, for example, was thought to be a reinforcer whether or not it was used to reinforce lever pressing. The response-deprivation hypothesis makes explicit the radically different idea that a reinforcer is produced by the instrumental contingency itself. How instrumental contingencies create reinforcers and increases in the instrumental response has remained a topic of great interest to behavioral scientists (e.g., Baum, 2012).

The Response Allocation Approach

The response-allocation approach considers the problem of reinforcement and instrumental conditioning from a broader perspective than the Premack principle or the response-deprivation hypothesis. Instead of just focusing on the instrumental and reinforcer responses, the response-allocation approach considers the broad range of activities that are always available to an individual. During the course of a day, you spend time getting dressed, eating, walking, driving, listening to music, talking to friends, going to class, studying, taking a nap, and so forth. Even while you are sitting in a class, you can listen to the professor, look at the slides on the screen, daydream about what you will do Saturday night, take notes, or sneak a peek at your text messages. Response allocation refers to how an individual distributes his or her responses among the various options that are available.

Courtesy of J. Allison

J. Allison

Scientists who employ the response-allocation approach examine how the distribution of responses is altered when an instrumental conditioning procedure is introduced and what factors determine the nature of the response reallocation (e.g., Allison, 1993; Timberlake, 1980, 1995). The starting point for these analyses is the *unconstrained baseline*. The unconstrained baseline is how the individual allocates his or her responses to various behavioral options when there are no restrictions and presumably reflects the individual's unique preferences. Think about how you might spend your time when you are on summer vacation and don't have to go to school. You may stay in bed, sleep later in the morning, play video games, visit friends, go fishing, or spend time getting a tan, but you probably will not spend much time reading textbooks or taking notes. That is the unconstrained baseline.

The unconstrained baseline becomes seriously disrupted when the new school year starts and you have to start attending classes again. Now you can no longer afford to sleep as late in the morning or spend as much time visiting friends. In addition, you are likely to devote more effort to studying and taking notes. In an analogous fashion, the introduction of an instrumental conditioning procedure disrupts an organism's unconstrained baseline and causes a redistribution of responses.

Consider, for example, how a high school student may distribute his or her activities between studying and interacting with friends on Facebook. Figure 7.7 represents time spent on Facebook on the vertical axis and time spent studying on the horizontal axis. In the absence of restrictions, the student will probably spend a lot more time on Facebook than studying. This is represented by the open circle in Figure 7.7 and is the unconstrained baseline in this situation. Without restrictions, the student spends 60 minutes on Facebook for every 15 minutes of studying. The unrestricted baseline is sometimes also called the **behavioral bliss point**. The term *bliss point* is borrowed from economics and refers to a preferred response allocation in the absence of restrictions.

Imposing an Instrumental Contingency   How would the introduction of an instrumental contingency between studying and being on Facebook disrupt the student's response allocation? The outcome depends on the nature of the contingency. Figure 7.7 shows a schedule line starting at the origin and increasing at a 45° angle. This line defines a schedule of reinforcement, according to which the student is allowed to be on Facebook for as long as he or she spends studying. If the student studies for 10 minutes, he or she will get 10 minutes on Facebook; if he or she studies for an hour, the student will get to be on Facebook for an hour. What might be the consequences of such a schedule constraint?

Individuals will generally defend their response allocations against challenges to the unrestricted baseline or bliss point condition. However, the interesting thing is that the baseline response allocation usually cannot be reestablished after an

FIGURE 7.7 Allocation of behavior between spending time on Facebook and studying. The open circle shows the optimal allocation, or behavioral bliss point, obtained when there are no constraints on either activity. The schedule line represents a schedule of reinforcement in which the student is required to study for the same amount of time that he or she spends on Facebook. Notice that once this schedule of reinforcement is imposed, it is no longer possible for the student to achieve the behavioral bliss point. The schedule deprives the student of time on Facebook and forces or motivates an increase in studying.

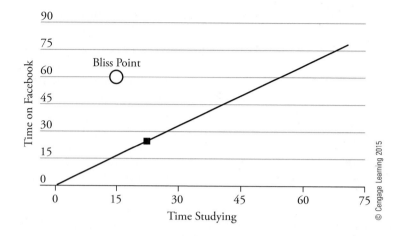

instrumental contingency has been introduced. In our example, the unrestricted baseline point was 60 minutes on Facebook for every 15 minutes of studying. Once the instrumental contingency is imposed, there is no way the student can be on Facebook for 60 minutes and only study for 15 minutes. If he or she insists on being on Facebook for 60 minutes, the student will have to tolerate adding 45 minutes to his or her studying time. On the other hand, if the student insists on spending only the 15 minutes on his or her studies (as in the baseline condition), he or she will have to make do with 45 minutes less on Facebook. Defending the baseline study time or defending the baseline Facebook time both have their disadvantages. That is often the dilemma posed by an instrumental contingency. How this dilemma is resolved is the central issue of the response-allocation approach.

Given that the instrumental contingency shown in Figure 7.7 makes it impossible to return to the unrestricted baseline, the redistribution of responses between the instrumental and contingent behaviors becomes a matter of compromise. The rate of one response is brought as close as possible to its preferred level without moving the other response too far away from its preferred level.

Staddon, for example, proposed a **minimum-deviation model** of behavioral regulation to solve the dilemma of schedule constraints (Staddon, 1983/2003). According to this model, introduction of a response-reinforcer contingency causes organisms to redistribute their behavior between the instrumental and contingent responses in a way that minimizes the total deviation of the two responses from the unrestricted baseline or bliss point. The minimum deviation point is shown by the dark symbol on the schedule line in Figure 7.7. For situations in which the free baseline cannot be achieved in the face of a schedule constraint, the minimum-deviation model provides one view of how organisms settle for the next best thing.

Explanation of Reinforcement Effects How are reinforcement effects produced according to the response allocation perspective? A reinforcement effect is identified by an increase in the occurrence of an instrumental response above the level of that behavior in the absence of the response–reinforcer contingency. The schedule line shown in Figure 7.7 involves restricting time on Facebook below the level specified by the baseline point. To move toward the preferred baseline level, the student has to increase his or her studying so as to gain more Facebook time. This is precisely what occurs in typical instrumental conditioning procedures. Access to the reinforcer is restricted; to gain more opportunity to engage in the reinforcer response, the individual has to perform more of the instrumental response. Thus, increased performance of the instrumental response (a reinforcement effect) results from a reallocation of responses that minimize deviations from the free baseline or bliss point.

BOX 7.2

The Response-Allocation Approach and Behavior Therapy

Considering instrumental conditioning as a matter of response allocation not only provides new insights into age-old theoretical issues concerning reinforcement but also suggests alternative approaches to behavior therapy (Farmer-Dougan, 1998; Timberlake & Farmer-Dougan, 1991). For example, it forces us to consider the broader behavioral context in which an instrumental contingency is introduced. Depending on that behavioral context, a reinforcement procedure may increase or decrease the target response. Thus, the response-allocation approach can provide insights into situations in which introducing a reinforcement procedure produces an unexpected decrease in the instrumental response.

One area of behavior therapy in which reinforcement procedures are surprisingly ineffective is the use of parental social reinforcement to increase a child's pro-social behavior. A parent whose child frequently misbehaves is encouraged to provide

more social approval for positive behavior on the assumption that low rates of parental reinforcement are responsible for the child's misbehavior. Viken and McFall (1994) pointed out that the common failure of such reinforcement procedures is predictable if we consider the unconstrained baseline or bliss point for the child.

Figure 7.8 shows the behavioral space for parental social reinforcement and positive child behavior. The open circle represents the child's presumed unconstrained or preferred baseline. Left to his or her own devices, the child prefers a lot of social reinforcement while emitting few positive behaviors. The dashed line represents the low rate of parental reinforcement in effect before a therapeutic intervention. According to this schedule line, the child has to perform two positive responses to receive each social reinforcer from the parent. The solid point on the line indicates the equilibrium point, where positive responses by the child and social

reinforcers earned are equally far from their respective bliss point values.

The therapeutic procedure involves increasing the rate of social reinforcement, let's say to a ratio of 1:1. This is illustrated by the solid line in Figure 7.8. Now the child receives one social reinforcer for each positive behavior. The equilibrium point is again illustrated by the filled data point. Notice that with the increased social reinforcement, the child can get more social reinforcers without having to make more positive responses. In fact, the child can increase his or her rate of social reinforcement while performing fewer positive responses. No wonder, then, that the therapeutic reinforcement procedure does not increase the rate of positive responses. The unexpected result of increased social reinforcement illustrated in Figure 7.8 suggests that solutions to behavior problems require careful consideration of the relation between the new instrumental contingency and prior reinforcement conditions.

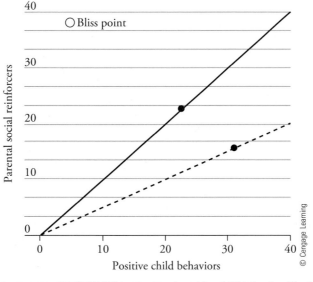

FIGURE 7.8 Hypothetical data on parental social reinforcement and positive child behavior. The behavioral bliss point for the child is indicated by the open circle. The dashed line represents the rate of social reinforcement for positive behavior in effect prior to introduction of a treatment procedure. The solid line represents the rate of social reinforcement for positive behavior set up by the behavior therapy procedure. The solid point on each line represents the equilibrium point for each schedule.

Viewing Reinforcement Contingencies in a Broader Behavioral Context The above explanation of how schedule constraints produce reinforcement effects considers only the instrumental and reinforcer responses (studying and being on Facebook). However, a student's environment most likely provides a much greater range of options. Instrumental contingencies do not occur in a behavioral vacuum. They occur in the context of all of the responses and reinforcers the participant has available. Furthermore, that broader behavioral context can significantly influence how the person adjusts to a schedule constraint. For example, if the student enjoys listening to his or her iPod as much as being on Facebook, restrictions of Facebook time may not increase studying behavior. Rather, the student may switch to listening to the iPod, playing a video game, or hanging out with friends. Any of these options will undermine the instrumental contingency. The student could listen to his or her iPod or hang out with friends in place of being on Facebook without increasing studying behavior.

This example illustrates that accurate prediction of the effects of an instrumental conditioning procedure requires considering the broader context of the organism's response options. Focusing on just the instrumental response and its antecedent and consequent stimuli (i.e., the associative structure of instrumental behavior) is not enough. The effect of a particular instrumental conditioning procedure depends on what alternative sources of reinforcement are available, how those other reinforcers are related to the particular one involved in the instrumental contingency, and the cost of obtaining those alternatives. These issues have been systematically examined with the application of economic concepts to the problem of response allocation.

Behavioral Economics

The response-allocation approach redefined the fundamental issue in reinforcement. It shifted attention away from the idea that reinforcers are special stimuli that enter into special associative relations with the instrumental response and its antecedents. With the response-allocation approach, the fundamental question is: *How is the allocation of behavior among an individual's response options altered by the constraints imposed by an instrumental conditioning procedure?*

Students who have studied economics may recognize a similarity here to problems addressed by economists. Economists, similar to psychologists, strive to understand changes in behavior in terms of preexisting preferences and restrictions on fulfilling those preferences. As Bickel, Green, and Vuchinich (1995) noted, "Economics is the study of the allocation of behavior within a system of constraint" (p. 258). In the economic arena, the restrictions on behavior are imposed by our income and the price of the goods that we want to purchase. In instrumental conditioning situations, the restrictions are provided by the number of responses an organism is able to make (its "income") and the number of responses required to obtain each reinforcer (the "price" of the reinforcer).

Psychologists have become interested in the similarities between economic restrictions in the marketplace and schedule constraints in instrumental conditioning. The analysis of response allocation in terms of economic concepts can be a bit complex. For the sake of simplicity, I will concentrate on the basic ideas that have had the most impact on understanding reinforcement. (For a more complete discussion see Hursh et al., 2013.)

Consumer Demand Fundamental to the application of economic concepts to the problem of reinforcement is the relation between the price of a commodity and how much of it is purchased. This relation is called the **demand curve**. Figure 7.9 shows three examples of demand curves. Curve A illustrates a situation in which the consumption of a commodity is very easily influenced by its price. This is the case with candy.

FIGURE 7.9 Hypothetical consumer demand curves illustrating high sensitivity to price (Curve A), intermediate sensitivity (Curve B), and low sensitivity (Curve C).

If the price of candy increases substantially, the amount purchased quickly drops. Other commodities are less responsive to price changes (Curve C in Figure 7.9). The purchase of gasoline, for example, is not as easily discouraged by increases in price. People continue to purchase gas for their cars even if the price increases, showing a small decline only at the highest prices.

The degree to which price influences consumption is called **elasticity of demand**. Demand for candy is highly elastic. The more candy costs, the less you will buy. In contrast, demand for gasoline is much less elastic. People continue to purchase gas even if the price increases a great deal.

The concept of consumer demand has been used to analyze a variety of major behavior problems including eating and drug abuse (e.g., Epstein, Leddy, Temple, & Faith, 2007). In a recent laboratory study, for example, 10- to 12-year-old children increased their purchases of healthy foods as the price of unhealthy alternatives was increased (Epstein et al., 2006). The selection of healthy food also increased in a study of food choices in a restaurant when the healthy alternatives were reduced in price (Horgen & Brownell, 2002). Interestingly, a decrease in price was more effective in encouraging the selection of healthy foods than messages encouraging patrons to eat healthy.

The concept of consumer demand has been used to analyze instrumental behavior by considering the number of responses performed (or time spent responding) to be analogous to money and the reinforcer obtained to be analogous to the commodity that is purchased. The price of a reinforcer then is the time or number of responses required to obtain the reinforcer. Thus, the price of the reinforcer is determined by the schedule of reinforcement. The goal is to understand how instrumental responding (spending) is controlled by instrumental contingencies (prices).

Johnson and Bickel (2006), for example, investigated the elasticity of demand for cigarettes and money in smokers with a mean age of 40 years who were not trying to quit. The apparatus had three plungers the participants could pull, each for a different reinforcer. The reinforcers were three puffs on a cigarette, 5¢, or 25¢. Only one of the plungers (and its assigned reinforcer) was available in a particular session. The response requirement for obtaining the reinforcer was gradually increased during each session. The ratio requirement started at an FR 3 and was then raised to FR 30, 60, 100, 300, 600, and eventually 6,000. The investigators wanted to determine at what point the

W. K. Bickel

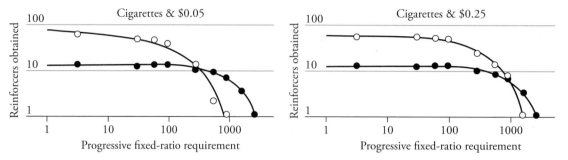

FIGURE 7.10 Demand curves for cigarettes (solid circles) and money (open circles) with progressively larger fixed-ratio requirements. The number of reinforcers obtained and the fixed-ratio requirements are both presented on logarithmic scales. (Based on Johnson & Bickel, 2006.)

participants would quit responding because the response requirement, or price, was too high. (None of the reinforcers could support responding on the FR 6,000 schedule.)

The results of the experiment are summarized in Figure 7.10. Data for the 5¢ reinforcer and the 25¢ reinforcer are presented in separate panels. Data for the cigarette reinforcer are reproduced in both panels for comparison. The greatest elasticity of demand occurred for the 5¢ monetary reinforcer. Here, the number of reinforcers obtained started decreasing as soon as more than three responses were required to obtain the 5¢ and dropped quickly when 100 or more responses were required. With the 25¢ reinforcer, the demand curve did not start to decline until the response requirement exceeded FR 300. As might be expected, the participants were most resistant to increases in the price of the cigarette reinforcer. With puffs at a cigarette, the number of reinforcers obtained did not start to decline until the response requirement was raised above an FR 600. These results show that the participants were willing to make many more responses for puffs at a cigarette than they were for the monetary rewards. No doubt the results would have been different if the experiment had been conducted with nonsmokers. (For a review of behavioral economic approaches to drug abuse, see Higgins, Heil, & Sigmon, 2013.)

Determinants of the Elasticity of Demand   The application of economic concepts to the analysis of instrumental conditioning would be of little value if it did not provide new insights into the mechanisms of reinforcement. As it turns out, economic concepts have helped to identify four major factors that influence how schedule constraints shape the reallocation of behavior. Each of these factors determines the degree of elasticity of demand, or the extent to which increases in price cause a decrease in consumption of that reinforcer.

(1) Availability of Substitutes   Perhaps the most important factor that influences the elasticity of demand is the availability of alternative reinforcers that can serve as substitutes for the reinforcer of interest. Whether increases in the price of one item cause a decline in consumption depends on the availability (and price) of other goods that can be used in place of the original item. The availability of substitutes increases the sensitivity of the original item to higher prices.

Newspaper subscriptions in the United States have seen a steep decline since news has become readily available on 24-hour cable channels and the Internet. This reflects the fact that cable and Internet sources are good substitutes for news obtained from newspapers. The availability of substitutes is also determining how often people go to the movies. Watching a movie on a rented or downloaded DVD is a reasonable substitute for going to the theater, especially now that surround sound is readily available in home-entertainment systems. Increases in the price of movie tickets at the theater encourage cost-conscious movie goers to wait for the release of the movie on DVD. In contrast, the amount of gasoline people buy is not as much influenced by price (especially in areas without mass transit) because there are few readily available substitutes for gasoline to fuel a car.

Contemporary analyses of drug abuse also recognize the importance of substitute reinforcers. Murphy, Correla, and Barnett (2007), for example, considered how one might reduce excessive alcohol intake among college students and concluded that "behavioral economic theory predicts that college students' decisions about drinking are related to the relative availability and price of alcohol, the relative availability and price of substance-free alternative activities, and the extent to which reinforcement from delayed substance-free outcomes is devalued relative to the immediate reinforcement associated with drinking" (p. 2573).

In an experimental study of individuals on a methadone maintenance program (Spiga, 2006, as cited in Hursh et al., 2013), the participants could obtain methadone by pressing a response lever on a progressively increasing FR schedule. In one condition, methadone was the only available drug. In another condition, the participants could obtain another opiate, hydromorphone, at a constant price (FR 32) by pressing a second lever. The investigators were interested in whether the availability of hydromorphone would influence the demand for methadone.

The results are presented in Figure 7.11. When methadone was the only reinforcer, increases in its price resulted in decreased consumption at the highest FR values. Less methadone was consumed if the other opiate, hydromorphone, was also available. Furthermore, responding for hydromorphone increased as the price of methadone increased. These results show that hydromorphone served as a substitute for methadone and because of that the availability of hydromorphone decreased the demand for methadone.

(2) Price Range   Another important determinant of the elasticity of demand is the price range of the commodity. Generally, an increase in price has less of an effect at low prices than at high prices. Consider, for example, the cost of candy. A 10% increase in the price from 50¢ to 55¢ is not likely to discourage consumption. But if the candy costs $5.00, a 10% increase to $5.50 might well discourage purchases.

Price effects on elasticity of demand are evident in Figure 7.10. Notice that at low prices there is little change in the number of reinforcers obtained as the price increases a bit. However, dramatic declines occur in the number of reinforcers obtained at the high end of the price range.

FIGURE 7.11 Number of doses of methadone obtained when only methadone was available at increasing prices (solid circles) and when methadone was available at increasing prices along with hydromorphone at a fixed low price (open circles). The number of doses of hydromorphone obtained is also shown as a function of the price of methadone (solid squares). Notice that consumption of hydromorphone increases as the price of methadone increased (based on Hursh et al., 2013).

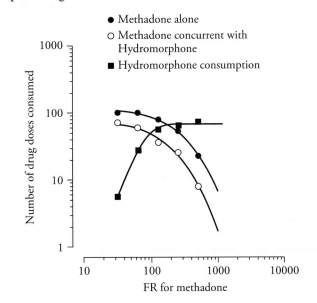

(3) Income Level   A third factor that determines elasticity of demand is the level of income. In general, the higher your income, the less deterred you will be by increases in price. This is also true for reinforcers obtained on schedules of reinforcement. In studies of instrumental conditioning, the number of responses or amount of time available for responding corresponds to income. These are resources an organism can use to respond to a schedule constraint. The more responses or time animals have available, the less their behavior is influenced by increases in the cost of the reinforcer (e.g., Silberberg, Warren-Bouton, & Asano, 1987; see also DeGrandpre, Bickel, Rizvi, & Hughes, 1993).

Income level also influences the choice of substitutes. In an interesting study of choice between healthy and unhealthy foods (Epstein et al., 2006), children aged 10–14 years were tested at three different income levels ($1, $3, and $5). At the low-income level, increases in the price of unhealthy foods (potato chips, cookies, pudding, and cola) led to increased choice of the healthy alternatives (apples, pretzels, yogurt, and milk). In contrast, at the high-income level, the children continued to purchase the unhealthy but preferred foods as the price of these foods went up. This left them with less money to buy the lower priced, healthier substitutes. Thus, at the high-income level, increases in the price of the junk food reduced the choice of healthy alternatives.

(4) Link to Complementary Commodity   The fourth factor that influences price sensitivity is the link of a reinforcer to a complementary commodity. Hot dogs and hot dog buns are complementary. People do not eat one without the other. Therefore, if the price of hot dogs drives down the number of hot dogs that are purchased, this will also decrease the purchase of hot dog buns. Numerous reinforcers are linked to complementary commodities. For individuals who both smoke and consume alcohol, these two reinforcers are typically linked, such that smoking increases with drinking and vice versa. Evidence suggests that among individuals on a methadone maintenance program, methadone and cigarettes are complementary commodities (Spiga et al., 2005). For rats, eating dry food and drinking water are complementary (Madden et al., 2007). The more food that is consumed, the more water is purchased.

Contributions of the Response-Allocation Approach and Behavioral Economics

Thinking about instrumental behavior as a problem of response allocation originated in considerations of the Premack principle and the response-deprivation hypothesis. Although challenges remain, this line of theorizing has made major contributions to how we think about the motivation of instrumental behavior. It is instructive to review some of these contributions.

- The response-allocation approach has moved us away from thinking about reinforcers as special kinds of stimuli or as special kinds of responses. We are now encouraged to look for the causes of reinforcement in how instrumental contingencies constrain the free flow of behavior. Reinforcement effects are regarded as the consequence of schedule constraints on an organism's ongoing activities.
- Instrumental conditioning procedures are no longer considered to "stamp in" or to strengthen instrumental behavior. Rather, instrumental conditioning is seen as creating a new distribution, or allocation, of responses. The resultant reallocation depends on tradeoffs between various options that are usefully characterized by behavioral economics.
- The response-allocation approach and behavioral economics provide new and precise ways of describing constraints that various instrumental conditioning procedures impose on an organism's behavioral repertoire. Most importantly, they emphasize

that instrumental behavior cannot be studied in a vacuum or behavioral test tube. Rather, all of the organism's response options at a given time must be considered as a system. Changes in one part of the system determine how other parts of the system can be altered. Constraints imposed by instrumental procedures are more or less effective depending on the nature of the constraint, the availability of substitutes, the organism's level of income, and linkages to complementary commodities. Given these complexities, response allocation and economic analyses are probably our best hope of understanding how instrumental behavior occurs in complex real-world environments.

Concluding Comments

Motivational processes in instrumental behavior have been addressed from two radically different perspectives and intellectual traditions, the associationist perspective rooted in Thorndike's law of effect and Pavlovian conditioning, and the response-allocation perspective rooted in Skinner's behavioral analysis. These two approaches differ in more ways than they are similar, making it difficult to imagine how they might be integrated. The fundamental concept in the associationist approach (the concept of an association) is entirely ignored in the response-allocation approach. Also, the mechanism of response allocation characterized by behavioral economics has no corresponding structure in the associationist approach. Both approaches have contributed significantly to our understanding of the motivation of instrumental behavior. Therefore, neither approach can be ignored in favor of the other.

One way to think about the two approaches is that they involve different levels of analysis. The associationist approach involves the molecular level and focuses on individual stimuli, responses, and their connections. In contrast, response allocation and behavioral economics operate at a molar level, considering the broader behavioral context in which an instrumental contingency is introduced. Thus, the response-allocation approach makes better contact with the complexities of an organism's ecology.

These alternative perspectives provide an exciting illustration of the nature of scientific inquiry. The inquiry has spanned intellectual developments from simple stimulus–response formulations to comprehensive considerations of how an organism's repertoire is constrained by instrumental contingencies and how organisms solve complex ecological problems. This area in the study of conditioning and learning, perhaps more than any other, has moved boldly to explore radically new conceptions when older ideas did not meet the challenges posed by new empirical findings.

Sample Questions

1. Describe what is an S–R association and what provides the best evidence for it.
2. Describe what is an S–O association and what research tactic provides the best evidence for it.
3. What investigative techniques are used to provide evidence of R–O associations? Why is it not possible to explain instrumental behavior by assuming only R–O association learning?
4. How do studies of the associative structure of instrumental conditioning help in understanding the nature of drug addiction?
5. Describe similarities and differences between the Premack principle and subsequent response allocation models.
6. What are the primary contributions of economic concepts to the understanding of the motivational bases of instrumental behavior?
7. Describe implications of modern concepts of reinforcement for behavior therapy.

Key Terms

behavioral bliss point The preferred distribution of an organism's activities before an instrumental conditioning procedure is introduced that sets constraints and limitations on response allocation.

consummatory-response theory A theory that assumes that species-typical consummatory responses (eating, drinking, and the like) are the critical features of reinforcers.

demand curve The relation between how much of a commodity is purchased and the price of the commodity.

differential probability principle A principle that assumes that reinforcement depends on how much more likely the organism is to perform the reinforcer response than the instrumental response before an instrumental conditioning procedure is introduced. The greater the differential probability of the reinforcer and instrumental responses during baseline conditions, the greater is the reinforcement effect of providing opportunity to engage in the reinforcer response after performance of the instrumental response. Also known as the *Premack principle*.

elasticity of demand The degree to which price influences the consumption or purchase of a commodity. If price has a large effect on consumption, elasticity of demand is high. If price has a small effect on consumption, elasticity of demand is low.

minimum-deviation model A model of instrumental behavior, according to which participants respond to a response–reinforcer contingency in a manner that gets them as close as possible to their behavioral bliss point.

Premack principle The same as *differential probability principle*.

response-deprivation hypothesis An explanation of reinforcement according to which restricting access to a response below its baseline rate of occurrence (response deprivation) is sufficient to make the opportunity to perform that response an effective positive reinforcer.

CHAPTER 8

Stimulus Control of Behavior

CHAPTER PREVIEW

This chapter focuses on the topic of stimulus control. Although most of the chapter deals with the ways in which instrumental behavior comes under the control of particular stimuli, the concepts are equally applicable to classical conditioning. The chapter begins with a definition of stimulus control and the basic concepts of stimulus discrimination and generalization. I then go on to discuss factors that determine the extent to which behavior comes to be restricted to particular stimuli. Along the way, I will describe special forms of stimulus control (intradimensional discrimination) and control by special categories of stimuli (interoceptive stimuli, configural stimuli, and contextual cues). The chapter concludes with a discussion of the learning of conditional relations in both instrumental and classical conditioning.

Both Thorndike and Skinner recognized that instrumental responses and reinforcers occur in the presence of particular stimuli which come to control those responses. As I described in Chapter 7, research on the associative structure of instrumental conditioning deals with how these stimuli come to determine whether or not the instrumental response is performed. The importance of antecedent stimuli has been examined further in studies of the stimulus control of instrumental behavior, which is the topic of this chapter.

The stimulus control of instrumental behavior is evident in many aspects of life. Studying, for example, is under the strong control of school-related stimuli. College students who fall behind in their course work may make determined resolutions to study a lot when they go home during a semester break. However, such good intentions are rarely carried out. The stimuli of semester breaks are very different from the stimuli students experience when classes are in session. Because of that, semester breaks do not engender effective studying behavior.

The proper fit between an instrumental response and the stimulus context in which the response is performed is so important that the failure of appropriate stimulus control is often considered abnormal. Getting undressed, for example, is acceptable instrumental behavior in the privacy of your bedroom. The same behavior on a public street will get you arrested. Staring at a computer screen is considered appropriate if the computer is turned on but not if it is blank. Talking is appropriate if someone is there to listen. Talking in the absence of an audience is considered strange and possibly evidence of psychopathology.

Identification and Measurement of Stimulus Control

To investigate the stimulus control of behavior, one first has to figure out how to identify and measure it. How can a researcher tell that an instrumental response has come under the control of certain stimuli?

Differential Responding and Stimulus Discrimination

Consider, for example, a classic experiment by Reynolds (1961). Two pigeons were reinforced on a variable-interval schedule for pecking a circular response key. Reinforcement for pecking was available whenever the response key was illuminated by a visual pattern consisting of a white triangle on a red background (Figure 8.1). Reynolds was interested in which of these stimulus components gained control over

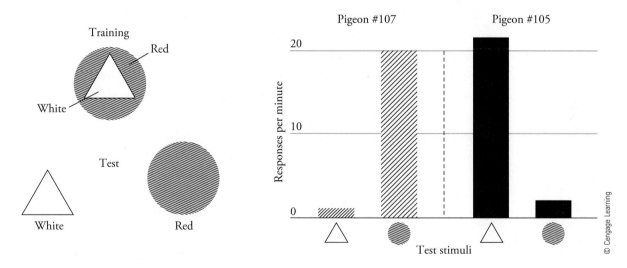

FIGURE 8.1 Summary of the procedure and results of an experiment by Reynolds (1961). Two pigeons were first reinforced for pecking whenever a compound stimulus consisting of a white triangle on a red background was projected on the response key. The rate of pecking was then observed with each pigeon when the white triangle and the red background stimuli were presented separately.

the pecking behavior. Were the pigeons pecking because they saw the white triangle or because they saw the red background?

After the pigeons learned to peck steadily at the triangle on the red background, Reynolds measured the amount of pecking that occurred when only one of the stimuli was presented. On some of the test trials, the white triangle was projected on the response key without the red background. On other test trials, the red background color was projected on the response key without the white triangle.

The results are summarized in Figure 8.1. One of the pigeons pecked more frequently when the response key was illuminated with the red light than when it was illuminated with the white triangle. This outcome shows that its pecking behavior was much more strongly controlled by the red color than by the white triangle. By contrast, the other pigeon pecked more frequently when the white triangle was projected on the response key than when the key was illuminated by the red light. Thus, for the second bird, the pecking behavior was more strongly controlled by the triangle. (For a similar effect in pigeon search behavior, see Cheng & Spetch, 1995.)

This experiment illustrates several important ideas. First, it shows how to experimentally determine whether instrumental behavior has come under the control of a particular stimulus. The stimulus control of instrumental behavior is demonstrated by variations in responding (differential responding) related to variations in stimuli. If an organism responds one way in the presence of one stimulus and in a different way in the presence of another stimulus, its behavior has come under the control of those stimuli. Such differential responding was evident in the behavior of both pigeons Reynolds tested.

Differential responding to two stimuli also indicates that the pigeons were treating each stimulus as different from the other. This is called **stimulus discrimination**. An organism is said to exhibit stimulus discrimination if it responds differently to two or more stimuli. Stimulus discrimination and stimulus control are two ways of considering the same phenomenon. One cannot have one without the other. If an organism does not discriminate between two stimuli, its behavior is not under the control of those cues.

Another interesting aspect of the results of Reynolds's experiment was that the pecking behavior of each bird came under the control of a different stimulus. The behavior of bird 107 came under the control of the red color, whereas the behavior of bird 105 came under the control of the triangle. The procedure used by Reynolds did not direct attention to one of the stimuli at the expense of the other. Therefore, it is not surprising that each bird came to respond to a different aspect of the situation. The experiment is comparable to showing a group of children a picture of a cowboy grooming a horse. Some of the children may focus on the cowboy; others may find the horse more interesting. In the absence of special procedures, one cannot always predict which of the various stimuli an organism experiences will gain control over its instrumental behavior.

Stimulus Generalization

Psychologists and physiologists have long been concerned with how organisms identify and distinguish different stimuli. In fact, some have suggested that this is the single most important question in psychology (Stevens, 1951). The problem is central to the analysis of stimulus control. As you will see, numerous factors are involved in the identification and differentiation of stimuli. Experimental analyses of the problem have relied heavily on the phenomenon of **stimulus generalization**. Stimulus generalization is the opposite of differential responding, or stimulus discrimination. An organism is said to show stimulus generalization if it responds in a similar fashion to two or more stimuli.

The phenomenon of stimulus generalization was first observed by Pavlov. He found that after one stimulus was used as a CS, his dogs would also make the conditioned

FIGURE 8.2 Stimulus generalization gradient for pigeons that were trained to peck in the presence of a colored light of 580-nm wavelength and were then tested in the presence of other colors. (From "Discriminability and Stimulus Generalization," by N. Guttman and H. I. Kalish, 1956, *Journal of Experimental Psychology, 51,* pp. 79–88.)

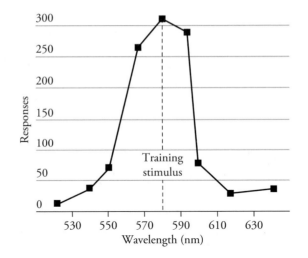

response to other, similar stimuli. That is, they failed to respond differentially to stimuli that were similar to the original CS. Since then, stimulus generalization has been examined in a wide range of situations and species. As Ghirlanda and Enquist (2003) noted, "Empirical data gathered in about 100 years of research establish generalization as a fundamental behavioral phenomenon, whose basic characteristics appear universal" (p. 27).

In a landmark study of stimulus generalization in instrumental conditioning, Guttman and Kalish (1956) first reinforced pigeons on a variable-interval schedule for pecking a response key illuminated by a yellow light with a wavelength of 580 nanometers (nm). After training, the birds were tested with a variety of other colors presented in a random order without reinforcement, and the rate of responding in the presence of each color was recorded.

The results of the experiment are summarized in Figure 8.2. The highest rate of pecking occurred in response to the original 580-nm color. But the birds also made substantial numbers of pecks when lights of 570-nm and 590-nm wavelength were tested. This indicates that responding generalized to the 570-nm and 590-nm stimuli. However, as the color of the test stimuli became increasingly different from the color of the original training stimulus, progressively fewer responses occurred. The results showed a gradient of responding as a function of how similar each test stimulus was to the original training stimulus. This is an example of a **stimulus generalization gradient**.

Stimulus generalization gradients are an excellent way to measure stimulus control because they provide precise information about how sensitive the organism's behavior is to systematic variations in a stimulus (Honig & Urcuioli, 1981; Kehoe, 2008). Consider, for example, the gradient in Figure 8.2. When the original 580-nm training stimulus was changed 10 nm (to 570 or 590 nm), responding did not change. However, when the 580 nm was changed 40 nm or more (to 520, 540, 620, or 640 nm) responding dropped off significantly. This aspect of the stimulus generalization gradient provides precise information about how much of a change in a stimulus is required for the pigeons to respond differently.

How do you suppose the pigeons would have responded if they had been color-blind? In that case, they could not have distinguished lights on the basis of color or wavelength. Therefore, they would have responded in much the same way regardless of what color was projected on the response key. Figure 8.3 presents hypothetical results of an experiment of this sort. If the pigeons did not respond on the basis of the color of the

FIGURE 8.3 Hypothetical stimulus generalization gradient for color-blind pigeons trained to peck in the presence of a colored light of 580-nm wavelength and then tested in the presence of other colors.

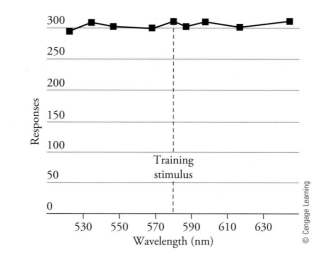

key light, similar high rates of responding would have occurred as different colors were projected on the key. Thus, the stimulus generalization gradient would have been flat.

A comparison of the results obtained by Guttman and Kalish and our hypothetical experiment with color-blind pigeons indicates that the steepness of a stimulus generalization gradient provides a precise measure of the degree of stimulus control. A steep generalization gradient (Figure 8.2) indicates strong control of behavior by the stimulus dimension that is tested. In contrast, a flat generalization gradient (Figure 8.3) indicates weak or nonexistent stimulus control. The primary question in this area of behavior theory is what determines the degree of stimulus control that is obtained. The remainder of this chapter is devoted to answering that question.

BOX 8.1

Generalization of Treatment Outcomes

Stimulus generalization is critical to the success of behavior therapy. Like other forms of therapy, behavior therapy is typically conducted in a distinctive environment (e.g., in a therapist's office). For the treatment to be maximally useful, what is learned during the treatment should generalize to other situations. An autistic child, for example, who is taught certain communicative responses in interactions with a particular therapist should also exhibit those responses in interactions with other people. The following techniques have been proposed to facilitate generalization of treatment outcomes (e.g., Schreibman,

Koegel, Charlop, & Egel, 1990; Stokes & Baer, 1977):

1. The treatment situation should be made as similar as possible to the natural environment of the client. If the natural environment provides reinforcement only intermittently, it is a good idea to reduce the frequency of reinforcement during treatment sessions as well. Another way to increase the similarity of the treatment procedure to the natural environment is to use the same reinforcers the client is likely to encounter in the natural environment.

2. Generalization also may be increased by conducting the treatment procedure in new settings. This strategy is called *sequential modification*. After a behavior has been modified or conditioned in one situation (a classroom), training is conducted in a new situation (the playground). If that does not result in sufficient generalization, training can be extended to a third environment (e.g., the school cafeteria).

3. Using numerous examples during training also facilitates generalization. In trying to extinguish fear of elevators, for example, training should be

Continued

BOX 8.1 (continued)

conducted in many different types of elevators.

4. Generalization may be also encouraged by conditioning the new responses to stimuli that are common to various situations. Language provides effective mediating stimuli. Responses conditioned to verbal or instructional cues are likely to generalize to new situations in which those instructional stimuli are encountered.

5. Another approach is to make the training procedure indiscriminable or incidental to other activities. In one study (McGee, Krantz, & McClannahan, 1986), the investigators took advantage of the interest that autistic children showed in specific toys during a play session to teach the children how to read the names of the toys.

6. Finally, generalization outside a training situation is achieved if

the training helps to bring the individual in contact with contingencies of reinforcement available in the natural environment (Baer & Wolf, 1970). Once a response is acquired through special training, the behavior often can be maintained by naturally available reinforcers. Reading, doing simple arithmetic, and riding a bicycle are all responses that are maintained by natural reinforcers once the responses have been acquired through special training.

An interesting study involved teaching 4- and 5-year-old children safety skills to prevent playing with firearms (Jostad et al., 2008). During the training sessions, a disabled handgun was deliberately left in places where the children would find it. If a child found the firearm, he or she was instructed not to touch it

and to report it to an adult. Praise and corrective feedback served as reinforcers. The unusual aspect of the study was that the training was conducted by children who were just a bit older (6 and 7 years old) than the research participants. This required training the peer trainers first.

The results were very encouraging. With many (but not all) of the participants, the safety behaviors generalized to new situations and were maintained as long as a year. The experiment was not designed to prove that peer trainers were critical in producing the generalized responding. However, accidents often occur when two or more children find and play with a firearm together. The fact that the safety training was conducted between one child and another should facilitate generalization of the safety behaviors to other situations in which two or more children find a gun.

Stimulus and Reinforcement Variables

In the experiment by Reynolds (1961) described at the beginning of the chapter, pigeons pecked a response key that had a white triangle on a red background. Such a stimulus obviously has two features, the color of the background and the shape of the triangle. Perhaps less obvious is the fact that all stimulus situations can be analyzed in terms of multiple features. Even if the response key only had the red background, one could characterize it in terms of its brightness, shape, or location in the experimental chamber in addition to its color.

Situations outside the laboratory are even more complex. During a football game, for example, cheering is reinforced by social approval if the people near you are all rooting for the same team as you are and if your team is doing well. The cues that accompany appropriate cheering include your team making a good play on the field, the announcer describing the play, cheerleaders dancing exuberantly, and the people around you cheering.

The central issue in the analysis of stimulus control is what determines which of the numerous features of a stimulus situation gains control over the instrumental behavior. Stimuli as complex as those found at a football game are difficult to analyze experimentally. Laboratory studies are typically conducted with stimuli that consist of more easily identifiable features. In this section, we will consider stimulus and reinforcement variables that determine which cues come to control behavior. In the following section, we will consider learning factors.

Sensory Capacity and Orientation

The most obvious variable that determines whether a particular stimulus feature controls responding is the organism's sensory capacity and orientation. Sensory capacity and orientation determine which stimuli are included in an organism's sensory world. People cannot see behind their back and cannot hear sounds whose pitch is above about 20,000 cycles per second (cps). Dogs, on the other hand, can hear whistles outside the range of human hearing and are also much more sensitive to odors. These differences make the sensory world of dogs very different from the sensory world of human beings.

Because sensory capacity sets a limit on what stimuli can control behavior, studies of stimulus control are often used to determine what an organism is, or is not, able to perceive (Heffner, 1998; Kelber, Vorobyev, & Osorio, 2003). Consider, for example, the question: Can horses see color? To answer that question, investigators used a training procedure in which horses had to select a colored stimulus over a gray one to obtain food reinforcement (Blackmore et al., 2008). The colored and gray stimuli were projected on separate stimulus panels placed side by side on a table in front of the horse. There was a response lever in front of each stimulus panel that the horse could push with its head to register its choice on that trial. Several shades of gray were tested with several shades of red, green, yellow, and blue.

If the horses could not detect color, they could not consistently select the colored stimulus in such a choice task. However, all the four horses in the experiment chose blue and yellow over gray more than 85% of the time. Three of the horses also did well on choices between green and gray. However, only one of the horses consistently selected the color when red was tested against gray. These results indicate that horses have good color vision over a large range of colors but have some difficulty detecting red. (For a similar experiment with giant pandas, see Kelling et al., 2006.)

Relative Ease of Conditioning Various Stimuli

Having the necessary sense organs to detect the stimulus being presented does not guarantee that the organism's behavior will come under the control of that stimulus. Stimulus control also depends on the presence of other cues in the situation. In particular, how strongly organisms learn about one stimulus depends on how easily other cues in the situations can become conditioned. This phenomenon is called **overshadowing**. Overshadowing illustrates competition among stimuli for access to the processes of learning.

Consider, for example, trying to teach a child to read by having him or her follow along as you read a children's book that has a big picture and a short sentence on each page. Learning about pictures is easier than learning words. Therefore, the pictures may well overshadow the words. The child will quickly memorize the story based on the pictures rather than the words and will not learn much about the words.

Pavlov (1927) was the first to observe that if two stimuli are presented at the same time, the presence of the more easily trained stimulus may hinder learning about the other one. In many of Pavlov's experiments, the two stimuli differed in intensity. The basic experimental design is illustrated in Table 8.1. During training, a relatively weak stimulus (designated as "*a*" in Table 8.1) is conditioned either by itself (in the control group) or in the presence of a more intense stimulus (designated as "*B*"). Subsequent tests reveal weaker conditioned responding to stimulus *a* in the overshadowed group than in the control group.

GROUP	TRAINING STIMULI	TEST STIMULUS	GENERALIZATION FROM TRAINING TO TEST
Overshadowing group	*aB*	*a*	Decrement
Control group	*a*	*a*	No decrement

TABLE 8.1   EXPERIMENTAL DESIGN FOR OVERSHADOWING

© Cengage Learning 2015

Overshadowing has been of considerable interest in contemporary studies of spatial navigation. People and other animals use a variety of different stimuli to find their way around (beacons, landmarks, and spatial or geographical cues). The availability of one type of cue (e.g., a prominent landmark) can sometimes overshadow learning about other types of spatial information (Horne & Pearce, 2011). Interestingly, whether landmark cues overshadow spatial cues differs between males and females (e.g., Rodríguez, Chamizo, & Mackintosh, 2011). (We will discuss spatial navigation in greater detail in Chapter 11. For other studies of overshadowing, see Dwyer, Haselgrove, & Jones, 2011; Jennings, Bonardi, & Kirkpatrick, 2007.)

Type of Reinforcement

The development of stimulus control also depends on the type of reinforcement that is used (Weiss, 2012). Certain types of stimuli are more likely to gain control over the instrumental behavior in appetitive than in aversive situations. This phenomenon was originally discovered in experiments with pigeons (see LoLordo, 1979).

In one study (Foree & LoLordo, 1973), two groups of pigeons were trained to press a foot treadle in the presence of a compound stimulus consisting of a red light and a tone whose pitch was 440 cps. When the light–tone compound was absent, responses were not reinforced. For one group of pigeons, reinforcement for treadle pressing was provided by food. For the other group, treadle pressing was reinforced by the avoidance of shock. If the avoidance group pressed the treadle in the presence of the light–tone compound stimulus, no shock was delivered on that trial; if they failed to respond during the light–tone stimulus, a brief shock was periodically applied until a response occurred.

Both groups of pigeons learned to respond during the light–tone compound. Foree and LoLordo then sought to determine which of the two elements of the compound stimulus was primarily responsible for the treadle-press behavior. Test trials were conducted during which the light and tone stimuli were presented one at a time. The results are summarized in Figure 8.4.

Pigeons conditioned with food reinforcement responded much more when tested with the light stimulus alone than when tested with the tone alone. In fact, their rate of treadle pressing in response to the isolated presentation of the red light was nearly as high as when the light was presented simultaneously with the tone. Therefore, the behavior of these birds was nearly exclusively controlled by the red light.

A contrasting pattern of results occurred with the pigeons that had been trained with shock-avoidance reinforcement. Those birds responded much more when tested with the tone alone than when tested with the light alone. Thus, with shock-avoidance reinforcement, the tone acquired more control over the treadle response than the red light (see also Schindler & Weiss, 1982).

The above findings indicate that stimulus control of instrumental behavior is determined in part by the type of reinforcement that is used. Subsequent research showed that the critical factor is whether the compound tone+light CS acquires positive or aversive properties (Weiss, Panlilio, & Schindler, 1993a, 1993b). Visual control predominates

Courtesy of Donald A. Dewsbury

V. M. LoLordo

FIGURE 8.4 Effects of the type of reinforcement on stimulus control. A treadle-press response in pigeons was reinforced in the presence of a compound stimulus consisting of a tone and red light. With food reinforcement, the light gained much more control over the behavior than the tone. With shock-avoidance reinforcement, the tone gained more control over behavior than the light (adapted from Foree & LoLordo, 1973).

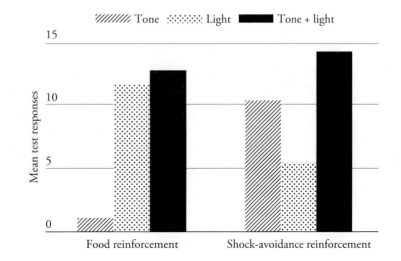

when the CS acquires positive or appetitive properties, and auditory control predominates when the CS acquires negative or aversive properties.

The dominance of visual control in appetitive situations and auditory control in aversive situations is probably related to the behavior systems that are activated in the two cases. A signal for food activates the feeding system. Food eaten by pigeons and rats is more likely to be identified by visual cues than by auditory cues. Therefore, activation of the feeding system is accompanied by increased attention to visual rather than auditory stimuli. In contrast, a signal for an aversive outcome activates the defensive behavior system. Responding to auditory cues may be particularly adaptive in avoiding danger.

Unfortunately, we do not know enough about the evolutionary history of pigeons or rats to be able to calculate the adaptive value of different types of stimulus control in feeding versus defensive behavior. We also do not know much about how stimulus control varies as a function of type of reinforcement in other species. One might predict, for example, that bats that forage for food using echolocation would show stronger control by auditory cues in a feeding situation than is observed with pigeons. Such questions remain fertile areas for future research.

Stimulus Elements Versus Configural Cues in Compound Stimuli

So far I have assumed that organisms treat the various components of a complex stimulus as distinct and separate elements. Thus, I treated the simultaneous presentation of a light and tone as consisting of separate visual and auditory cues. This way of thinking about a compound stimulus is known as the **stimulus-element approach** and has been dominant in learning theory going back about 80 years. An important alternative assumes that organisms treat a compound stimulus as an integral whole that is not divided into parts or elements. This is called the **configural-cue approach**. Although the configural-cue approach also has deep roots (in Gestalt psychology), its prominence in behavior theory is of more recent vintage.

According to the configural-cue approach, individuals respond to a compound stimulus in terms of the unique configuration of its elements. It is assumed that the elements are not treated as separate entities. In fact, they may not even be identifiable when the stimulus compound is presented. In the configural-cue approach, stimulus elements are important not because of their individuality but because of the way they contribute to the entire configuration of stimulation provided by the compound.

The concept of a configural cue may be illustrated by considering the sound of a symphony orchestra. The orchestral sound originates from the sounds of the individual instruments. However, the sound of the entire orchestra is very different from the sound of any of the individual instruments, some of which are difficult to identify when the entire orchestra is playing. We primarily hear the configuration of the sounds created by all the instruments that are playing.

In contemporary behavior theory, the configural-cue approach has been championed by John Pearce (Pearce, 1987, 1994, 2002), who showed that many learning phenomena are consistent with this framework. Let us consider, for example, the overshadowing effect (Table 8.1). As I noted earlier, an overshadowing experiment involves two groups of subjects and two stimulus elements, one of low intensity (*a*) and the other of high intensity (*B*). For the overshadowing group, the two stimuli are presented together (*aB*) as a compound cue and paired with reinforcement during conditioning. For the control group, only the low intensity stimulus (*a*) is presented during conditioning. Tests are then conducted for each group with the weaker stimulus element (*a*) presented alone. These tests show less responding to *a* in the overshadowing group than in the control group. Thus, the presence of *B* during conditioning disrupts control of behavior by the weaker stimulus *a*.

According to the configural-cue approach, overshadowing reflects different degrees of generalization decrement from training to testing (Pearce, 1987). There is no generalization decrement for the control group when it is tested with the weak stimulus *a* because that is the same as the stimulus it received during conditioning. In contrast, considerable generalization decrement occurs when the overshadowing group is tested with stimulus *a* after conditioning with the compound *aB*. For the overshadowing group, responding becomes conditioned to the *aB* compound, which is very different from *a* presented alone during testing. Therefore, responding conditioned to *aB* suffers considerable generalization decrement. According to the configural-cue approach, this greater generalization decrement is responsible for the overshadowing effect.

The configural-cue approach has enjoyed considerable success in generating new experiments and explaining the results of those experiments. However, other findings have favored analyses of stimulus control in terms of stimulus elements. At this point what is needed is a comprehensive theory that deals successfully with both types of results. Whether such a theory requires abandoning the fundamental concept of stimulus elements remains a heatedly debated theoretical issue (Harris et al., 2009; McLaren & Mackintosh, 2002; Pearce, 2002; Wagner & Brandon, 2001).

Learning Factors in Stimulus Control

The factors described in the preceding section set the preconditions for how human and nonhuman animals learn about the environmental stimuli they encounter. However, the fact that certain stimuli can be perceived does not ensure that those stimuli will come to control behavior. A young child, for example, may correctly identify a car as different from a bus but may not be able to distinguish between Hondas and Toyotas. A novice chess player may be able to look at two different patterns on a chess board without being able to identify which represents the more favorable configuration. Whether or not certain stimuli come to control behavior depends on what the individual has learned about those stimuli, not just whether the stimuli can be detected.

The suggestion that experience with stimuli may determine the extent to which those stimuli come to control behavior originated in efforts to explain the phenomenon of stimulus generalization. As I noted earlier, stimulus generalization refers to the fact that a response conditioned to one stimulus will also occur when other stimuli similar

J. M. Pearce

to the original cue are presented. Pavlov suggested that stimulus generalization occurs because learning about a CS gets transferred to other stimuli on the basis of the physical similarity of those test stimuli to the original CS.

In a spirited attack, Lashley and Wade (1946) took exception to Pavlov's proposal. Lashley and Wade argued that stimulus generalization reflects the *absence* of learning rather than the *transfer* of learning. More specifically, they proposed that stimulus generalization occurs if organisms have not learned to distinguish differences among the stimuli. Thus, in contrast to Pavlov, Lashley and Wade considered the shape of a stimulus generalization gradient to be determined primarily by the organism's previous learning experiences rather than by the physical properties of the stimuli tested.

Stimulus Discrimination Training

Courtesy of John Freeman

John Freeman

As it has turned out, Lashley and Wade were closer to the truth than Pavlov. Numerous studies have shown that stimulus control can be dramatically altered by learning experiences. Perhaps the most powerful procedure for bringing behavior under the control of a stimulus is **stimulus discrimination training** (Kehoe, 2008). Stimulus discrimination training can be conducted using either classical or instrumental conditioning procedures. For example, Campolattaro, Schnitker, and Freeman (2008, Experiment 3) used a discrimination training procedure in eyeblink conditioning with laboratory rats. A low-pitched tone (2,000 cps) and a high-pitched tone (8,000 cps) served as the CSs. Each session consisted of 100 trials. On half of the trials, one of the tones (A+) was paired with the US. On the remaining trials, the other tone (B–) was presented without the US. The results are presented in Figure 8.5. The rats showed progressive increases in eyeblink responding to the A+ tone that was paired with the US. By the 15th session, the rats responded to A+ more than 85% of the time. Responding to the B– also increased at first, but not as rapidly. Furthermore, after the 10th session, responding to the B– tone gradually declined. By the end of the experiment, the data showed very nice differential responding to the two tones.

The results presented in Figure 8.5 are typical for discrimination training in which the reinforced (A+) and nonreinforced (B–) stimuli are of the same modality. The conditioned responding that develops to A+ generalizes to B– at first, but with further training responding to B– declines and a clear discrimination becomes evident. It is as if the

FIGURE 8.5 Eyeblink conditioning in rats to a tone (A+) paired with the US and a different tone (B–) presented without the US (based on Campolattaro, Schnitker, & Freeman 2008).

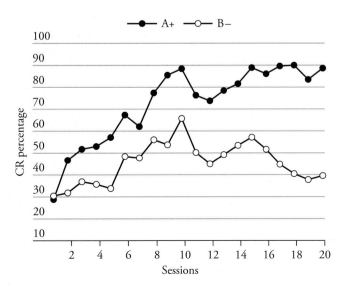

participants confuse A+ and B– at first but come to tell them apart with continued training. The same kind of thing happens when children are taught the names of different types of fruit. They may confuse oranges and tangerines at first, but with continued training they learn the distinction.

Stimulus discrimination training can also be conducted with instrumental conditioning procedures. This is the case when children are taught what to do at an intersection controlled by a traffic light. Crossing the street is reinforced with praise and encouragement when the traffic light is green but not when the light is red. The stimulus (the green light) that signals the availability of reinforcement for the instrumental response is technically called the S+ or S^D (pronounced "ess dee"). By contrast, the stimulus (the red light) that signals the lack of reinforcement for responding is called the S– or S^Δ (pronounced "ess delta").

As in Figure 8.5, initially a child may attempt to cross the street during both the S+ (green) and S– (red) lights. However, as training progresses, responding in the presence of the S+ persists and responding in the presence of the S– declines. The emergence of greater responding to the S+ than to the S– indicates differential responding to these stimuli. Thus, a **stimulus discrimination procedure** establishes control by the stimuli that signal when reinforcement is and is not available. Once the S+ and S– have gained control over the individual's behavior, they are called **discriminative stimuli**. The S+ is a discriminative stimulus for performing the instrumental response, and the S– is a discriminative stimulus for not performing the response. (For a laboratory example of discrimination training in instrumental conditioning, see Andrzejewski et al., 2007.)

In the discrimination procedures I described so far, the reinforced and nonreinforced stimuli (S+ and S–) were presented on separate trials. (Green and red traffic lights are never turned on simultaneously at a street crossing.) Discrimination training can also be conducted with the S+ and S– stimuli presented at the same time next to each other, with responses to S+ reinforced and responses to S– nonreinforced. Such a simultaneous discrimination procedure allows the participants to directly compare S+ and S– and makes discrimination training easier. For example, Huber, Apfalter, Steurer, and Prossinger (2005) examined whether pigeons can learn to tell the difference between male and female faces that were presented with the people's hair masked out. As you might imagine, this is not an easy discrimination. However, the pigeons learned the discrimination in a few sessions if the male and female faces were presented at the same time, and the birds were reinforced for pecking one of the face categories. If the faces were presented on successive trials, the pigeons had a great deal more difficulty with the task.

An instrumental conditioning procedure in which responding is reinforced in the presence of one stimulus (the S+) and not reinforced in the presence of another cue (the S–) is a special case of a **multiple schedule of reinforcement**. In a multiple schedule, a different schedule of reinforcement is in effect during different stimuli. For example, a VI schedule of reinforcement may be in effect when a light is turned on, and an FR schedule may be in effect when a tone is presented. With sufficient training with such a procedure, the pattern of responding during each stimulus will correspond to the schedule of reinforcement in effect during that stimulus. The participants will show a steady rate of responding during the VI stimulus and a stop-run pattern during the FR stimulus. (For a recent study of multiple-schedule performance of individuals with mild intellectual disabilities, see Williams, Saunders, & Perone, 2011.)

Stimulus discrimination and multiple schedules are common outside the laboratory. Nearly all reinforcement schedules that exist outside the laboratory are in effect only in the presence of particular stimuli. Playing a game yields reinforcement only in the presence of enjoyable or challenging partners. Driving rapidly is reinforced when you are on a freeway but not when you are on a crowded city street. Loud and boisterous discussion with your friends is reinforced at a party. The same type of behavior is frowned upon during a church service. Eating with your fingers is reinforced at a picnic but not when you are in a fine restaurant. Daily activities typically consist of going from one situation to another, each associated with its own schedule of reinforcement.

Effects of Discrimination Training on Stimulus Control Discrimination training brings the instrumental response under the control of the S+ and S–. How precise is the control that S+ acquires over the instrumental behavior, and what factors determine the precision of the stimulus control that is achieved? To answer these questions, it is not enough to observe differential responding to S+ versus S–. One must also find out how steep the generalization gradient is when the participants are tested with stimuli that systematically vary from the S+. Another important question is which aspect of the discrimination training procedure is responsible for the type of stimulus generalization gradient that is obtained. These issues were first addressed in classic experiments by Jenkins and Harrison (1960, 1962).

Jenkins and Harrison examined how auditory stimuli that differ in pitch can come to control the pecking behavior of pigeons reinforced with food. As I discussed earlier, when pigeons are reinforced with food, visual cues exert stronger stimulus control than auditory cues (Figure 8.4). However, as Jenkins and Harrison found out, with the proper training procedures, the behavior of pigeons can come under the control of auditory cues as well. They evaluated the effects of three different training procedures. In all three procedures, a 1,000-cps tone was present when pecking a response key was reinforced with access to food on a variable interval schedule.

One group of pigeons received a discrimination training procedure in which the 1,000-cps tone served as the S+ and the absence of the tone served as the S–. Pecking was reinforced on trials when the S+ was present but was not reinforced on trials when the tone was off (S–). A second group also received discrimination training. The 1,000-cps tone again served as the S+. However, this time the S– was a 950-cps tone. The third group of pigeons served as a control group and did not receive discrimination training. For them the 1,000-cps tone was continuously turned on, and they could always receive reinforcement for pecking during the experimental sessions.

Upon completion of the three different training procedures, each group was tested for pecking in the presence of tones of various frequencies to see how precisely pecking was controlled by pitch. Figure 8.6 shows the generalization gradients that were obtained. The control group, which did not receive discrimination training, responded nearly equally in the presence of all of the test stimuli. The pitch of the tones did not control their behavior; they acted tone deaf. Each of the other two training procedures produced more stimulus control by pitch. The steepest generalization gradient, and hence the strongest stimulus control, was observed in birds that were trained with the 1,000-cps tone as S+ and the 950-cps tone as S–. Pigeons that previously received discrimination training between the 1,000-cps tone (S+) and the absence of tones (S–) showed an intermediate degree of stimulus control by tonal frequency.

The Jenkins and Harrison experiment provides two important conclusions. First, it shows that discrimination training increases the stimulus control of instrumental behavior. Second, a particular stimulus dimension (such as tonal frequency) is most likely to gain control over responding if the S+ and S– differ along that stimulus dimension. The most precise control by tonal frequency was observed after discrimination training in which the S+ was a tone of one frequency (1,000 cps) and the S– was a tone of another frequency (950 cps). Weaker control by pitch occurred when the S+ was a 1,000-cps tone and the S– was the absence of tones. The discrimination between the presence and absence of the 1,000-cps tone could have been based on the loudness or timbre of the

FIGURE 8.6 Generalization gradients of responding to tones of different frequencies after various types of training. Each data point represents the percentage of all test responses that occurred to a particular test stimulus. Prior to testing, one group of pigeons received discrimination training in which a 1,000-cps tone served as the S+ and the absence of tones served as the S−. Another group received training in which a 1,000-cps tone served as the S+ and 950-cps tone served as the S−. The control group did not receive discrimination training before the generalization test. (From "Effects of Discrimination Training on Auditory Generalization," by H. M. Jenkins and R. H. Harrison, 1960, *Journal of Experimental Psychology, 59,* pp. 246–253; also from "Generalization Gradients of Inhibition Following Auditory Discrimination Learning," by H. M. Jenkins and R. H. Harrison, 1962, *Journal of Experimental Analysis of Behavior, 5,* pp. 435–441.)

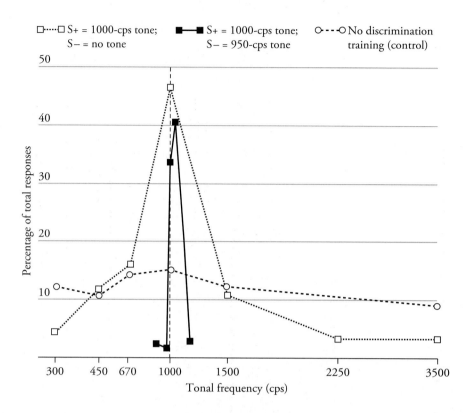

tone rather than its frequency. Hence, tonal frequency did not gain as much control in that case. (For further discussion of these and related issues, see Balsam, 1988; Kehoe, 2008; Lea & Wills, 2008.)

Discrimination Training Focused on Interoceptive Cues The experiment by Jenkins and Harrison demonstrates that discrimination training can be used to bring behavior under the control of environmental stimuli (auditory cues in this case) that would not ordinarily have such influence. Can this strategy be extended to the internal sensations we experience when we feel hungry or take a drug such as nicotine or alcohol? Can discrimination training bring overt behavior (pecking a response key in the case of pigeons) under the control of internal sensations created by a drug state or withdrawal from an addictive drug?

Internal sensations produced by a psychoactive drug (or other physiological manipulation such as food deprivation) are called *interoceptive cues*. The detection of interoceptive cues associated with drug withdrawal and the stimulus control that such cues may exert are prominent components of modern theories of drug addiction (Baker et al., 2004). Such theories gain substantial support from laboratory research on the stimulus control of instrumental behavior by drug-produced interoceptive cues.

Investigators in this area have inquired whether an organism can tell when it is under the influence of a sedative (pentobarbital) and whether other drugs (e.g., chlordiazepoxide, alcohol, and methamphetamine) produce sensations similar to those of sedatives. Discrimination training with drug stimuli and tests of stimulus generalization are used to provide answers to such questions (Stolerman et al., 2011). Interestingly, the mechanisms of stimulus control by drug stimuli seem to be remarkably similar to the mechanisms identified by Jenkins and Harrison (1960, 1962) for the control of key pecking by auditory cues in pigeons.

FIGURE 8.7

Responding as a function of cocaine dose for a pigeon before (left panel) and after (right panel) discrimination training in which 3.0 mg/kg of cocaine was present during S+ sessions and a saline injection (no drug) was given prior to S– sessions. (Based on Schaal et al., 1996. Discrimination of methadone and cocaine by pigeons without explicit discrimination training. *Journal of the Experimental Analysis of Behavior*, 66, p. 199.)

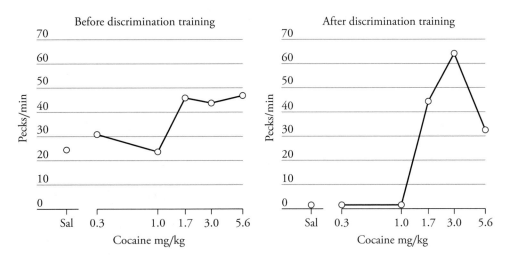

Schaal and his colleagues, for example, compared the strength of stimulus control by the interoceptive cues of cocaine before and after discrimination training (Schaal et al., 1996). Pigeons were reinforced for pecking a response key on a VI 2-min schedule of reinforcement. In the first phase of the experiment (no discrimination training), the birds were injected with 3.0 mg/kg of cocaine before each session. After responding stabilized, generalization tests were periodically interspersed between training sessions. During these tests, the pigeons received no drug (saline) or various doses of cocaine ranging from 0.3 to 5.6 mg/kg. (Responding was not reinforced during the test sessions.) The results obtained with one of the birds (P1) are presented on the left of Figure 8.7. Notice that the generalization gradient as a function of drug dose is fairly flat, indicative of weak stimulus control.

During the next phase of the experiment, the pigeons were trained to discriminate cocaine from the absence of the drug. Some sessions were preceded with an injection of cocaine (S+) as before, and pecking was reinforced. During other sessions, cocaine was not administered (S–) and pecking was not reinforced. The pigeons learned the discrimination, responding strongly during S+ sessions and much less during S– sessions. Once the discrimination was established, generalization tests were conducted as before.

The results of the tests are shown on the right panel of Figure 8.7 for pigeon P1. Notice that now the generalization gradient is much steeper, indicating much stronger control by the internal drug stimuli. The greatest level of responding occurred when the pigeon was tested with the 3.0 mg/kg of cocaine that had been used during reinforced sessions. Virtually no responding occurred during sessions with no drug or with just 0.3 or 1.0 mg/kg of cocaine. Interestingly, responding also declined a bit when the test dose was 5.6 mg/kg, which exceeded the training dose. Thus, as was the case with stimulus control of behavior by tonal frequency, discrimination training increased stimulus control by the internal sensations created by cocaine. (For a recent study of the role of muscarinic receptors in cocaine discrimination, see Thomsen et al., 2011.)

The fact that stimulus discrimination procedures can be used to bring behavior under the control of a wide variety of stimuli makes these procedures powerful tools for the investigation of how animals process information. Some impressive results of such experiments will be presented in discussions of contemporary research in comparative cognition in Chapters 11 and 12.

Discrimination Training Focused on Compound or Configural Cues As I described in the preceding section, one can use discrimination training to increase control of behavior by interoceptive cues. Another special category of stimuli involves configural

TABLE 8.2   TRIAL TYPES FOR POSITIVE AND NEGATIVE PATTERNING

POSITIVE PATTERNING	NEGATIVE PATTERNING
A–	C+
B–	D+
AB+	CD–

Note: A, B, C, and D are different stimuli. "+" indicates reinforcement and "–" indicates nonreinforcement.

cues that arise from the combination of two or more stimuli that are presented at the same time. Can discrimination procedures increase control by configural cues? Two different procedures have been designed with this question in mind, **positive patterning** and **negative patterning**. See Table 8.2.

In a positive patterning procedure, whenever each of two stimuli occur individually, they are not reinforced (A– and B– trials). However, reinforcement occurs whenever the two stimuli are presented simultaneously (AB+). To accurately predict reinforcement with such a procedure, the participant cannot respond on the basis of the presence of the individual cues but has to identify when the two cues are present at the same time (AB). The negative patterning procedure is similar except that the role of reinforced and nonreinforced trials is now reversed. This time reinforcement is available when the cues are presented individually (C+ and D+) but not when they appear simultaneously (CD–).

Although positive and negative patterning procedures are typically carried out with separate groups of participants, they can be also conducted concurrently, as in a recent study with laboratory rats (Harris et al., 2008). Four different CSs were used in the experiment (noise, tone, flashing light, and steady light). Each CS presentation lasted 30 seconds and reinforced trials ended with the delivery of food into a cup. Conditioned responding was nosing the food cup during the CS. The assignment of the auditory and visual cues was arranged so that each compound stimulus (AB and CD) was made up of one auditory and one visual cue. Training sessions consisted of six types of trials (A–, B–, AB+, C+, D+, and CD–) intermixed.

The results are presented in Figure 8.8. The first thing to note is that the rats were able to solve both discrimination problems. With the positive patterning procedure, they learned to respond whenever A and B were presented simultaneously but not when each

FIGURE 8.8 Conditioned goal tracking to reinforced (+) and nonreinforced (–) stimuli in a study of positive and negative patterning. Capital letters designate different stimuli and + and – designate reinforced and nonreinforced trials (based on Harris et al., 2008).

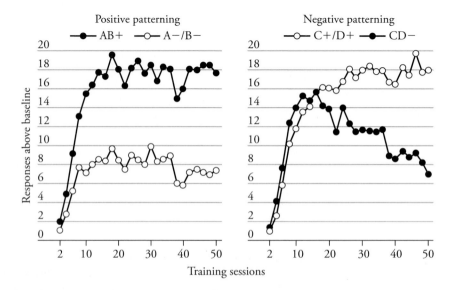

CS appeared alone. In the negative patterning procedure, they learned to withhold responding when C and D were presented simultaneously but responded to each of these cues when they were presented alone. Thus, the rats learned to respond to the combination of two cues in a manner that cannot be attributed to the sum of their responses to the individual cues. This is consistent with the interpretation that the stimulus configuration created by AB and CD acquired unique control over conditioned responding. The learning was not fast (especially in the case of negative patterning) but it was clearly evident. (For theoretical interpretations of positive and negative patterning, see Grand & Honey, 2008; Harris et al., 2009.)

What Is Learned in Discrimination Training?

Because of the profound effect that discrimination training has on stimulus control, investigators have been interested in what is learned during discrimination training. Consider the following relatively simple situation: Responses are reinforced whenever a red light is turned on (S+) and not reinforced whenever a loud tone is presented (S−). What strategies could an individual use to make sure that most of its responses were reinforced in this situation? One possibility is to learn to respond whenever the S+ is present and not respond otherwise. With this strategy, one would end up responding much more to S+ than to S− without having learned anything specific about S−. Another possibility is to learn to suppress responding during S− but respond whenever S− was absent. This strategy would also lead to more responding during S+ than S− but without learning anything specific about S+. A third possibility is to learn the significance of both S+ and S−, by learning to respond to S+ and suppress responding to S−.

Spence's Theory of Discrimination Learning

K. W. Spence

One of the first and most influential theories of discrimination learning was proposed by Kenneth Spence (1936). Although Spence's theory was formulated about 80 years ago, it remains influential in guiding research (Lazareva, 2012; Pearce et al., 2008; Wagner, 2008b). The basic idea of the theory elaborates on the last of the possibilities described above. The theory assumes that reinforcement of a response in the presence of the S+ conditions excitatory response tendencies to S+. By contrast, nonreinforcement of responding during S− conditions inhibitory properties to S− that serve to suppress the instrumental behavior. Differential responding to S+ and S− reflects both conditioned excitation to S+ and conditioned inhibition to S−.

The suggestion that discrimination training results in the conditioning of excitation to S+ is not controversial because excitation develops to a reinforced stimulus even in the absence of discrimination training. However, the proposition that inhibition becomes conditioned to S− is much less self-evident. One can respond more to S+ than to S− simply because S− is not excitatory. In principle S− does not have to be inhibitory to elicit less responding than S+. However, a number of experiments have shown that discrimination training does make S− inhibitory (e.g., Honig et al., 1963).

Kearns and colleagues (2005), for example, employed a summation test to determine if an S− comes to inhibit instrumental responding for cocaine following discrimination training. We previously encountered the summation test in Chapter 3 as a technique for measuring Pavlovian conditioned inhibition. According to the summation test, if S− acquires active inhibitory properties, it should suppress responding that is otherwise elicited by an S+. To test this prediction, Kearns and colleagues (2005) outfitted laboratory rats so that they could receive small doses of cocaine intravenously. The drug was delivered contingent on pressing a response lever on a variable-interval schedule. Reinforced trials were alternated with trials during which lever pressing was never reinforced.

FIGURE 8.9 Self-administration of cocaine by rats during tone-alone and tone+light test trials. The experimental group previously received discrimination training in which the tone occurred only on reinforced trials (S+) and the light occurred only on nonreinforced trials (S–). The control group received similar prior training, but for them the light occurred equally often on both reinforced and nonreinforced trials (based on Kearns et al., 2005).

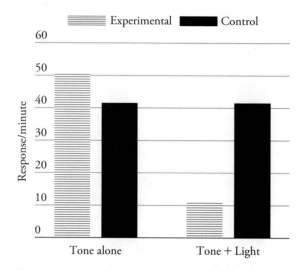

Two groups of rats were tested. For the experimental group, the reinforced trials were signaled by a tone half the time and a clicker the remaining times. Thus, both the tone and the clicker became S+ stimuli. A light was always presented during trials when reinforcement was not available, making the light an S–. The procedures were similar for the control group, except an effort was made to avoid having the light become an S–. This was accomplished by presenting the light half the time with the clicker (when cocaine was available) and half the time during the nonreinforced trials (when cocaine was not available). Because the light occurred equally on reinforced and nonreinforced trials, it was not expected to acquire inhibitory properties.

The summation test was conducted after the rats were well practiced on their procedures. In fact, the criterion for moving to the test phase was that lever pressing during reinforced trials had to exceed lever pressing during the nonreinforced trials by a factor of 7. Two trials were conducted during the summation test. In one trial, the tone was presented by itself. Because the tone was an S+ for both groups, both groups were expected to respond vigorously during the tone. During the second test, the tone was presented together with the light. Recall that the light was trained as an S– for the experimental group but not for the control group. Therefore, the light was expected to suppress responding only in the experimental group.

The results of the experiment are presented in Figure 8.9. As expected, both groups showed vigorous responding to the tone. Adding the light to the tone did not disrupt responding in the control group but produced a profound suppression of lever pressing in the experimental group. Note that the test phase was the first time the light was presented at the same time as the tone. The suppression of responding evident in the experimental group shows that a stimulus that is a signal for nonreinforcement (S–) in a discrimination procedure acquires active inhibitory properties, as predicted by Spence.

This experiment by Kearns and colleagues (2005) is interesting not only because of its relevance to theories of discrimination training but also because it suggests a novel approach to the treatment of drug abuse. The emphasis in analyses of drug abuse has been on identifying and moderating factors that lead to drug self-administration. On the whole, these involve various forms of excitatory conditioning. The study by Kearns and colleagues suggests that negative discriminative stimuli (S– cues) can exert a powerful inhibitory influence on drug seeking and drug self-administration behavior. Furthermore, this inhibitory influence transfers to counteract the excitatory effects of an S+ for drug administration. This suggests that drug seeking can be reduced by inhibition even if excitatory processes remain intact.

Interactions Between S+ and S–: The Peak-Shift Effect

So far I have described general characteristics of stimulus discrimination training under the assumption that what subjects learn about S+ is pretty much independent of what they learn about S–. This assumption is too simplistic. Learning is not so neatly compartmentalized. What you learn about S+ can influence your response to S– and vice versa. Such interactions are particularly likely if S+ and S– are related in some way.

S+ and S– may be related if they are similar except for one feature or attribute. This was the case in the Jenkins and Harrison experiment, whose results are presented in Figure 8.6. For one of the groups in that study, the S+ was a 1,000-cps tone and the S– was a 950-cps tone. Thus, the S+ and S– stimuli differed only slightly in pitch. A training procedure in which the S+ and S– differ only in terms of the value of one stimulus feature (in this case pitch) is called an **intradimensional discrimination**. The eyeblink stimulus discrimination procedure whose results are presented in Figure 8.5 was also an intradimensional discrimination. In that study, the CS+ and CS– stimuli were also tones differing in pitch (2,000 cps versus 8,000 cps).

Intradimensional discriminations are of particular interest because they are related to the issue of expert performance. Expert performance typically involves making subtle distinctions. Distinguishing stimuli that differ only in a single feature is more difficult than distinguishing stimuli that differ in many respects. It does not require much expertise to tell the difference between a compact car and a bus. In contrast, one has to be fairly sophisticated about cars to tell the difference between one version of the Honda Civic and another. Greater expertise is required to make finer distinctions. Two championship skaters may perform with equal skill as far as most people can tell, but expert judges are able to detect subtle but important differences that result in one performer getting higher marks than the other. Intradimensional discrimination is a form of expert performance because it requires detecting a single differentiating feature between S+ and S–.

Intradimensional discriminations are interesting because they can produce a counterintuitive phenomenon known as the **peak-shift effect**. This was demonstrated in a classic experiment by Hanson (1959). Hanson examined the effects of intradimensional discrimination training on the extent to which various colors controlled pecking behavior in pigeons. All the pigeons were reinforced for pecking in the presence of a light whose wavelength was 550 nm. However, independent groups differed in how similar the S– was to the S+ (how expert the pigeons had to become in telling the colors apart). One group received discrimination training in which the S– was a color of 590-nm wavelength, 40 nm away from the S+. For another group, the wavelength of the S– was 555 nm, only 5 nm away from the S+. The performance of these pigeons was compared to a control group that did not receive discrimination training but was also reinforced for pecking in the presence of the 550-nm stimulus. (Notice the similarity of this experiment to the study by Jenkins and Harrison shown in Figure 8.6. In both cases, the difficulty of the discrimination was varied across groups.)

After their various training experiences, all the birds were tested for their rate of pecking in the presence of test stimuli that varied in color. The results are shown in Figure 8.10. Consider first the performance of the control group that did not receive discrimination training. These pigeons responded most to the S+ stimulus and responded progressively less as the color of the test stimuli deviated from the color of S+. The control group showed a standard **excitatory generalization gradient** centered at the S+.

Different results were obtained after discrimination training with the 590-nm color as S–. These pigeons also responded at high rates to the 550-nm color that had served as the S+. However, they showed much more generalization of the pecking response to the 540-nm color. In fact, their rate of response was slightly higher to the 540-nm color than to the original 550-nm S+. This shift of the peak responding away from the original

FIGURE 8.10 Effects of intradimensional discrimination training on stimulus control. All three groups of pigeons were reinforced for pecking in the presence of 550-nm light (S+). One group received discrimination training in which the S– was a 590-nm light. For another group, the S– was a 555-nm light. The third group served as a control and did not receive discrimination training before the test for stimulus generalization. (From "Effects of Discrimination Training on Stimulus Generalization," by H. M. Hanson, 1959, *Journal of Experimental Psychology, 58,* pp. 321–333.)

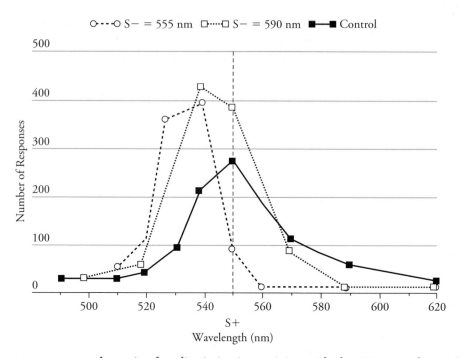

S+ was even more dramatic after discrimination training with the 555-nm color as S–. These birds showed much lower rates of responding to the original S+ (550 nm) than either of the other two groups. Furthermore, their highest response rates occurred to colors of 540- and 530-nm wavelength. This shift of the peak of the generalization gradient away from the original S+ is remarkable because in the earlier phase of discrimination training, responding was never reinforced in the presence of the 540-nm or 530-nm stimuli. Thus, the highest rates of pecking occurred to stimuli that had never even been presented during original training.

The shift of the peak of the generalization gradient away from the original S+ is called the peak-shift effect. It is important to note the two features of the peak-shift effect evident in Figure 8.10. First, the peak-shift effect is a result of intradimensional discrimination training. The control group, which did not receive intradimensional discrimination training, did not show the peak-shift effect. Second, the peak-shift effect was a function of the similarity of the S– to the S+ used in discrimination training. The biggest peak shift occurred after training in which the S– was very similar to the S+ (555 nm and 550 nm, respectively). Less of a peak shift occurred after discrimination training with more widely different colors (590 nm compared with 550 nm).

Similar results were evident in the Jenkins and Harrison experiment (Figure 8.6). A small peak-shift effect was evident in birds that received discrimination training with the 1,000-cps tone as S+ and the 950-cps tone as S–. Notice that for this group, the highest rate of responding occurred to a tonal frequency above 1,000 cps. No peak shift occurred for pigeons trained with the 1,000-cps tone as S+ and the absence of the tone as S–.

The peak-shift effect can result from any intradimensional discrimination not just pitch and color. The S+ and S– may be lines of different orientations, tones of different loudness, temporal cues, spatial stimuli, or facial cues. Furthermore, the effect has been observed in a variety of species, including people (e.g., Bizo & McMahon, 2007; Spetch, Chang, & Clifford, 2004; Russella & Kirkpatrick, 2007; Wisniewski, Church, & Mercado, 2009).

Spence's Explanation of Peak Shift   The peak-shift effect is remarkable because it shows that the S+, or reinforced stimulus, is not necessarily the one that produces the

For therapists interested in using learning principles, stimulus equivalence training is highly attractive because it results in new or emergent skills that are not specifically taught during training. Consider, for example, the scenario outlined in Table 8.3. During the reassignment phase, R3 is conditioned to stimuli in Set A and R4 is conditioned to stimuli in Set C. Stimuli from Sets B and D are never trained with R3 and R4. Nevertheless, because of the previously established equivalence of A and B (and C and D), the participants make R3 to stimuli in Set B and R4 to stimuli in Set D. These new stimulus-response relations are called *emergent relations* because they emerge as a consequence of the acquisition of equivalence without being directly trained.

Emergent relations are very useful in training verbal skills. For example, having trained a child to name a fruit upon seeing a picture of the fruit (Picture → Word), the child is likely to be able to pick out the picture when she is given the word (Word → Picture). This symmetry relation is an emergent skill that may not require direct training. Anther possibility is to teach a participant that a rose is a flower (Rose → Flower), and that a flower is a plant (Flower → Plant). Having learned these relationships, the participant should be able to correctly identify a rose as a plant (Rose → Plant) as an emergent transitive relation without direct training of the Rose → Plant relation.

Contextual Cues and Conditional Relations

So far we have been discussing the control of behavior by discrete stimuli, such as a tone or a light, presented individually or in combination with one another. A stimulus is said to be *discrete* if it is presented for a brief period, has a clear beginning and end, and can be easily characterized. Although studies with discrete stimuli have provided much information about the stimulus control of behavior, such studies do not tell the whole story. A more comprehensive analysis of the stimuli organisms experience during the course of conditioning indicates that discrete discriminative stimuli occur in the presence of background contextual cues. The contextual cues are various features (visual, auditory, and olfactory) of the room or place where the discrete discriminative stimuli are presented. Recent research indicates that contextual cues can provide an important additional source of control of learned behavior.

Control by Contextual Cues

Several of the examples of stimulus control I described at the beginning of this chapter involved the control of behavior by contextual cues. It is easier to concentrate on studying when you are in the college library rather than at home during holidays because of contextual control of studying behavior by stimuli experienced in the library. Getting undressed is appropriate in the context of your bedroom but not on a public street.

Contextual cues can come to control behavior in a variety of ways (e.g., Balsam & Tomie, 1985; Urcelay & Miller, 2010). In a study of sexual conditioning, for example, Akins (1998, Experiment 1) used contextual cues as a signal for sexual reinforcement in much the same way that a discrete CS might be used. Male domesticated quail served in the experiment, which was conducted in an apparatus made up of two adjacent compartments. One compartment had sand on the floor, and the walls and ceiling were painted orange. The other compartment had a wire-mesh floor, and the walls and ceiling were green. Before the start of the conditioning trials, the birds were allowed to move back and forth between the two compartments to determine their baseline preference of one compartment over the other. The nonpreferred compartment was then designated as the CS.

Conditioning trials consisted of placing a male bird in its CS context for 5 minutes, at which point a sexually receptive female was placed with them for another 5 minutes.

TABLE 8.3	**Common Response Training and Testing to Establish Stimulus Equivalence**

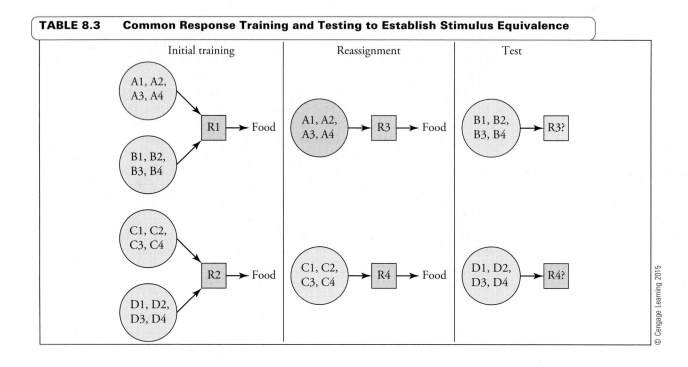

Set B became *equivalent* to those in Set A during original training, they should also come to elicit response R3 after the reassignment training. Following the same reasoning, stimuli in Set D should come to elicit R4 following the reassignment training of Set C. These predictions of stimulus equivalence are tested in the last phase of the experiment.

Experimental designs like that presented in Table 8.3 have been employed in numerous studies of stimulus equivalence training with both human and nonhuman participants (see Urcuioli, 2013, for a review). The basic idea is that training the same response to a set of physically different stimuli creates *functional equivalence* among those stimuli. Once this has occurred, a new response trained to a subset of those cues will generalize to other elements of the equivalence class that were not used during the reassignment phase.

A more formal definition of *equivalence class* was proposed by Sidman and his colleagues (Sidman, 1994; Sidman & Tailby, 1982). According to the Sidman definition, an equivalence class is said to exist if its members possess three properties: (1) reflexivity or sameness, (2) symmetry, and (3) transitivity. Consider, for example, an equivalence class consisting of three stimuli A, B, and C. *Reflexivity*, or sameness, refers to the relation A = A, B = B, and C = C. *Symmetry* is said to exist if a relationship is bidirectional. Thus, for example, if A leads to B (A → B), then symmetry requires that B leads to A (B → A). Finally, *transitivity* refers to the integration of two relationships into a third one. For example, given the relations A → B and B → C, transitivity requires that A → C. (For further discussions of these issues, see Lionello-DeNolf, 2009; Urcuioli & Swisher, 2012.)

Stimulus equivalence training has been of great interest in applied behavior analysis (e.g., Rehfeldt, 2011). As I noted, learning various forms of stimulus equivalence is critical in learning language. Therefore, equivalence training has been commonly used in efforts to increase the verbal repertoire of individuals with intellectual disabilities. Interestingly, the ability to use verbal labels facilitates equivalence class formation (e.g., Randell & Remington, 1999). However, language competence is not essential for the learning of stimulus equivalence classes (Carr, Wilkinson, Blackman, & McIlvane, 2000).

dissimilar physical stimuli all call for the same word. Such examples raise the provocative possibility that there are learning procedures that increase stimulus generalization. How might we construct such procedures?

In a discrimination procedure, stimuli are treated differently: They have different consequences. One stimulus (the S+) is associated with reinforcement, whereas the other (the S–) is not. This differential treatment leads organisms to respond to the stimuli as distinct from each other. What would happen if two stimuli were treated in the same or equivalent fashion? Would such a procedure lead to responding to them in the same fashion? The answer seems to be yes. Just as discrimination training encourages differential responding, equivalence training encourages generalized responding among a set of stimuli or the establishment of **stimulus equivalence**.

Several approaches are available to promote generalization rather than discrimination among stimuli. One involves linking each of several different stimuli to a common outcome and hence is called *common outcome training*. In an experiment by Honey and Hall (1989), for example, rats first received presentations of two different auditory cues, a noise and a clicker, paired with food. The common food outcome was expected to create functional equivalence between the noise and clicker stimuli. The control group also received presentations of the noise and the clicker, but for the control group only the clicker was paired with food. Both groups then had the noise paired with mild foot shock, resulting in the conditioning of fear to the noise. The main question was whether this conditioned fear of the noise would generalize to the clicker. Significantly more generalization occurred in the common outcome group than in the control group. The initial phase in which the clicker and noise were paired with the common food outcome served to make the clicker and noise equivalent for those animals.

In the experiment by Honey and Hall, equivalence was established by associating the two physically different stimuli (noise and clicker) with a common reinforcer (food). The equivalence class in this case had two members (the noise and the clicker). A larger equivalence class could have been created by pairing additional cues with the common food outcome. The critical factor is to associate all of the members of an equivalence class with a common event. The common event can be a reinforcer, such as food, or a common stimulus outcome (e.g., Delius, Jitsumori, & Siemann, 2000).

Perhaps the most widely used strategy for establishing stimulus equivalence is called *common response training* and involves training the same response to several physically different stimuli. This is essentially what is happening when parents teach their children to say the word "fruit" when they see grapes, coconuts, bananas, and watermelons. Even though the various types of fruit are physically different from each other, the common response ("fruit") is reinforced, and that creates the equivalence class called "fruit."

Experiments on common response training to establish stimulus equivalence often employ the experimental design illustrated in Table 8.3. The letters A, B, C, and D represent four different sets of stimuli. For example, Set A may consist of four arbitrary designs (A1 through A4), Set B may consist of a second set of arbitrary designs (B1 through B4), and so on. During initial training, the participants are reinforcing for making one response (R1) whenever stimuli from Set A or Set B are presented. Making this common response presumably establishes the A and B stimuli as an equivalence class. A similar procedure is carried out with stimuli from Sets C and D, but in that case the common reinforced response is R2. Once participants are well trained on the original discrimination problem (consistently making R1 on all A and B trials and R2 on all C and D trials), they are ready to move on to the reassignment phase of the experiment.

During the reassignment phase, the stimuli in Set A are trained with a new response R3 and the stimuli in Set C are trained with a new response R4. Notice that stimuli from Sets B and D are not used during the reassignment training phase. However, if stimuli in

P. Urcuioli

highest response rate. How can this be? Excitatory stimulus generalization gradients are supposed to peak at the S+. In an ingenious analysis, Spence (1937) proposed a theoretical approach that continues to command respect in contemporary research. Spence suggested that discrimination training leads to the learning of excitation to S+ and inhibition to S–. Furthermore, both of these were assumed to generalize to other similar cues, with the excitatory stimulus generalization gradient centered around S+ and the inhibitory gradient centered around S–. When S+ and S– are both colors, the generalization gradients of excitation and inhibition may overlap, with the degree of overlap depending on the degree of similarity between S+ and S–. Because of this overlap, inhibition to S– may generalize to S+ and suppress responding to S+, resulting in a peak-shift effect. More inhibition from S– to S+ is expected if S– is closer to S+, and this should result in a greater peak-shift effect. The data in Figure 8.10 conform to these predictions perfectly.

Spence's theory of discrimination learning has been remarkably successful (e.g., Hearst, 1968, 1969; Marsh, 1972), although the theory has not been able to explain all relevant data (e.g., Lazareva et al., 2008). Reflecting on the overall impact of Spence's theory, Pearce and colleagues (2008) noted that "the study of discrimination learning represents one of psychology's more enduring theoretical endeavors. Spence's theory has already made a significant contribution to this endeavor, and it seems likely that it will continue to do so for many years to come" (p. 198).

Alternative Accounts of Peak Shift   As we discussed earlier, studies of stimulus control can tell us a great deal about how organisms (human and nonhuman) view the world. An important question that has been a source of debate for decades is whether we view stimuli in terms of their individual and absolute properties or in terms of their relation to other stimuli that we experience (e.g., Köhler, 1939). The elemental versus configural analysis of control by stimulus compounds that I discussed earlier in this chapter is part of this long-standing debate. As with many such debates, evidence consistent with both approaches is available, suggesting that both types of mechanisms can operate, perhaps under different circumstances (e.g., Lazareva, 2012).

Spence's model of discrimination learning is an absolute stimulus learning model. It predicts behavior based on the net excitatory properties of individual stimuli. The alternative approach assumes that organisms learn to respond to a stimulus based on its relation to other cues in the situation. For example, when presented with an S+ that is a large circle and S– that is a smaller circle, the participant may respond to the S+ based on its relative size (in comparison to S–) rather than in terms of its absolute size. An interesting prediction of this approach is that the shape of a generalization gradient will change as a function of the range of test stimuli that are presented during the generalization test session. These and other predictions of the relational approach have been confirmed in studies with both human and nonhuman participants (e.g., Bizo & McMahon, 2007; Lazareva et al., 2008; Thomas, 1993).

Stimulus Equivalence Training

As we have seen, discrimination training dramatically increases the stimulus control of behavior (Figure 8.6) and can bring behavior under the control of interoceptive and configural cues. There are certainly situations where increased discrimination is highly desirable (deciding, for example, whether a mole on your skin is benign or cancerous). However, there are also situations where generalizing the same response to a variety of physically different stimuli is helpful. Language, for example, requires calling something an "apple" in response to a photograph of an apple, the presence of an apple on the kitchen counter, or the taste of an apple that you have just bitten into. These highly

Courtesy of Olga Lazareva

Olga Lazareva

FIGURE 8.10 Effects of intradimensional discrimination training on stimulus control. All three groups of pigeons were reinforced for pecking in the presence of 550-nm light (S+). One group received discrimination training in which the S– was a 590-nm light. For another group, the S– was a 555-nm light. The third group served as a control and did not receive discrimination training before the test for stimulus generalization. (From "Effects of Discrimination Training on Stimulus Generalization," by H. M. Hanson, 1959, *Journal of Experimental Psychology, 58,* pp. 321–333.)

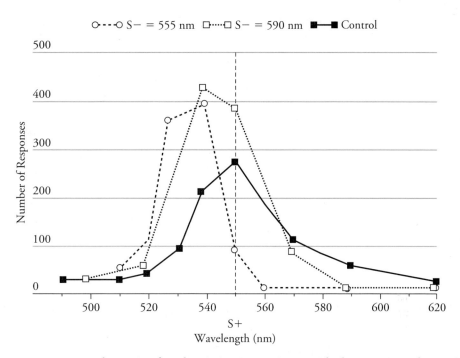

S+ was even more dramatic after discrimination training with the 555-nm color as S–. These birds showed much lower rates of responding to the original S+ (550 nm) than either of the other two groups. Furthermore, their highest response rates occurred to colors of 540- and 530-nm wavelength. This shift of the peak of the generalization gradient away from the original S+ is remarkable because in the earlier phase of discrimination training, responding was never reinforced in the presence of the 540-nm or 530-nm stimuli. Thus, the highest rates of pecking occurred to stimuli that had never even been presented during original training.

The shift of the peak of the generalization gradient away from the original S+ is called the peak-shift effect. It is important to note the two features of the peak-shift effect evident in Figure 8.10. First, the peak-shift effect is a result of intradimensional discrimination training. The control group, which did not receive intradimensional discrimination training, did not show the peak-shift effect. Second, the peak-shift effect was a function of the similarity of the S– to the S+ used in discrimination training. The biggest peak shift occurred after training in which the S– was very similar to the S+ (555 nm and 550 nm, respectively). Less of a peak shift occurred after discrimination training with more widely different colors (590 nm compared with 550 nm).

Similar results were evident in the Jenkins and Harrison experiment (Figure 8.6). A small peak-shift effect was evident in birds that received discrimination training with the 1,000-cps tone as S+ and the 950-cps tone as S–. Notice that for this group, the highest rate of responding occurred to a tonal frequency above 1,000 cps. No peak shift occurred for pigeons trained with the 1,000-cps tone as S+ and the absence of the tone as S–.

The peak-shift effect can result from any intradimensional discrimination not just pitch and color. The S+ and S– may be lines of different orientations, tones of different loudness, temporal cues, spatial stimuli, or facial cues. Furthermore, the effect has been observed in a variety of species, including people (e.g., Bizo & McMahon, 2007; Spetch, Chang, & Clifford, 2004; Russella & Kirkpatrick, 2007; Wisniewski, Church, & Mercado, 2009).

Spence's Explanation of Peak Shift The peak-shift effect is remarkable because it shows that the S+, or reinforced stimulus, is not necessarily the one that produces the

Interactions Between S+ and S−: The Peak-Shift Effect

So far I have described general characteristics of stimulus discrimination training under the assumption that what subjects learn about S+ is pretty much independent of what they learn about S−. This assumption is too simplistic. Learning is not so neatly compartmentalized. What you learn about S+ can influence your response to S− and vice versa. Such interactions are particularly likely if S+ and S− are related in some way.

S+ and S− may be related if they are similar except for one feature or attribute. This was the case in the Jenkins and Harrison experiment, whose results are presented in Figure 8.6. For one of the groups in that study, the S+ was a 1,000-cps tone and the S− was a 950-cps tone. Thus, the S+ and S− stimuli differed only slightly in pitch. A training procedure in which the S+ and S− differ only in terms of the value of one stimulus feature (in this case pitch) is called an **intradimensional discrimination**. The eyeblink stimulus discrimination procedure whose results are presented in Figure 8.5 was also an intradimensional discrimination. In that study, the CS+ and CS− stimuli were also tones differing in pitch (2,000 cps versus 8,000 cps).

Intradimensional discriminations are of particular interest because they are related to the issue of expert performance. Expert performance typically involves making subtle distinctions. Distinguishing stimuli that differ only in a single feature is more difficult than distinguishing stimuli that differ in many respects. It does not require much expertise to tell the difference between a compact car and a bus. In contrast, one has to be fairly sophisticated about cars to tell the difference between one version of the Honda Civic and another. Greater expertise is required to make finer distinctions. Two championship skaters may perform with equal skill as far as most people can tell, but expert judges are able to detect subtle but important differences that result in one performer getting higher marks than the other. Intradimensional discrimination is a form of expert performance because it requires detecting a single differentiating feature between S+ and S−.

Intradimensional discriminations are interesting because they can produce a counterintuitive phenomenon known as the **peak-shift effect**. This was demonstrated in a classic experiment by Hanson (1959). Hanson examined the effects of intradimensional discrimination training on the extent to which various colors controlled pecking behavior in pigeons. All the pigeons were reinforced for pecking in the presence of a light whose wavelength was 550 nm. However, independent groups differed in how similar the S− was to the S+ (how expert the pigeons had to become in telling the colors apart). One group received discrimination training in which the S− was a color of 590-nm wavelength, 40 nm away from the S+. For another group, the wavelength of the S− was 555 nm, only 5 nm away from the S+. The performance of these pigeons was compared to a control group that did not receive discrimination training but was also reinforced for pecking in the presence of the 550-nm stimulus. (Notice the similarity of this experiment to the study by Jenkins and Harrison shown in Figure 8.6. In both cases, the difficulty of the discrimination was varied across groups.)

After their various training experiences, all the birds were tested for their rate of pecking in the presence of test stimuli that varied in color. The results are shown in Figure 8.10. Consider first the performance of the control group that did not receive discrimination training. These pigeons responded most to the S+ stimulus and responded progressively less as the color of the test stimuli deviated from the color of S+. The control group showed a standard **excitatory generalization gradient** centered at the S+.

Different results were obtained after discrimination training with the 590-nm color as S−. These pigeons also responded at high rates to the 550-nm color that had served as the S+. However, they showed much more generalization of the pecking response to the 540-nm color. In fact, their rate of response was slightly higher to the 540-nm color than to the original 550-nm S+. This shift of the peak responding away from the original

FIGURE 8.11 Development of a preference for a distinctive context paired (or unpaired) with sexual reinforcement in male domesticated quail. Five conditioning trials were conducted between successive tests for the subjects in the paired group. (Based on "Context Excitation and Modulation of Conditioned Sexual Behavior," by C. K. Akins, *Animal Learning & Behavior, Vol. 26*, Figure 1, p. 419.)

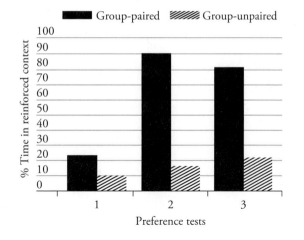

Thus, the birds received exposure to the CS context paired with sexual reinforcement. Birds in the control group received access to a female in their home cages 2 hours before being placed in the CS context, making the CS and US presentations unpaired.

In addition to the preference test conducted before the start of conditioning, preference tests were conducted after the 5th and 10th conditioning trials. The results of these tests are presented in Figure 8.11. Notice that the paired and unpaired groups showed similar low preferences for the CS compartment at the outset of the experiment. This low preference persisted in the control group. In contrast, the birds that received the CS context paired with sexual reinforcement came to prefer that context. Thus, the association of contextual cues with sexual reinforcement increased preference for those cues.

Experiments like the one by Akins illustrate that contextual cues can come to control behavior if they serve as a signal for a US or a reinforcer. This methodology is common in studies of drug-conditioned place preference. The conditioned place-preference technique is used to determine whether a drug has reinforcing effects. This question is particularly important in the development of new drugs because drugs that can condition a place preference have the potential of becoming drugs of abuse.

As in the study by Akins, the participants (usually laboratory rats or mice) in a conditioned place-preference experiment are first familiarized with two distinct contexts. One of these is then designated as the CS and paired with the administration of the drug under evaluation. After the conditioning phase, the participants are again tested for their preference between the two contexts to see if they now have a greater preference for the drug-paired context (see Tzschentke, 2007, for a review). Studies of fear conditioning also often employ contextual cues as CSs (e.g., McNally & Westbrook, 2006).

In the above experiments, contextual cues were used in the same way as discrete CSs. It is not surprising, therefore, that they gained control over behavior. Would contextual cues also come to control behavior when they do not signal reinforcement—when they are truly "background" cues that the organism is not specifically required to pay attention to? This is one of the fundamental questions in the stimulus control of instrumental behavior. Much work has been devoted to it, and the answer is clearly *yes*. Contextual cues do not have to signal reinforcement to gain control over behavior.

A classic experiment by Thomas, McKelvie, and Mah (1985) illustrates control by contextual cues that are not correlated with the availability of reinforcement. Pigeons were first trained on a line-orientation discrimination in which a vertical line (90°) served as the S+ and a horizontal line (0°) served as the S–. The birds were periodically reinforced with food for pecking on S+ trials and were not reinforced on S– trials. The training took place in a standard Skinner box (Context 1).

FIGURE 8.12 Generalization gradients obtained with various line-angle stimuli following training in two different contexts. In Context 1, the 90° stimulus served as the S+ and the 0° stimulus served as the S–. In Context 2, the 0° stimulus served as the S+ and the 90° stimulus served as the S–. (Based on "Context as a Conditional Cue in Operant Discrimination Reversal Learning," by D. R. Thomas, A. R. McKelvie, and W. L. Mah, 1985, *Journal of Experimental Psychology: Animal Behavior Processes, 11,* pp. 317–330.)

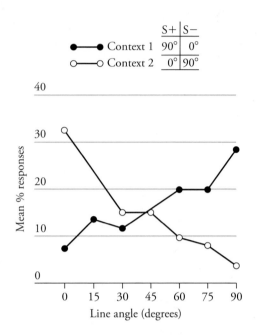

After the discrimination was well learned, the contextual cues of the experimental chamber were changed by altering both the lighting and the type of noise in the chamber. In the presence of these new contextual cues (Context 2), the discrimination training contingencies were reversed. Now, the horizontal line (0°) served as the S+ and the vertical line (90°) served as the S–. Notice that the pigeons were not specifically required to pay attention to the contextual cues. They were simply required to learn the new discrimination problem. (They could have learned this new problem had the contextual cues not been changed.)

After mastery of the reversal problem, the birds received generalization tests in which lines of various orientations between 0° and 90° were presented. One such generalization test was conducted in Context 1, and another was conducted in Context 2. The results of these tests are presented in Figure 8.12. Remarkably, the shape of the generalization gradient in each context was appropriate to the discrimination problem that was in effect in that context. Thus, in Context 1, the birds responded most to the 90° stimulus (which had served as the S+ in that context) and least to the 0° stimulus (which had served as the S–). The opposite pattern of results occurred in Context 2. Here, the pigeons responded most to the 0° stimulus and least to the 90° stimulus, appropriate to the reverse discrimination contingencies that had been in effect in Context 2. (For a similar result in human predictive learning, see Üngör & Lachnit, 2006.)

The findings presented in Figure 8.12 show that control by contextual cues can develop without one context being more strongly associated with reinforcement than another. The pigeons received reinforced (S+) and nonreinforced (S–) trials in both Context 1 and Context 2. One context was not a better signal for the availability of reinforcement than the other. (For a related recent study, see Bonardi & Jennings, 2009.)

How did Contexts 1 and 2 come to produce such contrasting responses to line angles? A likely possibility is that each context activated a different memory. Context 1 activated the memory of reinforcement with 90° and nonreinforcement with 0° (90+/0–). In contrast, Context 2 activated the memory of reinforcement with 0° and nonreinforcement with 90° (90–/0+). Instead of being associated with a particular stimulus, each context came to activate a different S+/S– contingency. Thus, the participants learned a **conditional relation**: If Context 1, then 90+/0–; if Context 2, then 90–/0+. The relationship between the line orientations and reinforcement was conditional upon the context in which the participants were located at the time.

BOX 8.2

Hippocampal Function and Long-Term Potentiation

One of our most remarkable abilities involves the rapid encoding of distinct episodes within our lives, providing a form of episodic memory. We can remember what we had for breakfast and where, a new acquaintance we met yesterday, and where we parked our car at the airport. To remember this type of information, we must encode a form of mental conjunction, a unique memory trace that records what, when, and where an event occurred. Research has shown that this ability depends on a portion of the forebrain, the *hippocampus*, a seahorse-shaped structure that lies under the cortical surface and is richly interconnected with it (EP-6 at the back of the book and Figure 8.13A). Over the last 50 years, researchers have elucidated both its function and how it biologically encodes new information (for recent reviews, see Buckner, 2010; Leuner & Gould, 2010; Wang & Morris, 2010).

Insights regarding hippocampal function first emerged from work with a patient, known during his lifetime as simply H.M. In the 1950s, he underwent bilateral removal of the hippocampus and the surrounding tissue to treat debilitating seizures (Squire & Wixted, 2011). While the surgery reduced his seizures, it also led to a devastating memory impairment that was studied by Brenda Milner. She found that his impairment had remarkable specificity. He could recognize objects and understand the meaning of words (*semantic memory*). He could also recall events that happened years ago (*long-term memory*) and temporarily remember new information (*short-term memory*), such as a phone number. However, he lost the capacity to transfer new information into long-term memory and later consciously recall it. He lost the ability to encode distinct episodes within his

life, a deficit in **episodic memory** that is also seen with the dementia of *Alzheimer's disease*, which causes a disruption in hippocampal function.

The role of the hippocampus in learning and memory has been extensively studied using laboratory animals and experimentally induced lesions. Because the hippocampus is richly interconnected with the overlying cortex, it receives input related to multiple dimensions, including color, sound, time, and location. By binding together the constellation of cues that define a particular moment in time, it can provide a snapshot that represents unique stimulus configurations. What distinguishes the hippocampus is that it accomplishes this feat in a rapid manner, incidentally in the absence of explicit reinforcement (O'Relly & Rudy, 2001; Rudy, 2009). When you enter a new room, you automatically encode what the room looks like with little or no mental effort. Likewise, a rat will encode the unique configuration of cues that define a new environment (context). This is readily shown using a Pavlovian task in which a rat is given a mild shock (the US) within a novel context. If the shock is given 2–3 minutes after the rat is placed in the environment, it will exhibit conditioned fear (freezing) when it is re-exposed to the context the next day. If, however, shock is given immediately after the rat is placed in the chamber, before it can presumably form a conjunctive representation of the context, it fails to associate the context with shock. This *immediate shock deficit* can be eliminated by simply exposing the rats to the context for 2–3 minutes the day before (Stote & Fanselow, 2004). It appears that rats must first encode the configuration of cues that define a context before the context can be associated with shock. Lesioning the

hippocampus eliminates this capacity (context conditioning). Importantly, it does so without affecting the capacity to learn that a discrete cue (e.g., a tone) predicts shock. As we saw earlier (Box 4.3), fear conditioning depends upon the basolateral region of the amygdala, where the cue (the CS) and shock (the US) are joined. The difference is that a simple cue provides a direct input to the amygdala, whereas context conditioning depends on the derivation of a conjunctive representation and output from the hippocampus.

Spatial learning also depends on a conjunction of cues. If you have good luck fishing on a lake, you will likely return to the same area. To do so, you need to remember your relative location given distant cues in your environment. As we will see in Chapter 11, rats are extremely good at this. For example, rats readily remember where they retrieved a food on a radial maze or the location of a submerged platform in water tank (*Morris water maze*). Research has shown that learning in these tasks requires an intact hippocampus. Likewise, rats will explore an object that is new or one that has been moved to a different location. If the hippocampus is lesioned, the rat will notice that an object has been changed (*object memory*) but not whether its location has been changed (*spatial memory*).

Given that the hippocampus has an important role in learning and memory, and its dysfunction contributes to dementia, researchers have worked to uncover the neurobiological mechanisms that allow it to encode new information. This work has revealed a cellular system for altering synaptic strength that is used throughout the nervous system. Electrophysiological studies by Bliss and Lomo (1973) showed that a strong neural input can strengthen

Continued

BOX 8.2 (continued)

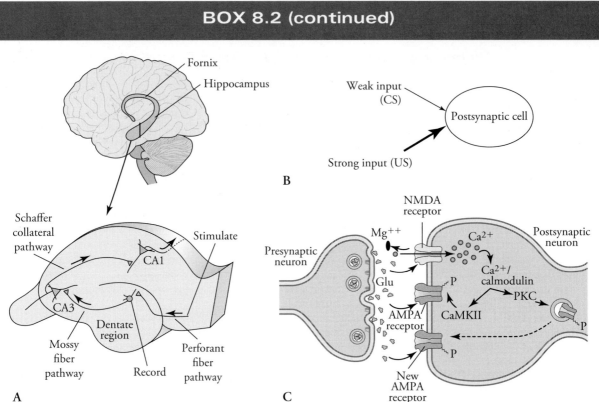

FIGURE 8.13 (A) A slice of the hippocampus. Bliss & Lomo (1973) stimulated the axons of the perforant path and recorded the response observed in the mossy fibers. They found that a strong input produced a long-lasting increase in the response elicited in the cells of the mossy fiber pathway. (B) A schematic of the neural relations that support associativity. One cell has weak input (the CS) while another has a strong connection (the US). The weak connection can be strengthened through paired presentation of both the weak and strong inputs (adapted from Kandel et al., 2013). (C) If a postsynaptic cell undergoes a sufficiently strong depolarization, it dislodges Mg^{++} from the NMDA channel, which allows Ca^{++} to enter the cell when the NMDA receptor is activated by glutamate (Glu). Ca^{++} entry engages a calmodulin-dependent protein kinase (CA^{++}/calmodulin [CaMKII]) that activates (phosphorylates) AMPA receptors. It also engages a protein kinase (PKC) that fosters the insertion of additional AMPA receptors into the active zone of the postsynaptic cell (adapted from Kandel et al., 2013).

the synaptic connection between two cells. In these studies, the authors lowered an electrode into a bundle of neurons in the hippocampus known as the *perforant path* and applied an electrical current (Figure 8.13A). The cells that form the perforant path synapse on hippocampal neurons called *mossy fibers*. By recording neural activity through electrodes placed near the mossy fiber cell bodies, Bliss and Lomo obtained a measure of synaptic strength. As we would expect, applying a moderate electrical stimulus to the perforant

path elicited moderate neural activity in the mossy fibers, and this response changed little over time. But if a strong input was provided, one that caused a very strong response (*depolarization*) in the mossy fibers, subsequent inputs produced a much larger response. This phenomenon is called **long-term potentiation (LTP)**. It appears that a strong input can effectively strengthen synaptic connections.

Interestingly, the impact of stimulation depends upon a variety of factors, including the frequency of

stimulation (Bear and Malenka, 1994; Habib & Dringenberg, 2010; Malenka and Bear, 2004). When a high-frequency stimulus (e.g., 100 Hz) is applied, LTP is typically observed. However, if a low frequency stimulus (e.g., 1 Hz) is given, an opponent-like phenomenon is induced, a *long-term depression (LTD)* that weakens the synaptic connections. In the absence of LTD, input to the hippocampus could saturate plasticity, which would prevent further learning.

LTP has a number of properties that suggest it plays a role in learning

Continued

BOX 8.2 (continued)

and memory (Dudai, 1989; Kandel et al., 2013). The most obvious is its *enduring nature*. Another important quality is *input specificity*: The modification is limited to those synapses that are concurrently active. LTP also exhibits a kind of *cooperativity*. The induction of LTP requires a strong response in the postsynaptic cell. This strong response does not have to come from just one input. Rather, a number of inputs can work together to drive the postsynaptic cell to the threshold for learning. Moreover, all the contributing inputs can benefit. A variation of this cooperativity yields the final, and most interesting property: *associativity* (Figure 8.13B). If a weak input is paired with a strong input, the latter will be sufficient to engage LTP at both connections. As a result, the weak input will acquire the capacity to drive a response in the postsynaptic cell, in much the same way that a CS acquires the ability to generate a CR as a result of being paired with a US.

A strong input could increase the strength of a chemical synapse and induce LTP by enhancing either the amount of transmitter released or the responsiveness of the postsynaptic cell. Research suggests that LTP is largely due to increased responsiveness of the postsynaptic cell. The presynaptic cell releases a neurotransmitter (*glutamate*) that can engage two types of receptors (AMPA and NMDA) on the postsynaptic cell (Figure 8.13C). Engaging the *AMPA receptor* allows Na^+ to enter the cell and initiates the chemical processes that produce an action potential (see Box 1.1). The **NMDA receptor** operates in a different manner and regulates the flow of Ca^{++} into the cell. At rest, the NMDA channel is blocked by the ion magnesium (Mg^{++}). For the NMDA receptor to work, this Mg^{++} must be displaced,

which requires a strong depolarization of the postsynaptic cell. This can be produced by strongly engaging the AMPA receptors at the same synapse or from a depolarization provided at another synapse on the same cell. In either case, when the Mg^{++} block is removed, the release of glutamate from the presynaptic cell engages the NMDA receptor and allows Ca^{++} to flow into the cell. This initiates biochemical processes within the cell that enhance AMPA receptor function. This is accomplished in two ways. One is by chemically altering (phosphorylating) the receptor, a modification that enhances the flow of positively charged ions into the cell. The other is by initiating the movement (trafficking) of additional AMPA receptors into the active region of the postsynaptic membrane (Malenka, 2003). Interestingly, trafficking can even turn on (awaken) a synapse that was silent because there were no AMPA receptors in the active zone. LTD is mediated by analogous chemical processes, but in the opposite direction.

Notice that the NMDA receptor acts as a kind of coincidence detector. For it to function, two conditions must be met—there must be both presynaptic release of glutamate and a strong depolarization. Also notice that the NMDA receptor is only needed for the induction of LTP (or LTD). Once the synapse has been changed, synaptic communication depends on the AMPA receptor alone. As a result, drug antagonists that disrupt NMDA function (e.g., MK-801 or APV) prevent the induction of LTP but not its maintenance.

To explore whether hippocampal LTP plays a functional role within the living organism (*in vivo*, Latin from "within the living"), researchers have examined whether treatment with an NMDA antagonist affects

learning and memory in tasks that depend upon hippocampal function. Supporting the proposed link, disrupting NMDA receptor function undermines fear conditioning to a context but not an embedded (discrete) cue. Similarly, the NMDA receptor antagonist MK-801 disrupts spatial learning within the Morris water maze. Importantly, in both cases, local infusion of the drug disrupts learning, but not memory retrieval. Research suggests that the NMDA receptor also contributes to learning and memory in other neural systems, including the cerebellum, amygdala, nucleus accumbens, and spinal cord (Boxes 3.2, 4.3, 7.1, and 10.1).

While the loss of hippocampal function with aging or disease can bring devastating memory impairments, there is reason to hope that this process may be slowed. Overturning the long-standing view that brain neurons do not regenerate, Gould and her colleagues have found evidence for the birth of new neurons (neurogenesis) within the hippocampus (Leuner & Gould, 2010). Exercise and environmental enrichment promote this process, whereas stress inhibits neurogenesis.

J. W. Grau

episodic memory   Memory for autobiographical events that occurred at a particular time and place.

long-term potentiation (LTP)   A lasting increase in neural excitability observed in a (postsynaptic) neuron that has been strongly depolarized. The induction of LTP has been linked to the activation of the NMDA receptor.

NMDA receptor   A specialized receptor that functions as a gated channel. Engaging the receptor requires both a strong depolarization (to displace the Mg^{++} ion blocking the channel) and the binding of the neurotransmitter glutamate.

Control by Conditional Relations

In much of the book so far, the emphasis has been on relations that involved just two events: a CS and US, or a response and a reinforcer. Relations between two events are called *binary relations*. Under certain circumstances, the nature of a binary relation is determined by a third event, called a **modulator**. In the previous experiment by Thomas and colleagues (1985), each context was a modulator. Whether or not a particular line-angle stimulus was associated with reinforcement depended on which contextual cues were present. The relation of a modulator to the binary relation that it signals is called a *conditional relation*. Numerous experiments have indicated that animals can learn to use modulators to tell when a particular binary relation is in effect (see reviews by Holland, 1984, 1992; Schmajuk & Holland, 1998; Swartzentruber, 1995).

We have already encountered some conditional relations without having identified them as such. One example is instrumental stimulus discrimination training. In an instrumental discrimination procedure, the organism is reinforced for responding during S+ but is not reinforced during S–. The discriminative stimuli S+ and S– are modulators that signal the relation between the response and the reinforcer. One response–reinforcer relation exists during S+ (positive reinforcement), and a different relation exists during S– (nonreinforcement). Thus, instrumental discrimination procedures involve conditional control of the relation between the response and the reinforcer.

Conditional Control in Pavlovian Conditioning   Conditional relations have been extensively investigated using Pavlovian conditioning procedures. Classical conditioning typically involves a binary relation between a CS and a US. The CS may be a brief auditory cue (white noise), and the US may be food. A strong relation exists between the CS and US if the food is presented immediately after each occurrence of the CS but not at other times. How could conditional control be established over such a CS–US relation?

Establishing a conditional relation requires introducing a third event (the modulator) that indicates when the presentation of the auditory CS will end in food. For example, a light could be introduced, in the presence of which the brief auditory CS would be followed by food. In the absence of the light, presentations of the auditory CS would be nonreinforced. This procedure is diagrammed in Figure 8.14. As in instrumental discrimination procedures, both reinforced and nonreinforced trials are conducted. During reinforced trials, the light is turned on for 15 seconds. Ten seconds into the light, a 5-second noise CS is turned on and is immediately followed by the food US. During nonreinforced trials, the noise CS is presented by itself and does not end in food.

The procedure I just described is similar to one that was conducted by Fetsko, Stebbins, Gallagher, and Colwill (2005) in a study with inbred mice. (There is great interest in adapting conditioning techniques for use with mice so that problems of learning and memory can be studied in genetically engineered knockout mice.) A light was used as the modulator on reinforced trials, and the target CS was a 5-second noise stimulus. Food was delivered into a food cup recessed in the wall of the experimental chamber. An infrared detector recorded each time the mouse poked its head into the food cup. As the

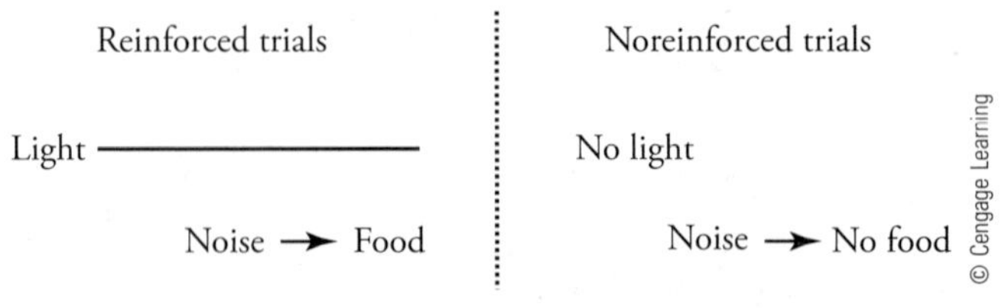

FIGURE 8.14 Procedure for establishing conditional stimulus control in classical conditioning. On reinforced trials, a light stimulus (modulator) is presented and the CS (noise) is paired with food. On nonreinforced trials, the modulator is absent and the CS (noise) is presented without food.

Reinforced trials	Noreinforced trials
Light ———————	No light
Noise → Food	Noise → No food

© Cengage Learning

FIGURE 8.15 Head entries into the food cup during a light and a noise stimulus when these stimuli were presented alone (L– and N–) without food and when the noise was presented at the end of the light stimulus and paired with food (L → N+) (based on Fetsko, Stebbins, Gallagher, & Colwill, 2005.)

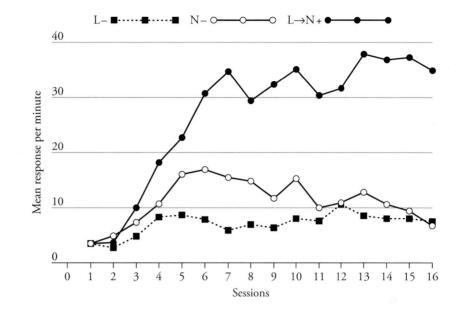

noise CS became associated with food, the mice showed increased head poking into the food cup during the CS. These anticipatory head pokes were measured as the conditioned response.

The results of the experiment are presented in Figure 8.15. The mice showed much more food-cup head entries during the noise CS when the CS was presented at the end of the light (L→N+) than on trials in which the noise CS was presented by itself (N–). The experiment also included trials with the light presented by itself (L–). The mice also showed low levels of responding during those trials. These results show that the modulator (L) facilitated responding to the noise CS. This occurred even though the modulator itself did not elicit responding. Just as a discriminative stimulus facilitates instrumental behavior, the modulator facilitated CS-elicited responding in this experiment.

Research on the modulation of conditioned responding in Pavlovian conditioning was pioneered by Peter Holland (Holland, 1985; Ross & Holland, 1981) and Robert Rescorla (Rescorla, 1985). Holland elected to call a Pavlovian modulator an *occasion setter* because the modulator sets the occasion for reinforcement of the target CS. Rescorla elected to call a Pavlovian modulator a *facilitator* because the modulator facilitates responding to the target CS. The terms **occasion setting** and **facilitation** have both been used in subsequent discussions of Pavlovian modulation.

It is interesting to note that the procedure outlined in Figure 8.14 is the converse of the standard procedure for inhibitory conditioning (Figure 3.11). To turn the procedure outlined in Figure 8.14 into one that will result in the conditioning of inhibitory properties to the noise, all one has to do is to reverse which type of trial has the light. Instead of presenting the light on reinforced trials, the light would be presented on nonreinforced trials in a conditioned inhibition procedure.

Presenting the light on nonreinforced trials would make the light a signal for nonreinforcement of the noise CS and might make the light a conditioned inhibitor (see Chapter 3). This example shows that the procedure for inhibitory Pavlovian conditioning involves a conditional relation, just as positive occasion setting and facilitation procedures do. This argument also suggests that conditioned inhibition may be the conceptual opposite of facilitation or positive occasion setting rather than the opposite of conditioned excitation (Rescorla, 1987).

Distinction Between Excitation and Modulation Studies of positive occasion setting or facilitation (e.g., Figure 8.14) are important not only because they illustrate that classical conditioning is subject to conditional control but also because they involve a new mechanism of learning. Positive occasion setting or facilitation is different from conditioned excitation.

As the results presented in Figure 8.14 show, the light stimulus was effective in facilitating responding to the noise CS on L→N+ trials but the light itself did not elicit responding on L– trials. This shows that a modulator need not have conditioned excitatory properties. In fact, conditioning excitatory properties to a stimulus does not make that stimulus function as a modulator (Holland, 1985; Rescorla, 1985).

Additional evidence for a distinction between modulation and conditioned excitation is based on the effects of extinction procedures. *Extinction* refers to a procedure in which a previously conditioned CS is presented repeatedly but now without the US. We will discuss extinction in greater detail in Chapter 9. The typical outcome of extinction is that conditioned responding declines. Interestingly, the same procedure (repeated nonreinforced stimulus presentations) carried out with a modulator often has no effect. Once a stimulus has become established to set the occasion for a CS–US relation, repeated presentations of the stimulus by itself usually do not reduce its ability to facilitate conditioned responding to the CS (e.g., Holland, 1989a; Rescorla, 1985).

The difference in the effects of an extinction procedure on conditioned excitatory stimuli and modulators is related to what is signaled. A conditioned excitatory stimulus signals the forthcoming presentation of the US. The absence of the US following presentation of the CS during extinction is a violation of that expectancy. Hence, the signal value of the CS has to be readjusted in extinction to bring it in line with the new reality. In contrast, a modulator signals a relation between a CS and a US. The absence of the US when the modulator is presented alone does not mean that the relation between the target CS and the US has changed. Thus, the information signaled by a modulator is not invalidated by presenting the modulator by itself during extinction. Therefore, the ability of the modulator to promote responding elicited by another CS remains intact during extinction.

Modulation Versus Configural Conditioning Not all discrimination procedures of the type illustrated in Figure 8.14 result in the learning of a conditional relation between the stimuli involved. On reinforced trials in this procedure, a compound stimulus was presented consisting of the light and the noise CS. As I noted earlier, organisms can respond to a compound stimulus either in terms of the elements that make up the compound or in terms of the unique stimulus configuration produced by the elements. For the light to serve as a signal that the noise will be paired with food, the light and noise cues have to be treated as independent events rather than as a combined configural cue (Holland, 1992).

To encourage organisms to treat stimulus compounds as consisting of independent elements, investigators have presented the elements one after the other rather than simultaneously. On reinforced trials, the modulator is usually presented first, followed by the target CS and reinforcement. This is how the procedure in Figure 8.14 was designed. The light started 10 seconds before the noise on each reinforced trial. In many of his experiments on occasion setting, Holland has even inserted a 5-second gap between the modulator and the target CS. Such a gap discourages the perception of a stimulus configuration based on the occasion setter and the target CS. If the modulator and the target CS are presented simultaneously, modulatory effects are often not observed (e.g., Holland, 1986).

Concluding Comments

Stimulus control refers to how precisely tuned an organism's behavior is to specific features of the environment. Therefore, the study of stimulus control is critical for understanding how an organism interacts with its environment. Stimulus control is measured in terms of the steepness of generalization gradients. A steep generalization gradient indicates that small variations in a stimulus produce large differences in responding. Weaker stimulus control is indicated by flatter generalization gradients.

The degree of stimulus control is determined by numerous factors, including the sensory capacity of the organism, the relative salience of other cues in the situation, and the type of reinforcement used. Importantly, stimulus control is also a function of learning. Discrimination training increases the stimulus control of behavior whether that training involves stimuli that differ in several respects (interdimensional discrimination) or stimuli that differ in only one respect (intradimensional discrimination). Intradimensional discrimination training produces more precise stimulus control and may lead to the counterintuitive outcome that the highest level of responding is shifted away from the reinforced stimulus. The converse of discrimination training is equivalence training, which increases the generalization of behavior to a variety of physically different stimuli because all those stimuli lead to the same outcome or occasion the same response.

Not only discrete stimuli but also background contextual cues can come to control behavior. Furthermore, stimulus control by contextual cues can develop even if attention to contextual cues is not required to optimize reinforcement. Finally, behavior can come under the control of conditional relations among stimuli, in which a stimulus activates an association between two other events.

Sample Questions

1. Describe the relationship between stimulus discrimination and stimulus generalization.
2. Describe the phenomenon of overshadowing, and describe how it may be explained by elemental and configural approaches to stimulus control.
3. Describe how the steepness of a generalization gradient may be altered by experience and learning.
4. Describe the difference between intradimensional and interdimensional discrimination training.
5. Describe the peak-shift effect and its determinants.
6. Describe the ways in which contextual cues can come to control behavior.
7. Compare and contrast conditioned excitation and modulatory or occasion-setting properties of stimuli.

Key Terms

conditional relation   A relation in which the significance of one stimulus or event depends on the status of another stimulus.

configural-cue approach   An approach to the analysis of stimulus control which assumes that organisms respond to a compound stimulus as an integral whole rather than a collection of separate and independent stimulus elements. (Compare with the *stimulus-element approach.*)

discriminative stimulus   A stimulus that controls the performance of instrumental behavior because it signals the availability (or nonavailability) of reinforcement.

excitatory generalization gradient   A gradient of responding that is observed when organisms are tested with the S+ from a discrimination procedure and with stimuli that increasingly differ from the S+. Typically the highest level of responding occurs to the S+; progressively less responding occurs to stimuli that increasingly differ from the S+. Thus, the gradient has an inverted-U shape.

facilitation   A procedure in which one cue designates when another cue will be reinforced. Also called *occasion setting.*

intradimensional discrimination A discrimination between stimuli that differ only in terms of the value of one stimulus feature, such as color, brightness, or pitch.

modulator A stimulus that signals the relation between two other events. A modulator may signal that a CS will be followed by a US or that an instrumental response will be reinforced. The modulator is part of a conditional relation in which the status of a binary relation depends on the status of the modulator.

multiple schedule of reinforcement A procedure in which different reinforcement schedules are in effect in the presence of different stimuli presented in succession. Generally, each stimulus comes to evoke a pattern of responding that corresponds to whatever reinforcement schedule is in effect during that stimulus.

negative patterning A discrimination procedure in which reinforcement is provided when each of two stimuli appear by themselves (A+ and B+) but not when the two stimuli appear simultaneously (AB−).

occasion setting Same as *facilitation.*

overshadowing Interference with the conditioning of a stimulus because of the simultaneous presence of another stimulus that is easier to condition.

peak-shift effect A displacement of the highest rate of responding in a stimulus generalization gradient away from the S+ in a direction opposite the S−.

positive patterning A discrimination procedure in which reinforcement is provided when two stimuli (A and B) are presented simultaneously (AB+) but not when those stimuli appear by themselves (A− and B−).

stimulus discrimination Differential responding in the presence of two or more stimuli.

stimulus discrimination training Training with a stimulus discrimination procedure that results in stimulus discrimination.

stimulus discrimination procedure (in classical conditioning) A classical conditioning procedure in which one stimulus (the CS+) is paired with the US on some trials and another stimulus (the CS−) is presented without the US on other trials. As a result of this procedure, the CS+ comes to elicit a conditioned response and the CS− comes to inhibit this response.

stimulus discrimination procedure (in instrumental conditioning) A procedure in which reinforcement for responding is available whenever one stimulus (the S+, or S^D) is present and not available whenever another stimulus (the S−, or S^Δ) is present.

stimulus-element approach An approach to the analysis of control by compound stimuli which assumes that participants respond to a compound stimulus in terms of the stimulus elements that make up the compound. (Compare with the *configural-cue approach.*)

stimulus equivalence Responding to physically distinct stimuli as if they were the same because of common prior experiences with the stimuli.

stimulus generalization Responding to test stimuli that are different from the cues that were present during training.

stimulus generalization gradient A gradient of responding that is observed if participants are tested with stimuli that increasingly differ from the stimulus that was present during training. (See also *excitatory generalization gradient.*)

CHAPTER **9**

Extinction of Conditioned Behavior

CHAPTER PREVIEW

This chapter represents a departure from previous chapters in that for the first time the focus is on procedures that produce a decline in responding. Extinction can only be conducted after a response or association has been established using Pavlovian or instrumental conditioning. Often the goal is to reverse the effects of acquisition. However, a true reversal of acquisition is rarely achieved and may not be possible. The phenomena of spontaneous recovery, renewal, reinstatement, and resurgence all attest to the fact that extinction does not erase what was learned previously. Additional evidence indicates that S–O and R–O associations survive extinction procedures. Rather than erasing old learning, extinction seems to involve learning a new inhibitory S–R association. The inhibition arises from the "frustrative" effects of the unexpected absence of reward. The frustration produced by nonreward is responsible for a number of paradoxical reward effects, including the partial-reinforcement extinction effect. Intermittent or partial reinforcement permits organisms to learn about nonreward so as to immunize them against the effects of extinction. That kind of resistance to change is also the subject of studies of behavioral momentum that are described at the end of the chapter.

So far, our discussion of classical and instrumental conditioning has centered on various aspects of the acquisition and maintenance of new associations and new responses. Learning is useful because the new responses that are acquired often facilitate adjustment to a changing environment. But changes in the environment can also favor the loss of conditioned behavior. Not many reinforcement schedules remain in effect forever. Responses that are successful at one point may cease to be effective later. Children are praised for drawing crude representations of people and objects in nursery school, but the same type of drawing is not rewarded if made by a high school student. Dating someone may be extremely pleasant and rewarding at first but stops being reinforcing when that person falls in love with someone else.

Acquisition of conditioned behavior involves procedures in which a reinforcing outcome occurs. In Pavlovian conditioning, the outcome or unconditioned stimulus (US) is presented as a consequence of a conditioned stimulus (CS). In instrumental conditioning, the reinforcing outcome is presented as a consequence of the instrumental response. **Extinction** involves omitting the US, or reinforcer. In classical conditioning, extinction involves repeated presentations of the CS without the US. In instrumental conditioning, extinction involves no longer presenting the reinforcer when the response occurs. With both types of procedures, conditioned responding declines. Thus, the behavior change that occurs in extinction is the reverse of what was observed in acquisition. Because of this, extinction appears to be the opposite of acquisition. Indeed, that is how extinction has been characterized in some theories of learning, such as the Rescorla–Wagner model (see Chapter 4). However, as the evidence described in the present chapter shows, this view of extinction is incorrect.

It is important to point out that the loss of conditioned behavior that occurs as a result of extinction is not the same as the loss of responding that may occur because of **forgetting**. Extinction is an active process produced by the omission of an expected US or the reinforcer. Forgetting, by contrast, is a decline in responding that may occur because of the passage of time and does not require nonreinforcement of the CS or the instrumental response.

Extinction is one of the most vigorous areas of research in learning today. Behavioral investigations of extinction are being pursued in both appetitive conditioning and aversive or fear conditioning paradigms, following both classical and instrumental conditioning (Bouton & Woods, 2008; Lattal & Lattal, 2012; Lattal et al., 2013). Extinction is also being studied at the level of brain structures, neurotransmitter systems, and cellular and genetic mechanisms. Impressive progress is being made in the neuroscience and neurobiology of extinction, especially in the case of conditioned fear (e.g., Peters, Kalivas, & Quirk, 2009; Stafford & Lattal, 2011).

Extinction is also one of the hottest areas for translational research that seeks to improve clinical practice based on laboratory findings (e.g., Bouton & Nelson, 1998; Gillihan & Foa, 2011). Social phobia, fear of flying, claustrophobia, and other pathological fears and phobias are typically treated with some form of exposure therapy (e.g., Meuret et al., 2012). Exposure therapy is basically an extinction procedure in which participants are exposed to cues that elicit fear in the absence of the aversive US. Exposure to the actual fearful stimulus is the best way to conduct exposure therapy, but that is often not practical. Having clients imagine being in the fearful situation can be helpful. However, more vivid and realistic exposure is now possible with the use of virtual reality techniques (e.g., Parsons & Rizzo, 2008). Exposure therapy is also employed in treating drug addiction, with the aim of extinguishing cues associated with drug-taking behavior. More careful consideration of the relevant basic research literature promises to substantially improve the effectiveness of exposure therapy in this area (Conklin & Tiffany, 2002; Kaplan,

Heinrichs, & Carey, 2011). (For translational research on extinction focused on neurobiological mechanisms, see Maren, 2011; Milad & Quirk, 2012.)

Effects of Extinction Procedures

What would you do if the key to your apartment unexpectedly did not work and you could not get in? Chances are you would not give up after the first attempt but would try several more times, perhaps jiggling the key in the lock in different ways each time. But, if none of those response variations worked, you would eventually quit trying. This illustrates two basic behavioral effects of extinction. The most obvious behavioral effect is that the target response decreases when the response no longer results in reinforcement. This is the primary behavioral effect of extinction and the outcome that has occupied most of the attention of scientists. Investigations of extinction have been concerned with how rapidly responding decreases and how long the response suppression lasts. If the key to your apartment no longer opens the door, you will give up trying. However, notice that before you give up entirely, you are likely to jiggle the key in various ways in an effort to make it work. This illustrates the second basic behavioral effect of extinction, namely that it produces an increase in response variability.

The two basic behavioral effects of extinction were nicely illustrated in a study with laboratory rats (Neuringer, Kornell, & Olufs, 2001). Two groups served in the experiment. The apparatus and procedure were set up to facilitate the measurement of response variability. The experimental chamber had two response levers on one wall and a round response key on the opposite wall. During the reinforcement phase, the rats had to make three responses in a row to obtain a food pellet. For example, they could press the left lever three times (LLL), press each lever and the response key once (RLK), or press the left lever twice and the key once (LLK). One group of rats was reinforced for varying its response sequences (Group Var). They got food only if the sequence of responses they made on a particular trial was different from what they did on earlier trials. Each participant in the second group was also required to make three responses to get reinforced, but for them, there was no requirement to vary how they accomplished that (Group Yoke). After responding was well established by the reinforcement contingencies in both groups, extinction was introduced, and food was no longer provided no matter what the rats did.

Figure 9.1 shows the results of the experiment for the last four sessions of the reinforcement phase and the first four sessions of the extinction phase. The left panel represents the variability in the response sequences each group performed; the right panel represents their rates of responding. Notice that reinforcement produced the expected difference between the two groups in terms of the variability of their response sequences. Participants reinforced for varying their responses (Group Var) showed much more variability than those that did not have to vary their behavior (Group Yoke). The second group responded somewhat faster, perhaps because they did not have to move as frequently from one manipulandum to another.

Extinction produced a decline in the rate of responding in both groups (see right panel of Figure 9.1). Interestingly, this decline in responding occurred in the face of an increase in the variability of the response sequences the participants performed (see left panel of Figure 9.1). Both groups showed a significant increase in the variability of the response sequences they performed during the extinction phase. The increase in response variability was evident during the first extinction session and increased during subsequent sessions. Thus, extinction produced a decline in the number of response sequences the participants completed, but it increased the variability of those sequences.

FIGURE 9.1 Effects of extinction on response variability (left panel) and response rates (right panel) for rats that were required to perform variable response sequences for reinforcement (Var) or received reinforcement regardless of their response sequence (Yoke). The open symbols represent the last four sessions of the reinforcement phase. The filled symbols represent the first four sessions of the extinction phase. (Response variability was measured in terms of the probability of meeting the variability criterion. Response rate was measured in terms of the number of three-response sequences that were completed per minute.) (Based on Neuringer et al. [2001]. *Journal of Experimental Psychology: Animal Behavior Processes, 27.* Figure 4, p. 84.)

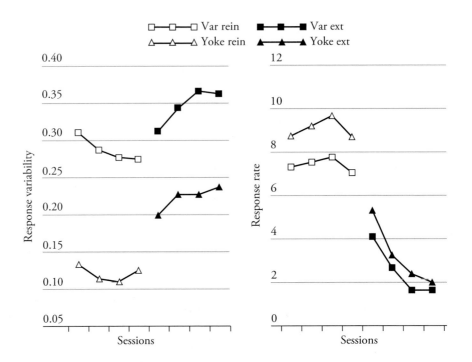

Aaron Blaisdell

M. R. Papini

Another interesting finding was that the increase in response variability that occurred during extinction did not come at the expense of the rats repeating response sequences that they had performed during the reinforcement phase. Response sequences that were highly likely to occur during the reinforcement phase continued to occur during extinction. But these were supplemented by other sequences that the participants rarely tried before. Subsequent studies have shown that increased response variability is not unique to extinction but is also obtained with procedures in which participants receive a low rate or magnitude of reinforcement (Stahlman & Blaisdell, 2011; Stahlman, Roberts, & Blaisdell, 2010).

In addition to the behavioral effects illustrated in Figure 9.1, extinction procedures also often produce strong emotional effects (Amsel, 1992; Papini, 2003). If an organism has become accustomed to receiving reinforcement for a particular response, it may become upset when reinforcers are no longer delivered. The emotional reaction induced by withdrawal of an expected reinforcer is called **frustration**. Frustrative nonreward energizes behavior. Under certain conditions, frustration may be intense enough to induce aggression. When a vending machine breaks down and no longer delivers the expected candy bar, you are likely to become annoyed and may pound and kick the machine. If your partner takes you on a date every Saturday evening, you will surely be very upset if he or she calls one Saturday afternoon to unexpectedly cancel the date.

Aggression induced by extinction was dramatically demonstrated by an experiment in which two pigeons were placed in the same Skinner box (Azrin, Hutchinson, & Hake, 1966). One of them was initially reinforced for pecking a response key, while the other bird was restrained in the back corner of the experimental chamber. After pecking was well established, the key-pecking bird experienced alternating periods of **continuous reinforcement (CRF)** and extinction. While reinforcement was available for pecking, the key-pecking bird largely ignored the other bird in the back of the chamber. However, when extinction was introduced, the previously rewarded pigeon attacked its innocent partner. Aggression was most likely early in each extinction period and subsided thereafter. Aggression also occurred if a stuffed model instead of a real pigeon was placed in the Skinner box. Extinction-induced aggression has been observed in studies with pigeon, rats, and people and can be a problem when extinction is used in behavior therapy. (For a recent review of extinction-induced aggression and other behaviors generated by extinction, see Lattal et al., 2013.)

Forms of Recovery From Extinction

Traditionally the focus of studies of extinction has been on the decline in conditioned behavior that is evident with continued exposure to an extinction procedure. Indeed, this decline is the main reason that extinction procedures are often used in therapeutic interventions. The decrease in behavior observed in extinction is the opposite of what occurs during acquisition, but extinction does not reverse or eliminate the effects of acquisition. Because extinction does not erase what was originally learned, the extinguished response reappears under various circumstances. The reappearance of the extinguished response is problematic for therapeutic applications designed to eliminate undesired behaviors. Therefore, a great deal of translational research has been devoted to studying the circumstances under which extinguished behavior occurs again. I will describe four lines of evidence that have attracted the most attention: studies of spontaneous recovery, renewal, reinstatement, and resurgence.

Spontaneous Recovery

The decline in conditioned behavior that occurs with extinction dissipates with time. If a rest period is introduced after extinction training, responding comes back. Because nothing specific is done during the rest period to produce the recovery, the effect is called **spontaneous recovery**. I previously described spontaneous recovery in Chapter 2 in connection with habituation. There, the term referred to recovery from the effects of habituation training. Procedurally, spontaneous recovery from extinction is similar in that it is also produced by a period of rest.

Spontaneous recovery was originally identified by Pavlov. However, the phenomenon has since been the focus of attention by numerous other investigators. The effect is illustrated by a particularly well-controlled experiment in which original acquisition was conducted with either a drop of sucrose or a solid food pellet delivered into cups recessed in one wall of the experimental chamber (Rescorla, 1997, 2004a). Infrared detectors identified each time the rat poked its head into the food cups. The experimental chamber was normally dark. One of the unconditioned stimuli was signaled by a noise CS and the other was signaled by a light CS. As conditioning progressed, each CS quickly came to elicit nosing the food cup (goal tracking), with the two CSs eliciting similar levels of responding. The left panel of Figure 9.2 shows the progress of acquisition, with data for the two CSs averaged together.

Two extinction sessions (of 16 trials each) were then conducted with each CS, followed by a series of four test trials. The experimental manipulation of primary interest was the interval between the end of extinction training and the test trials. For one of the conditioned stimuli (S1), an eight-day period separated extinction and testing. In contrast, for the other stimulus (S2) the test trials were started immediately after extinction training. The middle panel of the graph shows that during the course of extinction, responding declined in a similar fashion for S1 and S2. Responding remained suppressed during the test trials conducted immediately afterward with S2. However, responding substantially recovered for S1, which was tested eight days after extinction training.

FIGURE 9.2 Rate of rats poking their head into the food cup (goal tracking) for two different CSs. The left panel shows the original acquisition of responding to the two stimuli (averaged together) when each was paired with food. The middle panel shows loss of responding during the extinction phase. The final test trials were conducted right after extinction for S2 and eight days after extinction for S1. Note that the eight-day rest period resulted in a substantial recovery of the conditioned behavior. (From Rescorla, Learn. Mem. 2004. 11: 501–509 Copyright © 2004, by Cold Spring Harbor Laboratory press. Page 05.)

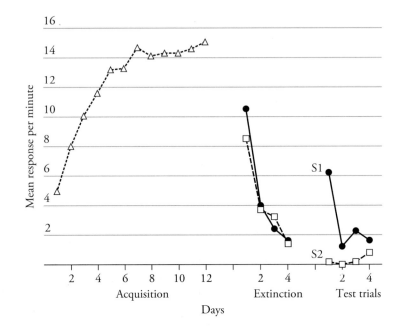

The recovery of responding observed to S1 represents *spontaneous recovery.* Notice that the recovery was not complete. At the end of the acquisition phase, the rate of head pokes into the food cup had been 15.6 responses per minute. During the first trial after the rest period, the mean response rate to S1 was about 6.2 responses per minute. (For a study of spontaneous recovery following the extinction of fear, see Leung & Westbrook, 2008.)

Spontaneous recovery is also a prominent phenomenon following extinction of instrumental behavior (see Lattal et al., 2013). Here again, the critical factor is introducing a period of rest between the end of extinction training and assessments of responding. The typical finding is that behavior that has become suppressed by extinction recovers with a period of rest.

Renewal of Conditioned Responding

Another strong piece of evidence that extinction does not result in permanent loss of conditioned behavior is the phenomenon of **renewal**, identified by Mark Bouton and his colleagues (see Bouton & Woods, 2008, for a review). Renewal refers to a recovery of conditioned responding when the contextual cues that were present during extinction are changed. In many renewal experiments, acquisition training is conducted in the presence of one set of contextual cues, designated A. The participants are then moved to a different context B where they receive extinction training. The contextual cues of extinction are then changed by returning the participants to context A. The shift from context B back to context A causes a reappearance of conditioned responding. Renewal has been of special interest for translational research because it suggests that clinical improvements that are achieved in the context of a therapist's office may not persist when the client returns home or goes to work where the original maladaptive behavior was acquired.

The phenomenon of renewal has been the subject of vigorous experimental research in a variety of learning situations. A recent study examined the renewal effect in extinction of instrumental lever-press responding in laboratory rats (Bouton et al., 2011). Standard Skinner boxes were modified to create distinctively different contexts for the different phases of the experiment. For one context, one wall and the ceiling of the

M. E. Bouton

chamber had black and white stripes, the floor was level, and the chamber was scented with the odor of an anise solution. For the other context, the floor was made uneven (by alternating metal rods of different diameters), one wall and the ceiling were covered with dark dots, and the odor cue was provided by a coconut extract. Each distinctive chamber was used equally often as context A and context B. The rats received five 30-minute sessions of acquisition during which lever pressing was reinforced with a pellet of food on a VI-30 second schedule of reinforcement in context A.

The results, presented in Figure 9.3, show that by the end of the acquisition phase, the rats were responding nearly 30 times per minute. As expected, responding declined during the next four sessions when extinction was introduced, and lever presses no longer produced food. The next day, the rats received two 10-minute test sessions, one in context A and the other in context B (with the order of the two tests counterbalanced). No reinforcement for lever pressing was available during either test. Notice that responding was near zero when the rats were tested in the extinction context B. In contrast, when they were tested in the original context A, responding recovered substantially. This recovery of responding with a change in context is called the **renewal effect**.

Another question addressed by this experiment was whether the renewal effect was due to possible excitatory properties acquired by context A during the original acquisition phase. To evaluate this possibility, one of the groups shown in Figure 9.3 was repeatedly exposed to context A without food (or the response lever) during the extinction phase so as to extinguish any excitatory properties context A might have acquired. As is evident from the results in Figure 9.3, extinction of context A did not alter the magnitude of the renewal effect. This suggests that the renewal effect is not due to context–reinforcer associations. (For further studies of the role of context conditioning in the renewal effect, see Laborda, Witnauer, & Miller, 2011.)

The data presented in Figure 9.3 illustrate the ABA renewal effect. Renewal of conditioned responding has been also observed when, after extinction in context B, participants are tested in a neutral context C, which was not previously associated with either acquisition or extinction. This is called ABC renewal and illustrates the general conclusion that conditioned responding reappears with any shift away from the context of where extinction was conducted. (For a recent study of ABC renewal in human participants, see Nelson et al., 2011.)

The renewal effect occurs under a wide range of circumstances. It has been obtained with extinction of both appetitive and aversively conditioned responding and in both

FIGURE 9.3 Renewal of extinguished lever pressing in rats reinforced by food. Acquisition was conducted in context A. Extinction was conducted in context B. The rats were then tested in both context A and context B. Group Exp also received extinction of context A during the extinction phase. Group NoExp did not receive this context extinction procedure (based on Bouton et al., 2011).

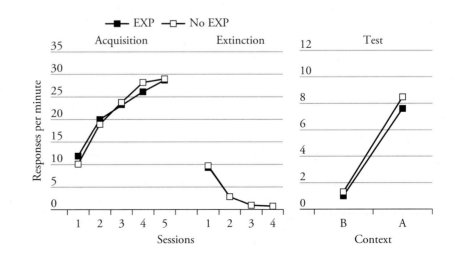

Pavlovian and instrumental conditioning. Interestingly, the phenomenon is evident not just with external contextual cues but also with contextual cues created by drug states (e.g., Bouton, Kenney, & Rosengard, 1990; Cunningham, 1979). Thus, contextual control of extinction can also occur with interoceptive cues.

The renewal effect shows that the memory of extinction is specific to the cues that were present during the extinction phase. Therefore, a shift away from the context of extinction disrupts retrieval of the memory of extinction, with the result that extinction performance is lost. But why should this restore behavior characteristic of original acquisition? To account for that, one has to make the added assumption that original acquisition performance generalizes from one context to another more easily than does extinction performance.

Why is it that original acquisition is less disrupted (if at all) by a change in context when extinction performance is highly context specific? Bouton (1993, 1994) has suggested that contextual cues serve to disambiguate the significance of a CS. This function is similar to the function of semantic context in disambiguating the meaning of a word. Consider the word *cut*. *Cut* could refer to the physical procedure of creating two pieces, as in "The chef cut the carrots." Alternatively, it could refer to dropping a player from a team, as in "Johnny was cut from the team after the first game." The meaning of the word depends on the semantic context. In an analogous fashion, a CS that has undergone excitatory fear conditioning and then extinction also has an ambiguous meaning in that the CS could signify that shock is about to occur (acquisition) or that shock won't occur (extinction). This ambiguity allows the CS to come under contextual control more easily. After just acquisition training, the CS is not ambiguous because it only signifies one thing (shock). Therefore, such a CS is not as susceptible to contextual control.

The renewal effect has important implications for behavior therapy, and unfortunately these implications are rather troubling. It suggests that even if a therapeutic procedure is effective in extinguishing a pathological fear or phobia in the relative safety of a therapist's office, the conditioned fear may easily return when the client encounters the fear CS in a different context. Equally problematic is the fact that the effects of excitatory conditioning readily generalize from one context to another. Thus, if you acquire a pathological fear in one situation, the fear is likely to plague you in a variety of other contexts. But if you overcome your fear, that benefit will not generalize as readily to new situations. Thus, the problems created by conditioning will have much more widespread effects than the solutions or remedies for those problems.

Reinstatement of Conditioned Responding

Another procedure that serves to restore responding to an extinguished CS is called **reinstatement**. Reinstatement refers to the recovery of conditioned behavior that occurs when the individual encounters the US again. Consider, for example, having learned an aversion to fish because you got sick after eating fish on a trip. Your aversion is then extinguished by nibbling on fish without getting sick on a number of occasions. In fact, you may learn to enjoy eating fish again because of this extinction experience. The phenomenon of reinstatement suggests that if you were to become sick again for some reason, your aversion to fish will return even if your illness had nothing to do with eating this particular food. (For an analogous study with laboratory rats, see Schachtman, Brown, & Miller, 1985.)

As with renewal, reinstatement is a challenging phenomenon for behavior therapy. Consider, for example, a client who suffers from anxiety and fear of intimacy acquired during the course of being raised by an abusive parent. Extensive therapy may be successful in providing relief from these symptoms. However, the phenomenon of reinstatement suggests that the fear and anxiety may return full blown if the client experiences an abusive encounter later in life. Because of reinstatement, responses that are successfully extinguished during the course of therapeutic intervention can reappear if the individual is exposed to the US again.

Although reinstatement was originally discovered in studies with laboratory rats (Rescorla & Heth, 1975), the phenomenon has since been documented in a variety of other situations as well. In one experiment, Yale undergraduates served as participants (LaBar & Phelps, 2005). The CS was a blue square presented on a computer screen for 4 seconds. On each acquisition trial, the CS ended with a 1-second burst of very loud noise (the US). This resulted in the conditioning of fear to the visual CS, which was measured by an increase in skin conductance (produced by mild sweating). Participants received four acquisition trials followed by eight extinction trials. Four reinstatement noise bursts were then presented either in the same test room or in a different room. After this, all the students were tested for fear of the CS in the original training context.

The results of the experiment are presented in Figure 9.4. As expected, conditioned fear (as measured by skin conductance) increased during the course of original acquisition and decreased during extinction. Subsequent US presentations in the same room resulted in recovery of the extinguished skin conductance response. US presentations in a different room did not produce this recovery. Thus, the reinstatement effect was context specific. (For reinstatement of human conditioned fear in fear-potentiated startle, see Norrholm et al., 2006.)

A great deal of research has been done on the reinstatement effect in the past 20 years (see Bouton & Wood, 2008). The results have indicated that context conditioning is important, but not because it permits summation of excitation. Rather, as was the case with renewal, the role of context is to disambiguate the significance of a stimulus that has a mixed history of conditioning and extinction. Context conditioning has relatively little effect on stimuli that do not have a history of extinction (e.g., Bouton, 1984).

Reinstatement of extinguished responding has also been the focus of interest in animal models of drug abuse. Laboratory rats, for example, can be conditioned to press a response lever for small intravenous injections of cocaine. Once such lever pressing has been established, the behavior declines if extinction is introduced and lever pressing no longer produces cocaine. However, a "free" shot of cocaine will cause a rapid resumption of the drug-reinforced instrumental behavior (e.g., Kelamangalath et al., 2009). Thus, exposure to the drug following extinction reverses the therapeutic gains produced by extinction. This has encouraged some to examine reinstatement as a possible model of relapse in the treatment of drug addiction (e.g., Epstein et al., 2006).

FIGURE 9.4 Fear conditioning in human participants as measured by increased skin conductance. All participants received acquisition followed by extinction, reinstatement USs, and tests of responding to the CS. The reinstatement USs were presented in either the same or a different context than the rest of the experiment. (Based on LaBar & Phelps, 2005.)

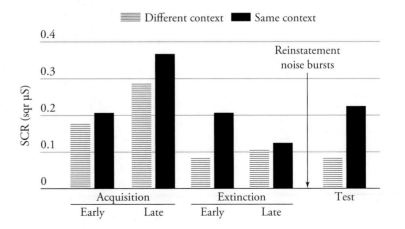

Resurgence of Conditioned Behavior

So far I have been discussing the effects of extinction with the focus on a single response that is initially conditioned or reinforced and is then extinguished. However, as I emphasized in Chapters 6 and 7, learning procedures do not occur in a behavioral test tube that has just one response option. Individuals can do a variety of things, and their experience with one response may influence how often they do something else. Such carry-over effects from one behavior to another also occur in extinction. The phenomenon of **resurgence** is a primary example.

Resurgence involves the reappearance of an extinguished target response when another reinforced response is extinguished. Consider a parent going shopping with a 3-year-old child. To make the supermarket excursion easier, the parent puts the child in the seat of the shopping cart. However, the child is not interested in shopping and starts to wiggle and squirm, trying to get the parent's attention. Not wanting to encourage this behavior, the parent admonishes the child and puts the behavior on extinction, ignoring the child whenever he or she wiggles and squirms. This works, but the parent feels bad about having the child just sit in the cart with little to do and gives the child a toy to play with. Things proceed smoothly for a while until the child gets bored with the toy and thus experiences extinction of the toy-playing response. This extinction of the second response will result in *resurgence* of the original wiggling and squirming behavior. (For an experimental study of resurgence in an infant care-giving task, see Bruzek, Thompson, & Peters, 2009.)

Resurgence has been frequently examined in studies of instrumental or operant conditioning (see review by Lattal & St. Peter Pipkin, 2009). As the above example indicates, the phenomenon involves two different responses. One response is initially conditioned and then extinguished. A second behavior is then also reinforced and extinguished. The point of interest is whether extinction of the second response increases the frequency of the first response.

In a recent study, for example, Winterbauer and Bouton (2011) trained rats with food reinforcement in an experimental chamber that had two retractable levers. Only one of the levers (L1) was in the chamber at first, and the rats were reinforced for pressing this lever on a variable interval schedule of reinforcement. Training sessions continued until responding exceeded 20 responses per minute. The rats then received extinction with L1 over three sessions, which reduced responding to below 2.5 responses per minute. Extinction of L1 continued in the next session. However, 15 minutes into the session, the second response lever (L2) was inserted into the experimental chamber. Responding on L2 was reinforced on a continuous reinforcement schedule until the rats obtained 20 reinforcers. At that point, extinction was introduced for L2 (and continued for L1). The results of this test session are presented in Figure 9.5.

Figure 9.5 shows responding on L1 during the final extinction/test session as a function of time before and after the reinforcement of L2, which is indicated by L2+. Some responding on L1 occurred at the start of the session, reflecting spontaneous recovery from the previous day's extinction session. However, L1 responding declined close to zero by the time reinforcement for L2 was introduced. When responding to L2 was put on extinction, L1 responding reappeared, illustrating the phenomenon of resurgence. The resurgence effect was fairly short-lived, as continued extinction of L1 reduced responding again (see also Winterbauer, Lucke, & Bouton, 2013).

At this point, the mechanisms of resurgence are not well understood. This is due, in part, to the fact that a variety of procedures have been used, and different procedures may produce resurgence by different mechanisms (e.g., Da Silva et al., 2008). Regardless of what mechanism may be responsible for resurgence, the phenomenon is of considerable

FIGURE 9.5 Rate of responding on lever 1 (L1) during a test of resurgence. L1 was never reinforced (L1−) during the test session. In the middle of the session (indicated by the two vertical lines), responding on lever 2 was reinforced (L2+). During the remaining session neither L2 nor L1 were reinforced (L1−, L2−). Notice that responding on L1 reappeared (resurged) when extinction was started for L2. The rate of responding on L2 is not shown. (Based on Winterbauer & Bouton, 2011.)

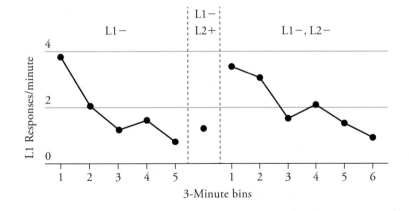

interest in translational research. One area of application in which resurgence is of concern is in *functional communications training* or FCT (Volkert et al., 2009). Individuals with developmental disabilities may engage in disruptive or self-injurious behavior in the classroom if they get frustrated working on an assignment because they lack communication skills to request a break or rest from the task. FCT involves reinforcing them for making an appropriate request for a break, by raising their hand, for example. This is successful in keeping disruptive and self-injurious behavior at a low level as long as the teacher is not too busy to reinforce the appropriate communication response. If the teacher becomes too busy and ignores the student's raised hand, resurgence of the disruptive behavior may occur.

Enhancing Extinction

The phenomena reviewed in the preceding section indicate that extinction does not erase what was originally learned and the extinguished behavior can reappear with the passage of time (spontaneous recovery), a change in context (renewal), reexposure to the US (reinstatement), or the extinction of another response (resurgence). This is bad news for various forms of exposure therapy that use extinction to eliminate problematic fears, phobias, and habits. Can the impact of extinction be increased so as to make extinction procedures more effective? This question is increasingly commanding the attention of scientists (Quirk et al., 2010). Figuring out ways to enhance extinction is of great contemporary interest in both basic and translational research in learning.

Number and Spacing of Extinction Trials

Perhaps the simplest way to increase the impact of extinction is to conduct more extinction trials. The use of larger numbers of extinction trials produces a more profound decrease in conditioned responding. This outcome has been found in a variety of learning situations, including eyeblink conditioning, taste-aversion learning, and context conditioning (e.g., Brooks et al., 2003; Leung et al., 2007; Weidemann & Kehoe, 2003).

Another important variable in extinction is the spacing of trials. I previously discussed this variable in the context of habituation of the startle response in Chapter 2. In a habituation procedure (Figure 2.10), presenting stimuli close together in time (massed) produces a greater decrement in startle responding than presenting the stimuli spread out in time (spaced). However, the habituation effect produced by massed trials shows significant spontaneous recovery, whereas habituation produced by spaced trials does not. Similar results occur in extinction.

Using a fear-conditioning procedure with mice, Cain, Blouin, and Barad (2003) found greater loss of fear during an extinction session with massed trials (intertrial interval of 6 seconds) than with spaced trials (intertrial interval of 600 seconds). However, a subsequent study showed that spaced trials produce a more enduring extinction effect. Extinction produced by trials spaced 600 seconds apart was much less subject to spontaneous recovery and renewal than extinction produced by trials spaced 6 seconds apart (see also Urcelay, Wheeler, & Miller, 2009). These results show that although massed extinction trials may produce a rapid immediate decrement in responding, the conditioned behavior is likely to return with a period of rest (spontaneous recovery) or a change in context (renewal). Such relapse is troublesome for exposure therapy, making spaced exposure trials preferable. (For a study of these issues in the extinction of fear of public speaking, see Tsao & Craske, 2000.)

Immediate Versus Delayed Extinction

The next manipulation to enhance extinction was inspired by research on the molecular neuroscience of memory **consolidation**. Memory consolidation is described in greater detail in Box 9.1 and in Chapter 11. For now, let it suffice to say that establishing a learning experience in long-term memory requires a process called memory consolidation. Memory consolidation takes time, which raises the possibility that introducing extinction before the memory of acquisition has been fully consolidated might change the memory and promote extinction performance. This hypothesis has stimulated studies of the effects of conducting extinction immediately after acquisition as compared with one or two days later.

This line of research has produced conflicting findings. However, the general picture is reminiscent of what we previously described for the effects of massed versus spaced extinction trials. Conducting extinction trials immediately after acquisition produces a more rapid loss of conditioned behavior than conducting extinction one day later. However, this enhanced decline of conditioned behavior is deceptive because with immediate extinction the behavior is more likely to show spontaneous recovery and renewal (Woods & Bouton, 2008; see also Chang & Maren, 2009). A more enduring loss of behavior occurs if extinction trials are delayed 24 hours after the end of acquisition. These findings are encouraging because they suggest that for exposure therapy to be effective, it need not be initiated right after the learning of a fear response.

Repetition of Extinction/Test Cycles

A relatively simple technique for reducing the reappearance of extinguished behavior is to repeat the extinction/test cycle. This approach has been examined most extensively with spontaneous recovery. A study involving goal tracking as the conditioned response (CR) illustrates the strategy (Rescorla, 2004). During the initial acquisition phase (not shown), a noise CS was paired with the presentation of food in a cup. As conditioning progressed, the rats came to poke their nose in the food cup when the CS was presented. Extinction was then introduced, with eight CS-alone trials conducted during each daily session.

The results of the extinction sessions are presented in Figure 9.6. The data are presented in two-trial blocks, with a break in the curve after each session. Notice that during each extinction session, responding was highest during the first two trials and then declined. When the rats were returned to the experimental chamber for the next session, responding was higher than it had been at the end of the preceding session, indicating

FIGURE 9.6 Effects of repeated extinction sessions on the magnitude of spontaneous recovery. There are breaks in the line connecting the data points to indicate the breaks between the end of one extinction session and the start of the next. Notice that the degree of spontaneous recovery gets progressively smaller across successive sessions. (From Rescorla, 2004. Learn. Mem. 2004. 11: 501–509 Copyright © 2004, by Cold Spring Harbor Laboratory Press.)

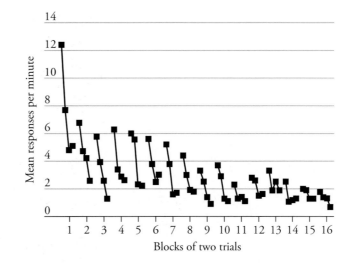

spontaneous recovery. However, the degree of recovery progressively declined with repeated extinction/test sessions.

Experiments such as that depicted in Figure 9.6 have not been conducted with renewal, reinstatement, and resurgence. However, one might predict similar results. From a therapeutic perspective, such results suggest that enduring therapeutic gains would be best achieved by periodic reapplications of the exposure therapy so as to reduce any conditioned responding that might have reappeared.

Conducting Extinction in Multiple Contexts

Another strategy for increasing the impact of extinction training is to conduct extinction in several different contexts. This strategy has been examined most often in efforts to eliminate the renewal effect. As you may recall, renewal refers to the recovery of responding that occurs when the individual is moved from the extinguished context either to a new context or back to the context of acquisition. In a sense, renewal can be attributed to lack of generalization of extinction performance from the extinction context to other situations. Conducting extinction in several different contexts may serve to increase the stimulus generalization of extinction.

Whether or not extinction in multiple contexts facilitates the generalization of extinction performance (and the reduction of the renewal effect) depends on the number of extinction trials that are conducted. This was demonstrated in a study of the extinction of fear using a conditioned suppression procedure (Thomas et al., 2009). Laboratory rats were first trained to press a response lever on a VI-60 second scheduled with a drop of sucrose as the reinforcer, to create a behavioral baseline for the measurement of conditioned suppression. Fear conditioning was then conducted in which an auditory CS (termination of the background noise for 2 minutes) was paired with a brief shock 10 times. Acquisition took place in a distinctive context designated as A. For the next phase of the experiment, the rats were moved out of the acquisition context and received either 36 or 144 extinction trials. For some animals, only one context (B) was used for all of the extinction trials, whereas for other groups three different contexts were used (B, C, and D). All the rats were then returned to the context of acquisition (A) and tested for renewal of conditioned fear.

The results of the extinction and renewal tests are presented in Figure 9.7. Notice that by the end of extinction training, all of the groups showed virtually no fear of the

FIGURE 9.7 Extinction and renewal of fear in a conditioned suppression procedure, with lower scores indicating more suppression and hence more fear. Data are shown for the beginning (B) and the end (E) of the first and last extinction session as well as the renewal test. Groups differed only during the renewal test. Group NE did not receive extinction training. 1C indicates that extinction was conducted in one context. 3C indicates extinction in three different contexts. 36 Ext indicates that 36 extinction trials were conducted. 144 Ext indicates that 144 extinction trials were conducted (based on Thomas et al., 2009).

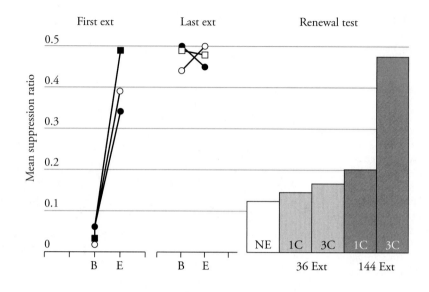

CS. However, fear reappeared when the rats were returned to context A. The renewal effect was evident for all of the groups except the one that received a large number of extinction trials (144) in three different contexts. Thus, elimination of the renewal effect required extensive extinction training in multiple contexts.

Conducting extinction in multiple contexts has also been observed to eliminate the renewal effect in experiments with human participants (e.g., Vansteenwegen et al., 2007) especially if the contexts of extinction are similar to the context of acquisition (Bandarian Balooch & Neumann, 2011). These findings suggest that the effectiveness of exposure therapy can be enhanced by conducting the therapy in a variety of different places. Conducting exposure therapy in the context of original acquisition may not be essential for reducing relapse through renewal.

Using multiple contexts for extinction has been examined primarily in studies of renewal. However, because the other forms of relapse from extinction (spontaneous recovery, reinstatement, and resurgence) have also been interpreted as possibly due to shifts away from the context of extinction, using multiple contexts for extinction may serve to reduce reappearance of conditioned behavior in those procedures as well. This is a hypothesis ripe for investigation.

Presenting Extinction Reminder Cues

As I noted earlier, many of the extinction relapse effects have been interpreted as due to the fact that extinction training does not generalize when the learned behavior is tested in a new place. One way to overcome this problem is to present retrieval cues for extinction during tests of recovery of extinguished behavior (Laborda & Miller, 2012). This strategy was first tested with spontaneous recovery. Investigators found that introducing cues that were present during extinction training can reduce spontaneous recovery and enhance extinction performance in taste aversion learning (Brooks et al., 1999) as well as in appetitive conditioning preparations (Brooks, 2000; Brooks & Bouton, 1993).

Extinction cues may similarly reduce the renewal effect by reactivating extinction performance in the renewal context. This prediction was initially confirmed in studies of appetitive conditioning with rats (Brooks & Bouton, 1994). Encouraging results were also found in a study of exposure therapy with people who were afraid of spiders (Mystkowski et al., 2006). Participants who were instructed to mentally recall the treatment context showed less fear of spiders in a novel situation than participants who did not engage in the reminder exercise. The reminder strategy can be applied more broadly to increase generalization of treatment outcomes by encouraging clients to carry a card, repeat a short phrase, or call a help line whenever they are concerned about relapsing. Participants of Alcoholics Anonymous carry a chip that designates their duration of sobriety. All these techniques provide reminders of the therapeutic context.

Compounding Extinction Stimuli

Yet another interesting approach involves presenting two stimuli at the same time that are both undergoing extinction. In fact, recent research has shown that presenting two extinguished stimuli at the same time can deepen the extinction of those cues (Leung, Reeks, & Westbrook, 2012; Rescorla, 2006a). Consider, for example, the experiment depicted in Table 9.1. The table outlines an instrumental conditioning experiment (Rescorla, 2006a, Experiment 3) in which rats were first conditioned to press a response lever during each of three different discriminative stimuli—a light (L) and noise (X) and tone (Y) stimuli. During initial acquisition training, lever pressing during these stimuli was reinforced on a VI 30-second schedule with food. Lever pressing was not reinforced when these stimuli were absent (between trials).

Following acquisition, the light, tone, and noise stimuli were each presented repeatedly by themselves with lever presses no longer reinforced. Responding during each of these cues declined to close to zero. However, some subthreshold tendency to respond may have remained. Compound extinction trials were introduced to evaluate that possibility. During this second extinction phase, the light was presented simultaneously with one of the auditory cues (X). The other auditory cue, Y, continued to be presented alone without reinforcement, as a control. The effects of compound extinction were evaluated at the end of the experiment by testing responding during X and Y, each presented by itself.

Figure 9.8 shows rates of responding at the end of the first phase of extinction, during the compound extinction trials, and during the final test trials. Responding was close to zero by the end of the first extinction phase. However, presenting L in compound with X during the next extinction phase (LX) resulted in a substantial elevation of responding. This represents summation of subthreshold responding that remained to the L and X stimuli despite their individual extinction treatments (Reberg, 1972). No such elevation was evident with control stimulus Y, which was presented by itself during the compound extinction phase.

TABLE 9.1   TEST OF COMPOUNDING EXTINCTION STIMULI

Acquisition	Element extinction	Compound extinction	Test
L+	L−	LX−	X
and	and	and	and
X+	X−	Y−	Y
and	and		
Y+	Y−		

FIGURE 9.8 Discriminative lever pressing in the presence of a light (L) and two auditory cues (a tone and a noise stimulus counterbalanced as X and Y) at the end of a series of extinction trials with each stimulus presented by itself, during a compound extinction phase in which L was presented simultaneously with X, and during a test phase conducted six days later. (Based on Rescorla, 2006a, Figure 3, page 139.)

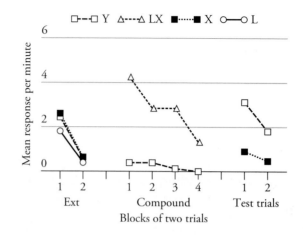

The data of greatest interest were obtained during the final tests with X and Y. This final test was conducted six days after the end of the compound extinction phase. The six-day rest period caused substantial spontaneous recovery of responding to Y. However, no such recovery occurred to stimulus X. This outcome shows that the compound extinction trials deepened the extinction of stimulus X. Other experiments have shown that this deepening of extinction also reduces the reinstatement effect and slows the rate of reacquisition of an extinguished stimulus (Rescorla, 2006a).

The fact that compounding two extinction cues deepens the extinction of the individual stimuli suggests that extinction operates at least in part by an error-correction process similar to the Rescorla–Wagner model. As I described in Chapter 4, according to the Rescorla–Wagner model, associative values are adjusted if the outcome of a trial is contrary to what is expected. Original acquisition creates an expectation that the US will occur. This expectation is violated when the US is omitted in extinction, and that *error* is corrected by reduced responding on subsequent extinction trials. Compounding two conditioned stimuli increases the resulting *error* when the trial ends without a reinforcer. This induces a larger correction and hence greater reduction of responding (for an alternative analysis in terms of the comparator hypothesis, see Witnauer & Miller, 2012).

The above reasoning predicts an entirely different outcome if an extinction cue is compounded with a conditioned inhibitor during extinction training. In that case, there should be an interference rather than a facilitation of the extinction process. Recall that a conditioned inhibitor is a signal for the absence of a US. In the fear system, a conditioned inhibitor is a safety signal indicating that the aversive US will not occur. If such a safety signal is compounded with a fear stimulus during extinction, the absence of the US will be fully predicted by the safety signal. Therefore, there won't be any error to encourage learning that the fear stimulus no longer ends in shock. Thus, the safety signal will block extinction of the fear stimulus. This prediction has been confirmed in laboratory studies with rats and pigeons (McConnell & Miller, 2010; Thomas & Ayres, 2004; Rescorla, 2003) as well as in human clinical research (e.g., Lovibond et al., 2009; Schmidt et al., 2006).

Priming Extinction to Update Memory for Reconsolidation

The presentation of a CS serves to activate the memory of acquisition. Once activated, the memory is in a labile or modifiable state in which it can be changed before the memory is reconsolidated and returned to long-term store. The period during which an activated

BOX 9.1

Consolidating Memories Requires Protein Synthesis

Stephen Lovekin/Getty Images

J. E. LeDoux

In exploring the neurobiological mechanisms that underlie learning so far, we have concentrated on the processes that occur during training. These processes depend on preexisting proteins that can bring about a rapid alteration in synaptic function. These changes typically decay within a matter of hours. To produce a lasting modification within a neural circuit requires a structural modification. This depends on inducing the synthesis of new proteins (Figure 9.9A), a process that can continue beyond the training period.

At a behavioral level, researchers have known for decades that events that occur after a training episode can impact long-term memory (McGaugh, 2000; Squire & Wixted, 2011). (We will discuss some of these phenomena in Chapter 11.) The implication is that memory depends on a period of *consolidation*, a process that may take hours to complete and likely involves **protein synthesis** (for reviews, see Dudai, 2004; McKenzie & Eichenbaum, 2011; Nader & Einarsson, 2010). For example, as we saw in Chapter 3, pairing a tone with a mild electric shock endows the tone with the capacity to elicit conditioned freezing in laboratory rats, a Pavlovian CR indicative of fear. Ordinarily, conditioned freezing is remembered for months after training. If, however, the rats are given a drug (e.g., anisomycin) that inhibits protein synthesis prior to the tone–shock pairings, they don't

remember the fear conditioning. They show amnesia. Further research has shown that the required protein synthesis occurs within the first hour or two of training; if protein synthesis is inhibited 4–6 hours after training, it has little effect on long-term memory (Figure 9.9B). Researchers have observed a similar effect across a range of learning paradigms (Hernandez & Abel, 2008), an observation that supports a common hypothesis: To produce a lasting change in neuronal function, learning must induce a structural modification (e.g., the growth of new synaptic connections), and this requires protein synthesis.

The fact that inhibiting protein synthesis 6 hours after training generally has little effect on long-term retention is important because drugs such as anisomycin have a broad range of effects and impact cellular function throughout the body. These secondary effects of drug treatment could indirectly disrupt the expression of the CR. Further, the physiological consequences of drug treatment could take a long time to decay and impact the expression of the CR at the time of testing. If either of these alternatives were operating, delaying the injection of anisomycin after training should (if anything) produce more memory loss because such a delay decreases the interval between drug treatment and testing (Figure 9.9B). However, the opposite is observed (Hernandez & Abel, 2008). Across a range of behavioral learning paradigms, administration of anisomycin soon after training disrupts the memory of conditioning while delayed drug treatment has little effect. This suggests that the drug has a temporally limited impact and disrupts memory by interfering with the mechanisms that underlie consolidation.

Researchers have also shown that anisomycin disrupts learning and memory when it is injected into regions

of the brain implicated in the long-term retention of a CR. As described in Box 4.3, fear conditioning depends on the basolateral region of the amygdala. Microinjection of a protein synthesis inhibitor into the basolateral amygdala disrupts consolidation in the usual time-dependent manner (Johansen, Cain, Ostroff, & LeDoux, 2011). That is, the greatest disruption occurs when the injection is given soon after training, and there is little effect if the injection occurs 6 hours later. Additional evidence that gene expression and protein synthesis are critical has been obtained using pharmacological and genetic techniques that target other aspects of translation or transcription (Hernandez & Abel, 2008). One reason that treatments designed to target protein synthesis may generally disrupt learning is that they affect processes involved in the maintenance of neural activity (Sharma et al., 2012).

Researchers have used these same manipulations to explore whether extinction requires protein synthesis, and, in general, parallel results have been obtained (Myers & Davis, 2007). Animals that undergo extinction treatment in the presence of a protein synthesis inhibitor later exhibit a robust CR, as if the extinction treatment had not occurred. Here too, if the drug is administered hours after the extinction treatment, it generally has little effect.

Interestingly, the nonreinforced presentation of a previously trained CS does not always weaken the CR. This effect was nicely illustrated by a series of experiments performed by LeDoux and his colleagues (Nader, Schafe, & LeDoux, 2000; Nader & Einarsson, 2010). Using a Pavlovian paradigm, rats received a single presentation of a tone paired with a mild shock. The next day, the rats were given a single exposure to the tone (Figure 9.9C). Reexposure to the previously trained cue activates the memory for the earlier training episode, and during this reminder, the memory

Continued

BOX 9.1 (continued)

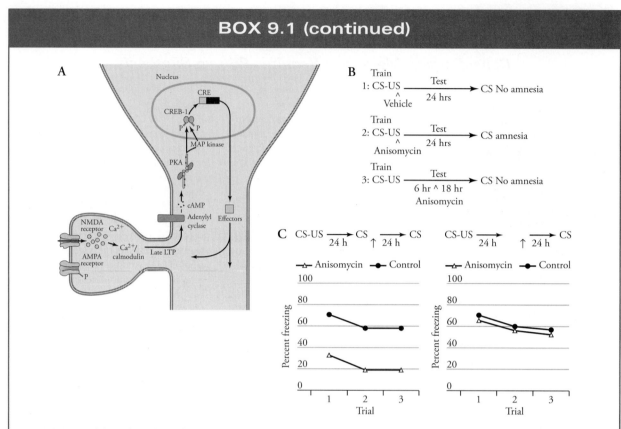

FIGURE 9.9 (A) With prolonged input, the activation of CaMKII can initiate a long-term LTP (late LTP) that requires protein synthesis. The signal pathway involves the activation of adeynl cyclase, which converts ATP to cAMP and engages a protein kinase (PKA). PKA in turn activates a mitogen-activated kinase (MAP kinase), which, in conjunction with PKA, engages a cAMP response element-binding protein (CREB). CREB then initiates the transcription of plasticity-related genes. The resultant mRNA is then translated into protein products (effectors) that can bring about structural changes in how the neuron functions (e.g., producing an increase in the number of synaptic connections) (adapted from Kandel et al., 2013). (B) Subjects (1: vehicle control) that receive a conditioned stimulus (CS) paired with a unconditioned stimulus (US) exhibit a conditioned response to the CS when it is presented 24 hours later. Subjects (2: immediate anisomycin) treated with the protein synthesis inhibitor anisomycin soon after training do not exhibit a conditioned response to the CS when it is presented 24 hours later. If drug treatment is delayed for 6 hours (3: delayed anisomycin), anisomycin has little effect. (© Cengage Learning 2015) (C) The left panel illustrates conditioned freezing in rats that received a single presentation of the CS 24 hours after training, followed by drug treatment. When the CS was presented the next day, rats that had received anisomycin exhibited amnesia. Drug treatment had no effect when the reminder CS was omitted (right panel) (adapted from Nader, Schafe, & LeDoux, 2000).

may be in an especially labile state (making it sensitive to disruption). Supporting this, presenting an amnesia-inducing event (e.g., an electroconvulsive shock) soon after the reminder treatment undermines retention of the previously learned response (Misani, Miller, & Lewis, 1968). These results suggest that once a memory has been retrieved, it has to be **reconsolidated** for subsequent retention. If this reconsolidation process is disrupted, the earlier memory may be erased. (For additional discussion of reconsolidation, see Chapter 11.)

LeDoux and Nader hypothesized that the process of reconsolidation depends on protein synthesis. To explore this possibility, they injected anisomycin into the basolateral amygdala immediately after rats received the reminder cue (Figure 9.9C). Other rats received the drug vehicle after the reminder cue or received these drug treatments alone (without the reminder cue). The rats were then tested with the CS the next day. Animals that had not received the reminder treatment exhibited a robust CR,

Continued

BOX 9.1 (continued)

whether or not they got anisomycin. In contrast, rats that received anisomycin after the reminder treatment exhibited a profound amnesia. This was not due to the presentation of the CS alone (extinction) because rats that received the reminder followed by the vehicle exhibited a normal CR. These observations suggest that reexposure to the CS had indeed placed the memory in a labile state and that, during this period, the maintenance of the memory required a second round of protein synthesis.

Further research showed that reconsolidation is disrupted when the drug is given soon after training, but not when it's given 6 hours later (Nader et al., 2000).

Work on reconsolidation has raised a host of questions that continue to drive empirical studies (see McKenzie & Eichenbaum, 2011; Nader & Einarsson, 2010; Routtenberg, 2008; Rudy, 2008). One basic question concerns the relation between extinction and reconsolidation. On the face of it, both involve a common manipulation: the nonreinforced presentation of a previously trained cue. Why then does inhibiting protein synthesis in one case (extinction) help preserve the CR while in the other (reconsolidation) it has an amnesic effect? One obvious difference concerns the number of stimulus presentations. Reminder treatments typically involve only a few CS presentations, whereas extinction typi-

cally involves extensive exposure to the CS alone. Another question concerns the locus of the protein synthesis. Although many scientists assumed that this occurs within the cell body, recent research suggests that the dendrites contain the biological machinery needed to locally synthesize proteins.

J. W. Grau

---

protein synthesis The cellular process used to make proteins (the biological molecules that form the structures of living organisms) from messenger RNA (mRNA).

reconsolidation A process whereby a previously consolidated memory is placed in a labile state by reactivating the memory trace.

Marie Monfils

memory can be modified is called the *reconsolidation window.* Generally, the reconsolidation window lasts less than 6 hours. Although limited, the interval is long enough for extinction training. This raises the possibility that the memory of acquisition might be substantially altered by conducting extinction trials during the reconsolidation window.

The above hypothesis was first tested in a series of experiments with rats (Monfils et al., 2009). Based on the success of those experiments, the strategy was also evaluated in human fear conditioning (Schiller et al., 2010). Participants first received fear conditioning in which a colored square was paired with mild shock to the wrist (a square of a different color was presented without shock). When the participants came back the next day, some received a single exposure to the fear-conditioned CS, followed by a series of extinction trials conducted either 10 minutes later (within the consolidation window) or 6 hours later (outside the consolidation window). A third group received extinction trials without a prior priming presentation of the CS. All the participants returned to the laboratory on day 3 for a test of spontaneous recovery of fear.

Conditioned fear was measured in terms of the skin conductance response. Higher scores on this measure indicate greater levels of fear. The results of the experiment are presented in Figure 9.10. All three groups showed substantial fear responses during acquisition and little fear at the end of the extinction phase. When they were tested again the next day, there was substantial spontaneous recovery of fear in the nonprimed control group and in the group that received extinction training outside the reconsolidation window (6 hours after the priming CS presentation). However, there was no spontaneous recovery if extinction training was conducted within the consolidation window (10 minutes after a priming exposure to the CS). These results show that fear memory is especially vulnerable to extinction training if extinction is conducted while the fear memory is in the reconsolidation window. Subsequent studies showed that these effects are evident as long as a year after original training

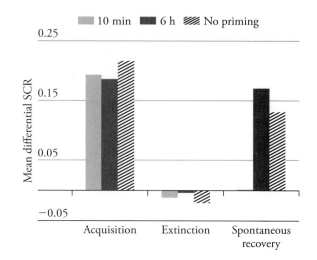

FIGURE 9.10 Conditioned fear (as measured by skin conductance), during acquisition, extinction, and a test of spontaneous recovery, in human participants who received a priming exposure to the CS 10 minutes or 6 hours before extinction training or did not receive priming. (Based on Schiller et al., 2010.)

and are specific to the fear CS that is used to initially prime memory retrieval (Schiller et al., 2010).

A major unanswered question in this area of research is why a priming exposure to the CS facilitates extinction far more than the first of a series of extinction trials. The answer is probably related to the fact that the priming exposure is followed by a longer interval (10 minutes in Schiller et al., 2010) than the subsequent extinction trials (which were spaced 10–12 seconds apart). However, so far that variable has not been explicitly evaluated.

Andrew Delamater

What Is Learned in Extinction?

Studies of spontaneous recovery, renewal, reinstatement, and resurgence all indicate that extinction does not involve *unlearning*. Other studies have shown that response–outcome (R–O) and stimulus–outcome (S–O) associations remain pretty much intact after extinction (e.g., Delamater, 2004, 2012). If these associations remain intact, what produces the response decrement? This question is the topic of continuing debate and empirical study. A fully satisfactory answer is not yet available, but investigators are considering the importance of inhibitory S–R associations motivated by the unexpected absence of the reinforcer in extinction. (For alternative perspectives, see Baum, 2012; Gallistel, 2012.)

Why should nonreinforcement produce an inhibitory S–R association? In answering this question, it is important to keep in mind that extinction involves a special type of nonreinforcement. It involves nonreinforcement after a history of conditioning with repeated presentations of the reinforcer. Nonreinforcement without such a prior history is not extinction but is more akin to habituation. This is an important distinction because the effects of nonreinforcement depend critically on the individual's prior history. If your partner never made you coffee in the morning, you would not be disappointed if the coffee was not ready when you got up. If you never received an allowance, you would not be disappointed when you didn't get one. It is only the omission of an expected reward that creates disappointment or frustration. In a similar fashion, the omission of an expected aversive event creates relief, which is not experienced without that expectation.

As I mentioned at the outset of the chapter, extinction involves both behavioral and emotional effects. The emotional effects stem from the frustration that is triggered when an expected reinforcer is not forthcoming. Nonreinforcement in the face of the expectation of reward is assumed to trigger an unconditioned aversive frustrative reaction (Amsel, 1958; Papini, 2003). This aversive emotion serves to discourage responding during the

TABLE 9.2 **DEVELOPMENT OF AN INHIBITORY S–R ASSOCIATION IN INSTRUMENTAL EXTINCTION (RESCORLA 1993A, EXPERIMENT 3)**

PHASE 1	PHASE 2	EXTINCTION	TEST
N: Rc → P	R1 → P	N: R1–	N: R1 or R2
L: Rc → P	R2 → P	L: R2–	L: R1 or R2

Note: N and L were noise and light discriminative stimuli. Rc was a common response (nose poking) for all subjects, P represents the food pellet reinforcer, and R1 and R2 were lever press and chain pull, counterbalanced across subjects.

course of extinction through the establishment of an inhibitory S–R association (Rescorla, 2001a).

The establishment of an inhibitory S–R association during the course of extinction is illustrated by an experiment whose procedures are outlined in Table 9.2. Laboratory rats first received discrimination training in which a common response (poking the nose into a hole) was reinforced with food pellets whenever a light or noise stimulus (L or N) was present. This training was conducted so that nonreinforcement in the presence of L or N would elicit frustration when extinction was introduced. The targets of extinction were lever-press and chain-pull responses (designated as R1 and R2, counterbalanced across subjects). R1 and R2 were first reinforced, again with food pellets. Notice that the reinforcement of R1 and R2 did not occur in the presence of the light and noise stimuli. Therefore, this reinforcement training was not expected to establish any S–R associations involving the light and noise.

Extinction was conducted in the third phase and consisted of presentations of L and N (to create the expectancy of reward) with either R1 or R2 available but nonreinforced. The extinction phase presumably established inhibitory S–R associations involving N-R1 and L-R2. The presence of these associations was tested by giving subjects the opportunity to perform R1 or R2 in the presence of the L and N stimuli. If an inhibitory N-R1 association was established during extinction, the subjects were predicted to make fewer R1 than R2 responses when tested with N. In a corresponding fashion, they were expected to make fewer R2 than R1 responses when tested with L. Notice that this differential response outcome cannot be explained in terms of changes in R–O or S–O associations because such changes should have influenced R1 and R2 equally.

The results of the experiment are presented in Figure 9.11. Responding is shown for the intertrial interval (ITI) and in the presence of the stimulus (L or N) with which the

FIGURE 9.11 Demonstration that extinction involves the acquisition of an inhibitory S–R association that is specific to the stimulus in the presence of which the response is nonreinforced (see procedure summarized in Table 9.2). A particular response occurred less often during the stimulus with which the response had been extinguished (Ext) than during an alternative stimulus (NotExt). ITI refers to the intertrial interval. (Based on "Inhibitory Associations between S and R in Extinction," by R. A. Rescorla, *Animal Learning & Behavior*, Vol. 21, Figure 7, p. 333, 1993.)

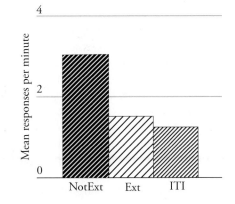

response had been extinguished or not. Responding during the stimulus with which the response had been extinguished was significantly less than responding during the alternate stimulus. Furthermore, the extinction stimulus produced responding not significantly higher than what occurred during the intertrial interval. These results indicate that the extinction procedure produced an inhibitory S–R association that was specific to a particular stimulus and response.

Paradoxical Reward Effects

If the decline in responding in extinction is due to the frustrative effects of an unexpected absence of reinforcement, then one would expect more rapid extinction following training that establishes greater expectations of reward. This is indeed the case and has led to a number of paradoxical effects. For example, the more training that is provided with continuous reinforcement, the stronger will be the frustration that occurs when extinction is introduced. That in turn produces more rapid extinction. This phenomenon is called the **overtraining extinction effect** (e.g., Ishida & Papini, 1997; Theios & Brelsford, 1964).

The overtraining extinction effect is paradoxical because it involves fewer responses in extinction after more extensive reinforcement training. Casually thinking, one might think that more extensive training should create a stronger response that would be more resistant to extinction. But, in fact, the opposite is the case, especially when training involves continuous reinforcement.

Another paradoxical reward effect that reflects similar mechanisms is the **magnitude reinforcement extinction effect**. This phenomenon refers to the fact that responding declines more rapidly in extinction following reinforcement with a larger reinforcer (Hulse, 1958; Wagner, 1961) and is also readily accounted for in terms of the frustrative effects of nonreward. Nonreinforcement is apt to be more frustrating if the individual expects a large reward than if the individual expects a small reward. Consider the following scenarios. In one you receive $100 per month from your parents to help with incidental expenses at college. In the other, you get only $20 a month. In both cases your parents stop the payments when you drop out of school for a semester. This nonreinforcement will be more aversive if you came to expect the larger monthly allowance.

The most extensively investigated paradoxical reward effect is the **partial-reinforcement extinction effect (PREE)**. A key factor that determines the magnitude of both the behavioral and emotional effects of an extinction procedure is the schedule of reinforcement that is in effect before the extinction procedure is introduced. Various subtle features of reinforcement schedules can influence the rate of extinction. However, the most important variable is whether the instrumental response was reinforced every time it occurred (*continuous reinforcement*) or only some of the times it occurred (*intermittent*, or *partial*, *reinforcement*). Extinction is much slower and involves fewer frustration reactions if partial reinforcement rather than continuous reinforcement was in effect before the introduction extinction. This phenomenon is called the *partial-reinforcement extinction effect*.

The partial reinforcement extinction effect has been invoked to explain the behavior of habitual gamblers, who persist in gambling even if they encounter a long string of failures (extinction). In an interesting recent study (Horsley et al., 2012), persistence in extinction was compared between individuals who rarely gamble and those who gamble frequently (more than three times a week). The instrumental conditioning task was a computer game in which the participants had to produce the correct combination of a lock that would open a pirate's treasure chest. The reinforcer was seeing the gold coins in the chest and getting a congratulatory laugh and verbal feedback ("Correct!"). Independent

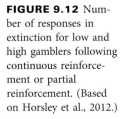

FIGURE 9.12 Number of responses in extinction for low and high gamblers following continuous reinforcement or partial reinforcement. (Based on Horsley et al., 2012.)

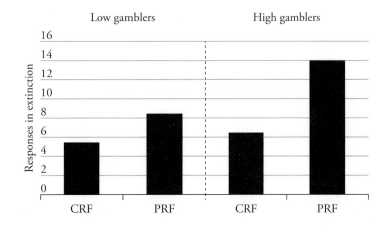

groups received either continuous reinforcement or 50% partial reinforcement until they made 20 correct responses. Thereafter, responding produced the message "Incorrect" and the sound of a jammed lock for 20 trials of extinction.

The number of responses in extinction is presented in Figure 9.12. The various groups made similar numbers of responses during acquisition. Among both the low and the high gamblers, partial reinforcement yielded more responses in extinction than continuous reinforcement. However, the magnitude of this partial-reinforcement extinction effect was greater among the high gamblers. Although this experiment shows a relationship between the propensity to gamble and the partial-reinforcement extinction effect, it does not identify the directionality of the effect. A stronger partial-reinforcement extinction effect may be a consequence of frequent prior gambling or a cause of frequent gambling.

The persistence in responding that is created by **intermittent reinforcement** is evident in many situations. Consider, for example, a child riding in a grocery cart while the parent is shopping. The child asks the parent to buy a piece of candy. The parent says no. The child asks again and again and then begins to throw a temper tantrum because the parent continues to say no. At this point, the parent is likely to give in to avoid public embarrassment. By finally giving the candy, the parent will have provided intermittent reinforcement for the child's repeated requests. The parent will also have reinforced the tantrum behavior. The intermittent reinforcement of the requests for candy will make the child very persistent (and obnoxious) in asking for candy during future shopping trips.

Although most studies of the partial-reinforcement extinction effect have employed instrumental conditioning procedures, the partial-reinforcement extinction effect has been also demonstrated in Pavlovian conditioning (e.g., Haselgrove, Aydin, & Pearce, 2004; Rescorla, 1999c). In early studies, the partial-reinforcement extinction effect was found only in studies that compared the effects of continuous and partial reinforcement training in separate groups of subjects. However, later studies have demonstrated that the effect can also occur in the same individuals if they experience continuous reinforcement in the presence of one set of cues and intermittent reinforcement in the presence of other stimuli (e.g., Nevin & Grace, 2005; Rescorla, 1999c; Svartdal, 2000).

Mechanisms of the Partial-Reinforcement Extinction Effect

Perhaps the most obvious explanation of the partial-reinforcement extinction effect is that the introduction of extinction is easier to detect after continuous reinforcement than after partial reinforcement. This explanation of the partial-reinforcement extinction effect is called the **discrimination hypothesis**. Although the discrimination hypothesis is plausible, the partial-reinforcement extinction effect is not so simple. In an ingenious test of the hypothesis, Jenkins (1962) and Theios (1962) first trained one group of animals with partial reinforcement and another with continuous reinforcement. Both groups then received a phase of continuous reinforcement before extinction was introduced. Because extinction was introduced immediately after continuous reinforcement for both groups, extinction should have been equally noticeable or discriminable for both. Nevertheless, the subjects that initially received partial reinforcement training responded more in extinction.

The results of Jenkins and Theios indicate that the response persistence produced by partial reinforcement does not come from greater difficulty in detecting the start of extinction. Rather, individuals learn something long lasting from partial reinforcement that is carried over even if they subsequently receive continuous reinforcement. Partial reinforcement seems to teach individuals not to give up in the face of failure, and this learned persistence is retained across an unbroken string of successes.

What is learned during partial reinforcement that creates persistence in the face of a run of bad luck or failure? Hundreds of experiments have been performed in attempts to answer this question. These studies indicate that partial reinforcement promotes persistence in two different ways. One explanation, **frustration theory**, is based on what individuals learn about the emotional effects of nonreward during partial reinforcement training. The other explanation, **sequential theory**, is based on what is learned about the memory of nonreward.

A. Amsel

Frustration Theory   Frustration theory was developed by Abram Amsel (e.g., 1958, 1992; see also Papini, 2003). According to frustration theory, persistence in extinction results from learning something counterintuitive, namely to continue responding when you expect to be nonreinforced or frustrated. This learning develops in stages. Intermittent reinforcement involves both rewarded and nonrewarded trials. Rewarded trials lead individuals to expect reinforcement, and nonrewarded trials lead them to expect the absence of reward. Consequently, intermittent reinforcement initially leads to the learning of two competing expectations. These two competing expectations lead to conflicting behaviors: the expectation of reward encourages responding, and the anticipation of nonreinforcement discourages responding. However, as training continues, this conflict is resolved in favor of responding.

The resolution of the conflict occurs because reinforcement is not predictable in the typical intermittent reinforcement schedule. Therefore, responding is reinforced some of the times when the participant expects nonreward. Because of such experiences, the instrumental response becomes conditioned to the expectation of nonreward or frustration. According to frustration theory, this is the key to persistent responding in extinction. With sufficient training, *intermittent reinforcement results in learning to make the instrumental response in the face of the expectation of nonreward*. This is observed in gamblers who continue to play even though they know that the odds are against winning. Once the responding has become conditioned to the expectation of nonreward, responding persists when extinction is introduced. By contrast, there is nothing about the experience of continuous reinforcement that encourages individuals to respond when they expect nonreward. Therefore, continuous reinforcement does not produce persistence in extinction.

E. J. Capaldi

Sequential theory   The major alternative to frustration theory, sequential theory, was proposed by Capaldi (e.g., 1967, 1971) and is stated in terms of memory concepts rather than the expectations of reward or frustration. Sequential theory assumes that individuals can remember whether or not they were reinforced for performing the instrumental response in the recent past. They remember both recent rewarded and nonrewarded trials. The theory assumes further that with intermittent reinforcement, the memory of nonreward becomes a cue for performing the instrumental response. Precisely how this happens depends on the sequence of rewarded (R) and nonrewarded (N) trials that are administered. That is why the theory is labeled *sequential theory*.

Consider the following sequence of trials: RNNRRNR. In this sequence, the individual is rewarded (R) on the first trial, not rewarded (N) on the next two trials, then rewarded twice, then not rewarded, and then rewarded again. The fourth and last trials are critical in this schedule and are therefore underlined. On the fourth trial, the individual is reinforced after receiving nonreward on the preceding two trials. Because of this, the memory of two nonrewarded trials becomes a cue for responding. Responding in the face of the memory of nonreward is again reinforced on the last trial. Here, the individual is reinforced for responding during the memory of one nonreinforced trial. With enough experiences of this type, the individual learns to respond whenever it remembers not having been reinforced on the preceding trials. This learning creates persistent responding in extinction (e.g., Capaldi et al., 1996; Capaldi et al., 1992; Haggbloom et al., 1990.)

Some considered frustration theory and sequential theory to be competing explanations of the partial-reinforcement extinction effect. However, since the two mechanisms were originally proposed, a large and impressive body of evidence has been obtained in support of each theory. Therefore, it is unlikely that one theory is correct and the other is wrong. A better way to think about them is that the two theories point out different ways in which partial reinforcement can promote responding during extinction. Memory mechanisms may make more of a contribution when training trials are scheduled close together and it is easier to remember what happened on the preceding trial. In contrast, the emotional learning described by frustration theory is less sensitive to intertrial intervals and thus provides a better explanation of the partial-reinforcement extinction effect when widely spaced training trials are used.

All the studies I have described in this section have involved appetitive conditioning because most of the experiments focusing on emotional effects of extinction and the learning of inhibitory S–R associations have been conducted in appetitive conditioning situations. However, one can construct analogous arguments and mechanisms for extinction in aversive situations. There, the unexpected omission of the aversive reinforcer should result in relief, and learning supported by such relief should lead to the inhibition of fear. Application of these ideas to aversive situations awaits future investigation.

Resistance to Change and Behavioral Momentum

Another way to think about response persistence in extinction is that it represents resistance to the change in reinforcement contingencies that occurs when the extinction procedure is introduced (Nevin, 2012; Nevin & Grace, 2005). Nevin and Grace have thought about resistance to change more broadly and have proposed the concept of **behavioral momentum** to characterize the susceptibility of behavior to disruptions (Grace & Nevin, 2004; Nevin & Grace, 2000). The term *behavioral momentum* is based on an analogy to physical momentum in Newtonian physics. The momentum of a physical object is the product of its weight (or mass) and its speed. A fast-moving bullet and a slow-moving freight train both have a great deal of momentum. In both cases, the product of weight × speed is large, making both the bullet and the train hard to stop, and hence resistant to change. By analogy (fleshed out by mathematical equations), the behavioral momentum hypothesis states that behavior that has a great deal of momentum will also be hard to "stop" or disrupt by various manipulations, including extinction.

Research on behavioral momentum has been conducted using multiple schedules of reinforcement. As was described in Chapter 8, a multiple schedule has two or more components. Each component is identified by a distinctive stimulus and its accompanying schedule of reinforcement. Multiple schedules are popular in studies of behavioral momentum because they enable investigators to compare the susceptibility of behavior to disruption under two different conditions in the same session and the same individual. One may be interested, for example, in whether adding free reinforcers to a schedule of reinforcement makes behavior more resistant to change. The question can be answered by using a multiple schedule in which each component has the same VI schedule but one of the components also includes extra reinforcers that are delivered independent of responding (Podlesnik & Shahan, 2008).

A number of different sources of disruption have been examined in studies of behavioral momentum. These have included providing extra food before the experimental session, providing extra food during intervals between components of the multiple schedule, and terminating reinforcement (extinction). Most of the experiments have been conducted with pigeons and rats. However, there is increasing interest in exploring the implications of behavioral momentum in applied behavior analysis because most applications of behavioral principles involve efforts to change behavior in some manner (Nevin & Shahan, 2011). (For an analysis of women's basketball games in terms of behavioral momentum, see Roane et al., 2004.)

Studies of behavioral momentum have encouraged two major conclusions. The first is that *behavioral momentum is directly related to the rate of reinforcement* (see Nevin & Grace, 2000; Nevin, 2012). Higher rates of reinforcement produce behavior that has greater momentum and is less susceptible to disruption. Another common (but not universal) finding is that behavioral momentum is unrelated to response rate. Thus, two behaviors that occur at similar rates do not necessarily have similar degrees of behavioral momentum (e.g., Nevin, Mandell, & Atak, 1983).

The primacy of reinforcement rate rather than response rate as the determinant of behavioral momentum has encouraged Nevin and Grace (2000) to attribute behavioral momentum primarily to Pavlovian conditioning or S–O associations (e.g., McLean, Campbell-Tie, & Nevin, 1996). An interesting corollary to this conclusion is that behavioral momentum should be increased by adding reinforcers to a component of a multiple schedule even if those reinforcers are not contingent on responding. This prediction was confirmed in a study with pigeons that I cited earlier (Podlesnik & Shahan, 2008) as well as in studies with children with developmental disabilities (Ahearn et al., 2003).

The effects of reinforcer rate on behavioral momentum are illustrated by a study conducted with 10 students with developmental disabilities who were between 7 and 19 years old (Dube et al., 2003). A variation of a video game was used that involved catching a moving icon or sprite by touching the screen with a finger or clicking on the sprite with a joystick. Two different sprites (1 and 2) were used during baseline training, and each was presented on separate trials. Thus, each sprite represented a component of a multiple schedule. Correct responses were reinforced with tokens, points, or money for different participants. In the presence of each sprite, a VI 12-second schedule of reinforcement was in effect. To increase the rate of reinforcement in one of the components of the multiple schedule, free reinforcers were added to the VI 12-second schedule at variable times averaging 6 seconds (VT 6 second). No responses were required to obtain the extra reinforcers. Thus, one sprite was associated with a higher rate of reinforcement (VI 12 second + VT 6 second) than the other sprite (VI 12 second). Responding was also trained in the presence of a third sprite, reinforced on a VI 8-second schedule. The third sprite was used at the end of the experiment to test for resistance to change.

After responding was well established to all the sprites, tests of behavioral momentum were conducted. During each of these tests, sprite 1 or sprite 2 was presented by itself as usual. However, during the tests the third sprite also appeared as a distracter. The question was how much of a disruption this would cause in responding to sprites

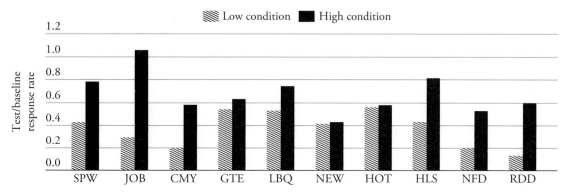

FIGURE 9.13 Relative rate of responding during two components of a multiple schedule that involved either a low or high rate of reinforcement during a test for behavioral momentum for 10 students identified by the letters on the horizontal axis. (From Dube et al., 2003. Figure 1, page 139.)

1 and 2 and whether the degree of disruption would be different depending on the rate of reinforcement that was associated with each of the first two sprites.

The results of the experiment are summarized separately for each participant in Figure 9.13. The data are presented in terms of responding that occurred during the momentum test (when sprite 3 appeared as a distracter) as a proportion of baseline responding (when sprites 1 and 2 appeared alone). A score of 1.0 indicates no disruption by sprite 3. Some disruption occurred in all of the participants. However, the major finding was that responding was less disrupted in the presence of the sprite that was associated with the higher reinforcement rate. This effect, which was predicted by the behavioral momentum hypothesis, was clear in 9 of the 10 participants.

Concluding Comments

Extinction is one of the most active areas of contemporary research in behavior theory. Although the phenomenon was identified by Pavlov more than a hundred years ago, much of what we know about extinction has been discovered in the last 30 years. A great deal of work was done earlier on the partial-reinforcement extinction effect. That line of work, and its contemporary counterpart in studies of behavioral momentum, was focused on factors that contribute to persistence in responding. In contrast, the emphasis in most other studies of extinction has been on conditions that promote the decline in conditioned responding and the circumstances under which responding recovers. These issues are of great interest for translational research because of their implications for exposure therapy and relapse. Unfortunately, there are no simple answers. As Bouton and Wood (2008) commented, "Extinction is a highly complex phenomenon, even when analyzed at a purely behavioral level" (p. 166).

Sample Questions

1. Describe the basic behavioral and emotional consequences of extinction.
2. Describe various conditions under which extinguished responding can reappear.
3. Describe how extinguishing one response may influence how often other responses occur.
4. Describe the various ways in which control of behavior by contextual cues is relevant to the behavioral effects of extinction.
5. Describe various ways in which extinction performance may be enhanced.
6. Describe evidence that identifies the development of inhibitory S–R associations in extinction.

7. Describe the partial-reinforcement extinction effect and major explanations of that phenomenon.

8. Describe the concept of behavioral momentum. What are the advantages and disadvantages of the concept?

Key Terms

behavioral momentum The susceptibility of responding to disruption by manipulations such as presession feeding, delivery of free food, or a change in the schedule of reinforcement.

consolidation The establishment of a memory in relatively permanent form so that it is available for retrieval a long time after original acquisition.

continuous reinforcement (CRF) A schedule of reinforcement in which every occurrence of the instrumental response produces the reinforcer.

discrimination hypothesis An explanation of the partial-reinforcement extinction effect according to which extinction is slower after partial reinforcement than continuous reinforcement because the onset of extinction is more difficult to detect following partial reinforcement.

extinction (in classical conditioning) Reduction of a learned response that occurs because the CS is no longer paired with the US. Also, the procedure of repeatedly presenting a CS without the US.

extinction (in instrumental conditioning) Reduction of the instrumental response that occurs because the response is no longer followed by the reinforcer. Also, the procedure of no longer reinforcing the instrumental response.

forgetting The loss of a learned response that occurs because information about training is irrevocably lost due to the passage of time. Forgetting is contrasted with extinction, which is produced by a specific procedure rather than the passage of time.

frustration An aversive emotional reaction that results from the unexpected absence of reinforcement.

frustration theory A theory of the partial-reinforcement extinction effect, according to which extinction is slower after partial reinforcement because the instrumental response becomes conditioned to the anticipation of frustrative nonreward.

intermittent reinforcement A schedule of reinforcement in which only some of the occurrences of the instrumental response are reinforced. The instrumental response is reinforced occasionally or intermittently. Also called *partial reinforcement.*

overtraining extinction effect Less persistence of instrumental behavior in extinction following extensive training with reinforcement (overtraining) than following only moderate levels of training. This effect is most prominent with continuous reinforcement.

magnitude reinforcement extinction effect Less persistence of instrumental behavior in extinction following training with a large reinforcer than following training with a small or moderate reinforcer. This effect is most prominent with continuous reinforcement.

partial-reinforcement extinction effect The term used to describe greater persistence in instrumental responding in extinction after partial (or intermittent) reinforcement training than after continuous reinforcement training.

reinstatement Reappearance of an extinguished response produced by exposure to the US or reinforcer.

renewal effect Reappearance of an extinguished response produced by a shift away from the contextual cues that were present during extinction. In ABA renewal, the shift is back to the context of acquisition. In ABC renewal, the shift is to a familiar context unrelated to either acquisition or extinction.

resurgence Reappearance of an extinguished response caused by the extinction of another behavior.

sequential theory A theory of the partial-reinforcement extinction effect according to which extinction is retarded after partial reinforcement because the instrumental response becomes conditioned to the memory of nonreward.

spontaneous recovery (in extinction) Reappearance of an extinguished response caused by the passage of time. (Compare with spontaneous recovery in habituation.)

CHAPTER 10

Aversive Control: Avoidance and Punishment

CHAPTER PREVIEW

This chapter deals with how behavior can be controlled by aversive stimulation. The discussion focuses on two types of instrumental conditioning: avoidance and punishment. Avoidance conditioning increases the performance of a target behavior, and punishment decreases the target response. In both cases, individuals learn to minimize their exposure to aversive stimulation. Because of this similarity, theoretical analyses of avoidance and punishment share some of the same concepts. Nevertheless, for the most part, experimental analyses of avoidance and punishment have proceeded independently of each other. I will describe the major empirical findings and theoretical puzzles in both areas of research.

Fear, pain, and disappointment are inevitable in life. It is not surprising, therefore, that there is considerable interest in how behavior is controlled by aversive stimuli. Two procedures have been extensively investigated in studies of aversive control: avoidance and punishment. In an **avoidance** procedure, the individual has to make a specific response to prevent an aversive stimulus from occurring. For example, you might grab a handrail to avoid slipping, or take an umbrella to avoid getting wet if it rains. An avoidance procedure involves a negative contingency between an instrumental response and the aversive stimulus. If the response occurs, the aversive stimulus is omitted. By contrast, **punishment** involves a positive contingency: the target response produces the aversive outcome. If you touch a hot stove, you will get burned.

Avoidance procedures increase the occurrence of instrumental behavior, whereas punishment procedures suppress instrumental responding. However, with both procedures, the final result is less contact with the aversive stimulus or longer periods of safety. In avoidance, safety is achieved by doing something. Hence, avoidance conditioning is sometimes referred to as *active avoidance*. With punishment, increased safety is achieved by not doing something. Hence, punishment is sometimes called *passive avoidance*.

Despite the similarities between them, different intellectual traditions have dominated considerations of avoidance and punishment. Research on avoidance behavior has focused primarily on theoretical issues. Investigators have been interested in the mechanisms that are responsible for behavior whose primary consequence is the absence of something. By contrast, scientists studying punishment have focused on practical and ethical considerations, such as which punishment procedures are effective in suppressing behavior and under what circumstances is it justified to use those procedures.

Avoidance Behavior

Avoidance learning has been studied for about 100 years. Most of the experiments have involved laboratory rats responding to avoid shock. However, numerous studies have been also conducted with human participants, and a variety of aversive stimuli have been tested including loss of points or money, white noise, invasion of Martians in a computer game, and time-out from positive reinforcement (e.g., Costa & Boakes, 2011; DeFulio & Hackenberg, 2007; Molet, Leconte, & Rosas, 2006).

Origins of the Study of Avoidance Behavior

To appreciate how scientists approach the study of avoidance behavior, one has to understand its historical roots. Experimental investigations of avoidance originated in studies of classical conditioning. The first avoidance experiments were conducted by the Russian psychologist Vladimir Bechterev (1913) as an extension of Pavlov's research. Unlike Pavlov, however, Bechterev was interested in studying associative learning in human participants. In one situation, individuals were instructed to place a finger on a metal plate. A warning stimulus (the conditioned stimulus [CS]) was then presented, followed by a brief shock (the unconditioned stimulus [US]) through the metal plate. As you might predict, the participants quickly lifted their finger when they were shocked. Pretty soon they also learned to lift their finger in response to the warning stimulus.

At first Bechterev's experiment was incorrectly viewed as a standard example of classical conditioning. However, in Bechterev's method the participants controlled whether or not they received the US. If they lifted their finger in response to the CS, they did not get the shock delivered through the metal plate. This aspect of the procedure constitutes a significant departure from Pavlov's methods because in standard classical conditioning making the conditioned response does not cancel (or change) the delivery of the US.

The fact that Bechterev did not use a standard classical conditioning procedure went unnoticed for many years. However, starting in the 1930s, several scientists started examining the difference between a standard classical conditioning procedure and a procedure that had an instrumental avoidance component added (e.g., Schlosberg, 1934, 1936). One of the most influential of these studies was performed by Brogden, Lipman, and Culler (1938).

Brogden and colleagues tested two groups of guinea pigs in a rotating wheel apparatus. A tone served as the CS, and shock served as the US. When the shock came on, the guinea pigs ran and rotated the wheel. For the classical conditioning group, the shock was always presented 2 seconds after the beginning of the tone. For the avoidance conditioning group, the shock also followed the tone when the animals did not rotate the wheel. However, if the avoidance animals moved the wheel during the tone CS, the scheduled

FIGURE 10.1

Panel A: Modern running wheel for rodents. Panel B: Percentage of trials when guinea pigs moved the running wheel on successive days of training. Such responses prevented shock delivery for the avoidance group but not for the classical group. (From "The Role of Incentive in Conditioning and Extinction" by W. J. Brogden, E. A. Lipman, and E. Culler, 1938. *American Journal of Psychology, 51,* pp. 109–117.)

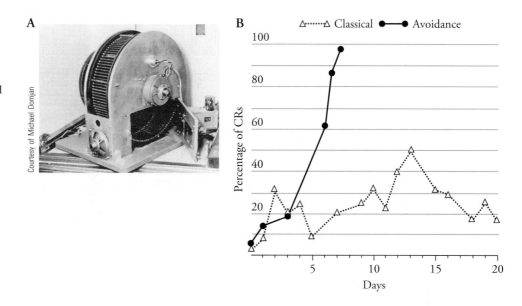

shock was omitted. Figure 10.1 shows the percentage of trials on which each group made the conditioned response. The avoidance group quickly learned to make the conditioned response and was responding on 100% of the trials within 8 days of training. With this high level of responding, these guinea pigs managed to avoid all scheduled shocks. In contrast, the classical conditioning group never achieved this high level of performance.

The results of Brogden and his collaborators proved that avoidance conditioning is different from standard classical conditioning and ushered in years of research on instrumental avoidance learning.

The Discriminated Avoidance Procedure

Although avoidance behavior is not just another case of classical conditioning, the classical conditioning heritage of the study of avoidance behavior has greatly influenced its experimental and theoretical analysis to the present day. Investigators have been concerned with the importance of the warning signal in avoidance procedures and the relation of the warning signal to the US and the instrumental response. Experimental questions of this type have been extensively investigated with procedures similar to that used by Brogden and his colleagues. This method is called **discriminated**, or **signaled**, **avoidance**. The standard features of the discriminated avoidance procedure are diagrammed in Figure 10.2.

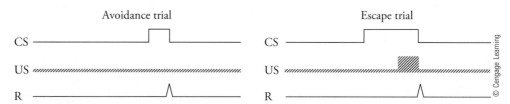

FIGURE 10.2 Diagram of the discriminated, or signaled, avoidance procedure. *Avoidance trial:* If the participant makes the response required for avoidance during the CS (the signal) but before the US (e.g., shock) is scheduled, the CS is turned off, and the US is omitted on that trial. *Escape trial:* If the participant fails to make the required response during the CS–US interval, the scheduled shock is presented and remains on until the response occurs, whereupon both the CS and the US are terminated.

The first thing to note about the discriminated avoidance procedure is that it involves discrete trials. Each trial is initiated by the warning stimulus or CS. What happens after that depends on what the participant does. If the participant makes the target response before the shock is delivered, the CS is turned off and the US is omitted on that trial. This is a successful **avoidance trial**. If the participant fails to make the required response during the CS–US interval, the scheduled shock is delivered and remains on until the response occurs, whereupon both the CS and the US are terminated. In this case, the instrumental response results in escape from the shock; hence, this type of trial is called an **escape trial**. During early stages of training, most of the trials are escape trials, but as training progresses, avoidance trials come to predominate.

Discriminated avoidance procedures are often conducted in a shuttle box similar to that shown in Figure 10.3. The shuttle box consists of two compartments separated by an opening at floor level. The animal (a rat or mouse) is placed on the left side of the apparatus. At the start of a trial, the CS is presented (e.g., a light or a tone). If the animal crosses over to the right side before the shock occurs, no shock is delivered and the CS is turned off. After an intertrial interval, the next trial is administered with the animal starting in the right compartment. On successive trials, the animal shuttles back and forth between the two sides of the apparatus, hence the name **shuttle avoidance**. (For an example of shuttle avoidance involving transgenic mice, see Nelson et al., 2012.)

There are two types of shuttle avoidance procedures. In the procedure just described, the animal moves from left to right on the first trial and then back the other way on the second trial. This type of procedure is technically called *two-way shuttle avoidance* because the animal moves in both directions on successive trials. In the second type of shuttle avoidance, the animal is placed on the same side of the apparatus at the start of each trial and always moves from there to the other side. This type of procedure is called *one-way avoidance*. Generally, one-way avoidance is easier to learn than the two-way procedure because the two-way procedure requires that the animal return to the side that was dangerous on the preceding trial.

Two-Process Theory of Avoidance

Avoidance procedures involve a negative contingency between a response and an aversive stimulus. If you make the appropriate avoidance response, you will not fall, get rained on, or drive off the road. No particular pleasure is derived from these experiences. You simply do not get hurt. The absence of the aversive stimulus is presumably the reason that avoidance responses occur. However, how can the absence of something

FIGURE 10.3 A shuttle box. The box has a metal grid floor and is separated into two compartments by an archway. The instrumental response consists of crossing back and forth (shuttling) from one side of the box to the other.

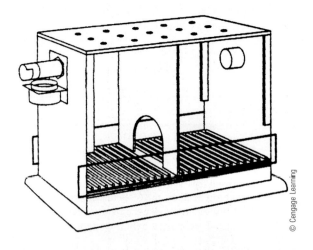

N. E. Miller

provide reinforcement for instrumental behavior? This is the fundamental question in the study of avoidance.

Mowrer and Lamoreaux (1942) pointed out more than a half century ago that "not getting something can hardly, in and of itself, qualify as rewarding" (p. 6). Since then, much intellectual effort has been devoted to figuring out what individuals "get" in avoidance conditioning procedures that might provide reinforcement for the avoidance response. In fact, the investigation of avoidance behavior has been dominated by this theoretical question. The first and most influential solution to the problem was the **two-process theory of avoidance**, proposed by Mowrer (1947) and elaborated by Miller (1951) and others (e.g., Levis & Brewer, 2001; McAllister & McAllister, 1995). (For a recent implementation and extension of two-process theory using reinforcement learning concepts from computer science, see Maia, 2010.)

As its name implies, two-process theory assumes that two mechanisms are involved in avoidance learning. The first is a classical conditioning process activated by pairings of the warning stimulus (CS) with the aversive event (US) on trials when the organism fails to make the avoidance response. Through these classical conditioning trials, the CS comes to elicit fear. Thus, the first component of two-process theory is the *classical conditioning of fear to the CS*. As I discussed in Chapters 3 and 9, considerable contemporary research is devoted to the mechanisms of fear conditioning and its extinction. Two-process theory treats conditioned fear as a source of motivation for avoidance learning.

Fear is an emotionally arousing, unpleasant state. As we discussed in Chapter 5, the termination of an unpleasant or aversive event provides negative reinforcement for instrumental behavior. The second process in two-process theory is based on such negative reinforcement. Mowrer proposed that the instrumental avoidance response is learned because the response terminates the CS and thereby reduces the conditioned fear elicited by the CS. Thus, the second component in two-process theory is *instrumental reinforcement of the avoidance response through fear reduction*.

There are several noteworthy aspects of this two-process theory. First, and perhaps most important, is that the classical and instrumental processes depend on each other. Instrumental reinforcement through fear reduction is not possible until fear has become conditioned to the CS. Therefore, the classical conditioning process has to occur first. Classical conditioning is an *establishing operation* that enables the reinforcement of the instrumental response through fear reduction. However, successful avoidance responses constitute extinction trials for the CS (because the US gets omitted). Thus, two-process theory predicts repeated interaction between classical and instrumental processes. Classical conditioning makes possible instrumental negative reinforcement, but successful instrumental avoidance responding can result in extinction of the classically conditioned fear.

Another important aspect of two-process theory is that it explains avoidance behavior in terms of escape from conditioned fear rather than in terms of the prevention of shock. The fact that the avoidance response prevents shock is seen as an incidental by-product in two-process theory and not the primary determinant of avoidance behavior. Escape from conditioned fear is the primary causal factor. Because of this, the instrumental response is reinforced by a tangible event (fear reduction) rather than merely the absence of something.

Experimental Analysis of Avoidance Behavior

Avoidance learning has been the subject of numerous experiments. Much of the research has been stimulated by efforts to prove or disprove two-process theory. Space does not permit reviewing all the evidence. However, I will consider several important findings that must be considered in understanding the mechanisms of avoidance behavior.

Escape From Fear Experiments

Escape From Fear Experiments   In the typical avoidance procedure, classical conditioning of fear and instrumental reinforcement through fear reduction occur intermixed across trials. However, if these two processes make separate contributions to avoidance learning, it should be possible to demonstrate their operation when the two types of conditioning are not intermixed. This is the goal of **escape from fear (EFF) procedure**.

The basic strategy is to first condition fear to a CS with a *pure* classical conditioning procedure in which the CS is paired with the US regardless of what the animal does. In the next phase of the procedure, the participants are periodically exposed to the fear-eliciting CS and allowed to perform an instrumental response to turn off the CS (and thereby reduce fear). No shocks are scheduled in the second phase.

EFF experiments have generally upheld the predictions of the two-process theory. That is, the termination of a conditioned aversive stimulus is an effective reinforcer for instrumental behavior. One study, by Esmorís-Arranz and colleagues (2003), for example, compared EFF learning after delayed and simultaneous conditioning in a shuttle box. During the initial phase of the experiment, rats were confined to one side of the shuttle box (called the *shock* side) and received 10 Pavlovian trials during each of three sessions. The CS was a 15-second audiovisual cue, and the US was 15 seconds of mild foot shock. The delayed conditioning group always got the US at the end of the CS. The simultaneous conditioning group got the US at the same time as the CS. A third group served as a control and got the CS and the US unpaired.

After the fear-conditioning phase, the barrier to the other side of the shuttle box was removed and the rats were tested for escape from fear. Each trial started with the rat placed on the shock side with the CS turned on. If the rat moved to the other side within a minute, it turned off the CS and was allowed to stay on the other side for 30 seconds. The next trial was then initiated. Rats that did not move to the safe side within a minute were removed and placed in a holding box before starting their next trial. The latency to escape to the safe side is summarized in Figure 10.4. Both the delayed conditioning group and the simultaneous conditioning group showed decreased latencies to escape from the fear stimulus across trials, indicating learning to escape from fear. No systematic changes in latency to escape were evident in the unpaired control group. These results show clear EFF learning, as predicted by two-process theory.

This type of experiment was first conducted more than 60 years ago (e.g., Brown & Jacobs, 1949) but remains of considerable contemporary interest (see Cain & LeDoux, 2007, for an extensive discussion). EFF is attracting renewed interest in contemporary clinical work because it represents a transition from a passive fear reaction to an active coping strategy that helps to overcome fear and anxiety attendant to trauma (LeDoux & Gorman, 2001; van der Kolk, 2006).

Independent Measurement of Fear During Acquisition of Avoidance Behavior

Independent Measurement of Fear During Acquisition of Avoidance Behavior
Another important strategy that has been used in investigations of avoidance behavior involves independent measurement of fear and instrumental avoidance responding. This approach is based on the assumption that if fear motivates avoidance responding and if fear reduction is reinforcing, then the conditioning of fear and the conditioning of instrumental avoidance behavior should go hand in hand. Contrary to this prediction, however, conditioned fear and avoidance responding tend to be correlated only early in training. After that, avoidance responding may persist without much fear being exhibited when the CS or warning signal occurs (Mineka, 1979).

Fairly early in the study of avoidance learning, Solomon and his associates noticed that dogs become less fearful as they become proficient in performing an avoidance response (Solomon, Kamin, & Wynne, 1953; Solomon & Wynne, 1953). Subsequently, more systematic measurements of fear and avoidance behavior have confirmed this

Courtesy of Donald A. Dewsbury

S. Mineka

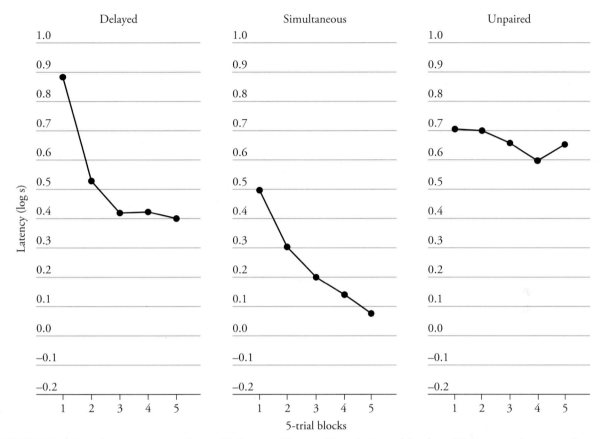

FIGURE 10.4 Mean latencies to escape from a CS that was either conditioned using a delayed conditioning procedure, a simultaneous conditioning procedure, or was presented unpaired with the US (based on Esmorís-Arranz, Pardo-Vázquez, & Vázquez-Garciá, 2003).

observation (e.g., Kamin et al., 1963; Mineka & Gino, 1980). Many of these studies were done with laboratory rats conditioned in a shuttle avoidance task, with fear measured using the conditioned suppression technique. A similar dissociation between fear and avoidance learning is observed in people.

In an experiment by Lovibond and colleagues (2008), college students received conditioning with three different stimuli, designated as A, B, and C. The stimuli were colored blocks presented on a computer screen. The US was shock to the index finger at an intensity that was uncomfortable but not painful. On trials with Stimulus A, an avoidance conditioning procedure was in effect. Stimulus A was presented for 5 seconds, followed by shock 10 seconds later (A+). However, if the participant pressed the correct button during the CS, shock was omitted on that trial. Stimulus B received only Pavlovian conditioning as a comparison. Each presentation of B was followed by shock (B+) without the opportunity to avoid. Stimulus C was a control cue and was never followed by shock (C−). To track the effect of these procedures, the participants were asked to rate their expectation that shock would occur, and their skin conductance responses were recorded as an index of fear. Ratings of shock expectancy were obtained during the 10-second delay between the CS and the scheduled US.

The results of the experiment are summarized in Figure 10.5. The left graph shows changes in skin conductance as a measure of fear. Fear was always low for Stimulus C, as would be expected because C never ended in shock. Fear increased across trials for the Pavlovian Stimulus B, which ended in shock on each trial (B+). In contrast, fear

FIGURE 10.5 Changes in skin conductance and expectancy of shock across trials for a warning stimulus in an avoidance procedure (A+), a Pavlovian CS paired with shock (B+), and a stimulus never paired with shock (C−) (based on Lovibond et al., 2008).

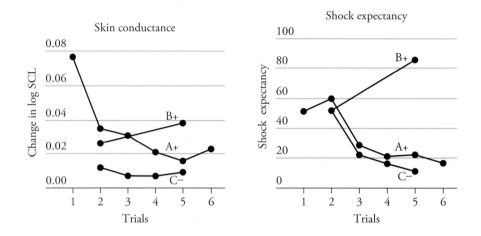

decreased across trials for the avoidance stimulus (A+). The changes in fear to Stimuli A and B were paralleled by changes in the expectancy of shock. Shock expectancy increased across trials for the Pavlovian Stimulus B but decreased for the avoidance Stimulus A. Subsequent test trials indicated that the participants were not afraid of Stimulus A because they had learned to prevent shock on A trials. If their avoidance response was blocked, their fear returned, as did their expectation that shock would occur again. These findings illustrate that successful avoidance behavior is associated with low levels of fear and low expectations of danger.

Extinction of Avoidance Behavior Through Response Blocking and CS-Alone Exposure   Early in the study of avoidance, the extinction procedure used for avoidance conditioning involved disconnecting the shock generator so that responses were no longer required to avoid the shock. However, responding still resulted in termination of the warning stimulus or CS. Under these conditions, avoidance responding persisted for a long time. In a classic experiment conducted with dogs, Solomon, Kamin, and Wynne (1953) described one participant that performed the avoidance response on 650 successive trials after only a few avoidance conditioning trials. Given such persistence, how might avoidance behavior be extinguished? The answer to this question is very important not only for theoretical analyses of avoidance but also for the treatment of clinically troublesome or pathological avoidance responses.

The most effective extinction procedure for avoidance behavior involves extensive exposure to the CS without the US. However, to achieve extensive CS exposure, the participants cannot be permitted to terminate the CS prematurely, as occurred in the study by Solomon, Kamin, and Wynne (1953). Rather, the apparatus has to be altered so that the avoidance response is blocked. This is called **response blocking**. In a shuttle box, for example, a barrier can be inserted to prevent the participant from going to the safe side when the CS comes on. By blocking the avoidance response, the participants can be exposed to the CS for a long time, or "flooded" with the CS (Baum, 1970). Hence this procedure is sometimes called **flooding**. (For discussion of a related procedure, called *implosive therapy*, see Levis, 1995; Levis & Brewer, 2001.)

Longer exposures to the CS without the US lead to more successful extinction of avoidance responding. This was demonstrated in a classic experiment by Schiff, Smith, and Prochaska (1972). Rats were trained to avoid shock in response to an auditory CS by going to a safe compartment. After acquisition, the safe compartment was blocked off by a barrier, and the rats received various amounts of exposure to the CS without shock. Different groups received 1, 5, or 12 blocked trials, and on each of these trials the CS was presented for 1, 5, 10, 50, or 120 seconds. The barrier blocking the avoidance response was then removed to test for extinction. At the start of each test trial, the animal was placed in the apparatus and the CS was presented until the animal crossed into the safe compartment. Shocks never occurred during the test trials, and each animal was tested until it took at least 120 seconds to cross into the safe compartment on three consecutive trials. The strength of the avoidance response was measured by the number of trials required to reach this extinction criterion.

The results of the experiment are summarized in Figure 10.6. As expected, exposure to the CS facilitated extinction of the avoidance response. Furthermore, this effect was determined mainly by the total duration of CS exposure. The number of flooding trials administered (1, 5, or 12) facilitated extinction only because each trial added to the total CS exposure time. Increases in the total duration of blocked exposure to the CS resulted in more extinction (see also Baum, 1969; Weinberger, 1965).

Research on extinction procedures has also shown that blocking access to the avoidance response can facilitate extinction of avoidance in its own right, even if response blocking does not increase the duration of the CS (e.g., Katzev & Berman, 1974). In the study of fear conditioning in college students by Lovibond and colleagues (2008) that I described earlier, fear and expectancy of shock declined with successful avoidance training, but both quickly returned during test trials when the opportunity to make the avoidance response was blocked. Procedures in which the avoidance response is blocked may be especially effective in extinguishing avoidance behavior because they permit the return of fear and thereby make fear more accessible to extinction. Response blocking in extinction also makes it clear that failure to make the avoidance response is no longer dangerous, which should disconfirm previously acquired shock expectancies (Lovibond, 2011).

Nondiscriminated (Free-Operant) Avoidance Two-process theory places great emphasis on the role of the warning signal, or CS, in avoidance learning. Clear warning signals are often evident in pathological avoidance behavior, as when someone shies away from intimacy after an abusive relationship. Can individuals also learn an

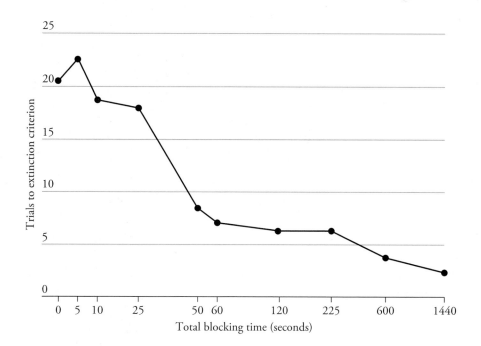

FIGURE 10.6 Trials to an extinction criterion for independent groups of animals that previously received various durations of blocked exposure to the CS. (From "Extinction of Avoidance in Rats as a Function of Duration and Number of Blocked Trials" by R. Schiff, N. Smith, and J. Prochaska, 1972, *Journal of Comparative and Physiological Psychology, 81,* pp. 356–359.)

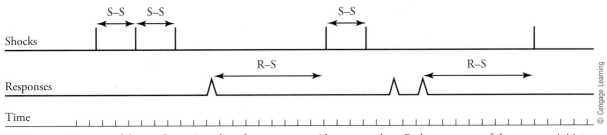

FIGURE 10.7 Diagram of the nondiscriminated, or free-operant, avoidance procedure. Each occurrence of the response initiates a period without shock, as set by the R–S interval. In the absence of a response, the next shock occurs a fixed period after the last shock, as set by the S–S interval. Shocks are not signaled by an exteroceptive stimulus and are usually brief and inescapable.

avoidance response if there is no external warning stimulus in the situation? Within the context of two-factor theory, this is a heretical question. However, progress in science requires posing bold questions, and Sidman (1953a, 1953b, 1966) did just that. He devised an avoidance conditioning procedure that did not involve a warning stimulus. The procedure has come to be called **nondiscriminated** or **free-operant avoidance**.

In a free-operant avoidance procedure, the aversive stimulus (e.g., shock) is scheduled to occur periodically without warning (e.g., every 10 seconds). Each time the participant makes the avoidance response, it obtains a period of safety (let's say 20 seconds long), during which shocks do not occur. Repetition of the avoidance response before the end of the shock-free period serves to start the safe period over again.

A free-operant avoidance procedure is constructed using two time intervals (Figure 10.7). One of these is the interval between shocks in the absence of a response. This is called the **S–S (shock–shock) interval**. The other critical time period is the interval between the avoidance response and the next scheduled shock. This is called the **R–S (response–shock) interval**. The R–S interval is the period of safety created by each response. In our example, the S–S interval was 10 seconds and the R–S interval was 20 seconds. Another important feature is that no matter when it occurs, an avoidance response will always reset the R–S interval (hence the term *free-operant avoidance*). By responding before the end of each R–S interval, the individual can always reset the R–S interval and thereby prolong its period of safety indefinitely.

Demonstrations of Free-Operant Avoidance Learning   Most of the research on free-operant avoidance learning has been conducted with laboratory rats and brief foot shock as the aversive stimulus. However, experiments have been also conducted with human participants and more "natural" aversive stimuli. For example, in one study, four college students served as the participants, and air enriched with carbon dioxide (CO_2) was the aversive US (Lejuez et al., 1998). CO_2 rather than shock was used because the investigators wanted to produce symptoms related to panic attacks. CO_2 inhalation produces respiratory distress, increased heart rate (tachycardia), and dizziness similar to what occurs during a panic attack.

Potential participants for the experiment were first screened to make sure they did not have a history of respiratory problems. During the experiment, the students were asked to wear a mask that usually provided room air. To deliver the aversive stimulus, the room air was switched to 20% CO_2 for 25 seconds. Each CO_2 delivery was followed by a 65-second rest period to permit resumption of normal breathing. The instrumental response was operating a plunger. Three seconds after the rest period, a hit of CO_2 was provided without warning if the participant did not pull the plunger (S–S interval = 3 seconds). Following a response, the next CO_2 delivery was scheduled 10 seconds later (R–S interval = 10 seconds). In addition, each occurrence of the avoidance response reset the R–S interval. If the participants never responded, they could get as many as 22 CO_2 deliveries in each session. However, they could avoid all CO_2 deliveries by responding before the end of the first S–S interval and then before the end of each subsequent R–S interval. Sessions during which the avoidance contingency was in effect were alternated with control sessions during which responding had no effect and the participants received a CO_2 delivery on average every 6 minutes.

The results of the experiment are summarized in Figure 10.8. The left side of the figure shows the response rates of the four students during the avoidance and control sessions. The right side of the figure shows the number of CO_2 deliveries the participants

FIGURE 10.8 Rate of responding and rate of CO_2 presentations for four college students in a study of free-operant avoidance. Open symbols represent data obtained during sessions when the avoidance contingency was in effect. Closed symbols represent data obtained during control sessions when the avoidance response was not effective and the subjects received a CO_2 delivery every 6 minutes (based on C. W. Lejuez, et al. [1998]. Avoidance of 20% carbon dioxide–enriched air within humans. *Journal of the Experimental Analysis of Behavior, 70,* pp. 79–86.).

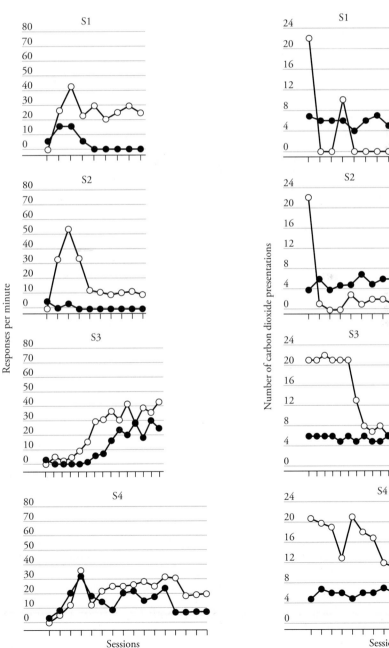

received during the two types of sessions. Notice that response rates were higher during the avoidance sessions than during the control sessions. Furthermore, as the participants acquired the avoidance response, the number of CO_2 presentations they received declined. These behavior changes (and consequences) occurred even though the CO_2 presentations were not signaled by an explicit warning stimulus.

No explicit instructions were provided at the beginning of the experiment concerning the response plunger. Students S1 and S2 discovered the avoidance contingency without much difficulty on their own. In contrast, students S3 and S4 had a bit of trouble at first and were given a hint before their sixth and seventh sessions, respectively. The hint was, "The only thing that you can do by pulling the plunger is sometimes change the number of times you receive carbon-dioxide-enriched air. It is even possible for you to sometimes receive no deliveries of carbon dioxide." This hint was enough to get S3 and S4 to respond effectively during subsequent avoidance sessions. However, notice that the instructions did not provide clues about the difference between the avoidance and control sessions or the timing of the CO_2 deliveries. Nevertheless, S3 and S4 responded more vigorously during the avoidance sessions than during the control sessions by the end of the experiment. Thus, the difference in response levels (and CO_2 presentations) that occurred during avoidance versus control sessions cannot be attributed to how well any of the participants followed the instructions. They all had to discover when the avoidance contingency was in effect and when it was not in effect without help.

Free-operant avoidance behavior has been investigated in numerous studies with rats and other laboratory animals and with brief shock as the aversive stimulus (see Hineline, 1977; Hineline & Rosales-Ruiz, 2013). The fact that rats do not respond to verbal instructions simplifies interpreting the results. These experiments have shown that the rate of responding is controlled by the length of the S–S and R–S intervals. The more frequently shocks are scheduled in the absence of responding (the S–S interval), the more likely the participant is to learn the avoidance response. Increasing the duration of safety produced by the response (the R–S interval) also promotes avoidance responding. In addition, the relative value of the S–S and R–S intervals is important. The safe period produced by each response (R–S interval) has to be longer than the interval between shocks that would occur without responding (S–S interval).

Efficient free-operant avoidance responding requires skill in keeping track of time. Avoiding shocks with minimal effort requires responding close to the end of each R–S interval. Because there are no external cues to signal when the R–S interval is about to end, internal temporal cues have to be used. This makes free-operant avoidance a useful procedure for testing an organism's ability to keep track of time. We will discuss learning about temporal cues in greater detail in Chapter 12.

P. N. Hineline

Alternative Theoretical Accounts of Avoidance Behavior

Studies of free-operant avoidance behavior have encouraged consideration of mechanisms of avoidance that go beyond the factors identified by the classic two-process theory of avoidance. In two-process theory, reinforcement for the avoidance response is assumed to be provided by reduction of conditioned fear. This is a case of negative reinforcement: reinforcement due to removal of an aversive stimulus. Several subsequent theoretical treatments have proposed that avoidance procedures also provide for positive reinforcement of the avoidance response, whereas others have suggested that neither negative nor positive reinforcement is important in avoidance learning.

Positive Reinforcement Through Conditioned Inhibition of Fear or Conditioned Safety Signals   Performance of an avoidance response always results in distinctive stimuli, such as spatial cues involved in going from one side to the other in a shuttle box or

tactile and other cues involved in pressing a response lever. The stimuli that are produced by making a skeletal response are called response feedback cues. Because the avoidance response produces a period of safety in all avoidance conditioning procedures, response feedback stimuli may acquire conditioned inhibitory properties and become signals for the absence of aversive stimulation. Such stimuli are called **safety signals**. According to the *safety-signal hypothesis*, the safety signals that accompany avoidance responses may provide positive reinforcement for avoidance behavior.

In most avoidance experiments, no special cues are introduced as response feedback cues that could acquire safety signal functions. Free-operant avoidance procedures in particular do not involve any special response feedback cues provided by the experimenter. However, the act of making the instrumental response provides spatial, tactile, and proprioceptive stimuli (internal cues related to muscle contractions) that inevitably accompany the avoidance response. These cues could become safety signals (Dinsmoor, 2001b). In addition, any avoidance procedure can be easily modified to include a distinctive stimulus (a brief light or tone) after each occurrence of the avoidance response. The safety-signal hypothesis predicts that introducing an explicit feedback stimulus will facilitate the learning of an avoidance response. Numerous experiments have found this to be true (e.g., Bolles & Grossen, 1969; Cándido, Maldonado, & Vila, 1991; D'Amato, Fazzaro, & Etkin, 1968).

Other studies have shown that, during the course of avoidance training, a response feedback stimulus becomes a conditioned inhibitor of fear (e.g., Cándido, González, & de Brugada, 2004; Morris, 1974; Rescorla, 1968). Furthermore, there is also direct evidence that a feedback stimulus that has been conditioned to inhibit fear during avoidance training is an effective positive reinforcer for new responses (Morris, 1975; Weisman & Litner, 1972). Thus, there is considerable evidence for safety signals as sources of positive reinforcement in avoidance learning (see Dinsmoor, 2001b, and ensuing commentary).

The safety-signal hypothesis is particularly well suited to explain free-operant avoidance behavior. Participants often experience numerous unsignaled shocks during the initial stages of free-operant avoidance training. This makes it highly likely that the experimental context becomes conditioned to elicit fear. Because shocks never occur for the duration of the R–S interval after a response is made, the proprioceptive and tactile stimuli that accompany the avoidance response can become conditioned inhibitors of fear. Thus, response-associated feedback cues can come to provide positive reinforcement for the free-operant avoidance response (Dinsmoor, 1977, 2001a,b; Rescorla, 1968).

Reinforcement of Avoidance Through Reduction of Shock Frequency   Positive reinforcement through conditioned inhibition can occur alongside the negative reinforcement mechanism of two-process theory. In contrast, another reinforcement mechanism, **shock-frequency reduction**, has been proposed as a radical alternative to two-process theory (deVilliers, 1974; Herrnstein, 1969; Herrnstein & Hineline, 1966). By definition, avoidance responses prevent the delivery of shock and thereby reduce the frequency of shocks an organism receives. The theories of avoidance we have discussed so far have viewed the reduction of shocks as a secondary by-product rather than as a primary cause of avoidance behavior. In contrast, the shock-frequency reduction hypothesis views the reduction of shocks to be critical to the reinforcement of avoidance behavior.

Shock-frequency reduction as the cause of avoidance behavior was encouraged by studies of free-operant avoidance learning that challenged two-process theory (Herrnstein & Hineline, 1966). However, several experiments have shown that animals can learn to make an avoidance response even if the response does not reduce the frequency of shocks delivered (Gardner & Lewis, 1976; see also Hineline, 1981). Responding in these studies delayed the onset of the next scheduled shock but did not prevent its delivery. Thus, overall shock frequency was unchanged. This evidence suggests that shock-frequency reduction is not necessary for avoidance learning. However, notice that in any procedure where responding postpones the next shock, response feedback cues can acquire safety signal properties that may reinforce the instrumental response.

Avoidance and Species-Specific Defense Reactions

In the theories discussed so far, the emphasis was on how the events that precede and follow the avoidance response control avoidance behavior. The exact nature or form of the response itself was not of concern. In addition, the reinforcement mechanisms assumed by the theories all required some time to develop. Before fear reduction can be an effective reinforcer, fear first must be conditioned to the CS; before response feedback cues can come to serve as reinforcers, they must become signals for the absence of shock; and before shock-frequency reduction can work, organisms must experience enough shocks to be able to calculate shock frequencies. Therefore, these theories tell us little about the organism's behavior during the first few trials of avoidance training.

Lack of concern with what an organism does during the first few trials of avoidance conditioning is a serious weakness of any theory. For an avoidance mechanism to be useful under natural conditions, the mechanism has to generate successful avoidance responses quickly. Consider, for example, a mouse trying to avoid being caught by a hawk. An avoidance mechanism that requires numerous training trials is of no use in this case. If the mouse fails to avoid attack by the hawk during its initial encounter, it may not survive for future training trials. Bolles (1970, 1971) recognized this problem and focused on what controls an organism's behavior during the early stages of avoidance training.

Courtesy of Donald A. Dewsbury

R. C. Bolles

Bolles assumed that aversive stimuli and situations elicit strong unconditioned, or innate, responses. These innate responses are assumed to have evolved because during the course of evolution they were successful in defense against pain and injury. Therefore, Bolles called these **species-specific defense reactions (SSDRs)**. In rats, for example, prominent SSDRs include flight (running), freezing (remaining vigilant but motionless, except for breathing), and defensive fighting. Other reactions to danger include thigmotaxis (approaching walls), defensive burying (covering up the source of aversive stimulation), and seeking out dark areas.

Bolles proposed that the configuration of the environment determines which particular SSDR occurs. For example, flight may predominate when an obvious escape route is available, and freezing may predominate if there is no way out of the situation. This is indeed the case (Blanchard, 1997; Sigmundi, 1997). Defensive fighting, for example, is not possible without an opponent, and defensive burying is not possible without something like sand or wood shavings to bury the source of danger. Even freezing, a response that one might think does not require stimulus support, only occurs in relatively safe places (near a wall or in a corner) rather than in the middle of an arena. If a rat finds itself in the middle of an arena when it encounters danger, it will move to a corner or a familiar safe enclosure before freezing (De Oca, Minor, & Fanselow, 2007).

A major prediction of the SSDR theory is that instrumental responses similar to SSDRs will be learned more easily in avoidance experiments than responses that are unrelated to SSDRs. Consistent with this prediction, Bolles (1969) found that rats can rapidly learn to run in a running wheel to avoid shock. In contrast, their performance of a rearing response (standing on the hind legs) does not improve much during the course of avoidance training. Presumably, running is learned faster because it is closer to the rat's SSDRs in the running wheel. (For a related finding in EFF learning, see Cain and LeDoux, 2007.)

Predatory Imminence and Defensive and Recuperative Behaviors

By focusing on ecological and evolutionary influences on defensive behavior, SSDR theory significantly advanced our thinking about fear and avoidance learning. The role of ecological and

M. S. Fanselow

evolutionary factors was developed further by Fanselow and his associates, who formulated the concept of a *predatory imminence continuum* (Fanselow & Lester, 1988; Fanselow, 1997; Rau & Fanselow, 2007). According to the **predatory imminence** continuum, different defensive responses occur depending on the level of danger faced by an animal.

Consider, for example, a small rodent (e.g., a rat) that is a potential source of food for coyotes, snakes, and other predators. The rat is presumably safest in its nest in a burrow, but it has to go out periodically to forage for food. When it is out foraging, it is not in much danger as long as no snakes or coyotes are around. When a snake appears, the rat's level of danger increases, but not by much if the snake is far away. However, as the snake gets closer, the level of danger rises. The situation is very dangerous when the snake is close enough to strike, and danger is at its peak when the strike actually occurs. This progression of increasing levels of danger is the predatory imminence continuum and is illustrated in Figure 10.9.

Different species typical defense responses are assumed to occur at different levels of predatory imminence. If a rat is forced to forage for food in a location where it periodically encounters snakes, it will leave its burrow only rarely but will eat larger meals during each excursion (Fanselow, Lester, & Helmstetter, 1988). Thus, the response to a low level of predatory imminence is an adjustment in meal patterns. Rats also show increased locomotor behavior and increased preference for dark places as a part of their preencounter defensive behavior (Goodsil & Fanselow, 2004). When a snake appears but is not about to strike, the rat's defensive behavior is likely to change to freezing. Freezing will reduce the chance that a predator will see or hear the rat. Many predators will strike only at moving prey. Freezing by the prey also may result in the predator shifting its attention to something else (Suarez & Gallup, 1981).

When the snake actually touches the rat, the rat is likely to leap into the air. It is as if the rat's prior freezing behavior prepares it to explode into the air when it is touched. This is called the *circa strike response*. The explosive leap is likely to get the rat away from the snake's mouth. However, if the rat does not successfully escape the predator at this point, it is likely to engage in defensive aggression. If the defensive behavior is successful and the rat manages to get away from the snake, it will gradually shift to recuperative responses (such as grooming) that promote healing from injuries.

Like SSDR theory, the predatory-imminence hypothesis assumes that defensive behavior initially occurs as unconditioned responding. Defensive responses can also come to be elicited by a CS if that CS becomes associated with an aversive event. Which defensive response occurs to the CS will depend on the temporal relation of the CS to the unconditioned aversive stimulus. If the CS precedes the US (as in delayed conditioning), the defensive behavior will be one level lower on the predatory-imminence scale than the response elicited by the US. Thus, if the US elicits a circa strike response,

FIGURE 10.9 The predatory-imminence continuum (based on "Neurobiological and neuroethological perspectives on fear and anxiety" by V. Rau and M. S. Fanselow, in L. J. Kirmayer, R. Lemelson, and M. Barad [Eds.], *Understanding trauma: Integrating biological, clinical, and cultural perspectives* [pp. 27–40]).

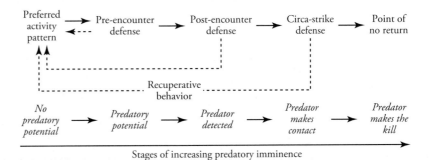

Stages of increasing predatory imminence

the CS is likely to elicit freezing behavior. In contrast, if the CS and US are presented at the same time (as in simultaneous conditioning), the defensive response will be more similar to the response to the US (Esmorís-Arranz et al., 2003).

Studies with laboratory rats and human participants have shown that different degrees of predatory imminence are associated with a corresponding cascade of neurobiological states. Low levels of predatory imminence engage forebrain cortical areas, whereas high levels of predatory imminence activate evolutionarily older midbrain areas, including the central nucleus of the amygdala (Mobbs et al., 2010; Maren, 2007; Rau & Fanselow, 2007). Evidently, evolution has created powerful and specialized behavioral and neurobiological processes that enable us to deal effectively with different levels of danger. These processes were no doubt essential to survival during our ancestral history. However, they can go awry and be inappropriately activated, resulting in posttraumatic stress disorder and other disorders of stress and coping (e.g., Kirmayer, Lemelson, & Barad, 2007).

The predatory imminence formulation does not include an instrumental conditioning component and was not intended to explain the diverse array of experimental findings that scientists have accumulated in their many decades of research on avoidance learning. However, predatory imminence is important because it involves the innate coping mechanisms that come into play whenever the defensive behavior system is activated. Predatory imminence also determines the outcome of conditioning procedures.

Given the roots of defensive behavior (and its neurobiological substrates) in our evolutionary past, the predatory imminence concept can be also used to analyze human reactions to danger. Consistent with this idea, Craske (1999) characterized human fear and anxiety reactions in terms of the imminence of the perceived danger. The lowest level of perceived danger leads to worry. The next higher level leads to fear and vigilance (similar to freezing in rats). The highest level of perceived threat leads to panic (which is analogous to the circa strike response). Interestingly, men and women respond differently to the stress of perceived danger. Whereas men have a flight-or-fight response, women have a tend-and-befriend response (Taylor et al., 2000). When stressed, women are more likely to protect and care for their offspring and seek out social support rather than fight or flee.

Expectancy Theory of Avoidance   The theories of avoidance behavior that we have considered so far have employed fairly low-level conditioning mechanisms that do not require conscious awareness. In contrast, investigators of avoidance learning with human participants have been especially interested in the role of shock expectancies in avoidance behavior. Unlike laboratory rats, human participants can be questioned about their expectancies of shock, and one can then see how these expectancies are related to their avoidance behavior.

According to expectancy theory, encounters with aversive events trigger a conscious process of threat appraisal that generates expectations of future threat (or lack of threat) based on cues and responses. Cues that are paired with shock elicit expectations of shock, and responses that turn off these cues and prevent shock elicit expectations of no-shock or safety (Lovibond, 2011). Thus, expectancy theory acknowledges the Pavlovian and instrumental components of avoidance procedures but treats the cognitive expectancies that these generate as the primary cause of avoidance behavior.

Studies of avoidance learning with human participants have generally confirmed predictions of expectancy theory (e.g., Declercq et al., 2008; Lovibond et al., 2009). An early success of the theory was explaining why avoidance behavior persists when shocks can no longer occur because the shock generator has been disabled. According to expectancy theory, participants come to expect that making the avoidance response will not be followed by shock. Because this expectation continues to be confirmed when the shock generator is disabled, the avoidance behavior persists (Seligman & Johnson, 1973). However, the persistence of avoidance responding in extinction also can be explained by an extension of the two-process theory without postulating cognitive expectancies (Maia, 2010). This raises the question whether expectancies are the primary cause of human avoidance responses or develop in parallel with more primitive conditioning mechanisms. A definitive answer to this question is likely to challenge investigators for some time to come (e.g., McAndrew et al., 2012).

The Avoidance Puzzle: Concluding Comments

We have learned a great deal about avoidance behavior since Mowrer and Lamoreaux (1942) questioned how *not getting something* can motivate avoidance responses. As we saw, numerous creative answers to this puzzle have been offered. Two-process theory, conditioned inhibition reinforcement, and shock-frequency-reduction reinforcement all provide different views of what happens after an avoidance response to reinforce it. By contrast, the SSDR account focuses on unconditioned aspects of defensive behavior, which are further elaborated through the concept of predatory imminence.

None of the major theories can explain everything that occurs in aversive conditioning situations. However, each provides ideas that are useful for understanding various aspects of avoidance behavior. For example, two-process theory is uniquely suited to explain the results of escape from fear experiments. The safety-signal theory is particularly useful in explaining free-operant avoidance learning and the role of response-feedback stimuli in avoidance conditioning. The concept of predatory imminence provides the most useful account of what happens during the early stages of avoidance training, and expectancy theory is useful in dealing with the cognitive aspects of human avoidance behavior. Given the complexities of various avoidance learning paradigms, we should not be surprised that several conceptual frameworks are needed to explain all the available data.

Punishment

J. ALBERT DIAZ KRT/Newscom

N. H. Azrin

Although most of us engage in all sorts of avoidance responses every day, as a society, we are not particularly concerned about what is involved in avoidance learning. This may be because procedures that generate active avoidance are rarely used in organized efforts to change or control someone's behavior. By contrast, punishment has always been in the public eye (see Repp & Singh, 1990). As a society, we use punishment as a form of retribution for egregious criminal acts. Punishment is also used to encourage adherence to religious and civil codes of conduct. Many institutions and rules have evolved to ensure that punishment is administered in ways that are ethical and just. What constitutes acceptable punishment in the criminal justice system, in childrearing, or in the treatment of individuals with developmental disabilities is a matter of continual debate.

Despite long-standing societal concerns about punishment, for many years experimental psychologists did not devote much attention to the topic. On the basis of a few experiments, Thorndike (1932) and Skinner (1938, 1953) concluded that punishment was not an effective method for controlling behavior and had only temporary effects (see also Estes, 1944). This claim was not seriously challenged until the 1960s, when punishment began to be more extensively investigated (Azrin & Holz, 1966; Church, 1963). We now know that punishment can be a highly effective technique for modifying behavior. With the appropriate punishment procedure, responding can be totally suppressed in just one or two trials. However, if punishment is misapplied, the suppression of behavior may be incomplete, responding may recover, and the procedure may have unintended collateral effects.

Consider, for example, a child who accidentally sticks a metal fork in an electric outlet. The resultant shock is likely to discourage repetition of that response for the rest of the child's life. Contrast that with getting a ticket for driving 10 miles above the speed limit. Will that produce the same dramatic suppression of the punished response? Not likely. Systematic laboratory experiments have taught us a great deal about the circumstances under which punishment does and does not work (Hineline & Rosales-Ruiz, 2013). However, numerous questions remain to be answered in efforts to translate this knowledge to therapeutic interventions (Lerman & Vorndran, 2002).

Experimental Analysis of Punishment

The basic punishment procedure is simple: An aversive stimulus is presented after a target instrumental response. If the procedure is effective, the target response becomes suppressed. Because punishment involves the suppression of behavior, it can be observed only with responses that are likely to occur in the first place. This prerequisite is easily met in therapeutic situations where the target of punishment is a harmful activity that occurs more often than one would like. Vorndran and Lerman (2006), for example, documented the effectiveness of punishment in two participants with developmental disabilities. One of the participants engaged in frequent hyperventilation, and the other engaged in self-injurious mouthing of his hand. The target responses were successfully suppressed by punishment in both cases.

Laboratory studies of punishment usually begin with a preliminary phase in which the target response is first established with positive reinforcement. A pigeon, for example, may be reinforced with food for pecking a response key. A punishment procedure is then superimposed on the schedule of positive reinforcement. This sets up a conflict between responding to obtain positive reinforcement and withholding the response to avoid punishment. The degree of response suppression that occurs is determined both by variables related to presentation of the aversive stimulus and by variables related to the availability of positive reinforcement. The interplay of these two factors can be complicated and can make it difficult to predict what will happen.

Characteristics of the Aversive Stimulus and Its Method of Introduction   A great variety of aversive stimuli have been used in punishment experiments, including electric shock, a sudden burst of air, loud noise, verbal reprimands, a physical slap, a squirt of lemon juice in the mouth, and a cue previously conditioned with shock (e.g., Hake & Azrin, 1965; Reed & Yoshino, 2008; Sajwaj, Libet, & Agras, 1974). Other response-suppression procedures have involved the loss of positive reinforcement, time out from positive reinforcement, overcorrection, and manual restraint (Foxx & Azrin, 1973; Lerman et al., 1997; Trenholme & Baron, 1975).

Time out refers to removal of the opportunity to obtain positive reinforcement. Time out is often used to punish children, as when a child is told to sit in a time-out chair in the back of a classroom. Sitting in a chair is not inherently aversive. A time-out chair suppresses behavior because it prevents the child from doing other things that he or she may enjoy more. **Overcorrection** involves requiring a person not only to rectify what was done badly but to overcorrect for the mistake. For example, a child who has placed an object in his mouth may be asked to remove the object and also to wash out his mouth with an antiseptic solution.

A convenient aversive stimulus in human studies of punishment is point loss. For example, in one study (O'Donnell et al., 2000), college students pressed a response lever to obtain points that could be exchanged for money at the end of the experiment. Two discriminative stimuli (lines of different lengths) were used. During the baseline phase, only one of the lines (the S^D) was presented, and responses were reinforced on a variable interval (VI) schedule. After that, the S^D was alternated with the other discriminative stimulus, which served as the $S^D{}_P$. Responding continued to be reinforced according to

FIGURE 10.10 Lever-press responding of college students reinforced on a VI schedule with points that could be exchanged for money at the end of the experiment. During the baseline phase, only the reinforced discriminative stimulus (S^D) was presented. During the next phase, the S^D was presented in alternation with a punishment stimulus (S^D_P), during which the VI schedule remained in effect but each response was also punished by point loss. Each panel presents data from a different subject (based on J. O'Donnell, et al. [2000]. Stimulus control and generalization of point-loss punishment with humans. *Journal of the Experimental Analysis of Behavior, 73*, Figure 1, p. 266.).

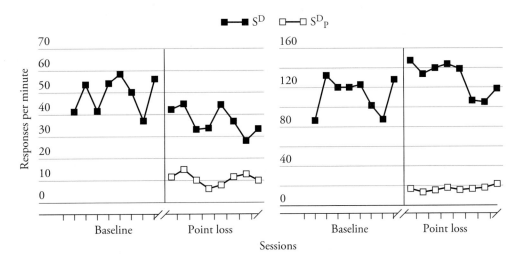

the VI schedule during the S^D_P, but now a point-loss punishment contingency was also in effect. With each response, points were subtracted from the total the subject had obtained.

The results of the experiment are summarized in Figure 10.10. Responding was well maintained during the S^D in the baseline phase. In the subsequent punishment phase, responding continued at substantial levels during the S^D but was suppressed during the S^D_P. (For an analogue to point loss in a study of punishment in pigeons, see Raiff, Bullock, & Hackenberg, 2008.)

The response suppression produced by punishment depends in part on features of the aversive stimulus. The effects of various characteristics of the aversive event have been most extensively investigated in studies with laboratory rats and pigeons. Shock is usually employed as the aversive stimulus in these experiments because the duration and intensity of shock can be precisely controlled. As one might predict, more intense and longer shocks are more effective in punishing responding (Azrin & Holz, 1966; Church, 1969). Low-intensity punishment produces only moderate suppression of behavior. Even more problematic is the fact that responding often recovers with continued punishment with mild shock (e.g., Azrin, 1960). Individuals habituate to mild punishment. By contrast, if the aversive stimulus is of high intensity, responding will be completely suppressed for a long time (Azrin, 1960).

Another very important factor in punishment is how the aversive stimulus is introduced. If a high intensity of shock is used from the outset of punishment, the instrumental response will be severely suppressed. However, if the high-intensity punishment is reached only after a gradual increase, much less suppression of behavior will occur (Azrin et al., 1963; Banks, 1976; Miller, 1960). This is a very important finding. It shows that exposure to low intensity of punishment builds resistance and makes the individual immune to the effects of more severe punishment. Spending a month in jail is not a disturbing experience for a repeat offender who has become accustomed to shorter periods of incarceration.

The preceding findings suggest that how organisms respond during their *initial exposure* to punishment determines how they will respond to punishment subsequently (Church, 1969). This idea has an interesting implication. Suppose an individual is first exposed to intense shock that results in strong response suppression. If the shock intensity is subsequently reduced, the severe suppression of behavior should persist. Thus, after exposure to intense shock, mild shock should be more effective in suppressing behavior than if the mild shock had been used from the beginning. Such findings were obtained

FIGURE 10.11 Top panel: Effects of a history of mild punishment (Phase 1) on later responding during intense punishment (Phase 2). Bottom panel: Effects of a history of intense punishment (Phase 1) on later responding to mild punishment (Phase 2). (Hypothetical data.) (From Domjan, *The Essentials of Learning and Conditioning*, 3e. © 2005 Cengage Learning.)

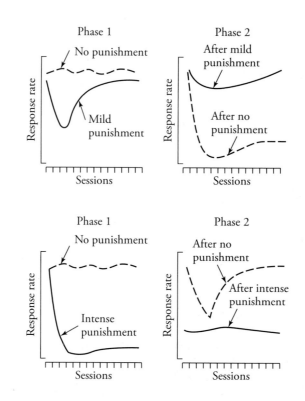

by Raymond (reported in Church, 1969). Taken together, the evidence indicates that initial exposure to mild aversive stimulation that does not disrupt behavior reduces the effects of later intense punishment. By contrast, initial exposure to intense aversive stimulation increases the suppressive effects of later mild punishment (see Figure 10.11).

Response-Contingent Versus Response-Independent Aversive Stimulation   Another very important variable that determines the effectiveness of punishment is whether the aversive stimulus is presented contingent on the target response or independently of behavior. Response-independent aversive stimulation can result in some suppression of instrumental behavior. (We saw this to be the case in the conditioned suppression effect, described in Chapter 3.) However, significantly more suppression of behavior occurs if the aversive stimulus is triggered by the instrumental response (e.g., Bolles et al., 1980; Camp et al., 1967).

One study of the importance of the response contingency in punishment (Goodall, 1984) compared lever-press responding in rats in the presence of two different stimuli (a tone and a light). One of the stimuli was used with a punishment procedure (the PUN cue), and the other stimulus was used with a conditioned suppression procedure (the CER cue). Lever pressing was always reinforced on a VI 60-second food-reinforcement schedule. Once baseline responding was well established, the PUN cue and the CER cue were presented periodically. During the PUN cue, the rats received a brief shock after every third lever press. Thus, punishment was delivered on an FR 3 schedule. Each CER trial was yoked to the preceding punishment trial, so that the rats received the same number and distribution of shocks during the CER cue as they got during the immediately preceding PUN cue. However, shocks during the CER cue were always delivered independent of the lever-press behavior.

The results of the experiment are presented in Figure 10.12 in terms of suppression of lever pressing during the CER and punishment cues. Given the brief and mild shocks that were used (0.5 mA, 0.5 seconds), not much suppression of behavior was evident

FIGURE 10.12 Suppression of lever pressing during punishment and CER stimuli during 10 successive sessions. During the punishment cue, lever pressing was punished on an FR 3 schedule. During the CER cue, the same number and distribution of shocks was delivered independent of behavior. (Based on "Learning Due to the Response-Shock Contingency in Signaled Punishment" by G. Goodall, 1984, *The Quarterly Journal of Experimental Psychology*, 36B, pp. 259–279.)

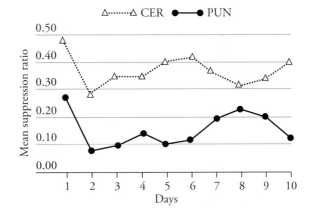

during the CER stimulus. By contrast, the same number and distribution of shocks substantially suppressed responding during the punishment stimulus. This difference illustrates that delivering shocks contingent on an instrumental response is more effective in suppressing that response than delivering the aversive stimulus independent of behavior. (For a related study of punishment with loss of money as the aversive stimulus in human participants, see Pietras, Brandt, & Searcy, 2010.)

Effects of Delay of Punishment Another critical factor in punishment is the interval between the target response and the aversive stimulus. Increasing the delay of punishment results in less suppression of behavior (e.g., Baron, 1965; Camp et al., 1967). This relation is particularly important in practical applications of punishment. Inadvertent delays can occur if the undesired response is not detected right away, if it takes time to investigate who is actually at fault for an error, or if preparing the aversive stimulus requires time. Such delays can make punishment totally ineffective. If you cannot punish the target response right away, you might as well not punish it at all.

Effects of Schedules of Punishment Just as positive reinforcement does not have to be provided for each occurrence of the instrumental response, punishment may also be delivered only intermittently, as we saw in the experiment by Goodall. In that study, punishment was delivered on an FR 3 schedule. More systematic studies have shown that the degree of response suppression produced by punishment depends on the proportion of responses that are punished.

In an early study of FR punishment by Azrin and his colleagues (1963), pigeons were first reinforced with food on a VI schedule for pecking a response key. Punishment was then introduced. Various FR punishment procedures were tested while the VI reinforcement schedule remained in effect. The results are summarized in Figure 10.13. When every response was shocked (FR 1 punishment), key pecking ceased entirely. Higher FR schedules allowed more responses to go unpunished. Not surprisingly, therefore, higher rates of responding occurred when higher FR punishment schedules were used. Remarkably, however, some suppression of behavior was observed even when only every 1,000th response was followed by shock.

Effects of Schedules of Positive Reinforcement In most punishment situations, the target response is simultaneously maintained by a schedule of positive reinforcement. A high school student who is punished for violating the school's dress code is being simultaneously reinforced for breaking the rules by social approval from his or her peers. In this case the alternative source of reinforcement is obvious. In other instances, such as

FIGURE 10.13
Cumulative records of pecking by a pigeon when the response was not punished and when the response was punished according to various fixed-ratio schedules of punishment. The oblique slashes indicate the delivery of punishment. Responding was reinforced on a VI 3-minute schedule. (Based on "Fixed-Ratio Punishment" by N. H. Azrin, W. C. Holz, and D. R. Hake, 1963, *Journal of the Experimental Analysis of Behavior, 6,* pp. 141–148.)

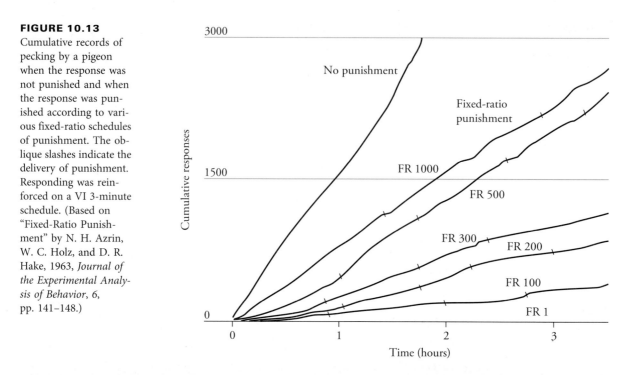

BOX 10.1

Instrumental Learning Within the Spinal Cord

The vertebrate central nervous system is composed of a forebrain, brainstem, cerebellum, and **spinal cord** (Figure 1.C). Traditionally, researchers assumed that learning was mediated by higher neural structures within the forebrain, and, indeed, we have seen that structures such as the amygdala and hippocampus play a critical role in emotional (Box 4.3) and spatial learning (Box 8.2). We have also seen that lower-level neural mechanisms within the midbrain play an instructive role and that neurons within the cerebellum mediate learning and memory for delayed eyeblink conditioning (Box 3.2). The latter observation suggests that the forebrain is not required. A more radical question is whether the brain is needed. Can neurons in the spinal cord support learning (Patterson & Grau, 2001)?

On first blush, the idea that spinal neurons can learn would seem a strange question because a major function of the spinal cord is to relay neural signals between the periphery and the brain. This capacity depends upon the axons that form the neural tracts that line the outer region of spinal tissue. Because these axons have a *myelin* coating (a form of electrical insulation that speeds neural conduction), they appear white, and for this reason, the outer band of neurons in the spinal cord is known as the *white matter* (Figure 10.14A). When neural conduction in these axons is disrupted by injury, the brain loses the ability to communicate with parts of the body below the injury, causing an inability to sense stimuli and a disruption in the individual's capacity to execute a voluntary response.

What is sometimes forgotten is that there is also an inner region of tissue in the spinal cord, a butterfly-shaped structure (the *central gray*) composed of neurons and supporting cells (*glia*). The central gray contains hundreds of thousands of neurons, far more than the entire nervous system of invertebrates that can learn (Box 2.2).

Neurons within the dorsal (upper) central gray of the spinal cord play a role in processing the sensory signals relayed to the brain. Neurons within the ventral (lower) portion help to organize behavioral responses, including complex movement such as stepping (Kandel et al., 2013). Moreover, sensory input to the spinal cord can initiate a behavioral response (a spinal reflex) in the absence of input from the brain. For example, if you step on a thorn, a reflexive withdrawal (flexion) response is elicited that lifts the foot away from the source of irritation. We know that this response does not require any input from the brain because it can be elicited after communication with the

Continued

BOX 10.1 (continued)

brain has been experimentally disrupted.

Spinal reflexes demonstrate that neurons within the spinal cord can organize unconditioned (unlearned) responses to stimuli. Can these neurons also support learning? Groves and Thompson (1970) were among the first to explore this issue, showing that a spinal reflex becomes weaker (habituates) when a stimulus is repeatedly presented. In addition, they found that intense stimulation can sensitize behavioral reactivity, providing the foundation for the dual process theory of nonassociative learning described in Chapter 2. Thompson and his collaborators also provided evidence that spinal neurons are sensitive to stimulus–stimulus (Pavlovian) relations (Patterson, 2001).

More recently, Grau and his colleagues have shown that neurons within the spinal cord can support a simple form of instrumental learning (reviewed in Grau et al., 2012). In these studies, communication with the brain was disrupted by cutting the spinal cord below the shoulders. The rats were then trained using a shock that elicited a hind-limb flexion response. One group (the master rats) received leg shock whenever the leg was extended. Animals in a yoked group were experimentally coupled to the master rats. Each time a master rat received shock, its yoked partner did too. Master rats quickly learned to hold their leg up, effectively minimizing exposure to shock (Figure 10.14B). In contrast, the yoked rats that received shock independent of leg position failed to learn. This difference between the master and yoked rats indicates that neurons within the spinal cord are sensitive to instrumental (response-reinforcer) relations.

Master and yoked rats were then tested under common conditions with controllable shock. As you would expect, master rats learned faster than the control group that previously had not received shock. In contrast, the yoked rats failed to learn (Figure 10.14B). This behavioral deficit resembles the phenomenon of *learned helplessness* (Maier & Seligman, 1976). As observed in intact animals (see Box 5.5), exposure to controllable shock also has an immunizing effect that can protect the spinal cord from the adverse effect of uncontrollable stimulation.

Neurobiological studies have revealed that learning within the spinal cord depends upon a form of N-methyl-D-aspartate (NMDA)-receptor-mediated plasticity (Grau et al., 2012), the same neurochemical system that underlies learning and memory within the hippocampus (Box 8.2). Moreover, physiological phenomena linked to learning and memory (e.g., long-term potentiation and depression) have been observed in spinal neurons. Combined with the behavioral studies, this research shows that spinal neurons can learn.

Just as the study of the retina and optic nerve have helped us to understand vision, an analysis of spinal processing has begun to inform us about learning processes. At a functional level, studies of spinal learning can help reveal what is a basic or inherent property of any system that can learn. To explore this issue, let's consider the kind of learning that might be involved. Does response-contingent shock cause an increase in flexion duration because a downward movement of the leg coincides with shock onset (punishment) or because an upward movement is contiguous with shock termination (escape)? This issue can be addressed by delaying either the onset or offset of shock. Delaying the onset of shock by just 100 milliseconds eliminated learning, whereas delaying offset had no effect (Grau et al., 2012). This suggests that the key reinforcer is linked to shock onset and that the learning reflects a form of punishment. The corollary to this is that escape learning may require more sophisticated (brain-dependent) neural systems.

Instrumental learning depends on a response–outcome (R–O) relation. For shock onset (the outcome) to matter, it must occur in the presence of a cue that provides information about leg position (the response). Physiological studies have revealed that sensory receptors within the muscles and joints provide a sensory signal that indicates current limb position (a form of *proprioception*). This proprioceptive cue yields an index of limb position (the response) at the time of shock onset (the outcome), which would allow for a form of R–O learning. From this perspective, the cue for leg position is linked to shock onset and, as a result of this learning, gains the capacity to drive a flexion response (Figure 10.14C). This analysis relates to a more general issue in learning: Does Pavlovian conditioning contribute to instrumental learning? In the present case, the answer may be yes, for the learning appears to depend upon the relation between a proprioceptive cue (the CS) and shock onset (the US).

We have a tendency to think of instrumental learning as a motoric effect, with the organism executing an adaptive behavior in response to sensory input. In many cases, this may be how learning proceeds. However, studies of spinal learning suggest an alternative. If, as posited by Grau and colleagues (2012), spinal neurons can encode that there is a regular relationship between an index of limb position (the R) and cutaneous stimulation (the O), this learning could transform the signal relayed to

Continued

BOX 10.1 (continued)

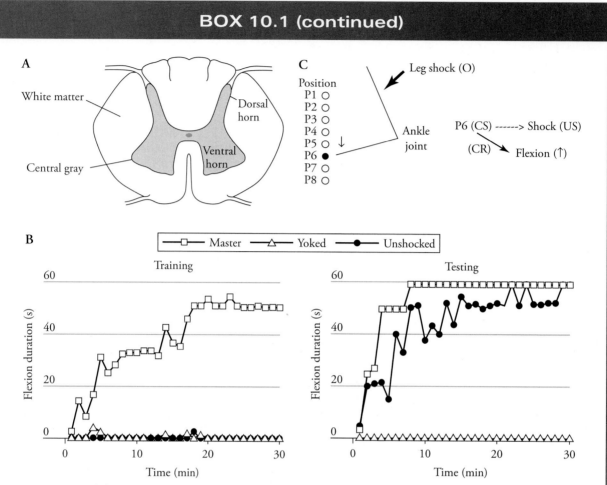

FIGURE 10.14 (A) A cross-section of the spinal cord. The inner region (central gray) is composed of cell bodies, inter-neurons, and glia. It is surrounded by a band of axons (the white matter) that relay signals to and from the brain, segments of the cord, and the periphery (adapted from Martin, 1996). (B) Training with response-contingent shock (left panel). Master rats receive shock whenever one leg is extended. Even though the spinal cord has been surgically disconnected from the brain, they learn to hold their leg up (an increase in flexion duration) to minimize net shock exposure. Yoked rats that receive the same amount of shock independent of leg position fail to learn. When all subjects are subsequently tested (right panel) with response-contingent shock, master rats quickly re-learn the required response. Yoked rats that had previously received shock independent of leg position fail to learn (adapted from Grau & Joynes, 2001). (C) A hypothetical model of the processes that underlie spinal instrumental learning. It is assumed that proprioceptive cues (P) provide an afferent signal of limb position. In instrumental training, shock onset (the effective reinforcer) always occurs at the same position (e.g., P6). It is suggested that the index of limb position (P6) can function as a Pavlovian conditioned stimulus (CS) and that shock onset acts as an unconditioned stimulus (US). As a result of the CS-US pairing, the CS (P6) may acquire the capacity to elicit a flexion response (the conditioned response, CR) (adapted from Grau et al., 2012).

the brain, allowing the organism to *directly perceive* some instrumental (R–O) relations. If you repeatedly tap your finger on a hard surface, your brain receives information about both the response being performed and its outcome. In this case, the R–O relation

may be directly perceived in the same way depth within a visual field can be derived from variation in retinal size (texture gradient; Gibson, 1979).

A final consideration concerns the limits of instrumental learning within the spinal cord. As we have

seen, learning is often biologically constrained. Nonetheless, we can train a normal rat to perform a variety of behaviors (e.g., pull a chain, press a bar) using a wide range of reinforcers (sugar water, food pellets). In contrast, both the response and the

Continued

range of outcomes available seem highly constrained in spinal learning. We cannot, for example, arbitrarily train a spinally transected rat to exhibit either a leg flexion or extension using the same outcome. Nor are there many outcomes available. More generally, the learning appears tied to preexisting reflexive behavior. Spinal mechanisms can encode R–O relations, but they do so using a simple system that is highly constrained. Brain processes bring a level of flexibility that allows the organism to integrate information across sensory modalities, time, and response alternatives. In both cases, learning depends upon an R–O relation, but the functional mechanisms differ. Likewise, multiple systems within the central nervous system can encode stimulus–stimulus (Pavlovian) relations, but here too, the functional properties of the systems may vary. For example, the cerebellum can support delayed eyeblink conditioning but to span a gap in time (trace conditioning) requires a hippocampus.

These observations suggest that a common environmental puzzle (e.g., encoding an R–O relation) can be solved in multiple ways and that alternative mechanisms may vary in both their sophistication and operational range. For these reasons, Grau and Joynes (2005) have argued for a functional approach to the study of learning (**neurofunctionalism**), suggesting that a process-level description of the mechanisms can be used to link neurobiological observations to behavior (also see the Functional Neurology section, Chapter 1).

Independent of how we characterize spinal learning, the work remains important because it has implications for recovery after spinal injury. For example, exposure to uncontrollable stimulation not only impairs spinal learning, it also undermines behavioral and physiological recovery after a *contusion injury* (a bruising of the spinal tissue that emulates the most common type of human injury). Conversely, instrumental training can foster behavioral recovery (Edgerton,

Tillakaratne, Bigbee, & de Leon, 2004; Hook and Grau, 2007; Musienko et al., 2012). More generally, consider the aim of physical therapy—to retrain the patient to perform some essential activities. The hope is that training will have a lasting effect, yielding a form of memory that will improve function. Rehabilitation remains the most effective treatment after spinal injury, and its aim is to inspire a form of instrumental learning.

J. W. Grau

---

spinal cord   The tubular portion of the central nervous system that extends from the lower brain (brainstem) and serves to relay signals to and from the periphery, organize simple behaviors, and integrate local sources of information.

neurofunctionalism   An approach to the study of learning and behavior that assumes environmental puzzles can be solved in multiple ways and that detailing the functional processes involved will facilitate the identification of the underlying neurobiological mechanisms.

---

self-injurious behavior in a person with developmental disabilities, the source of reinforcement may not be easy to identify but is just as important (Hagopian et al., 2013). The effects of punishment always depend on the reinforcer that maintains the target response. This relationship is dramatic in the case of drug reinforcers. One of the hallmarks of severe drug addiction is that the individual continues to seek and take the drug even if the addiction causes the person to lose his or her job, family, house, and health.

Only recently have scientists succeeded in developing a satisfactory animal model of drug addiction that incorporates the resistance of drug-seeking behavior to punishment. Pelloux, Everitt, and Dickinson (2007) trained rats to obtain a hit of cocaine using a two-lever task (see also Xe, Steketee, & Sun, 2012). The first lever was the drug-seeking lever and the second one was the drug-taking lever. At the beginning of each trial, the *seeking* lever was extended into the experimental chamber. Responding on this lever on a VI 120-second schedule resulted in the appearance of the *taking* lever. One response on the *taking* lever produced a hit of cocaine (delivered intravenously). Rats received either a moderate amount of training on this task (about eight sessions) or extensive training (an additional 14 sessions). Punishment was then introduced. On half of the trials, responding on the *seeking* lever ended in a brief shock and no cocaine was delivered. On the rest of the trials, there was no shock and cocaine was available as usual. (A control group continued being trained without punishment.)

FIGURE 10.15 Rate of responding to seek cocaine (left panel) or sucrose (right panel) during a baseline period and during a period when punishment occurred on half the trials. Different groups of rats received either moderate or extended training. Subjects receiving extended training with cocaine were further segregated depending on whether they were sensitive or resistant to the effects of punishment. A control group with cocaine reinforcement was tested without punishment. (Based on Pelloux, Everitt, & Dickinson, 2007.)

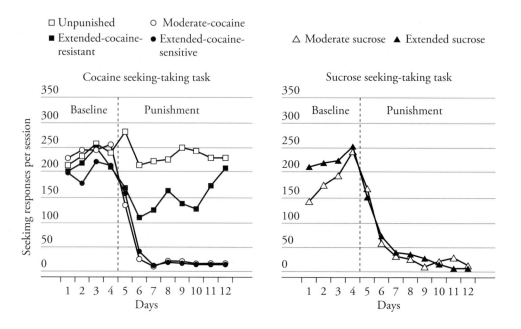

The results of the baseline and punishment phase of the experiment are summarized in the left panel of Figure 10.15. During the baseline phase, the rats made 200–250 seeking responses per session. Responding continued at this level for the rats that were not punished. The introduction of punishment produced a decrement in behavior. However, the decrement depended on the extent of training on the drug-reinforcement task. Punishment was highly effective for the moderately trained rats. The results were mixed for the rats that got extensive training on cocaine self-administration. Some of the extensively trained rats behaved just like those that were moderately trained. Punishment suppressed their drug-seeking behavior. In contrast, the remaining extensively trained rats (5 out of 21) were resistant to the effects of punishment. These punishment-resistant rats showed an initial drop in responding when punishment was introduced, but their drug-seeking behavior subsequently recovered in the face of continued punishment.

Ordinarily scientists are discouraged when they find that a manipulation is effective in only a subset of their research participants. However, in this instance, the fact that punishment did not work for a subset of the extended-cocaine rats is good news because that makes this a better model of human addiction. Only a subset of people who try drugs or use drugs on a regular basis develop the kind of severe addiction that leads them to continue their addictive behaviors at the expense of their marriage, job, or house. Other investigators have shown that resistance to punishment, persistence in drug-seeking behavior in extinction, and motivation to obtain the drug (as measured by a progressive ratio schedule) are all correlated with drug-induced relapse (Deroche-Gamonet, Belin, & Piazza, 2004).

Is the resistance to punishment a consequence of extensive use of cocaine as the reinforcer, or are such effects also observed following training with other reinforcers? Pelloux and colleagues (2007) addressed that question by training rats with sucrose as the reinforcer, using procedures identical to what was used with the cocaine-reinforced rats. The results of punishing sucrose-seeking behavior are summarized in the right panel of Figure 10.15. Sucrose seeking was suppressed by punishment whether the rats received moderate or extended training. None of the sucrose rats showed evidence of being so addicted to sucrose that they became resistant to punishment. Only cocaine produced that result.

Availability of Alternative Reinforced Responses   Punishment has dramatically different outcomes depending on whether the individual is able to obtain reinforcement by engaging in some other activity. If the punished response is the only activity available for obtaining reinforcement, punishment will be much less effective than if an alternative reinforced response is made available with the introduction of punishment. This is very important in practical applications of punishment.

The impact of alternative sources of reinforcement was demonstrated in an early study of adult male smokers conducted by Herman and Azrin (1964). The participants were seated facing two response levers. Pressing either lever was reinforced with a ciga-rette on a VI schedule. Once lever pressing occurred at a stable rate, responding on one of the levers was punished by a brief obnoxious noise. In one experimental condition, only one response lever was available during the punishment phase. In another condi-tion, both response levers were available, but the punishment procedure was only in effect for one of the levers. Figure 10.16 shows the results. When the punished response was the only way to obtain cigarettes, punishment produced a moderate suppression of behavior. By contrast, when the alternative response lever was available, responding on the punished lever ceased altogether. Thus, the availability of an alternative response for obtaining positive reinforcement greatly increased the suppressive effects of punishment.

Similar results have been obtained in other situations. For example, children pun-ished for playing with certain toys are much less likely to play with these if they are allowed to play with other toys instead (Perry & Parke, 1975). Reinforcement for alterna-tive behavior also increases the effectiveness of mild punishment in suppressing self-injurious behavior in individuals with severe developmental disabilities (Thompson, Iwata, Conners, & Roscoe, 1999). In another study (with a student with high-functioning autism), the availability of an alternative preferred activity made the word "no" more effective in suppressing a target response (Mace et al., 2011).

Effects of a Discriminative Stimulus for Punishment   As we saw in Chapter 8, if positive reinforcement is available for responding in the presence of a distinctive stimu-lus but is not available in its absence, the individual will learn to respond only when the stimulus is present. The suppressive effects of punishment can also be brought under stimulus control. This occurs if responding is punished in the presence of a discrimina-tive stimulus but is not punished when the stimulus is absent. Such a procedure is called **discriminative punishment**. With discriminative punishment training, the suppressive

FIGURE 10.16

Cumulative record of responding when responses were not punished, when responses were punished and there was no alter-native source of rein-forcement, and when responses were punished but an alternative rein-forced response was available. (Based on "Fixed-Ratio Punish-ment" by N. H. Azrin and W. C. Holz, in W. K. Honig (Ed.), 1966, *Operant Behavior*.)

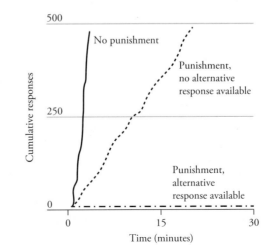

effects of punishment will come to be limited to the presence of the discriminative stimulus (Dinsmoor, 1952).

Discriminative punishment was used in the study whose results are summarized in Figure 10.10. The college students who served in this experiment could earn points for responding during one discriminative stimulus, the S^D. In the presence of another discriminative stimulus, the S^D_P, responding was also punished by loss of points. As Figure 10.10 illustrates, the suppressive effects of punishment were largely limited to the S^D_P.

The fact that the suppressive effects of punishment can be limited to the presence of a discriminative stimulus can be problematic in applications of punishment. In many situations, the person who administers the punishment also serves as a discriminative stimulus for punishment, with the result that the undesired behavior is suppressed only as long as the monitor is present. For example, children learn which teachers are strict about discipline and learn to suppress their rambunctious behavior only with those teachers. A highway patrol car is a discriminative stimulus for punishment for speeding. Drivers stay at or below the speed limit where they see patrol cars but exceed the speed limit on unpatrolled stretches of highway.

Punishment as a Signal for the Availability of Positive Reinforcement Under certain circumstances, people seem to seek out punishment. How can that be? Isn't punishment supposed to suppress behavior? Experimental evidence suggests that individuals may seek punishment if positive reinforcement is available only when the instrumental response is also punished. In such circumstances, punishment becomes a signal, or discriminative stimulus, for the availability of positive reinforcement. When this occurs, punishment will increase rather than suppress responding.

Punishment as a cue for reinforcement was discovered in a study with pigeons that were first trained to peck a response key for food reinforcement on a VI schedule (Holz & Azrin, 1961). Each response was then punished by a mild shock sufficient to reduce the response rate by about 50%. In the next phase of the experiment, periods in which the punishment procedure was in effect were alternated with periods with no punishment. In addition, the pecking response was reinforced with food only during the punishment periods. A critical feature of the procedure was that the punishment and safe periods were not signaled by an environmental stimulus, such as a light or a tone. The only way for the pigeons to tell whether reinforcement was available was to see whether they were punished for pecking. Under these circumstances, higher rates of pecking occurred during punishment periods than during safe periods. Punishment became a discriminative stimulus for food reinforcement. (For other examples of punishment-seeking behavior, see Brown, 1969; Brown & Cunningham, 1981; Dean & Pittman, 1991.)

Theories of Punishment

In contrast to the study of avoidance behavior, investigations of punishment, by and large, have not been motivated by theoretical considerations. Most of the evidence about the effects of punishment has been the product of empirical curiosity. Investigators were interested in finding out how punishment is influenced by various manipulations rather than in testing specific theoretical formulations. In fact, there are few systematic theories of punishment, and most of these were formulated some time ago (see Spradlin, 2002). I will describe three of the most prominent theories.

The Conditioned Emotional Response Theory of Punishment One of the first theories of punishment was proposed by Estes (1944) and is based on the observation by Estes and Skinner (1941) that a CS that has been paired with shock will suppress the performance of food-reinforced instrumental behavior. We discussed this conditioned

BOX 10.2

When Punishment Doesn't Work

Sometimes children are brought to a therapist because their behavior is out of control. A child may be unruly and unresponsive to the disciplinary practices of parents or teachers. Punishment may be tried as a last resort, but without much success. The parents or teachers may note that punishing the child only makes the behavior worse. It is not uncommon for children with a severe problem of this type to be diagnosed as hyperactive or emotionally disturbed. These labels suggest there is something fundamentally wrong with the child. Behavior therapists, however, have found that in some cases the problem may be nothing more than the result of mismanaged discipline. The parents or teachers may have inadvertently established punishment as a discriminative stimulus for positive reinforcement. Instead of decreasing some undesirable behavior, punishment increases it.

Let us consider the hypothetical case of Johnny, who lives in a home with two busy parents. Johnny, like most children, is rather active. If he is quietly playing in his room, the parents are likely to ignore him and do their own thing. By contrast, if Johnny behaves badly or makes demands, the parents are forced to pay attention to him. The parents may be giving Johnny attention only when he is misbehaving or making demands. Any time he is not being a problem, the parents may be thankfully relieved to have a moment's peace. Thus, rather than reinforcing cooperative or peaceful behavior, the parents may be ignoring Johnny at these times. What we have then is a vicious circle. The more Johnny misbehaves, the less attention he is given for nondisruptive behavior because the parents increasingly come to cherish quiet moments as a chance to do something on their own. Misbehavior becomes Johnny's main means of

obtaining attention. The punishments and reprimands that go with the behavior signal to him that his parents are caring and attentive to him.

In actuality, the therapist does not have the opportunity to observe how behavior problems of this type originate. The explanation in terms of the *discriminative value of punishment* is supported by the outcome of attempts to change the situation. The hypothesis suggests that if one changes the attention patterns of the parents, the behavior problem can be alleviated. Indeed, clinical psychologists often show parents how to attend to appropriate and constructive activities and how to administer punishment with a minimum of attention directed toward the child. In many cases, dramatic improvement ensues when parents are able to positively reinforce cooperative behavior with their attentions and ignore disruptive activities as much as possible.

suppression procedure earlier in this chapter as well as in Chapter 3. Conditioned suppression involves a suppression of ongoing behavior elicited by a stimulus that has been associated with aversive stimulation. The behavioral suppression occurs primarily because a fear-conditioned stimulus elicits freezing, which then interferes with other activities.

Estes (1944) proposed that punishment suppresses behavior through the same mechanism that produces conditioned suppression (see also Estes, 1969). In contrast to the usual conditioned suppression experiment, however, punishment procedures usually do not involve an explicit CS that signals the impending delivery of the aversive stimulus. Estes suggested that the various stimuli an individual experiences just before making the punished response serve this function. Consider, for example, how an invisible fence works to keep a dog in its yard. An invisible or electronic fence detects when the dog goes to the edge of its yard and administers a brief shock to the dog through a remote-sensing collar if the dog crosses this boundary. The punished response (going too far) is associated with various cues of the boundary of the yard. When the dog is punished, the visual and other spatial cues of the yard borders become paired with shock. According to the conditioned emotional response theory, as these cues acquire conditioned aversive properties, they will elicit freezing (the behavioral manifestation of fear), which is incompatible with the punished behavior. Thus, the punished response will become suppressed.

The Avoidance Theory of Punishment An alternative to the conditioned emotional response theory regards punishment as a form of avoidance behavior. This theory is most closely associated with Dinsmoor (1954, 1998) and follows the tradition of the two-process theory of avoidance. Dinsmoor accepted the idea that the stimuli that accompany the instrumental response acquire aversive properties when the response is punished. He went on to propose that organisms learn to escape from the conditioned aversive stimuli related to the punished response by engaging in some other behavior that is incompatible with the punished activity. Performance of the alternative activity results in suppression of the punished behavior. Thus, the avoidance theory explains punishment in terms of the acquisition of incompatible avoidance responses.

The avoidance theory of punishment is an ingenious proposal. It suggests that all changes produced by aversive instrumental conditioning, be they an increase or a decrease in the likelihood of a response, can be explained by similar avoidance learning mechanisms. Suppression of behavior is not viewed as reflecting the weakening of the punished response. Rather, it is explained in terms of the strengthening of competing avoidance responses.

Despite its cleverness and parsimony, the avoidance theory of punishment has been controversial. Because it explains punishment in terms of avoidance mechanisms, all the theoretical problems that have burdened the analysis of avoidance behavior become problems in the analysis of punishment. Another challenge for the theory is that its critical elements are not stated in a way that makes them easy to prove or disprove (Rachlin & Herrnstein, 1969; Schuster & Rachlin, 1968). The stimuli that are assumed to acquire conditioned aversive properties are not under the direct control of the experimenter. Rather, they are events that an organism is assumed to experience when it is about to make the punished response. The avoidance responses that are presumably acquired as alternatives to the punished behavior are also ill specified. The theory cannot predict what these responses will be or how we might identify and measure them.

Punishment and the Negative Law of Effect   The third and last explanation of punishment that I will describe is also the oldest. Thorndike (1911) originally proposed that positive reinforcement and punishment involve symmetrically opposite processes. Just as positive reinforcement strengthens behavior, so punishment weakens it. In later years, Thorndike abandoned the idea that punishment weakens behavior (Thorndike, 1932), but the belief that there is a negative Law of Effect that is comparable but opposite of a positive Law of Effect has remained with us (e.g., Azrin & Holz, 1966; Rachlin & Herrnstein, 1969).

Contemporary research related to a possible negative Law of Effect has employed concurrent schedules of reinforcement in which one component includes a punishment contingency (e.g., Critchfield, Paletz, MacAleese, & Newland, 2003). As I described in Chapter 6, a concurrent schedule is one in which participants have two responses available at the same time, and each is reinforced on a different schedule. The results of such experiments are typically analyzed using the generalized matching law that characterizes how the relative rate of responding on one alternative is related to the relative rate of reinforcement on that alternative. As I noted in Chapter 6, the generalized matching law includes parameters for response bias and sensitivity to relative rates of reinforcement (see page 169). Punishment can change these parameters.

An interesting question related to the negative Law of Effect is whether a punisher and a reinforcer have equal but opposite effects. This question was addressed by Rasmussen and Newland (2008) in a study with college students (for a related study with children with attention deficit hyperactivity disorder [ADHD], see Carlson & Tamm, 2000). College students worked on a concurrent schedule that involved clicking on moving targets on a computer screen. Two different targets were available at the same time, and clicking on each was reinforced according to a different VI schedule. The reinforcer was gaining

4¢ and the punisher was losing 4¢. After responding stabilized on a concurrent schedule that involved only reinforcement in each component, a punishment contingency was added to one of the components (also on a VI schedule). Each participant was tested on nine variations of the concurrent schedules, and the results were analyzed using the generalized matching law, with special emphasis on the bias and sensitivity parameters.

One might not predict that gaining and losing 4¢ would motivate much behavior among college students, but the results were dramatic. Imposing a punishment procedure in one component of the concurrent schedule created a large bias in favor of responding on the nonpunished alternative. In addition, the punishment contingency caused a reduction in sensitivity to relative reinforcement rates. Most interestingly, punishment was three times more effective in changing response preference than reinforcement. Rasmussen and Newland concluded that "losing a penny is three times more punishing than earning that same penny is reinforcing" (p. 165).

Punishment Outside the Laboratory

As we have seen, punishment can be a highly effective procedure for rapidly suppressing behavior and can cause a major shift in favor of alternative responses that are reinforced. However, the effectiveness of punishment in laboratory studies is not sufficient to justify its application outside the laboratory. Punishment procedures are easily misused. Even if the procedures are administered appropriately, there are serious ethical constraints on their application, and they can have troublesome side effects.

Punishment is typically not applied in an effective manner. Often punishment is first introduced at low intensities (e.g., a reprimand for the first offense). The aversive stimulus may not be administered rapidly after the target response but delayed until it is convenient to administer it ("Wait until I tell your parents about this"). Punishment is usually administered on an intermittent schedule, and the chances of getting caught may not be high. (How often do drivers who exceed the speed limit get a ticket?) Punishment is rarely instituted with specific alternative sources of reinforcement set up, because it is much easier to react to transgressions than to systematically train appropriate behavior. Often there are clear discriminative stimuli for punishment. The behavior targeted for punishment may be monitored only at particular times or by a particular person, making it likely that the response will be suppressed only at those times. Finally, punishment may be the only source of attention for someone, making punishment a discriminative stimulus for positive reinforcement.

The preceding problems with the use of punishment outside the laboratory can be overcome. However, it is difficult to guard against these pitfalls in common interpersonal interactions. When you yell at your child or rudely hang up on your girlfriend, you are likely doing so out of frustration and anger. A frustrative act of punishment is likely to violate many of the guidelines for the effective use of punishment. Punishing someone in an act of anger and frustration is a form of abuse, not a form of systematic training.

The use of punishment in parenting has been the subject of extensive research. Consistent with the implications of laboratory research, a review of the literature on parental corporal punishment concluded that punishment is strongly associated with increased immediate compliance on the part of a child (Gershoff, 2002, 2008). However, the same analysis showed that corporal punishment is also associated with unintended consequences, such as aggression, mental health issues, and parent–child relationship difficulties. In addition, parental punishment is related to delinquent and antisocial behavior and increased incidence of aggressive behavior in adulthood. (For a cross-cultural study of these issues, see Gershoff et al., 2010.) However, it is difficult to isolate the causal role of parental punishment in these effects because most of the evidence is based on correlational data. Parents who are apt to use punishment may be cold and aloof in their relationship with their children and less likely to reward them for good behavior. Or they may be harsh and punitive in a variety of ways, only one of which is corporal punishment.

Parental use of corporal punishment has been outlawed in a number of countries (Zolotor & Puzia, 2010), and many states in the USA have adopted laws limiting the use of corporal punishment by teachers and guardians. However, punishment can be justified and may be even imperative if the target response is likely to be injurious and the behavior has to be suppressed immediately (Lerman & Vorndran, 2002). If a child is about to chase a ball into a busy street, there is no time for shaping and positive reinforcement of appropriate behavior.

Sample Questions

1. What is the fundamental problem in the analysis of avoidance behavior, and how is this problem resolved by two-process theory?
2. How is avoidance responding related to conditioned fear and the expectation of aversive stimulation?
3. Compare and contrast discriminated and free-operant avoidance procedures.
4. How can the concept of a safety signal be used to explain free-operant avoidance learning?
5. What are species-specific defense reactions, and why is it important to consider them in avoidance and punishment situations?
6. Describe factors that enhance the effectiveness of punishment in suppressing behavior.
7. In what ways is punishment similar to positive reinforcement? In what ways is it different?

Key Terms

avoidance An instrumental conditioning procedure in which the participant's behavior prevents the delivery of an aversive stimulus.

avoidance trial A trial in a discriminated avoidance procedure in which an avoidance response is made and prevents the delivery of the aversive stimulus.

discriminated avoidance An avoidance conditioning procedure in which occurrences of the aversive stimulus are signaled by a CS. Responding during the CS terminates the CS and prevents the delivery of the aversive US. Also called *signaled avoidance*.

discriminative punishment A procedure in which responding is punished in the presence of a particular stimulus and not punished in the absence of that stimulus.

escape trial A trial during discriminated avoidance training in which the required avoidance response is not made and the aversive US is presented. Performance of the instrumental response during the aversive stimulus results in termination of the aversive stimulus. Thus, the organism is able to escape from the aversive stimulus.

escape from fear (EFF) procedure Situation in which subjects learn an instrumental response to escape from or terminate a conditioned stimulus that elicits fear. Escape from fear is predicted by the two-process theory

of avoidance and provides a coping mechanism for individuals suffering from excessive fear.

flooding A procedure for extinguishing avoidance behavior in which the CS is presented while the participant is prevented from making the avoidance response.

free-operant avoidance Same as *nondiscriminated avoidance*.

nondiscriminated avoidance An avoidance conditioning procedure in which occurrences of the aversive stimulus are not signaled by an external stimulus. The aversive stimulus is presented periodically, as set by the S–S interval. Each occurrence of the avoidance response creates (or resets) a period of safety determined by the S–R interval during which the aversive stimulus is not presented. Also called *free-operant avoidance*; originally called *Sidman avoidance*.

overcorrection A procedure for discouraging behavior in which the participant is not only required to correct or rectify a mistake but is also required to go beyond that by, for example, extensively practicing the correct response alternative.

predatory imminence The perceived likelihood of being attacked by a predator. Different species-typical defense responses occur with different degrees of predatory imminence.

punishment   An instrumental conditioning procedure in which there is a positive contingency between the instrumental response and an aversive stimulus. If the participant performs the instrumental response, it receives the aversive stimulus; if the participant does not perform the instrumental response, it does not receive the aversive stimulus. Punishment typically suppresses instrumental behavior.

R–S interval   The interval between the occurrence of an avoidance response and the next scheduled presentation of the aversive stimulus in a nondiscriminated avoidance procedure. Thus, the R–S interval sets the duration of safety created by each avoidance response in a nondiscriminated avoidance procedure.

response blocking   Blocking the opportunity to make the avoidance response so that the subject is exposed to a fear stimulus without being able to escape from it. Usually used in connection with *flooding*.

safety signal   A stimulus that signals the absence of an aversive event.

shock-frequency reduction   A hypothesis according to which reduction in the frequency of shock serves to reinforce avoidance behavior.

shuttle avoidance   A type of avoidance conditioning procedure in which the required instrumental response consists of going back and forth (shuttling) between two sides of an experimental apparatus on successive trials.

signaled avoidance   Same as *discriminated avoidance.*

species-specific defense reactions (SSDRs)   Species-typical responses animals perform in an aversive situation. The responses may involve freezing, fleeing, or fighting.

S–S interval   The interval between successive presentations of the aversive stimulus in a nondiscriminated avoidance procedure when the avoidance response is not performed.

time out   A period during which the opportunity to obtain positive reinforcement is removed. This may involve removal of the participant from the situation where reinforcers are available.

two-process theory of avoidance   A theory originally developed to explain discriminated avoidance learning that presumes the operation of two mechanisms: classical conditioning of fear to the warning signal or CS and instrumental reinforcement of the avoidance response through termination of the warning signal and consequent fear reduction.

CHAPTER 11

Comparative Cognition I: Memory Mechanisms

CHAPTER PREVIEW

The study of comparative cognition dates back to Darwin's writings about the evolution of intelligence, but the best research on comparative cognition has been done in the past 40 years. This chapter begins with a general characterization of comparative cognition and then moves onto the most important topic in this area of research, namely memory mechanisms. I start by describing the relationship between learning and memory and the distinctions among several different forms of memory. I then discuss several prominent paradigms for the study of working memory in animals. The next section describes research relevant to three different stages of information processing: acquisition, retention, and retrieval. Forgetting and various sources of memory failure are described after that, including the phenomenon of retrograde amnesia. The chapter ends with a discussion of contemporary views of memory retrieval and consolidation and the implication of these views for the permanence and accuracy of memories.

As we discussed in Chapter 1, interest in comparative cognition dates back to the founding of the field of animal learning in the second half of the nineteenth century. Early experimental efforts to study comparative cognition employed animal learning

T. Zentall

E. A. Wasserman

paradigms. However, the study of animal learning soon came to have a life of its own. Through much of the twentieth century, learning was investigated in animals for what it told us about behavior in general rather than for what it told us about a particular species or what it told us about the evolution of learning mechanisms. This approach continues today, especially in studies of the neurobiology of learning. However, in contemporary research, the general-process approach to learning is accompanied by a robust interest in comparative cognition (e.g., Shettleworth, 2010; Zentall & Wasserman, 2012).

Comparative cognition is an approach to the study of animal behavior that focuses on "the mechanisms by which animals acquire, process, store, and act on information from the environment" (Shettleworth, 2010, p. 4). This makes comparative cognition a very broad topic that includes topics such as perception and attention, learning, memory, spatial navigation, timing and counting, learning of perceptual and abstract concepts, problem solving, and tool use. In addition to providing important new information about how different species deal with various types of information, studies of comparative cognition address the kind of theoretical questions about the evolution of intelligence that captivated Darwin. Exploring the cognitive skills of animals tells us about the uniqueness of various human cognitive skills, just as exploring other planets can reveal the uniqueness of our terrestrial habitat. As Wasserman (1993) put it, "Comparing the intelligence of many species of animals may help us know better what it means to be human" (p. 211). Studies of comparative cognition are also important because they provide model systems for the investigation of the neurophysiological bases of cognitive functions. Memory-enhancing drugs, for example, cannot be developed without first developing animal model systems for the study of memory mechanisms (e.g., Gold, 2008). Studies of the mechanisms of cognition in nonhuman animals may also help us in designing intelligent machines and robots (e.g., Asada et al., 2008; Gnadt & Grossberg, 2007).

Comparative Cognition, Consciousness, and Anthropomorphism

The word *cognition* comes from the Latin meaning *knowledge* or *thinking* and is commonly used to refer to thought processes. In casual discourse, we regard thinking as voluntary, deliberate, and conscious reflection on some topic, usually involving language. For comparative cognition, a more important characteristic of thinking is that it can lead to actions that cannot be explained on the basis of the external stimuli an individual experiences at the time. For example, on your way to work, you may start thinking that you did not lock the door to your apartment when you left home. This idea may prompt you to return home to check whether the door is locked. Your returning cannot be explained by the external stimuli you encountered on your way to work. You come across those stimuli every day without going back to check the door. Rather, your behavior is attributed to the thought that you might have left your apartment unlocked.

There is some controversy about what the domain of comparative cognition should be. Advocates of **cognitive ethology** claim that animals are capable of conscious thought and intentionality (Griffin, 1992; Ristau, 1991). According to cognitive ethologists, comparative cognition should encompass the full range of issues that are included in considerations of human cognition. The claim that nonhuman animals are capable of consciousness and intentionality is based on the complexity, flexibility, and cleverness of various examples of animal behavior. The argument is that conscious intent is the likely source of such clever and flexible behavior. This is basically an argument from design, an argument that has been debated and rejected by philosophers for centuries (Blumberg & Wasserman, 1995). In addition to such philosophical arguments, it is also important to consider the serious limitations of conscious intent as an adequate explanation of human behavior (Bargh & Morsella, 2008; Wegner, 2002). If conscious intent cannot adequately characterize important features of human behavior, why should we assume that the concept will be useful in explaining the behavior of nonhuman organisms?

In contrast to cognitive ethologists, experimental psychologists use the term *comparative cognition* in a more restricted sense. They follow H. S. Jennings (1904/1976) who argued more than a century ago that "objective evidence cannot give a demonstration either of the existence or of the non-existence of consciousness, for consciousness is precisely that which cannot be perceived objectively." Jennings went on to say that "no statement concerning consciousness in animals is open to refutation by observation and experiment" (pp. 335–336).

Contemporary experimental psychologists tie cognitive mechanisms closely to behavioral predictions. That way, cognitive inferences can be supported or refuted by experimental evidence. Experimental psychologists make inferences about the internal or cognitive machinery that mediates behavior in cases where simple S–R or reflex mechanisms are insufficient. However, they are careful to accept only those hypothesized cognitive processes that lead to unambiguous behavioral predictions. Thus, for experimental psychologists, comparative cognition does not imply anything about awareness, consciousness, or verbal reasoning. Rather, **comparative cognition** refers to theoretical constructs and models used to explain aspects of behavior that cannot be readily characterized in terms of simple S–R mechanisms.

A critical feature of comparative cognition is that it employs the simplest possible explanations that are consistent with the data. Consider the following description of behavior:

> *At first, the allure is weak; there is a vague yearning and a mild agitation. Ultimately, the strength of desire grows irresistible; its head turns sharply and it skitters across the uneven floor to caress the objects of its affection with consummate rapture.* (Zentall & Wasserman, 2012, p. 1)

Whose behavior is being described here? As it turns out, this is a poetic description of a coin being drawn to a magnet. We regard such elaborate descriptions as preposterous when applied to a coin because we have come to accept that physical objects don't have an essence that is capable of rich emotional experience. Unfortunately, adopting a similar dispassionate scientific perspective toward the behavior of nonhuman animals is much more difficult because we have been raised on Disney cartoons and other animated films whose entertainment value is based on attributing a rich mental life (and extensive linguistic skills) to ordinary and fictitious animals.

When we make casual inferences about the rich mental life of a bird or squirrel, we are projecting our own thoughts, emotions, and intentions on them. This is called **anthropomorphism**. Anthropomorphic explanations hamper knowledge of comparative cognition because they overemphasize human experience and they prejudge the conclusions that we may reach through systematic research. These pitfalls of overinterpreting animal behavior were pointed out more than a century ago by C. Lloyd Morgan (1894) but are just as relevant today.

Cognitive mechanisms involve an internal representation or "mental" record of something and rules for manipulating that mental record. Internal representations may encode various types of information, such as particular features of stimuli or relations between stimuli. Internal representations and their manipulations cannot be investigated directly by looking into the brain. Rather, they have to be inferred from behavior. Thus, a cognitive mechanism is a theoretical construct inferred from behavior, just as magnetic force is a theoretical construct inferred from the behavior of objects that are attracted to each other. Neither requires any assumptions about consciousness or intentionality.

Memory: Basic Concepts

One of the largest areas of comparative cognition is the study of memory mechanisms (e.g., Spear & Riccio, 1994; Urcelay & Miller, 2008). The term **memory** is commonly used to refer to the ability to respond on the basis of information that was acquired earlier. We are said to remember what happened in our childhood if we talk about our childhood experiences, and we are said to remember someone's name if we call that person by the correct name. Unfortunately, such tests of memory are impractical with nonhuman animals. We cannot ask a pigeon to tell us what it did last week. Instead, we have to use the bird's nonverbal responses as clues to its memory.

If your cat goes out of the house but finds its way back, you might conclude that it remembered where you live. If your dog greets you with unusual exuberance after a long vacation, you might conclude that it remembered you. These and similar examples illustrate that the existence of memory in animals is identified by the fact that *their current behavior is based on some aspect of their earlier experiences.* Any time an animal's behavior is determined by past events, we can conclude that some type of memory is involved.

You may notice that this definition of memory is very similar to the definition of learning stated in Chapter 1. There, learning was defined as an enduring change in responding to a particular situation as a result of prior experience with that type of situation. Thus, evidence of learning is also identified on the basis of changes in behavior due to earlier experiences. Indeed, learning is not possible without memory. How, then, are studies of memory to be distinguished from studies of learning?

Stages of Information Processing

The differences between learning and memory may be clarified by considering the three stages of information processing that are common to both learning and memory experiments (see Table 11.1). The first stage in both types of experiments is that the participants are exposed to certain kinds of stimuli or information. This stage is termed **acquisition**. The information that was acquired is then retained for some time, a period called the **retention interval**. At the end of the retention interval, the participants are tested for their memory of the original experience, which requires **retrieval** or reactivation of the information encountered during acquisition. Thus, studies of learning and studies of memory all involve stages of acquisition, retention, and retrieval.

Consider, for example, riding a bicycle. To be a skilled rider, you first have to be trained to balance, pedal, and steer the bike (acquisition). You then have to remember those training experiences (retention). When you get on a bicycle again a week later, you have to reactivate what you learned earlier to ride successfully again (retrieval).

TABLE 11.1	COMPARISON OF LEARNING AND MEMORY EXPERIMENTS	
PHASE	**STUDIES OF LEARNING**	**STUDIES OF MEMORY**
Acquisition	Varied	Constant
Retention	Constant (long)	Varied (short and long)
Retrieval	Constant	Varied

© Cengage Learning

In studies of learning, the focus is on the acquisition stage. Learning experiments deal with the kind of information we acquire and the ways in which we acquire it. Thus, *learning experiments involve manipulations of the conditions of acquisition.* The retention interval typically is not varied in learning experiments and is always fairly long (a day or longer) because short-term changes in behavior are not considered instances of learning. Because the emphasis is on the conditions of acquisition, the conditions of retrieval are also kept constant. All participants in a given experiment are tested for what they learned using the same test procedures.

In contrast, *studies of memory focus on the conditions of retention and retrieval.* Acquisition is of interest only to the extent that it is relevant to retention and retrieval. The retention interval is often varied in studies of memory to determine how the availability of the acquired information changes with time. Unlike studies of learning, which employ only long retention intervals, studies of memory can employ retention intervals of both short and long duration. In fact, many studies of animal memory evaluate performance at several retention intervals.

Studies of memory also focus on the circumstances of retrieval. Consider, for example, taking a vocabulary test on a set of technical terms in a college course. You may miss many items if the test consists of a series of fill-in-the-blank questions for which you have to provide the technical terms. In contrast, you are likely to do better if you are provided with a list of the technical terms and are merely required to match each term with its definition. These different forms of the test involve different conditions of retrieval.

Types of Memory

Memory mechanisms have been classified in various ways depending on what is remembered (the contents of memory), how long the memory lasts (the retention interval), and the mechanisms involved in the memory. Schachter and Tulving (1994), for example, identified five types of human learning and memory: procedural memory, perceptual memory, semantic memory, primary or working memory, and episodic or declarative memory. Not all these forms of memory have their counterparts in research with nonhuman subjects.

Much of the research on classical and instrumental conditioning that we discussed in earlier chapters involved **procedural memory**. Procedural memory reflects knowledge about relationships among features of the environment and mediates the learning of behavioral and cognitive skills that are performed automatically, without the requirement of conscious control. Procedural memory is memory for what to do and how to do it. Studies of comparative cognition have also begun to examine **episodic memory**. Episodic memory is memory for specific events or memory for what, when, and where something happened. I will have much more to say about episodic memory in Chapter 12.

Another distinction that has been particularly important in comparative cognition is the distinction between **working memory** and **reference memory**. That is the topic we turn to next.

Working and Reference Memory

Working memory is operative when information has to be retained only long enough to complete a particular task, after which the information is best discarded because it is no longer needed or because it may interfere with successful completion of the next task. A mechanic changing the oil in a car has to remember which steps of the job have already been finished, but only as long as that particular car is being serviced. In cooking a good stew, you have to remember which spices you have already put in before adding others, but once the stew is finished, you can forget this information. These are all examples of working memory.

Working memory *is the retention of recently acquired information just long enough to complete a task.* However, such information is useful only in the context of more enduring knowledge. The working memory that a cook uses in keeping track of what spices he or she has put into a stew requires long-term knowledge about the names and tastes of spices, where to obtain spices, what different spices look like, how they are measured, and generally how much is appropriate for a particular type of stew. These pieces of information remain useful after flavoring a particular pot of stew. Such memory is called *reference memory* (Honig, 1978).

Reference memory is *long-term retention of information necessary for the successful use of incoming and recently acquired information.* Information about what a mechanic has done recently is useful only in the context of general knowledge about cars and lubrication procedures. All successful uses of working memory require appropriate reference memories.

Increasingly sophisticated techniques have been developed for the study of working memory in various animal species. I will describe several of these. The first procedure, delayed matching to sample, is a laboratory procedure that was developed without much regard for the behavioral predispositions of animals and can be adapted to the study of how animals remember a variety of different events. The other techniques that we will consider were developed to test spatial memory or memory for particular locations and these take advantage of species-specific behavioral specializations.

Delayed Matching to Sample

The **delayed-matching-to-sample procedure** was initially developed to study short-term memory for visual cues in pigeons (Blough, 1959). However, since then it has been adopted for use with a variety of species and stimuli. In a recent review of this area of research, White (2013) noted that "delayed matching to sample is the most frequently used procedure in the study of nonhuman short-term remembering."

In a delayed-matching-to-sample procedure, the participant is presented with a sample stimulus that designates which response will be correct at the end of the trial. This stimulus is then removed for a retention period. The participant is then given a memory test consisting of two cues, one of which is the original sample. Choice of the sample stimulus during the memory test is the correct response and is reinforced.

Figure 11.1 shows stimuli that were used in a study of working memory in human participants with first-episode schizophrenia (Lencz et al., 2003). The stimuli consisted of complex patterns of dark and light voxels. The sample stimulus was presented for 500 milliseconds, followed by the choice alternatives. Responding to the choice alternative that was the same as the sample was the correct response. The correct choice alternative could appear on the left or the right. Therefore, the location of a choice alternative could not be used as a basis for making the correct choice. In addition, different sample stimuli were used on successive trials so that a particular one was not always the correct choice.

During the first phase of training, the test stimuli appeared immediately after the sample and remained available until the participant made a choice. Once the participants learned to select the matching choice alternative more than 80% of the time, a 4- or 8-second delay was introduced between the sample and choice stimuli as a test of memory. The experiment was also carried out with a nonclinical sample of individuals for comparison. The two groups performed equally well when the matching task did not involve a delay. However, participants with schizophrenia showed a deficit in performance when trials included a 4- or 8-second delay between the sample stimulus and

FIGURE 11.1

Example of stimuli used in a matching-to-sample procedure with human subjects. The sample stimulus is presented initially, followed by the choice alternatives. Response to the choice alternative that is the same as the sample is reinforced. Delays introduced between exposure to the sample and presentation of the choice alternatives provide a test of memory (based on Lencz et al., 2003).

Sample

Choice
alternatives

the choice alternatives. The fact that performance differed between the two groups only in the delay conditions indicates that schizophrenia includes a deficit in working memory. (For other studies of delayed matching to sample in relation to schizophrenia, see Koychev, 2010; Quee et al., 2011.)

Successful performance in delayed matching to sample requires both working and reference memory. Working memory is involved in retaining information from the initial presentation of the sample to the choice test at the end of the trial. Reference memory is involved in remembering the basic structure of the task from one trial to the next. Delayed matching to sample has been employed in experiments with a wide range of species, including rats, monkeys, chimpanzees, dolphins, sea lions, harbor seals, and goldfish (e.g., D'Amato, 1973; Forestell & Herman, 1988; Iversen, 1993; Kastak & Schusterman, 1994; Mauk & Dehnhardt, 2005; Steinert, Fallon, & Wallace, 1976). In addition, the procedure has been adapted to investigate how animals remember a variety of stimuli, including shapes, numbers of responses performed, presence or absence of reward, the spatial location of stimuli, the order of two successively presented events, or which particular response the participant recently performed (e.g., D'Amato, 1973; Maki, Moe, & Bierley, 1977; MacDonald, 1993; Mercado et al., 1998; Wilkie & Summers, 1982).

Procedural Determinants of Delayed Matching to Sample Several aspects of the matching-to-sample procedure determine how accurately the participants perform. One of these is the nature of the stimulus that serves as the sample. Some types of sample stimuli are more effective than others (e.g., Wilkie & Summers, 1982). Other important factors are the duration of exposure to the sample stimulus at the start of the trial and the delay interval after the sample (Grant, 1976). Generally, sample stimuli that are presented for a longer period lead to better performance. In addition, as might be expected, participants make more mistakes if they are confronted with a longer delay between the sample stimulus and the choice test at the end of a trial.

The fact that memory performance is worse with longer retention intervals is a common finding in memory experiments and fits with common experience. You are less likely to do well on a test if the test is on material you heard in a lecture a month ago than if you heard the lecture earlier that day. There are many reasons why memory is

Courtesy of D. S. Grant

D. S. Grant

worse with longer retention intervals. A popular early explanation was based on the concept of a stimulus trace. The idea was that presentation of a stimulus creates a stimulus trace in the brain that automatically fades with time, leading to more memory errors (e.g., Roberts & Grant, 1976). This idea was simple and highly appealing, but unfortunately it has turned out to be incorrect. Memory does not fade automatically as a function of time. Numerous factors contribute to memory failure, some of which we will consider later in this chapter. Interestingly, one of the major factors that determines the rate of forgetting is the retention interval used during training. Training with longer retention intervals improves memory performance.

The importance of the retention interval used during training was demonstrated in a provocative experiment by Sargisson and White (2001). Investigators who employ the delayed-matching-to-sample task typically begin training with no delay between the sample and the choice stimuli on each trial. Presenting the choice alternatives without a delay makes the task a bit easier and facilitates learning. After the participants have mastered the task with no delay, memory trials are conducted in which various delays are introduced between the sample and the choice alternatives. Sargisson and White (2001) departed from this standard method by introducing different delay intervals from the outset to see if better memory could be trained by using longer delay intervals from the beginning of training.

Each trial began with either a red or green sample stimulus projected on a pecking key for pigeons, followed by a choice between the two colors. Which color was the sample on a given trial and whether the sample appeared on the left or the right during the choice test varied from trial to trial. For one group of pigeons, the delay between the sample and choice stimuli was always 2 seconds during training. For other groups, this delay was 4 or 6 seconds. For comparison, a control group was trained with the usual procedure of getting the choice test immediately after the sample. Training was continued until each group performed correctly on at least 80% of the trials. All of the birds were then tested with delays ranging from 0 to 10 seconds to determine their forgetting functions. The results of these tests are presented in Figure 11.2.

FIGURE 11.2
Accuracy of matching-to-sample performance as a function of delay between the sample and choice stimuli for independent groups of pigeons that were previously trained with delays of 0, 2, 4, or 6 seconds. (Based on "Forgetting Functions," by R. J. Sargisson & K. G. White, 2001, *Animal Learning & Behavior*, 29, pp. 193–207.)

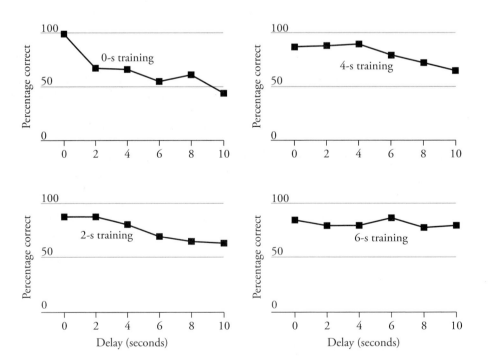

M. Spetch

The control group, which had been trained with a 0-second sample–choice delay, showed the standard forgetting function. Their correct choices declined steadily as the delay between the sample and choice stimuli was increased from 0 to 10 seconds. In contrast, no such decline was evident in pigeons that had been trained with a 6-second delay between the sample and choice stimuli. These birds performed equally well at all test delays. The other groups showed results between these two extremes. Importantly, for all groups the most accurate performance occurred when the delay used in the test was the same as the delay that they received during training.

The results presented in Figure 11.2 clearly show that forgetting functions do not simply reflect the decay or fading of memory for the sample stimulus as a function of time. Rather, test performance depends on the similarity between the conditions of testing and the conditions of training (see also Spetch, 1987; Rayburn-Reeves & Zentall, 2009). The common finding that memory gets worse with the passage of time reflects the fact that participants are usually not trained with longer delay intervals.

The delay interval used in training is just one training variable that influences delayed-matching-to-sample performance. Matching is basically instrumental-choice behavior motivated by the reinforcer provided at the end of the trial. Therefore, it should not be surprising that various factors that influence choice behavior are also relevant in the analysis of matching-to-sample performance. For example, pigeons show better memory performance if they receive a signal during the retention interval that the correct response will be reinforced with a large rather than a small reward. Interestingly, memory performance is also better if the signal for reward size is switched from small to large halfway through the retention interval. Correspondingly, switching the reward signal from large to small impairs memory (White & Brown, 2011). This is one of a growing number of findings showing that memory is not a passive process but matches the requirements of the environment. You remember things when there is significant payoff for remembering and forget things when the payoff is poor.

General Versus Specific Rule Learning   The term *matching to sample* suggests that this procedure trains participants to select a choice stimulus that is the same as the sample presented at the start of that trial. As it turns out that is just one possible mechanism of matching performance. Picking the choice stimulus that is the same as the prior sample involves use of a general "same-as" rule or concept. Another possibility is that the participants learn a series of specific rules or stimulus–response relations. In the experiment by Sargisson and White (2001), for example, there were just two possible sample stimuli, red and green. Therefore, the pigeons may have learned two specific rules: "Select red after exposure to red" and "Select green after exposure to green." Most matching-to-sample procedures employ more than just two possible sample stimuli. But, if the potential pool of sample stimuli is relatively small (six to eight items, for example), the participants can solve the matching problem by learning a series of specific stimulus–response or S–R relations.

How can we decide whether participants learn specific S–R relations or a general same-as rule? The key is to see how matching performance transfers to new stimuli. After training with one set of stimuli, the participants have to be tested with a matching problem that involves new sample and choice stimuli. If they learned a series of S–R relations (e.g., "select red after exposure to red"), they will have a hard time when tested with novel stimuli (e.g., blue sample and blue and yellow choice stimuli). In contrast, general rule learning predicts considerable transfer of matching performance to novel stimuli because the general same-as rule can be used to solve any matching-to-sample problem. Thus, in tests of transfer from one matching-to-sample problem to another, general-rule learning should produce better performance than specific-rule learning.

In a study with infant chimpanzees, Oden, Thompson, and Premack (1988) first provided training on a matching-to-sample task with just one pair of stimulus objects—a stainless steel measuring cup and a brass bolt lock. One of the objects was presented at the start of the trial, followed by a choice of both objects. If the chimp selected the matching object, it was reinforced with effusive praise, tickling, cuddling, or an edible treat, depending on its preference. After the chimps learned the task with the two training stimuli, they were tested with a variety of other stimulus objects. Remarkably, with most of the test objects, the transfer performance was better than 80% accurate. Thus, the chimps seemed to have learned a general same-as rule with just two training stimuli.

Chimpanzees are more likely to show evidence of generalized matching than pigeons and other species. However, the preponderance of evidence suggests that both general-rule learning and specific stimulus–response learning can occur as a result of matching-to-sample training in a variety of species. Which type of learning predominates is related to the size of the stimulus set that is used in the matching-to-sample procedure. Experiments that employ relatively few (six to eight) different sample stimuli tend to result in the learning of specific stimulus–response relations. By contrast, procedures that employ a couple of hundred possible samples promote the learning of a general same-as rule (e.g., Bodily, Katz, & Wright, 2008).

The greatest variation in possible samples occurs in what is called a **trials-unique procedure**. In a trials-unique procedure, a different stimulus serves as the sample on each trial and is paired with another stimulus during the choice phase (Wright et al., 1988). Because a given sample stimulus is not presented on more than one trial, accurate performance with a trials-unique procedure is possible only if the participant learns to respond on the basis of a general same-as rule. (Other approaches to learning the same-as concept will be discussed in Chapter 12.)

A. A. Wright

Spatial Memory in Mazes

The matching-to-sample procedure can be adapted to investigate how animals (human and otherwise) remember a variety of stimuli. The next set of tasks we will consider are more specialized but focus on a very important type of memory: memory for places. One of the major frustrations of being in a new place is that you don't know where things are. We get around comfortably in our hometown because we have learned how the streets are laid out. In addition, as we go someplace, we can remember where we have been and which streets we still have to take to reach to our destination.

The Morris Water Maze A procedure that has been popular in neuroscience research on spatial memory is the Morris water maze, named after its inventor (Morris, 1981; Sharma, Rakoczy, & Brown-Borg, 2010). The water maze is typically used with laboratory rats or mice. It consists of a circular tank, about 1–2 meters in diameter (smaller for mice), filled with water high enough to force the animals to swim. A platform is submerged somewhere in the tank, just below the surface of the water. Rats and mice don't like to swim. Therefore, they are motivated to find the platform. The water is colored (by adding nontoxic paint or milk) so that the platform is not visible as the animals swim around. This forces them to use spatial cues.

The first time the participants are placed in the water tank, they swim around until they find the platform and are then allowed to remain there for 15–20 seconds. This platform time allows them to learn where the platform is located in relation to the various spatial cues of the room. (Spatial cues include things like windows, doors, corners, long and short walls, etc.) On subsequent trials, the participants will have to find the platform just on the basis of these spatial cues because the platform is not visible above the surface of the water. Training trials begin with the animal placed in the water near the edge of the tank. The start position is varied randomly from one trial to the next so that the platform cannot be found by always swimming in the same direction (e.g., left of the start point). If the animal does not find the platform in 60 seconds, it is gently guided to it to end the trial.

The results of a study conducted with laboratory rats are summarized in Figure 11.3. The rats received four trials per day. Learning progressed fairly rapidly. As they learned the task, the rats took less time to find the platform and took more direct routes to the platform. The largest improvements in performance occurred from the first to the second day of training (Blokland, Geraerts, & Been, 2004).

The Radial Arm Maze   The Morris water maze has been a useful technique for the study of the neural bases of spatial memory, but it is not a task that rats or mice are likely to encounter in their natural environment. A self-respecting rat or mouse that finds itself in a pool of water will quickly learn to avoid falling into the water again. Therefore, it is not likely to have to remember information about the location of a submerged platform. A more ecologically valid laboratory technique for the study of spatial memory is the radial arm maze, which takes advantage of evolved strategies for finding food in an animal's environment.

In many environments, once food has been eaten at one location, it is not available there again for some time. Therefore, animals have to remember where they last obtained food while foraging and avoid that location until the food there is replenished. For example, the Hawaiian amakihi honeycreeper (*Loxops virens*) feeds on the nectar of mamane flowers. After feeding on a cluster of flowers, these birds have to avoid returning to the same flowers for about an hour. By delaying their return to clusters they recently visited, the birds increase their chances of finding nectar in the flowers they search. They appear to remember the spatial location of recently visited flower clusters (Kamil, 1978; see also Healy & Hurly, 1995).

The radial arm maze was developed to test memory for places where an animal recently obtained food and depleted that food source. Although the procedure was originally designed for use with laboratory rats (Figure 11.4), analogous procedures have been

FIGURE 11.3 Time required to find a submerged platform in the Morris water maze as a function of days of training. Subjects received four trials each day (based on Blokland, Geraerts, & Been, 2004).

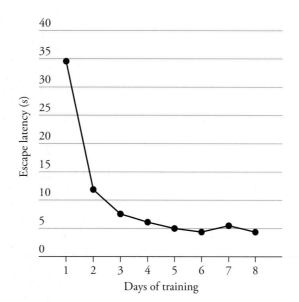

FIGURE 11.4 Rat foraging on an elevated radial maze.

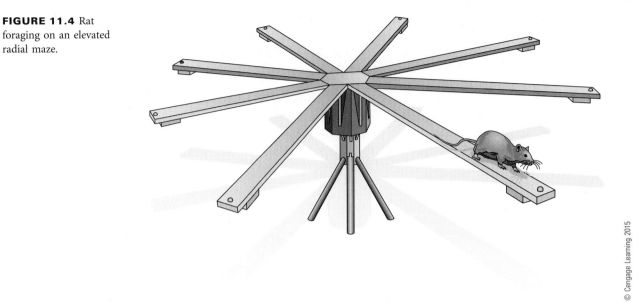

© Cengage Learning 2015

Courtesy of Donald A. Dewsbury

D. S. Olton

developed for other species, including pigeons (Roberts & Van Veldhuizen, 1985) and college students (Kesner & DeSpain, 1988). There is even a report of radial maze performance in the tortoise (*Geochelone carbonaria*). The tortoise navigated the maze rather slowly but showed evidence of spatial learning (Wilkinson, Chan, & Hall, 2007).

A radial arm maze typically has eight arms radiating from a central choice area, with a food cup at the end of each arm (Olton & Samuelson, 1976). Before the start of each trial, a pellet of food is put into each food cup. The rat is then placed in the center of the maze and allowed to go from one arm to another and pick up all the food. Once a food pellet has been consumed, that arm of the maze remains empty for the rest of the trial. Given this arrangement, the most efficient way for a rat to get all eight pellets is to enter only those arms of the maze that it had not yet visited. That is, in fact, what rats do.

The results of an experiment conducted by David Olton (who developed this technique) are summarized in Figure 11.5. Entering an arm that had not been visited previously was considered to be a correct choice. Figure 11.5 summarizes the number of correct choices the rats made during the first eight choices of successive tests. During the first five test runs after familiarization with the maze, the rats made a mean of nearly seven correct choices during each test. With continued practice, the mean number of correct choices was consistently above seven, indicating that the animals rarely entered an arm they had previously chosen on that trial.

Rats do not require much training to perform efficiently in the radial maze because the task takes advantage of foraging tactics that rats acquired through their evolutionary history. Rats live in burrows, from which they venture out periodically to find food. While out foraging, they follow preexisting trails and move about without returning to recently visited places. In fact, their tendency to avoid recently visited places is so strong that they don't return to recently visited arms in a maze even if the maze arms have no food (FitzGerald et al., 1985; Timberlake & White, 1990). These results suggest that radial maze performance has deep evolutionary roots. (For additional experiments on the ecological basis of radial arm maze performance, see Brown, Farley, & Lorek, 2007; Hoffman et al., 1999; Timberlake, Leffel, & Hoffman, 1999.)

There are several mechanisms by which rats could choose to enter only previously unselected arms of a maze without necessarily remembering which arms they had

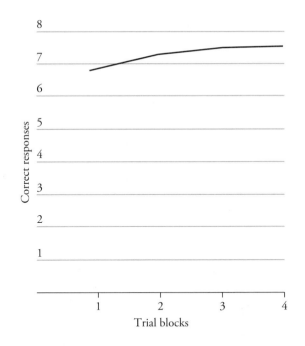

FIGURE 11.5 Mean number of correct responses rats made in the first eight choices during blocks of five test trials in an eight-arm radial maze (Based on D. S. Olton, 1978.)

already visited. For example, they could mark each arm they visit with a drop of urine and then avoid maze arms that had this odor marker. Another strategy would be to select arms in a fixed sequence, such as always entering successive arms in a clockwise order. However, they do not appear to use either of these tactics (e.g., Olton & Samuelson, 1976; Zoladek & Roberts, 1978). Rather, rats appear to use distinctive features of the environment, such as a window, door, or corner of the room, as landmarks and locate maze arms relative to these landmarks. If the landmarks are moved relative to the maze, the rats treat the maze arms as being in new locations (Suzuki, Augerinos, & Black, 1980). Thus, under ordinary circumstances, spatial location is identified relative to distal room cues, not in relation to local cues inside the maze. (Rats use similar spatial cues for successful performance in the Morris water maze.)

Because radial maze performance usually depends on memory for recently visited locations, the radial maze procedure has become a popular technique for the study of memory processes, both at the behavioral and neurobiological levels. The memory capacity revealed by the technique is impressive. By adding more arms to the end of a radial maze, investigators have explored the limits of working memory. These and other spatial memory tests have indicated that rats are able to remember 16–24 spatial locations in a food-depletion working memory task (Cole & Chappell-Stephenson, 2003). This is far more than the classic claim that human working memory has a capacity for 7 ± 2 items (Miller, 1956).

The duration of spatial working memory is also remarkable. To determine how long rats can remember where they have been, the basic radial maze procedure has been modified to include a retention interval. In the modified procedure, rats are allowed to enter four arms of the maze and obtain the food located at the end of those arms. The animals are then detained in their home cages for a retention interval before being returned to the maze and allowed to pick up the food pellets in the remaining four arms. If the rats remember where they previously obtained food, they will not reenter those arms.

Crystal and Babb (2008) tested rats with this interruption procedure, comparing two retention intervals. On some test trials, a 1-hour retention interval was inserted between

FIGURE 11.6 Proportion of correct maze choices in an eight-arm radial maze following a 1-hour or a 25-hour retention interval after the first four arm entries. Independent groups of rats were trained with either a 24-hour or a 48-hour intertrial interval (ITI). Chance performance is indicated by the dashed line.

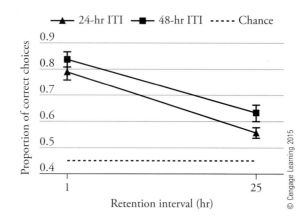

the rats' first four choices in the maze and their subsequent choices. On other test trials, the retention interval was 25 hours. Two groups of rats were tested. For one group, each trial began 48 hours after the end of the preceding trial. For the second group, each trial began 24 hours after the end of the preceding trial. The results are presented in Figure 11.6.

As is usually the case, performance was better for the rats trained with the longer intertrial interval. In addition, the rats were more likely to respond correctly (avoiding previously entered arms) if the retention interval was only 1 hour rather than 25 hours. This shows that working memory deteriorates with time, as one might expect. However, even with the 25-hour retention interval, performance was significantly above chance. Thus, the rats had some memory of which four arms they entered 25 hours earlier. (For an example of how this behavioral paradigm can be used to test drugs that may enhance memory, see Wise et al., 2007.)

BOX 11.1

Genes and Learning

The mechanisms that mediate changes in synaptic strength operate in phases. Initially, local molecular mechanisms produce short-term and rapid changes in synaptic strength. Additional processes are then activated that result in lasting memories. Establishing a long-term memory depends on the activation of *genes* that manufacture new protein products that produce a lasting change in how a synapse works (Figure 9.9A).

Using drugs that block protein synthesis, early observations suggested that the manufacture of new proteins contributes to the formation of long-term memories (Davis & Squire, 1984; see Box 9.1). More

recently, it has been established that the same is true for the lasting forms of long-term potentiation (LTP) and long-term depression (LTD) (Mayford & Kandel, 1999). Even learning in the invertebrate Aplysia (see Box 2.2) depends on gene expression (Hawkins, Kandel, & Bailey, 2006).

Modern molecular biology has given us a host of new techniques that allow researchers to uncover the genes involved in learning. These studies have revealed that a variety of learning mechanisms depend on the induction of common genetic codes, genes that encode some biological universals that have been well con-

served through evolution. Just as the mechanisms that underlie the generation of a neural signal (the action potential) are well conserved across species, so too may be the mechanisms that underlie synaptic plasticity.

Modern genetics has also given us new tools for studying the role of gene expression in learning. We can read the genetic code, identify the locus of the relevant genes, and experimentally manipulate how those genes operate. If we believe that a particular protein plays an essential role in learning, we can test this by using mice in which the relevant gene has been knocked out. This provides a new and unique window into the

Continued

BOX 11.1 (continued)

molecular mechanisms that underlie learning (Nakajima & Tang, 2005).

Silva and his colleagues were among the first to use this approach to study learning, creating genetically engineered mice that exhibit specific deficits in the way they learn and remember (Silva & Giese, 1998; Lee & Silva, 2009). Early studies addressed this issue by manipulating a protein known as *calmodulin-dependent protein kinase II (CaMKII)*. One way a synapse can be strengthened is by allowing calcium (Ca^{++}) into the postsynaptic cell. Ca^{++} is an electrically charged particle that normally has a higher concentration outside of the neuron than inside. When Ca^{++} is allowed into the neuron by the *N-methyl-D-aspartate* (NMDA) receptor (Figure 8.13C), it engages CaMKII, which enhances synaptic efficacy by modifying the α-amino-3-hydroxy- 5-methyl-4-isoxazolepropionic acid (AMPA) receptors that mediate the neural signal. Silva created mice that lacked the gene that underlies the production of CaMKII within the hippocampus. From other studies, Silva knew that the hippocampus plays a critical role in learning about spatial relations (see Box 8.2). He reasoned that if CaMKII is critical for learning, then **knockout** mice that lack this gene should have difficulty remembering where a hidden platform is in a Morris water maze. That is precisely what occurred, providing a link between learning and a particular protein product (Wayman, Lee, Tokumitsu, Silva, & Soderling, 2008).

A difficulty with studies of knockout mice is that the mice may not develop normally. When a gene is missing, other biochemical mechanisms can be enlisted that help the organism compensate for its deficiency. This could yield a brain that differs in a variety of ways from a normal brain. The abnormal neural

environment can make it difficult to interpret the consequences of the genetic manipulation. Neuroscientists are solving this problem by making mice in which the expression of a gene can be experimentally controlled. An interesting application of this technology involves the creation of a **transgenic** mouse. Instead of losing a gene (a knockout), the transgenic mouse has an extra gene that makes a new protein product.

In one example, mice were engineered that made a mutant version of CaMKII that did not work properly. The expression of this gene was placed under the control of a bacterial promoter that is regulated by *tetracycline transactivator (tTA)*. Because tTA is not normally present, its gene was also inserted, coupled to a promoter that was engaged within brain neurons late in development (Figure 11.7). Because the mutated CaMKII would only be expressed in cells that make tTA, limiting the expression of tTA assured that the mutated gene was only manufactured within the brain. What makes this transgenic system so powerful is that tTA can be inactivated by adding the chemical *doxycycline (DOX)* to the animal's food. As long as DOX is present, tTA is inactivated and the mutated gene is silenced. Under these conditions, the mutated mice exhibited LTP and normal learning in a Morriz water maze (Wayman et al., 2008). When DOX was removed, the mutated CaMKII was expressed, and shortly thereafter both LTP and spatial learning were disrupted.

Researchers are also exploring the possibility that modifying gene expression might improve memory. A good example is provided by a genetically engineered mouse named *doogie* (Lee & Silva, 2009). As discussed in Box 8.2, the induction of LTP depends on the NMDA receptor.

This receptor is formed from components (subunits), one of which changes with development. Early in development, animals have a subunit called NR2B which appears to promote the induction of LTP. In adults, this subunit is replaced by an alternative form (NR2A) that downregulates LTP. The change from the juvenile form (NR2B) to the adult form (NR2A) could make it more difficult for an adult animal to learn about new environmental relations. To explore this possibility, Tsein and his colleagues created mice that continued to make the juvenile form of the subunit (NR2B) into adulthood. As expected, these mice showed stronger LTP as adults. The mice also exhibited enhanced learning in an object recognition task and improved spatial memory in the Morris water maze. Across a range of tests, *doogie* mice seemed smarter.

Advances in genetic engineering are providing us with the tools needed to answer questions that were previously unanswerable. For example, it was suggested earlier that the hippocampus encodes the conjunction of features that define a context (Box 8.2). From this perspective, a configuration of cues is represented by a subset of neurons within the hippocampus. Supporting this proposal, it has been shown that lesioning the hippocampus disrupts context conditioning, which suggests that this structure plays a *necessary* role. To strengthen the hypothesized link, it would be useful to show that engaging these hippocampal neurons is sufficient to activate the contextual memory. We cannot do this by simply activating the hippocampus with an excitatory chemical or electrical stimulation because that would engage hippocampal neurons in a nonselective manner. Instead, we need a technique that would engage

Continued

BOX 11.1 (continued)

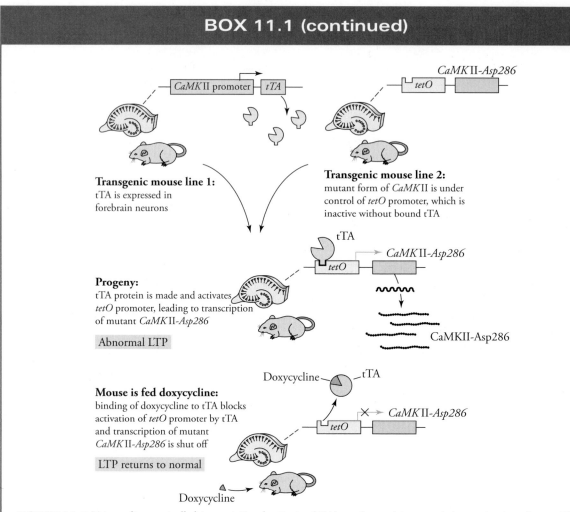

Transgenic mouse line 1:
tTA is expressed in forebrain neurons

Transgenic mouse line 2:
mutant form of *CaMK*II is under control of *tetO* promoter, which is inactive without bound tTA

Progeny:
tTA protein is made and activates *tetO* promoter, leading to transcription of mutant *CaMK*II-*Asp286*

Abnormal LTP

Mouse is fed doxycycline:
binding of doxycycline to tTA blocks activation of *tetO* promoter by tTA and transcription of mutant *CaMK*II-*Asp286* is shut off

LTP returns to normal

FIGURE 11.7 Tetracycline-controlled transcriptional activator (tTA) can be used to control the production of a modified gene. In this example, a transgenic line of mice was made that would manufacture a mutated version of the CaMKII gene under the control of the tetO promoter. This promoter is engaged by the protein tTA, which is normally not found in animals. Thus, to engage the tetO promoter, another line of mice was generated that would make tTA. In these mice, the production of tTA was placed under the control of a subunit of CaMKII, one that is highly expressed relatively late in development within the hippocampus. Offspring from these two lines of mice made tTA in the hippocampus, which engaged the tetO promoter and led to the production of the mutated CaMKII gene. The production of the mutated gene can be turned off by feeding the animals the chemical doxycycline, which inactivates tTA. (Adapted from Kandel et al., 2013.)

only those neurons that are activated by a particular context.

The solution was provided by combining the transgenic approach with a *viral vector*. A virus infects cells by binding to the cell membrane and depositing genes that the cell mistakes for its own, causing it to produce a foreign protein. This provides

researchers with another tool for inserting a gene into a cell. In the present case, a virus was used that would deliver the gene for *channel-rhodopsin (ChR2)*, a light-sensitive protein that is inserted into the neural membrane. Similar to the rhodopsin found in our retina, ChR2 is light sensitive; when illuminated by blue

light it allows positively charged ions (e.g., Na^+) to enter the cell, which chemically activates the neuron. The expression of the ChR2 gene was placed under the control of the tTA promoter. As a result, ChR2 would only be made if tTA was present and here too, its expression could be silenced by feeding the animals DOX.

Continued

BOX 11.1 (continued)

Because this approach combines optical and genetic techniques, it is known as **optogenetics** (Garner & Mayford, 2012; Johansen, Wolff, Lüthi, & LeDoux, 2012).

Liu and colleagues (2012) microinjected the ChR2-containing virus into a region of the hippocampus (the dentate gyrus) using mice that contained the gene for tTA. The expression of tTA was linked to another gene (*c-fos*) that is engaged by neuronal activity. We now have an animal that expresses tTA in active neurons and, within the dentate gyrus, this engages the expression of ChR2. We can then activate these cells with blue light provided by an optical fiber inserted into the dentate gyrus. Using this preparation, Liu and colleagues silenced the expression of ChR2 by feeding the animals DOX and then habituated the mice to one

context (A). They then removed DOX from the diet and presented a shock in a novel context (B). Their hypothesis was that exposure to the novel context (B) would engage cellular activity (*c-fos* expression) within the hippocampal cells that encode that context, causing ChR2 to be expressed within those cells. They then stopped further ChR2 expression by giving the mice DOX. Finally, the mice were returned to the pre-training context (A) and observed. In the absence of stimulation, the animals exhibited no evidence of fear (freezing). When blue light was presented through the optical fiber, it elicited freezing behavior—as if it had engaged the memory of the shock context. Importantly, mice that were treated the same but never received shock did not exhibit light-induced freezing. Thus, optical activation of

hippocampal cells that were active during context conditioning elicited freezing behavior. This implies that engaging cells involved in the formation of a memory is *sufficient* to induce the behavioral expression of that memory.

J. W. Grau

---

knockout mouse   A genetically engineered mouse in which the code for a particular gene has been disrupted.

optogenetics   A neurobiological approach wherein the genetic code for a light-sensitive channel is inserted into a neuron, allowing researchers to control neural activity using a light source (e.g., an optical fiber).

transgenic mouse   A genetically engineered mouse that has had new gene inserted into its genome.

Memory Mechanisms

The preceding section provided descriptions of several prominent techniques for the study of memory processes in animals and some of the results of that research. Next, we turn to a discussion of factors that determine what we remember and how well we remember it. As I noted earlier, memory processes involve three phases: acquisition, retention, and retrieval (see Table 11.1). What we remember and how well we remember it depends on all three of these phases, often in combination with each other. In this part of the chapter, I will discuss research with nonhuman animals relevant to each of the three phases of information processing.

Acquisition and the Problem of Stimulus Coding

Obviously, we cannot remember the winning play in a championship game if we did not see the game. Memory depends on our having experienced an event and having made some kind of record of that experience. However, even when our memory is excellent, it is not because we retain a perfect or literal record of the earlier experience.

Experiences cannot be recorded in a literal sense, even by machines. A digital camera can do an excellent job recording the winning play in a championship game, but even that is not a literal record. Rather, digital cameras create a record of an event in the form of a series of zeros and ones, or digital bits of information. The coded record bears no resemblance to the actual event. In a similar sense, we do not have a literal record of our past experiences in memory. Rather, our experiences are coded in the nervous system in some way for the purposes of retention and retrieval. What we recall later depends on how an experience was coded and how that code is retrieved at a later time. Thus, **stimulus coding** is a critical feature of the acquisition phase of memory.

Investigators have been interested in several aspects of the problem of coding. Consider, for example, rats foraging for food in a radial maze (Figure 11.4). The animals have to enter the various arms of the maze to obtain the food located at the end of each arm. So as not to waste effort, they have to select only the arms they have not yet tried that day. As we have seen, rats rely on their memory to do this. But what do they keep in mind? How is memory coded?

Cognitive Maps and Other Navigational Codes   One possibility is that the animals make a serial list of the maze arms they visit, adding an item to the list with each new arm visited. Given the excellent performance of rats on mazes with 16 or more arms (Cole & Chappell-Stephenson, 2003), this would involve a rather long list. Such extensive list learning seems unlikely because even humans have difficulty maintaining that many items in working memory at one time. Another possibility is that the animals form a mental map or mental representation of how the maze and the food cups are arranged. They then use this cognitive map to decide which arm of the maze to enter next (e.g., O'Keefe & Nadel, 1978; Jacobs & Schenk, 2003).

The idea that animals form a *cognitive map* which then guides their spatial navigation has been a prominent hypothesis for many years, but it calls for further specification. Potentially, maps can represent a variety of different types of information (distance, height or topography, presence of particular landmarks, compass direction, etc.). To claim that animals form a cognitive map does not tell us precisely what information is contained in such a map and how animals use that information. Such questions have led investigators to focus on more specific mechanisms that enable subjects to find a particular location in space. A number of mechanisms have been examined (see reviews by Shettleworth, 2010; Spetch & Kelly, 2006).

Consider a rat trying to find food hidden in the corner of a rectangular arena, such as the one depicted in Figure 11.8. Rats can easily learn to find the food in this situation by using spatial cues. What might these be? Notice that the food is hidden at the base of a small pyramid. A rat could find the food by heading toward the pyramid. This would be an example of using a *beacon* to locate the goal object. Beacons are cues at the location of the goal. Beacon following is a fairly simple navigational tactic, requiring little more than learning an association between the beacon and the goal object. Sign-tracking behavior described in Chapter 3 is an example of beacon following (see especially Figure 3.5). To determine whether animals are using a beacon to find a particular location, test trials have to be conducted in which the location of the beacon is changed.

FIGURE 11.8

Diagram of a spatial task in which food is hidden in corner 2 of a rectangular arena. Notice the beacon near the goal object and a landmark some distance away from the goal object.

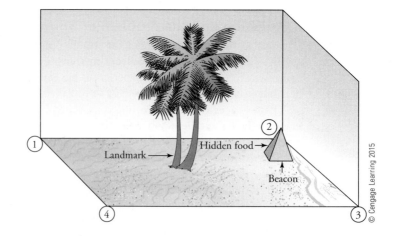

If the animal searches in the new location of the beacon, one may conclude that its search was controlled by the beacon. (For other experiments on the use of beacons, see Shettleworth & Sutton, 2005; Timberlake, Sinning, & Leffel, 2007.)

Another form of spatial learning involves using landmarks. A *landmark* is a distinctive stimulus that is not at the goal location but has a fixed relation to the goal. In Figure 11.8, the food is hidden to the right of a distinctive landmark. Note that for successful use of the landmark, the participant has to learn both the direction and the distance of the goal object from the landmark. To determine whether animals are using a landmark, the landmark has to be moved to a new location to see how that influences where the individuals focus their search for the food. (For examples of landmark use, see Chamizo, Rodrigo, & Mackintosh, 2006; Fiset, 2007.)

The arena in Figure 11.8 also allows rats to use *geometric cues* to locate the hidden food. Geometric cues are provided by the shape of the arena. In our example, the arena has a rectangular shape. The four corners of the rectangle are numbered 1–4. The food is hidden in corner 2, which has a long wall to the left and a short wall to the right. If the animals are using this geometric information to locate the goal, they will search in other corners that have these same geometric features. Corner 4 has the same geometric features as corner 2 (a long wall to the left and a short wall to the right.) Therefore, if the rats are using geometric information, they will confuse corner 4 and corner 2. Evidence of such confusion errors has been obtained in numerous studies of spatial learning in various species (see reviews by Chang & Newcomb, 2005; Kelly & Spetch, 2012).

On the basis of the associative learning mechanisms we discussed in Chapter 4, one might predict that animals would be more likely to use geometric cues in spatial learning when salient beacons and landmarks are either unavailable or difficult to use. However, evidence on this question remains controversial. The dominant issue in contemporary research on the coding of spatial information is how animals use information from multiple sources including beacons, landmarks, and geometric features to guide their spatial search behavior. Investigators are examining how learning about one spatial feature influences learning about other spatial cues (e.g., Gibson & Shettleworth, 2003; Pearce, 2009; Timberlake, Sinning, & Leffel, 2007), how learning about different types of spatial cues is integrated into a comprehensive spatial representation (e.g., Chamizo, Rodrigo, & Mackintosh, 2006), and how these interactions are best characterized theoretically (e.g., Chang & Newcombe, 2005; Miller & Shettleworth, 2007, 2008).

Retrospective and Prospective Coding

The studies of spatial learning we have discussed so far have been concerned with the nature of the information that is acquired or coded to guide future spatial navigation. Another issue that has become highly prominent in contemporary research is whether the information retained in memory deals with events that occurred in the past or events or actions that are planned for the future. On the face of it, the idea that memory is about something in the future may seem odd because we usually think about memory as information about the past. In fact, our definition of memory was that it reflected current control of behavior by a past event or experience. However, many things that we keep in mind or remember involve plans for future action.

When a quarterback calls a play in the huddle, the player is activating both memories for past events and plans for future action. The players on the team have to remember what they learned about the play during prior practice sessions. That involves **retrospective coding**. However, to execute the play during a game, the players also have to remember what they are supposed to do as the play unfolds on the field. That involves **prospective coding**. Calling the play in the huddle essentially activates a plan for future action. Executing the play requires that team members remember what they are supposed to do next based on the play the quarterback called in the huddle.

Prospection, or imagining the future, has captivated the attention of scientists studying human memory because the brain mechanisms involved in human future thinking or prospection turn out to be similar to the brain mechanisms of **retrospection**, or thinking about past events (Schachter et al., 2012). The overlap in brain mechanisms is not complete, but it is striking, suggesting that thinking about the future and thinking about the past involve similar processes. This, in turn, suggests that there may be a unitary cognitive mechanism that allows people to move either forward or backward in time, imagining future experiences and reliving past experiences. Mentally moving forward or backward in time is referred to as **mental time travel**.

Scientists working in comparative cognition initially studied prospective versus retrospective coding in an effort to better understand what information animals use in performing memory tasks. Consider, for example, a rat collecting food pellets in a radial arm maze. As we previously discussed, rats in such a task obtain the food available at the end of each maze arm, without going back to any arms they previously visited. What are they keeping in mind in doing this? Are they remembering which arms they have already entered (retrospective coding) or which arms they have yet to visit (prospective coding)? Early investigators attempted to answer this question by analyzing the mistakes that rats make at various stages of completing the maze. The pattern of these errors suggested that when the rats first start going through the maze they use retrospective coding and keep track of arms they have already entered. However, when the list of previously visited arms gets long, the rats switch to prospective coding and keep track of the few arms that remain to be visited (Cook, Brown, & Riley, 1985; for a similar study with college students, see Kesner & DeSpain, 1988).

In the radial-maze experiment described earlier, error rates were used to infer whether the rats were using retrospective or prospective coding. Recent interest in future thinking and mental time travel has encouraged scientists working in comparative cognition to develop procedures that provide more direct evidence of future thinking and mental time travel. These efforts have yielded convincing evidence of prospection or future thinking in various species of birds and primates as well as the proverbial laboratory rat (e.g., Crystal, 2012; Roberts, 2012; Zentall, 2010).

One approach to the study of future thinking involves a form of "saving room for dessert." If you go to a pot-luck dinner and see numerous delectable desserts on the buffet table, you might decide to eat less of the main course so that you will have room for dessert. Evidently, animals also display such future thinking. In one experiment, chickadees were given access to sunflower seeds for 5 minutes, followed after a delay by a dish containing mealworms (Feeney, Roberts, & Sherry, 2011). These birds much prefer mealworms to sunflower seeds. The experimenters wanted to find out if the chickadees would learn to hold back on eating sunflower seeds so as to have more room for mealworms. The delay between access to the sunflower seeds and the mealworms was 5 minutes during the first 15 trials and was then increased to 10 minutes and then 30 minutes. A control group was only given the sunflower seeds without the mealworm dessert later.

Evidence of planning for the future was obtained at all delay intervals. Figure 11.9 shows how many sunflower seeds each group of chickadees ate in the last phase of the experiment when the sunflower seeds were followed 30 minutes later by access to mealworms for birds in the experimental group. Clearly the chickadees in the experimental group were "saving room for dessert." They ate fewer sunflower seeds than birds in the control group in anticipation of the more delectable mealworms they were to get 30 minutes later.

FIGURE 11.9 Mean number of sunflower seeds eaten by chickadees that did not get more preferred mealworms later (control group) and chickadees that got mealworms 30 minutes later (experimental group).

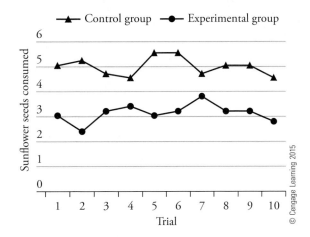

Another behavioral paradigm that has been used to examine the nature of memory coding is the matching-to-sample procedure (e.g., Roitblat, 1980). This type of problem can be solved either using retrospective or prospective memory. Beran and colleagues (2012) modified the procedure so as to encourage prospective coding. The experiment was conducted with rhesus and capuchin monkeys. The monkeys previously served in numerous experiments that required them to manipulate a joystick to move a cursor on a computer screen. Thus, they were expert at doing that. At the outset of each trial in the present experiment, a sample stimulus was presented in the center of the computer screen, with four possible choice cues arranged around the sample (Figure 11.10). The stimuli were selected from a set of 500 different images. If the monkeys selected the choice alternative that matched the center sample, they received a bit of food. The sample image varied from trial to trial, and where the sample appeared among the choice alternatives at the corners of the display also varied from trial to trial. To force the monkeys to plan their future actions, the choice alternatives were masked as soon as they started to move the cursor. Thus, to get the cursor to the correct corner of the display, the monkeys had to remember where they intended to move the cursor. An added wrinkle was that the monkeys had to move the cursor to the sample stimulus before moving it to the corner where they had previously seen the correct match.

As you might imagine, this was not an easy task for the monkeys to learn. However, four of the capuchins and five of the rhesus monkeys became very skillful in performing the task. Subsequent experiments showed that they continued to select the correct masked alternative even if they had to perform a "filler" task after contacting the sample. The purpose of this filler task was to prevent the monkeys from visually fixating on the

FIGURE 11.10 Matching-to-sample task used in a test of prospective coding with monkeys. The sample stimulus appeared in the center of the display, and the choice alternatives appeared on the corners (left panel). The monkeys had to move the cursor to the sample first and then to the location of the correct corner. However, as soon as they moved the cursor, the choice alternatives were masked (right panel). (Based on Beran et al. 2012a).

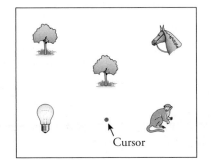

Michael Beran

position of the correct choice alternative once the choices were masked. (For additional studies of prospective coding in primates, see Evans & Beran, 2012; Beran et al., 2012b.)

Retention and the Problem of Rehearsal

The second phase of memory processes is retention. With working-memory tasks, a prominent issue involving retention is **rehearsal**. Rehearsal refers to keeping information in an active state, readily available for use. If someone tells you a phone number, you may rehearse the number by repeating it to yourself over and over until you get to a phone. If someone gives you directions to a popular club, you may try to create a mental image of the route and imagine yourself following the route a number of times. Such rehearsal strategies facilitate keeping newly acquired information readily at hand, available to guide behavior. (For a recent theoretical treatment of rehearsal processes in human learning and memory, see Laming, 2009.)

Rehearsal processes were first investigated in animal memory as they relate to the learning of new associations. Models of learning and memory typically assume that associations are formed between two events (e.g., a CS and a US) provided that the two events are rehearsed at the same time (e.g., Wagner, 1976, 1981). Given this assumption, learning should be disrupted by manipulations that disrupt rehearsal. Early studies of rehearsal processes in animal memory focused on such manipulations and their effects on the learning of new associations (e.g., Wagner, Rudy, & Whitlow, 1973). More recently, the focus of research has been on the role of rehearsal in working memory paradigms. An important line of evidence for rehearsal processes in working memory comes from studies of **directed forgetting**.

Studies of human memory have shown that the accuracy of recall can be modified by cues or instructions indicating that something should (or should not) be remembered (e.g., Bjork, 1972; Hourlhan & Taylor, 2006; Johnson, 1994). In this research, participants are first exposed to a list of items. Some of the items are accompanied by a remember cue (R-cue), indicating that the item will appear later in a test of memory. Other items are accompanied by a forget cue (F-cue), indicating that the item will not be included in the memory test. Probe trials are occasionally included in which memory is tested for an item that was accompanied by the F-cue. The results of these probe trials indicate that memory is disrupted by F-cues.

Demonstrations of directed forgetting are important because they provide evidence that memory is an active process that can be brought under stimulus control. Research on directed forgetting in people has sparked interest in finding analogous effects with non-human animals. How might we devise a procedure to study directed forgetting in animals?

Directed forgetting has been examined in numerous studies with pigeons employing variations of the delayed-matching-to-sample procedure. The procedure used in a study by Milmine, Watanabe, and Colombo (2008) is outlined in Figure 11.11. The experimental chamber had three pecking keys arranged in a row. The center key was used to display the sample stimulus (a red or white light), and the two side keys were used during tests of memory, which involved a choice between the sample and the alternate color. Five different types of trials could take place. On R-cue trials, the sample was followed by a 2-second high-pitched tone, followed by a 3-second silent period and the choice test. If the pigeon pecked the matching choice stimulus, it was reinforced with food. On F-cue trials, presentation of the sample was followed by a low-pitched tone and a delay period, but then the trial ended without a test. Thus, pigeons did not have to keep anything in mind during the delay period on F-cue trials.

The third type of trial was a free-reward (F-r) trial, which also ended without a choice test. However, on free-reward trials, the pigeons received food at the end of the

FIGURE 11.11 Outline of types of trials used in a study of directed forgetting in pigeons. Each trial started with a sample stimulus presented on the center key. This was followed by different auditory cues that served as the R-cue, F-cue, or free-reward (F-r) cue. Probe trials evaluated the impact of the F-cue and F-r cue on memory. (From "Neural Correlates of Directed Forgetting in the Avian Prefrontal Cortex," by M. Milmine.)

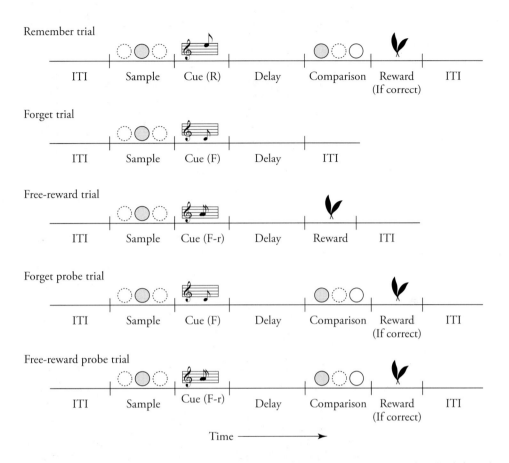

delay interval. The free-reward trials were included because previous studies had found that the anticipation of food at the end of the trial can serve to encourage memory for the sample stimulus. Free-reward trials were signaled by a pulsing auditory cue of intermediate pitch presented after the sample stimulus.

The first three trial types served to establish the functions of the R-cue, F-cue, and F-r cue. How effective were these cues in actually controlling memory? Memory was assessed on each R-cue trial because all R-cue trials ended with the choice test. To assess memory on F-cue and free-reward trials, a choice test was included as a probe on some of those trials as well. These probe trials are outlined as the last two trial types in Figure 11.11.

Two pigeons served in the experiment. The results provided by each bird are presented in Figure 11.12. Most accurate matching performance occurred on R-cue trials. As expected, the pigeons did poorly on the F-cue trials, indicating that the F-cue disrupted memory. Notice that because the forget instruction was provided after the sample stimulus, one cannot argue that the F-cue disrupted attention to the sample. Rather, the F-cue altered memory rehearsal during the delay interval.

Memory was also good on free-reward probe trials, indicating that the anticipation of reward can also facilitate memory. This effect is consistent with the results of an experiment by White and Brown (2011) that we mentioned earlier in the chapter. In that experiment, pigeons showed better matching-to-sample performance if they receive a signal during the retention interval that the correct response would be reinforced with a large rather than a small reward. Evidently, the anticipation of reward helps to keep recently experienced events in memory, and larger rewards produce greater improvements in memory.

FIGURE 11.12

Accuracy in delayed matching to sample in pigeons EZ2 and T19 on R-cue, F-cue, and free-reward trials. (Based on "Neural Correlates of Directed Forgetting in the Avian Prefrontal Cortex," by M. Milmine, A. Watanabe, and M. Colombo, 2008, *Behavioral Neuroscience*, 122, 199–209.)

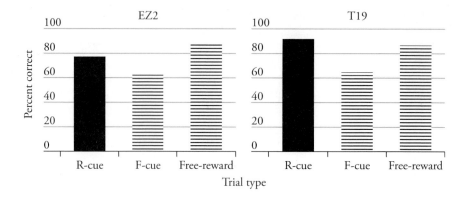

Milmine and colleagues (2008) also measured the activity of individual neurons in a part of the pigeon brain that is analogous to the mammalian prefrontal cortex because of suggestions that directed forgetting involves executive control. Consistent with that hypothesis, they found sustained increased single-cell activity during the delay interval on R-cue trials and suppressed activity during F-cue trials. Neuronal activity during the delay interval on free-reward trials was similar to the activity on R-cue trials. Thus, the single-cell neuronal activity in the avian analogue of the prefrontal cortex corresponded to the behavioral data, suggesting that these neurons were involved in the control of memory processes.

In the experiment by Milmine et al. (2008), the F-cue was correlated with nonreinforcement during training because the choice test was omitted on F-cue training trials. As it turns out, this is not critical. F-cues can be trained even if the procedure includes reinforcement on F-cue trials (Roper, Kaiser, & Zentall, 1995; Kaiser, Sherburne, & Zentall, 1997). The key factor is to omit a test for memory on F-cue training trials.

Once trained, F-cues can have broad impact. For example, an F-cue trained in one matching-to-sample problem can control memory in a different matching problem (Roper, Chaponis, & Blaisdell, 2005). These experiments demonstrate the phylogenetic generality of directed forgetting and provide laboratory paradigms for studying the neural mechanisms of how memory processes are subject to stimulus control.

Retrieval

In the third phase of memory processes, retrieval, stored information is recovered so that it can be used to guide behavior. Whereas problems of coding and rehearsal are primarily being investigated in working-memory paradigms, research on retrieval has focused on reference memory and, more specifically, on memory for learned associations. Retrieval processes are of special interest because many instances of memory failure reflect deficits in the recovery of information—**retrieval failure**—rather than loss of the information from the memory store (Urcelay & Miller, 2008).

During the course of our daily lives, we learn all sorts of things, which are somehow stored in the brain. Which aspect of our extensive knowledge we think of at a particular time depends on which pieces of information are retrieved from our long-term memory store. At any moment, we recall only a tiny portion of what we know. Retrieval processes are triggered by reminders, or **retrieval cues**. If you are discussing what you did at summer camp with your friends, the things they say will serve as retrieval cues that remind you of other events you experienced at the camp.

Retrieval cues are effective in reminding you of a past experience because they are associated with the memory of that experience. A song may remind you of the concert you attended on your first date. Balancing on a bicycle will remind you of what you have to do to ride a bicycle. The sensations of sinking in a swimming pool will remind you of what you learned about swimming, and the voice of a friend you have not seen for a long time will stimulate retrieval of other information about that friend.

Retrieval Cues and Memory for Instrumental Behavior in Human Infants

Various stimuli that are present during acquisition of a memory can serve as retrieval cues for that memory. Borovsky and Rovee-Collier (1990), for example, investigated retrieval of the memory for instrumental conditioning in six-month-old infants. The infants were trained in their own homes, in playpens whose sides were covered with a cloth liner. Some of these liners were striped and others had a square pattern. The investigators were interested in whether the cloth liner might serve as a retrieval cue for the instrumental response.

A mobile was mounted above the playpen. Each infant was seated in the playpen in a reclining baby seat so that he or she could see the mobile. One end of a satin ribbon was looped around the infant's ankle and the other end was attached to the stand that supported the mobile. With this arrangement, each kick by the infant made the mobile move. The instrumental response was kicking the leg, and the reinforcer was movement of the mobile. The kicking response was conditioned in two short training sessions. The infants then received a test session 24 hours later.

The cues present during the test session were varied for different groups. Some of the babies were tested in a crib with the same cloth liner that had been present during the training sessions (Group Same). Others were tested with the alternate cloth liner that was new to them (Group Diff, for "different"). For a third group, the alternate cloth liner was familiar but had not been present during the training trials (Group Diff-Fam). Finally, a fourth group of babies was tested without a liner and could look around their familiar playroom (None-Fam).

The results of the experiment are summarized in Figure 11.13. The best retention performance was evident in the group that was tested with the same crib liner that had been present during conditioning. Each of the other groups showed significantly worse memory performance. A change in the crib liner from what was used during original acquisition resulted in worse recall even if the liner used during testing was familiar. The inferior performance of Group Diff-Fam as compared to Group Same provides strong evidence that the cloth liner served as a retrieval cue for the instrumental kicking behavior.

Courtesy of C. Rovee-Collier

C. Rovee-Collier

FIGURE 11.13
Retention scores of six-month-old infants in a test of instrumental conditioning. Group Same was tested in a playpen with the same cloth liner that had been present during conditioning. Group Diff was tested with a new cloth liner. Group Diff-Fam was tested with a familiar cloth liner that was different from the one in the playpen during conditioning. Group None-Fam was tested without a cloth liner but in a familiar playpen in a familiar room. (Based on "Contextual Constraints on Memory Retrieval at Six Months" by D. Borovsky and C. Rovee-Collier, 1990, *Child Development*, 61, pp. 1569–1583.)

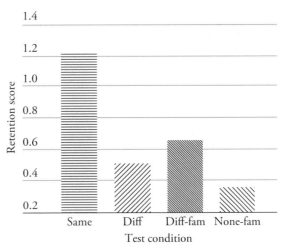

The results presented in Figure 11.13 illustrate the importance of contextual cues for memory retrieval. Contextual cues are stimuli incidental to a learning task that are present during original acquisition of the task. In the above experiment, these were visual cues provided by the crib liner. Studies with infants have shown that incidental auditory and olfactory cues can also become important contextual cues for memory retrieval (Daman-Wasserman et al., 2006; Schroers, Prigot, & Fagen, 2007). In general, memory is most successful if the contextual cues at retrieval are the same as the contextual cues that were present during original learning. That is why a football team preparing for a big game will practice with prerecorded crowd noise piped in rather than in an empty stadium or practice field. That is also why you should not study lying down in bed because you will have to be sitting upright in class when you are tested for what you learned.

Courtesy of N. E. Spear

N. E. Spear

The Generality of Retrieval Cues   We now know a great deal about the facilitation of memory by the presentation of retrieval cues (e.g., Spear & Riccio, 1994). As we have seen, contextual cues are especially effective in stimulating memory retrieval. Retrieval can be also enhanced by presenting just one component of the original learning task, such as the *unconditioned stimulus* (MacArdy & Riccio, 1995), the *reinforced conditioned stimulus* (CS+) (Gisquet-Verrier & Alexinsky, 1990), or a *nonreinforced conditioned stimulus* (CS–) (Miller, Jagielo, & Spear, 1992). Furthermore, such reminder treatments can be used to reverse many instances of memory loss (Gisquet-Verrier & Riccio, 2012; Urcelay & Miller, 2008).

Reminder treatments can remind older animals (and babies) of forgotten early-life experiences (e.g., Galluccio & Rovee-Collier, 1999; Rovee-Collier & Barr, 2008). Reminder treatments can counteract stimulus-generalization decrements that occur when learned behavior is tested in a new context (Millin & Riccio, 2004). Reminder treatments also have been observed to increase the low levels of conditioned responding that typically occur in latent inhibition, overshadowing, and blocking procedures (see Urcelay & Miller, 2008).

Retrieval Cues and Memory Priming   In the above examples, retrieval cues were presented at the time of testing to enhance retrieval and memory performance. Facilitation of recall by retrieval cues is just one example of various ways in which retrieval processes can be enhanced. Another procedure that has attracted considerable contemporary interest is called memory priming. In memory priming, the retrieval cue is presented at the end of a long retention interval, but memory is not tested until the next day. Thus, the question is whether reactivating a memory after a long retention period can increase how long something is remembered.

Infants tend to forget things faster than adults, which makes them good candidates for studying procedures that might increase the duration of memory. In a recent experiment (Suss, Gaylord, & Fagen, 2012), three-month-old babies were first trained to kick their legs to move a mobile in the presence of the odor of cherry or coconut. The babies were then tested for their instrumental responding a week later in the presence of the same distinctive odor. Ordinarily, three-month-old babies do not retain the conditioned leg-kick response over a seven-day retention interval. The investigators were interested in whether they could extend successful retention to seven days by providing a priming treatment one day before the retention test.

The priming treatment involved returning the babies to the experimental crib for a short period with the mobile moved by the experimenter rather than the infant. Such a procedure is not effective in conditioning the leg-kick response, but it can reactivate the memory of earlier training. For one group of babies, the priming procedure was

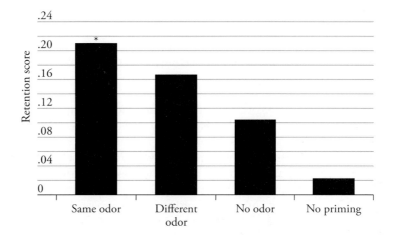

conducted in the presence of the odor that had been used during original training. For another group, the odor present during priming was changed (from cherry to coconut or vice versa). Finally, babies in the control groups were either not given an odor during priming or did not receive the priming treatment. (Keep in mind that the training context odor was present during the final retention test for all groups.)

The results of the experiment are summarized in Figure 11.14. The group that did not receive a priming treatment showed no memory for the mobile leg-kick task, confirming that three-month-old babies cannot remember this task over a seven-day retention interval. Babies who received the priming procedure six days after training showed much better retention on day 7. However, the priming procedure had to be conducted in the presence of the same context odor as had been used during training. In fact, the only group that showed significant retention on day 7 was the group that received priming in the odor context of original training.

Studies of priming demonstrate that retention can be significantly enhanced by reactivating a memory during the retention interval. Priming reactivates a previously learned memory without providing additional training. However, for best effect the priming should be conducted in the context of original training. (For additional studies of priming, see DeFrancisco & Rovee-Collier, 2008; Rovee-Collier & Barr, 2008).

Forgetting and Sources of Memory Failure

Forgetting is the flip side of memory. We are said to exhibit **forgetting** when memory fails and we don't respond in accordance with past experience or learning. However, as Kraemer and Golding (1997) have argued, forgetting should not be viewed simply as the absence of remembering. Rather, forgetting should be considered an important phenomenon in its own right (see also White, 2001). In our personal experience, forgetting is often unpleasant, as we suffer the consequences of having forgotten an appointment or someone's name. However, forgetting can also be adaptive and useful. One of the goals of treatment for posttraumatic stress disorder is to somehow erase or overwrite the memory of the trauma (Maren, 2011). Forgetting can increase behavioral variability as you search for the missing information. Forgetting can also reduce the context specificity of learning and thereby permit learned behavior to occur in a broader range of situations (Jasnow, Cullen, & Riccio, 2012).

The common experience is that failures of memory become more likely as time passes after a learning episode. However, it is not informative to view time as a *cause* of forgetting. As Piaget is reputed to have said, "Time is not a cause but a vehicle of

Stephen Maren

causes." And there may be a variety of causes of forgetting. As we have discussed, many things determine whether you perform successfully on a test of memory. Some of these concern coding and the acquisition of information. Others involve rehearsal and the retention of information. Still others involve processes of retrieval. Things can go wrong at any point along the way. Therefore, failures of memory, or forgetting, can occur for a variety of reasons.

As we saw in the infant memory experiments that were described earlier in this chapter, failures of memory do not always reflect the loss of previously learned information. The results presented in Figure 11.13 indicated poor memory for previous learning in infants who were tested with a crib liner that was different from what they saw during original learning. This poor memory performance did not reflect loss of the learned information but rather a failure to retrieve that information. The retrieval failure was easily corrected by using the same crib liner during testing as had been used during training. The forgetting that was evident when three-month-old infants were tested seven days after training (Figure 11.14) also did not reflect the loss of that information but its inaccessibility. In that case, memory was successfully reactivated if the infants received a priming treatment one day before the memory test. These examples illustrate that what we colloquially refer to as "forgetting" may not reflect the irreversible loss of stored information but some other mechanism that causes poor performance. The term **memory failure** is preferable in referring to these instances of poor performance on tests of memory.

Failures of memory have been extensively investigated in the context of interference effects and retrograde amnesia. We turn to these phenomena next.

Proactive and Retroactive Interference

The most common sources of memory disruption arise from exposure to prominent stimuli either before or after the event that you are trying to remember. Consider meeting people at a party. If the only new person you meet is Alice, chances are you will not have much trouble remembering her name. However, if you are introduced to a number of new people before or after meeting Alice, you may find it much harder to recall her name.

There are numerous well-documented and analyzed situations in which memory for something is disrupted by earlier exposure to other information. In these cases, the interfering information acts forward to disrupt the memory of a future target event. Therefore, the disruption of memory is called **proactive interference**. In other cases, memory for something is disrupted by subsequent exposure to competing information. In these situations, the interfering stimulus acts backward to disrupt the memory of a preceding target event. Therefore, the disruption of memory is called **retroactive interference**.

The mechanisms of proactive and retroactive interference have been extensively investigated in studies of human memory (Postman, 1971; Slamecka & Ceraso, 1960; Underwood, 1957). Proactive and retroactive interference have also been investigated in various animal memory paradigms. (For examples of proactive interference, see Grant, 2000; White et al., 2004; and Wright, Katz, & Ma, 2012. For examples of retroactive interference, see Escobar & Miller, 2003; Harper & Garry, 2000; and Killeen, 2001.)

Retrograde Amnesia

Sadly, a frequent source of memory failure is severe head injury. People who receive a concussion in a car accident, for example, may suffer memory loss or **amnesia**. However, the amnesia is likely to be selective. They may forget how the injury occurred, which car crashed into them, or whether the traffic light was green or amber. But they will continue to remember their name and address, where they grew up, and what they prefer to eat for dessert. Thus, there is a gradient of memory loss, with forgetting limited to events that occurred close to the accident. This phenomenon is called **retrograde amnesia** (Russell & Nathan, 1946). The farther back you go from the time of injury, the better the memory. (For a discussion of the human literature on retrograde amnesia, see Squire, 2006.)

Retrograde amnesia has been extensively investigated in studies with laboratory animals during the past 50 years. The research has demonstrated that retrograde amnesia can be produced not only by closed-head injury but also a variety of other disturbances of the nervous system. These have included electroconvulsive shock, anesthesia, temporary cooling of the body, and injection of drugs that inhibit protein synthesis (for reviews, see McGaugh & Herz, 1972; Spear & Riccio, 1994; Riccio, Millin, & Bogart, 2006).

Retrograde Amnesia for Extinction   Studies of retrograde amnesia typically examine amnesia for recently learned information. As we saw in Chapter 9, extinction is a form of new learning. If that is true, then extinction should also be susceptible to retrograde amnesia. This prediction was tested by Briggs and Riccio (2007) in a fear-conditioning paradigm, with cooling of the body, or hypothermia, used as the amnesic agent. Laboratory rats were conditioned in a shuttle box that had a white and a black compartment separated by a door. Conditioning was accomplished in a single trial. The rats were placed in the white compartment and the door to the black compartment was then opened. As soon as the rats walked into the black compartment the door behind them closed and they got two inescapable shocks. This single punishment episode made the rats reluctant to enter the black compartment again, and that was used as the measure of conditioning.

Extinction was conducted the day after conditioning and consisted of putting the rats in the black compartment without shock for 12 minutes. Following the extinction procedure, some of the rats were immersed in cold water to substantially reduce their body temperature. This hypothermia treatment was provided either immediately after the extinction treatment (when it would disrupt consolidation of the extinction experience) or 30 or 60 minutes after extinction. The next day the rats were put back into the white compartment to see how long they would take to enter the black compartment (which had been paired with shock). The test was terminated after 600 seconds if the rat still had not entered the black compartment.

The results of the experiment are summarized in Figure 11.15. The first bar in the figure is for a group of rats that received the conditioning procedure but not the extinction treatment. These rats spent nearly 600 seconds in the white side of the shuttle box, indicating strong fear of the black compartment. The second bar is for a group of rats that received the extinction procedure but was not subjected to hypothermia. They lost their fear of the black compartment, entering it after about 200 seconds. The next three bars were from rats that received the hypothermia treatment immediately (Hypo-0) or 30 or 60 minutes after extinction (Hypo-30 and Hypo-60). Notice that rats in the Hypo-0 group behaved as if they never got extinction. They took more than 500 seconds to enter the black compartment. Similar results were obtained with the rats in the Hypo-30 group. Thus, these two groups showed retrograde amnesia for the extinction treatment. However, delaying the hypothermia 60 minutes after extinction did not produce the amnesic effect. Rats in the Hypo-60 group responded like those in the normal extinction group, entering the black compartment in about 200 seconds.

D. C. Riccio

FIGURE 11.15 Time for rats to enter the black compartment of a shuttle box after having been shocked there. The first group received only fear conditioning. The second group received extinction after the conditioning trial. Groups Hypo-0, Hypo-30, and Hypo-60 received hypothermia to induce amnesia 0, 30, or 60 minutes after the extinction procedure. (Based on Briggs & Riccio, 2007, Figure 1, p. 134.)

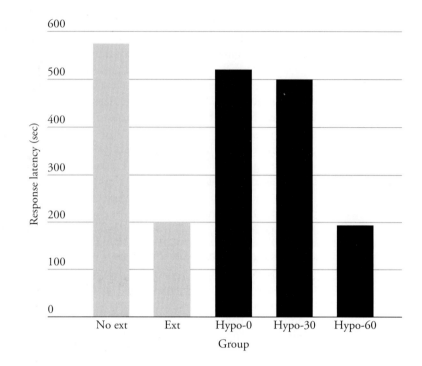

The fact that hypothermia disrupted the memory of extinction only if it occurred within 30 minutes or less after the extinction treatment indicates that the extinction memory was at first malleable and subject to modification. However, after this initial period of plasticity, the memory became immune to modification by hypothermia. The transformation of a memory from a flexible and modifiable state to a more stable state is called **memory consolidation**. Retrograde amnesia has attracted a great deal of experimental attention because it has become the primary method for the investigation of memory consolidation. Numerous experiments have shown that various memory disruptors such as drugs that inhibit protein synthesis are effective only if they are administered during a limited period soon after a memory is activated. This limited period is called the **consolidation window**.

Explanations of Retrograde Amnesia   Why do various interventions during the consolidation window produce memory failure or amnesia? According to the traditional explanation, a neural insult during the consolidation window disrupts the consolidation process and interferes with establishing a long-term record of the learning experience (see McGaugh & Herz, 1972). According to this explanation, when a stimulus is first encountered, it enters a short-term, or temporary, memory store. While in short-term memory, the information is vulnerable and can be lost because of interfering stimuli or neurophysiological disturbances. However, if the proper conditions are met, the information gradually becomes consolidated into a relatively permanent form in what is called long-term memory.

If an intervention such as hypothermia disrupts the consolidation process, then the memory is never properly recorded in the long-term memory store and therefore can never be retrieved during subsequent memory tests. This is called the *consolidation failure* explanation of retrograde amnesia. The consolidation failure account attributes the amnesia to a disruption in the original acquisition of the memory. A major alternative

interpretation is that amnesic agents cause a failure to retrieve information that was experienced close in time to the neurophysiological disturbance (Miller & Matzel, 2006; Miller & Springer, 1973; Riccio & Richardson, 1984). This explanation is called the *retrieval failure hypothesis.* According to the retrieval failure hypothesis, an amnesic agent alters the coding of new memories so as to make them more difficult to recover. Thus, the amnesia is attributed to a problem in the retrieval phase of information processing rather than the acquisition phase.

What kind of evidence would help decide between the memory-consolidation and retrieval-failure interpretations? If information is lost because of a failure of consolidation, it cannot ever be recovered. By contrast, the retrieval-failure view assumes that amnesia can be reversed if the proper procedure is found to reactivate the memory. Thus, to decide between the alternatives, we have to find techniques that can reverse the effects of amnesic agents. As we saw in studies of memory in infants, contextual cues of acquisition and exposure to the reinforcer (or US) are good potential candidates to reactivate memories. Such reminder treatments have been also found to be successful in overcoming retrograde amnesia (e.g., Gordon, 1981; Riccio & Richardson, 1984; Spear & Riccio, 1994; Urcelay & Miller, 2008).

Consider, for example, the experiment I described earlier on retrograde amnesia for extinction that was produced by hypothermia (Figure 11.15). These rats received the hypothermia treatment after extinction. Therefore, their memory of extinction may have been encoded in the context of a low body temperature. If that is true, then the memory of extinction should be reactivated if the rats again receive the hypothermia treatment.

Briggs and Riccio (2007) repeated the experiment I described earlier, but this time they added three groups whose body temperatures were recooled for the memory test.

FIGURE 11.16 Time for rats to enter the black compartment of a shuttle box after having been shocked there. The first group received only conditioning. The second group received extinction after the conditioning trial. The remaining groups received a hypothermia treatment right after extinction and were tested the next day. Group Exp/Hypo was tested without being recooled. Groups Recool 30, Recool 33, and Recool 37 were recooled before the memory test and were allowed to warm up to body temperatures of 30, 33, and 37°C for the test session (based on Briggs & Riccio, 2007, Figure 2, p. 136).

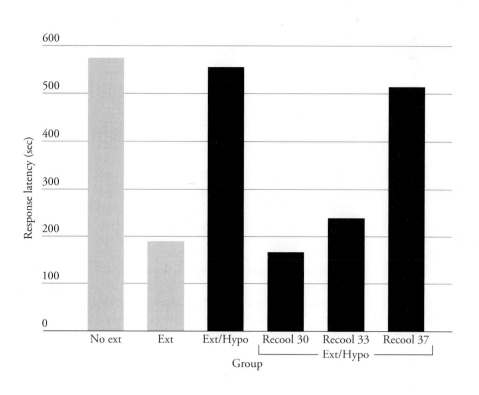

The results for these groups are summarized in Figure 11.16. Recall that the rats were first conditioned to avoid stepping into the black compartment. They then received a session of extinction followed by a memory test the next day. The first two groups in Figure 11.16 (No Ext and Ext) received the same procedures as in the first experiment without hypothermia and yielded the same results: great reluctance to enter the black compartment in the No Ext group and more rapid entry in the Ext group. All of the other groups received hypothermia right after the extinction treatment, which should have caused amnesia for extinction. That was the outcome in the Ext/Hypo group, which was tested the day after hypothermia at normal body temperature.

The next three groups in Figure 11.16 were given the same hypothermia treatment just before the memory test that they received after the extinction and were then tested at different points as their bodies warmed up. The normal body temperature for a rat is 37°C. The first of the recooled groups (Recool 30) was tested when its body temperature was 30°C, which is still pretty cold. This reactivated the memory of extinction, and these rats showed rapid entry into the black compartment. The next group (Recool 33) was allowed to warm up to 33°C after recooling and also showed some evidence of extinction. The final group (Recool 37) was allowed to warm up to normal body temperature (37°C) after recooling. This group showed no evidence of the memory of extinction.

These results show that amnesia caused by hypothermia can be reversed by returning the subjects to the body temperature they had right after the extinction procedure. Thus, in this case, the amnesic treatment did not disrupt consolidation of the memory of extinction. Rather, cues provided by hypothermia became incorporated into the extinction memory so that extinction performance was only evident when these cues were available during the memory test. The implication of this type of experiment is that retrograde amnesia after a car accident might also be overcome by reenacting many of the elements of the accident.

Consolidation, Reconsolidation, and Memory Updating

Although scientists have debated for decades whether retrograde amnesia is a failure of consolidation or a failure of retrieval, the fundamental concept of memory consolidation is firmly established in memory research. The centrality of the concept of consolidation is rooted in the fact that amnesic agents or physiological manipulations are effective in disrupting memory only during a limited period after that memory has been activated. After this period of vulnerability (the consolidation window) has ended, the memory becomes immune to disruption or modification. Consolidation remains the dominant concept to explain this shift in the modifiability of memory.

A great deal of progress has been made in elucidating the neural mechanisms of memory consolidation. These investigations have identified several forms of consolidation that may be roughly separated into two categories. *Synaptic consolidation* refers to changes in synaptic efficacy that presumably underlie learning. Synaptic consolidation is a fairly rapid process, occurring on a time scale of minutes and involves changes at the cellular and molecular level, including the synthesis of new proteins (e.g., Hernandez & Abel, 2008). Memory also becomes consolidated in changes at the level of neural circuits and neural systems. This process is called *systems consolidation* and involves changes in how memory is represented in hippocampal or cortical circuits (e.g., McKenzie & Eichenbaum, 2011). Systems consolidation is a much slower process than synaptic consolidation and can take days or weeks.

Reconsolidation

Research on consolidation has focused not only on how memories are initially established but also how memories may be updated. Interest in the updating of memories was encouraged by experiments showing that retrograde amnesia occurs not only with memories that are learned the first time but also with previously learned memories that have become reactivated. Experiments have shown that a reactivated memory is just as unstable and is just as susceptible to disruptions by amnesic agents as a newly learned memory. This phenomenon was discovered nearly 50 years ago (Misanin, Miller, & Lewis, 1968; Schneider & Sherman, 1968) but was reintroduced to the neuroscience community more recently by Karim Nader and his colleagues (Nader, Schafe, & LeDoux, 2000).

The tremendous advances that have been made in sophisticated neuroscience techniques have stimulated extensive investigations of the neural mechanisms of reconsolidation. The results of these studies have encouraged the conclusion that consolidation and **reconsolidation** fundamentally involve the same processes (McKenzie & Eichenbaum, 2011; Nader & Hardt, 2009). This conclusion has broad implications for how we think about the formation and maintenance of memories. In fact, the claim that reconsolidation is the same as original consolidation is revolutionizing our basic conceptions of memory.

The contrast between the traditional and contemporary views of memory processes is illustrated in Figure 11.17. The traditional view made a distinction between short-term and long-term memories (STM and LTM). Initially, information was assumed to enter the short-term memory state. Information in short-term memory was assumed to be lost unless it was successfully consolidated, which moved the memory to a long-term state. Once in the long-term state, the memory could be reactivated and returned to the short-term state. However, long-term memory was considered to be a type of "read-only" memory. It was like a read-only PDF file. You can access such files and read some or all of them. But you cannot modify them, and thoughts or reactions you have to them do not become a part of the file once you close it.

The contemporary view of memory processes also distinguishes between two memory states, but it calls these "active" and "inactive" forms of memory. These terms are preferred so that one does not have to worry about how brief "short" is and when "short" becomes "long." The critical issue is not the duration of these

FIGURE 11.17
Contrasting views of memory storage and recall. In the traditional view, information first entered short-term memory (STM) and was then consolidated for transfer to long-term memory (LTM). Memory activation served to return the information to short-term memory but did not change the memory. In the contemporary view, memory is either in an active or inactive state. Active memories can always be consolidated for transfer to the inactive state, whether the information is in the active state because of original learning or because of the activation of an old memory.

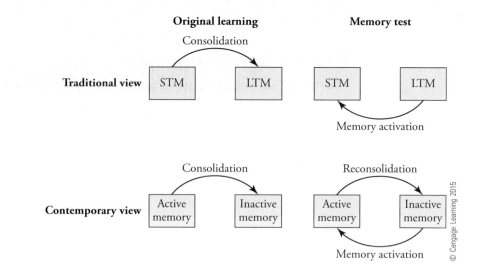

memory states but whether the memory is active or inactive. If a memory is in the active state, then it is assumed to be unstable and potentially modifiable. In contrast, if the memory is inactive, then it is not subject to modification. Another way to think about this is that an active memory is in the consolidation window, whereas an inactive memory is not.

A second important feature of the contemporary view is that the only way to move information from the active to the inactive state is through the process of consolidation. If the active memory was recently acquired, this shift to an inactive state will be the first time the memory is consolidated. If the memory is in the active state because it was previously learned and is now reactivated, then return to the inactive state will involve the process of reconsolidation. This means that reactivated memories are not read-only memories. Rather, activation of a memory returns it to a state in which it can be modified by current thoughts and experiences. Given that memories are reconsolidated after each recollection, the cumulative effect of these reconsolidations can substantially modify the original memory. According to this view, there is no permanent record or read-only PDF file of the original experience.

The contemporary view suggests that no matter how well a memory may have been consolidated originally, with repeated recollections all we have are the various altered versions of that original memory. There is no permanent record or pure undistorted memory. Although this may be a bit disturbing to contemplate, there are two advantages. First, memories can be updated so that they are responsive to new information. In fact, such updates allow for improvements in performance with repeated practice. Second, reconsolidation can serve to strengthen memories and may allow for the priming effect that we described earlier in this chapter.

The contemporary view is consistent with recent neuroimaging data that indicate that similar neural circuits are involved in the original learning of a task and the recollection of that task (Danker & Anderson, 2010). Another major advantage of the contemporary view is that it provides a neurobiological foundation for understanding numerous well-documented instances of false and distorted memories in research with human participants (Hardt, Einarsson, & Nader, 2010). If reactivated memories have to be reconsolidated each time before they return to an inactive state, then it is easy to understand how memories can be significantly altered by new information that is encountered during a recollection. Evidently, when we recall something we are not accessing what we originally experienced but how we previously remembered that experience.

Concluding Comments

The study of memory processes is central to the understanding of comparative cognition. Memory processes involve (1) acquisition and coding of information, (2) rehearsal and retention, and (3) retrieval. Difficulties in any of these phases, or problems involving interactions among them, can result in failures of memory, or forgetting. Several ingenious techniques for the study of memory processes in animals have been developed in the past 40 years. These techniques have told us much about the coding of information, rehearsal processes, and retrieval processes. This information has, in turn, allowed us to better understand failures of memory that occur in interference paradigms and in retrograde amnesia. Contemporary research has also substantially changed our conception of memory from a read-only type of process to an active process that involves continual updates and modifications of memories.

Sample Questions

1. Compare and contrast working and reference memory.
2. Describe the delayed matching-to-sample procedure and alternative strategies that can be used to respond accurately in such a procedure. How can these response strategies be distinguished experimentally?
3. Describe spatial learning tasks and mechanisms that have been used to explain efficient performance in such situations.
4. Describe how retrospective and prospective coding can be differentiated experimentally.
5. Describe the phenomenon of directed forgetting and what it tells us about memory processes.
6. Describe the memory consolidation and retrieval failure explanations of retrograde amnesia and what evidence can be used to support one or the other hypothesis.
7. Compare and contrast traditional and contemporary views of memory storage and recall and the implications of these views for the accuracy of recollections.

Key Terms

acquisition The initial stage of information processing in which something is learned for the first time.

amnesia Loss of memory. (See also *retrograde amnesia*.)

anthropomorphism Interpretation of complex behavior in nonhuman animals based on the assumption that these animals have the same thoughts, emotions, and intentions as people might have under similar circumstances. Anthropomorphic explanations hamper understanding because they overemphasize conscious human experience and are often accepted without experimental proof.

cognitive ethology A branch of ethology that assumes that consciousness, awareness, and intentionality can be inferred from the complexity, flexibility, and cleverness of certain forms of behavior.

comparative cognition Theoretical constructs and models used to explain aspects of behavior in various animal species that cannot be readily characterized in terms of simple S–R mechanisms. These mechanisms do not presume the existence of consciousness, awareness, or intentionality.

consolidation window A limited period after the activation of a memory during which the memory is subject to modification by new information or neural or pharmacological interventions.

delayed-matching-to-sample procedure A procedure in which participants are reinforced for selecting a test stimulus that is the same as a sample stimulus that was presented at the start of the trial some time earlier.

directed forgetting Forgetting that occurs because of a stimulus (a forget cue) that indicates that working memory will not be tested on that trial. Directed forgetting is of interest because it is an example of the stimulus control of memory.

episodic memory Memory for a specific event or episode that includes information about what occurred and when and where the event took place, as contrasted with memory for general facts or ways of doing things.

forgetting Failure to remember previously acquired information because the information is no longer stored in the nervous system.

memory A term used to characterize instances in which an organism's current behavior is determined by some aspect of its previous experience.

memory consolidation The establishment of a memory in a relatively permanent form or the transfer of information from an active or short-term state to an inactive or long-term state.

memory failure The inability to accurately recall something from memory. Memory failure can occur because the information was never acquired in the first place (acquisition deficit), because it was lost during the retention interval (retention deficit or forgetting), or because it cannot be retrieved (retrieval deficit).

mental time travel The ability to project one's experience into the future (prospection) or the past (retrospection).

proactive interference Disruption of memory caused by exposure to stimuli before the event to be remembered.

procedural memory Memory for learned behavioral and cognitive skills that are performed automatically, without the requirement of conscious control, often reflecting knowledge about invariant relationships in the environment, such as CS–US contiguity (classical conditioning) or response–reinforcer contiguity (instrumental conditioning).

prospection   Same as *prospective coding.*

prospective coding   Memory code for an expected future event or response.

reconsolidation   The process of stabilizing or consolidating a reactivated memory. The disruption of this reconsolidation can lead to the modification or loss of the original memory.

reference memory   Long-term retention of background information necessary for successful use of incoming and recently acquired information. (Compare with *working memory.*)

rehearsal   Maintaining information in an active state, available to influence behavior or influence the processing of other information.

retention interval   The time between acquisition of information and a test of memory for that information.

retrieval   The recovery of information from a memory store.

retrieval cues   Stimuli related to an experience that facilitate the recall of other information related to that experience.

retrieval failure   A deficit in recovering information from a memory store.

retroactive interference   Disruption of memory caused by exposure to stimuli following the event to be remembered.

retrograde amnesia   A gradient of memory loss going back in time from the occurrence of brain injury or disturbance of the nervous system. Amnesia is greatest for events that took place closest to the time of injury and less for events experienced earlier.

retrospection   Same as *retrospective coding.*

retrospective coding   Memory code for a previously experienced event or response. Also called *retrospection.*

stimulus coding   How a stimulus is represented in memory.

trials-unique procedure   A matching-to-sample procedure in which different sample and comparison stimuli are used on each trial.

working memory   Temporary retention of information that is needed for successful responding on the task at hand but not on subsequent (or previous) similar tasks. (Compare with *reference memory.*)

CHAPTER **12**

Comparative Cognition II: Special Topics

Food Caching and Recovery

Spatial Memory in Food Caching and Recovery

Episodic Memory in Food Caching and Recovery

Timing

Techniques for Studying the Temporal Control of Behavior

Properties of Temporally Controlled Behavior

Models of Timing

Serial Order Learning

Possible Bases of Serial Order Performance

Techniques for the Study of Serial Order Learning

Categorization and Concept Learning

Perceptual Concept Learning

Learning Higher-Level Concepts

Learning Abstract Concepts

Tool Use in Nonhuman Animals

Language Learning in Nonhuman Animals

Early Attempts at Language Training

Language Training Procedures

Components of Linguistic Skill

Evidence of "Grammar" in Great Apes

Sample Questions

Key Terms

CHAPTER PREVIEW

The final chapter explores a diversity of contemporary research areas in comparative cognition. We begin with research on the remarkable ability of some bird species to retrieve food that they previously stored in various locations. Studies of food caching are a major source of information about spatial memory and episodic memory in nonhuman species. We next turn to how behavior can become organized in time, a ubiquitous feature of the environment, and how organisms learn about the serial order of stimuli, which is a prerequisite for numerical skill. Research on categorization and concept learning in nonhuman species is described next. This rich area of research ranges from studies of perceptual concepts to studies of higher level and abstract concepts, all of which are required for language. I then describe research on tool use, with emphasis on recent research on tool use in New Caledonian crows. The chapter concludes with what may be the most complex of cognitive behaviors, language. As we will see, language is actually a collection of cognitive skills, some of which are clearly evident in a number of nonhuman species.

The various aspects of behavior discussed in this chapter are not all reflections of a common underlying mechanism, nor are they all involved in the solution of a common behavioral problem or challenge to survival. Rather, they involve major contemporary areas of research in animal cognition that have stimulated a great deal of interest. The cognitive processes involved in these phenomena were originally considered to be characteristic primarily of human behavior. In addition, each of these areas of research has stimulated considerable controversy.

The controversies have centered on whether complex cognitive processes have to be postulated to explain the various skills that investigators have uncovered in birds and mammals. Opponents of cognitive interpretations have argued that the phenomena could be explained by traditional forms of associative learning. By contrast, proponents of cognitive interpretations have argued that cognitive mechanisms provide simpler explanations for the phenomena and are more productive in stimulating new research. The work in this area has amply borne out this latter justification. Without a cognitive perspective, much of the research described in this chapter would not have been done, and many of the phenomena would never have been discovered.

The phenomena described in this chapter are just examples of prominent areas of contemporary research in comparative cognition. In fact, one of the major challenges in summarizing recent developments has been to select among the numerous topics that are currently under investigation. Many important topics such as attention, causal reasoning, observational learning, social intelligence, and metacognition had to be omitted in the interest of space. For more comprehensive discussions of comparative cognition, see Shettleworth (2010) and Zentall and Wasserman (2012).

Food Caching and Recovery

We begin with research on food caching and recovery. Numerous avian and mammalian species store food in various places during times of plenty and visit these caches later to recover the stored food items (e.g., De Kort et al., 2012; Kamil & Gould, 2008; Sherry, 1985). One remarkable example of cache recovery is provided by the Clark's nutcracker (*Nucifraga columbiana*) (Balda & Turek, 1984; Kamil & Balda, 1990). These birds live in alpine areas of the western United States and harvest seeds from pine cones in late summer and early autumn. They hide the seeds in underground caches and recover them months later in the winter and spring when other food sources are scarce. A nutcracker may store as many as 33,000 seeds in caches of four or five seeds each and recover several thousand of these during the next winter.

Caching behavior is related to ecological factors and varies considerably among species and within different populations of the same species. Pravosudov and Clayton (2002), for example, compared food caching and recovery in two populations of black-capped chickadees (*Poecile atricapilla*): those living in Colorado and those living in Alaska. Although both environments have harsh winters, the weather in Alaska is more challenging. Chickadees from both populations were brought into the laboratory and tested under common conditions. The Alaska chickadees stored more food items and were more efficient in their cache recovery. They also performed better on a noncaching spatial memory task but were not better than the Colorado chickadees on a nonspatial learning task.

Food caching and recovery involves many different factors. First, you have to decide what food items to cache. Storing perishable foods is not useful unless you intend to recover them soon. Nonperishable items will remain edible over a longer storage duration. Then you have to decide where to store the food because the location has to be recalled at the time of recovery. Caching also involves a social component: Storing food is only useful if you, rather than a competitor, get to eat what you stored. The decision of whether or not to cache can be influenced by the presence of a competitor who might steal the food (Dally, Emery, & Clayton, 2006). The cache location chosen may also depend on how easy that location is for competitors to find.

Similar issues arise at the time of recovery. You have to decide where to look for stored food, whether to look in the presence of a competitor, which foods to retrieve first, and whether to eat what you recover or store it someplace else. Given the species differences that exist in food-caching behavior and the complexity of the processes involved, many different types of questions can be examined using this behavior system. Therefore, food caching and recovery has become a rich source of information about comparative cognition (De Kort et al., 2012; Kamil & Gould, 2008).

Spatial Memory in Food Caching and Recovery

Laboratory studies of cache recovery are typically designed to isolate one or two variables to permit close examination of how those variables contribute to food caching and recovery. Numerous studies have focused on questions related to spatial learning and spatial memory (e.g., Kamil & Gould, 2008). The theoretical ideas and experimental controls required to study spatial memory in food caching and recovery are similar to those I discussed in Chapter 11 for other forms of spatial memory. Before one can accept the conclusion that memory for specific spatial locations is involved, other possibilities have to be ruled out.

One possibility is that birds find caches by searching randomly among possible cache sites. Another possibility is that they store food only in particular types of locations and then go back to these favored places to recover the food items without specifically remembering that they had put food there. They may also mark food-storage sites somehow and then look for these markings when it comes time to recover the food. Yet another possibility is that they are able to smell or see the stored food and identify caches by smell.

Ruling out nonmemory interpretations has required carefully controlled laboratory experiments (e.g., Kamil & Balda, 1990; Sherry, 1984; Sherry, Krebs, & Cowie, 1981; Shettleworth & Krebs, 1986). In one such laboratory study, for example, Kamil and Balda (1985) tested Clark's nutcrackers in a room that had a special floor with 180 recessed cups of sand (see left panel of Figure 12.1). After habituation to the experimental situation and while they were hungry, the birds were given three sessions during which they could store pinyon pine seeds in the sand cups. During each caching session, only 18 cups were available; the rest of the cups were covered with lids. This procedure forced the birds to store food in cups selected at random by the experimenter rather than in cups or locations the birds might have found especially attractive.

Starting 10 days after the seeds had been stored by the nutcrackers, four recovery sessions were conducted on successive days. During recovery sessions none of the 180 sand cups was covered with a lid, but seeds were located only in the cups where the birds had previously stored seeds. The results are summarized on the right side of Figure 12.1. Notice that, on average, the birds performed much better than chance in going to the cups where they had previously stored food. The correct locations could not be identified by disturbed sand because the experimenters raked the sand smooth at the start of each recovery session. Other tests showed that the correct locations were not identified by the smell of the seeds buried in the sand because the birds visited places where they had previously stored food even if the experimenter removed the food before the test session. These control studies indicate that cache recovery reflects spatial memory. In other experiments, Balda and Kamil (1992) found that memory of nutcrackers for

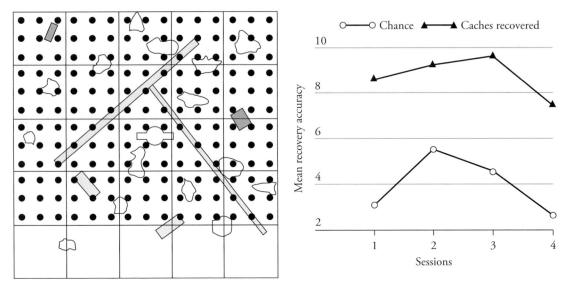

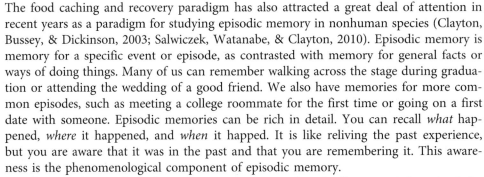

FIGURE 12.1 Left panel: Floor plan of the apparatus used by Kamil and Balda (1985) to test the spatial memory of Clark's nutcrackers. Filled circles represent sand cups. Other symbols represent rocks, logs, and a feeder in the middle. Right panel: Recovery accuracy, compared to chance, during four successive recovery sessions started 10 days after the birds stored pine seeds (after Kamil & Balda, 1985).

the spatial location of cached food lasts as long as 285 days (the longest retention interval tested).

Episodic Memory in Food Caching and Recovery

N. S. Clayton

The food caching and recovery paradigm has also attracted a great deal of attention in recent years as a paradigm for studying episodic memory in nonhuman species (Clayton, Bussey, & Dickinson, 2003; Salwiczek, Watanabe, & Clayton, 2010). Episodic memory is memory for a specific event or episode, as contrasted with memory for general facts or ways of doing things. Many of us can remember walking across the stage during graduation or attending the wedding of a good friend. We also have memories for more common episodes, such as meeting a college roommate for the first time or going on a first date with someone. Episodic memories can be rich in detail. You can recall *what* happened, *where* it happened, and *when* it happed. It is like reliving the past experience, but you are aware that it was in the past and that you are remembering it. This awareness is the phenomenological component of episodic memory.

Comparative psychologists were energized to study episodic memory in animals by claims that episodic memory is a uniquely human trait (e.g., Tulving, 1983). Starting with Darwin, the claim that something is uniquely human has been a *call to arms* for scientists studying comparative cognition—or at least it has been a call to examine the claim with ingenious experiments with nonhuman species. It is unlikely that scientists will ever find ways to establish that nonhuman species experience the phenomenological aspect of episodic memory (the feelings of remembering). However, science can establish whether nonhuman species exhibit the other features of episodic memory. What are those other features?

Clayton, Bussey, and Dickinson (2003) have argued that episodic memory in nonhuman species has to have certain *content*. More specifically, the memory has to include information about *what* happened, *when* it happened, and *where* it happened. Furthermore, the what, when, and where information has to be *integrated* into a coherent

A. Dickinson

representation rather than being independent bits of information. Finally, this integrated representation of the past episode has to be available for *flexible use* in dealing with new problems. Given the complexity of these issues, it is not surprising that there have been debates about the criteria for episodic memory and whether any of the available evidence satisfactorily meets these criteria (e.g., Roberts, 2002; Zentall, 2005). However, studies employing the food caching and recovery paradigm provide some of the best evidence to date on episodic memory in nonhuman species (Salwiczek, Watanabe, & Clayton, 2010). (For related studies with rats and rhesus monkeys, see Crystal, 2010; Hoffman, Beran, & Washburn, 2009).

The western scrub jay is an ideal species for studying questions related to episodic memory because it caches both perishable and nonperishable food, engages in caching behavior all year round, and readily performs these activities in the laboratory. How might one take advantage of these traits to study episodic memory? If you store several different food items in a number of places, why should you care about which type of food is stored where? If you find all of the food items equally acceptable, then there is no reason to keep track of where specific foods were stored. However, if you prefer one food over another, then knowing the location of each type of food will be useful because you can retrieve the more preferred items first. Thus, by varying the palatability of the food, one can examine memory for *what* was stored *where*. Remembering *when* the food was stored becomes important if the food item is perishable because perishable foods are not worth retrieving if a long time has passed and the item is no longer good to eat.

Western scrub jays prefer to eat worms over peanuts. However, worms are perishable and deteriorate if they are stored a long time. Clayton and Dickinson (1999) first gave jays practice trials in which they were allowed to store worms and peanuts in the compartments of an ice cube tray (Figure 12.2). A different tray was used for each type of food. The trays were made distinctive by placing different objects around them. To permit hiding the foods, the compartments of each ice tray were filled with sand. Each trial consisted of two storage or caching episodes (one for peanuts and the other for worms, in a counterbalanced order). A recovery period was then conducted 4 hours or 124 hours later with both food trays available (Figure 12.3). On training trials with a 4-hour retention interval, neither food deteriorated by the time the recovery or choice test occurred. In contrast, on trials with the 124-hour retention interval, the worms were in pretty bad shape by the time of recovery.

As training progressed, the birds learned to select the worms during the recovery period if recovery was scheduled 4 hours after caching. If recovery occurred 124 hours after caching, the birds selected the peanuts instead. However, this behavior could have been cued by the sight or smell of the peanut and worm caches during the recovery

FIGURE 12.2 Food caching by a western scrub jay. Food items were cached in compartments of an ice cube tray filled with sand. One tray was used for caching worms; another was used to cache peanuts. To make the trays distinctive, each tray was located near a distinctive set of Legos.

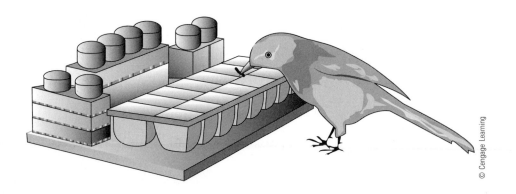

FIGURE 12.3 Procedure used to train scrub jays to remember what, where, and when they stored worms and peanuts (based on Clayton & Dickinson, 1999).

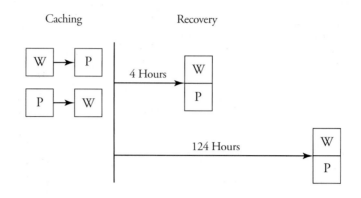

period. To prevent responding on the basis of visual or olfactory cues, test trials were conducted at the end of the experiment during which fresh sand was put in the trays and all food was removed. The results of those test trials are summarized in Figure 12.4. Data for the scrub jays that learned that worms deteriorate if stored for 124 hours are presented in the left panel. (This was the *deteriorate* group.) As expected, these birds searched more in the worm tray than the peanut tray if the choice test occurred 4 hours after caching. In contrast, they searched more in the peanut tray than in the worm tray if the worms had been stored 124 hours earlier.

The right panel shows the results for a second group of jays (*replenish*) that received a different training history. For the *replenish* group, fresh worms were always provided during the recovery or choice periods of the training trials. Therefore, these birds did not get a chance to learn that worms deteriorate with time. Consistent with their training history, the *replenish* group showed a preference for worms whether the worms had been stored 4 or 124 hours before the recovery or choice period.

The scrub jays in the Clayton and Dickinson study could not have located the compartments in which food had been stored if they did not remember *where* they had

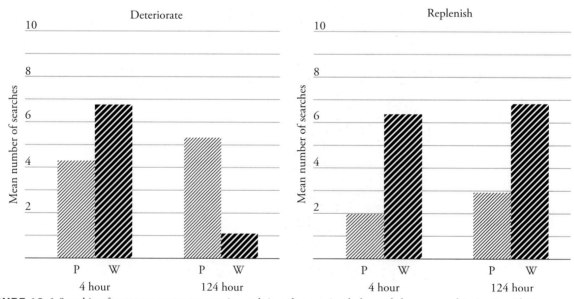

FIGURE 12.4 Searching for worms versus peanuts in scrub jays that previously learned that worms deteriorate with time (*deteriorate* group, left panel) and scrub jays for which worms were always replenished during training (*replenish* group, right panel). The choice tests were conducted 4 or 124 hours after the caching of worms (based on Clayton & Dickinson, 1999).

stored the food items. The fact that the birds distinguished between the worm and peanut storage sites indicates that they remembered *what* type of food was stored in each site. The fact that the *deteriorate* group changed its choice depending on how long ago the worms had been stored indicates that they also remember *when* the food had been stored. Thus, these results indicate that scrub jays are able to remember *what*, *where*, and *when* they stored particular food items.

Some have argued that loss of preference for the cached worms following a 124-hour retention interval in the *deteriorate* group reflects decay of memory for the worms rather than knowledge of *when* the caching took place. To answer this criticism, de Kort, Dickinson, and Clayton (2005) conducted an experiment in which the quality of the worms improved as a function of time. This is analogous to fruit ripening and getting better with longer retention intervals. The jays in this experiment received training trials involving caching worms and peanuts, followed by retrieval opportunities 4 or 28 hours later. The quality of the peanuts remained the same regardless of the retention interval, but the experimenters put better worms in the cache sites at the 28-hour retention interval than at the 4-hour retention interval. Under these circumstances, the jays preferred peanuts at the short retention interval and worms at the longer interval. (For other studies of the structure and flexibility of memory for caching episodes, see Salwiczek, Watanabe, & Clayton, 2010.)

Studies with food-storing birds have provided a great deal of information about episodic-like features of memory in a nonhuman species. It is unlikely that these results reflect specializations of the food caching and recovery system. Indeed, studies with rats and monkeys that were inspired by the scrub jay experiments have shown memory for what, when, and where in these mammalian species as well (Crystal, 2010; Hoffman et al., 2009). In addition, the strategy used in these experiments with nonhuman species can be also extended to examine episodic-like features of memory in human infants who are too young to make verbal reports about what they remember (e.g., Clayton & Russell, 2009; Salwiczek et al., 2010). The scrub jay experiments opened up an exciting new area of research that is challenging the notion that episodic memory is a unique feature of human cognition that depends on language. (For other approaches to the comparative study of episodic memory, see Eichenbaum et al., 2012; Zentall, Singer, & Stagner, 2008.)

Timing

The next topic we turn to is timing. Timing is relevant to virtually all aspects of behavior. Everything occurs across time. Some events occur closely together; others are separated by longer intervals. In either case, the effects of stimuli and events are determined by their durations and distribution in time.

Our earlier discussions of conditioning and learning involved many phenomena that reflect the timing of events. Habituation, sensitization, and spontaneous recovery from habituation (Chapter 2) are all time-dependent effects. Pavlovian conditioning critically depends on the temporal relation between conditioned and unconditioned stimuli (Chapter 3), instrumental conditioning depends on the temporal relation between response and reinforcer (Chapter 5), and some schedules of reinforcement involve important temporal factors (Chapter 6). There are also major time-dependent effects in extinction (Chapter 9), avoidance and punishment (Chapter 10), and memory (Chapter 11).

In the past 40 years, behavioral and cognitive mechanisms responsible for the temporal control of behavior have been the subject of vigorous empirical research and theoretical debate (Church, 2012; Crystal, 2012; Josefowiez & Staddon, 2008; Lejeune & Wearden, 2006). Investigators are also working on identifying the neural circuits involved in timing and are studying how temporal control of behavior is influenced by

Warren Meck

neurotransmitter systems and pharmacological agents (see Buhusi & Meck, 2005; Coull, Cheng, & Meck, 2011; Galtress, Marshall, & Kirkpatrick, 2012).

Time intervals that are significant for biological systems vary a great deal in scale. The 24-hour day–night cycle is one of the most important time cycles for biological systems. Other important time intervals operate on the order of fractions of a second (e.g., different components of the heartbeat). Intervals in the range of seconds (and occasionally minutes) are important in conditioning procedures. Timing on this order, referred to as *interval timing*, has been the focus of learning investigators. (For contrast, see Pizzo & Crystal, 2007, for a study of rats learning to time a two-day interval.)

A critical methodological requirement in studies of timing is to make sure that the passage of time is not correlated with an external stimulus, such as the noise of a clock ticking or the gradual increase in light that occurs as the sun comes up in the morning. Experimental situations have to be set up carefully to eliminate time-related external stimuli that might inadvertently tip off the organism and permit accurate responding without the use of an internal timing process. This methodological requirement is similar to what we encountered in tests for memory. Similar to tests for memory, tests for timing have to be designed to be sure that the behavior is mediated by the internal cognitive process of interest rather than external cues or signals.

Techniques for Studying the Temporal Control of Behavior

Various powerful techniques have been developed to investigate timing in human and nonhuman animals. Some tasks involve **duration estimation**. A duration estimation task is basically a discrimination procedure in which the discriminative stimulus is the duration of an event. One study (Fetterman, 1995), for example, employed a modified matching-to-sample procedure. Pigeons were trained in an experimental chamber that had three pecking keys arranged in a row. The sample stimulus at the start of the trial was an amber light presented on the center key for either 2 seconds or 10 seconds. The sample was followed by illumination of one side key with a red light and the other side key with a green light. If the sample was short (the 2-second stimulus), pecks on the red key were reinforced. If the sample was long (the 10-second stimulus), pecks on the green key were reinforced. Pigeons, rats, and humans can learn to perform accurately in such tasks without too much difficulty. Once the temporal discrimination is well established, one can examine the limits of the discrimination by testing the participants with sample durations that are more similar than the training durations. (For related studies, see de Carvalho & Machado, 2012; Santi, Hoover, & Simmons, 2011).

Another major technique for the study of timing, the **peak procedure**, involves **duration production** instead of duration estimation. Each trial begins with the presentation of a discriminative stimulus—a noise or a light. After a specified time interval, a food pellet is set up, or made ready for delivery. Once the food pellet has been set up, the participant can obtain it by performing a designated instrumental response. Thus, the peak procedure is a discrete-trial variation of a fixed-interval schedule. (Fixed-interval schedules were introduced in Chapter 6.)

A classic study by Roberts (1981) nicely illustrates the use of the peak procedure to investigate timing in laboratory rats. The participants were tested in a standard lever-press chamber housed in a sound-attenuating enclosure to minimize extraneous stimuli. Some trials began with a light; other trials began with a noise. In the presence of the light, food was set up after 20 seconds; in the presence of the noise, food was set up after 40 seconds. Most of the trials ended when the rats responded and obtained the food pellet. However, some of the trials were designated as test trials and continued for 80 seconds or more and ended without food reward. These extra-long trials were

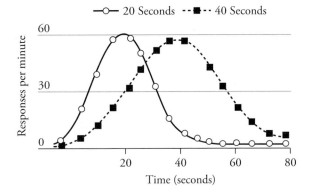

FIGURE 12.5 Rate of responding at various times during nonreinforced test trials. During training, food became available for delivery after 20 seconds in the presence of one stimulus (solid line) and after 40 seconds in the presence of another stimulus (dashed line). (Based on "Isolation of an Internal Clock" by S. Roberts, 1981, *Journal of Experimental Psychology: Animal Behavior Processes, 7*, pp. 242–268.)

included to see how the rats would respond after the usual time of reinforcement had passed.

Figure 12.5 summarizes the results of the experiment in terms of rates of responding at various points during the test trials. During the 20-second signal, the highest rate of responding occurred around 20 seconds into the trial. By contrast, during the 40-second signal, the highest rate of responding occurred around 40 seconds into the trial. The results were remarkably orderly. The peak response rates occurred near the times that food became available during training, with lower response rates evident before and after that point. These features make the peak procedure especially useful in studies of timing. However, it should be noted that results like those shown in Figure 12.5 emerge only after extensive training and are based on averaging together numerous nonreinforced test trials. (For a more detailed analysis, see Balci et al., 2009.)

A variation of the peak procedure that involves less training has become popular in recent years. In this procedure, free food is delivered into a food cup at a fixed time (e.g., 40 seconds) after the start of each trial. The rats learn this predictable interval and check the food cup with increasing frequency as the time for the next food delivery gets closer. (We discussed this type of conditioning in Chapter 3.) Temporal control of behavior is evident in the frequency of head pokes into the food cup rather than lever presses reinforced with food (e.g., Kirkpatrick & Church, 2003). Peak responding again occurs near the time of food delivery.

Properties of Temporally Controlled Behavior

Numerous interesting questions have been examined in efforts to better understand the temporal control of behavior. One important question is whether organisms respond to time intervals in terms of their absolute or relative durations. Consider, for example, distinguishing between 3 and 9 seconds. If we treated the intervals in terms of their absolute values, we would consider 9 seconds to be 6 seconds longer than 3 seconds. In contrast, if we treated the intervals in terms of their relative values, we would consider 9 seconds to be three times as long as 3 seconds. Numerous studies have shown that organisms respond to the relative values of time intervals. Thus, a discrimination between 3 and 9 seconds is similar in difficulty to a discrimination between 9 and 27 seconds. If the relative value of the time intervals is preserved, the tasks are equivalent. The units of a time scale are invariant as long as each unit is the same proportion of the interval being measured. This property is called **scalar invariance**. (For a review of scalar invariance, see Lejeune & Wearden, 2006.)

Let us consider again the results presented in Figure 12.5. As I noted earlier, during one stimulus, responding was reinforced 20 seconds into the trial, whereas during the

FIGURE 12.6 Rate of responding as a function of time during a signal in the presence of which food was set up after 40 seconds. On some trials, the signal was interrupted for a 10-second blackout period (dashed line). On other trials, no blackout occurred (solid line). (Based on "Isolation of an Internal Clock" by S. Roberts, 1981, *Journal of Experimental Psychology: Animal Behavior Processes, 7,* pp. 242–268.)

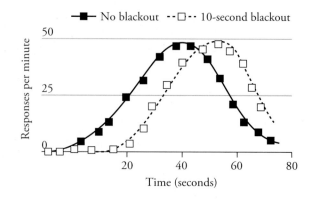

other stimulus, responding was reinforced at 40 seconds. Scalar invariance emphasizes the proportional relation between the 20- and 40-second stimuli. Because the longer stimulus was twice the value of the shorter one, the peak responding occurred at approximately twice the duration for the longer stimulus. In examining Figure 12.5, you will also notice that the 40-second curve was about twice as wide as the 20-second curve. That is another manifestation of scalar invariance. The variability in response rates is proportional to the value of the interval being timed.

Another question investigators have been interested in is what happens when a temporal interval is interrupted. Does the timing process continue during the interruption, or is it also interrupted? Roberts (1981) conducted one of the first experiments that addressed this question. The experimental chamber used was ordinarily dark. Each trial started with the onset of a light, and food was set up 40 seconds after the start of the trial. On special test trials without food reinforcement, the light was turned off for 10 seconds, starting 10 seconds after the start of the trial. Roberts was interested in how the interruption influenced when the rats showed their peak responding.

Figure 12.6 shows the resulting distributions of response rates at various times during trials with and without the 10-second break. Introducing the 10-second break shifted the peak response rate to the right by a bit more than 10 seconds (13.3 seconds, to be exact). These results suggest that the timing process was interrupted when the break was introduced. Some information about elapsed time was lost during the break, but when the light was turned back on, the timing process continued from where it had left off. If the break had reset the timing process to zero, the peak responding would have been shifted to the right by 20 seconds on trials with the break. (For a recent study of gap effects in peak procedure timing, see Swearingen & Buhusi, 2010.)

Models of Timing

What might be the details of a mechanism that permits organisms to respond on the basis of temporal information? This has been one of the thorniest theoretical questions in behavior theory. The question has been vigorously examined and debated for more than 40 years (e.g., Church, 2012; Cheng & Crystal, 2008; Machado, Malheiro, & Erlhagen, 2009). Time is not a physical reality. It is a human invention that helps us characterize certain aspects of our environment. One cannot see a time interval; one can only see the events that start and end the interval. Given that time itself is a conceptual abstraction, models of timing also tend to be fairly abstract.

Scalar Expectancy Theory   The most influential account of timing is an information processing model proposed by Gibbon and Church (1984) known as *scalar expectancy*

FIGURE 12.7

Diagram of scalar expectancy theory of timing. (Based on "Sources of Variance in an Information Processing Theory of Timing" by J. Gibbon and R. M. Church, in H. L. Roitblat, T. G. Bever, & H. S. Terrace (Eds.), 1984, *Animal Cognition.*

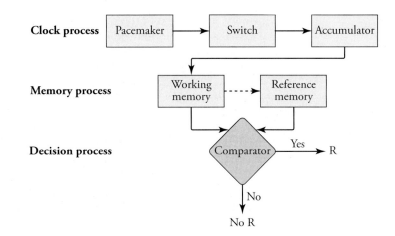

R. M. Church

theory (SET) (see Church, 2003, for a summary). This model has served as the standard against which other models are evaluated. Different components of the model are diagrammed in Figure 12.7, but the model is formally stated in mathematical rather than conceptual terms. A major feature of the model is that it incorporates the property of scalar invariance we discussed earlier. As Figure 12.7 illustrates, the model considers temporally controlled behavior to be the result of three independent processes: a clock process, a memory process, and a decision process.

The clock process provides information about the duration of elapsed time. A key component of the clock process is a pacemaker that generates pulses at a certain rate (something like a metronome). The pacemaker pulses are fed to a switch, which is opened at the start of the interval to be timed. Opening the switch allows the pacemaker pulses to go to an accumulator that counts how many pulses come through. When the interval to be timed ends, the switch closes, thereby blocking any further accumulations of pacemaker pulses. Thus, the accumulator adds up the number of pulses that occurred during the timed interval. The greater the number of accumulated pulses, the longer the interval.

The number of accumulated pulses is then relayed to the memory process. The memory process thereby obtains information about the duration of the current stimulus. This information is stored in working memory. The memory process is also assumed to have information about the duration of similar stimuli in reference memory from past training. The contents of working and reference memory are then compared in the decision process, and this comparison provides the basis for the individual's response. For example, in the peak procedure, if the time information in working memory matches the information in reference memory concerning availability of reinforcement, the decision is to respond. If information in working and reference memory does not match closely enough, the decision is to not respond. This mechanism produces a peak response rate close to the time when reinforcement is set up.

SET has been highly successful in stimulating research and guiding analyses of fine-grained details of timing behavior (e.g., Church, Meck, & Gibbon, 1994). The model has also guided investigations of the neural mechanisms of timing (Buhusi & Meck, 2005) and has been the stepping stone for pocket theory, which spells out in greater detail how the cognitive mechanisms of timing generate specific patterns of responding (Kirkpatrick, 2002; Kirkpatrick & Church, 2003). However, the theory has not been without its critics, and efforts continue to formulate alternatives. Some of these alternatives emphasize behavioral mechanisms that avoid the elaborate cognitive processes of SET

Kim Kirkpatrick

(clock, memory, and decision processes). Others strive to model timing behavior without using a pacemaker or an accumulator. Investigators are examining whether the temporal control of behavior can be the result of biological decay or growth processes or oscillators that do not require accumulating pulses.

Behavioral Theory of Timing   A prominent alternative to the Gibbon–Church information processing model or SET was offered by Killeen and Fetterman (1993; Killeen, Fetterman, & Bizo, 1997; see also Machado, 1997; Arantes & Machado, 2008) who characterized the timing process in more behavioral terms. This behavioral theory of timing (BET) follows the Gibbon–Church model in postulating the existence of a pacemaker. However, the role of the pacemaker in behavioral theory of timing is quite different. Behavioral theory of timing also characterizes the memory and decision processes differently (see Machado et al., 2009).

The behavioral theory of timing is based on the observation that systematic time-related behaviors emerge in situations where the primary basis for the delivery of a reinforcer is the passage of time. These activities are akin to the pacing or finger tapping that people engage in during periods of forced waiting. In experimental situations, these activities have been called **adjunctive behaviors**. Adjunctive behaviors are not specifically required to pass the time but seem to emerge automatically when organisms are forced to wait for something important.

Clear examples of adjunctive behavior are evident in situations in which food is presented periodically at predictable intervals, say every 15 seconds. As I described in Chapter 5 (see discussion of *Skinner's superstition experiment*, pp. 144–145), the feeding system (and its accompanying foraging responses) are activated in food-deprived animals that are given small portions of food at fixed intervals. Behavior under these circumstances reflects preorganized species-typical foraging and feeding activities (Silva & Timberlake, 1998; Silva & Timberlake, 2005). Different behaviors occur depending on when food was last delivered and when food is going to occur again. Just after the delivery of food, the organism is assumed to display *post-food focal search* responses that involve activities near the food cup. In the middle of the interval between food deliveries (when the subjects are least likely to get food), *general search* responses are evident that take the subject away from the food cup. As time for the next food delivery approaches, subjects exhibit *prefood focal search* responses that bring the subject back to the food cup.

The behavioral theory of timing focuses on the successive behavioral states that are activated when food is predictably delivered after a fixed duration of time. Because different responses emerge at different intervals in a forced waiting period, these contrasting responses can be used to tell time. The successive adjunctive responses or behavioral states take on the role of a clock process. According to the behavioral theory of timing, participants in a timing experiment learn to use their temporally organized behavioral states as discriminative stimuli for the experimentally required timing responses. Thus, instead of reading an internal clock, participants are assumed to "read" their adjunctive behavior states to tell time.

An interesting contrast between the information processing theory of timing and the behavioral theory of timing is that one is retrospective whereas the other is prospective. In the information processing model (SET), the decision to respond is made only after the target time interval has elapsed, not in anticipation of that time interval. Thus, SET assumes that timing is entirely retrospective, providing information about the duration of an interval that has been completed. In contrast, the behavioral theory of timing allows animals to anticipate how long an interval will be based on the signal that starts a timing trial. If the interval to be timed is short, behavioral states appropriate to a short interval are activated (involving focal search responses). In contrast, if the interval to be

P. R. Killeen

A. Machado

timed is long, behavioral states appropriate to a long interval are activated (involving general search responses). Thus, the behavior theory of timing operates prospectively, in anticipation of the duration of the interval being timed. Interestingly, recent experimental evidence is consistent with such prospective rather than retrospective mechanisms (Fetterman & Killeen, 2010). (For additional studies of behavioral versus information processing factors in timing, see Galtress, Marshall, & Kirkpatrick, 2012; Jozefowiez, Staddon, & Cerutti, 2009; Machado et al., 2009.)

J. D. Crystal

Oscillators Instead of Pacemakers   A second major alternative approach to SET is based on the idea that temporally organized behavior is mediated by oscillators rather than pacemakers (Crystal, 2012; Cheng & Crystal, 2008; Silver et al., 2011). An oscillator is like a pendulum rather than an hourglass. An oscillator cycles through a predictable sequence of events, over and over again. It goes through repeated cycles that have a fixed period. Different time points are associated with different points in the cycle. Oscillators can operate over a long time scale, such as the rotations of the earth around its axis, which have a periodicity of 24 hours, or the trajectory of the earth around the sun, which has a periodicity of a year. Oscillators can also operate over a short time scale, such as the bouncing of a weight on a spring, which can have a periodicity on the order of a second or less.

Most species show daily variations in activity and body temperature. These are referred to as circadian rhythms. Humans are diurnal and are more active during the day than at night. In contrast, rats are nocturnal and are more active at night than during the day. Such circadian rhythms have been explained using the concept of an oscillator that has the periodicity of about a day. Evidence for such an oscillator is provided by results showing that circadian fluctuations of activity and body temperature persist even if individuals are put in a constant-light environment. Using this strategy, Crystal and Baramidze (2007) demonstrated that the periodicity of food-cup entries generated by delivering food at fixed intervals (e.g., every 48 seconds) persists after the food is no longer provided. Such results are not predicted by SET and suggest that short interval timing is based at least in part on the entrainment of a self-sustaining endogenous oscillator. This raises the possibility that theories of timing employing oscillators can be formulated that will provide an integrated account of timing over a broad range of time intervals (Crystal, 2012).

Serial Order Learning

Time is one ubiquitous characteristic of events in the environment. Another is serial order. Events rarely occur randomly or independently of each other. Rather, many aspects of the environment are organized in orderly sequences. One thing leads to the next in a predictable fashion. Stimuli are arranged in orderly sequences as you walk from one end of a street to the other, as you work to open a package, or as you eat a plate of spaghetti from a full plate initially, to one that is half full, and finally one that is empty. Stimulus order is also very important in language. "The hunters ate the bear" is very different from "The bear ate the hunters." It is also important in dialing a phone number, entering your pin number at an ATM machine, or using a keypad for text messaging. All of these are examples of **serial order performance**. Investigators have been interested in how various species achieve serial order performance, how they form representations of serial order, and how they use those representations in new situations.

Possible Bases of Serial Order Performance

There are several possible ways in which to respond to a series of stimuli. By way of illustration, consider playing through a six-hole miniature golf course, a schematic of

BOX 12.1

Neurobiology of Time

Learning allows us to derive regularities within our environment across space and time, enhancing our capacity to predict the future. For example, by providing an informed guess as to where and when a food may be found, the organism gains an adaptive advantage. While space and time represent the two dimensions over which our lives unfold, we know considerably more about how the brain represents space than how it represents time. In part, this may be because researchers find it easier to study spatial relations—we can "see" the three-dimensional structure of our environment and readily manipulate it. Time, in contrast, has a more intangible quality. It is like air, always present but not immediately perceived.

As we have seen (Box 8.2), researchers have discovered that particular brain regions (e.g., the hippocampus) are especially adept at encoding spatial relations and can do so over a wide range of values, from centimeters to kilometers. In contrast, the processes that underlie the encoding of time are more widely distributed across the central nervous system and the system employed varies with temporal duration (Buhusi & Meck, 2005). Daily rhythms are modulated by a circadian clock that has been linked to neural activity within the suprachiasmatic nucleus. At the other extreme are neural computations that require millisecond-level timing to sequence motor actions and govern the development of synaptic plasticity (e.g., long-term potentiation [Box 8.2]). Timing at the millisecond level requires a local solution and is an inherent feature of neural function. Indeed, timing of this nature does not require a brain; even spinal neurons

are sensitive to temporal relations (Grau et al., 2012).

The idea that the neural mechanisms used to time vary depending upon the nature of the timing task is supported by imaging studies with humans. Using *functional magnetic resonance imaging (fMRI)* (see Box 6.3), researchers have found that timing on the order of milliseconds elicits neural activity within the cerebellum, whereas timing with longer intervals engages a thalamo-cortical-striatal circuit (EP-7 at the back of the book) that includes the basal ganglia, prefrontal cortex, and posterior parietal cortex (Buhusi & Meck, 2005; Coull, Cheng, & Meck, 2011). The basal ganglia represent a group of neural structures that includes the striatum, nucleus accumbens, globus pallidus, substantia nigra, and subthalamic nuclei (EP-7 at the back of the book). It has been suggested that neurons within the striatum monitor activity within the thalamo-cortico-striatal circuit and derive coincident patterns of activity that encode time.

Further evidence for two modes of timing has been derived using a technique known as **transcranial magnetic stimulation (TMS)**. TMS is a noninvasive procedure that can be used to explore brain function in humans. The procedure relies on electromagnetic induction to create a weak electrical current. Placing the inducing current near a particular brain region engages ion flow in the underlying neural tissue, which initiates some action potentials followed by a period of deactivation. The period of deactivation likely reflects the induction of inhibitory neurons and can be used to examine whether a neural region plays an essential role. Using this technique, researchers

have shown that TMS applied over the cerebellar region impairs timing on subsecond, but not suprasecond, tasks. Conversely, when TMS is applied over the right prefrontal cortex, it impairs performance on timing tasks that involve suprasecond durations but not those in the subsecond range.

Further evidence that a thalamo-cortical-striatal circuit is involved in interval timing comes from clinical disorders that affect these neural structures. For example, Parkinson's disorder is associated with a degeneration of function in the basal ganglia, and this is accompanied by a disruption in interval timing. Another disorder that affects timing is schizophrenia, which involves multiple symptoms, including delusions and hallucinations, social withdrawal or lack of motivation, and deficits in working memory and attention. There is a remarkable overlap in the neural structures implicated in timing and schizophrenia. Given this overlap, it is not surprising that patients with schizophrenia exhibit a disruption in timing (Buhusi & Meck, 2005; Coull et al., 2011). Indeed, some psychotic symptoms may arise because patients have difficulty deriving the temporal structure of events, causing a disorientation that could contribute to the breakdown of reality.

Schizophrenia appears to be due, in part, to an increase in how some neurons respond to the transmitter *dopamine*. Neurons that release dopamine project to a region of the basal ganglia (the *striatum*) where they can engage either the D1 or D2 receptor. In schizophrenic patients, dopamine appears to have an exaggerated effect at the D2 receptor and, for this reason, administration of a

Continued

BOX 12.1 (continued)

FIGURE 12.8 Impact of lesioning the caudate putamen on responding with the peak procedure. Prior to lesion (left panel), animals exhibit a distribution of responses that peaks at the expected time of rein-forcement. Lesioning the caudate putamen elimi-nates time-dependent responding (right panel) (adapted from Coull et al., 2011).

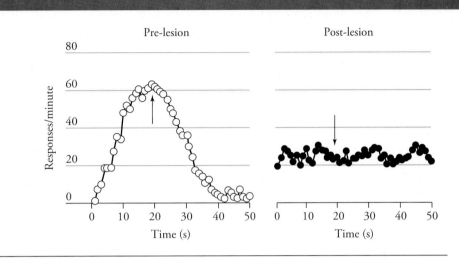

dopamine D2 antagonist (*haloperidol*) attenuates psychotic symptoms. Importantly, haloperidol also improves timing accuracy. Conversely, administration of a dopamine agonist (e.g., methamphetamine) induces a distortion in time and, with continued use, can cause psychotic-like symptoms.

Researchers have studied the neurobiology of interval timing in animals using the peak procedure (Coull et al., 2011). As discussed in the text, this involves training rats to bar-press for food that occurs at a particular temporal interval. On probe trials, subjects exhibit a distri-bution of responding that peaks at the expected time of reward. Administration of a dopamine ago-nist (e.g., amphetamine or cocaine) causes a leftward shift in this func-tion, as if the drug caused the inter-nal clock to speed up. Conversely, administration of a D2 antagonist (haloperidol) causes a rightward shift. In addition, researchers have shown that lesioning the primary source of dopaminergic input to the basal ganglia (from the *caudate putamen*) eliminates the capacity for

timing on the peak procedure (Figure 12.8).

Additional evidence that dopa-mine is involved in timing comes from studies using a transgenic mouse model of schizophrenia (Ward, Kellendonk, Kandel, & Balsam, 2012; Ward, Simpson, Kandel, & Balsam, 2011). To produce hyperreactivity within the dopamine system, Kellendonk and colleagues (2006) placed a copy of the dopamine D2 receptor gene under the control of the tetO promotor (Box 11.1), which could be activated by the chemical tTA. These mice were crossbred with another line that was engineered to express tTA in a tissue-specific manner. The result was a strain of mice (D2OE) that overexpressed the D2 receptor within the striatum at a level that was, fortuitously, equivalent to the 15% enhancement observed in schizophrenic patients. To determine whether the overexpression of the D2 receptor influenced timing, D2OE mice were tested using a temporal bisection procedure in which the duration of a signal (e.g., 2 versus 8 seconds) indicated

whether reinforcement was available for pressing the response lever on the right or the left. When the long cue had a moderate duration (8 seconds), D2 overexpressing mice responded as accurately as the non-transgenic controls. However, when the duration of the long cue was increased to 20 seconds, D2OE mice were much less accurate. This sug-gests a deficit in processing temporal information over longer temporal intervals, which could reflect a problem in working memory or attention.

Temporal behavior has been modeled using operational com-ponents such as a pacemaker, accumulator, and comparator (see Figure 12.7), a framework that implies a kind of localization of function. However, neurobiological studies generally have not supported this view, suggesting instead that interval timing depends upon a dis-tributed circuit and cortical oscilla-tors (Buhusi & Meck, 2005). From this perspective, medium spiny neu-rons within the striatum that receive cortical input encode coincident patterns of activation related to

Continued

temporal intervals. Earlier (Box 7.1) we reviewed electrophysiological studies that showed that neural activity within dopaminergic neurons is regulated by reward expectation (Schultz, 2006). Further work has shown that when the probability of reward is manipulated, these neurons exhibit a burst of activity at trial onset, sustained activity during the trial, and a burst at the expected time of reward. The pulse of dopamine at the start of a to-be-timed interval

could provide a signal that the spiny neurons should start monitoring cyclic cortical input. The second pulse at the time of reward would cause the neurons to store the current pattern of activity, providing a memory of the temporal interval (Ward et al., 2012). An interesting feature of this model is that it relies on a form of spike counting to derive a sense of time. This has led researchers to suggest that the same system may underlie judgments of

numerosity and quantity (Buhusi & Meck, 2005).

J. W. Grau

---

transcranial magnetic stimulation (TMS) A noninvasive experimental procedure wherein magnetic pulses are applied over the skull, producing an electrical current in the underlying neural tissue. The procedure can be used to temporarily disrupt cortical activity.

which is shown to the left in Figure 12.9. Each hole involves a unique set of stimuli and may be represented by letters of the alphabet: A, B, C, D, E, and F. Each hole also requires a unique response, a unique way in which the ball must be hit to get it into the hole. Let's label the responses R1, R2, ... , R6. In playing the course, you have to go in order from the first to the last hole, A → F. In addition, you have to make the correct response on each hole: R1 on hole A, R2 on B, and so on.

How might you learn to play the course successfully? The simplest way would be to learn which response goes with which stimulus. In the presence of A, you would automatically make R1, which would get you to stimulus B; in the presence of B, you would automatically make R2, which would get you to C, and so on. This would be learning a set of S–R associations: A–R1, B–R2, ... , F–R6. Such a mechanism is called a **response chain**. In a response chain, each response produces the stimulus for the next response in the sequence, and correct responses occur because the organism has learned a series of S–R associations.

Although a response chain can result in responding appropriately to a series of stimuli, it does not require actually learning the stimulus sequence or forming a mental representation of the order in which the stimuli or responses occur. Response chains do not require cognitive mechanisms any more complex than S–R associations. A response-chain strategy works perfectly well on the usual miniature golf course because the successive holes are laid out so that one is forced to go through them in the correct sequence, A → F.

FIGURE 12.9 Two possible layouts of a six-hole miniature golf course. A sequential arrangement is shown on the left, and a simultaneous arrangement is shown on the right.

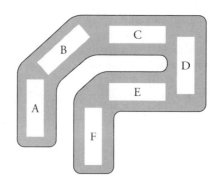

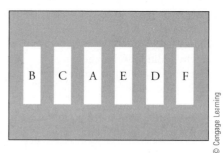

© Cengage Learning

Now, let us consider a course with a different layout, as shown on the right of Figure 12.9. The rules are the same; you again have to play in order from A to F. However, with this course layout you are not forced to go in order from A to F. After having played hole A, for example, your movement would not be restricted to hole B. You could go to any other hole next. To earn points, however, you would still have to play B after having finished with A, and then go to C, then D, and so forth. Learning a series of S–R associations (A–R1, B–R2, and so on) would not be enough to succeed on such a course. Even if someone got you started at A, after playing hole A, you would not know where to go next because you would be confronted with the full array of possibilities, not just hole B.

With the holes laid out as in the right panel of Figure 12.9, you would be forced to learn the required order of the stimuli. You could get by with just knowing the order of successive pairs of stimuli. You could learn that A is followed by B, B is followed by C, and so forth. These would be a set of independent S–S associations (A–B, B–C, C–D, and so on). This type of mechanism is called **paired-associate learning**. Once you know the correct independent paired associates, having played hole A, you would know to go to B; having played B, you would know to go to C; and so on until you had completed the course.

Obviously, learning more than just the order of successive pairs of stimuli would also enable you to perform the task accurately. At the extreme, you might form a mental representation of the entire sequence: A → B → C → D → E → F. This alternative is called **serial-representation learning**. By learning a serial representation of the entire sequence, you would know the ordinal position of each stimulus. You would know that stimulus A is in position 1, B is in position 2, and so forth.

Techniques for the Study of Serial Order Learning

Several different techniques have been developed to study the learning of serial representations in animals. Each of them employs some variation of the altered miniature golf course presented in the right panel of Figure 12.9. The stimuli the participants have to respond to are all available at the same time, just as the numbers on a cell phone. To call someone, you have to enter the numbers in the correct order, but all of the possible numbers are available when each response is made. The keypad does not dictate the order in which the numbers are entered. This type of procedure is called a **simultaneous chain procedure** because it requires a series of responses but all of the response options are always available.

In a method developed by Stephen Fountain, rats are tested in an experimental chamber that is built in the shape of an octagon. Each of the eight walls of the chamber has a response lever, and the rats are reinforced for pressing the levers in an order specified by the experimenter (see Fountain et al., 2012). For example, if the levers are numbered 1 → 8, the specified order of presses may be 123234345456567678.

Courtesy of S. B. Fountain

S. B. Fountain

The method developed by Fountain has been particularly useful for studying how animals process the structure of a stimulus sequence. The above-mentioned sequence (123234345456567678) has an internal structure that consists of three adjacent levers (123, 234, 345, 456, and so on). These three-response units are called *chunks*. In general, sequences that are organized into chunks are learned more easily than ones that do not have any organization (e.g., Brown, 2012). Phone numbers in the United States, for example, have three chunks. The first is a three-digit area code. The second is a three-digit exchange, and the third is a four-digit chunk that is unique to the number being called. Fountain and his colleagues have found that rats readily learn response sequences in the octagonal chamber and show great sensitivity to the internal structure of those sequences. Sequences made up of smaller chunks (like the above example) are

H. S. Terrace

M. Colombo

learned much more easily than sequences that have no structure or sequences in which the internal structure is more complicated. Evidence of the importance of sequence structure has been found in other species as well, including chickens and horses (e.g., Kundey et al., 2010.)

Another widely used method for studying serial order learning was developed by Herbert Terrace and his colleagues and tests responses to a series of visual stimuli (see Terrace, 2012). As the numbers on a cell phone, the visual stimuli are presented all at the same time, but the participants are required to respond to each in a prescribed order by touching the correct stimulus. This method has been particularly useful in studies of comparative cognition because it can be adapted for use with a variety of species. The simultaneous chain procedure has been tested with pigeons, various nonhuman primates, and *Homo sapiens*. These experiments have shown that the learning and representation of serial order is remarkably similar across this broad range of species.

In an effort to specifically compare the performance of college students on a simultaneous chain procedure with that of monkeys, Colombo and Frost (2001) designed their procedures based on the previous studies with Cebus monkeys by D'Amato and Colombo (1988). The research participants had to learn a five-stimulus sequence. The stimuli were icons presented on a touch screen. The icons were either representational or abstract, but that did not influence the results (Figure 12.10). All five icons were presented at the same time at the start of a trial, but the participants had to press them in a set order ($A \rightarrow B \rightarrow C \rightarrow D \rightarrow E$). The position of each icon on the screen changed randomly from one trial to the next. Therefore, the participants could not perform the task by learning a sequence of spatial positions. The task was like having the numbers on your phone replaced by pictures and having the position of each picture change each time you went to dial a new phone number. It turns out that both college students and monkeys can learn this task with sufficient training.

The next question is, how do college students and monkeys represent the stimulus order that they learned? To answer this question, investigators typically examine how participants respond when they are tested with subsets of the original stimuli. Following training with the five-element array, Colombo and Frost (2001) tested the participants with subsets consisting of just two or three elements. Consider, for example, a subset consisting of elements B, D, and E. Keep in mind that these could appear in any position on the screen. If the participants formed a representation of the order of the original five-element series, they would respond to B first, D next, and E last. That would count as a correct response to the subset.

Figure 12.10 shows the results of tests with all possible three-element subsets of the five-element serial order task. Both college students and monkeys responded with a high degree of accuracy on nearly all of the subsets, and responding was always well above chance. This indicates that the participants were not responding on the basis of a chain of S–R or S–S associations. Simple associations would have left the participants in the dark with any subset that did not include stimulus A or had adjacent elements missing.

Further evidence for the learning of a representation of serial order was provided by examining the latency of the first response to three-element subsets (Figure 12.11). If the three-element subset included stimulus A, the participants responded very quickly. Their latency to make the first response was longer if the triplet started with B (BCD, BDE, or BCE), and the longest latencies occurred if the triplet started with C (CDE). Why take longer to get started with triples starting with B or C? Presumably when the participants were tested with a triplet like BDE, they mentally started through the full sequence (ABCDE) and made their first response when they came to B. Their first response was delayed further when they were tested with CDE because it took them longer to reach C in their mental rehearsal of the sequence. Thus, these latency data are predicted by the

Training sequences

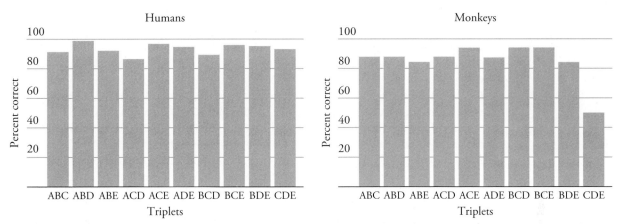

FIGURE 12.10 Examples of stimuli used in training college students to respond on a five-element simultaneous chain, and test data for subsets of three stimuli for college students and Cebus monkeys. Chance responding would have resulted in about 10% correct responses (from "Representation of serial order in humans: A comparison to the findings with monkeys (*Cebus apella*)," by M. Colombo and N. Frost, 2001, *Psychonomic Bulletin & Review*, 8, 262–269).

FIGURE 12.11
Latency to respond to the first item of a three-item test, when the first item was A, B, or C, in college students and Cebus monkeys (from "Representation of serial order in humans: A comparison to the findings with monkeys (*Cebus apella*)," by M. Colombo and N. Frost, 2001, *Psychonomic Bulletin & Review*, 8, 262–269).

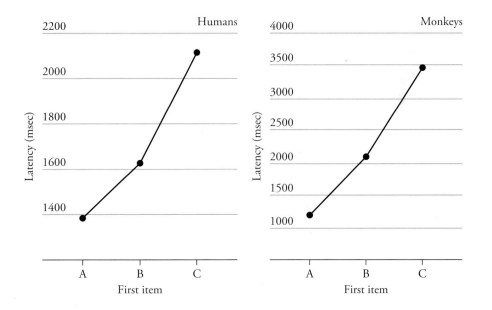

assumption that the participants formed a mental representation of the five-element sequence and rehearsed this when they were tested with the three-element subsets.

Another interesting line of evidence is provided by looking at the latency of the second response to three-element subsets. With some triplets, the second item was adjacent to the first, as in ABD and BCD. In other cases, the second item followed one missing item, as in ACD, and BDE. Finally, sometimes the second item followed two missing items, as in ADE. If the participant was going through the full five-element sequence mentally, the latency of its second response would be greatest with the greatest number of missing items. This is exactly what was found with both college students and Cebus monkeys (Figure 12.12). Taking longer to respond to the next item as a function of the number of missing items is called the *symbolic distance effect*. The symbolic distance effect provides further evidence that the participants learned a representation of the five-element series.

The simultaneous chain procedure has turned out to be a powerful technique for the study of complex cognition in nonverbal organisms. Terrace, Son, and Brannon (2003), for example, taught monkeys to respond to four different seven-element simultaneous chains. These might be represented as A1 → A2 → A3 → … A7, B1 → B2 → B3 → … B7, C1 → C2 → C3 → … C7, and D1 → D2 → D3 … D7. After the monkeys were responding with high levels of accuracy on each seven-element series, tests with various pairs of stimuli were introduced. As one would expect, performance was highly accurate when the two stimuli of a pair come from the same list (e.g., A3A5, or C2C6). Remarkably, the monkeys also responded with about 90% accuracy when the two stimuli of a test pair came from different lists. Consider, for example, test pairs made up of A5C6. The correct response here would be to select A5 first and C6 next. To respond so well on cross-list pairs, the monkeys had to have learned the position of each element in each list and then integrated that knowledge across lists. (For additional studies of serial order learning, see Beran & Parrish, 2012; Koba et al., 2012; Merritt & Terrace, 2011; Scarf & Colombo, 2010).

Study of serial order learning is not only telling us about learning and memory for lists of items. It also opens the window to studying the cognitive foundations of arithmetic (Terrace, 2012). Arithmetic knowledge is built on an abstract serial order that puts one before two, which is before three, and so on. When the monkeys were responding to a specific icon as the fifth in a series, they were essentially telling us that they knew the order of the icons. If those icons had just been Arabic numerals, the participants would have been counting from one to five. Of course, arithmetic involves more than establishing a serial order among arbitrary symbols. Those symbols also refer to different quantities. Exciting new research is ongoing using the simultaneous chain procedure and other techniques to examine how birds and various nonhuman primates learn

Elizabeth Brannon

FIGURE 12.12

Latency to respond to the second item of a three-item test in college students and Cebus monkeys as a function of the number of items missing between the first and second item (from "Representation of serial order in humans: A comparison to the findings with monkeys (*Cebus apella*)," by M. Colombo and N. Frost, 2001, *Psychonomic Bulletin & Review, 8*, 262–269).

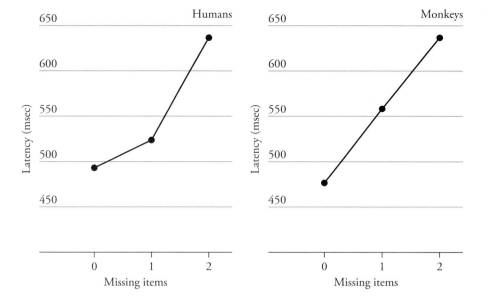

The chimpanzee Lana working on a computer counting task.

quantitative information and quantitative reasoning (e.g., Beran, Evans, & Hoyle, 2011; Harris et al., 2010; Roberts, 2010). This line of research is beginning to reveal the evolutionary origins of human arithmetic skills (Merritt, DeWind, & Brannon, 2012).

Categorization and Concept Learning

Organisms experience a great variety of stimuli during their lifetime. In fact, in the natural environment, no stimulus ever occurs the same way twice. Fortunately, we do not have to respond to each stimulus as an independent and isolated event. Serial pattern learning represents one type of cognitive organization. An even more basic form of cognitive organization involves perceptual concept learning. Stimuli that vary in their physical properties can be grouped together and associated with a single response through categorization or concept learning. Consider, for example, your favorite chair in the living room. Each time you see the chair, the sensory input you get varies depending on the amount of light in the room, whether you are seeing the chair from the front or the back, and how far away it is. Additional variations are provided by whether you are looking at the chair or sitting in it and feeling its firmness and shape. Instead of treating each unique view of the chair as a separate entity, we form a perceptual category that includes all of the different views and treats them as equivalent in identifying a particular chair.

The above example illustrates a basic-level perceptual category. Basic-level perceptual categorization permits us to recognize our car as the same vehicle regardless of our angle of view or how dirty the car might be. It also allows us to recognize a person as being the same individual whether we see him or her from the front, back or side. Categorization can occur at the level of individual objects or people. It can also occur at the level of broader classes of objects. A specific chair can be considered a member of a broader category that includes chairs of all sizes, shapes, and designs. Chairs in turn can be considered as instances of all things that are furniture or all things that are human made. These higher-level categories are more abstract, and there are fewer physical similarities among the members of the category. People also form more abstract categories such as *same* versus *different*. One of the major issues in comparative cognition has been whether nonhuman species are also capable of categorization and concept learning and whether they are capable of learning abstract categories.

Perceptual Concept Learning

Much of the comparative research on categorization has involved demonstrations of perceptual concept learning and explorations of the mechanisms of such learning (e.g., Huber & Aust, 2012; Jitzumori, 2012). What constitutes evidence that a nonverbal organism has learned a perceptual concept? Perceptual categorization represents a balance between stimulus discrimination and stimulus generalization. You recognize your cat as the same animal even though, strictly speaking, the visual image the cat projects on your retina is different every time you see it. However, you distinguish your cat from your neighbor's cat and from your parakeet. As this example illustrates, perceptual concepts have two important and complementary characteristics, *generalization within a category* or set of stimuli and *discrimination between categories* or sets of stimuli.

Early comparative studies of perceptual concept learning employed go/no-go discrimination procedures. For example, Herrnstein, Loveland, and Cable (1976) presented color pictures of various natural scenes as stimuli in a discrimination procedure with pigeons. If the scene included a tree or some part of a tree, the pigeons were reinforced with food for pecking the response key. If the picture did not include a tree (or any part of one), pecking was not reinforced. Each experimental session consisted of 80 slide presentations, about 40 of which included a tree. The stimuli for any given training session were selected from 500–700 pictures depicting various scenes from all four seasons of the year in New England. The pigeons learned the task without much difficulty and pecked at much higher rates in the presence of pictures that included a tree or part of a tree than in the presence of pictures without trees.

Did this discrimination performance reflect the learning of a perceptual concept? An alternative interpretation is that the pigeons memorized what the reinforced and non-reinforced pictures looked like without paying particular attention to the presence or absence of trees. Although this may seem unlikely, pigeons are capable of memorizing more than 800 pictures (e.g., Cook et al., 2005). A common tactic for ruling out the role of memorization of the training stimuli is to test for transfer of performance to stimuli that did not appear during training. Herrnstein and colleagues (1976) did this by presenting a new set of photos at the end of the experiment. The pigeons performed nearly as accurately on the new pictures as on those used during prior training. Such evidence of *generalization to novel exemplars* is critical for demonstrations of perceptual concept learning.

In an interesting recent example, Grainger and colleagues (2012) inquired whether baboons (*Papio papio*) can learn to identify a sequence of four letters as a word in the English language as opposed to just a random collection of letters. English speakers easily distinguish between letter sequences that constitute words or nonwords based on the relative probability of certain letters occurring next to each other in English words. This is called *orthographic* information. Some have suggested that the ability to use orthographic information is a language-specific skill preliminary to reading. If that is true, then baboons who are unfamiliar with the English language should not be able to distinguish English words from nonwords.

Six baboons were tested in the experiment. Each training trial started with the presentation of a four-letter word or nonword (presented in all capital letters). This was followed by two symbols, one associated with word stimuli and other with nonword stimuli. If the baboon selected the symbol associated with the correct category, it was reinforced with a bit of food. Each session consisted of 100 trials. Twenty-five of these were presentations of a novel word to learn, 25 were words previously learned, and 50 trials were nonwords. A specific word reappeared until the participant classified it correctly at least 80% of the time. Nonwords were generated randomly and did not reappear.

The baboons received in excess of 40,000 training trials, and different baboons learned from 81 to 308 words. Accuracy among the baboons on word trials ranged from 73% to 80% (with 50% being chance performance). Correctly identifying nonword trials ranged from 66% to 80%. Thus, the baboons mastered discriminating words from nonwords during training. However, as I noted earlier, the critical evidence is whether the training generalizes to novel instances of the categories "word" and "nonword."

Performance on trials in which the baboons saw the last 50 word and nonword stimuli for the first time is summarized in Figure 12.13. The data in the figure show the percentage of "nonword" responses for each baboon. The baboons were highly accurate in classifying nonword stimuli, responding "nonword" about 80% of the time that such stimuli were first encountered. They were less accurate in identifying word stimuli, but even here they responded to these as nonwords less than 50% of the time. Furthermore, each baboon responded "nonword" less often for word stimuli than for nonword stimuli. These results show that the ability to distinguish words from nonwords generalized to novel examples of each category. Other aspects of the data indicated that the baboons discriminated words from nonwords on the basis of orthographic information or the relative probabilities of various letter combinations in English words.

A great deal of research has been done on the learning of perceptual concepts since this area of research was initiated by Herrnstein and his associates half a century ago. In the tradition set by Herrnstein, much of the research has been done with pigeons categorizing complex visual stimuli. However, as the study of word perception indicates,

FIGURE 12.13 Percent nonword responses among six baboons tested for the first time with four-letter stimuli that were words or nonwords. Each shading pattern represents data for one baboon (based on Grainger et al., 2012).

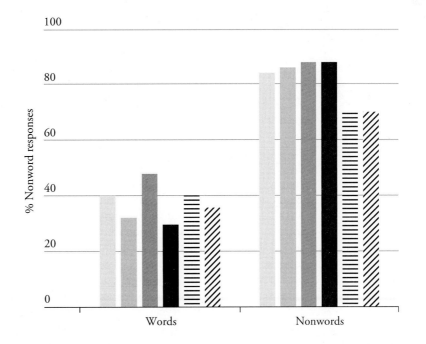

various primates and other species have been also tested. In addition, a large variety of stimulus categories have been examined. Pigeons have been trained to categorize the presence versus absence of water in various forms (lakes, oceans, puddles, and so on), the presence or absence of a particular person (in various types of clothing, in various situations, and engaged in various activities), pictures of male versus female human faces, or pictures of individual pigeons taken from various perspectives (e.g., Aust & Huber, 2003; Loidolt et al., 2006; Nakamura, Croft, & Westbrook, 2003). Pigeons can also categorize stimuli based on their speed of rotation (Cook, Beale, & Koban, 2011).

In all these cases, the participants learned to respond similarly to stimuli belonging to the category in question even though members of the category differed in numerous respects. Perceptual concept learning is a form of stimulus equivalence learning (see Chapter 8, pp. 231–234). Because responding to various examples of the category has the same (or equivalent) reinforcing consequence, participants learn to treat physically different members of the category in the same manner (or equivalently).

Mechanisms of Perceptual Concept Learning Perceptual concept learning is a well-established phenomenon. How animals manage to do this, however, remains a lively topic of debate. The issue is complex because of the complexity of the stimuli that are involved. The pictures that included a tree or a part of a tree in the experiment by Herrnstein and colleagues (1976) differed in numerous respects. What aspect(s) of the tree photographs led the pigeons to classify those photographs differently from the non-tree photographs? Were there specific colors, shapes, or textures in the photographs that were critical, or was it the overall brightness or sharpness of the pictures? Answers to such questions required both technological and theoretical advances.

Progress in categorization research has been facilitated by advances in computer image analysis and image production. Investigators can now examine how organisms learn perceptual categories by using computer-generated images that permit control over specific visual features (e.g., Jitsumori, 2012). Such advances also enable investigators to test participants with systematic variations of natural images to determine what features are related to categorical responding.

Aust and Huber (2003), for example, trained pigeons to discriminate between photographs that included a person and ones that did not have anyone in the natural scene. The pictures were of a wide range of settings, and if they included a person, the person could be of either sex or any race, age, and size, and they could appear anywhere in the picture. After the pigeons learned to categorize the photographs, they were tested with specially altered photos in which the body parts of the people were rearranged in various ways. The types of rearrangements tested are illustrated schematically in Figure 12.14.

The pigeons were less likely to identify a photo as including a person if the person's body parts were rearranged than if that the photo showed the person in a normal configuration. However, responses to these rearranged figures were considerably higher than responses to photos that did not include a person. These findings indicate that the pigeons used the normal relative position of body parts to judge whether an image was that of a person. In addition, the pigeons also used smaller visual features, which remained intact under the various body rearrangements. Attending to those smaller visual features allowed the birds to respond more to the rearranged photos than to photos that did not include a person (for a more detailed discussion, see Huber & Aust, 2012).

Studies in which visual features are systematically modified suggest that perceptual categorization depends on learning about various stimulus elements that members of a category have in common. These common elements create what might be called family

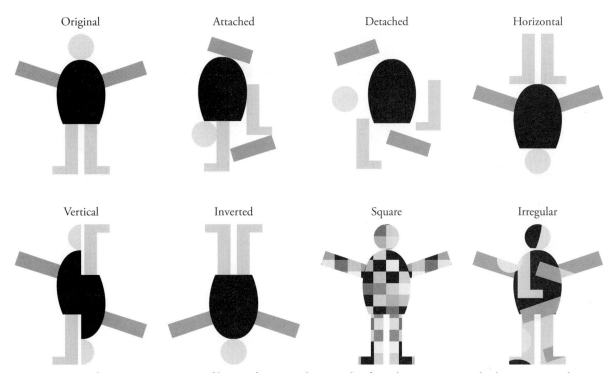

Original	Attached	Detached	Horizontal

Vertical	Inverted	Square	Irregular

FIGURE 12.14 Schematic representation of human figures used in a study of people-present or people-absent perceptual concept learning in pigeons (based on Aust & Huber, 2003). *Original* represents the normal images used in training. All the other cartoons represent rearrangements of a normal image used in testing.

resemblance among the individual members of a perceptual category. The common elements can be a small part of the image (a curve in a line or a patch of color) or more global aspects of the scene (overall brightness or contrast). Early investigators of perceptual concept learning rejected explanations of categorization based on common elements because they had difficulty identifying the shared features or combination of features that created family resemblance among photos of natural scenes that belonged to the same category. However, theories of categorization based on common elements are making a comeback.

This resurgence of interest in the common elements approach is encouraged by results from experiments that use carefully designed test stimuli that have preset statistical properties or stimulus features that have been altered using image morphing, blurring, or other manipulations (e.g., Jitsumori, 2006; Herbranson, Fremouw, & Shimp, 2002; Martin-Malivel et al., 2006). The renewed interest in the common elements approach is also fueled by new theoretical work by Soto and Wasserman (2010, 2012b) that has shown that major phenomena of categorization can be simulated by an error-correction learning model (such as the Rescorla–Wagner model we discussed in Chapter 4) that assumes that members of a perceptual category have a number of shared or common stimulus elements.

The assumption of shared stimulus elements does not require that all members of a category have a critical stimulus feature or combination of features. Rather, as illustrated in Figure 12.15, each exemplar or member of the category may have a different combination of these elements. The theoretical approach developed by Soto and Wasserman is particularly powerful because it does not require identifying the common stimulus elements empirically. Without identifying what those elements may be, the model makes

FIGURE 12.15

Schematic representation of potential common stimulus elements among members of a category. Each row in the top panel represents a member or exemplar of a perceptual category. The 10 circles in each row represent potential stimulus elements or features that exemplars have in common. Whether an exemplar has a particular stimulus feature is indicated by the dark shading of the corresponding circle. The bottom panel shows the probability that a particular stimulus element will appear among all the members of the category (based on Soto & Wasserman, 2010).

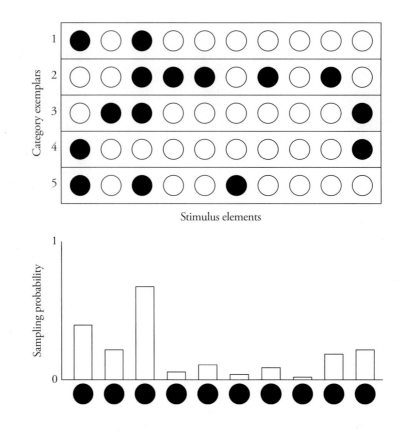

novel predictions about category learning that have been verified by experimental data (e.g., Soto & Wasserman, 2012a).

Learning Higher-Level Concepts

So far we have discussed basic-level perceptual categories that correspond to the naming of objects such as chairs and flowers. Chairs and flowers also may be categorized in terms of a higher level concept: artificial versus natural. Studies with pigeons and other animals have demonstrated higher level categorization (e.g., Roberts & Mazmanian, 1988). In fact, animals can learn to categorize stimuli at both a basic and superordinate level at the same time.

In one study (Lazareva, Freiburger, & Wasserman, 2004), for example, pigeons were trained with pictures of cars, flowers, persons, and chairs. On some trials, four reporting keys were available (one at each corner of the display screen), and each reporting key was assigned to one of the basic-level categories. Responding on the key assigned to cars was reinforced if the picture on that trial showed a car, responding on the chair key was reinforced if the picture on that trial showed chair, and so on.

The basic-level categorization trials were intermixed with superordinate categorization trials. On these trials, two new reporting keys were available (to the left or right of the display screen). Responding on one reporting key was reinforced if the picture on that trial was an artificial object (cars or chairs), and responding on the other key was reinforced if the picture on that trial showed a natural object (a person or a flower).

The pigeons readily learned both the basic and superordinate categories, although learning the category *artificial* took a bit longer than learning the category *natural.* The pigeons continued to respond correctly at both the basic and superordinate levels

when tested with novel pictures of cars, flowers, persons, and chairs. However, their performance on the novel stimulus trials was a bit lower than with the training stimuli. Investigators have yet to explore whether the processes involved in learning superordinate categories are the same as those responsible for basic categories, but a good bet is that general concept learning processes are involved in both cases.

Learning Abstract Concepts

Superordinate categories like *natural* versus *artificial* are fairly abstract but refer to objects in the real world. We also have concepts that do not represent things in the real world. They exist only in our minds. Consider, for example, the concept of *same* versus *different.* These are not attributes of objects in the real world. A chair cannot be described as same or different. These terms refer to a judgment we make in comparing two objects or images. Are nonhuman species capable of learning such abstract concepts?

A great deal of research has been done on how pigeons, various primate species, and other animals learn the concepts *same* and *different* (Cook & Wasserman, 2012). In one approach to same/different learning (e.g., Wright & Katz, 2006, 2007), pigeons, rhesus monkeys, and capuchin monkeys were presented with two pictures on each trial (Figure 12.16). If the two pictures were the same, the participants had to touch or peck the lower picture to obtain food reinforcement. If the two pictures were different, they had to touch or peck a reporting key to the side of the pictures to get reinforced. Training started with a set of eight pictures, but the stimulus set was doubled each time the participants responded correctly about 80% of the time. As in other concept formation studies, learning of the same/different concept was evaluated by testing the participants with novel stimuli.

Performance on the transfer trials improved with increases in the number of pictures used in training. The number of trials required to reach criterion performance also decreased with additions to the training stimuli. The monkeys learned the same/different concept in fewer trials than the pigeons. However, the fact that performance improved for each species with increases in the number of stimuli used suggests that the monkeys and pigeons used similar concept learning mechanisms (see also Wright & Katz, 2007; Wright & Lickteig, 2010). Other studies have indicated that the degree of variability in the objects that appear on a visual display determines whether pigeons respond to visual scenes as being the same or different. Although the degree of stimulus variability is also relevant in human performance, more detailed comparative studies are beginning to reveal some interesting differences in how people and pigeons make same/different judgments (Wasserman & Castro, 2012).

FIGURE 12.16 Diagram of procedure for training a same/different discrimination. On *same* trials, two of the pictures in the stimulus panels are the same and participants are reinforced for touching or pecking the lower panel. On *different* trials, the pictures are different and participants are reinforced for touching or pecking the response button to the right of the pictures. (Photographs rather than drawings were used in the study by Wright and Katz, 2007.)

Same trial

Different trial

Tool Use in Nonhuman Animals

In this section and the next, we turn to two of the most controversial topics in comparative cognition, tool use and language learning in nonhuman animals. Ever since Köhler (1927) observed a chimpanzee putting one box on top of another to reach a piece of food, scientists interested in comparative cognition have been fascinated with tool use in animals. This interest was motivated by the assumption that the construction and use of tools requires complex cognitive processes (e.g., Vaesen, 2012). However, that basic assumption may not apply to all instances of tool use. How animals learn to make and use tools and what behavioral and cognitive processes are responsible for this type of behavior remain major issues in comparative cognition.

Numerous species have been observed to use tools in various ways (e.g., Bentley-Condit & Smith, 2010). Much of the research on nonhuman tool use has been conducted with chimpanzees and other primates (e.g., Boesch & Boesch, 1990; Visalberghi & Fragaszy, 2012). Given all of what we have learned about the cognitive abilities of these species, the fact that they use tools does not greatly challenge our view of them. More provocative are reports of extensive tool use and tool fabrication by various species of birds (Lefebvre, Nicolakakis, & Boire, 2002).

Some of the more provocative examples of tool use involve crows that live on the island of New Caledonia in the western Pacific (*Corvus moneduloides*). New Caledonian crows modify twigs, leaves, cardboard, and feathers to use as tools to obtain food from crevices and other places they cannot reach with their beak. To study tool use in this species more systematically, a colony of these birds was established at Oxford University by Alex Kacelnik and his colleagues (e.g., Bluff et al., 2007; Kacelnik et al., 2006). In one experiment, for example, two wild-caught crows were given access to food placed in a clear horizontal plastic tube that had one end open. The food was positioned at different distances from the opening of the tube, and twigs of different lengths were available for the birds to use to poke out the food (Chappell & Kacelnik, 2002). The crows readily used the twigs that were provided (Figure 12.17). More importantly, they selected twigs of the appropriate length on each trial at a rate that far exceeded chance (see also, Hunt, Rutledge, & Gray, 2006).

In another study (Weir & Kacelnik, 2006), Betty, one of the wild-caught crows, was tested with food placed in a miniature bucket that was lowered into a clear plastic tube. To get the food, Betty had to fashion a hook out of a piece of metal and use that to grab

FIGURE 12.17 Betty, a New Caledonian crow, selecting a stick of the appropriate length to get food out of a long tube in a study by Chappell & Kacelnik, 2002.

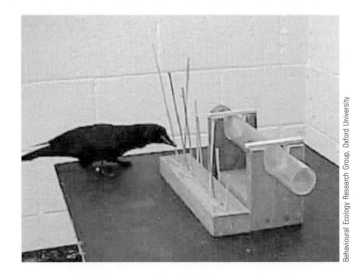

Behavioural Ecology Research Group, Oxford University

FIGURE 12.18 Betty, a New Caledonian crow, pulling up a bucket with food after fashioning a hook to use as a tool.

Behavioural Ecology Research Group, Oxford University

the handle of the bucket so that the bucket could be pulled up to provide the food (Figure 12.18). Betty was given metal strips of different shapes. Without much difficulty, Betty figured out how to modify each one in a unique fashion to serve as an effective hook.

A major issue in the study of tool use is how the behavior is acquired. Studies of New Caledonian crows in their natural habitat indicate that juveniles do not achieve adult-like competence in tool use until the end of their first year of life. Thus, tool use is learned over a long period of time. Juveniles seem to learn by observing how their parents use tools. This observational learning complements what they learn through their own individual experiences with potential tools (Holzhaider, Hunt, & Gray, 2010).

Laboratory studies of hand-reared crows in captivity have shown that modeling tool use facilitates learning but is not necessary (Kenward et al., 2005; Kenward et al., 2006). Crows can figure out on their own that they can obtain pieces of food by using twigs to prod out the food. However, this type of tool use is preceded by other behaviors involving manipulating twigs. Evidently, New Caledonian crows have a predisposition to pick up nonfood objects and handle them in various ways. Such manipulatory behavior then makes it possible for them to learn to use the objects as tools.

Tool use in nonhuman species has been theoretically provocative because it appears to be very clever and may reflect advanced intelligence. An alternative interpretation is that tool fabrication and use is a form of instrumental behavior, reinforced by food items that are obtained using the tools. The importance of this distinction is illustrated by a recent comparison of tool use between apes and corvids involving the same type of task (Albiach-Serrano, Bugnyar, & Call, 2012). The apes generally performed better than the corvids, but the corvids also showed tool use. More importantly, special tests indicated that the behavior of the apes reflected causal knowledge of the task. In contrast, evidence of causal knowledge was not observed in the corvids. Such results demonstrate that "tool use" is not a homogeneous behavioral category. Rather, various instances of tool use may reflect different behavioral and cognitive mechanisms.

Language Learning in Nonhuman Animals

Perhaps the most complex cognitive skill is linguistic competence. In fact, historically, the dominant view was that language is so complex and specialized that it is a uniquely human skill. According to this view, linguistic ability depends on certain innate neural modules that have evolved only in our own species (e.g., Chomsky, 1972; Lennenberg, 1967). By contrast, others have proposed that human beings are able to use language because they are especially intelligent and have experiences that permit language acquisition. This second view suggests that nonhuman organisms may also acquire language

skills if they are sufficiently intelligent and encounter the requisite experiences. Encouraged by this possibility, investigators have tried to teach language skills to various species (e.g., Hillix & Rumbaugh, 2004).

Early language-training efforts attempted to determine whether nonhuman animals are capable of language. However, it soon became evident that this is not an answerable question (Roitblat, Harley, & Helweg, 1993). Language is not a unitary entity that one either does or does not have. Rather, it consists of a number of component skills. A human infant's language abilities, for example, improve gradually as the infant acquires and integrates increasingly sophisticated language skills. In this developmental sequence, there is no one point at which the young child graduates from not having language to having it.

If the goal is no longer to demonstrate human-like linguistic competence in nonhuman species, what is the goal of this type of research? There are several goals. One is to use language training as a vehicle to study the cognitive abilities of nonhuman species. This is the basic objective of the program of work directed by Irene Pepperberg (e.g., 1999, 2010), who has been studying the cognitive abilities of gray parrots since 1977. A related sentiment was expressed by Louis Herman, who directed language studies in dolphins: "The animal language work can help us to identify with more surety those processes in humans that may derive from general cognitive structures rather than from language-specific structures" (Herman & Uyeyama, 1999, p.22). Research on language learning in nonhuman species can also tell us about the cognitive prerequisites and components of language competence and provide information about how best to teach linguistic skills. This information can then be put to use in language instruction for persons with cognitive or developmental disabilities.

Early Attempts at Language Training

Most efforts to teach animals language have involved chimpanzees because chimpanzees have many characteristics in common with human beings. Despite these similarities, however, chimpanzees do not learn to speak when they are given the same types of experiences that children have as they learn to speak. Cathy and Keith Hayes, for example, raised a chimpanzee named Viki with the explicit intent of teaching her to talk (Hayes & Hayes, 1951). Despite several years of training, Viki learned to say only three words: *mama, papa,* and *cup.* The search for linguistic competence in chimpanzees did not progress significantly until the innovative work of Allen and Beatrice Gardner and their students (Gardner & Gardner, 1969, 1975, 1978) who taught the chimpanzee, Washoe, American Sign Language rather than vocal speech.

American Sign Language uses manual gestures rather than vocal sounds. Although chimpanzees make a number of distinct vocalizations that have linguistic properties (e.g., Taglialatela, Savage-Rumbaugh, & Baker, 2003), they can make a much broader range of hand movements and gestures. Washoe was a good student. She learned to sign well over 100 words. The success of the Gardners with Washoe encouraged other language-training efforts with chimpanzees, as well as with other species, including a gorilla (Patterson, 1978), dolphins (Herman, 1987), sea lions (Gisiner & Schusterman, 1992; Schusterman & Gisiner, 1988), and African grey parrots (Pepperberg, 1990).

Language Training Procedures

A variety of procedures have been employed to train language skills. For example, in the program of research on African grey parrots directed by Irene Pepperberg (1999, 2010), an observational learning procedure known as the **model–rival technique** is used. In this technique, one research assistant acts as a trainer and the other acts as a rival student

Ethologist Irene Pepperberg with Alex, her African gray parrot

who competes with the parrot for the attention of the trainer. The trainer may present an object of interest to the parrot and ask what color it is. The person acting as the student then responds, sometimes correctly and sometimes incorrectly. An incorrect response results in a reprimand from the trainer and temporary removal of the object. A correct response results in praise and a chance to manipulate the object. The parrot observes these interactions and attempts to gain the attention of the trainer (and obtain the object) by responding correctly before the rival human student does so.

The longest-running and most informative language training project was developed by Duane Rumbaugh and his colleagues at the Language Research Center at Georgia State University. Instead of employing sign language, the words used in this project were simple visual designs of various shapes and colors (Rumbaugh, 1977; see also Savage-Rumbaugh, 1986). These symbols, called lexigrams, were presented on a board (Figures 12.19 and 12.20). A number of chimpanzees and their close relatives, the bonobos (*Pan paniscus*), participated in this project. Bonobos are more similar to human beings than chimpanzees, but they are rare both in the wild and in captivity.

The participants were raised in a language-rich environment with human contact all day every day. They could communicate with their caretakers by pointing to or pressing particular lexigrams on the board. Portable versions of the lexigram board permitted the participants to use the lexigrams when they moved around the compound in which they lived. Computer records of these lexigram responses provide detailed information about the linguistic performance of the participants. One particular bonobo, Kanzi, became famous for having learned language without explicit instruction and for providing unusually good evidence of linguistic skill (Savage-Rumbaugh et al., 1993; Savage-Rumbaugh et al., 1990).

During the first 2.5 years of his life, Kanzi lived with his mother, Matata, who was born in the wild and started language training at the Language Research Center of Georgia State University when Kanzi was six months old. Matata was trained with standard procedures in which she had to indicate the lexigram names of food objects to obtain those foods. For several years, Kanzi observed these training sessions but did not participate in them. Matata was then removed for a period for breeding purposes. During this separation, Kanzi began to interact with the lexigram board spontaneously. The investigators took advantage of this spontaneous use of the lexigram board and

FIGURE 12.19

Examples of lexigrams used at the Language Research Center of Georgia State University. Courtesy of Duane Rumbaugh, Language Research Center, Georgia State University.

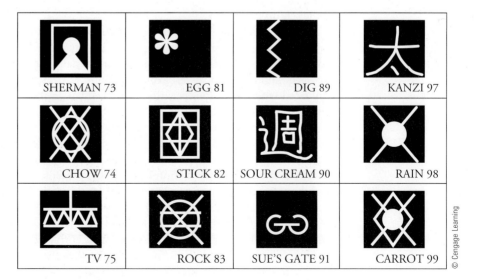

SHERMAN 73 | EGG 81 | DIG 89 | KANZI 97
CHOW 74 | STICK 82 | SOUR CREAM 90 | RAIN 98
TV 75 | ROCK 83 | SUE'S GATE 91 | CARROT 99

© Cengage Learning

FIGURE 12.20
Panzee working with a lexigram board.

Courtesy of Michael Beran

allowed Kanzi to continue to use it in addition to communicating with manual gestures. The caretakers also allowed Kanzi to continue to learn language skills by listening to spoken English and observing humans communicating with gestures and lexigrams.

Every effort was made to provide Kanzi with as rich and as natural an environment as possible. He was allowed to go on excursions in a 50-acre wooded area adjacent to the laboratory. The woods were provisioned with food stations at fixed locations. Excursions in the woods provided numerous opportunities for conversation concerning which food site to visit, what to take along, and so on. Kanzi was also allowed to visit various areas of the laboratory, including areas in which other apes were housed, and periodically he was taken on car rides.

Spoken and lexical language were incorporated into Kanzi's daily activities, such as diaper changes, food preparation, and various games. The hope was that Kanzi would acquire language incidentally during his normal daily activities, as children do. No explicit language training sessions were conducted, and Kanzi's use of language was not explicitly reinforced with food. However, the reinforcement contingencies inherent in social interactions were probably important in Kanzi's language learning (Sundberg, 1996).

In addition to spontaneously learning lexigrams, Kanzi also learned to recognize spoken English words. Kanzi, like other chimpanzees, could not produce the sounds of English words, but he appeared to know their meaning. Savage-Rumbaugh and her colleagues evaluated this comprehension by presenting the sound of words through headphones and then allowing Kanzi to select the corresponding lexigram from a choice of three alternatives (Savage-Rumbaugh et al., 1986) (See Figure 12.21). The experimenter did not see the possible lexigram choices and thus could not inadvertently prompt the correct response. Kanzi responded correctly on nearly every trial.

The results obtained with Kanzi indicate that the ability to discriminate phonemes in human speech is not unique to *Homo sapiens*. The limits of speech perception in chimpanzees was tested further with Panzee, another chimpanzee that was raised in an environment rich with human speech (Heimbauer, Beran, & Owren, 2011). In these tests, the acoustic features of words were severely degraded. Human listeners find normally spoken words easier to identify than crudely synthesized word sounds. Panzee showed similar results but responded more accurately than chance even with the degraded auditory stimuli.

Components of Linguistic Skill

There is no longer any doubt that great apes and other species (e.g., grey parrots, dolphins, and sea lions) can learn numerous vocabulary items. Chimpanzees and bonobos raised in a language-rich social environment typically acquire a vocabulary on the order of one or two hundred words. But that is probably not the limit of their ability to learn words. In an impressive demonstration, a border collie named Chaser learned the names of 1,022 different objects that she was encouraged to retrieve (Pilley & Reid, 2011). Such demonstrations make clear that vocabulary learning is not a uniquely human skill. As impressive as Chaser's vocabulary was, learning the meaning of words is just one component of linguistic skill.

Chaser correctly retrieved the object that was named on a given trial from a field of eight familiar objects, but she did not learn about word combinations and did not use her vocabulary in a flexible fashion to respond to more complex commands or to communicate about objects and events to someone else. Language involves arrangement of words into sequences according to certain rules of grammar or syntax. Hence, a major issue in language research has been whether the participants display evidence of using grammatical rules. Another major issue is whether language-trained animals limit their use of language to making requests rather than also using language to communicate about objects and events without a specific goal or reinforcer. (For further discussion of these and related issues, see Washburn, 2007). There has been considerable debate about this, and the debate is ongoing (e.g., Kako, 1999; Roitblat, 2007).

FIGURE 12.21 The bonobo chimpanzee Kanzi participating in a test of English comprehension. Words were presented to him through the earphones, and he had to respond by pressing lexigrams on the panel in the background.

Evidence of "Grammar" in Great Apes

Early studies of language production in the chimpanzee failed to provide convincing evidence of responding on the basis of some kind of grammar or set of rules for word combinations (Terrace, 1979; Terrace et al., 1979). The chimpanzee Nim, who was taught sign language by Terrace and his associates, performed sequences of signs, but these appeared to be imitations of the trainer and included meaningless repetitions. For example, Nim's most common four-sign combination was *eat–drink–eat–drink*. More convincing evidence of the development of grammatical word sequences was obtained initially in studies with Kanzi (Greenfield & Lyn, 2007; Greenfield & Savage-Rumbaugh, 1990; see also Savage-Rumbaugh et al., 1990). Subsequent analyses included data from Kanzi as well as Kanzi's half-sister Panbanisha and a chimpanzee named Panpanzee (Lyn, Greenfield, & Savage-Rumbaugh, 2011).

Analyses of thousands of utterances made by Kanzi and the other great apes indicated that the vast majority involved a single word. Only about 10–15% of their utterances included two or more words, and most of those were only two-word sequences. This contrasts with the language performance of children at a comparable stage of development, whose utterances include two or more words more than 50% of the time (Lyn et al., 2011a). When they occurred, two-word utterances among the great apes usually involved a request of some sort. For example, 96% of Kanzi's two-word utterances were requests.

Even though two-word utterances were not common with the great apes, when they occurred, the words did not appear in random order. This was most obvious with utterances that included a lexigram and a gesture. In these cases, the lexigram response was usually made first, followed by the gesture. The lexigram response preceded the gesture 91% of the time for Panpanzee, 88% of the time for Panbanisha, and 81% of the time for Kanzi.

Analysis of instances in which the two words were both lexigram responses also showed some evidence of a preferred order (Lyn et al., 2011a). But the preferred order was not uniform among the three apes studied. For example, if one lexigram referred to an object and the other to an action, Kanzi put the action before the object most of the time. However, the other two apes did not show an order preference in these cases. In contrast, if the lexigrams involved an action and a goal, Panpanzee and Panbanisha invariably put the action first, but Kanzi did not. As these examples illustrate, the word-order preferences of Panpanzee matched those of Panbanisha more often than they matched those of Kanzi. This may have been related to the fact that Panpanzee and Panbanisha had been raised together.

As I noted earlier, many of the two-word sequences of the great apes involved various types of requests. Such imperative goal-oriented use of language is common in children as well. However, people also use language to express or declare something without an intended consequence. Such declarative language use does not occur as often among great apes. Lyn and colleagues (2011b) found that about 5% of the utterances of great apes are declarative as compared with about 40% for children.

Declarative statements made by great apes refer more often to events in the past or the future than the statements of children, and they include fewer declarations about the names of things. However, in other ways the content of the declarative statements are not unusual. For example, Lyn and colleagues (2011b) described an episode in which Panbanisha ate a strawberry and then indicated the word "strawberry" on the lexigram board while looking at the caretaker, who agreed that she was eating a strawberry. Notice that this episode represents communication since Panbanisha used the lexigram board and looked at the experimenter. Panbanisha did not pick a word at random because the selected lexigram corresponded to what she was eating. Furthermore, the communication was not a request for a strawberry since she had already eaten the fruit. Thus, she was making a declarative statement. (For additional data and discussion, see Lyn et al., 2011b).

Studies of language training in great apes have come a long way since the pioneering efforts of Cathy and Keith Hayes. Several great apes have shown language competence far beyond what early investigators might have hoped to see. Although we have not figured out how to communicate with great apes with the ease and richness of content that characterize human language interactions, the research has vindicated Darwin's belief that seemingly unique human language abilities do not reflect a discontinuity in the animal kingdom.

Sample Questions

1. Describe food-caching behavior and what factors experimenters have to rule out before concluding that the behavior is mediated by working memory.
2. Describe how the behavior of food storing in birds can be used to provide evidence of episodic memory.
3. Describe the peak procedure and how results obtained with the peak procedure may be explained by scalar expectancy theory.
4. Compare and contrast the scalar expectancy model of timing and the behavioral theory of timing.
5. Explain why tests with subsets of items from a simultaneous array are useful in assessing the mechanisms of serial pattern learning.
6. Compare and contrast perceptual and abstract concept learning.
7. Describe instances of tool use in avian species and discuss how tool use may be acquired.
8. Describe similarities and differences in language learning among chimpanzees and human children.

Key Terms

adjunctive behaviors   Systematic activities or responses that occur when reinforcers are delivered at fixed intervals. Different adjunctive behaviors develop at different points in the interval between reinforcers.

duration estimation   A discrimination procedure in which the discriminative stimulus is the duration of an event.

duration production   A procedure in which participants learn to respond a set time after the onset of a stimulus or the start of a trial.

model–rival technique   An observational learning procedure in which the participant observes a trainer teaching a student and tries to compete with that student for the trainer's attention.

paired-associate learning   Learning of associations between successive pairs of an ordered list of stimuli.

peak procedure   A discrete-trial variation of a fixed interval schedule used to study timing in animals. Each trial begins with a stimulus. The reinforcer is set up a fixed time after the onset of the stimulus and is delivered when the participant responds. After training, nonreinforced test trials are provided during which the trial stimulus is extended substantially past the usual time of reinforcement. Responding during these test trials shows a peak at the fixed interval value of the training schedule.

response chain   A consecutively ordered series of responses in which each response produces the cue for the next response in the sequence.

scalar invariance   A property of the temporal control of behavior that emphasizes that participants respond to time intervals in terms of their relative or proportional durations rather than their absolute durations.

serial-representation learning The learning of a mental representation of the order of a list or series of stimuli.

serial order performance Learning to respond to a set of stimuli in a specified order. Serial order performance can be achieved by learning a series of S-R or S-S associations or by forming a mental representation of the order of the stimuli.

simultaneous chain procedure A procedure for studying the learning of serial order in which all of the stimuli in the series are presented at the same time and the participant has to select the stimuli in a specified order.

References

Abramson, L. Y., Metalsky, G. I., & Alloy, L. B. (1989). Hopelessness depression: A theory-based subtype of depression. *Psychological Review, 96,* 358–372.

Ahearn, W. H., Clark, K. M., Gardenier, N. C., Chung, B. I., & Dube, W. V. (2003). Persistence of stereotypic behavior: Examining the effects of external reinforcers. *Journal of Applied Behavior Analysis, 36,* 439–448.

Akin-Little, K. A., Eckert, T. L., Lovett, B. J., & Little, S. G. (2004). Extrinsic reinforcement in the classroom: Bribery or best practice. *School Psychology Review, 33,* 344–362.

Akins, C. K. (1998). Context excitation and modulation of conditioned sexual behavior. *Animal Learning & Behavior, 26,* 416–426.

Akins, C. K. (2000). Effects of species-specific cues and the CS-US interval on the topography of the sexually conditioned response. *Learning and Motivation, 31,* 211–235.

Akins, C. K., & Domjan, M. (1996). The topography of sexually conditioned behaviour: Effects of a trace interval. *Quarterly Journal of Experimental Psychology, 49B,* 346–356.

Albert, M., & Ayres, J. J. B. (1997). One-trial simultaneous and backward excitatory fear conditioning in rats: Lick suppression, freezing, and rearing to CS compounds and their elements. *Animal Learning & Behavior, 25,* 210–220.

Albiach-Serrano, A., Bugnyar, T., & Call, J. (2012). Apes (*Gorilla gorilla, Pan paniscus, P. troglodytes, Pongoabelii*) versus corvids (*Corvuscorax, C. corone*) in a support task: The effect of pattern and functionality. *Journal of Comparative Psychology, 126,* 355–367.

Allam, M. D.-E., et al. (2010). Long-lasting memory for an odor acquired at the mother's breast. *Developmental Science, 13,* 849–863.

Allan, L. G. (2005, with additional articles from pp. 131–263). Learning of contingent relationships. *Special Issue of Learning & Behavior, 33,* 127–130.

Allan, R. W., & Zeigler, H. P. (1994). Autoshaping the pigeon's gape response: Acquisition and topography as a function of reinforcer type and magnitude. *Journal of the Experimental Analysis of Behavior, 62,* 201–223.

Allison, J. (1993). Response deprivation, reinforcement, and economics. *Journal of the Experimental Analysis of Behavior, 60,* 129–140.

Altevogt, B. M., Pankevich, D. E., Shelton-Davenport, M. K., & Kahn, J. P. (Eds.). (2011). *Chimpanzees in biomedical and behavioral research: Assessing the necessity.* Washington, DC: Institute of Medicine and the National Research Council of the National Academy of Sciences.

Alvarez, V. A., & Sabatini, B. L. (2007). Anatomical and physiological plasticity of dendritic spines. *Annual Review of Neuroscience, 30,* 79–87.

Amat, J., Matus-Amat, P., Watkins, L. R., & Maier, S. F. (1998). Escapable and inescapable stress differentially alter extracellular levels of 5-HT in the basolateral amygdala of the rat. *Brain Research, 812,* 113–120.

Amsel, A. (1958). The role of frustrative nonreward in noncontinuous reward situations. *Psychological Bulletin, 55,* 102–119.

Amsel, A. (1992). *Frustration theory.* Cambridge, UK: Cambridge University Press.

Amundson, J. C., & Miller, R. R. (2008). CS-US temporal relations in blocking. *Learning & Behavior, 36,* 92–103.

Anderson, M. C., & Shettleworth, S. J. (1977). Behavioral adaptation to fixed-interval and fixed-time food delivery in golden hamsters. *Journal of the Experimental Analysis of Behavior, 25,* 33–49.

Andrzejewski, M. E., Cardinal, C. D., Field, D. P., Flannery, B. A., Johnson, M., Bailey, K., & Hineline, P. N (2005). Pigeons' choices between fixed-interval and random-interval schedules: Utility of variability? *Journal of the Experimental Analysis of Behavior, 83,* 129–145.

Andrzejewski, M. E., Ryals, C. D., Higgins, S., Sulkowski, J., Doney, J., Kelley, A. E., & Bersh, P. J. (2007). Is extinction the hallmark of operant discrimination? Reinforcement and S^Δ effects. *Behavioural Processes, 74,* 49–63.

Anger, D. (1963). The role of temporal discrimination in the reinforcement of Sidman avoidance behavior. *Journal of the Experimental Analysis of Behavior, 6,* 477–506.

Arentes, J., & Machado, A. (2008). Context effects in a temporal discrimination task: Further tests of the scalar expectancy theory and learning learning-to-time models. *Journal of the Experimental Analysis of Behavior, 90,* 33–51.

Asada, M., Hallam, J. C. T., Meyer, J.-A., & Tani, J. (Eds.) (2008). *From animals to animats 10.* Proceedings of the 10th International Conference on simulations of adaptive behavior, Osaka, Japan. Berlin: Springer-Verlag.

Ator, N. A., & Griffiths, R. R. (2003). Principles of drug abuse liability assessment in laboratory animals. *Drug and Alcohol Dependence, 70,* S55–S72.

Audrain-McGovern, J., Rodriguez, D., Epstein, L. H., Cuevas, J., Rodgers, K., & Wileyto, E. P. (2009). Does delay discounting play an etiological role in smoking or is it a consequence of smoking? *Drug and Alcohol Dependence, 103,* 99–106.

Aust, U., & Huber, L. (2003). Elemental versus configural perception in a people-present/people-absent discrimination task by pigeons. *Learning & Behavior, 31,* 213–234.

Ayres, J. J. B. (1998). Fear conditioning and avoidance. In W. O'Donohue (Ed.), *Learning and behavior therapy* (pp. 122–145). Boston: Allyn Bacon.

Ayres, J. J. B. (2012). Conditioned suppression. In N. M. Seel (Ed.), *Encyclopedia of the Sciences of Learning* (pp. 749–751). New York: Springer Science.

Azorlosa, J. L., & Cicala, G. A. (1986). Blocking of conditioned suppression with 1 or 10 compound trials. *Animal Learning & Behavior, 14,* 163–167.

Azrin, N. H. (1956). Some effects of two intermittent schedules of immediate and non-immediate punishment. *Journal of Psychology, 42,* 3–21.

Azrin, N. H. (1959). Punishment and recovery during fixed ratio performance. *Journal of the Experimental Analysis of Behavior, 2,* 301–305.

Azrin, N. H. (1960). Effects of punishment intensity during variable interval reinforcement. *Journal of the Experimental Analysis of Behavior, 3,* 123–142.

Azrin, N. H., & Holz, W. C. (1961). Punishment during fixed-interval reinforcement. *Journal of the Experimental Analysis of Behavior, 4,* 343–347.

Azrin, N. H., & Holz, W. C. (1966). Punishment. In W. K. Honig (Ed.), *Operant behavior: Areas of research and application* (pp. 380–447). New York: Appleton-Century-Crofts.

Azrin, N. H., Holz, W. C., & Hake, D. F. (1963). Fixed-ratio punishment. *Journal of the Experimental Analysis of Behavior, 6,* 141–148.

Azrin, N. H., Hutchinson, R. R., & Hake, D. F. (1966). Extinction induced aggression. *Journal of the Experimental Analysis of Behavior, 9,* 191–204.

Babkin, B. P. (1949). *Pavlov: A biography.* Chicago: University of Chicago Press.

Baer, D. M., & Wolf, M. M. (1970). The entry into natural communities of reinforcement. In R. Ulrich, T. Stachnik, & J. Mabry (Eds.), *Control of human behavior* (Vol. 2, pp. 319–324). Glenview, IL: Scott Foresman.

Baerends, G. P. (1988). Ethology. In R. C. Atkinson, R. J. Herrnstein, G. Lindzey, & R. D. Luce (Eds.), *Stevens' handbook of experimental psychology* (Vol. 1, pp. 765–830). New York: Wiley.

Bailey, C. H., & Kandel, E. R. (2008). Synaptic remodeling, synaptic growth and the storage of long-term memory in *Aplysia. Progress in Brain Research, 169,* 179–198.

Baillargeon, R. (2008). Innate ideas revisited. *Perspectives in Psychological Science, 3,* 2–13.

Baker, T. B., et al. (2004). Addiction motivation reformulated: An affective processing model of negative reinforcement. *Psychological Review, 111,* 33–51.

Balci, F., et al. (2009). Acquisition of peak responding: What is learned? *Behavioural Processes, 80,* 67–75.

Balda, R. P., & Turek, R. J. (1984). The cache-recovery system as an example of memory capabilities in Clark's nutcracker. In H. L. Roitblat, T. G. Bever, & H. S. Terrace (Eds.), *Animal cognition* (pp. 513–532). Hillsdale, NJ: Erlbaum.

Balleine, B. W., & Ostlund, S. B. (2007). Still at the choice point. *Annals of the New York Academy of Sciences, 1104,* 147–171.

Balsam, P. D. (1985). The functions of context in learning and performance. In P. D. Balsam & A. Tomie (Eds.), *Context and learning* (pp. 1–21). Hillsdale, NJ: Erlbaum.

Balsam, P. D. (1988). Selection, representation, and equivalence of controlling stimuli. In R. C. Atkinson, R. J. Herrnstein, G. Lindzey, & R. D. Luce (Eds.), *Stevens' handbook of experimental psychology, Vol. 2: Learning and cognition* (pp. 111–166). New York: Wiley.

Balsam, P. D., & Gallistel, C. R. (2009). Temporal maps and informativeness in associative learnig. *Trends in Neuroscience, 32,* 73–78.

Balsam, P. D., Drew, M. R., & Gallistel, C. R. (2010). Time and associate learning. *Comparative Cognition & Behavior Reviews, 5,* 1–22.

Balsam, P. D., & Tomie, A. (Eds.). (1985). *Context and learning.* Hillsdale, NJ: Erlbaum.

Balsam, P. D., Deich, J. D., Ohyama, T., & Stokes, P. D. (1998). Origins of new behavior. In W. O'Donohue (Ed.), *Learning and behavior therapy* (pp. 403–420). Boston: Allyn and Bacon.

Balsam, P. D., Drew, M. R., & Yang, C. (2001). Timing at the start of associative learning. *Learning and Motivation, 33,* 141–155.

Balsam, P., Sanchez-Castillo, H., Taylor, K., Van Volkinburg, H., & Ward, R. D. (2009). Timing and anticipation: Conceptual and methodological approaches. *European Journal of Neuroscience, 30,* 1749–1755.

Bandarian Balooch, S., & Neumann, D. L. (2011). Effects of multiple contexts and context similarity on the renewal of extinguished conditioned behaviour in an ABA design with humans. *Learning and Motivation, 42,* 53–63.

Banks, R. K. (1976). Resistance to punishment as a function of intensity and frequency of prior punishment experience. *Learning and Motivation, 7,* 551–558.

Baratta, M. V., Christianson, J. P., Gomez, D. M., Zarza, C. M., Amat, J., Masini, C. V., Watkins, L. R. Maier, S. F. (2007). Controllable versus uncontrollable stressors bi-directionally modulate conditioned but not innate fear. *Neuroscience, 146,* 1495–1503.

Bargai, N., Ben-Shakhar, G., & Shalev, A. Y. (2007). Posttraumatic stress disorder and depression in battered women: The mediating role of learned helplessness. *Journal of Family Violence, 22,* 267–275.

Bargh, J. A., & Morsella, E. (2008). The unconscious mind. *Perspectives in psychological science, 3,* 73–79.

Barlow, D. H. (1988). *Anxiety and its disorders.* New York: Guilford Press.

Barnet, R. C., & Miller, R. R. (1996). Second-order excitation mediated by a backward conditioned inhibitor. *Journal of Experimental Psychology: Animal Behavior Processes, 22,* 279–296.

Baron, A. (1965). Delayed punishment of a runway response. *Journal of Comparative and Physiological Psychology, 60,* 131–134.

Baron, A., & Herpolsheimer, L. R. (1999). Averaging effects in the study of fixed ratio response patterns. *Journal of the Experimental Analysis of Behavior, 71,* 145–153.

Barrett, D. (2010). *Supernormal stimuli.* New York: W. W. Norton.

Bashinski, H., Werner, J., & Rudy, J. (1985). Determinants of infant visual attention: Evidence for a two-process theory. *Journal of Experimental Child Psychology, 39,* 580–598.

Bateson, P., & Mameli, M. (2007). The innate and the acquired: Useful clusters or a residual distinction from folk biology? *Developmental Psychobiology, 49,* 818–837

Batsell, W. R., & Paschall, G. Y. (2009). Mechanisms of overshadowing and potentiation in flavor-aversion conditioning. In S. Reilly & T. R. Schachtman (Eds.), *Conditioned taste aversion: Behavioral and neural processes* (pp. 179–195). Oxford/New York: Oxford University Press.

Batsell, W. R., Jr., Paschall, G. Y., Gleason, D. I., & Batson, J. D. (2001). Taste preconditioning augments odor-aversion learning. *Journal of Experimental Psychology: Animal Behavior Processes, 27,* 30–47.

Batson, J. D., & Batsell, W. R., Jr. (2000). Augmentation, not blocking, in an A+/AX+ flavor-conditioning procedure. *Psychonomic Bulletin & Review, 7,* 466–471.

Baum, M. (1969). Extinction of avoidance response following response prevention: Some parametric investigations. *Canadian Journal of Psychology, 23,* 1–10.

Baum, M. (1970). Extinction of avoidance responding through response prevention (flooding). *Psychological Bulletin, 74,* 276–284.

Baum, W. (2012). Rethinking reinforcement: Allocation, induction, and contingency. *Journal of the Experimental Analysis of Behavior, 97,* 101–124.

Baum, W. M. (1974). On two types of deviation from the matching law: Bias and undermatching. *Journal of the Experimental Analysis of Behavior, 22,* 231–242.

Baum, W. M. (1979). Matching, undermatching, and overmatching in studies of choice. *Journal of the Experimental Analysis of Behavior, 32,* 269–281.

Baum, W. M. (1993). Performances on ratio and interval schedules of reinforcement: Data and theory. *Journal of the Experimental Analysis of Behavior, 59,* 245–264.

Baum, W. M. (2002). From molecular to molar: A paradigm shift in behavior analysis. *Journal of the Experimental Analysis of Behavior, 78,* 95–116.

Baum, W. M. (2012). Extinction as discrimination: The molar view. *Behavioural Processes, 90,* 101–110.

Bear, M. F., & Malenka, R. C. (1994). Synatic plasticity: LTP and LTD. *Current Opinion in Neurobiology, 4,* 389–399.

Bechterev, V. M. (1913). *La psychologie objective.* Paris: Alcan.

Begley, S. (2001, Feb 12). How it all starts inside your brain. *Newsweek, 137*(7), 40–42.

Belin, D., Jonkman, S., Dickinson, A., Robbins, T. W., & Everitt, B. J. (2009). Parallel and interactive learning processes within the basal ganglia: Relevance for the understanding of addiction. *Behavioural Brain Research, 199,* 89–102.

Belke, T. W., & Hancock, S. D. (2003). Responding for sucrose and wheel-running reinforcement: Effects of sucrose concentration and wheel-running reinforcer duration. *Journal of the Experimental Analysis of Behavior, 79,* 243–265.

Bentley-Condit, V. K., & Smith, E. O. (2010). Animal tool use: Current definitions and an updated comprehensive catalog. *Behaviour, 147,* 185–221.

Beran, M. J., et al. (2012, (a)). Prospective memory in a language-trained chimpanzee (*Pan troglodytes*). *Learning and Motivation, 43,* 192–199.

Beran, M. J., et al. (2012, (b)). Rhesus monkeys (*Macaca mulatta*) and capuchin monkeys (*Cebus apella*) remember future responses in a computerized task. *Journal of Experimental Psychology: Animal Behavior Processes, 38,* 233–243.

Beran, M. J., Evans, T. A., & Hoyle, D. (2011). Numerical judgments by chimpanzees (*Pan troglodytes*) in a token economy. *Journal of Experimental Psychology: Animal Behavior Processes, 37,* 165–174.

Beran, M. J., & Parrish, A. E. (2012). Sequential responding and planning in capuchin monkeys (*Cebus apella*). *Animal Cognition, 15,* 1085–1094.

Bernstein, I. L., & Borson, S. (1986). Learned food aversion: A component of anorexia syndromes. *Psychological Review, 93,* 462–472.

Berridge, K. C., & Krinelbach, M. L. (2008). Affective neuroscience of pleasure: Reward in humans and animals. *Psychopharmacology, 199,* 457–480.

Bernstein, I. L., & Webster, M. M. (1980). Learned taste aversions in humans. *Physiology and Behavior, 25,* 363–366.

Berridge, K. C., & Robinson, T. E. (2003). Parsing reward. *Trends in Neuroscience, 26,* 507–513.

Berridge, K. C., Robinson, T. E., & Aldridge, J. W. (2009). Dissecting components of reward: 'liking', 'wanting', and learning. *Current Opinion in Pharmacology, 9,* 65–73.

Best, M. R., Dunn, D. P., Batson, J. D., Meachum, C. L., & Nash, S. M. (1985). Extinguishing conditioned inhibition in flavour-aversion learning: Effects of repeated testing and extinction of the excitatory element. *Quarterly Journal of Experimental Psychology, 37B,* 359–378.

Bevins, R. A., McPhee, J. E., Rauhut, A. S., & Ayres, J. J. B. (1997). Converging evidence for one-trial context fear conditioning with an immediate shock: Importance of shock potency. *Journal of Experimental Psychology: Animal Behavior Processes, 23,* 312–324.

Bickel, W. K., Green, L., & Vuchinich, R. E. (1995). Behavioral economics. *Journal of the Experimental Analysis of Behavior, 64,* 257–262.

Bickel, W. K., Miller, M. L., Yi, R., Kowal, B. P., Lindquist, D. M., & Pitcock, J. A. (2007). Behavioral and neuroeconomics of drug addiction: Competing neural systems and temporal discounting processes. *Drug and Alcohol Dependence, 90,* S85–91.

Bizo, L. A., & McMahon, C. V. (2007). Temporal generalization and peak shift in humans. *Learning & Behavior, 35,* 123–130.

Bjork, R. A. (1972). The updating of human memory. In G. H. Bower (Ed.), *The psychology of learning and motivation*

(Vol. 12, pp. 235–259). New York: Academic Press.

Blackman, D. (1977). Conditioned suppression and the effects of classical conditioning on operant behavior. In W. K. Honig & J. E. R. Staddon (Eds.), *Handbook of operant behavior* (pp. 340–363). Englewood Cliffs, NJ: Prentice Hall.

Blackmore, T. L., Foster, T. M., Sumpter, C. E., & Temple, W. (2008). An investigation of colour discrimination with horses (*Equus caballus*). *Behavioural Processes, 78,* 387–396.

Blaisdell, A. P., Gunther, L. M., & Miller, R. R. (1999). Recovery from blocking through deflation of the blocking stimulus. *Animal Learning & Behavior, 27,* 63–76.

Blakemore, C., & Cooper, G. F. (1970). Development of the brain depends on visual environment. *Science, 228,* 477–478.

Blanchard, D. C. (1997). Stimulus, environmental, and pharmacological control of defensive behaviors. In M. E. Bouton & M. S. Fanselow (Eds.), *Learning, motivation, and cognition* (pp. 283–303). Washington, DC: American Psychological Association.

Blass, E. M., Ganchrow, J. R., & Steiner, J. E. (1984). Classical conditioning in newborn humans 2-48 hours of age. *Infant Behavior and Development, 7,* 223–235.

Bliss, T. V. P., & Lomo, T. (1973). Long-lasting potentiation of synaptic transmission in the dentate area of the anesthetized rabbit following stimulation of the perforant path. *Journal of Physiology, 232,* 331–356.

Blokland, A., Geraerts, E., & Been, M. (2004). A detailed analysis of rats' spatial memory in a probe trial of a Morris task. *Behavioural Brain Research, 154,* 71–75.

Blough, D. S. (1959). Delayed matching in the pigeon. *Journal of the Experimental Analysis of Behavior, 2,* 151–160.

Bluff, L. A., Weir, A. A. S., Rutz, C., Wimpenny, J. H., & Kacelnik, A. (2007). Tool-related cognition in New Caledonian Crows. *Comparative Cognition & Behavior Reviews, 2,* 1–25.

Blumberg, M. S., & Wasserman, E. A. (1995). Animal mind and the argument from design. *American Psychologist, 50,* 133–144.

Boakes, R. A. (1984). *From Darwin to behaviourism.* Cambridge: Cambridge University Press.

Boddez, Y., Baeyens, F., Hermans, D., & Beckers, T. (2011). The hide-and-seek of retrospective revaluation: Recovery from blocking is context dependent in human causal learning. *Journal of Experimental Psychology: Animal Behavior Processes, 37,* 230–240.

Bodily, K. D., Katz, J. S., & Wright, A. A. (2008). Matching-to-sample abstract concept learning by pigeons. *Journal of Experimental Psychology: Animal Behavior Processes, 34,* 178–184.

Boesch, C., & Boesch, H. (1990). Tool use and tool making in wild chimpanzees. *Folia Primatologica: International Journal of Primatology, 54,* 86–99.

Boice, R. (1973). Domestication. *Psychological Bulletin, 80,* 215–230.

Boice, R. (1977). Burrows of wild and albino rats: Effects of domestication, outdoor raising, age, experience, and maternal state. *Journal of Comparative and Physiological Psychology, 91,* 649–661.

Boice, R. (1981). Behavioral comparability of wild and domesticated rats. *Behavior Genetics, 11,* 545–553.

Bolles, R. C. (1969). Avoidance and escape learning: Simultaneous acquisition of different responses. *Journal of Comparative and Physiological Psychology, 68,* 355–358.

Bolles, R. C. (1970). Species-specific defense reactions and avoidance learning. *Psychological Review, 71,* 32–48.

Bolles, R. C. (1971). Species-specific defense reaction. In F. R. Brush (Ed.), *Aversive conditioning and learning* (pp. 183–233). New York: Academic Press.

Bolles, R. C., & Fanselow, M. S. (1980). A perceptual defensive-recuperative model of fear and pain. *Behavioral and Brain Sciences, 3,* 291–323.

Bolles, R. C., & Grossen, N. E. (1969). Effects of an informational stimulus on the acquisition of avoidance behavior in rats. *Journal of Comparative and Physiological Psychology, 68,* 90–99.

Bolles, R. C., Holtz, R., Dunn, T., & Hill, W. (1980). Comparisons of stimulus learning and response learning in a punishment situation. *Learning and Motivation, 11,* 78–96.

Borovsky, D., & Rovee-Collier, C. (1990). Contextual constraints on memory retrieval at six months. *Child Development, 61,* 1569–1583.

Borrero, J. C., Crisolo, S. S., Tu, Q., Rieland, W. A., Ross, N. A., Francisco, M. T., et al. (2007). An application of the matching law to social dynamics. *Journal of Applied Behavior Analysis, 40,* 589–601.

Bouton, M. E. (1984). Differential control by context in the inflation and reinstatement paradigms. *Journal of Experimental Psychology: Animal Behavior Processes, 10,* 56–74.

Bouton, M. E. (1993). Context, time, and memory retrieval in the interference paradigms of Pavlovian learning. *Psychological Bulletin, 114,* 80–99.

Bouton, M. E. (1994). Conditioning, remembering, and forgetting. *Journal of Experimental Psychology: Animal Behavior Processes, 20,* 219–231.

Bouton, M. E. (2001). Classical conditioning and clinical psychology. In N. J. Smelser & P. B. Baltes (Eds.), *Encyclopedia of the Social and Behavioral Sciences.* New York: Elsevier Science.

Bouton, M. E., & Bolles, R. C. (1980). Conditioned fear assessed by freezing and by the suppression of three different baselines. *Animal Learning & Behavior, 8,* 429–434.

Bouton, M. E., & King, D. A. (1983). Contextual control of the extinction of conditioned fear: Tests for the associative value of the context. *Journal of Experimental Psychology: Animal Behavior Processes, 9,* 248–265.

Bouton, M. E., & Ricker, S. T. (1994). Renewal of extinguished responding in a second context. *Animal Learning & Behavior, 22,* 317–324.

Bouton, M. E., & Woods, A. M. (2008). Extinction: Behavioral mechanisms and their implications. In R. Menzel (Ed.), *Learning theory and behavior. In J. Byrne (Ed.), Learning and Memory: A comprehensive reference* (Vol. 1, pp. 151–172). Oxford: Elsevier.

Bouton, M. E., Kenney, F. A., & Rosengard, C. (1990). State-dependent fear extinction with two benzodiazepine tranquilizers. *Behavioral Neuroscience, 104,* 44–55.

Bouton, M. E., Todd, T. P., Vurbic, D., & Winterbauer, N. E. (2011). Renewal after the extinction of free operant behavior. *Learning & Behavior, 39,* 57–67.

Bouton, M. E., Woods, A. M., Moody, E. W., Sunsay, C., & Garcia-Gutiérrez, A. (2006). Counteracting the context-dependence of extinction: Relapse and tests of some relapse prevention methods. In M. G. Craske, D. Hermans, & D. Vansteenwegen (Eds.), *Fear and learning* (pp. 175–196). Washington, DC: American Psychological Association.

Bowe, C. A., Miller, J. D., & Green, L. (1987). Qualities and locations of stimuli and responses affecting discrimination learning of chinchillas (*Chinchilla laniger*) and pigeons (*Columba livia*). *Journal of Comparative Psychology, 101,* 132–138.

Bradfield, L., & McNally, G. P. (2008). *Journal of Experimental Psychology: Animal Behavior Processes, 34,* 256–265.

Bradley, M. M., Moulder, B., & Lang, P. J. (2005). When good things go bad: The reflex physiology of defense. *Psychological Science, 16,* 468–473.

Brakke, K. E., & Savage-Rumbaugh, E. S. (1995). The development of language skills in bonobo and chimpanzee. I. Comprehension. *Language & Communication, 15,* 121–148.

Breland, K., & Breland, M. (1961). The misbehavior of organisms. *American Psychologist, 16,* 681–684.

Briggs, J. F., & Riccio, D. C. (2007). Retrograde amnesia for extinction: Similarities with amnesia for original acquisition memories. *Learning & Behavior, 35,* 131–140.

Brogden, W. J., Lipman, E. A., & Culler, E. (1938). The role of incentive in conditioning and extinction. *American Journal of Psychology, 51,* 109–117.

Brooks, D. C. (2000). Recent and remote extinction cues reduce spontaneous recovery. *Quarterly Journal of Experimental Psychology, 53B,* 25–58.

Brooks, D. C., & Bouton, M. E. (1993). A retrieval cue for extinction attenuates spontaneous recovery. *Journal of Experimental Psychology: Animal Behavior Processes, 19,* 77–89.

Brooks, D. C., & Bouton, M. E. (1994). A retrieval cue for extinction attenuates response recovery caused by a return to the conditioning context. *Journal of Experimental Psychology: Animal Behavior Processes, 20,* 366–379.

Brooks, D. C., Bowker, J. L., Anderson, J. E., & Palmatier, M. I. (2003). Impact of brief or extended extinction of a taste aversion in inhibitory associations: Evidence from summation, retardation,

and preference tests. *Learning & Behavior, 31,* 69–84.

Brooks, D. C., Palmatier, M. I., Garcia, E. O., & Johnson, J. L. (1999). An extinction cue reduces spontaneous recovery of a conditioned taste aversion. *Animal Learning & Behavior, 27,* 77–88.

Brown, G. S., & White, K. G. (2005). On the effects of signaling reinforcer probability and magnitude in delayed matching to sample. *Journal of the Experimental Analysis of Behavior, 83,* 119–128.

Brown, J. S. (1969). Factors affecting self-punitive behavior. In B. Campbell & R. M. Church (Eds.), *Punishment and aversive behavior.* New York: Appleton-Century-Crofts.

Brown, J. S., & Cunningham, C. L. (1981). The paradox of persisting selfpunitive behavior. *Neuroscience & Biobehavioral Reviews, 5,* 343–354.

Brown, J. S., & Jacobs, A. (1949). The role of fear in the motivation and acquisition of responses. *Journal of Experimental Psychology, 39,* 747–759.

Brown, K. L., & Woodruff-Pak, D. S. (2011). Eyeblink conditioning in animal models and humans. *Animal Models of Behavioral Analysis: Neuromethods, 50,* 1–27.

Brown, M. F. (2012). Spatial patterns: Behavioral control and cognitive representation. In T. R. Zentall & E. A. Wasserman (Eds.), *The Oxford Handbook of Comparative Cognition* (pp. 579–593). New York/Oxford: Oxford University Press.

Brown, M. F., Farley, R. F., & Lorek, E. J. (2007). Remembrance of places you passed: Social spatial working memory in rats. *Journal of Experimental Psychology: Animal Behavior Processes, 33,* 213–224.

Brown, P. L., & Jenkins, H. M. (1968). Autoshaping the pigeon's key peck. *Journal of the Experimental Analysis of Behavior, 11,* 1–8.

Bruzek, J. L., Thompson, R. H., & Peters, L. C. (2009). Resurgence of infant caregiving responses. *Journal of the Experimental Analysis of Behavior, 92,* 327–343.

Buckner, R. L. (2010). The role of the hippocampus in prediction and imagination. *Annual Review of Psychology, 61,* 28–48.

Budzynski, C. A., & Bingman, V. P. (1999). Time-of-day discriminative learning in

homing pigeons. *Columba Livia. Animal Learning & Behavior, 27,* 295–302.

Buhusi, C. V., & Meck, W. H. (2005). What makes us tick? Functional and neural mechanisms of interval timing. *Nature Reviews Neuroscience, 6,* 755–765.

Bulow, P. J., & Meller, P. J. (1998). Predicting teenage girls' sexual activity and contraception use: An application of matching law. *Journal of Community Psychology, 26,* 581–596.

Burghardt, G. M. (2009). Darwin's legacy to comparative psychology and ethology. *American Psychologist, 64,* 102–110.

Burns, M., & Domjan, M. (1996). Sign tracking versus goal tracking in the sexual conditioning of male Japanese quail (*Coturnix japonica*). *Journal of Experimental Psychology: Animal Behavior Processes, 22,* 297–306.

Burns, M., & Domjan, M. (2000). Sign tracking in domesticated quail with one trial a day: Generality across CS and US parameters. *Animal Learning & Behavior, 28,* 109–119.

Burns, M., & Domjan, M. (2001). Topography of spatially directed conditioned responding: Effects of context and trial duratin. *Journal of Experimental Psychology: Animal Behavior Processes, 27,* 269–278.

Busoniu, L., Babuska, R., De Schutter, B., & Ernst, D. (2010). *Reinforcement learning and dynamic programming using function approximations.* Boca Raton, FL: CRC Press.

Byrne, J. H. (Ed.). (2008). *Learning and Memory: A comprehensive Reference* (Vols. 1–4). Oxford: Elsevier.

Byron, K., & Khazanchi, S. (2012). Rewards and creative performance: A meta-analytic test of theoretically derived hypotheses. *Psychological Bulletin, 138,* 809–830.

Cain, C. K., & LeDoux, J. E. (2007). Escape from fear: A detailed behavioral analysis of two atypical responses reinforced by CS termination. *Journal of Experimental Psychology: Animal Behavior Processes, 33,* 451–463.

Cain, C. K., Blouin, A. M., & Barad, M. (2003). Temporally massed CS presentations generate more fear extinction than spaced presentations. *Journal of Experimental Psychology: Animal Behavior Processes, 29,* 323–333.

Calvert, A. L., Green, L., & Myerson, J. (2011). Discounting in pigeons when the choice is between two delayed rewards: Implications for species comparisons. *Frontiers in Neuroscience, 5* (article 96), 1–10. Doi:10:3389/fnins.2011.00096

Cameron, J., Banko, K. M., & Pierce, W. D. (2001). Pervasive negative effects of rewards on intrinsic motivation: The myth continues. *The Behavior Analyst, 24,* 1–44.

Camhi, J. M. (1984). *Neuroethology.* Sunderland, MA: Sinauer.

Camp, D. S., Raymond, G. A., & Church, R. M. (1967). Temporal relationship between response and punishment. *Journal of Experimental Psychology, 74,* 114–123.

Campolattaro, M. M., Schnitker, K. M., & Freeman, J. H. (2008). Changes in inhibition during differential eyeblink conditioning with increased training. *Learning & Behavior, 36,* 159–165.

Cándido, A., González, F., & de Brugada, I. (2004). Safety signals from avoidance learning but not from yoked classical conditioning training pass both summation and retardation tests of inhibition. *Behavioural Processes, 66,* 153–160.

Cándido, A., Maldonado, A., & Vila, J. (1991). Effects of duration of feedback on signaled avoidance. *Animal Learning & Behavior, 19,* 81–87.

Capaldi, E. J., Alptekin, S., & Birmingham, K. M. (1996). Instrumental performance and time between reinforcements: Intimate relation to learning or memory retrieval? *Animal Learning & Behavior, 24,* 211–220.

Capaldi, E. D., Hunter, M. J., & Lyn, S. A. (1997). Conditioning with taste as the CS in conditioned flavor preference learning. *Animal Learning & Behavior, 25,* 427–436.

Capaldi, E. J. (1967). A sequential hypothesis of instrumental learning. In K. W. Spence & J. T. Spence (Eds.), *The psychology of learning and motivation* (Vol. 1, pp. 67–156). New York: Academic Press.

Capaldi, E. J. (1971). Memory and learning: A sequential viewpoint. In W. K. Honig & P. H. R. James (Eds.), *Animal memory* (pp. 115–154). New York: Academic Press.

Capaldi, E. J., Alptekin, S., & Birmingham, K. M. (1996). Instrumental performance and time between reinforcements: Intimate relation to learning or memory retrieval? *Animal Learning & Behavior, 24,* 211–220.

Capaldi, E. J., Alptekin, S., Miller, D. J., & Barry, K. (1992). The role of instrumental responses in memory retrieval in a T-maze. *Quarterly Journal of Experimental Psychology, 45B,* 65–76.

Carlson, C. L., & Tamm, L. (2000). Responsiveness of children with attention deficit-hyperactivity disorder to reward and response cost: Differential impact on performance and motivation. *Journal of Consulting and Clinical Psychology, 68,* 73–83.

Carr, D., Wilkinson, K. M., Blackman, D., & McIlvane, W. J. (2000). Equivalence classes in individuals with minimal verbal repertoires. *Journal of the Experimental Analysis of Behavior, 74,* 101–114.

Carroll, M. E., Anker, J. J., Mach, J. L., Newman, J. L., & Perry, J. L. (2010). Delay discounting as a predictor of drug abuse. In G. J. Madden & W. K. Bickel (Eds.), *Impulsivity: The behavioral and neurological science of discounting* (pp. 243–271). Washington, DC: American Psychological Association.

Carter, M. M., Hollon, S. D., Carson, R., & Shelton, R. C. (1995). Effects of a safe person on induced distress following a biological challenge in panic disorder with agoraphobics. *Journal of Abnormal Psychology, 104,* 156–163.

Chamizo, V. D., Rodrigo, T., & Mackintosh, N. J. (2006). Spatial integration with rats. *Learning & Behavior, 34,* 348–354.

Champagne, F. A. (2010). Early adversity and developmental outcomes: Interaction between genetics, epigenetics, and social experiences across the life span. *Perspectives in Psychological Science, 5,* 564–574.

Chance, P. (1999). Thorndike's puzzle boxes and the origins of the experimental analysis of behavior. *Journal of the Experimental Analysis of Behavior, 72,* 433–440.

Chang, C., & Maren, S. (2009). Early extinction after fear conditioning yields a context-independent and short-term suppression of conditional freezing in rats. *Learning and Memory, 16,* 62–68.

Chang, R. C., Blaisdell, A. P., & Miller, R. R. (2003). Backward conditioning: Mediation by context. *Journal of Experimental Psychology: Animal Behavior Processes, 29,* 171–183.

Chappell, J., & Kacelnik, A. (2002). Tool selectivity in a non-primate, the New

Caledonian crow (*Corvus moneduloides*). *Animal Cognition, 5,* 71–78.

Charlop, M. H., Kurtz, P. F., & Casey, F. G. (1990). Using aberrant behaviors as reinforcers for autistic children. *Journal of Applied Behavior Analysis, 23,* 163–181.

Chase, A. R. (2001). Music discrimination by carp (*Cyprinus carpio*). *Animal Learning & Behavior, 29,* 336–353.

Cheng, K., & Crystal, J. D. (2008). Learning to time intervals. In R. Menzel (Ed.), Learning theory and behavior. Vol. 1 of J. Byrne (Ed.), *Learning and memory: A comprehensive reference* (pp. 341–364). Oxford: Elsevier.

Cheng, K., & Newcombe, N. S. (2005). Is there a geometric module for spatial orientation? Squaring theory and evidence. *Psychonomic Bulletin & Review, 12,* 1–23.

Cheng, K., & Spetch, M. L. (1995). Stimulus control in the use of landmarks by pigeons in a touchscreen task. *Journal of the Experimental Analysis of Behavior, 63,* 187–201.

Chomsky, N. (1972). *Language and mind.* New York: Harcourt Brace Jovanovich.

Christensen, D. R., & Grace, R. C. (2010). A decision model for steady-state choice in concurrent chains. *Journal of the Experimental Analysis of Behavior, 94,* 227–240.

Christianson, J. P. & Maier, S. F. (2008). The sensory insular cortex mediates the stress buffering effects of safety signals but not behavioral control. *Journal of Neuroscience, 28,* 13703–13711.

Church, R. M. (1963). The varied effects of punishment on behavior. *Psychological Review, 70,* 369–402.

Church, R. M. (1969). Response suppression. In B. A. Campbell & R. M. Church (Eds.), *Punishment and aversive behavior* (pp. 111–156). New York: Appleton Century-Crofts.

Church, R. M. (2003). A concise introduction to scalar timing theory. In W. H. Meck (Ed.), *Functional and neural mechanisms of interval timing* (pp. 2–21). Boca Raton, FL: CRC Press.

Church, R. M. (2012). Behavioristic, cognitive, biological, and quantitative explanations of timing. In T. R. Zentall & E. A. Wasserman (Eds.), *The Oxford handbook of comparative cognition* (pp. 409–433). New York/Oxford: Oxford University Press.

Church, R. M., Meck, W. H., & Gibbon, J. (1994). Application of scalar timing theory to individual trials. *Journal of Experimental Psychology: Animal Behavior Processes, 20,* 135–155.

Clark, R. E., & Squire, L. R. (1998). Classical conditioning and brain systems: The role of awareness. *Science, 280,* 77–81.

Clayton, N. S., & Dickinson, A. (1999). Scrub jays (*Aphelocoma coerulescens*) remember the relative time of caching as well as the location and content of their caches. *Journal of Comparative Psychology, 113,* 403–416.

Clayton, N. S., & Russell, J. (2009). Looking for episodic memory in animals and young children: Propsects for a new minimalism. *Neuropsychologia, 47,* 2330–2340.

Clayton, N. S., Bussey, T. J., & Dickinson, A. (2003). Can animals recall the past and plan for the future? *Nature Reviews Neuroscience, 4,* 685–691.

Cole, M. R. (1994). Response-rate differences in variable-interval and variable ratio schedules: An old problem revisited. *Journal of the Experimental Analysis of Behavior, 61,* 441–451.

Cole, M. R. (1999). Molar and molecular control in variable-interval and variable-ratio schedules. *Journal of the Experimental Analysis of Behavior, 71,* 319–328.

Cole, M. R., & Chappell-Stephenson, R. (2003). Exploring the limits of spatial memory in rats, using very large mazes. *Learning & Behavior, 31,* 349–368.

Cole, R. P., Barnet, R. C., & Miller, R. R. (1997). An evaluation of conditioned inhibition as defined by Rescorla's two-test strategy. *Learning and Motivation, 28,* 323–341.

Colombo, J., & Mitchell, D. W. (2009). Infant visual habituation. *Neurobiology of Learning and Memory, 92,* 225–234.

Colombo, M., & Frost, N. (2001). Representation of serial order in humans: A comparison to the findings with monkeys (*Cebus apella*). *Psychonomic Bulletin & Review, 8,* 262–269.

Colwill, R. M., & Motzkin, D. K. (1994). Encoding of the unconditioned stimulus in Pavlovian conditioning. *Animal Learning & Behavior, 22,* 384–394.

Colwill, R. M., & Rescorla, R. A. (1986). Associative structures in instrumental learning. In G. H. Bower (Ed.), *The psychology of learning and motivation* (Vol. 20, pp. 55–104). Orlando, FL: Academic Press.

Colwill, R. M., & Rescorla, R. A. (1990). Evidence for the hierarchical structure of instrumental learning. *Animal Learning & Behavior, 18,* 71–82.

Conklin, C. A., & Tiffany, S. T. (2002). Applying extinction research and theory to cue-exposure addiction treatments. *Addiction, 97,* 155–167.

Conn, P. M., & Parker, J. (1998). Animal rights: Reaching the public. *Science, 282,* 1417.

Cook, R. G., & Wasserman, E. A. (2012). Relational discrimination learning in pigeons. In T. R. Zentall & E. A. Wasserman (Eds.), *The Oxford handbook of comparative cognition* (pp. 533–551). New York/Oxford: Oxford University Press.

Cook, R. G., Beale, K., & Koban, A. (2011). Velocity-based motion categorization by pigeons. *Journal of Experimental Psychology: Animal Behavior Processes, 37,* 175–188.

Cook, R. G., Brown, M. F., & Riley, D. A. (1985). Flexible memory processing by rats: Use of prospective and retrospective information in the radial maze. *Journal of Experimental Psychology: Animal Behavior Processes, 11,* 453–469.

Cook, R. G., Levison, D. G., Gillett, S. R., & Blaisdell, A. P. (2005). Capacity and limits of associative memory in pigeons. *Psychonomic Bulletin & Review, 12,* 350–358.

Costa, D. S. J., & Boakes, R. A. (2011). Varying temporal contiguity and intereference in a human avoidance task. *Journal of Experimental Psychology: Animal Behavior Processes, 37,* 71–78.

Coull, J. T., Cheng, R.-K., & Meck, W. H. (2011). Neuroanatomical and neurochemical substrates of timing. *Neuropsychopharmacology Reviews, 36,* 3–25.

Courville, A. C., Daw, N. D., & Touretzky, D. S. (2006). Bayesian theories of conditioning in a changing world. *Trends in Cognitive Sciences, 10,* 294–300.

Craig, W. (1918). Appetites and aversions as constituents of instinct. *Biological Bulletin, 34,* 91–107.

Craske, M. G. (1999). *Anxiety disorders: Psychological approaches to theory and treatment.* Boulder, CO: Westview Press.

Craske, M. G., Glover, D., & DeCola, J. (1995). Predicted versus unpredicted panic attacks: Acute versus general distress. *Journal of Abnormal Psychology, 104,* 214–223.

Craske, M. G., Hermans, D., & Vansteenwegen, D. (Eds.). (2006). *Fear and learning.* Washington, DC: American Psychological Association.

Crespi, L. P. (1942). Quantitative variation in incentive and performance in the white rat. *American Journal of Psychology, 55,* 467–517.

Critchfield, T. S., & Kollins, S. H. (2001). Temporal discounting: Basic research and the analysis of socially important behavior. *Journal of Applied Behavior Analysis, 34,* 101–122.

Critchfield, T. S., & Lattal, K. A. (1993). Acquisition of a spatially defined operant with delayed reinforcement. *Journal of the Experimental Analysis of Behavior, 59,* 373–387.

Critchfield, T. S., Haley, R., Sabo, B., Colbert, J., & Macropoulis, G. (2003). A half century of scalloping in the work habits of the United States Congress. *Journal of Applied Behavior Analysis, 36,* 465–486.

Critchfield, T. S., Paletz, E. M., MacAleese, K. R., & Newland, M. C. (2003). Punishment in human choice: Direct or competitive suppression? *Journal of the Experimental Analysis of Behavior, 80,* 1–27.

Cronin, P. B. (1980). Reinstatement of post response stimuli prior to reward in delayed-reward discrimination learning by pigeons. *Animal Learning & Behavior, 8,* 352–358.

Crossman, E. K., Bonem, E. J., & Phelps, B. J. (1987). A comparison of response patterns on fixed-, variable-, and random-ratio schedules. *Journal of the Experimental Analysis of Behavior, 48,* 395–406.

Crown, E. D., & Grau, J. W. (2001). Preserving and restoring behavioral potential within the spinal cord using an instrumental training paradigm. *Journal of Neurophysiology, 86,* 845–855.

Crystal, J. D. (2006). Sensitivity to time: Implications for the representation of time. In E. A. Wasserman & T. R. Zentall (Eds.), *Comparative cognition* (pp. 270–284). Oxford, UK: Oxford University Press.

Crystal, J. D. (2010). Episodic-like memory in animals. *Behavioural Brain Research, 215,* 235–243.

Crystal, J. D. (2012). Prospective cognition in rats. *Learning and Motivation, 43,* 181–191.

Crystal, J. D. (2012). Sensitivity to time: Implications for the representation of time. In T. R. Zentall & E. A. Wasserman (Eds.), *The Oxford handbook of comparative cognition* (pp. 434–450). New York/Oxford: Oxford University Press.

Crystal, J. D., & Babb, S. J. (2008). Spatial memory in rats after 25 hours. *Learning and Motivation, 39*, 278–284.

Crystal, J. D., & Baramidze, G. T. (2007). Endogenous oscillations in short-interval timing. *Behavioural Processes, 74*, 152–158.

Cumming, W. W. (1999). A review of Geraldine Jonçich's the sane positivist: A biography of Edward L. Thorndike. *Journal of the Experimental Analysis of Behavior, 72*, 429–432.

Cunningham, C. L. (1979). Alcohol as a cue for extinction: State dependency produced by conditioned inhibition. *Animal Learning & Behavior, 7*, 45–52.

Cusato, B., & Domjan, M. (1998). Special efficacy of sexual conditioned stimuli that include species typical cues: Tests with a CS preexposure design. *Learning and Motivation, 29*, 152–167.

Cusato, B., & Domjan, M. (2000). Facilitation of appetitive conditioning with naturalistic conditioned stimuli: CS and US factors. *Animal Learning and Behavior, 28*, 247–256.

Cusato, B., & Domjan, M. (2012). Naturalistic conditioned stimuli facilitate sexual conditioning because of their similarity with the unconditioned stimulus. *International Journal of Comparative Psychology, 25*, 166–179.

D'Amato, M. R. (1973). Delayed matching and short-term memory in monkeys. In G. H. Bower (Ed.), *The psychology of learning and motivation* (Vol. 7, pp. 227–269). New York: Academic Press.

D'Amato, M. R., & Colombo, M. (1988). Representation of serial order in monkeys (*Cebus apella*). *Journal of Experimental Psychology: Animal Behavior Processes, 14*, 131–139.

D'Amato, M. R., & Salmon, D. P. (1982). Tune discrimination in monkeys (*Cebus apella*) and in rats. *Animal Learning & Behavior, 10*, 126–134.

D'Amato, M. R., Fazzaro, J., & Etkin, M. (1968). Anticipatory responding and avoidance discrimination as factors in avoidance conditioning. *Journal of Comparative and Physiological Psychology, 77*, 41–47.

da Silva, S. P., Maxwell, & Lattal, K. A. (2008). Concurrent resurgence and behavioral history. *Journal of the Experimental Analysis of Behavior, 90*, 313–331.

Dallery, J., & Soto, P. L. (2013). Quantitative description of environment-behavior relations. In G. J. Madden (Ed.), *APA Handbook of Behavior Analysis, Vol. 1* (pp. 219–249). Washington, DC: American Psychological Association.

Dally, J. M., Emery, N. J., & Clayton, N. S. (2006). Food caching Western scrub-jays keep track of who was watching when. *Science, 312*, 1662–1665.

Daman-Wasserman, M., Brennan, B., Radcliffe, F., Prigot, J., & Fagen, J. (2006). Auditory-visual context and memory retrieval in 3–month-old infants. *Infancy, 10*, 201–220.

Danker, J. F., & Anderson, J. R. (2010). The ghosts of brain states past: Remembering reactives the brain regions engaged during encoding. *Psychological Bulletin, 136*, 87–102.

Darwin, C. (1897). *The descent of man and selection in relation to sex.* New York: Appleton-Century-Crofts.

Davey, G. C. L., & Cleland, G. G. (1982). Topography of signal-centered behavior in the rat: Effects of deprivation state and reinforcer type. *Journal of the Experimental Analysis of Behavior, 38*, 291–304.

Davey, G. C. L., Phillips, S., & Cleland, G. G. (1981). The topography of signal-centered behaviour in the rat: The effects of solid and liquid food reinforcers. *Behaviour Analysis Letters, 1*, 331–337.

Davidson, T. L., Flynn, F. W., & Jarrard, L. E. (1992). Potency of food deprivation intensity cues as discriminative stimuli. *Journal of Experimental Psychology: Animal Behavior Processes, 18*, 174–181.

Davis, H. P., & Squire, L. R. (1984). Protein synthesis and memory: A review. *Psychological Bulletin, 96*, 518–559.

Davis, M. (1974). Sensitization of the rat startle response by noise. *Journal of Comparative and Physiological Psychology, 87*, 571–581.

Davis, M. (1989). Sensitization of the acoustic startle reflex by footshock. *Behavioral Neuroscience, 103*, 495–503.

Davis, M. (1997). The neurophysiological basis of acoustic startle modulation: Research on fear motivation and sensory gating. In P. J. Lang, R. F. Simons, & M. T. Balaban (Eds.), *Attention and orienting: Sensory and motivational processes* (pp. 69–96). Mahwah, NJ: Erlbaum.

Davis, M., Antoniadis, E. A., Amaral, D. G., & Winslow, J. T. (2008). Acoustic startle in rhesus monkeys: A review. *Reviews in the Neurosciences, 19*, 171–185.

Davis, R. L. (1996). Physiology and biochemistry of Drosophila learning mutants. *American Physiological Society, 76*, 299–317.

Davison, M., & Baum, W. M. (2003). Every reinforcer counts: Reinforcer magnitude and local preference. *Journal of the Experimental Analysis of Behavior, 80*, 95–129.

Davison, M., & McCarthy, D. (1988). *The matching law: A research review.* Hillsdale, NJ: Erlbaum.

Davison, M., & Nevin, J. A. (1999). Stimuli, reinforcers, and behavior: An integration. *Journal of the Experimental Analysis of Behavior, 71*, 439–482.

De Carvalho, M. P., & Machado, A. (2012). Relative versus absolute stimulus control in the temporal bisection task. *Journal of the Experimental Analysis of Behavior, 98*, 23–44.

De Houwer, J. (2011). Evaluative conditioning: A review of functional knowledge. In T. R. Schachtman & S. Reilly (Eds.), *Associative learning and conditioning theory: Human and non-human applications* (pp. 399–416). Oxford and New York: Oxford University Press.

de Kort, S. R., Dickinson, A., & Clayton, N. S. (2005). Retrospective cognition by food-caching Western scrub-jays. *Learning and Motivation, 36*, 159–176.

de Kort, S. R., Emery, N. J., & Clayton, N. S. (2012). Corvid caching: The role of cognition. In T. R. Zentall & E. A. Wasserman (Eds.), *The Oxford handbook of comparative cognition* (pp. 390–406). New York/Oxford: Oxford University Press.

De la Casa, Marquez, R., & Lubow, R. E. (2009). Super-latent inhibition of conditioned taste preference with a long retention interval. *Learning and Motivation, 40*, 329–342.

De Oca, B. M., Minor, T. R., & Fanselow, M. S. (2007). Brief flight to a familiar enclosure in response to a conditioned stimulus in rats. *Journal of General Psychology, 134*, 153–172.

Dean, S. J., & Pittman, C. M. (1991). Self-punitive behavior: A revised analysis. In M. R. Denny (Ed.), *Fear, avoidance and phobias* (pp. 259–284). Hillsdale, NJ: Erlbaum.

Declercq, M., De Houwer, J., & Baeyens, F. (2008). Evidence for an expectancy-based theory of avoidance behaviour. *Quarterly Journal of Experimental Psychology, 61,* 1803–1812.

DeFrancisco, B. S., & Rovee-Collier, C. (2008). The specificity of priming effects over the first year of life. *Developmental Psychobiology, 50,* 486–501.

DeFulio, A., & Hackenberg, T. D. (2007). Discriminated timeout avoidance in pigeons: The roles of added stimuli. *Journal of the Experimental Analysis of Behavior, 88,* 51–71.

DeGrandpre, R. J., Bickel, W. K., Rizvi, S. A. T., & Hughes, J. R. (1993). Effect of income on drug choice in humans. *Journal of the Experimental Analysis of Behavior, 59,* 483–500.

Deich, J. D., Allan, R. W., & Zeigler, H. P. (1988). Conjunctive differentiation of gape during food-reinforced keypecking in the pigeon. *Animal Learning & Behavior, 16,* 268–276.

Delamater, A. R. (1996). Effects of several extinction treatments upon the integrity of Pavlovian stimulus– outcome associations. *Animal Learning & Behavior, 24,* 437–449.

Delamater, A. R. (2004). Experimental extinction in Pavlovian conditioning: Behavioural and neuroscience perspectives. *Quarterly Journal of Experimental Psychology, 57B,* 97–132.

Delamater, A. R. (2012). Issues in extinction of specific stimulus-outcome associations in Pavlovian conditioning. *Behavioural Processes, 90,* 9–19.

Delamater, A. R., Campese, V., LoLordo, V. M., & Sclafani, A. (2006). Unconditioned stimulus devaluation effects in nutrientconditioned flavor preferences. *Journal of Experimental Psychology: Animal Behavior Processes, 32,* 295–306.

Delameter, A. R., & Holland, P. C. (2008). The influence of CS-US interval on several different indices of learning in appetitive conditioning. *Journal of Experimental Psychology: Animal Behavior Processes, 34,* 202–222.

Delius, J. D., Jitsumori, M., & Siemann, M. (2000). Stimulus equivalencies through discrimination reversals. In C. Heyes & L. Huber (Eds.), *The evolution of cognition* (pp. 103–122). Cambridge, MA: Bradford/MIT Press.

Denniston, J. C., Blaisdell, A. P., & Miller, R. R. (2004). Temporal coding in conditioned inhibtion: Analysis of associative structure of inhibition. *Journal of Experimental Psychology: Animal Behavior Processes, 30,* 190–202.

Denniston, J. C., Savastano, H. I., & Miller, R. R. (2001). The extended comparator hypothesis: Learning by contiguity, responding by relative strength. In R. R. Mowrer & S. B. Klein (Eds.), *Handbook of contemporary learning theories* (pp. 65–117). Mahwah, NJ: Erlbaum.

Deroche-Gamonet, V., Belin, D., & Piazza, P. V. (2004). Evidence for addiction-like behavior in the rat. *Science, 305,* 1014–1017.

deVilliers, P. A. (1974). The law of effect and avoidance: A quantitative relationship between response rate and shock-frequency reduction. *Journal of the Experimental Analysis of Behavior, 21,* 223–235.

DeVito, P. L., & Fowler, H. (1987). Enhancement of conditioned inhibition via an extinction treatment. *Animal Learning & Behavior, 15,* 448–454.

Dickinson, A., & Brown, K. J. (2007). Flavor-evaluative conditioning is unaffected by contingency knowledge during training with color-flavor compounds. *Learning & Behavior, 35,* 36–42.

Dickinson, A., Balleine, B., Watt, A., Gonzalez, F., & Boakes, R. A. (1995). Motivational control after extended instrumental training. *Animal Learning & Behavior, 23,* 197–206.

Dickinson, A., Nicholas, D. J., & Macintosh, N. J. (1983). A reexamination of one-trial blocking in conditioned suppression. *Quarterly Journal of Experimental Psychology, 35,* 67–79.

Dickinson, A., Watt, A., & Griffiths, W. J. H. (1992). Free-operant acquisition with delayed reinforcement. *The Quarterly Journal of Experimental Psychology, 45B,* 241–258.

Didden, R., Prinsen, H., & Sigafoos, J. (2000). The blocking effect of pictorial prompts on sight-word reading. *Journal of Applied Behavior Analysis, 33,* 317–320.

Dinsmoor, J. A. (1952). A discrimination based on punishment. *Quarterly Journal of Experimental Psychology, 4,* 27–45.

Dinsmoor, J. A. (1954). Punishment: I. The avoidance hypothesis. *Psychological Review, 61,* 34–46.

Dinsmoor, J. A. (1977). Escape, avoidance, punishment: Where do we stand? *Journal of the Experimental Analysis of Behavior, 28,* 83–95.

Dinsmoor, J. A. (1998). Punishment. In W. O'Donohue (Ed.), *Learning and behavior therapy* (pp. 188–204). Boston: Allyn Bacon.

Dinsmoor, J. A. (2001a). Still no evidence for temporally extended shockfrequency reduction as a reinforcer. *Journal of the Experimental Analysis of Behavior, 75,* 367–378.

Dinsmoor, J. A. (2001b). Stimuli inevitably generated by behavior that avoids electric shock are inherently reinforcing. *Journal of the Experimental Analysis of Behavior, 75,* 311–333.

Dittlinger, L. H., & Lerman, D. C. (2011). Further analysis of picture interference when teaching word recognition to children with autism. *Journal of Applied Behavior Analysis, 44,* 341–349.

Dixon, M. R., et al. (1998). Using a self-control training procedure to increase appropriate behavior. *Journal of Applied Behavior Analysis, 31,* 203–210.

Dixon, M. R., & Holcomb, S. (2000). Teaching self-control to small groups of dually diagnosed adults. *Journal of Applied Behavior Analysis, 33,* 611–614.

Dobrzecka, C., Szwejkowska, G., & Konorski, J. (1966). Qualitative versus directional cues in two forms of differentiation. *Science, 153,* 87–89.

Dollard, J., Miller, N. E., Doob, L. W., Mowrer, O. H., & Sears, R. R. (1939). *Frustration and aggression.* New Haven, CT: Yale University Press.

Domjan, M. (1980). Ingestional aversion learning: Unique and general processes. In J. S. Rosenblatt, R. A. Hinde, C. Beer, & M. Busnel (Eds.), *Advances in the study of behavior* (Vol. 11). New York: Academic Press.

Domjan, M. (1983). Biological constraints on instrumental and classical conditioning: Implications for general process theory. In G. H. Bower (Ed.), *The psychology of learning and motivation* (Vol. 17). New York: Academic Press.

Domjan, M. (1987). Animal learning comes of age. *American Psychologist, 42,* 556–564.

Domjan, M. (1993). *Principles of learning and behavior* (3rd ed.). Belmont, CA: Wadsworth.

Domjan, M. (1997). Behavior systems and the demise of equipotentiality:

Historical antecedents and evidence from sexual conditioning. In M. E. Bouton & M. S. Fanselow (Eds.), *Learning, motivation, and cognition: The functional behaviorism of Robert C. Bolles* (pp. 31–51). Washington, DC: American Psychological Association.

Domjan, M. (2005). Pavlovian conditioning: A functional perspective. *Annual Review of Psychology, 56,* 179–206.

Domjan, M. (2008). Adaptive specializations and generality of the laws of classical and instrumental conditioning. In R. Menzel (Ed.), *Learning theory and behavior.* Vol. 1 of J. Byrne (Ed.), *Learning and memory: A comprehensive reference* (pp. 327–340). Oxford: Elsevier.

Domjan, M. (2012). Learning and instinct. In N. M. Seel (Ed.), *Encyclopedia of the Sciences of Learning* (pp. 1790–1793). New York: Springer Science.

Domjan, M., & Akins, C. K. (2011). Applications of pavlovian conditioning to sexual behavior and reproduction. In T. R. Schachtman & S. Reilly (Eds.), *Associative learning and conditioning theory: Human and non-human applications* (pp. 507–531). New York: Oxford University Press.

Domjan, M., Cusato, B., & Krause, M. (2004). Learning with arbitrary versus ecological conditioned stimuli: Evidence from sexual conditioning. *Psychonomic Bulletin & Review, 11,* 232–246.

Domjan, M., Mahometa, M. J., & Matthews, R. N. (2012). Learning in intimate connections: Conditioned fertility and its role in sexual competition. *Socioaffective Neuroscience & Psychology, 2,* 17333. Doi:10.3402/snp.v2i0.17333.

Donaldson, J. M., & Vollmer, T. R. (2011). An evaluation and comparison of time-out procedures with and without release contingencies. *Journal of Applied Behavior Analysis, 44,* 693–705.

Doyere, V., Debiec, J., Monfils, M.-H., Schafe, G. E., & LeDoux, J. E. (2007). Synapse-specific reconsolidation of distinct fear memories in the lateral amygdala. *Nature Neuroscience, 10,* 414–416.

Dube, W. V., & McIlvane, W. J. (2001). Behavioral momentum in computer-presented discriminations in individuals with severe mental retardation. *Journal of the Experimental Analysis of Behavior, 75,* 15–23.

Dube, W. V., McIlvane, W. J., Mazzitelli, K., & McNamara, B. (2003). Reinforcer rate effects and behavioral momentum in individuals with developmental disabilities. *American Journal on Mental Retardation, 108,* 134–143.

Dudai, Y. (1989). *The neurobiology of memory: Concepts, findings, trends.* Oxford University Press: Oxford.

Dudai, Y. (2004). The neurobiology of consolidation, or, how stable is the engram? *Annual Review of Psychology, 55,* 51–86.

Dudeney, J. E., Olsen, K. N., & Kehoe, E. J. (2007). Time-specific extinction and recovery of the rabbit's (*Oryctolagus cuniculus*) conditioned nictitating membrane response using mixed interstimulus intervals. *Behavioral Neuroscience, 121,* 808–813.

Dunsmoor, J. E., White, A. J., & LaBar, K. S. (2011). Conceptual similarity promotes generalization of higher order fear learning. *Learning & Memory, 18,* 156–160.

Dweck, C. S., & Wagner, A. R. (1970). Situational cues and correlation between conditioned stimulus and unconditioned stimulus as determinants of the conditioned emotional response. *Psychonomic Science, 18,* 145–147.

Dwyer, D. M., Haselgrove, M., & Jones, P. M. (2011). Cue interactions in flavor preference learning: A configural analysis. *Journal of Experimental Psychology: Animal Behavior Processes, 37,* 41–57.

Eagleman, D. (2011). *Incognito: The secret lives of the brain.* New York: Pantheon Books.

Edgerton, V. R., Tillakaratne, N. J. K., Bigbee, A. J., de Leon, R. D., & Roy, R. R. (2004). Plasticity of the spinal neural circuitry after injury. *Annual Review of Neuroscience, 27,* 145–167.

Eichenbaum, H., et al. (2012). A comparative analysis of episodic memory. In T. R. Zentall & E. A. Wasserman (Eds.), *The Oxford handbook of comparative cognition* (pp. 305–321). New York/Oxford: Oxford University Press.

Eisenberger, R., & Adornetto, M. (1986). Generalized self-control of delay and effort. *Journal of Personality and Social Psychology, 51,* 1020–1031.

Eisenberger, R., Karpman, M., & Trattner, J. (1967). What is the necessary and sufficient condition for reinforcement in the contingency situation? *Journal of Experimental Psychology, 74,* 342–350.

Eisenberger, R., & Shanock, L. (2003). Rewards, intrinsic motivation, and creativity: A case study of conceptual and methodological isolation. *Creativity Research Journal, 15,* 121–130.

Eisenberger, R., Karpman, M., & Trattner, J. (1967). What is the necessary and sufficient condition for reinforcement in the contingency situation? *Journal of Experimental Psychology, 74,* 342–350.

Emmerton, J., & Renner, J. C. (2006). Scalar effects in the visual discrimination of numerosity by pigeons. *Learning & Behavior, 34,* 176–192.

Epstein, D. H., Preston, K. L., Stewart, J., & shaham, Y. (2006). Toward a model of drug relapse: An assessment of the validity of the reinstatement procedure. *Psychopharmacology, 189,* 1–16.

Epstein, L. H., Handley, E. A., Dearing, K. K., Cho, D. D., Roemmich, J. N., Paluch, R. A., et al. (2006). Purchases of food in youth. *Psychological Science, 17,* 82–89.

Epstein, L. H., Leddy, J. J., Temple, J. L., & Faith, M. S. (2007). Food reinforcement and eating: A multilevel analysis. *Psychological Bulletin, 133,* 884–906.

Epstein, L. H., Paluch, R., & Coleman, K. J. (1996). Differences in salivation to repeated food cues in obese and nonobese women. *Psychosomatic Medicine, 58,* 160–164.

Epstein, L. H., Robinson, J. L., Temple, J. L., Roemmich, J. N., Marusewski, A., & Nadbrzuch, R. (2008). Sensitization and habituation of motivated behavior in overweight and nonoverweight children. *Learning and Motivation, 39,* 243–255.

Epstein, L. H., Rodefer, J. S., Wisniewski, L., & Caggiula, A. R. (1992). Habituation and dishabituation of human salivary response. *Physiology & Behavior, 51,* 945–950.

Epstein, L. H., Saad, F. G., Giacomelli, A. M., & Roemmich, J. N. (2005). Effects of allocation of attention on habituation to olfactory and visual food stimuli in children. *Physiology & Behavior, 84,* 313–319.

Epstein, L. H., Saad, F. G., Handley, E. A., Roemmich, J. N., Hawk, L. W., & McSweeney, F. K. (2003). Habituation of salivation and motivated responding for food in children. *Appetite, 41,* 283–289.

Epstein, L. H., Temple, J. L., Roemmich, J. N., & Bouton, M. E. (2009). Habituation as a determinant of human food intake. *Psychological Review, 116,* 384–407.

Escobar, M., & Miller, R. R. (2003). Timing in retroactive interference. *Learning & Behavior, 31,* 257–272.

Esmorís-Arranz, F. J., Pardo-Vázquez, J. L., & Vázquez-Garcia, G. A. (2003). Differential effects of forward or simultaneous conditioned stimulus-unconditioned stimulus intervals on the defensive behavior system of the Norway rat (*Rattus Norvegicus*). *Journal of Experimental Psychology: Animal Behavior Processes, 29,* 334–340.

Estes, W. K. (1943). Discriminative conditioning: I. A discriminative property of conditioned anticipation. *Journal of Experimental Psychology, 32,* 150–155.

Estes, W. K. (1944). An experimental study of punishment. *Psychological Monographs, 57*(3, Whole No. 263).

Estes, W. K. (1948). Discriminative conditioning: II. Effects of a Pavlovian conditioned stimulus upon a subsequently established operant response. *Journal of Experimental Psychology, 38,* 173–177.

Estes, W. K. (1969). Outline of a theory of punishment. In B. A. Campbell & R. M. Church (Eds.), *Punishment and aversive behavior* (pp. 57–82). New York: Appleton-Century-Crofts.

Estes, W. K., & Skinner, B. F. (1941). Some quantitative properties of anxiety. *Journal of Experimental Psychology, 29,* 390–400.

Ettenberg, A. (2004). Opponent process properties of self-administered cocaine. *Neuroscience and Biobehavioral Reviews, 27,* 721–728.

Evans, T. A., & Beran, M. J. (2012). Monkeys exhibit prospective memory in a computerized task. *Cognition, 125,* 131–140.

Everitt, B. J., & Robbins, T. W. (2005). Neural systems of reinforcement for drug addiction: From actions to habits to compulsion. *Nature Neuroscience, 8,* 1481–1489.

Fanselow, M. S. (1997). Species-specific defense reactions: Retrospect and prospect. In M. E. Bouton & M. S. Fanselow (Eds.), *Learning, motivation, and cognition* (pp. 321–341). Washington, DC: American Psychological Association.

Fanselow, M. S. (1998). Pavlovian conditioning, negative feedback, and blocking: Mechanisms that regulate

association formation. *Neuron, 20,* 625–627.

Fanselow, M. S. (1999). Learning theory and neuropsychology: Configuring their disparate elements in the hippocampus. *Journal of Experimental Psychology: Animal Behavior Processes, 25,* 275–283.

Fanselow, M. S., & Lester, L. S. (1988). A functional behavioristic approach to aversively motivated behavior: Predatory imminence as a determinant of the topography of defensive behavior. In R. C. Bolles & M. D. Beecher (Eds.), *Evolution and learning* (pp. 185–212). Hillsdale, NJ: Erlbaum.

Fanselow, M. S., & Poulos, A. M. (2005). The neuroscience of mammalian associative learning. *Annual Review of Psychology, 56,* 207–234.

Fanselow, M. S., Lester, L. S., & Helmstetter, F. J. (1988). Changes in feeding and foraging patterns as an antipredator defensive strategy: A laboratory simulation using aversive stimulation in a closed economy. *Journal of the Experimental Analysis of Behavior, 50,* 361–374.

Farmer-Dougan, V. (1998). A disequilibrium analysis of incidental teaching determining reinforcement effects. *Behavior Modification, 22,* 78–95.

Feeney, M. C., Roberts, W. A., & Sherry, D. F. (2011). Black-capped chickadees (*Poecile atricapillus*) anticipate future outcomes of foraging choices. *Journal of Experimental Psychology: Animal Behavior Processes, 37,* 30–40.

Felton, M., & Lyon, D. O. (1966). The post-reinforcement pause. *Journal of the Experimental Analysis of Behavior, 9,* 131–134.

Ferster, C. B., & Skinner, B. F. (1957). *Schedules of Reinforcement*. New York: Appleton-Century-Crofts.

Fetsko, L. A., Stebbins, H. E., Gallagher, K. K., & Colwill, R. M. (2005). Acquisition and extinction of facilitation in the C57BL/6J mouse. *Learning & Behavior, 33,* 479–500.

Fetterman, J. G. (1995). The psychophysics of remembered duration. *Animal Learning & Behavior, 23,* 49–62.

Fetterman, J. G. (1996). Dimensions of stimulus complexity. *Journal of Experimental Psychology: Animal Behavior Processes, 22,* 3–18.

Fetterman, J. G., & Killeen, P. R. (2010). Prospective and retrospective timing by pigeons. *Learning & Behavior, 38,* 119–125.

Fiser, J. (2009). Perceptual learning and representational learning in humans and animals. *Learning & Behavior, 37,* 141–153.

Fiset, S. (2007). Landmark-based search memory in the domesticated dog (*Canis familiaris*). *Journal of Comparative Psychology, 121,* 345–353.

FitzGerald, R. E., Isler, R., Rosenberg, E., Oettinger, R., & Battig, K. (1985). Maze patrolling by rats with and without food reward. *Animal Learning & Behavior, 13,* 451–462.

Flagel, S. B., Akil, H., & Robinson, T. E. (2009). Individual differences in the attribution of incentive salience to reward-related cues: Implications for addiction. *Neuropharmacology, 56* (supplement 1), 139–148.

Flagel, S. B., et al. (2011). A selective role for dopamine in stimulus-reward learning. *Nature, 469,* 53–57.

Flaherty, C. F. (1996). *Incentive relativity.* Cambridge, UK: Cambridge University Press.

Flaten, M. A., & Blumenthal, T. D. (1999). Caffeine-associated stimuli elicit conditioned responses: An experimental model of the placebo effect. *Psychopharmacology, 145,* 105–112.

Foa, E. B., Zinbarg, R., & Rothbaum, B. O. (1992). Uncontrollability and unpredictability in post-traumatic stress disorder: An animal model. *Psychological Review, 112,* 218–238.

Foltin, R. W. (1999). Food and cocaine self-administration by baboons: Effects of alternatives. *Journal of the Experimental Analysis of Behavior, 72,* 215–234.

Foree, D. D., & LoLordo, V. M. (1973). Attention in the pigeon: The differential effects of food-getting vs. shock avoidance procedures. *Journal of Comparative and Physiological Psychology, 85,* 551–558.

Forestell, P. H., & Herman, L. M. (1988). Delayed matching of visual materials by a bottlenosed dolphin aided by auditory symbols. *Animal Learning & Behavior, 16,* 137–146.

Forgeard, M. J. C., Haigh, E. A. P., Beck, A. T., Davidson, R. J., Henn, F. A., Maier, S. F., Mayberg, H. S., & Seligman, M. E. P. (2011). Beyond depression: Towards a process-based approach to research, diagnosis, and treatment. *Clinical Psychology, 18,* 275–299.

Fountain, S. B., et al. (2012). The organization of sequential behavior:

Conditioning, memory, and abstraction. In T. R. Zentall & E. A. Wasserman (Eds.), *The Oxford handbook of comparative cognition* (pp. 594–614). New York/Oxford: Oxford University Press.

Foxx, R. M., & Azrin, N. H. (1973). The elimination of aubstic selfstimulatory behavior by overcorrection. *Journal of Applied Behavioral Analysis, 6,* 1–14.

France, K. G., & Hudson, S. M. (1990). Behavior management of infant sleep disturbance. *Journal of Applied Behavior Analysis, 23,* 91–98.

Franklin, S., & Hall, G. (2011). Analysis of US-preexposure effects in appetitive conditioning. *Journal of Experimental Psychology: Animal Behavior Processes, 37,* 495–500.

Freeman, J. H., & Nicholson, D. A. (2004). Developmental changes in the neural mechanisms of eyeblink conditioning. *Behavioral and Cognitive Neuroscience Reviews, 3,* 3–13.

Freeman, J. H., & Steinmetz, A. B. (2011). Neural circuitry and plasticity mechanisms underlying delayed eyeblink conditioning. *Learning & Memory, 18,* 666–677.

Fremouw, T., Herbranson, W. T., & Shimp, C. P. (2002). Dynamic shifts of avian local/global attention. *Animal Cognition, 5,* 233–243.

Friedman, B. X., Blaisdell, A. P., Escobar, M., & Miller, R. R. (1998). Comparator mechanisms and conditioned inhibition: Conditioned stimulus preexposure disrupts Pavlovian conditioned inhibition but not explicitly unpaired inhibition. *Journal of Experimental Psychology: Animal Behavior Processes, 24,* 453–466.

Frisher, M., & Beckett, H. (2006). Drug use desistance. *Criminology and criminal justice, 6,* 127–145.

Gallistel, C. R. (2012). Extinction from a rationalist perspective. *Behavioural Processes, 90,* 66–80.

Gallistel, C. R., & Gibbon, J. (2000). Time, rate, and conditioning. *Psychological Review, 107,* 289–344.

Gallistel, C. R., & Gibbon, J. (2001). Computational versus associative models of simple conditioning. *Current Directions in Psychological Science, 10,* 146–150.

Gallistel, C. R., & Matzel, L. D. (2013). The neuroscience of learning: Beyond the

Hebbian synapse. *Annual Review of Psychology, 64,* 169–200.

Galluccio, L., & Rovee-Collier, C. (1999). Reinstatement effects on retention at 3 months of age. *Learning and Motivation, 30,* 296–316.

Gallup, G. G., Jr., & Suarez, S. D. (1985). Alternatives to the use of animals in psychological research. *American Psychologist, 40,* 1104–1111.

Galtress, T., Marshall, A. T., & Kirkpatrick, K. (2012). Motivation and timing: Clues for modeling the reward system. *Behavioural Processes, 90,* 142–153.

Gámez, A. M., & Rosas, J. M. (2007). Associations in human instrumental conditioning. *Learning & Motivation, 38,* 242–261.

Gamzu, E. R., & Williams, D. R. (1973). Associative factors underlying the pigeon's key pecking in autoshaping procedures. *Journal of the Experimental Analysis of Behavior, 19,* 225–232.

Gantt, W. H. (1966). Conditional or conditioned, reflex or response? *Conditioned Reflex, 1,* 69–74.

Garcia, J., & Koelling, R. A. (1966). Relation of cue to consequence in avoidance learning. *Psychonomic Science, 4,* 123–124.

Garcia, J., Ervin, F. R., & Koelling, R. A. (1966). Learning with prolonged delay of reinforcement. *Psychonomic Science, 5,* 121–122.

Gardner, E. T., & Lewis, P. (1976). Negative reinforcement with shockfrequency increase. *Journal of the Experimental Analysis of Behavior, 25,* 3–14.

Gardner, R. A., & Gardner, B. T. (1969). Teaching sign language to a chimpanzee. *Science, 165,* 664–672.

Gardner, R. A., & Gardner, B. T. (1975). Early signs of language in child and chimpanzee. *Science, 187,* 752–753.

Gardner, R. A., & Gardner, B. T. (1978). Comparative psychology and language acquisition. *Annals of the New York Academy of Science, 309,* 37–76.

Garner, A., & Mayford, M. (2012). New approaches to neural circuits in behavior. *Learning & Memory, 19,* 385–390.

Gasbarri, A., & Tomaz, C. (2013). Habit formation. In N. M. Seel (Ed.), *Encyclopedia of the Sciences of Learning* (pp. 1409–1410). New York: Springer Science.

Gemberling, G. A., & Domjan, M. (1982). Selective association in one-day-old

rats: Taste-toxicosis and texture-shock aversion learning. *Journal of Comparative and Physiological Psychology, 96,* 105–113.

Gershoff, E. T. (2002). Parental corporal punishment and associated child behaviors and experiences: A meta-analytic and theoretical review. *Psychological Bulletin, 128,* 539–579.

Gershoff, E. T. (2008). *Report on Physical Punishment in the United States.* Columbus, OH: Center for Effective Discipline.

Gershoff, E. T., Grogan-Kaylor, A., Lansford, J. E., Chang, L., Zelli, A., Deater-Deckard, K., et al. (2010). Parent discipline practices in an international sample: Associations with child behaviors and moderation by perceived normativeness. *Child Development, 81,* 487–502.

Ghirlanda, S., & Enquist, M. (2003). A century of generalization. *Animal Behaviour, 66,* 15–36.

Gibbon, J., & Balsam, P. (1981). Spreading association in time. In C. M. Locurto, H. S. Terrace, & J. Gibbon (Eds.), *Autoshaping and conditioning theory* (pp. 219–253). New York: Academic Press.

Gibbon, J., & Church, R. M. (1984). Sources of variance in an information processing theory of timing. In H. L. Roitblat, T. G. Bever, & H. S. Terrace (Eds.), *Animal cognition.* Hillsdale, NJ: Erlbaum.

Gibson, B. M., & Shettleworth, S. J. (2003). Competition among spatial cues in a naturalistic food-carrying task. *Learning & Behavior, 31,* 143–159.

Gibson, J. (1979). *The ecological approach to visual perception.* Boston: Houghton Mifflin.

Gilbert, D. (2006). *Stumbling on happiness.* New York: Afred A. Knopf.

Gillan, D. J., & Domjan, M. (1977). Taste-aversion conditioning with expected versus unexpected drug treatment. *Journal of Experimental Psychology: Animal Behavior Processes, 3,* 297–309.

Gillihan, S. J., & Foa, E. B. (2011). Fear extinction and emotional processing theory: A critical review. In T. R. Schachtman & S. Reilly (Eds.), *Associative learning and conditioning theory: Human and non-human applications* (pp. 27–43). New York: Oxford University Press.

Gisiner, R., & Schusterman, R. J. (1992). Sequence, syntax, and semantics: Responses of a language-trained sea lion (*Zalophus californianus*) to novel sign combinations. *Journal of Comparative Psychology, 106,* 78–91.

Gisquet-Verrier, P., & Alexinsky, T. (1990). Facilitative effect of a pretest exposure to the CS: Analysis and implications for the memory trace. *Animal Learning & Behavior, 18,* 323–331.

Gisquet-Verrier, P., & Riccio, D. C. (2012). Memory reactivation effects independent of reconsolidation. *Learning & Memory, 19,* 401–409.

Glanzman, D. L. (2006). The cellular mechanisms of learning in *Aplysia*: Of blind men and elephants. *Biological Bulletin, 210,* 271–279.

Glanzman, D. L. (2008). New tricks for an old slug: The critical role of postsynaptic mechanisms in learning and memory in *Aplysia. Progress in Brain Research, 169,* 277–292.

Glover, E. M., et al. (2011). Tools for translational neuroscience: PTSD is associated with heightened fear responses using acoustic startle but not skin conductance measures. *Depression and Anxiety, 28,* 1058–1066.

Gnadt, W., & Grossberg, S. (2007). SOVEREIGN: An autonomous neural system for incrementally learning planned action sequences to navigate toward a rewarded goal. *Neural Networks, 21,* 699–758.

Godsil, B. P., & Fanselow, M. S. (2004). Light stimulus change evokes an activity response in the rat. *Learning & Behavior, 32,* 299–310.

Gold, P. (2008). Memory enhancing drugs. In H. Eichenbaum (Ed.), *Learning and memory: A comprehensive reference, Vol. 3: Memory systems* (pp. 555–576). Oxford: Elsevier.

Goodall, G. (1984). Learning due to the response-shock contingency in signalled punishment. *Quarterly Journal of Experimental Psychology, 36B,* 259–279.

Gordon, W. C. (1981). Mechanisms for cue-induced retention enhancement. In N. E. Spear & R. R. Miller (Eds.), *Information processing in animals: Memory mechanisms.* Hillsdale, NJ: Erlbaum.

Gormezano, I., Kehoe, E. J., & Marshall, B. S. (1983). Twenty years of classical conditioning research with the rabbit. In J. M. Prague & A. N. Epstein (Eds.), *Progress in psychobiology and physiological psychology* (Vol. 10). New York: Academic Press.

Grace, R. C. (1999). The matching law and amount-dependent exponential discounting as accounts of selfcontrol choice. *Journal of the Experimental Analysis of Behavior, 71,* 27–44.

Grace, R. C., & Hucks, A. D. (2013). The allocation of operant behavior. In G. J. Madden (Ed.), *APA Handbook of Behavior Analysis, Vol. 1: Methods and Principles* (pp. 307–338). Washington, DC: American Psychological Association.

Grace, R. C., & Nevin, J. A. (2004). Behavioral momentum and Pavlovian conditioning. *Behavioral and Brain Sciences, 27,* 695–697.

Graeff, F. G., Viana, M. B., & Mora, P. O. (1997). Dual role of 5-HT in defense and anxiety. *Neuroscience and Biobehavioral Reviews, 21,* 791–799.

Grainger, J., Dufau, S., Montant, M., Ziegler, J. C., & Fagot, J. (2012). Orthographic processing in baboons (*Papio papio*). *Science, 336,* 245–248.

Grand, C., & Honey, R. C. (2008). Solving XOR. *Journal of Experimental Psychology: Animal Behavior Processes, 34,* 486–493.

Grant, D. S. (1976). Effect of sample presentation time on long-delay matching in the pigeon. *Learning and Motivation, 7,* 580–590.

Grant, D. S. (2000). Influence of intertrial interval duration on the intertrial agreement effect in delayed matching-to-sample with pigeons. *Animal Learning & Behavior, 28,* 288–297.

Grau, J. W., & Joynes, R. L. (2001). Spinal cord injury: From animal research to human therapy. In M. E. Carroll & J. B. Overmier (Eds.), *Animal research and human health: Advancing human welfare through behavioral science* (pp. 209–226). Washington, DC: American Psychological Association.

Grau, J. W., & Joynes, R. L. (2005). A neural-functionalist approach to learning. *International Journal of Comparative Psychology, 18,* 1–22.

Grau, J. W., Crown, E. D., Ferguson, A. R., Washburn, S. N., Hook, M. A., & Miranda, R. C. (2006). Instrumental learning within the spinal cord: Underlying mechanisms and implications for recovery after injury.

Behavioral and Cognitive Neuroscience Reviews, 5, 1–48.

Grau, J. W., Huie, J. R., Garraway, S. M., Hook, M. A., Crown, E. D., Baumbauer, K. M., Lee, K. H., Hoy, K. C., & Ferguson, A. F. (2012). Impact of behavioral control on the processing of nociceptive stimulation. *Frontiers in Integrative Physiology, 3,* 1–21.

Greenfield, P. M., & Savage-Rumbaugh, E. S. (1990). Grammatical combination in *Pan paniscus*: Processes of learning and invention in the evolution and development of language. In S. T. Parker & K. R. Gibson (Eds.), *Language and intelligence in monkeys and apes* (pp. 540–578). Cambridge: Cambridge University Press.

Greenfield, P., & Lyn, H. (2007). Symbol combination in *Pan*: Language, Action, and Culture. In D. A. Washburn (Ed.), *Primate perspectives on behavior and cognition* (pp. 255–267). Washington, DC: American Psychological Association.

Grice, G. R. (1948). The relation of secondary reinforcement to delayed reward in visual discrimination learning. *Journal of Experimental Psychology, 38,* 1–16.

Griffin, D. R. (1992). *Animal minds.* Chicago: University of Chicago Press.

Grigson, P. S., et al. (2009). Drug-induced suppression of CS intake: Reward, aversion, and addiction. In S. Reilly & T. R. Schachtman (Eds.), *Conditioned taste aversion: Behavioral and neural processes* (pp. 74–91). Oxford/New York: Oxford University Press.

Groves, P. M., & Thompson, R. F. (1970). Habituation: A dual-process theory. *Psychological Review, 77,* 419–450.

Groves, P. M., Lee, D., & Thompson, R. F. (1969). Effects of stimulus frequency and intensity on habituation and sensitization in acute spinal cat. *Physiology and Behavior, 4,* 383–388.

Guttman, N., & Kalish, H. I. (1956). Discriminability and stimulus generalization. *Journal of Experimental Psychology, 51,* 79–88.

Habib, D., & Dringenberg, H. C. (2010). Low-frequency induced potentiation: A paradigm shift in the field of memory-related plasticity mechanisms? *Hippocampus, 20,* 29–35.

Haggbloom, S. J., Lovelace, L., Brewer, V. R., Levins, S. M., & Owens, J. D. (1990). Replacement of event-generated memories of nonreinforcement with signal-generated memories of reinforcement during partial reinforcement training: Effects on resistance to extinction. *Animal Learning & Behavior, 18,* 315–322.

Hagopian, L. P., Dozier, C. L., Rooker, G. W., & Jones, B. A. (2013). Assessment and treatment of severe problem behavior. In G. J. Madden (Ed.), *APA Handbook of Behavior Analysis, Vol. 2: Translating Principles into Practice* (pp. 353–386). Washington, DC: American Psychological Association.

Hake, D. F., & Azrin, N. H. (1965). Conditioned punishment. *Journal of the Experimental Analysis of Behavior, 8,* 279–293.

Halberstandt, A. L., & Geyer, M. A. (2009). Habituation and sensitization of acoustic startle: Opposite influences of dopamine D1 and D2-family receptors. *Neurobiology of Learning and Memory, 92,* 243–248.

Hall, G. (1991). *Perceptual and associative learning.* Oxford, UK: Clarendon Press.

Hall, G. (2009). Preexposure to the US in nausea-based aversion learning. In S. Reilly & T. R. Schachtman (Eds.), *Conditioned taste aversion: Behavioral and neural processes* (pp. 58–73). Oxford/New York: Oxford University Press.

Hall, G., Kaye, H., & Pearce, J. M. (1985). Attention and conditioned inhibition. In R. R. Miller & N. E. Spear (Eds.), *Information processing in animals: Conditioned inhibition.* Hillsdale, NJ: Erlbaum.

Hallam, S. C., Grahame, N. J., Harris, K., & Miller, R. R. (1992). Associative structures underlying enhanced negative summation following operational extinction of a Pavlovian inhibitor. *Learning and Motivation, 23,* 43–62.

Hammack, S., Cooper, M. A., & Lezak, L. R. (2012). Overlapping neurobiology of learned helplessness and conditioned defeat: Implications for PTSD and mood disorders. *Neuropharmacology, 62,* 565–575.

Hanley, G. P., Iwata, B. A., Thompson, R. H., & Lindberg, J. S. (2000). A component analysis of "stereotypy as reinforcement" for alternative behavior. *Journal of Applied Behavioral Analysis, 33,* 285–297.

Hanson, H. M. (1959). Effects of discrimination training on stimulus generalization. *Journal of Experimental Psychology, 58,* 321–333.

Hardt, O., Einarsson, E. Ö., & Nader, K. (2010). A bridge over troubled water: Reconsolidation as a link between cognitive and neuroscientific memory research traditions. *Annual Review of Psychology, 61,* 141–167.

Harlow, H. F. (1969). Age-mate or peer affectional system. In D. S. Lehrman, R. H. Hinde, & E. Shaw (Eds.), *Advances in the study of behavior* (Vol. 2). New York: Academic Press.

Harper, D. N., & Garry, M. (2000). Postevent cues bias recognition performance in pigeons. *Animal Learning & Behavior, 28,* 59–67.

Harris, E. H., Gulledge, J. P., Beran, M. J., & Washburn, D. A. (2010). What do Arabic numerals mean to macaques (Macaca mulatta)? *Journal of Experimental Psychology: Animal Behavior Processes, 36,* 66–76.

Harris, J. A., Gharaei, S., & Moore, C. A. (2009). Representations of single and compound stimuli in negative and positive patterning. *Leaning & Behavior, 37,* 230–245.

Harris, J. A., Jones, M. L., Bailey, G. K., & Westbrook, R. F. (2000). Contextual control over conditioned responding in an extinction paradigm. *Journal of Experimental Psychology: Animal Behavior Processes, 26,* 174–185.

Harris, J. A., Livesey, E. J., Gharaei, S., & Westbrook, R. F. (2008). Negative patterning is easier than a biconditional discrimination. *Journal of Experimental Psychology: Animal Behavior Processes, 34,* 494–500.

Harvey, L., Inglis, S. J., & Espie, C. A. (2002). Insomniac's reported use of CBT components and relationship to long-term clinical outcome. *Behavioural Research and Therapy, 40,* 75–83.

Haselgrove, M., & Hogarth, L. (2012). *Clinical applications of learning theory.* Hove and New York: Psychology Press.

Haselgrove, M., Aydin, A., & Pearce, J. M. (2004). A partial reinforcement extinction effect despite equal rates of reinforcement during Pavlovian conditioning. *Journal of Experimental Psychology: Animal Behavior Processes, 30,* 240–250.

Hawkins, R. D., & Kandel, E. R. (1984). Is there a cell-biological alphabet for simple forms of learning? *Psychological Review, 91,* 375–391.

Hawkins, R. D., Kandel, E. R., & Bailey, C. H. (2006). Molecular mechanisms of memory storage in Aplysia. *Biological Bulletin, 210,* 174–191.

Hayes, K. J., & Hayes, C. (1951). The intellectual development of a homeraised chimpanzee. *Proceedings of the American Philosophical Society, 95,* 105–109.

Healy, S. D., & Hurly, R. A. (1995). Spatial memory in rufous hummingbirds (Selasphorus rufus): A field test. *Animal Learning & Behavior, 23,* 63–68.

Hearst, E. (1968). Discrimination learning as the summation of excitation and inhibition. *Science, 162,* 1303–1306.

Hearst, E. (1969). Excitation, inhibition, and discrimination learning. In N. J. Mackintosh & W. K. Honig (Eds.), *Fundamental issues in associative learning.* Halifax: Dalhousie University Press.

Hearst, E. (1975). Pavlovian conditioning and directed movements. In G. Bower (Ed.), *The psychology of learning and motivation* (Vol. 9). New York: Academic Press.

Hearst, E., & Jenkins, H. M. (1974). *Sign-tracking: The stimulusreinforcer relation and directed action.* Austin, TX: Psychonomic Society.

Hebb, D. O. (1949). *The Organization of Behavior.* New York: Wiley.

Heffner, H. E. (1998). Auditory awareness. *Applied Animal Behavioural Science, 57,* 259–268.

Heimbauer, L. A., Beran, M. J., & Owren, M. J. (2011). A chimpanzee recognizes synthetic speech with significantly reduced acoustic cues to phonetic content. *Current Biology, 21,* 1210–1214.

Herbranson, W. T., Fremouw, T., & Shimp, C. P. (2002). Categorizing a moving target in terms of its speed and direction. *Journal of the Experimental Analysis of Behavior, 78,* 249–270.

Herman, L. M. (1987). Receptive competencies of language-trained animals. In J. S. Rosenblatt, C. Beer, M.-C. Busnel, & P. J. B. Slater (Eds.), *Advances in the study of behavior* (Vol. 17, pp. 1–60). Orlando, FL: Academic Press.

Herman, L. M., & Uyeyama, R. K. (1999). The dolphin's grammatical competency: Comments on Kako (1999). *Animal Learning & Behavior, 27,* 18–23.

Herman, L. M., Pack, A. A., & Morrel-Samuels, P. (1993). Representational and conceptual skills of dolphins.

In H. L. Roitblat, L. M. Herman, & P. E. Nachtigall (Eds.), *Language and communication: Comparative perspectives* (pp. 403–442). Hillsdale, NJ: Erlbaum.

Herman, R. L., & Azrin, N. H. (1964). Punishment by noise in an alternative response situation. *Journal of the Experimental Analysis of Behavior, 7,* 185–188.

Hernandez, P. J., & Abel, T. (2008). The role of protein synthesis in memory consolidation: Progress amid decades of debate. *Neurobiology of Learning and Memory, 89,* 293–311.

Herrnstein, R. J. (1961). Relative and absolute strength of response as a function of frequency of reinforcement. *Journal of the Experimental Analysis of Behavior, 4,* 267–272.

Herrnstein, R. J. (1969). Method and theory in the study of avoidance. *Psychological Review, 76,* 49–69.

Herrnstein, R. J. (1970). On the law of effect. *Journal of the Experimental Analysis of Behavior, 13,* 243–266.

Herrnstein, R. J. (1997). In H. Rachlin & D. I. Laibson (Eds.), *The matching law.* New York: Russell Sage; and Cambridge: Harvard University Press.

Herrnstein, R. J., & Hineline, P. N. (1966). Negative reinforcement as shock-frequency reduction. *Journal of the Experimental Analysis of Behavior, 9,* 421–430.

Herrnstein, R. J., Loveland, D. H., & Cable, C. (1976). Natural concepts in pigeons. *Journal of Experimental Psychology: Animal Behavior Processes, 2,* 285–301.

Herzog, H. A., Jr. (1988). The moral status of mice. *American Psychologist, 43,* 473–474.

Hespos, S. J., Ferry, A. L., & Rips, L. J. (2009). Five-month-old infants have different expectations for solids and liquids. *Psychological Science, 20,* 603–611.

Heyman, G. M., & Herrnstein, R. J. (1986). More on concurrent interval-ratio schedules: A replication and review. *Journal of the Experimental Analysis of Behavior, 46,* 331–351.

Higgins, S. T., Heil, S. H., & Sigmon, S. C. (2012). Voucher-based contingency management in the treatment of substance use disorder. In G. J. Madden (Ed.), *APA Handbook of Behavior Analysis, Vol. 2: Translating Principles into Practice* (pp. 281–500). Washington, DC: American Psychological Association.

Hilliard, S. H., Domjan, M., Nguyen, M., & Cusato, B. (1998). Dissociation of conditioned appetitive and consummatory sexual behavior: Satiation and extinction tests. *Animal Learning & Behavior, 26,* 20–33.

Hillix, W. A., & Rumbaugh, D. (2004). *Animal bodies, human minds: Ape, dolphin, and parrot language skills.* New York: Kluwer academic/Plenum.

Hineline, P. N. (1977). Negative reinforcement and avoidance. In W. K. Honig & J. E. R. Staddon (Eds.), *Handbook of operant behavior.* Englewood Cliffs. NJ: Prentice-Hall.

Hineline, P. N. (1981). The several roles of stimuli in negative reinforcement. In P. Harzem & M. D. Zeiler (Eds.), *Predictability, correlation, and contiguity.* Chichester, UK: Wiley.

Hineline, P. N., & Rosales-Ruiz, J. (2013). Behavior in relation to aversive events: Punishment and negative reinforcement. In G. J. Madden (Ed.), *APA Handbook of Behavior Analysis, Vol. 1: Methods and Principles* (pp. 483–512). Washington, DC: American Psychological Association.

Hoffman, C. M., Timberlake, W., Leffel, J., & Gont, R. (1999). How is radial arm maze behavior in rats related to locomotor search tactics? *Animal Learning & Behavior, 27,* 426–444.

Hoffman, H. S., & Fleshler, M. (1964). An apparatus for the measurement of the startle-response in the rat. *American Journal of Psychology, 77,* 307–308.

Hoffmann, H. (2011). Hot and bothered: Classical conditioning of sexual incentives in humans. In T. R. Schachtman & S. Reilly (Eds.), *Associative learning and conditioning theory: Human and non-human applications* (pp. 532–550). Oxford, UK: Oxford University Press.

Hoffman, M. L., Beran, M. J., & Washburn, D. A. (2009). Memory for "what," "where," and "when" information in rhesus monkeys (*Macaca mulatta*). *Journal of Experimental Psychology: Animal Behavior Processes, 35,* 143–152.

Hoffmann, W., De Houwer, J., Perugini, M., Baeyens, F., & Crombez, G. (2010). Evaluative conditioning in humans: A meta-analysis. *Psychological Bulletin, 136,* 390–421.

Hogarth, L., & Chase, H. W. (2011). Parallel goal-directed and habitual control of human drug-seeking: Implications for dependence vulnerability. *Journal of Experimental Psychology: Animal Behavior Processes, 37,* 261–276.

Hogarth, L., Dickinson, A., & Duka, T. (2010). Selective attention to conditioned stimuli in human discrimination learning: Untangling the effects of outcome prediction, valence, arousal, and uncertainty. In C. J. Mitchell & M. E. Le Pelley (Eds.), *Attention and associative learning* (pp. 71–97). Oxford, UK: Oxford University Press.

Hogarth, L., Dickinson, A., & Duka, T. (2010). The associative basis of cue-elicited drug taking in humans. *Psychopharmacology, 208,* 337–351.

Hogarth, L., Dickinson, A., Wright, A., Kouvaraki, M., & Duka, T. (2007). The role of drug expectancy in the control of human drug seeking. *Journal of Experimental Psychology: Animal Behavior Processes, 33,* 484–496.

Holland, P. C. (1984). Origins of behavior in Pavlovian conditioning. In G. H. Bower (Ed.), *The psychology of learning and motivation* (Vol. 18, pp. 129–174). Orlando, FL: Academic Press.

Holland, P. C. (1985). The nature of conditioned inhibition in serial and simultaneous feature negative discriminations. In R. R. Miller & N. E. Spear (Eds.), *Information processing in animals: Conditioned inhibition.* Hillsdale, NJ: Erlbaum.

Holland, P. C. (1986). Temporal determinants of occasion setting in feature-positive discriminations. *Animal Learning and Behavior, 14,* 111–120.

Holland, P. C. (1989). Feature extinction enhances transfer of occasion setting. *Animal Learning & Behavior, 17,* 269–279.

Holland, P. C. (1992). Occasion setting in Pavlovian conditioning. In D. L. Medin (Ed.), *The psychology of learning and motivation* (Vol. 28, pp. 69–125). San Diego, CA: Academic Press.

Holland, P. C. (2000). Trial and intertrial durations in appetitive conditioning in rats. *Animal Learning & Behavior, 28,* 121–135.

Holland, P. C. (2004). Relations between pavlovian-instrumental transfer and reinforcer devaluation. *Journal of Experimental Psychology: Animal Behavior Processes, 30,* 104–117.

Holland, P. C., & Gallagher, M. (1999). Amygdala circuitry in attentional and representational processes. *Trends in Cognitive Science, 3,* 65–73.

Holland, P. C., & Kenmuir, C. (2005). Variations in unconditioned stimulus processing in unblocking. *Journal of Experimental Psychology: Animal Behavior Processes, 31,* 155–171.

Holland, P. C., & Maddux, J.-M. (2010). Brain systems of attention in associative learning. In C. J. Mitchell & M. E. Le Pelley (Eds.), *Attention and associative learning* (pp. 305–349). Oxford, UK: Oxford University Press.

Holland, P. C., & Rescorla, R. A. (1975). The effect of two ways of devaluing the unconditioned stimulus after first-and second-order appetitive conditioning. *Journal of Experimental Psychology: Animal Behavior Processes, 1,* 355–363.

Hollis, K. L. (1997). Contemporary research on Pavlovian conditioning: A "new" functional analysis. *American Psychologist, 52,* 956–965.

Hollis, K. L., Cadieux, E. L., & Colbert, M. M. (1989). The biological function of Pavlovian conditioning: A mechanism for mating success in the blue gourami (*Trichogaster trichopterus*). *Journal of Comparative Psychology, 103,* 115–121.

Holmes, N. M., Marchand, A. R., & Coutureau, E. (2010). Pavlovian to instrumental transfer: A neurobehavioural perspective. *Neuroscience and Biobehavioral Reviews, 34,* 1277–1295.

Holz, W. C., & Azrin, N. H. (1961). Discriminative properties of punishment. *Journal of the Experimental Analysis of Behavior, 4,* 225–232.

Holzhaider, J. C., Hunt, G. R., Gray, R. D. (2010). Social learning in New Caledonian crows. *Learning & Behavior, 38,* 206–219.

Honey, R. C., & Hall, G. (1989). Acquired equivalence and distinctiveness of cues. *Journal of Experimental Psychology: Animal Behavior Processes, 15,* 338–346.

Honig, W. K. (1978). Studies of working memory in the pigeon. In S. H. Hulse, H. Fowler, & W. K. Honig (Eds.), *Cognitive processes in animal behavior.* (pp. 221–248). Hillsdale, NJ: Erlbaum.

Honig, W. K., Boneau, C. A., Burstein, K. R., & Pennypaker, H. S. (1963). Positive and negative generalization gradients obtained under equivalent training conditions. *Journal of Comparative and Physiological Psychology, 56,* 111–116.

Honig, W. K., & Urcuioli, P. J. (1981). The legacy of Guttman and Kalish (1956): 25 years of research on stimulus generalization. *Journal of the Experimental Analysis of Behavior, 36,* 405–445.

Hook, M. A., & Grau, J. W. (2007). An animal model of functional electrical stimulation: Evidence that the central nervous system modulates the consequences of training. *Spinal Cord, 45,* 702–712.

Horgen, K. B., & Brownell, K. D. (2002). Comparison of price change and health message interventions in promoting healthy food choices. *Health Psychology, 21,* 505–512.

Horne, M. R., & Pearce, J. M. (2011). Potentiation and overshadowing between landmarks and environmental geometric cues. *Learning & Behavior, 39,* 371–382.

Horsley, R. R., Osborne, M., Norman, C., & Wells, T. (2012). High-frequency gamblers show increased resistance to extinction following partial reinforcement. *Behavioural Brain Research, 229,* 428–442.

Hourlhan, K. L., & Taylor, T. L. (2006). Case remembering: Control processes in directed forgetting. *Journal of Experimental Psychology: Human Perception and Performance, 32*(6), 1354–1365.

Hu, C. J., et al. (2003). Trace but not delay fear conditioning requires attention and the anterior cingulate cortex. *Proceedings of the National Academy of Sciences, 100,* 13087–13092.

Huber, L., & Aust, U. (2006). A modified feature theory as an account of pigeon visual categorization. In E. A. Wasserman & T. R. Zentall (Eds.), *Comparative cognition* (pp. 325–342). Oxford, UK: Oxford University Press.

Huber, L., & Aust, U. (2012). A modified feature theory as an account of pigeon visual categorization. In T. R. Zentall & E. A. Wasserman (Eds.), *The Oxford handbook of comparative cognition* (pp. 497–512). New York/Oxford: Oxford University Press.

Huber, L., Apfalter, W., Steurer, M., & Prossinger, H. (2005). A new learning paradigm elicits fast visual discrimination in pigeons. *Journal of Experimental Psychology: Animal Behavior Processes, 31,* 237–246.

Hull, C. L. (1930). Knowledge and purpose as habit mechanisms. *Psychological Review, 30,* 511–525.

Hull, C. L. (1931). Goal attraction and directing ideas conceived as habit phenomena. *Psychological Review, 38,* 487–506.

Hulse, S. H. (1958). Amount and percentage of reinforcement and duration of goal confinement in conditioning and extinction. *Journal of Experimental Psychology, 56,* 48–57.

Hunt, G. R., Rutledge, R. B., & Gray, R. D. (2006). The right tool for the job: What stratetgies do wild New Caledonian crows use? *Animal Cognition, 9,* 307–316.

Hunter, W. S. (1913). The delayed reaction in animals and children. *Behavior Monographs, 2,* serial #6.

Hursh, S. R., Madden, G. J., Spiga, R., DeLeon, I., & Francisco, M. T. (2013). The translational utility of behavioral economics: The experimental analysis of consumption and choice. In G. J. Madden (Ed.), *APA Handbook of Behavior Analysis, Vol. 2: Translating Principles into Practice* (pp. 191–224). Washington, DC: American Psychological Association.

Hyman, S. E., Malenka, R. C., & Nestler, E. J. (2006). Neural mechanisms of addiction: The role of reward-related learning and memory. *Annual Review of Neuroscience, 29,* 565–598.

Innis, N. K., Simmelhag-Grant, V. L., & Staddon, J. E. R. (1983). Behavior induced by periodic food delivery: The effects of interfood interval. *Journal of the Experimental Analysis of Behavior, 39,* 309–322.

Irwin, M. R., Cole, J. C., & Nicassio, P. M. (2006). Comparative metaanalysis of behavioral interventions for insomnia and their efficacy in middle-aged adults and in older adults 55+ years of age. *Health Psychology, 25,* 3–14.

Ishida, M., & Papini, M. R. (1997). Massedtrial overtraining effects on extinction and reversal performance in turtles (*Geoclemys reevesii*). *Quarterly Journal of Experimental Psychology, 50B,* 1–16.

Iversen, I. H. (1993). Acquisition of matching-to-sample performance in rats using visual stimuli on nose keys. *Journal of the Experimental Analysis of Behavior, 59,* 471–482.

Ivkovich, D., Collins, K. L., Eckerman, C. O., Krasnegor, N. A., & Stanton, M. E. (1999). Classical delay eyeblink conditioning in 4- and 5-month-old human infants. *Psychological Science, 10,* 4–8.

Jackson, R. L., & Minor, T. R. (1988). Effects of signaling inescapable shock on subsequent escape learning: Implications for theories of coping and "learned helplessness." *Journal of Experimental Psychology: Animal Behavior Processes, 14,* 390–400.

Jackson, R. L., Alexander, J. H., & Maier, S. F. (1980). Learned helplessness, inactivity, and associative deficits: Effects of inescapable shock on response choice escape learning. *Journal of Experimental Psychology: Animal Behavior Processes, 6,* 1–20.

Jacobs, E. A., Borrero, J. C., & Vollmer, T. R. (2013). Translational applications of quantitative choice models. In G. J. Madden (Ed.), *APA Handbook of Behavior Analysis, Vol. 2: Translating Principles into Practice* (pp. 165–190). Washington, DC: American Psychological Association.

Jacobs, L. F., & Schenk, F. (2003). Unpacking the cognitive map: The parallel map theory of hippocampal function. *Psychological Review, 110,* 285–315.

Jacobs, N. S., Cushman, J. D., & Fanselow, M. S. (2010). The accurate measurement of fear memory in Pavlovian conditioning: Resolving the baseline issue. *Journal of Neuroscience Methods, 190,* 235–239.

Jasnow, A. M., Cullen, P. K., & Riccio, D. C. (2012). Remembering another aspect of forgetting. *Frontiers in Psychology, 3,* article 175. Doi:10.3389/fpsyg.2012 .00175

Jenkins, H. M. (1962). Resistance to extinction when partial reinforcement is followed by regular reinforcement. *Journal of Experimental Psychology, 64,* 441–450.

Jenkins, H. M., & Harrison, R. H. (1960). Effects of discrimination training on auditory generalization. *Journal of Experimental Psychology, 59,* 246–253.

Jenkins, H. M., & Harrison, R. H. (1962). Generalization gradients of inhibition following auditory discrimination learning. *Journal of the Experimental Analysis of Behavior, 5,* 435–441.

Jenkins, H. M., & Moore, B. R. (1973). The form of the autoshaped response with food or water reinforcers. *Journal of the Experimental Analysis of Behavior, 20,* 163–181.

Jenkins, H. M., Barnes, R. A., & Barrera, F. J. (1981). Why auto-shaping depends on trial spacing. In C. M. Locurto, H. S. Terrace, & J. Gibbon (Eds.), *Autoshaping and conditioning theory* (pp. 255–284). New York: Academic Press.

Jennings, D. J., Bonardi, C., & Kirkpatrick, K. (2007). Overshadowing and stimulus duration. *Journal of Experimental Psychology: Animal Behavior Processes, 33,* 464–475.

Jennings, H. E. (1976). *Behavior of lower organisms.* Bloomington, IN: Indiana University Press. (Originally published 1904.)

Ji, R.-R., Kohno, T., Moore, K. A., & Woolf, C. J. (2003). Central sensitization and LTP: Do pain and memory share similar mechanisms? *Trends in Neuroscience, 26,* 696–705.

Jiao, C., Knight, P. K., Weerakoon, P., & Turman, A. B. (2007). Effects of visual erotic stimulation on vibrotactile detection thresholds in men. *Archives of Sexual Behavior, 36,* 787–792.

Jimenez-Gomez, C., & Shahan, T. A. (2012). Concurrent-chain schedules as a method to study choice between alcohol-associated conditioned reinforcers. *Journal of the Experimental Analysis of Behavior, 97,* 71–83.

Jimura, K., et al. (2011). Domain independence and stability in young and older adults' discounting of delayed rewards. *Behavioural Processes, 87,* 253–259.

Jitsumori, M. (2006). Category structure and typicality effects. In E. A. Wasserman & T. R. Zentall (Eds.), *Comparative cognition* (pp. 343–362). Oxford, UK: Oxford University Press.

Jitsumori, M. (2012). Artificial categories and prototype effects in animals. In T. R. Zentall & E. A. Wasserman (Eds.), *The Oxford handbook of comparative cognition* (pp. 513–532). New York/ Oxford: Oxford University Press.

Jitsumori, M., Shimada, N., & Inoue, S. (2006). Family resemblance facilitates formation and expansion of functional equivalence classes in pigeons. *Learning & Behavior, 34,* 162–175.

Job, R. F. S. (2002). The effects of uncontrollable, unpredictable aversive and appetitive events: Similar effects warrant similar, but not identical, explanations? *Integrative Psychological and Behavioral Science, 37,* 59–81.

Johansen, J. P., Cain, C. K., Ostroff, L. E., & LeDoux, J. E. (2011). Molecular mechanisms of fear learning and memory. *Cell, 147,* 509–524.

Johansen, J. P., Wolff, S. B. E., Lüthi, A., & LeDoux, J. E. (2012). Controlling the elements: An optogenetic approach to understanding the neural circuits of fear. *Biological Psychiatry, 71,* 1053–1060.

Johnson, H. M. (1994). Processes of successful intentional forgetting. *Psychological Bulletin, 116,* 274–292.

Johnson, J. W., Munk, D. D., van Laarhoven, T., Repp, A. C., & Dahlquist, C. M. (2003). Classroom applications of the disequilibrium model of reinforcement. *Behavioral Interventions, 18,* 63–85.

Johnson, M. W., & Bickel, W. K. (2006). Replacing relative reinforcing efficacy with behavioral economic demand curves. *Journal of the Experimental Analysis of Behavior, 85,* 73–93.

Jones, B. M. (2003). Quantitative analyses of matching-to-sample performance. *Journal of the Experimental Analysis of Behaivor, 79,* 323–350.

Jostad, C. M., Miltenberger, R. G., Kelso, P., & Knudson, P. (2008). Peer tutoring to prevent firearm play: Acquisition, generalization, and long-term maintenance of safety skills. *Journal of Applied Behavior Analysis, 41,* 117–123.

Jozefowiez, J., & Staddon, J. E. R. (2008). Operant behavior. In R. Menzel (Ed.), *Learning theory and behavior.* Vol. 1 of J. Byrne (Ed.), *Learning and Memory: A comprehensive reference* (pp. 75–102). Oxford: Elsevier.

Jozefowiez, J., Staddon, J. E. R., & Cerutti, D. T. (2009). The behavioral economics of choice and interval timing. *Psychological Review, 116,* 519–539.

Kacelnik, A., Chappell, J., Kenward, B., & Weir, A. A. S. (2006). Cognitive adaptations for tool-related behavior in New Caledonian crows. In E. A. Wasserman & T. R. Zentall (Eds.), *Comparative cognition* (pp. 515–528). Oxford, UK: Oxford University Press.

Kaiser, D. H., Sherburne, L. M., & Zentall, T. R. (1997). Directed forgetting in pigeons resulting from reallocation of memory-maintaining processes on forget-cue trials. *Psychonomic Bulletin & Review, 4,* 559–565.

Kako, E. (1999). Elements of syntax in the systems of three language trained animals. *Animal Learning & Behavior, 27,* 1–14.

Kalat, J. W. (2009). *Biological Psychology.* Belmont, CA: Wadsworth.

Kalmbach, B. E., Ohyama, T., Kreider, J. C., Riusech, F., & Mauk, M. D. (2009). Interactions between prefrontal cortex and cerebellum revealed by trace eyelid conditioning. *Learning & Memory, 16,* 86–95.

Kamil, A. C. (1978). Systematic foraging by a nectarfeeding bird, the amakihi (*Loxops virens*). *Journal of Comparative and Physiological Psychology, 92*, 388–396.

Kamil, A. C., & Balda, R. P. (1985). Cache recovery and spatial memory in Clark's nutcrackers (*Nucifraga columbiana*). *Journal of Experimental Psychology: Animal Behavior Processes, 11*, 95–111.

Kamil, A. C., & Balda, R. P. (1990). Spatial memory in seed-caching corvids. In G. H. Bower (Ed.), *The psychology of learning and motivation* (Vol. 26, pp. 1–25). San Diego: Academic Press.

Kamil, A. C., & Gould, K. L. (2008). Memory in food caching animals. In R. Menzel (Ed.), *Learning theory and behavior*. Vol. 1 of J. Byrne (Ed.), *Learning and memory: A comprehensive reference* (pp. 419–440). Oxford: Elsevier.

Kamin, L. J., Brimer, C. J., & Black, A. H. (1963). Conditioned suppression as a monitor of fear of the CS in the course of avoidance training. *Journal of Comparative and Physiological Psychology, 56*, 497–501.

Kamin, L. J. (1965). Temporal and intensity characteristics of the conditioned stimulus. In W. F. Prokasy (Ed.), *Classical conditioning* (pp. 118–147). New York: Appleton-Century-Crofts.

Kamin, L. J. (1968). "Attention-like" processes in classical conditioning. In M. R. Jones (Ed.), *Miami Symposium on the Prediction of Behavior: Aversive stimulation* (pp. 9–31). Miami: University of Miami Press.

Kamin, L. J. (1969). Predictability, surprise, attention, and conditioning. In B. A. Campbell & R. M. Church (Eds.), *Punishment and aversive behavior* (pp. 279–296). New York: Appleton-Century-Crofts.

Kandel, E. R. (1976). *Cellular basis of behaviour*. San Francisco: Freeman.

Kandel, E. R., & Schwartz, J. H. (1982). Molecular biology of learning: Modulation of transmitter release. *Science, 218*, 433–443.

Kandel, E. R., Schwartz, J. H., & Jessell, T. M. (2000). *Principles of neural science*. New York: McGraw-Hill.

Kandel, E. R., Schwartz, J. H., Jessell, T. M., Siegelbaum, S. A., & Hudspeth, A. J. (2013). *Principles of neural science*. New York: McGraw Hill.

Kaplan, G. B., Heinrichs, S. C., & Carey, R. J. (2011). Treatment of addiction and anxiety using extinction approaches: Neural mechanisms and their treatment implications. *Pharmacology Biochemistry & Behavior, 97*, 619–625.

Kastak, D., & Schusterman, R. J. (1994). Transfer of visual identity matching-to-sample in two California sea lions (*Zatophus californianus*). *Animal Learning & Behavior, 22*, 427–435.

Kastak, D., & Schusterman, R. J. (1998). Low-frequency amphibious hearing in pinnipeds: Methods, measurement, noise, and ecology. *Journal of the Acoustical Society of America, 103*, 2216–2228.

Kastak, D., Schusterman, R. J., Southall, B. L., & Reichmuth, C. J. (1999). Underwater temporary threshold shift induced by octave-band noise in three species of pinniped. *Journal of the Acoustical Society of America, 106*, 1142–1148.

Katz, J. S., & Wright, A. A. (2006). Same/Different abstract-concept learning by pigeons. *Journal of Experimental Psychology: Animal Behavior Processes, 32*, 80–86.

Katzev, R. D., & Berman, J. S. (1974). Effect of exposure to conditioned stimulus and control of its termination in the extinction of avoidance behavior. *Journal of Comparative and Physiological Psychology, 87*, 347–353.

Kaufman, L. W., & Collier, G. (1983). Cost and meal pattern in wild-caught rats. *Physiology and Behavior, 30*, 445–449.

Kearns, D. N., Weiss, S. J., Schindler, C. W., & Panlilio, L. V. (2005). Conditioned inhibition of cocaine seeking in rats. *Journal of Experimental Psychology: Animal Behavior Processes, 31*, 247–253.

Kehoe, E. J. (2008). Discrimination and generalization. In R. Menzel (Ed.), *Learning theory and behavior*. Vol 1 of J. Byrne (Ed.), *Learning and memory: A comprehensive reference* (pp. 123–150). Oxford: Elsevier.

Kehoe, E. J., & White, N. E. (2004). Overexpectation: Response loss during sustained stimulus compounding in the rabbit nictitating membrane response. *Learning & Memory, 11*, 476–483.

Kelamangalath, L., Seymour, C. M., & Wagner, J. J. (2009). D-Serine facilitates the effects of extinction to reduce cocaine-primed reinstatement of drug-seeking behavior. *Neurobiology of Learning and Memory, 92*, 544–551.

Kelber, A., Vorobyev, M., & Osorio, D. (2003). Animal colour vision: Behavioural tests and physiological concepts. *Biological Reviews, 78*, 81–118.

Kellendonk, C., Simpson, E. H., Polan, H. J., Malleret, G., Vronskaya, S., Winiger, V., Moore, H. M., & Kandel, E. R. (2006). Transient and selective overexpression of dopamine D2 receptors in the striatum causes persistent abnormalities in prefrontal cortex functioning. *Neuron, 49*, 603–615.

Kelling, A. S., Snyder, R. J., Marr, M. J., Bloomsmith, M. A., Gardner, W., & Maple, T. L. (2006). Color vision in the giant panda (*Ailuropoda melanoleuca*). *Learning & Behavior, 34*, 154–161.

Kelly, D. M., & Spetch, M. L. (2012). Comparative spatial cognition. In T. R. Zentall & E. A. Wasserman (Eds.), *The Oxford handbook of comparative cognition* (pp. 366–389). New York/Oxford: Oxford University Press.

Kenward, B., Rutz, C., Weir, A. A. S., & Kacelnik, A. (2006). Development of tool use in New Caledonian crows: Inherited action patterns and social influences. *Animal Behaviour, 72*, 1329–1343.

Kenward, B., Weir, A. A. S., Rutz, C., & Kacelnik, A. (2005). Tool manufacture by naïve juvenile crows. *Nature, 433*, 121.

Kesner, R. P., & DeSpain, M. J. (1988). Correspondence between rats and humans in the utilization of retrospective and prospective codes. *Animal Learning & Behavior, 16*, 299–302.

Kesner, R. P., & Martinez, J. L. (2007). *Neurobiology of learning and memory*. Boston: Academic Press.

Killeen, P. R. (2001). Writing and overwriting short-term memory. *Psychonomic Bulletin & Review, 8*, 18–43.

Killeen, P. R., & Fetterman, J. G. (1993). The behavioral theory of timing: Transition analyses. *Journal of the Experimental Analysis of Behavior, 59*, 411–422.

Killeen, P. R., Fetterman, J. G., & Bizo, L. A. (1997). Time's causes. In C. M. Bradshaw & E. Szabadi (Eds.), *Time and behaviour: Psychological and neurobiological analyses* (pp. 79–239). Amsterdam: Elsevier Science.

Kim, J. J., Krupa, D. J., et al. (1998). Inhibitory cerebello-olivary projections and blocking effect in classical conditioning. *Science, 279*, 570–573.

Kim, S. D., Rivers, S., Bevins, R. A., & Ayres, J. J. B. (1996). Conditioned stimulus determinants of conditioned response form in Pavlovian fear conditioning. *Journal of Experimental Psychology: Animal Behavior Processes, 22,* 87–104.

Kimble, G. A. (1961). *Hilgard and Marquis' conditioning and learning* (2nd ed.). New York: Appleton.

Kimble, G. A., & Ost, J. W. P. (1961). A conditioned inhibitory process in eyelid conditioning. *Journal of Experimental Psychology, 61,* 150–156.

King, K. M., Fleming, C. B., Monahan, K. C., & Catalano, R. F. (2011). Changes in self-control problems and attention problems during middle school predict alcohol, tobacco, and marijuana use in high school. *Psychology of Addictive Behaviors, 25,* 69–79.

Kinloch, J. M., Foster, T. M., & McEwan, J. S. A. (2009). Extinction-induced variability in human behavior. *Psychological Record, 59,* 347–370.

Kirby, K. N. (2009). One-year temporal stability of delay-discounting. *Psychonomic Bulletin & Review, 16,* 457–462.

Kirby, K. N., Winston, G. C., & Santiesteban, M. (2005). Impatience and grades: Delay-discount rates correlate negatively with college GPA. *Learning and Individual Differences, 15,* 213–222.

Kirkpatrick, K. (2002). Packet theory of conditioning and timing. *Behavioural Processes, 57,* 89–106.

Kirkpatrick, K., & Church, R. M. (2000). Independent effects of stimulus and cycle duration in conditioning: The role of timing processes. *Animal Learning & Behavior, 28,* 373–388.

Kirkpatrick, K., & Church, R. M. (2003). Tracking of the expected time to reinforcement in temporal conditioning procedures. *Learning & Behavior, 31,* 3–21.

Kirkpatrick, K., & Church, R. M. (2004). Temporal learning in random control procedures. *Journal of Experimental Psychology: Animal Behavior Processes, 30,* 213–228.

Kirmayer, L. J., Lemelson, R., & Barad, M. (Eds.). (2007). *Understanding trauma: Integrating biological, clinical, and cultural perspectives.* Cambridge, UK: Cambridge University Press.

Klein, B. G., LaMon, B., & Zeigler, H. P. (1983). Drinking in the pigeon (*Columba livia*): Topography and spatiotemporal organization. *Journal*

of Comparative Psychology, 97, 178–181.

Knight, D. C., Waters, N. S., King, M. K., & Bandettini, P. A. (2010). Learning-related diminution of unconditioned SCR and fMRI signal responses. *NeuroImage, 49,* 843–848.

Koba, R., Takemoto, A., Miwa, M., & Nakamura, K. (2012). Characteristics of serial order learning in common marmosets (*Callithrix jacchus*). *Journal of Comparative Psychology, 126,* 279–287.

Köhler, W. (1927). *The mentality of apes.* London: Routledge & Kegan Paul.

Köhler, W. (1939). Simple structural functions in the chimpanzee and in the chicken. In W. D. Ellis (Ed.), *A source book of Gestalt psychology* (pp. 217–227). New York: Harcourt Brace Jovanovich.

Koob, G. F. (1999). Drug reward and addiction. In L. S. Squire, F. E. Bloom, S. K. McConnell, J. L. Roberts, N. C. Spitzer, & M. J. Zigmond (Eds.), *Fundamental neuroscience.* New York: Academic Press.

Koob, G. F. (2009). Neurobiological substrates for the dark side of compulsivity and addiction. *Neuropharmacology, 56,* 18–31.

Koob, G. F., & Le Moal, M. (2008). Addiction and the brain antireward system. *Annual Review of Psychology, 59,* 29–53.

Koychev, I., El-Deredy, W., Haenschel, C., & Deakin, J. F. W. (2010). Visual information processing deficits as biomarkers of vulnerability to schizophrenia: An event-related potential study in schizotypy. *Neuropsychologia, 48,* 2205–2214.

Kraemer, P. J., & Golding, J. M. (1997). Adaptive forgetting in animals. *Psychonomic Bulletin & Review, 4,* 480–491.

Krägeloh, C. U., Davison, M., & Elliffee, D. M. (2005). Local preference in concurrent schedules: The effects of reinforcer sequences. *Journal of the Experimental Analysis of Behavior, 84,* 37–64.

Krank, M. D., O'Neill, S. K., & Jacob, J. (2008). Goal- and signal-directed incentive: Conditioned approach, seeking, and consumption established with unsweetened alcohol in rats. *Psychopharmacology, 196,* 397–405.

Krieckhaus, E. E., & Wolf, G. (1968). Acquisition of sodium by rats: Interaction of innate and latent learning.

Journal of Comparative and Physiological Psychology, 65, 197–201.

Kruschke, J. (2008). Bayesian approaches to associative learning: From passive to active learning. *Learning & Behavior, 36,* 210–226.

Kruse, J. M., Overmier, J. B., Konz, W. A., & Rokke, E. (1983). Pavlovian conditioned stimulus effects upon instrumental choice behavior are reinforcer specific. *Learning and Motivation, 14,* 165–181.

Kundey, S. M. A., Strandell, B., Mathis, H., & Rowan, J. D. (2010). Learning of monotonic and nonmonotonic sequences in domesticated horses (*Equus callabus*) and chickens (*Gallus domesticus*). *Learning and Motivation, 41,* 213–223.

Kyonka, E. G. E., & Grace, R. C. (2010). Rapid acquisition of choice and timing and the provenance of the terminal-link effect. *Journal of the Experimental Analysis of Behavior, 94,* 209–225.

LaBar, K. S., & Phelps, E. A. (2005). Reinstatement of conditioned fear in humans is context dependent and impaired in amnesia. *Behavioral Neuroscience, 119,* 677–686.

Laborda, M. A., & Miller, R. R. (2012). Reactivated memories compete for expression after Pavlovian extinction. *Behavioural Processes, 90,* 20–27.

Laborda, M. A., Witnauer, J. E., & Miller, R. R. (2011). Contrasting AAC and ABC renewal: The role of context associations. *Learning & Behavior, 39,* 46–56.

Laming, D. (2009). Failure to recall. *Psychological Review, 116,* 157–186.

Lansdell, H. (1988). Laboratory animals need only humane treatment: Animal "rights" may debase human rights. *International Journal of Neuroscience, 42,* 169–178.

Lanuza, E., Nader, K., & LeDoux, J. E. (2004). Unconditioned stimulus pathways to the amygdala: Effects of posterior thalamic and cortical lesions on fear conditioning. *Neuroscience, 125,* 305–315.

Lashley, K. S., & Wade, M. (1946). The Pavlovian theory of generalization. *Psychological Review, 53,* 72–87.

Lattal, K. A. (1998). A century of effect: Legacies of E. L. Thorndike's animal intelligence monograph. *Journal of the Experimental Analysis of Behavior, 70,* 325–336.

Lattal, K. A. (2010). Delayed reinforcement of operant behavior. *Journal of the Experimental Analysis of Behavior, 93,* 129–139.

Lattal, K. A. (2013). The five pillars of the experimental analysis of behavior. In G. J. Madden (Ed.), *APA Handbook of Behavior Analysis, Vol. 1: Methods and Principles* (pp. 33–63). Washington, DC: American Psychological Association.

Lattal, K. A., & Neef, N. A. (1996). Recent reinforcement-schedule research and applied behavior analysis. *Journal of Applied Behavior Analysis, 29,* 213–230.

Lattal, K. A., & St. Peter Pipkin, C. (2009). Resurgence of previously reinforced responding: Research and application. *The Behavior Analyst Today, 10,* 254–266.

Lattal, K. A., St. Peter Pipkin, C., & Escobar, R. (2013). Operant extinction: Elimination and generation of behavior. In G. J. Madden (Ed.), *APA Handbook of Behavior Analysis. Vol 2: Translating Principles into Practice* (pp. 77–107). Washington, DC: American Psychological Association.

Lattal, K. M. (1999). Trial and intertrial durations in Pavlovian conditioning: Issues of learning and performance. *Journal of Experimental Psychology: Animal Behavior Processes, 25,* 433–450.

Lattal, K. M., & Lattal, K. A. (2012). Facets of Pavlovian and operant extinction. *Behavioural Processes, 90,* 1–8.

Lattal, K. M., & Nakajima, S. (1998). Overexpectation in appetitive Pavlovian and instrumental conditioning. *Animal Learning & Behavior, 26,* 351–360.

Lazareva, O. F. (2012). Relational learning in a context of transposition: A review. *Journal of the Experimental Analysis of Behavior, 97,* 231–248.

Lazareva, O. F., Freiburger, K. L., & Wasserman, E. A. (2004). Pigeons concurrently categorize photographs at both basic and superordinate levels. *Psychonomic Bulletin & Review, 11,* 1111–1117.

Lazareva, O. F., Freiburger, K. L., & Wasserman, E. A. (2006). Effects of stimulus manipulations on visual categorization in pigeons. *Behavioural Processes, 72,* 224–233.

Lazareva, O. F., Miner, M., Wasserman, E. A., & Young, M. E. (2008). Multiple-pair training enhances transposition in pigeons. *Learning & Behavior, 36,* 174–187.

Lea, S. E. G., & Wills, A. J. (2008). Use of multiple dimensions in learned discriminations. *Comparative Cognition & Behavior Reviews, 3,* 115–133.

Leaton, R. N. (1976). Long-term retention of the habituation of lick suppression and startle response produced by a single auditory stimulus. *Journal of Experimental Psychology: Animal Behavior Processes, 2,* 248–259.

LeDoux, J. E., & Gorman, J. M. (2001). A call to action: Overcoming anxiety through active coping. *American Journal of Psychiatry, 158,* 1953–1955.

Lee, D., Seo, H., & Jung, M. W. (2012). Neural basis of reinforcement learning and decision making. *Annual Review of Neuroscience, 35,* 287–308.

Lee, Y.-S., & Silva, A. J. (2009). The molecular and cellular biology of enhanced cognition. *Nature Reviews: Neuroscience, 10,* 126–140.

Lefebvre, L., Nicolakakis, N., & Boire, D. (2002). Tools and brains in birds. *Behaviour, 139,* 939–973.

Leising, K. J., Sawa, K., & Blaisdell, A. P. (2007). Temporal integration in Pavlovian appetitive conditioning in rats. *Learning & Behavior, 35,* 11–18.

Lejeune, H., & Wearden, J. H. (2006). Scalar properties in animal timing: Conformity and violations. *Quarterly Journal of Experimental Psychology, 59,* 1875–1908.

Lejuez, C. W., Eifert, G. H., Zvolensky, M. J., & Richards, J. B. (2000). Preference between onset predictable and unpredictable administrations of 20% carbon-dioxide-enriched air: Implications for better understanding the etiology and treatment of panic disorder. *Journal of Experimental Psychology: Applied, 6,* 349–358.

Lejuez, C. W., O'Donnell, J., Wirth, O., Zvolensky, M. J., & Eifert, G. H. (1998). Avoidance of 20% carbon dioxide-enriched air with humans. *Journal of the Experimental Analysis of Behavior, 70,* 79–86.

Lencz, T., Bilder, R. M., Turkel, E., Goldman, R. S., Robinson, D., Kane, J. M., et al. (2003). Impairments in perceptual competency and maintenance on a visual delayed match-to-sample test in first-episode schizophrenia. *Archives of General Psychiatry, 60,* 238–243.

Lennenberg, E. H. (1967). *Biological foundations of language.* New York: Wiley.

Lerman, D. C., & Vorndran, C. M. (2002). On the status of knowledge for using punishment: Implications for treating behavior disorders. *Journal of Applied Behavior Analysis, 35,* 431–464.

Lerman, D. C., Iwata, B. A., Shore, B. A., & DeLeon, I. G. (1997). Effects of intermittent punishment on self-injurious behavior: An evaluation of schedule thinning. *Journal of Applied Behavioral Analysis, 30,* 187–201.

Leslie, A. M. (2001). Learning: Association or computation? Introduction to special section. *Psychological Science, 10,* 124–127.

Leuner, B., & Gould, E. (2010). Structural plasticity and hippocampal function. *Annual Review of Psychology, 61,* 111–140.

Leung, H. T., & Westbrook, R. F. (2008). Spontaneous recovery of extinguished fear response deepens their extinction: A role for error-correction mechanisms. *Journal of Experimental Psychology: Animal Behavior Processes, 34,* 461–474.

Leung, H. T., Reeks, L. M., & Westbrook, R. F. (2012). Two ways to deepen extinction and the difference between them. *Journal of Experimental Psychology: Animal Behavior Processes, 38,* 394–406.

Leung, H. T., Bailey, G. K., Laurent, V., & Westbrook, R. F. (2007). Rapid reacquisition of fear to a completely extinguished context is replaced by transient impairment with additional extinction training. *Journal of Experimental Psychology: Animal Behavior Processes, 33,* 299–313.

Levenson, D. H., & Schusterman, R. J. (1999). Dark adaptation and visual sensitivity in shallow and deepdiving pinnipeds. *Marine Mammal Science, 15,* 1303–1313.

Levis, D. J. (1995). Decoding traumatic memory: Implosive theory of psychopathology. In W. O'Donohue & L. Krasner (Eds.), *Theories of behavior therapy* (pp. 173–207). Washington, DC: American Psychological Association.

Levis, D. J., & Brewer, K. E. (2001). The neurotic paradox: Attempts by two-factor fear theory and alternative avoidance models to resolve the issues associated with sustained avoidance responding in extinction. In R. R. Mowrer & S. B. Klein (Eds.),

Handbook of contemporary learning theories (pp. 561–597). Mahwah, NJ: Erlbaum.

Lieberman, D. A., McIntosh, D. C., & Thomas, G. V. (1979). Learning when reward is delayed: A marking hypothesis. *Journal of Experimental Psychology: Animal Behavior Processes, 5,* 224–242.

Lieberman, D. A., Sunnucks, W. L., & Kirk, J. D. J. (1998). Reinforcement without awareness: I. Voice level. *Quarterly Journal of Experimental Psychology, 51B,* 301–316.

Lindberg, J. S., Iwata, B. A., Kahng, S. W., & DeLeon, I. G. (1999). DRO Contingencies: An analysis of variable-momentary schedules. *Journal of Applied Behavior Analysis, 32,* 123–136.

Lionello-DeNolf, K. M. (2009). The search for symmetry: 25 years in review. *Learning & Behavior, 37,* 188–203.

Liu, X., Ramirez, S., Pang, P. T., Puryear, C. B., Govindarajan, A., Deisseroth, K., & Tonegawa, S. (2012). Optogenetic stimulation of hippocampal engram activates fear memory recall. *Nature, 484,* 381–385.

LoBue, V., & DeLoache, J. S. (2010). Superior detection of threat-relevant stimuli in infancy. *Developmental Science, 13,* 221–228.

LoBue, V., & DeLoache, J. S. (2011). What's so special about slithering serpents? Children and adults rapidly detect snakes based on their simple features. *Visual Cognition, 19,* 129–143.

Lockard, R. B. (1968). The albino rat: A defensible choice or a bad habit? *American Psychologist, 23,* 734–742.

Loeb, J. (1900). *Comparative physiology of the brain and comparative psychology.* New York: G. P. Putman.

Logue, A. W. (1985). Conditioned food aversion learning in humans. *Annals of the New York Academy of Sciences, 433,* 316–329.

Logue, A. W. (1988). A comparison of taste aversion learning in humans and other vertebrates: Evolutionary pressures in common. In R. C. Bolles & M. D. Beecher (Eds.), *Evolution and learning* (pp. 97–116). Hillsdale, NJ: Erlbaum.

Logue, A. W. (1995). *Self-control: Waiting until tomorrow for what you want today.* Englewood Cliffs, NJ: Prentice-Hall.

Logue, A. W., Ophir, I., & Strauss, K. E. (1981). The acquisition of taste aversions in humans. *Behaviour Research and Therapy, 19,* 319–333.

Loidolt, M., Aust, U., Steurer, M., Troje, N. F., & Huber, L. (2006). Limits of dynamic object perception in pigeons: Dynamic stimulus presentation does not enhance perception and discrimination of complex shape. *Learning & Behavior, 34,* 71–85.

LoLordo, V. M. (1979). Selective associations. In A. Dickinson & R. A. Boakes (Eds.), *Mechanisms of learning and motivation* (pp. 367–398). Hillsdale, NJ: Erlbaum.

LoLordo, V. M., & Fairless, J. L. (1985). Pavlovian conditioned inhibition: The literature since 1969. In R. R. Miller & N. E. Spear (Eds.), *Information processing in animals: Conditioned inhibition.* Hillsdale, NJ: Erlbaum.

LoLordo, V. M., & Overmier, J. B. (2011). Trauma, learned helplessness, its neuroscience, and implications for posttraumatic stress disorder. In T. R. Schachtman & S. Reilly (Eds.), *Associative learning and conditioning theory: Human and non-human applications* (pp. 121–151). Oxford and New York: Oxford University Press.

LoLordo, V. M., Jacobs, W. J., & Foree, D. D. (1982). Failure to block control by a relevant stimulus. *Animal Learning & Behavior, 10,* 183–193.

Losey, G. S., & Sevenster, P. (1995). Can three-spined sticklebacks learn when to display? Rewarded displays. *Animal Behaviour, 49,* 137–150.

Lovibond, P. F. (1983). Facilitation of instrumental behavior by a Pavlovian appetitive conditioned stimulus. *Journal of Experimental Psychology: Animal Behavior Processes, 9,* 225–247.

Lovibond, P. F. (2011). Learning and anxiety: A cognitive perspective. In T. R. Schachtman & S. Reilly (Eds.), *Associative learning and conditioning theory: Human and non-human applications* (pp. 104–120). New York: Oxford University Press.

Lovibond, P. F., Mitchell, C. J., Minard, E., Brady, A., & Menzies, R. G. (2009). Safety behaviours preserve threat beliefs: Protection from extinction of human fear conditioning by an avoidance response. *Behavioural Research and Therapy, 47,* 716–720.

Lovibond, P. F., Mitchell, C. J., Minard, E., Brady, A., & Menzies, R. G. (2009). Safety behaviours preserve threat beliefs; protection from extinction of human fear conditioning by an avoidance response. *Behavioural Research and Therapy, 47,* 716–720.

Lovibond, P. F., Saunders, J. C., Weidemann, G., & Mitchell, C. J. (2008). Evidence for expectancy as a mediator of avoidance and anxiety in a laboratory model of human avoidance learning. *Quarterly Journal of Experimental Psychology, 61,* 1199–1216.

Lubow, R. E. (1989). *Latent inhibition and conditioned attention theory.* Cambridge, UK: Cambridge University Press.

Lubow, R. E. (2011). Aberrant attentional processes in schizophrenia as reflected in latent inhibition data. In T. R. Schachtman & S. Reilly (Eds.), *Associative learning and conditioning theory: Human and non-human applications* (pp. 152–167). New York: Oxford University Press.

Lubow, R. E., & Moore, A. U. (1959). Latent inhibition: The effect of non-reinforced preexposure to the conditioned stimulus. *Journal of Comparative and Physiological Psychology, 52,* 415–419.

Lubow, R., & Weiner, I. (Eds.). (2010). *Latent inhibition: Cognition, Neuroscience and applications to schizophrenia.* Cambridge, UK: Cambridge University Press.

Lussier, J. P., Heil, S. H., Mongeon, J. A., Badget, G. J., & Higgins, S. T. (2006). A meta-analysis of voucher-based reinforcement therapy for substance abuse disorder. *Addiction, 101,* 192–203.

Lyn, H., Greenfield, P. M., & Savage-Rumbaugh, E. S. (2011a). Semiotic combinations in Pan: A comparison of communication in a chimpanzee and two bonobos. *First Language, 31,* 300–325.

Lyn, H., Greenfield, P. M., Savage-Rumbaugh, S. E., Gillespie-Lynch, K., & Hopkins, W. D. (2011b). Nonhuman primates do declare! A comparison of declarative symbol and gesture use in two children, two bonobos, and a chimpanzee. *Language & Communication, 31,* 63–74.

Lynch, M. A. (2004). Long-term potentiation and memory. *Physiological Reviews, 125,* 87–136.

Lysle, D. T., & Fowler, H. (1985). Inhibition as a "slave" process: Deactivation of conditioned inhibition through extinction of conditioned excitation. *Journal of Experimental Psychology: Animal Behavior Processes, 11,* 71–94.

MacArdy, E. A., & Riccio, D. C. (1995). Time-dependent changes in the effectiveness of a noncontingent footshock reminder. *Learning and Motivation, 26,* 29–42.

MacDonald, S. E. (1993). Delayed matching-to-successive-samples in pigeons: Short-term memory for item and order information. *Animal Learning & Behavior, 21,* 59–67.

MacDonall, J. S. (2000). Synthesizing concurrent interval performances. *Journal of the Experimental Analysis of Behavior, 74,* 189–206.

MacDonall, J. S. (2005). Earning and obtaining reinforcers under concurrent interval scheduling. *Journal of the Experimental Analysis of Behavior, 84,* 167–183.

Mace, F. C., Pratt, J. L., Prager, K. L., & Pritchard, D. (2011). An evaluation of three methods of saying "no" to avoid an escalating response class hierarchy. *Journal of Applied Behavior Analysis, 44,* 83–94.

Machado, A. (1997). Learning the temporal dynamics of behavior. *Psychological Review, 104,* 241–265.

Machado, A., Malheiro, M. T., & Erlhagen, W. (2009). Learning to time: A perspective. *Journal of the Experimental Analysis of Behavior, 92,* 423–458.

MacKillop, J., et al. (2011). Delayed reward discounting and addictive behavior: A meta-analysis. *Psychopharmacology, 216,* 305–321.

Mackintosh, N. J. (1974). *The psychology of animal learning.* London: Academic Press.

Mackintosh, N. J. (1975). A theory of attention: Variations in the associability of stimuli with reinforcement. *Psychological Review, 82,* 276–298.

Mackintosh, N. J., Bygrave, D. J., & Picton, B. M. B. (1977). Locus of the effect of a surprising reinforcer in the attenuation of blocking. *Quarterly Journal of Experimental Psychology, 29,* 327–336.

Mackintosh, N. J., & Dickinson, A. (1979). Instrumental (Type II) conditioning. In A. Dickinson & R. A. Boakes (Eds.), *Mechanisms of learning and motivation* (pp. 143–169). Hillsdale, NJ: Erlbaum.

McNally, G. P., Johansen, J. P., & Blair, H. T. (2011). Placing prediction into the fear circuit. *Trends in Neuroscience, 34,* 283–292.

Madden, G. J. (Eds.). (2013). *APA Handbook of behavior analysis, Vol. 2: Translating principles into practice.* Washington, DC: American Psychological Association.

Madden, G. J., & Bickel, W. K. (1999). Abstinence and price effects on demand for cigarettes: A behavioral-economic analysis. *Addiction, 94,* 577–588.

Madden, G. J., & Bickel, W. K. (2010). *Impulsivity: The behavioral and neurological science of discounting.* Washington, DC: American Psychological Association.

Madden, G. J., Peden, B. F., & Yamaguchi, T. (2002). Human group choice: Discrete-trial and free-operant tests of the ideal free distribution. *Journal of the Experimental Analysis of Behavior, 78,* 1–15.

Madden, G. J., Petry, N. M., Badger, G. J., & Bickel, W. K. (1997). Impulsive and self-control choices in opioid-dependent patients and nondrug-using control participants: Drug and monetary rewards. *Experimental and Clinical Psychopharmacology, 5,* 256–262.

Madden, G. J., Smethells, J., Ewan, E. E., & Hursh, S. R. (2007). Tests of behavioral economic assessments of relative reinforcer efficacy II. Economic complements. *Journal of the Experimental Analysis of Behavior, 88,* 355–367.

Maia, T. V. (2010). Two-factor theory, the actor-critic model, and conditioned avoidance. *Learning & Behavior, 38,* 50–67.

Maier, S. F., & Seligman, M. E. P. (1976). Learned helplessness: Theory and evidence. *Journal of Experimental Psychology: General, 105,* 3–46.

Maier, S. F., Jackson, R. L., & Tomie, A. (1987). Potentiation, overshadowing, and prior exposure to inescapable shock. *Journal of Experimental Psychology: Animal Behavior Processes, 13,* 260–270.

Maier, S. F., Rapaport, P., & Wheatley, K. L. (1976). Conditioned inhibition and the UCS-CS interval. *Animal Learning and Behavior, 4,* 217–220.

Maier, S. F., Seligman, M. E. P., & Solomon, R. L. (1969). Pavlovian fear conditioning and learned helplessness. In B. A. Campbell & R. M. Church (Eds.), *Punishment and aversive behavior.* New York: Appleton-Century-Crofts.

Maier, S. F., & Watkins, L. R. (1998). Stressor controllability, anxiety, and serotonin. *Cognitive Therapy and Research, 6,* 595–613.

Maier, S. F., & Watkins, L. R. (2005). Stressor controllability and learned helplessness: The roles of the dorsal raphe nucleus, serotonin, and corticotropin-releasing factor. *Neuroscience and Biobehavioral Reviews, 29,* 829–841.

Maier, S. F., & Watkins, L. R. (2010). Role of the medial prefrontal cortex in coping and resilience. *Brain Research, 1355,* 52–60.

Maki, W. S., Moe, J. C., & Bierley, C. M. (1977). Short-term memory for stimuli, responses, and reinforcers. *Journal of Experimental Psychology: Animal Behavior Processes, 3,* 156–177.

Malenka, R. C. (2003). Synaptic plasticity and AMPA receptor trafficking. *Annual Review of the New York Academy of Sciences, 1003,* 1–11.

Malenka, R. C., & Bear, M. F. (2004). LTP and LTD: An embarrassment of riches. *Neuron, 44,* 5–21.

Malenka, R. C., & Nicoll, R. A. (1999). Long-term potentiation—a decade of progress? *Science, 285,* 1870–1874.

Marchand, A. R., & Kamper, E. (2000). Time course of cardiac conditioned responses in restrained rats as a function of the trace CS-US interval. *Journal of Experimental Psychology: Animal Behavior Processes, 26,* 385–398.

Maren, S. (2007). The threatened brain. *Science, 317,* 1043–1044.

Maren, S. (2011). Seeking a spotless mind: Extinction, deconsolidation, and erasure of fear memory. *Neuron, 70,* 830–845.

Marsh, G. (1972). Prediction of the peak shift in pigeons from gradients of excitation and inhibition. *Journal of Comparative and Physiological Psychology, 81,* 262–266.

Martin-Malivel, J., Mangini, M. C., Fagot, J., & Biederman, I. (2006). Do humans and baboons use the same information when categorizing human and baboon faces? *Psychological Science, 17,* 599–607.

Martin, S. J., Grimwood, P. D., & Morris, R. G. M. (2000). Synaptic plasticity and memory: An evaluation of the hypothesis. *Annual Review of Neuroscience, 23,* 649–711.

Marx, B. P., Heidt, J. M., & Gold, S. D. (2005). Perceived uncontrollability and unpredictability, self-regulation, and sexual revictimization. *Review of General Psychology, 9,* 67–90.

Matthews, R. N., Domjan, M., Ramsey, M., & Crews, D. (2007). Learning effects on sperm competition and reproductive fitness. *Psychological Science, 18,* 758–762.

Mauk, B., & Dehnhardt, G. (2005). Identity concept formation during visual multiple-choice matching in a harbor seal (*Phoca vitulina*). *Learning & Behavior, 33,* 428–436.

Mauk, M. D., & Buonomano, D. V. (2004). The neural basis of temporal processing. *Annual Review of Neuroscience, 27,* 307–340.

Mayford, M., & Kandel, E. R. (1999). Genetic approaches to memory storage. *Trends in Genetics, 125,* 463–470.

Mayford, M., Bach, M. E., Huang, Y.-Y., Wang, L., Hawkins, R. D., & Kandel, E. R. (1996). Control of memory formation through regulated expression of a CaMKII transgene. *Science, 125,* 1678–1683.

Mazur, J. E. (1987). An adjusting procedure for studying delayed reinforcement. In M. L. Commons, J. E. Mazur, J. A. Nevin, & H. Rachlin (Eds.), *Quantitative analyses of behavior, Vol. 5: The effect of delay and intervening events on reinforcement value* (pp. 55–73). Hillsdale, NJ: Erlbaum.

Mazur, J. E. (2006). Choice between single and multiple reinforcers in concurrent-chains schedules. *Journal of the Experimental Analysis of Behavior, 86,* 211–222.

McAllister, W. R., & McAllister, D. E. (1995). Two-factor fear theory: Implications for understanding anxiety-based clinical phenomena. In W. O'Donohue & L. Krasner (Eds.), *Theories of behavior therapy* (pp. 145–171). Washington, DC: American Psychological Association.

McAndrew, A., Jones, F. W., McLaren, R. P., & McLaren, I. P. L. (2012). Dissociating expectancy of shock and changes in skin conductance: An investigation of the Perruchet effect using an electrodermal paradigm. *Journal of Experimental Psychology: Animal Behavior Processes, 38,* 203–208.

McCarthy, D. E., Baker, T. B., Minami, H. M., & Yeh, V. M. (2011). Applications of contemporary learning theory in the treatment of drug abuse. In T. R. Schachtman & S. Reilly (Eds.), *Associative learning and conditioning theory: Human and non-human*

applications (pp. 235–269). New York: Oxford University Press.

McClure, S. M., York, M. K., & Montague, P. R. (2004). The neural substrates of reward processing in humans: The modern role of fMRI. *The Neuroscientist, 10,* 260–268.

McConnell, B. L., & Miller, R. R. (2010). Protection from extinction provided by a conditioned inhibitor. *Learning & Behavior, 38,* 68–79.

McConnell, B.L., Urushihara, K., & Miller, R.R. (2010). Contrasting predictions of the extended comparator hypothesis and acquisition-focused models of learning concerning retrospective revaluation. *Journal of Experimental Psychology: Animal Behavior Processes, 36,* 137–147.

McCrink, K., & Wynn, K. (2007). Ratio abstraction by 6-month-old infants. *Psychological Science, 18,* 740–745.

McGaugh, J. L. (2000). Memory—a century of consolidation. *Science, 287,* 248–251.

McGaugh, J. L., & Herz, M. J. (1972). *Memory consolidation.* San Francisco: Albion.

McGee, G. G., Krantz, P. J., & McClannahan, L. E. (1986). An extension of incidental teaching procedures to reading instruction for autistic children. *Journal of Applied Behavior Analysis, 19,* 147–157.

McKenzie, S., & Eichenbaum, H. (2011). Consolidation and reconsolidation: Two lives of memories? *Neuron, 71,* 224–233.

McLaren, I. P. L., & Mackintosh, N. J. (2000). An elemental model of associative learning: I. Latent inhibition and perceptual learning. *Animal Learning & Behavior, 28,* 211–246.

McLaren, I. P. L., & Mackintosh, N. J. (2002). Associative learning and elemental representation: II. Generalization and discrimination. *Animal Learning & Behavior, 30,* 177–200.

McLean, A. P., Campbell-Tie, P., & Nevin, J. A. (1996). Resistance to change as a function of stimulus-reinforcer and location-reinforcer contingencies. *Journal of the Experimental Analysis of Behavior, 66,* 169–191.

McNally, G. P., & Westbrook, R. F. (2006). A short intertrial interval facilitates acquisition of context-conditioned fear and a short retention interval facilitates its expression. *Journal of Experimental Psychology: Animal Behavior Processes, 32,* 164–172.

McNish, K. A., Betts, S. L., Brandon, S. E., & Wagner, A. R. (1997). Divergence of conditioned eyeblink and conditioned fear in backward Pavlovian training. *Animal Learning & Behavior, 25,* 43–52.

McSweeney, F. K., & Murphy, E. S. (2009). Sensitization and habituation regulate reinforcer effectiveness. *Neurobiology of learning and memory, 92,* 189–198.

McSweeney, F. K., & Swindell, S. (1999). General-process theories of motivation revisited: The role of habituation. *Psychological Bulletin, 125,* 437–457.

Mercado, E. I. I. I., Murray, S. O., Uyeyama, R. K., Pack, A. A., & Herman, L. M. (1998). Memory for recent actions in the bottlenosed dolphin (*Tursiops truncates*): Repetition of arbitrary behaviors using an abstract rule. *Animal Learning & Behavior, 26,* 210–218.

Merritt, D. J., & Terrace, H. S. (2011). Mechanisms of inferential order judgments in humans (*Homo sapiens*) and Rhesus monkeys (*Macaca mulatta*). *Journal of Comparative Psychology, 125,* 227–238.

Merritt, D. J., DeWind, N. K., & Brannon, E. M. (2012). Comparative cognition of number representation. In T. R. Zentall & E. A. Wasserman (Eds.), *The Oxford handbook of comparative cognition* (pp. 451–476). New York/Oxford: Oxford University Press.

Meuret, A. E., Wolitzky-Taylor, K., Twohig, M. P., & Craske, M. G. (2012). Coping skills and exposure therapy in panic disorder and agoraphobia: Latest advances and future directions. *Behavior Therapy, 43*(2), 271–284.

Miguez, G., Witnauer, J. E., & Miller, R. R. (2012). The role of contextual associations in producing the partial reinforcement acquisition deficit. *Journal of Experimental Psychology: Animal Behavior Processes, 38,* 40–51.

Milad, M. R., & Quirk, G. J. (2012). Fear extinction as a model for translational neuroscience: Ten years of progress. *Annual Review of Psychology, 63,* 129–151.

Miller, C. A., & Sweatt, J. D. (2006). Amnesia or retrieval deficit? Implications of a molecular approach to the question of reconsolidation. *Learning and Memory, 13,* 498–505.

Miller, G. A. (1956). The magic number seven plus or minus two: Some limits on our capacity for processing

information. *Psychological Review, 63,* 81–97.

Miller, J. S., Jagielo, J. A., & Spear, N. E. (1990). Alleviation of shortterm forgetting: Effects of the CS– and other conditioning elements in prior cueing or as context during test. *Learning and Motivation, 21,* 96–109.

Miller, J. S., Jagielo, J. A., & Spear, N. E. (1992). The influence of the information value provided by prior-cuing treatment on the reactivation of memory in preweanling rats. *Animal Learning & Behavior, 20,* 233–239.

Miller, N. E. (1951). Learnable drives and rewards. In S. S. Stevens (Ed.), *Handbook of experimental psychology.* New York: Wiley.

Miller, N. E. (1960). Learning resistance to pain and fear: Effects of overlearning, exposure, and rewarded exposure in context. *Journal of Experimental Psychology, 60,* 137–145.

Miller, N. E., & Dollard, J. (1941). *Social learning and imitation.* New Haven, CT: Yale University Press.

Miller, N. Y., & Shettleworth, S. J. (2007). Learning about environmental geometry: An associate model. *Journal of Experimental Psychology: Animal Behavior Processes, 33,* 191–212.

Miller, N. Y., & Shettleworth, S. J. (2008). An associative model of geometry learning: A modified choice rule. *Journal of Experimental Psychology: Animal Behavior Processes, 34,* 419–422.

Miller, R. R., & Matzel, L. D. (1988). The comparator hypothesis: A response rule for the expression of associations. In G. H. Bower (Ed.), *The psychology of learning and motivation* (pp. 51–92). Orlando, FL: Academic Press.

Miller, R. R., & Matzel, L. D. (2006). Retrieval failure vs. memory loss in experimental amnesia: Definitions and processes. *Learning and Memory, 13,* 491–497.

Miller, R. R., & Springer, A. D. (1973). Amnesia, consolidation, and retrieval. *Psychological Review, 80,* 69–79.

Miller, R. R., Barnet, R. C., & Grahame, N. J. (1995). Assessment of the Rescorla-Wagner model. *Psychological Bulletin, 117,* 363–386.

Miller, R. R., Kasprow, W. J., & Schachtman, T. R. (1986). Retrieval variability: Sources and consequences. *American Journal of Psychology, 99,* 145–218.

Miller, V., & Domjan, M. (1981). Selective sensitization induced by lithium malaise and footshock in rats. *Behavioral and Neural Biology, 31,* 42–55.

Millin, P. M., & Riccio, D. C. (2004). Is the context shift effect a case of retrieval failure? The effects of retrieval enhancing treatments on forgetting under altered stimulus conditions in rats. *Journal of Experimental Psychology: Animal Behavior Processes, 30,* 325–334.

Milmine, M., Watanabe, A., & Colombo, M. (2008). Neural correlates of directed forgetting in the avian prefrontal cortex. *Behavioral Neuroscience, 122,* 199–209.

Mineka, S. (1979). The role of fear in theories of avoidance learning, flooding, and extinction. *Psychological Bulletin, 86,* 985–1010.

Mineka, S., & Gino, A. (1980). Dissociation between conditioned emotional response and extended avoidance performance. *Learning and Motivation, 11,* 476–502.

Mineka, S., & Henderson, R. (1985). Controllability and predictability in acquired motivation. *Annual Review of Psychology, 36,* 495–530.

Mineka, S., & Öhman, A. (2002). Phobias and preparedness: The selective, automatic, and encapsulated nature of fear. *Biological Psychiatry, 52,* 927–937.

Minor, T. R., Dess, N. K., & Overmier, J. B. (1991). Inverting the traditional view of "learned helplessness." In M. R. Denny (Ed.), *Fear, avoidance and phobias* (pp. 87–133). Hillsdale, NJ: Erlbaum.

Minor, T. R., Trauner, M. A., Lee, C.-Y., & Dess, N. K. (1990). Modeling signal features of escape response: Effects of cessation conditioning in "learned helplessness" paradigm. *Journal of Experimental Psychology: Animal Behavior Processes, 16,* 123–136.

Misanin, J. R., Miller, R. R., & Lewis, D. J. (1968). Retrograde amnesia produced by electroconvulsive shock after reactivation of a consolidated memory trace. *Science, 160,* 554–555.

Mischel, H. N., Ebbesen, E. B., & Zeiss, A. R. (1972). Cognitive and attentional mechanisms in delay of gratification. *Journal of Personality and Social Psychology, 21,* 204–218.

Mitchell, C. J., & Le Pelley, M. E. (Eds.). (2010). *Attention and associative learning.* Oxford, UK: Oxford University Press.

Mitchell, C. J., Lovibond, P. F., Minard, E., & Lavis, Y. (2006). Forward blocking in human learning sometimes reflects the failure to encode a cue-outcome relationship. *Quarterly Journal of Experimental Psychology, 59,* 830–844.

Mitchell, W. S., & Stoffelmayr, B. E. (1973). Application of the Premack principle to the behavioral control of extremely inactive schizophrenics. *Journal of Applied Behavior Analysis, 6,* 419–423.

Mobbs, D., Yu, R., Rowe, J. B., Eich, H., FeldmanHall, O., & Dalgleish, T. (2010). Neural activity associated with monitoring the oscillating threat value of a tarantula. *Proceedings of the National Academy of Sciences, 107*(47), 20582–20586.

Moffitt, T. E., et al. (2011). A gradient of childhood self-control predicts health, wealth, and public safety. *Proceedings of the National Academy of Sciences, 108*(7), 2693–2698.

Molet, M., Leconte, C., & Rosas, J. M. (2006). Acquisition, extinction, and temporal discrimination in human conditioned avoidance. *Behavioural Processes, 73*(2), 199–208.

Monfils, M., Cowansaage, K. K., Klann, E., & LeDoux, J. E. (2009). Extinction-reconsolidation boundaries: Key to persistent attenuation of fear memories. *Science, 324,* 951–955.

Montague, P. R., King-Casas, B., & Cohen, J. D. (2006). Imaging valuation models in human choice. *Annual Review of Neuroscience, 29,* 417–448.

Moody, E. W., Sunsay, C., & Bouton, M. E. (2006). Priming and trial spacing in extinction: Effects on extinction performance, spontaneous recovery, and reinstatement in appetitive conditioning. *Quarterly Journal of Experimental Psychology, 59,* 809–929.

Morgan, C. L. (1894). *An introduction to comparative psychology.* London: Scott.

Morgan, C. L. (1903). *Introduction to comparative psychology* (Rev. Ed.). New York: Scribner.

Morgan, D. L. (2010). Schedules of reinforcement at 50: A retrospective appreciation. *Psychological Record, 60,* 151–172.

Morris, R. G. M. (1974). Pavlovian conditioned inhibition of fear during shuttlebox avoidance behavior. *Learning and Motivation, 5,* 424–447.

Morris, R. G. M. (1975). Preconditioning of reinforcing properties to an exteroceptive

feedback stimulus. *Learning and Motivation, 6,* 289–298.

Morris, R. G. M. (1981). Spatial localization does not require the presence of local cues. *Learning and Motivation, 12,* 239–260.

Morris, R. G. M., Anderson, E., Lynch, G. S., & Baudry, M. (1986). Selective impairment of learning and blockade of long-term potentiation by an N-methyl-D-aspartate receptor antagonist, AP5. *Nature, 319,* 774–776.

Mowrer, O. H. (1947). On the dual nature of learning: A reinterpretation of "conditioning" and "problem-solving." *Harvard Educational Review, 17,* 102–150.

Mowrer, O. H., & Lamoreaux, R. R. (1942). Avoidance conditioning and signal duration: A study of secondary motivation and reward. *Psychological Monographs, 54*(Whole No. 247).

Mowrer, R. R., & Klein, S. B. (Eds.). (2001). *Handbook of contemporary learning theories.* Mahwah, NJ: Erlbaum.

Mui, R., Haselgrove, M., McGregor, A., Futter, J., Heyes, C., & Pearce, J. M. (2007). The discrimination of natural movement by budgerigars (*Melopsittacus undulates*) and pigeons (*Columba livia*). *Journal of Experimental Psychology: Animal Behavior Processes, 33,* 371–380.

Mukerjee, M. (1997, February). Trends in animal research. *Scientific American, 276,* 86–93.

Murphy, J. G., Correla, C. J., & Barnett, N. P. (2007). Behavioral economic approaches to reduce college student drinking. *Addictive Behaviors, 32,* 2573–2585.

Musienko, P., Heutschi, J., Friedli, L., van den Brand, R., & Courtine, G. (2012). Multi-system neurorehabilitative strategies to restore motor functions following severe spinal cord injury. *Experimental Neurology, 235,* 100–109.

Myers, K. M., & Davis, M. (2007). Mechanisms of fear extinction. *Molecular Psychiatry, 12,* 120–150.

Myers, K. M., Ressler, K. J., & Davis, M. (2006). Different mechanisms of fear extinction dependent on length of time since fear acquisition. *Learning and Memory, 13,* 216–223.

Mystkowski, J. L., Craske, M. G., Echiverri, A. M., & Labus, J. S. (2006). Mental reinstatement of context and return of fear in spider-fearful participants. *Behaviour Therapy, 37,* 49–60.

Nader, K., & Einarsson, E. O. (2010). Memory consolidation: An update. *Annals of the New York Academy of Sciences, 1191,* 27–41.

Nader, K., & Hardt, O. (2009). A single standard for memory: The case for reconsolidation. *Nature Reviews Neuroscience, 10,* 224–234.

Nader, K., Schafe, G. E., & LeDoux, J. E. (2000). Fear memories require protein synthesis in the amygdala for reconsolidation after retrieval. *Nature, 406,* 722–726.

Nader, K., Schafe, G., & LeDoux, J. E. (2000). Reconsolidation: The labile nature of consolidation theory. *Nature Reviews Neuroscience, 1,* 216–219.

Nakajima, A., & Tang, Y.-P. (2005). Genetic approaches to the molecular/neuronal mechanisms underlying learning and memory in the mouse. *Journal of Pharmacological Sciences, 125,* 1–5.

Nakamura, T., Croft, D. B., & Westbrook, R. F. (2003). Domestic pigeons (*Columba livia*) discriminate between photographs of individual pigeons. *Learning & Behavior, 31,* 307–317.

Nakamura, T., Ito, M., Croft, D. B., & Westbrook, R. F. (2006). Domestic pigeons (*Columba livia*) discriminate between photographs of male and female pigeons. *Learning & Behavior, 34,* 327–339.

Neill, J. C., & Harrison, J. M. (1987). Auditory discrimination: The Konorski quality-location effect. *Journal of the Experimental Analysis of Behavior, 48,* 81–95.

Nelson, A. B., Hang, G. B., Grueter, B. A., Pascoli, V., Luscher, C., Malenka, R. C., et al. (2012). A comparison of striatal-dependent behaviors in wild-type and hemizygous Drd1a and Drd2 BAC transgenic mice. *Journal of Neuroscience, 32,* 9119–9123.

Nelson, J. B., & del Carmen Sanjuan, M. (2006). A context-specific latent inhibition effect in a human conditioned suppression task. *Quarterly Journal of Experimental Psychology, 59,* 1003–1020.

Nelson, J. B., del Carmen Sanjuan, M., Vadillo-Ruiz, S., Prez, J., & Len, S. P. (2011). Experimental renewal in human participants. *Journal of Experimental Psychology: Animal Behavior Processes, 37,* 58–70.

Neuringer, A. (2004). Reinforced variability in animals and people: Implications for adaptive action. *American Psychologist, 59,* 891–906.

Nueringer, A., & Jensen, G. (2010). Operant variability and voluntary action. *Psychological Review, 117,* 972–993.

Neuringer, A., Kornell, N., & Olufs, M. (2001). Stability and variability in extinction. *Journal of Experimental Psychology: Animal Behavior Processes, 27,* 79–94.

Nevin, J. A. (2012). Resistance to extinction and behavioral momentum. *Behavioural Processes, 90,* 89–97.

Nevin, J. A., & Grace, R. C. (2000). Behavioral momentum and the law of effect. *Behavioral and Brain Sciences, 23,* 73–130.

Nevin, J. A., & Grace, R. C. (2005). Resistance to extinction in the steady state and in transition. *Journal of Experimental Psychology: Animal Behavior Processes, 31,* 199–212.

Nevin, J. A., & Shahan, T. A. (2011). Behavioral momentum theory: Equations and applications. *Journal of Applied Behavior Analysis, 44,* 877–895.

Nevin, J. A., Mandell, G., & Atak, J. R. (1983). The analysis of behavioral momentum. *Journal of the Experimental Analysis of Behavior, 39,* 49–59.

Norrholm, S. D., et al. (2006). Conditioned fear extinction and reinstatement in a human fear-potentiated startle paradigm. *Learning and Memory, 13,* 681–685.

O'Donnell, J., Crosbie, J., Williams, D. C., & Saunders, K. J. (2000). Stimulus control and generalization of point-loss punishment with humans. *Journal of the Experimental Analysis of Behavior, 73,* 261–274.

O'Donohue, W. (1998). Conditioning and third-generation behavior therapy. In W. O'Donohue (Ed.), *Learning and behavior therapy* (pp. 1–14). Boston: Allyn and Bacon.

O'Keefe, J., & Nadel, L. (1978). *The hippocampus as a cognitive map.* Oxford, UK: Oxford University Press.

Oden, D. L., Thompson, R. K. R., & Premack, D. (1988). Spontaneous transfer of matching by infant chimpanzees (*Pan troglodytes*). *Journal of Experimental Psychology: Animal Behavior Processes, 14,* 140–145.

Odum, A. L., & Baumann, A. A. L. (2010). Delay discounting: State and trait variable. In G. J. Madden & W. K. Bickel (Eds.), *Impulsivity: The behavioral and neurological science of discounting*

(pp. 39–65). Washington, DC: American Psychological Association.

Oehlberg, K., & Mineka, S. (2011). Fear conditioning and attention to threat: An integrative approach to understanding the etiology of anxiety disorders. In T. R. Schachtman & S. Reilly (Eds.), *Associative learning and conditioning theory: Human and non-human applications* (pp. 44–78). Oxford and New York: Oxford University Press.

Öhman, A., & Mineka, S. (2001). Fear, phobias, and preparedness: Towards an evolved module of fear and fear learning. *Psychological Review, 108,* 483–522.

Öhman, A., & Soares, J. J. F. (1998). Emotional conditioning to masked stimuli: Expectancies for aversive outcomes following nonrecognized fear-irrelevant stimuli. *Journal of Experimental Psychology: General, 127,* 69–82.

Öhman, A., Carlsson, K., Lundqvist, D., & Ingvar, M. (2007). On the unconscious subcortical origin of human fear. *Physiology & Behavior, 92,* 180–185.

Ohyama, T., & Mauk, M. D. (2001). Latent acquisition of timed responses in cerebellar cortex. *Journal of Neuroscience, 21,* 682–690.

Ohyama, T., Nores, W. L., Murphy, M., & Mauk, M. D. (2003). What the cerebellum computes. *Trends in Neuroscience, 26,* 222–227.

Okouchi, H. (2009). Response acquisition by humans with delayed reinforcement. *Journal of the Experimental Analysis of Behavior, 91,* 377–390.

Olton, D. S. (1978). Characterization of spatial memory. In S. H. Hulse, H. Fowler, & W. K. Honig (Eds.), *Cognitive processes in animal behavior* (pp. 341–374). Hillsdale, NJ: Erlbum.

Olton, D. S., & Samuelson, R. J. (1976). Remembrance of places passed: Spatial memory in rats. *Journal of Experimental Psychology: Animal Behavior Processes, 2,* 97–116.

O'Reilly, R. C., & Rudy, J. W. (2001). Conjunctive representations in learning and memory: Principles of cortical and hippocampal function. *Psychological Review, 108,* 311–345.

Ortega, L. A., Daniel, A. M., Davis, J. B., Fuchs, P. N., & Papini, M. R. (2011). Peripheral pain enhances the effects of incentive downshifts. *Learning and Motivation, 42,* 203–209.

Ost, J. W. P., & Lauer, D. W. (1965). Some investigations of salivary conditioning in the dog. In W. F. Prokasy (Ed.), *Classical conditioning.* New York: Appleton-Century-Crofts.

Ostlund, S. B., & Balleine, B. W. (2007). Selective reinstatement of instrumental performance depends on the discriminative stimulus properties of the mediating outcome. *Learning & Behavior, 35,* 43–52.

Ostlund, S. B., Winterbauer, N. E., & Balleine, B. W. (2008). Theory of reward systems. In R. Menzel (Ed.), *Learning theory and behavior.* Vol 1 of J. Byrne (Ed.), *Learning and memory: A comprehensive reference* (pp. 701–720). Oxford: Elsevier.

Otto, M. W., Tolin, D. F., Simon, N. M., Pearlson, G. D., Basden, S., Meunier, S. A., et al. (2010). Efficacy of D-cycloserine for enhancing response to cognitive-behavior therapy for panic disorder. *Biological Psychiatry, 67,* 365–370.

Overmier, J. B. (2002). On learned helplessness. *Integrative Physiological and Behavioral Science, 37,* 4–8.

Overmier, J. B., & Seligman, M. E. P. (1967). Effects of inescapable shock upon subsequent escape and avoidance learning. *Journal of Comparative and Physiological Psychology, 63,* 23–33.

Page, S., & Neuringer, A. (1985). Variability as an operant. *Journal of Experimental Psychology: Animal Behavior Processes, 11,* 429–452.

Panagiotaropoulos, T., Diamantopoulou, A., Stamatakis, A., Dimitropoulou, M., & Stylianopoulou, F. (2009). Learning of a T-maze by rat pups when contact with the mother is either permitted or denied. *Neurobiology of Learning and Memory, 91,* 2–12.

Papini, M. R. (2003). Comparative psychology of surprising nonreward. *Brain, Behavior and Evolution, 62,* 83–95.

Papini, M. R. (2008). *Comparative psychology* (2nd ed.). London: Taylor Francis.

Parsons, T. D., & Rizzo, A. A. (2008). Affective outcomes of virtual reality exposure therapy for anxiety and specific phobias: A meta-analysis. *Journal of Behavior Therapy and Experimental Psychiatry, 39,* 250–261.

Patterson, F. G. (1978). The gestures of a gorilla: Language acquisition in another pongid. *Brain and Language, 5,* 56–71.

Patterson, M. M. (2001). Classical conditioning of spinal reflexes: The first seventy years. In J. E. Steinmetz, M. A. Gluck, & P. R. Solomon (Eds.), *Model systems and the neurobiology of associative learning.* Mahwah, NJ: Erlbaum.

Patterson, M. M., & Grau, J. W. (Eds.). (2001). *Spinal cord plasticity: Alterations in reflex function.* Boston: Kluwer Academic Publishers.

Pavlov, I. P. (1927). *Conditioned reflexes* (G. V. Anrep, Trans.). London: Oxford University Press.

Pearce, J. M. (1987). A model for stimulus generalization in Pavlovian conditioning. *Psychological Review, 94,* 61–73.

Pearce, J. M. (1994). Similarity and discrimination: A selective review and a connectionistic model. *Psychological Review, 101,* 587–607.

Pearce, J. M. (2002). Evaluation and development of a connectionist theory of configural learning. *Animal Learning & Behavior, 30,* 73–95.

Pearce, J. M. (2009). The 36th Sir Frederick Bartlett Lecture: An associative analysis of spatial learning. *Quarterly Journal of Experimental Psychology, 62,* 1665–1684.

Pearce, J. M., & Bouton, M. E. (2001). Theories of associative learning. *Annual Review of Psychology, 52,* 111–139.

Pearce, J. M., Esber, G. R., & George, D. N. (2008). The nature of discrimination learning in pigeons. *Learning & Behavior, 36,* 188–199.

Pearce, J. M., & Hall, G. (1980). A model for Pavlovian learning: Variations in the effectiveness of conditioned but not of unconditioned stimuli. *Psychological Review, 87,* 532–552.

Pecina, S., Smith, K. S., & Berridge, K. C. (2006). Hedonic hot spots in the brain. *The Neuroscientist, 12,* 500–511.

Pelchat, M. L., & Rozin, P. (1982). The special role of nausea in the acquisition of food dislikes by humans. *Appetite, 3,* 341–351.

Pelloux, Y., Everitt, B. J., & Dickinson, A. (2007). Compulsive drug seeking by rats under punishment: Effects of drug taking history. *Psychopharmacology, 194,* 127–137.

Pepperberg, I. M. (1990). Some cognitive capacities of an African grey parrot (*Psittacus erithacus*). In P. J. B. Slater, J. S. Rosenblatt, & C. Beer (Eds.), *Advances in the study of behavior* (Vol. 19, pp. 357–409). San Diego: Academic Press.

Pepperberg, I. M. (1993). Cognition and communication in an African grey parrot (*Psittacus erithacus*): Studies on

a nonhuman, nonprimate, nonmammalian subject. In H. L. Roitblat, L. M. Herman, & P. E. Nachtigall (Eds.), *Language and communication: Comparative perspectives* (pp. 221–248). Hillsdale, NJ: Erlbaum.

Pepperberg, I. M. (1999). Rethinking syntax: A commentary on E. Kako's "elements of syntax in the systems of three language-trained animals." *Animal Learning & Behavior, 27*, 15–17.

Pepperberg, I. M. (1999). *The Alex studies: Cognitive and communicative abilities of Grey Parrots.* Cambridge, MA: Harvard University Press.

Pepperberg, I. M. (2010). Vocal learning in Grey parrots: A brief review of perception, production, and cross-species comparisons. *Brain & Language, 115*, 81–91.

Perry, D. G., & Parke, R. D. (1975). Punishment and alternative response training as determinants of response inhibition in children. *Genetic Psychology Monographs, 91*, 257–279.

Perry, J. L., & Dess, N. K. (2012). Laboratory animal research ethics: A practical educational approach. In S. J. Knapp (Ed.), *APA Handbook of ethics in psychology, Vol. 2: Practice, teaching, and research* (pp. 423–440). Washington, DC: American Psychological Association.

Peters, J., Kalivas, P. W., & Quirk, G. J. (2009). Extinction circuits for fear and addition overlap in prefrontal cortex. *Learning and Memory, 16*, 279–288.

Peterson, G. B., Ackil, J. E., Frommer, G. P., & Hearst, E. S. (1972). Conditioned approach and contact behavior toward signals for food and brain-stimulation reinforcement. *Science, 177*, 1009–1011.

Peterson, C., Maier, S. F., & Seligman, M. E. P. (1993). *Learned helplessness: A theory for the age of personal control.* New York: Oxford University Press.

Peterson, G. B., & Trapold, M. A. (1980). Effects of altering outcome expectancies on pigeons' delayed conditional discrimination performance. *Learning and Motivation, 11*, 267–288.

Pietras, C. J., Brandt, A. E., & Searcy, G. D. (2010). Human responding on random-interval schedules of response-cost punishment: The role of reduced reinforcement density. *Journal of Experimental Analysis of Behavior, 93*, 5–26.

Pilley, J. W., & Reid, A. K. (2011). Border collie comprehends object names as verbal referents. *Behavioural Processes, 86*, 184–195.

Pizzo, M. J., & Crystal, J. D. (2007). Temporal discrimination of alternative days in rats. *Learning & Behavior, 35*, 165–168.

Ploog, B. O. (2001). Effects of primary reinforcement on pigeons' initial-link responding under a concurrent chains schedule with nondifferential terminal links. *Journal of the Experimental Analysis of Behavior, 76*, 75–94.

Ploog, B. O., & Zeigler, H. P. (1996). Effects of food-pellet size on rate, latency, and topography of auto-shaped key pecks and gapes in pigeons. *Journal of the Experimental Analysis of Behavior, 65*, 21–35.

Podlesnik, C. A., & Shahan, T. A. (2008). Response-reinforcer relations and resistance to change. *Behavioural Processes, 77*, 109–125.

Poling, A., Nickel, M., & Alling, K. (1990). Free birds aren't fat: Weight gain in captured wild pigeons maintained under laboratory conditions. *Journal of the Experimental Analysis of Behavior, 53*, 423–424.

Polivy, J., Herman, C. P., & Girz, L. (2011). Learning to eat: The influence of food cues on what, when, and how much we eat. In T. R. Schachtman & S. Reilly (Eds.), *Associative learning and conditioning theory: Human and nonhuman applications* (pp. 290–304). Oxford and New York: Oxford University Press.

Postman, L. (1971). Transfer, interference, and forgetting. In J. W. Kling & L. A. Riggs (Eds.), *Woodworth and Schlosberg's experimental psychology* (3rd ed.). New York: Holt, Rinehart and Winston.

Prados, J. (2011). Blocking and overshadowing in human geometry learning. *Journal of Experimental Psychology: Animal Behavior Processes, 37*, 121–126.

Pravosudov, V. V., & Clayton, N. S. (2002). A test of the adaptive specialization hyothesis: Population differences in caching, memory, and the hippocampus in black-capped chickadees (*Poecile atricapilla*). *Behavioral Neuroscience, 116*, 515–522.

Premack, D. (1965). Reinforcement theory. In D. Levine (Ed.), *Nebraska Symposium on Motivation* (Vol. 13, pp. 123–180). Lincoln: University of Nebraska Press.

Premack, D. (1971a). Catching up with common sense, or two sides of a generalization: Reinforcement and punishment. In R. Glaser (Ed.), *The nature of reinforcement.* New York: Academic Press.

Premack, D. (1971b). Language in chimpanzee? *Science, 172*, 808–822.

Premack, D. (1976). *Intelligence in ape and man.* Hillsdale, NJ: Erlbaum.

Prescott, T. J., Bryson, J. J., & Seth, A. K. (2007). Modelling natural action selection. *Philosophical Transactions of the Royal Society, 362B*, 1521–1529.

Preston, K. L., Umbricht, A., Wong, C. J., & Epstein, D. H. (2001). Shaping cocaine abstinence by successive approximations. *Journal of Consulting and Clinical Psychology, 69*, 43–654.

Prus, A. (2014). *An introduction to drugs and the neuroscience of behavior.* Belmont, CA: Wadsworth.

Pryce, C. R., et al. (2011). Helplessness: A systematic translational review of theory and evidence for its relevance to understanding and treating depression. *Pharmacology & Therapeutics, 132*, 242–267.

Quee, P. J., Eling, P. A. T. M., van der Heijden, F. M. M. A., & Hildebrandt, H. (2011). Working memory in schizophrenia: A systematic study of specific modalities and processes. *Psychiatry Research, 185*, 54–59.

Quirk, G. J., & Mueller, D. (2008). Neural mechanisms of extinction learning and retrieval. *Neuropsychopharmacology, 33*, 56–72.

Quirk, G. J., et al. (2010). Erasing fear memories with extinction training. *Journal of Neuroscience, 30*, 14993–14997.

Rachlin, H. (1976). *Behavior and learning.* San Francisco: W. H. Freeman.

Rachlin, H. (2000). *The science of self-control.* Cambridge, MA: Harvard University Press.

Rachlin, H. (2006). Notes on discounting. *Journal of the Experimental Analysis of Behavior, 85*, 425–435.

Rachlin, H. C., & Green, L. (1972). Commitment, choice, and selfcontrol. *Journal of the Experimental Analysis of Behavior, 17*, 15–22.

Rachlin, H. C., & Herrnstein, R. L. (1969). Hedonism revisited: On the negative law of effect. In B. A. Campbell & R. M. Church (Eds.), *Punishment and aversive behavior.* New York: Appleton Century-Crofts.

Radke, A. K., Rothwell, P. E., & Gewirtz, J. C. (2011). An anatomical basis for opponent process mechanisms of opiate withdrawal. *Journal of Neuroscience, 31,* 7533–7539.

Raia, C. P., Shillingford, S. W., Miller, H. L., Jr., & Baier, P. S. (2000). *Journal of the Experimental Analysis of Behavior, 74,* 265–281.

Raiff, B. R., Bullock, C. E., & Hackenberg, T. D. (2008). Response-cost punishment with pigeons: Further evidence of response suppression via token loss. *Learning & Behavior, 36,* 29–41.

Randell, T., & Remington, B. (1999). Equivalence relations between visual stimuli: The functional role of naming. *Journal of the Experimental Analysis of Behavior, 71,* 395–415.

Randich, A., & LoLordo, V. M. (1979). Associative and non-associative theories of the UCS preexposure phenomenon: Implications for Pavlovian conditioning. *Psychological Bulletin, 86,* 523–548.

Rankin, C. H., et al. (2009). Habituation revisited: An updated and revised description of the behavioral characteristics of habituation. *Neurobiology of Learning and Memory, 92,* 135–138.

Rasmussen, E. B., & Newland, M. C. (2008). Asymmetry of reinforcement and punishment in human choice. *Journal of the Experimental Analysis of Behavior, 89,* 157–167.

Rau, V., & Fanselow, M. S. (2007). Neurobiological and neuroethological prespectives on fear and anxiety. In L. J. Kirmayer, R. Lemelson, & M. Barad (Eds.), *Understanding trauma: Integrating biological, clinical, and cultural perspectives* (pp. 27–40). Cambridge, UK: Cambridge University Press.

Rauhut, A. S., Thomas, B. L., & Ayres, J. J. B. (2001). Treatments that weaken Pavlovian conditioned fear and thwart its renewal in rats: Implications for treating human phobias. *Journal of Experimental Psychology: Animal Behavior Processes, 27,* 99–114.

Rayburn-Reeves, R., & Zentall, T. R. (2009). Animal memory: The contribution of generalization decrement to delayed conditional discrimination retention functions. *Learning & Behavior, 37,* 299–304.

Raymond, J. L., Lisberger, S. G., & Mauk, M. D. (1996). The cerebellum: A neuronal learning machine? *Science, 272,* 1126–1131.

Reberg, D. (1972). Compound tests for excitation in early acquisition and after prolonged extinction of conditioned suppression. *Learning and Motivation, 3,* 246–258.

Reed, D. D., Critchfield, T. S., & Martins, B. K. (2006). The generalized matching law in elite sport competition: Football play calling as operant choice. *Journal of Applied Behavior Analysis, 39,* 281–297.

Reed, P. (2007a). Human sensitivity to reinforcement feedback functions. *Psychonomic Bulletin & Review, 14,* 653–657.

Reed, P. (2007b). Response rate and sensitivity to the molar feedback function relating response and reinforcement rate on VI+ schedules of reinforcement. *Journal of Experimental Psychology: Animal Behavior Processes, 33,* 428–439.

Reed, P., & Yoshino, T. (2008). Effect of contingent auditory stimuli on concurrent schedule performance: An alternative punisher to electric shock. *Behavioural Processes, 78,* 421–428.

Reger, M. L., et al. (2012). Concussive brain injury enhances fear learning and excitatory processes in the amygdala. *Biological Psychiatry, 71,* 335–343.

Rehfeldt, R. A. (2011). Toward a technology of derived stimulus relations: An analysis of articles published in the Journal of Applied Behavior Analysis, 1992–2009. *Journal of Applied Behavior Analysis, 44,* 109–119.

Reilly, S., & Schachtman, T. R. (Eds.). (2009). *Conditioned taste aversion: Behavioral and neural processes.* Oxford/New York: Oxford University Press.

Repp, A. C., & Singh, N. N. (Eds.). (1990). *Perspectives on the use of nonaversive and aversive interventions for persons with developmental disabilities.* Sycamore, IL: Sycamore.

Rescorla, R. A. (1967a). Inhibition of delay in Pavlovian fear conditioning. *Journal of Comparative and Physiological Psychology, 64,* 114–120.

Rescorla, R. A. (1967b). Pavlovian conditioning and its proper control procedures. *Psychological Review, 74,* 71–80.

Rescorla, R. A. (1968). Pavlovian conditioned fear in Sidman avoidance learning. *Journal of Comparative and Physiological Psychology, 65,* 55–60.

Rescorla, R. A. (1969a). Conditioned inhibition of fear resulting from negative CS-US contingencies. *Journal of Comparative and Physiological Psychology, 67,* 504–509.

Rescorla, R. A. (1969b). Pavlovian conditioned inhibition. *Psychological Bulletin, 72,* 77–94.

Rescorla, R. A. (1980). *Pavlovian second-order conditioning.* Hillsdale, NJ: Erlbaum.

Rescorla, R. A. (1985). Conditioned inhibition and facilitation. In R. R. Miller & N. E. Spear (Eds.), *Information processing in animals: Conditioned inhibition.* Hillsdale, NJ: Erlbaum.

Rescorla, R. A. (1986). Extinction of facilitation. *Journal of Experimental Psychology: Animal Behavior Processes, 12,* 16–24.

Rescorla, R. A. (1987). Facilitation and inhibition. *Journal of Experimental Psychology: Animal Behavior Processes, 13,* 250–259.

Rescorla, R. A. (1992). Association between an instrumental discriminative stimulus and multiple outcomes. *Journal of Experimental Psychology: Animal Behavior Processes, 18,* 95–104.

Rescorla, R. A. (1993a). Inhibitory associations between S and R in extinction. *Animal Learning & Behavior, 21,* 327–336.

Rescorla, R. A. (1993b). Preservation of response-outcome associations through extinction. *Animal Learning & Behavior, 21,* 238–245.

Rescorla, R. A. (1996a). Preservation of Pavlovian associations through extinction. *Quarterly Journal of Experimental Psychology, 49B,* 245–258.

Rescorla, R. A. (1996b). Response-outcome associations remain functional through interference treatments. *Animal Learning & Behavior, 24,* 450–458.

Rescorla, R. A. (1997). Response-inhibition in extinction. *Quarterly Journal of Experimental Psychology, 50B,* 238–252.

Rescorla, R. A. (1997a). Spontaneous recovery after Pavlovian conditioning with multiple outcomes. *Animal Learning & Behavior, 25,* 99–107.

Rescorla, R. A. (1997b). Spontaneous recovery of instrumental discriminative responding. *Animal Learning & Behavior, 27,* 485–497.

Rescorla, R. A. (1999a). Summation and overexpectation with qualitatively different outcomes. *Animal Learning & Behavior, 27,* 50–62.

Rescorla, R. A. (1999b). Within-subject partial reinforcement extinction effect in autoshaping. *Quarterly Journal of Experimental Psychology, 52B,* 75–87.

Rescorla, R. A. (2000). Extinction can be enhanced by a concurrent excitor. *Journal of Experimental Psychology: Animal Behavior Processes, 26,* 251–260.

Rescorla, R. A. (2001). Retraining of extinguished Pavlovian stimuli. *Journal of Experimental Psychology: Animal Behavior Processes, 27,* 115–124.

Rescorla, R. A. (2003). Protection from extinction. *Learning & Behavior, 31,* 124–132.

Rescorla, R. A. (2004a). Spontaneous recovery. *Learning and Memory, 11,* 501–509.

Rescorla, R. A. (2004b). Spontaneous recovery varies inversely with the training-extinction interval. *Learning & Behavior, 32,* 401–408.

Rescorla, R. A. (2006a). Deepened extinction from compound stimulus presentation. *Journal of Experimental Psychology: Animal Behavior Processes, 32,* 135–144.

Rescorla, R. A. (2006b). Stimulus generalization of excitation and inhibition. *Quarterly Journal of Experimental Psychology, 59,* 53–67.

Rescorla, R. A. (2008). Evaluating conditioning of related and unrelated stimuli using a compound test. *Learning & Behavior, 36,* 67–74.

Rescorla, R. A., & Furrow, D. R. (1977). Stimulus similarity as a determinant of Pavlovian conditioning. *Journal of Experimental Psychology: Animal Behavior Processes, 3,* 203–215.

Rescorla, R. A., & Heth, C. D. (1975). Reinstatement of fear to an extinguished conditioned stimulus. *Journal of Experimental Psychology: Animal Behavior Processes, 104,* 88–96.

Rescorla, R. A., & Solomon, R. L. (1967). Two-process learning theory: Relationships between Pavlovian conditioning and instrumental learning. *Psychological Review, 74,* 151–182.

Rescorla, R. A., & Wagner, A. R. (1972). A theory of Pavlovian conditioning: Variations in the effectiveness of reinforcement and nonreinforcement.

In A. H. Black & W. F. Prokasy (Eds.), *Classical conditioning II: Current research and theory* (pp. 64–99). New York: Appleton-Century-Crofts.

Revusky, S. H., & Garcia, J. (1970). Learned associations over long delays. In G. H. Bower & J. T. Spence (Eds.), *The psychology of learning and motivation* (Vol. 4). New York: Academic Press.

Reynolds, G. S. (1961). Attention in the pigeon. *Journal of the Experimental Analysis of Behavior, 4,* 203–208.

Reynolds, G. S. (1975). *A primer of operant conditioning.* Glenview, IL: Scott Foresman.

Riccio, D. C., & Richardson, R. (1984). The status of memory following experimentally induced amnesias: Gone, but not forgotten. *Physiological Psychology, 12,* 59–72.

Riccio, D. C., MacArdy, E. A., & Kissinger, S. C. (1991). Associative processes in adaptation to repeated cold exposure in rats. *Behavioral Neuroscience, 105,* 599–602.

Riccio, D. C., Millin, P. M., & Bogart, A. R. (2006). Reconsolidation: A brief history, a retrieval view, and some recent issues. *Learning and Memory, 13,* 536–544.

Ristau, C. A. (Ed.). (1991). *Cognitive ethology.* Hillsdale, NJ: Erlbaum.

Robbins, S. J. (1990). Mechanisms underlying spontaneous recovery in autoshaping. *Journal of Experimental Psychology: Animal Behavior Processes, 16,* 235–249.

Roberts, S. (1981). Isolation of an internal clock. *Journal of Experimental Psychology: Animal Behavior Processes, 7,* 242–268.

Roberts, W. A. (1998). *Animal cognition.* Boston: McGraw-Hill.

Roberts, W. A. (2010). "Counting" serially presented stimuli by human and non-human primates and pigeons. *Learning and Motivation, 41,* 241–251.

Roberts, W. A. (2012). Evidence for future cognition in animals. *Learning and Motivation, 43,* 169–180.

Roberts, W. A., & Grant, D. S. (1976). Studies of short-term memory in the pigeon using the delayed matching to sample procedure. In D. L. Medin, W. A. Roberts, & R. T. Davis (Eds.), *Processes of animal memory.* Hillsdale, NJ: Erlbaum.

Roberts, W. A., & Grant, D. S. (1978). An analysis of light-induced retroactive inhibition in pigeon short term

memory. *Journal of Experimental Psychology: Animal Behavior Processes, 4,* 219–236.

Roberts, W. A., & Mazmanian, D. S. (1988). Concept learning at different levels of abstraction by pigeons, monkeys, and people. *Journal of Experimental Psychology: Animal Behavior Processes, 14,* 247–260.

Roberts, W. A., & Van Veldhuizen, N. (1985). Spatial memory in pigeons on a radial maze. *Journal of Experimental Psychology: Animal Behavior Processes, 11,* 241–260.

Roberts, W. A. (2002). Are animals stuck in time? *Psychological Bulletin, 128,* 473–489.

Robinson, T. E., & Berridge, K. C. (2003). Addiction. *Annual Review of Psychology, 54,* 25–53.

Rodriguez, C. A., Chamizo, V. D., & Mackintosh, N. J. (2011). Overshadowing and blocking between landmark learning and shape learning: The importance of sex differences. *Learning & Behavior, 39,* 324–335.

Roesch, M. R., Esber, G. R., Li, J., Daw, N. D., & Schoenbaum, G. (2012). Surprise! Neural correlates of Pearce-Hall and Rescorla-Wagner coexist within the brain. *European Journal of Neuroscience, 35,* 1190–1200.

Roitblat, H. L. (1980). Codes and coding processes in pigeon short-term memory. *Animal Learning & Behavior, 8,* 341–351.

Roitblat, H. L. (2007). A comparative psychologist looks at language. In D. A. Washburn (Ed.), *Primate perspectives on behavior and cognition* (pp. 235–242). Washington, DC: American Psychological Association.

Roitblat, H. L., Harley, H. E., & Helweg, D. A. (1993). Cognitive processing in artificial language research. In H. L. Roitblat, L. M. Herman, & P. E. Nachtigall (Eds.), *Language and communication: Comparative perspectives* (pp. 1–23). Hillsdale, NJ: Erlbaum.

Roll, J. M., & Newton, T. (2008). Methamphetamines. In S. T. Higgins, K. Silverman, & S. H. Heil (Eds.), *Contingency management in substance abuse treatment* (pp. 80–98). New York: Guilford Press.

Romanes, G. J. (1882). *Animal intelligence.* New York: Appleton.

Romaniuk, C. B., & Williams, D. A. (2000). Conditioning across the duration of a backward conditioned stimulus. *Journal of Experimental Psychology: Animal Behavior Processes, 26,* 454–461.

Roane, H. S., Kelley, M. E., Trosclair, N. M., & Hauer, L. S. (2004). Behavioral momentum in sports: A partial replication with women's basketball. *Journal of Applied Behavior Analysis, 37,* 385–390.

Roper, K. L., Chaponis, D. M., & Blaisdell, A. P. (2005). Transfer of directed-forgetting cues across discrimination tasks with pigeons. *Psychonomic Bulletin & Review, 12,* 1005–1010.

Roper, K. L., Kaiser, D. H., & Zentall, T. R. (1995). True directed forgetting in pigeons may occur only when alternative working memory is required on forget-cue trials. *Animal Learning & Behavior, 23,* 280–285.

Rosellini, R. A., & DeCola, J. P. (1981). Inescapable shock interferes with the acquisition of a low-activity response in an appetitive context. *Animal Learning & Behavior, 9,* 487–490.

Ross, C., & Neuringer, A. (2002). Reinforcement of variations and repetitions along three independent response dimensions. *Behavioural Processes, 57,* 199–209.

Ross, R. T., & Holland, P. C. (1981). Conditioning of simultaneous and serial feature-positive discriminations. *Animal Learning & Behavior, 9,* 293–303.

Routtenberg, A. (2008). The substrate for long-lasting memory: If not protein synthesis, then what? *Neurobiology of Learning and Memory, 89,* 225–233.

Rovee-Collier, C., & Barr, R. (2008). Infant learning and memory. In B. J. Gavin & A. Fogel (Eds.), *Blackwell handbook of infant development* (pp. 139–168). Oxford: Blackwell.

Rovee-Collier, C., & Giles, A. (2010). Why a neuromaturational model of memory fails: Exuberant learning in early infancy. *Behavioural Processes, 83,* 197–206.

Rudy, J. W. (2008a). Is there a baby in the bathwater? Maybe: Some methodological issues for the de novo protein synthesis hypothesis. *Neurobiology of Learning and Memory, 89,* 219–224.

Rudy, J. W. (2008b). *The neurobiology of learning and memory.* Sunderland, Mass: Sinauer Associates.

Rudy, J. W. (2009). Context representations, context functions, and the parahippocampal-hippocampal system. *Learning & Memory, 16,* 573–584.

Rumbaugh, D. M. (Eds.). (1977). *Language learning by a chimpanzee: The Lana project.* New York: Academic Press.

Russell, M. S., & Burch, R. L. (1959). *The principles of humane experimental technique.* London: Methuen.

Russell, W. R., & Nathan, P. W. (1946). Traumatic amnesia. *Brain, 69,* 280–300.

Russella, R., & Kirkpatrick, K. (2007). The role of temporal generalization in a temporal discrimination task. *Behavioural Processes, 74,* 115–125.

Saddoris, M., Gallagher, M., & Schoenbaum, G. (2005). Rapid associative encoding in basolateral amygdala depends on connections with orbitofrontal cortex. *Neuron, 46,* 321–331.

Sajwaj, T., Libet, J., & Agras, S. (1974). Lemon-juice therapy: The control of life-threatening rumination in a six-month-old infant. *Journal of Applied Behavior Analysis, 7,* 557–563.

Salwiczek, L. H., Watanabe, A., & Clayton, N. S. (2010). Ten years of research into avian models of episodic-like memory and its implications for developmental and comparative cognition. *Behavioural Brain Research, 215,* 221–234.

Sanabria, F., Sitomer, M. T., & Killeen, P. R. (2006). Negative automaintenance omission training is effective. *Journal of the Experimental Analysis of Behavior, 86,* 1–10.

Santi, A., Hoover, C., & Simmons, S. (2011). Rats' memory for time and relational responding in the duration-comparison procedure. *Learning and Motivation, 42,* 173–184.

Sargisson, R. J., & White, K. G. (2001). Generalization of delayed matching to sample following training at different delays. *Journal of the Experimental Analysis of Behavior, 75,* 1–14.

Savage-Rumbaugh, E. S. (1986). *Ape language.* New York: Columbia University Press.

Savage-Rumbaugh, E. S., McDonald, K., Sevcik, R. A., Hopkins, W. D., & Rubert, E. (1986). Spontaneous symbol acquisition and communicative use by pigmy chimpanzees (*Pan paniscus*). *Journal of Experimental Psychology: General, 115,* 211–235.

Savage-Rumbaugh, E. S., Murphy, J., Sevcik, R. A., Brakke, K. E., Williams, S. L., & Rumbaugh, D. M. (1993). Language comprehension in ape and child. *Monographs of the Society for Research in Child Development, 58*(Nos. 3–4, Serial No. 233).

Savage-Rumbaugh, E. S., Sevcik, R. A., Brakke, K. E., & Rumbaugh, D. M. (1990). Symbols: Their communicative use, comprehension, and combination by bonobos (*Pan paniscus*). In C. Rovee-Collier & L. P. Lipsitt (Eds.), *Advances in infancy research* (Vol. 6, pp. 221–278). Norwood, NJ: Ablex.

Savage-Rumbaugh, S., Shanker, S. G., & Taylor, T. J. (1998). *Apes, language, and the human mind.* New York: Oxford University Press.

Savastano, H. I., & Fantino, E. (1996). Differences in delay, not ratios, control choice in concurrent chains. *Journal of the Experimental Analysis of Behavior, 66,* 97–116.

Savastano, H., & Fantino, E. (1994). Human choice in concurrent ratio-interval schedules of reinforcement. *Journal of the Experimental Analysis of Behavior, 61,* 453–463.

Savastano, H. I., & Miller, R. R. (1998). Time as content in Pavlovian conditioning. *Behavioural Processes, 44,* 147–162.

Sawa, K., Nakajima, S., & Imada, H. (1999). Facilitation of sodium aversion learning in sodium-deprived rats. *Learning and Motivation, 30,* 281–295.

Scalera, G. (2002). Effects of conditioned food aversions on nutritional behavior in humans. *Nutritional Neuroscience, 5,* 159–188.

Scalera, G., & Bavieri, M. (2009). Role of conditioned taste aversion on the side effects of chemotherapy in cancer patients. In S. Reilly & T. R. Schachtman (Eds.), *Conditioned taste aversion: Behavioral and neural processes* (pp. 513–541). Oxford/New York: Oxford University Press.

Scarf, D., & Colombo, M. (2010). Representation of serial order in pigeons (*Columba livia*). *Journal of Experimental Psychology: Animal Behavior Processes, 36,* 423–429.

Scavio, M. J., Jr., & Gormezano, I. (1974). CS intensity effects on rabbit nictitating membrane conditioning, extinction and generalization. *Pavlovian Journal of Biological Science, 9,* 25–34.

Schaal, D. W. (2013). Behavioral neuroscience. In G. J. Madden (Ed.), *APA Handbook of Behavior Analysis, Vol. 1: Methods and Principles* (pp. 339–360). Washington, DC: American Psychological Association.

Schachter, D. L., et al. (2012). The future of memory: Remembering, imagining, and the brain. *Neuron, 76,* 677–694.

Schachter, D. L., & Tulving, E. (1994). What are the memory systems of 1994? In D. L. Schachter & E. Tulving (Eds.), *Memory systems 1994* (pp. 1–38). Cambridge, MA: MIT Press.

Schachtman, T. R., & Reilly, S. (Eds.). (2011). *Associative learning and conditioning theory: Human and non-human applications*. Oxford and New York: Oxford University Press.

Schachtman, T. R., Brown, A. M., & Miller, R. R. (1985). Reinstatement-induced recovery of a taste-LiCl association following extinction. *Animal Learning & Behavior, 13*, 223–227.

Schachtman, T. R., Walker, J., & Fowler, S. (2011). Effects of conditioning in advertising. In T. R. Schachtman & S. Reilly (Eds.), *Associative learning and conditioning theory: Human and non-human applications* (pp. 481–506). Oxford and New York: Oxford University Press.

Schafe, G. E., & LeDoux, J. E. (2000). Memory consolidation of auditory Pavlovian fear conditioning requires protein synthesis and protein kinase A in the amygdala. *Journal of Neuroscience, 20*, RC96, 1–5.

Schiff, R., Smith, N., & Prochaska, J. (1972). Extinction of avoidance in rats as a function of duration and number of blocked trials. *Journal of Comparative and Physiological Psychology, 81*, 356–359.

Schiller, D., Monfils, M. H., Raio, C. M., Johnson, D. C., LeDoux, J. E., & Phelps, E. A. (2010). Preventing the return of fear in humans using reconsolidation update mechanisms. *Nature, 463*, 49–54.

Schindler, C. W., & Weiss, S. J. (1982). The influence of positive and negative reinforcement on selective attention in the rat. *Learning and Motivation, 13*, 304–323.

Schlinger, H., Blakely, E., & Kaczor, T. (1990). Pausing under variable ratio schedules: Interaction of reinforcer magnitude, variable-ratio size, and lowest ratio. *Journal of the Experimental Analysis of Behavior, 53*, 133–139.

Schlosberg, H. (1934). Conditioned responses in the white rat. *Journal of Genetic Psychology, 45*, 303–335.

Schlosberg, H. (1936). Conditioned responses in the white rat: II. Conditioned responses based upon shock to the foreleg. *Journal of Genetic Psychology, 49*, 107–138.

Schmajuk, N. A. (2010). *Mechanisms in classical conditioning: A computational approach*. Cambridge, UK: Cambridge University Press.

Schmajuk, N. A., & Holland, P. C. (Eds.). (1998). *Occasion setting: Associative learning and cognition in animals*. Washington, DC: American Psychological Association.

Schmidt, N. B., Anthony, R. J., Maner, J. K., & Woolaway-Bickel, K. (2006). Differential effects of safety in extinction of anxious responding to a CO_2 challenge in patients with panic disorder. *Journal of Abnormal Psychology, 115*, 341–350.

Schneider, A. M., & Sherman, W. (1968). Amnesia: A function of the temporal relation of footshock to electroconvulsive shock. *Science, 159*, 219–221.

Schneiderman, N., & Gormezano, I. (1964). Conditioning of the nictitating membrane of the rabbit as a function of CS-US interval. *Journal of Comparative and Physiological Psychology, 57*, 188–195.

Schner, G., & Thelen, E. (2006). Using dynamic field theory to rethink infant habituation. *Psychological Review, 113*, 273–299.

Schreibman, L., Koegel, R. L., Charlop, M. H., & Egel, A. L. (1990). Infantile autism. In A. S. Bellack, M. Hersen, & A. E. Kazdin (Eds.), *International handbook of behavior modification and therapy* (pp. 763–789). New York: Plenum.

Schreurs, B. G. (1998). Long-term memory and extinction of rabbit nictitating membrane trace conditioning. *Learning and Motivation, 29*, 68–82.

Schroers, M., Prigot, J., & Fagen, J. (2007). The effect of a salient odor context on memory retrieval in young infants. *Infant Behavior & Development, 30*, 685–689.

Schultz, W. (2006). Behavioral theories and the neurophysiology of reward. *Annual Review of Psychology, 57*, 87–115.

Schultz, W. (2007). Multiple dopamine functions at different time courses. *Annual Review of Neuroscience, 30*, 259–288.

Schultz, W., Dayan, P., & Montaque, P. R. (1997). A neural substrate of prediction and reward. *Science, 275*, 1593–1599.

Schuster, R. H., & Rachlin, H. (1968). Indifference between punishment and free shock: Evidence for the negative law of effect. *Journal of the Experimental Analysis of Behavior, 11*, 777–786.

Schusterman, R. J., & Gisiner, R. (1988). Artificial language comprehension in dolphins and sea lions: The essential cognitive skills. *Psychological Record, 38*, 311–348.

Schwartz, B. (1988). The experimental synthesis of behavior: Reinforcement, behavioral stereotypy, and problem solving. In G. H. Bower (Ed.), *The psychology of learning and motivation* (Vol. 22, pp. 93–138). Orlando, FL: Academic Press.

Schweitzer, J. B., & Sulzer-Azaroff, B. (1988). Self-control: Teaching tolerance for delay in impulsive children. *Journal of the Experimental Analysis of Behavior, 50*, 173–186.

Seligman, M. E. P., & Johnston, J. C. (1973). A cognitive theory of avoidance learning. In F. J. McGuigan & D. B. Lumsden (Eds.), *Contemporary approaches to conditioning and learning* (pp. 69–110). Washington, DC: Winston.

Seligman, M. E. P., & Maier, S. F. (1967). Failure to escape traumatic shock. *Journal of Experimental Psychology, 74*, 1–9.

Sevenster, P. (1973). Incompatibility of response and reward. In R. A. Hinde & J. Stevenson-Hinde (Eds.), *Constraints on learning* (pp. 265–284). London: Academic Press.

Sharma, S., Rakoczy, S., & Brown-Borg, H. (2010). Assessment of spatial memory in mice. *Life Sciences, 87*, 521–536.

Sheffield, F. D., Roby, T. B., & Campbell, B. A. (1954). Drive reduction versus consummatory behavior as determinants of reinforcement. *Journal of Comparative and Physiological Psychology, 47*, 349–354.

Sherry, D. F. (1984). Food storage by black-capped chickadees: Memory for the location and contents of caches. *Animal Behaviour, 32*, 451–464.

Sherry, D. F. (1985). Food storage by birds and mammals. *Advances in the study of behavior, 15*, 153–188.

Sherry, D. F., Krebs, J. R., & Cowie, R. J. (1981). Memory for the location of stored food in marsh tits. *Animal Behaviour, 29*, 1260–1266.

Shettleworth, S. J. (1975). Reinforcement and the organization of behavior in golden hamsters: Hunger, environment, and food reinforcement. *Journal of Experimental Psychology: Animal Behavior Processes, 1*, 56–87.

Shettleworth, S. J. (2010). *Cognition, evolution, and behavior* (2nd ed.). New York: Oxford University Press.

Shettleworth, S. J., & Krebs, J. R. (1986). Stored and encountered seeds: A comparison of two spatial memory tasks in marsh tits and chickadees. *Journal of Experimental Psychology: Animal Behavior Processes, 12,* 248–257.

Shettleworth, S. J., & Sutton, J. E. (2005). Multiple systems for spatial learning: Dead reckoning and beacon homing in rats. *Journal of Experimental Psychology: Animal Behavior Processes, 31,* 125–141.

Shimp, C. P. (1969). Optimum behavior in free-operant experiments. *Psychological Review, 76,* 97–112.

Shimp, C. P., Herbranson, W. T., Fremouw, T., & Froehlich, A. L. (2006). Rule learning, memorization strategies, switching attention between local and global levels of perception, and optimality in avian visual categorization. In E. A. Wasserman & T. R. Zentall (Eds.), *Comparative cognition* (pp. 388–404). Oxford, UK: Oxford University Press.

Shors, T. J. (2006). Stressful experience and learning across the lifespan. *Annual Review of Psychology, 57,* 55–85.

Shuwairi, S. M., Albert, M. K., & Johnson, S. P. (2007). Discrimination of possible and impossible objects in infancy. *Psychological Science, 18,* 303–307.

Sidman, M. (1953a). Avoidance conditioning with brief shock and no exteroceptive warning signal. *Science, 118,* 157–158.

Sidman, M. (1953b). Two temporal parameters of the maintenance of avoidance behavior by the white rat. *Journal of Comparative and Physiological Psychology, 46,* 253–261.

Sidman, M. (1960). *Tactics of scientific research.* New York: Basic Books.

Sidman, M. (1966). Avoidance behavior. In W. K. Honig (Ed.), *Operant behavior.* New York: Appleton-Century-Crofts.

Sidman, M. (1994). *Equivalence relations and behavior: A research story.* Boston: Authors Cooperative.

Sidman, M. (2000). Equivalence relations and the reinforcement contingency. *Journal of the Experimental Analysis of Behavior, 74,* 127–146.

Sidman, M., & Tailby, W. (1982). Conditional discrimination vs. matching to sample: An expansion of the testing paradigm. *Journal of the Experimental Analysis of Behavior, 37,* 5–22.

Siegel, S. (1984). Pavlovian conditioning and heroin overdose: Reports by overdose victims. *Bulletin of the Psychonomic Society, 22,* 428–430.

Siegel, S. (1999). Drug anticipation and drug addiction. The 1998 H. David Archibald lecture. *Addiction, 94,* 1113–1124.

Siegel, S. (2005). Drug tolerance, drug addiction, and drug anticipation. *Current Directions in Psychological Science, 14,* 296–300.

Siegel, S. (2008). Learning and the wisdom of the body. *Learning & Behavior, 36,* 242–252.

Siegel, S., & Allen, L. G. (1996). The widespread influence of the Rescorla-Wagner model. *Psychonomic Bulletin & Review, 3,* 314–321.

Siegel, S., Baptista, M. A. S., Kim, J. A., McDonald, R. V., & Weise-Kelly, L. (2000). Pavlovian psychopharmacology: The associative basis of tolerance. *Experimental and Clinical Psychopharmacology, 8,* 276–293.

Siegel, S., & Domjan, M. (1971). Backward conditioning as an inhibitory procedure. *Learning and Motivation, 2,* 1–11.

Siegel, S., Hinson, R. E., Krank, M. D., & McCully, J. (1982). Heroin "overdose" death: Contribution of drug associated environmental cues. *Science, 216,* 436–437.

Sigmundi, R. A. (1997). Performance rules for problem-specific defense reactions. In M. E. Bouton & M. S. Fanselow (Eds.), *Learning, motivation, and cognition* (pp. 305–319). Washington, DC: American Psychological Association.

Sigmundi, R. A., & Bolles, R. C. (1983). CS modality, context conditioning, and conditioned freezing. *Animal Learning & Behavior, 11,* 205–212.

Sigurdsson, T., Doyere, V., Cain, C. K., & LeDoux, J. E. (2007). Long-term potentiation in the amygdala: A cellular mechanism of fear learning and memory. *Neuropharmacology, 52,* 215–227.

Silberberg, A., Warren-Boulton, F. R., & Asano, T. (1987). Inferior-good and Giffen-good effects in monkey choice behavior. *Journal of Experimental Psychology: Animal Behavior Processes, 13,* 292–301.

Silva, A. J., & Giese, K. P. (1998). Gene tageting: A novel window into the biology of learning and memory. In J. L. Martinez & R. P. Kesner (Eds.), *Neurobiology of learning and memory* (pp. 89–142). San Diego: Academic Press.

Silva, K. M., & Timberlake, W. (1997). A behavior systems view of conditioned states during long and short CS-US intervals. *Learning and Motivation, 28,* 465–490.

Silva, K. M., & Timberlake, W. (1998). The organization and temporal properties of appetitive behavior in rats. *Animal Learning & Behavior, 26,* 182–195.

Silva, K. M., & Timberlake, W. (2005). A behavior systems view of the organization of multiple responses during a partially or continuously reinforced interfood clock. *Learning & Behavior, 33,* 99–110.

Silver, R., Balsam, P. D., Butler, M. P., & LeSauter, J. (2011). Food anticipation depends on oscillators and memories in both body and brain. *Physiology & Behavior, 104,* 562–571.

Simons, R. C. (1996). *Boo! Culture, experience, and the startle reflex.* New York: Oxford University Press.

Singh, N. N., & Solman, R. T. (1990). A stimulus control analysis of the picture-word problem in children who are mentally retarded: The blocking effect. *Journal of Applied Behavior Analysis, 23,* 525–532.

Sissons, H. T., & Miller, R. R. (2009). Overexpectation and trial massing. *Journal of Experimental Psychology: Animal Behavior Processes, 35,* 186–196.

Skinner, B. F. (1938). *The behavior of organisms.* New York: Appleton-Century-Crofts.

Skinner, B. F. (1948). "Superstition" in the pigeon. *Journal of Experimental Psychology, 38,* 168–172.

Skinner, B. F. (1953). *Science and human behavior.* New York: Macmillan.

Slamecka, N. J., & Ceraso, J. (1960). Retroactive and proactive inhibition of verbal learning. *Psychological Bulletin, 57,* 449–475.

Small, W. S. (1899). An experimental study of the mental processes of the rat: 1. *American Journal of Psychology, 11,* 133–164.

Small, W. S. (1900). An experimental study of the mental processes of the rat: 11. *American Journal of Psychology, 12,* 206–239.

Smeets, P. M., & Barnes-Holmes, D. (2005). Establishing equivalence classes in preschool children with one-to-many and many-to-one training protocols. *Behavioural Processes, 69,* 281–293.

Smith, C. N., Clark, R. E., Manns, J. R., & Squire, L. R. (2005). Acquisition of differential delay eyeblink classical conditioning is independent of awareness. *Behavioral Neuroscience, 119*, 78–86.

Smith, J. C., & Roll, D. L. (1967). Trace conditioning with X-rays as an aversive stimulus. *Psychonomic Science, 9*, 11–12.

Smith, M. C., Coleman, S. R., & Gormezano, I. (1969). Classical conditioning of the rabbit's nictitating membrane response at backward, simultaneous, and forward CS-US intervals. *Journal of Comparative and Physiological Psychology, 69*, 226–231.

Smith, M. T., Perlis, M. L., Park, A., Smith, M. S., Pennington, J., Giles, D. E., et al. (2002). Comparative meta-analysis of pharmacotherapy and behavior therapy for persistent insomnia. *American Journal of Psychiatry, 159*, 5–11.

Solomon, R. L., & Corbit, J. D. (1974). An opponent-process theory of motivation: I. The temporal dynamics of affect. *Psychological Review, 81*, 119–145.

Solomon, R. L., & Wynne, L. C. (1953). Traumatic avoidance learning: Acquisition in normal dogs. *Psychological Monographs, 125*(Whole No. 354).

Solomon, R. L., Kamin, L. J., & Wynne, L. C. (1953). Traumatic avoidance learning: The outcomes of several extinction procedures with dogs. *Journal of Abnormal and Social Psychology, 48*, 291–302.

Soto, F. A., & Wasserman, E. A. (2010). Error-driven learning in visual categorization and object recognition: A common-elements model. *Psychological Review, 117*, 349–381.

Soto, F. A., & Wasserman, E. A. (2012a). A category-overshadowing effect in pigeons: Support for the common elements model of object categorization learning. *Journal of Experimental Psychology: Animal Behavior Processes, 38*, 322–328.

Soto, F. A., & Wasserman, E. A. (2012b). Visual object categorization in birds and primates: Integrating behavioral, neurobiological, and computational evidence within a "general process" framework. *Cognitive, Affective, and Behavioral Neuroscience, 12*, 220–240.

Spear, N. E., & Riccio, D. C. (1994). *Memory: Phenomena and principles.* Boston: Allyn and Bacon.

Spence, K. W. (1936). The nature of discrimination learning in animals. *Psychological Review, 43*, 427–449.

Spence, K. W. (1937). The differential response in animals to stimuli varying within a single dimension. *Psychological Review, 44*, 430–444.

Spence, K. W. (1956). *Behavior theory and conditioning.* New Haven, CT: Yale University Press.

Spetch, M. L. (1987). Systematic errors in pigeons' memory for event duration: Interaction between training and test delays. *Animal Learning & Behavior, 15*, 1–5.

Spetch, M. L., & Kelly, D. M. (2006). Comparative spatial cognition: Processes in landmark and surface based place finding. In E. A. Wasserman & T. R. Zentall (Eds.), *Comparative cognition* (pp. 210–228). Oxford, UK: Oxford University Press.

Spetch, M. L., Cheng, K., & Clifford, C. W. G. (2004). Peak shift but not range effects in recognition of faces. *Learning and Motivation, 35*, 221–241.

Spetch, M. L., Wilkie, D. M., & Pinel, J. P. J. (1981). Backward conditioning: A reevaluation of the empirical evidence. *Psychological Bulletin, 89*, 163–175.

Spetch, M. L., Wilkie, D. M., & Skelton, R. W. (1981). Control of pigeons' keypecking topography by a schedule of alternating food and water reward. *Animal Learning & Behavior, 9*, 223–229.

Spiga, R. (2006). *Using behavioral economics to understand reinforcer interactions: Human methadone, hydromorphone and valium self-administration.* Invited paper presented at the Symposium on Behavioral Economics and Drugs, 32nd Annual Convention of the Association of Behavior Analysis, Atlanta, GA.

Spiga, R., et al. (2005). Methadone and nicotine self-administration in humans: A behavioral economic analysis. *Psychopharmacology, 178*, 223–231.

Spoormaker, V. I., Andrade, K. C., Schrter, M. S., Sturm, A., Goya-Maldonado, R., Smann, P. G., et al. (2011). The neural correlates of negative prediction error signaling in human fear conditioning. *Neuroimage, 54*, 2250–2256.

Spradlin, J. E. (2002). Punishment: A primary process? *Journal of Applied Behavior Analysis, 35*, 457–477.

Squire, L. R. (2006). Lost forever or temporarily misplaced? The long debate about the nature of memory impairment. *Learning and Memory, 13*, 522–529.

Squire, L. R., & Wixted, J. T. (2011). The cognitive neuroscience of human memory since H.M. *Annual Review of Neuroscience, 34*, 258–288.

Squire, L. R., et al. (Eds.). (2003). *Fundamental Neuroscience* (2nd ed.). San Diego, CA: Academic Press.

Staddon, J. (2001). *The new behaviorism: Mind, Mechanism, and Society.* Philadelphia: Taylor Fracis, Psychology Press.

Staddon, J. E. R. (1983/2003). *Adaptive behavior and learning.* Cambridge: Cambridge University Press.

Staddon, J. E. R. (1988). Quasidynamic choice models: Melioration and ratio invariance. *Journal of the Experimental Analysis of Behavior, 49*, 303–320.

Staddon, J. E. R. (2001). *Adaptive dynamics.* Cambridge, Massachusetts: MIT Press.

Staddon, J. E. R., & Cerutti, D. T. (2003). Operant conditioning. *Annual Review of Psychology, 54*, 115–144.

Staddon, J. E. R., & Simmelhag, V. L. (1971). The "superstition" experiment: A reexamination of its implications for the principles of adaptive behavior. *Psychological Review, 78*, 3–43.

Stafford, D., & Branch, M. N. (1998). Effects of step size and break point criterion on progressive-ratio performance. *Journal of the Experimental Analysis of Behavior, 70*, 123–138.

Stafford, J. M., & Lattal, K. M. (2011). Is an epigenetic switch the key to persistent extinction? *Neurobiology of Learning and Memory, 96*, 35–40.

Stahlman, W. D., & Blaisdell, A. P. (2011). The modulation of operant variation by the probability, magnitude, and delay of reinforcement. *Learning and Motivation, 42*, 221–236.

Stahlman, W. D., Roberts, S., & Blaisdell, A. P. (2010). Effect of reward probability on spatial and temporal variation. *Journal of Experimental Psychology: Animal Behavior Processes, 36*, 77–91.

Stahlman, W. D., Young, M. E., & Blaisdell, A. P. (2010). Response variability in pigeons in a Pavlovian task. *Learning & Behavior, 38*, 111–118.

Stasiak, M., & Masterton, R. B. (1996). Auditory quality cues are more effective than auditory location cues in a R-no R (go-no go) differentiation: The extension of the rule to primitive mammals (American opposum Didelphis virginiana). *Acta Neurobiologica Experimentalis, 56*, 949–953.

Steel, P. (2007). The nature of procrastination: A meta-analysis and theoretical review of quintessential self-regulatory failure. *Psychological Bulletin, 133,* 65–94.

Steinert, P., Fallon, D., & Wallace, J. (1976). Matching to sample in goldfish (*Carassuis auratus*). *Bulletin of the Psychonomic Society, 8,* 265.

Steinmetz, J. E., Gluck, M. A., & Solomon, P. R. (2001). *Model systems and the neurobiology of associative learning: A festschrift in honor of Richard F. Thompson.* Hillsdale, NJ: Erlbaum.

Steinmetz, J. E., Tracy, J. A., & Green, J. T. (2001). Classical eyeblink conditioning: Clinical models and applications. *Integrative Physiological and Behavioral Science, 36,* 220–238.

Stevens, S. S. (1951). Mathematics, measurement and psychophysics. In S. S. Stevens (Ed.), *Handbook of experimental psychology* (pp. 1–49). New York: Wiley.

Stewart, J., & Wise, R. A. (1992). Reinstatement of heroin self-administration habits: Morphine prompts and naltrexone discourages renewed responding after extinction. *Psychopharmacology, 108,* 79–84.

Stokes, P. D. (2006). *Creativity from constraints.* New York: Springer.

Stokes, P. D., Mechner, F., & Balsam, P. D. (1999). Effects of different acquisition procedures on response variability. *Animal Learning & Behavior, 27,* 28–41.

Stokes, T. F., & Baer, D. M. (1977). An implicit technology of generalization. *Journal of Applied Behavior Analysis, 10,* 349–367.

Stolerman, I. P., Childs, E., Ford, M. M., & Grant, K. A. (2011). Role of training dose in drug discrimination: A review. *Behavioural Pharmacology, 22,* 415–429.

Storsve, A. B., McNally, G. P., & Richardson, R. (2012). Renewal and reinstatement of the conditioned but not the unconditioned response following habituation of the unconditioned stimulus. *Behavioural Processes, 90,* 58–65.

Stote, D. L., & Fanselow, M. S. (2004). NMDA receptor modulation of incidental learning in Pavlovian context conditioning. *Behavioral Neuroscience, 118,* 253–257.

Stout, S., Escobar, M., & Miller, R. R. (2004). Trial number and compound stimuli temporal relationships as joint determinants of second-order conditioning and conditioned inhibition. *Learning & Behavior, 32,* 230–239.

Stout, S. C., & Miller, R. R. (2007, Correction published in 2008, Psychological Review, 115, 82.). Sometimes-competing retrieval (SOCR): A formalization of the comparator hypothesis. *Psychological Review, 114,* 759–783.

Suarez, S. D., & Gallup, G. G. (1981). An ethological analysis of open-field behavior in rats and mice. *Learning and Motivation, 12,* 342–363.

Sumpter, C. E., Temple, W., & Foster, T. M. (1998). Response form, force, and number: Effects on concurrent schedule performance. *Journal of the Experimental Analysis of Behavior, 70,* 45–68.

Sundberg, M. L. (1996). Toward granting linguistic competence to apes: A review of Savage Rumbaugh et al.'s *Language comprehension in ape and child. Journal of the Experimental Analysis of Behavior, 65,* 477–492.

Sunsay, C., & Bouton, M. E. (2008). Analysis of the trial-spacing effect with relatively long intertrial intervals. *Learning & Behavior, 36,* 104–115.

Suss, C., Gaylord, S., & Fagen, J. (2012). Odor as a contextual cue in memory reactivation in young infants. *Infant Behavior & Development, 35,* 580–583.

Sutherland, A. (2008). *What Shamu taught me about life, love, and marriage.* New York: Random House.

Sutton, R. S., & Barto, A. G. (1998). *Reinforcement learning: An Introduction.* Cambridge, Mass: MIT Press.

Suzuki, S., Augerinos, G., & Black, A. H. (1980). Stimulus control of spatial behavior on the eight-arm maze in rats. *Learning and Motivation, 11,* 1–18.

Svartdal, F. (2000). Persistence during extinction: Conventional and reversed PREE under multiple schedules. *Learning and Motivation, 31,* 21–40.

Swartzentruber, D. (1995). Modulatory mechanisms in Pavlovian conditioning. *Animal Learning & Behavior, 23,* 123–143.

Swartzentruber, D. (1997). Modulation by the stimulus properties of excitation. *Journal of Experimental Psychology: Animal Behavior Processes, 23,* 434–440.

Swearingen, J. E., & Buhusi, C. V. (2010). The pattern of responding in the peak-interval procedure with gaps: An individual-trials analysis. *Journal of Experimental Psychology: Animal Behavior Processes, 36,* 443–455.

Taglialatela, J. P., Savage-Rumbaugh, S., & Baker, L. A. (2003). Vocal production by a language competent *Pan paniscus. International Journal of Primatology, 24,* 1–15.

Tait, R. W., & Saladin, M. E. (1986). Concurrent development of excitatory and inhibitory associations during backward conditioning. *Animal Learning & Behavior, 14,* 133–137.

Takeuchi, S. A. (2006). On the matching phenomenon in courtship: A probability matching theory of mate selection. *Marriage & Family Review, 40,* 25–51.

Tang, Y.-P., Shimizu, E., Dube, G. R., Rampon, C., Kerchner, G. A., Zhuo, M., et al. (1999). Genetic enhancement of learning and memory in mice. *Nature, 401,* 63–69.

Tanno, T., & Sakagami, T. (2008). On the primacy of molecular processes in determining response rates under variable-ratio and variable-interval schedules. *Journal of the Experimental Analysis of Behavior, 89,* 5–14.

Taylor, K. M., Joseph, V. T., Balsam, P. D., & Bitterman, M. E. (2008). Target-absent controls in blocking experiments with rats. *Learning & Behavior, 36,* 145–148.

Taylor, S. E., Klein, L. C., Lewis, B. P., Gruenewald, T. L., Gurung, R. A. R., & Updegraff, J. A. (2000). Biobehavioral responses to stress in females: Tend-and-befriend, not fight-or-flight. *Psychological Review, 107,* 411–429.

Terrace, H. (2012). The comparative psychology of ordinal knowledge. In T. R. Zentall & E. A. Wasserman (Eds.), *The Oxford handbook of comparative cognition* (pp. 615–551). New York/ Oxford: Oxford University Press.

Terrace, H. S. (1979). *Nim.* New York: Knopf.

Terrace, H. S., Petitto, L. A., Sanders, R. J., & Bever, T. G. (1979). Can an ape create a sentence? *Science, 206,* 891–1201.

Terrace, H. S., Son, L. K., & Brannon, E. M. (2003). Serial expertise of rhesus macaques. *Psychological Science, 14,* 66–73.

Theios, J. (1962). The partial reinforcement effect sustained through blocks of continuous reinforcement. *Journal of Experimental Psychology, 64,* 1–6.

Theios, J., & Brelsford, J. (1964). Overlearning-extinction effect as an incentive phenomena. *Journal of Experimental Psychology, 67,* 463–467.

Thomas, B. L., & Ayres, J. J. B. (2004). Use of the ABA fear renewal paradigm to assess the effects of extinction with co-present fear inhibitors or excitors: Implications for theories of extinction and for treating human fears and phobias. *Learning and Motivation, 35*, 22–52.

Thomas, B. L., Vurbic, D., & Novak, C. (2009). Extensive extinction in multiple contexts eliminates the renewal of conditioned fear in rats. *Learning and Motivation, 40*, 147–159.

Thomas, D. R. (1993). A model for adaptation-level effects on stimulus generalization. *Psychological Review, 100*, 658–673.

Thomas, D. R., McKelvie, A. R., & Mah, W. L. (1985). Context as a conditional cue in operant discrimination reversal learning. *Journal of Experimental Psychology: Animal Behavior Processes, 11*, 317–330.

Thomas, G. V., & Lieberman, D. A. (1990). Commentary: Determinants of success and failure in experiments on marking. *Learning and Motivation, 21*, 110–124.

Thompson, R. F. (1986). The neurobiology of learning and memory. *Science, 233*, 941–947.

Thompson, R. F. (1993). *The brain: A neuroscience primer. W. H.* Freeman: New York.

Thompson, R. F. (2005). In search of memory traces. *Annual Review of Psychology, 56*, 1–23.

Thompson, R. F. (2009). Habituation: A history. *Neurobiology of Learning and Memory, 92*, 127–134.

Thompson, R. F., & Spencer, W. A. (1966). Habituation: A model phenomenon for the study of neuronal substrates of behavior. *Psychological Review, 73*, 16–43.

Thompson, R. F., Groves, P. M., Teyler, T. J., & Roemer, R. A. (1973). A dual-process theory of habituation: Theory and behavior. In H. V. S. Peeke & M. J. Herz (Eds.), *Habituation*. New York: Academic Press.

Thompson, R. H., Iwata, B. A., Conners, J., & Roscoe, E. M. (1999). Effects of reinforcement for alternative behavior during punishment of self-injury. *Journal of Applied Behavior Analysis, 32*, 317–328.

Thomsen, M., Lindsley, C. W., Conn, P. J., Wessell, J. W., Fulton, B. S., Wess, J., et al. (2011). Contribution of both M1 and M4 receptors to muscarinic agonist-mediated attenuation of the cocaine discriminative stimulus in mice. *Psychopharmacology, 220*(4), 673–685.

Thorndike, E. L. (1898). Animal intelligence: An experimental study of the association processes in animals. *Psychological Review Monograph, 2*(Whole No. 8).

Thorndike, E. L. (1911). *Animal intelligence: Experimental studies.* New York: Macmillan.

Thorndike, E. L. (1932). *The fundamentals of learning.* New York: Teachers College, Columbia University.

Timberlake, W. (1980). A molar equilibrium theory of learned performance. In G. H. Bower (Ed.), *The psychology of learning and motivation* (Vol. 14). New York: Academic Press.

Timberlake, W. (1983). Rats' responses to a moving object related to food or water: A behavior-systems analysis. *Animal Learning & Behavior, 11*, 309–320.

Timberlake, W. (1990). Natural learning in laboratory paradigms. In D. A. Dewsbury (Ed.), *Contemporary issues in comparative psychology* (pp. 31–54). Sunderland, MA: Sinauer.

Timberlake, W. (1995). Reconceptualizing reinforcement: A causal-system approach to reinforcement and behavior change. In W. O'Donohue & L. Krasnerr (Eds.), *Theories of behavior therapy* (pp. 59–96). Washington, DC: American Psychological Association.

Timberlake, W. (2001). Motivational modes in behavior systems. In R. R. Mowrer & S. B. Klein (Eds.), *Handbook of contemporary learning theories* (pp. 155–209). Mahwah, NJ: Erlbaum.

Timberlake, W., & Allison, J. (1974). Response deprivation: An empirical approach to instrumental performance. *Psychological Review, 81*, 146–164.

Timberlake, W., & Farmer Dougan, V. A. (1991). Reinforcement in applied settings: Figuring out ahead of time what will work. *Psychological Bulletin, 110*, 379–391.

Timberlake, W., & Grant, D. S. (1975). Auto-shaping in rats to the presentation of another rat predicting food. *Science, 190*, 690–692.

Timberlake, W., & Lucas, G. A. (1985). The basis of superstitious behavior: Chance contingency, stimulus substitution, or appetitive behavior? *Journal of the Experimental Analysis of Behavior, 44*, 279–299.

Timberlake, W., & Lucas, G. A. (1989). Behavior systems and learning: From misbehavior to general principles. In S. B. Klein & R. R. Mowrer (Eds.), *Contemporary learning theories: Instrumental conditioning and the impact of biological constraints on learning* (pp. 237–275). Hillsdale, NJ: Erlbaum.

Timberlake, W., & White, W. (1990). Winning isn't everything: Rats need only food deprivation and not food reward to efficiently traverse a radial arm maze. *Learning and Motivation, 21*, 153–163.

Timberlake, W., Leffel, J., & Hoffman, C. M. (1999). Stimulus control and function of arm and wall travel by rats on a radial arm floor maze. *Animal Learning & Behavior, 27*, 445–460.

Timberlake, W., Sinning, S. A., & Leffel, J. K. (2007). Beacon training in a water maze can facilitate and compete with subsequent room cue learning in rats. *Journal of Experimental Psychology: Animal Behavior Processes, 33*, 225–243.

Timberlake, W., Wahl, G., & King, D. (1982). Stimulus and response contingencies in the misbehavior of rats. *Journal of Experimental Psychology: Animal Behavior Processes, 8*, 62–85.

Tinbergen, N. (1951). *The study of instinct.* Oxford: Oxford University Press, Clarendon Press.

Tinbergen, N., & Perdeck, A. C. (1950). On the stimulus situation releasing the begging response in the newly hatched herring gull chick (*Larus argentatus argentatus Pont*). *Behaviour, 3*, 1–39.

Tindell, A. J., Smith, K. S., Pecina, S., Berridge, K. C., & Aldridge, J. W. (2006). Ventral pallidum firing codes hedonic reward: When a bad taste turns good. *Journal of Neurophysiology, 96*, 2399–2409.

Todes, D. P. (1997). From the machine to the ghost within: Pavlov's transition from digestive physiology to conditioned reflexes. *American Psychologist, 52*, 947–955.

Tomie, A., Grimes, K. L., & Pohorecky, L. A. (2008). Behavioral characteristics and neurobiological substrates shared by Pavlovian sign-tracking and drug abuse. *Brain Research Reviews, 58*, 121–135.

Trenholme, I. A., & Baron, A. (1975). Immediate and delayed punishment of human behavior by loss of reinforcement. *Learning and Motivation, 6*, 62–79.

Trosclair-Lasserre, N. M., Lerman, D. C., Call, N. A., Addison, L. R., & Kodak, T.

(2008). Reinforcement magnitude: An evaluation of preference and reinforcer efficacy. *Journal of Applied Behavior Analysis, 41*, 203–220.

Tsao, J. C. I., & Craske, M. G. (2000). Timing of treatment and return of fear: Effects of massed, uniform- and expanding-spaced exposure schedules. *Behavior Therapy, 31*, 479–497.

Tsien, J. Z. (2000). Building a brainier mouse. *Scientific American, 282*, 62–69.

Tulving, E. (1983). *Elements of Episodic Memory.* New York: Clarendon Press.

Turati, C., Bulf, H., & Simion, F. (2008). Newborns' face recognition over changes in viewpoint. *Cognition, 106*, 1300–1321.

Turkkan, J. S. (1989). Classical conditioning: The new hegemony. *The Behavioral and Brain Sciences, 12*, 121–179.

Twitmyer, E. B. (1974). A study of the knee jerk. *Journal of Experimental Psychology, 103*, 1047–1066.

Tzschentke, T. M. (2007). Measuring reward with the conditioned place preference (CPP) paradigm: Update of the last decade. *Addictive Biology, 12*, 227–262.

Underwood, B. J. (1957). Interference and forgetting. *Psychological Review, 64*, 49–60.

Üngör, M., & Lachnit, H. (2006). Contextual control in discrimination reversal learning. *Journal of Experimental Psychology: Animal Behavior Processes, 32*, 441–453.

Urcelay, G. P., & Miller, R. R. (2008). Retrieval from memory. In R. Menzel (Ed.), *Learning theory and behavior.* Vol 1 of J. Byrne (Ed.), *Learning and memory: A comprehensive reference* (pp. 53–74). Oxford: Elsevier.

Urcelay, G. P., & Miller, R. R. (2010). Two roles of the context in Pavlovian fear conditioning. *Journal of Experimental Psychology: Animal Behavior Processes, 36*, 268–280.

Urcelay, G. P., Wheeler, D. S., & Miller, R. R. (2009). Spacing extinction trials alleviates renewal and spontaneous recovery. *Learning & Behavior, 37*, 60–73.

Urcuioli, P. J. (2005). Behavioral and associative effects of differential outcomes in discrimination learning. *Learning & Behavior, 33*, 1–21.

Urcuioli, P. J. (2006). Responses and acquired equivalence classes. In E. A. Wasserman & T. R. Zentall (Eds.), *Comarative cognition* (pp. 405–421). New York: Oxford University Press.

Urcuioli, P. J. (2008). The nature of the response in Simon discriminations by pigeons. *Learning & Behavior, 36*, 200–209.

Urcuioli, P. J. (2013). Stimulus control and stimulus class formation. In G. J. Madden (Ed.), *APA Handbook of Behavior Analysis, Vol. 1: Methods and Principles* (pp. 361–386). Washington, DC: American Psychological Association.

Urcuioli, P. J., & Kasprow, W. J. (1988). Long-delay learning in the T-maze: Effects of marking and delay-interval location. *Learning and Motivation, 19*, 66–86.

Urcuioli, P. J., & Swisher, M. (2012). Emergent identity matching after successive matching training. II: Reflexivity or transitivity. *Journal of the Experimental Analysis of Behavior, 97*, 5–27.

Vaesen, K. (2012). The cognitive bases of human tool use. *Behavioral and Brain Sciences, 35*, 203–262.

Vaidyanathan, U., Patrick, C. J., & Cuthbert, B. N. (2009). Linking dimensional models of internalizing psychopathology to neurobiological systems: Affect-modulated startle as an indicator of fear and distress disorder and affiliated traits. *Psychological Bulletin, 135*, 909–942.

van der Kolk, B. A. (2006). Clinical implications of neuroscience research in PTSD. *Annals of the New York Academy of Sciences, 1071*, 277–293.

Vansteenwegen, D., Dirikx, T., Hermans, D., Vervliet, B., & Eelen, P. (2006). Renewal and reinstatement of fear: Evidence from human conditioning research. In M. G. Craske, D. Hermans, & D. Vansteenwegen (Eds.), *Fear and learning* (pp. 197–215). Washington, DC: American Psychological Association.

Vansteenwegen, D., Vervliet, B., Iberico, C., Baeyens, F., Van den Bergh, O., & Hermans, D. (2007). The repeated confrontation with videotapes of spiders in multiple contexts attenuates renewal of fear in spider-anxious students. *Behaviour Research and Therapy, 45*, 1169–1179.

Vaughan, W., Jr. (1981). Melioration, matching, and maximizing. *Journal of the Experimental Analysis of Behavior, 36*, 141–149.

Vicken, R. J., & McFall, R. M. (1994). Paradox lost: Implications of contemporary

reinforcement theory for behavior therapy. *Current Directions in Psychological Science, 4*, 121–125.

Visalberghi, E., & Fragaszy, D. (2012). What is challenging about tool use? The capuchin's perspective. In T. R. Zentall & E. A. Wasserman (Eds.), *The Oxford handbook of comparative cognition* (pp. 795–817). New York: Oxford University Press.

Vogel, E. H., Castro, M. E., & Saavedra, M. A. (2004). Quantitative models of Pavlovian conditioning. *Brain Research Bulletin, 63*, 173–202.

Volkert, V. M., Lerman, D. C., Call, N. A., & Trosclair-Lasserre, N. (2009). An evaluation of resurgence during treatment with functional communication training. *Journal of Applied Behavior Analysis, 42*, 145–160.

Vollmer, T. R., & Bourret, J. (2000). An application of the matching law to evaluate the allocation of two and three-point shots by college basketball players. *Journal of Applied Behavior Analysis, 33*, 137–150.

Vorndran, C. M., & Lerman, D. C. (2006). Establishing and maintaining treatment effects with less intrusive consequences via a pairing procedure. *Journal of Applied Behavior Analysis, 39*, 35–48.

Vuchinich, R. E., & Tucker, J. A. (2006). Behavioral economic concepts in the analysis of substance abuse. In F. Rotgers, J. Morgenstern, & S. T. Walters (Eds.), *Treating substance abuse: Theory and technique* (pp. 217–247). New York: Guilford Press.

Wade-Galuska, T., Perone, M., & Wirth, O. (2005). Effects of past and upcoming response-force requirements on fixed-ratio pausing. *Behavioural Processes, 68*, 91–95.

Waddell, J., Morris, R. W., & Bouton, M. E. (2006). Effects of bed nucleus of the *stria terminalis* lesions conditioned anxiety: Conditioning with long-duration conditional stimuli and reinstatement of extinguished fear. *Behavioral Neuroscience, 120*, 324–336.

Wagner, A. R. (1961). Effects of amount and percentage of reinforcement and number of acquisition trials on conditioning and extinction. *Journal of Experimental Psychology, 62*, 234–242.

Wagner, A. R. (1976). Priming in STM: An information processing mechanism for self-generated or retrieval generated depression in performance.

In T. J. Tighe & R. N. Leaton (Eds.), *Habituation: Perspectives from child development, animal behavior, and neurophysiology*. Hillsdale, NJ: Erlbaum.

Wagner, A. R. (1981). SOP: A model of automatic memory processing in animal behavior. In N. E. Spear & R. R. Miller (Eds.), *Information processing in animals: Memory mechanisms* (pp. 5–47). Hillsdale, NJ: Erlbaum.

Wagner, A. R. (2008b). Some observations and remembrances of Kenneth W. Spence. *Learning & Behavior, 36*, 169–173.

Wagner, A. R., & Brandon, S. E. (2001). A componential theory of Pavlovian conditioning. In R. R. Mowrer & S. B. Klein (Eds.), *Handbook of contemporary learning theories* (pp. 23–64). Mahwah, NJ: Erlbaum.

Wagner, A. R., Logan, F. A., Haberlandt, K., & Price, T. (1968). Stimulus selection in animal discrimination learning. *Journal of Experimental Psychology, 76*, 171–180.

Wagner, A. R., & Rescorla, R. A. (1972). Inhibition in Pavlovian conditioning: Application of a theory. In R. A. Boakes & M. S. Halliday (Eds.), *Inhibition and learning*. London: Academic Press.

Wagner, A. R., Rudy, J. W., & Whitlow, J. W. (1973). Rehearsal in animal conditioning. *Journal of Experimental Psychology, 97*, 407–426.

Walters, E. T. (1994). Injury related behavior and neuronal plasticity: An evolutionary perspective on sensitization, hyperalgesia, and analgesia. *International Review of Neurobiology, 36*, 325–427.

Wang, S. H., & Morris, R. G. (2010). Hippocampal-neocortical interactions in memory formation, consolidation, and reconsolidation. *Annual Review of Psychology, 61*, 49–79.

Ward, R. D., Kellendonk, C., Kandel, E. R., & Balsam, P. D. (2012). Timing as a window on cognition in schizophrenia. *Neuropharmacology, 62*, 1175–1181.

Ward, R. D., Simpson, E. H., Kandel, E. R., & Balsam, P. D. (2011). Modeling motivational deficits in mouse models of schizophrenia: Behavior analysis as a guide for neuroscience. *Behavioural Processes, 87*, 149–156.

Washburn, D. A. (Ed.). (2007). *Primate perspectives on behavior and cognition*. Washington, DC: American Psychological Association.

Wasserman, E. A. (1993). Comparative cognition: Beginning the second century of the study of animal intelligence. *Psychological Bulletin, 113*, 211–228.

Wasserman, E. A., & Castro, L. (2012). Categorical discrimination in humans and animals: All different and yet the same? *Psychology of Learning and Motivation, 56*, 145–184.

Watanabe, S., Sakamoto, J., & Wakita, M. (1995). Pigeons' discrimination of paintings by Monet and Picasso. *Journal of the Experimental Analysis of Behavior, 63*, 165–174.

Watson, J. B., & Rayner, R. (1920). Conditioned emotional reactions. *Journal of Experimental Psychology, 3*, 1–14. Reprinted in 2000 *American Psychologist, 55*, 313–317.

Wayman, G. A., Lee, Y.-S., Tokumitsu, H., Silva, A., & Soderling, T. R. (2008). Calmodulin-kinases: Modulators of neuronal development and plasticity. *Neuron, 59*, 914–931.

Wegner, D. M. (2002). *The illusion of conscious will*. Cambridge, Mass: MIT Press.

Weidemann, G., & Kehoe, E. J. (2003). Savings in classical conditioning in the rabbit as a function of extended extinction. *Learning & Behavior, 31*, 49–68.

Weinberger, N. (1965). Effect of detainment on extinction of avoidance responses. *Journal of Comparative and Physiological Psychology, 60*, 135–138.

Weir, A. A. S., & Kacelnik, A. (2006). A New Caledonian crow (Corvus moneduloides) creatively re-designs tools by bending or unbending aluminium strips. *Animal Cognition, 9*, 317–334.

Weisman, R. G., & Litner, J. S. (1972). The role of Pavlovian events in avoidance training. In R. A. Boakes & M. S. Halliday (Eds.), *Inhibition and learning*. London: Academic Press.

Weiss, S. J. (2012). Selective associations. In (Ed.), *Encyclopedia of the Sciences of Learning* (pp. 2983–2987). New York: Springer Science.

Weiss, S. J., Panlilio, L. V., & Schindler, C. W. (1993a). Selective associations produced solely with appetitive contingencies: The stimulus-reinforcer interaction revisited. *Journal of the Experimental Analysis of Behavior, 59*, 309–322.

Weiss, S. J., Panlilio, L. V., & Schindler, C. W. (1993b). Single incentive selective associations produced solely as a function of compound-stimulus conditioning context. *Journal of Experimental Psychology: Animal Behavior Processes, 19*, 284–294.

Wernig, A., Muller, S., Nanassy, A., & Cagol, E. (1995). Laufband therapy based on "rules of spinal locomotion" is effective in spinal cord injured persons. *European Journal of Neuroscience, 7*, 823–829.

Wheeler, D. S., Sherwood, A., & Holland, P. C. (2008). Excitatory and inhibitory learning with absent stimuli. *Journal of Experimental Psychology: Animal Behavior Processes, 34*, 247–255.

White, K. G. (2001). Forgetting functions. *Animal Learning & Behavior, 29*, 193–207.

White, K. G. (2013). Remembering and forgetting. In G. J. Madden (Ed.), *Handbook of Behavior Analysis, Vol. 1* (pp. 411–437). Washington, DC: American Psychological Association.

White, K. G., & Brown, G. S. (2011). Reversing the signaled magnitude effect in delayed matching to sample: Delay-specific remembering? *Journal of the Experimental Analysis of Behavior, 96*, 7–15.

White, K. G., Parkinson, A. E., Brown, G. S., & Wixted, J. T. (2004). Local proactive interference in delayed matching to sample: The role of reinforcement. *Journal of Experimental Psychology: Animal Behavior Processes, 30*, 83–95.

Wiers, R. W., & Stacy, A. W. (2006). Implicit cognition and addiction. *Current directions in psychological science, 15*, 292–296.

Wilkie, D. M., & Summers, R. J. (1982). Pigeons' spatial memory: Factors affecting delayed matching of key location. *Journal of the Experimental Analysis of Behavior, 37*, 45–56.

Wilkinson, A., Chan, H.-M., & Hall, G. (2007). Spatial learning and memory in the tortoise (Geochelone carbonaria). *Journal of Comparative Psychology, 121*, 412–418.

Williams, B. A. (1994). Reinforcement and choice. In N. J. Mackintosh (Ed.), *Animal learning and cognition* (pp. 81–108). San Diego: Academic Press.

Williams, B. A. (1991). Marking and bridging versus conditioned reinforcement. *Animal Learning & Behavior, 19*, 264–269.

Williams, B. A. (1999). Associative competition in operant conditioning: Blocking the response-reinforcer association.

Psychonomic Bulletin & Review, 6, 618–623.

Williams, B. A. (2001). The critical dimensions of the response-reinforcer contingency. *Behavioural Processes, 54,* 111–126.

Williams, D. A., & Hurlburt, J. L. (2000). Mechanisms of second order conditioning with a backward conditioned stimulus. *Journal of Experimental Psychology: Animal Behavior Processes, 26,* 340–351.

Williams, D. A., Johns, K. W., & Brindas, M. (2008). Timing during inhibitory conditioning. *Journal of Experimental Psychology: Animal Behavior Processes, 34,* 237–246.

Williams, D. A., Overmier, J. B., & LoLordo, V. M. (1992). A reevaluation of Rescorla's early dictums about Pavlovian conditioned inhibition. *Psychological Bulletin, 111,* 275–290.

Williams, D. C., Saunders, K. J., & Perone, M. (2011). Extended pausing by humans on multiple fixed-ratio schedules with varied reinforcer magnitude and response requirements. *Journal of the Experimental Analysis of Behavior, 95,* 203–220.

Willis, W. D. (2001). Mechanisms of central sensitization of nociceptive dorsal horn neurons. In M. M. Patterson & J. W. Grau (Eds.), *Spinal cord plasticity: Alterations in reflex function* (pp. 127–161). Boston: Kluwer Academic Publishers.

Winter, J., & Perkins, C. C. (1982). Immediate reinforcement in delayed reward learning in pigeons. *Journal of the Experimental Analysis of Behavior, 38,* 169–179.

Winterbauer, N. E., & Bouton, M. E. (2011). Mechanisms of resurgence II: Response-contingent reinforcers can reinstate a second extinguished behavior. *Learning and Motivation, 42,* 154–164.

Winterbauer, N. E., Lucke, S., & Bouton, M. E. (2013). Some factors modulating the strength of resurgence after extinction of an instrumental behavior. *Learning and Motivation, 44,* 60–71.

Wise, L. E., Iredale, P. A., Stokes, R. J., & Lichtman, A. H. (2007). Combination of rimonabant and donepezil prolongs spatial memory duration. *Neuropsychopharmacology, 32,* 1805–1812.

Wisniewski, M. G., Church, B. A., & Mercado III, E. (2009). Learning-related shifts in generalization gradients for complex sounds. *Learning & Behavior, 37,* 325–335.

Witcher, E. S., & Ayres, J. J. B. (1984). A test of two methods for extinguishing Pavlovian conditioned inhibition. *Animal Learning & Behavior, 12,* 149–156.

Witnauer, J. E., & Miller, R. R. (2011). Some determinants of second-order conditioning. *Learning & Behavior, 39,* 12–26.

Witnauer, J. E., & Miller, R. R. (2012). Associative status of the training context determines the effectiveness of compound extinction. *Journal of Experimental Psychology: Animal Behavior Processes, 38,* 52–65.

Wolpe, J. (1990). *The practice of behavior therapy* (4th ed.). New York: Pergamon.

Wood, W., & Neal, D. T. (2007). A new look at habits and the habit-goal interface. *Psychological Review, 114,* 843–863.

Woodruff-Pak, D. S., & Disterhoft, J. F. (2008). Where is the trace in trace conditioning? *Trends in Neuroscience, 31,* 105–112.

Woodruff Pak, D. S., Seta, S., Roker, L. A., & Lehr, M. A. (2007). Effects of age and inter-stimulus interval in delay and trace eyeblink classical conditioning in rabbits. *Learning & Memory, 14,* 287–294.

Woods, A. M., & Bouton, M. E. (2008). Immediate extinction causes a less durable loss of performance than delayed extinction following either fear or appetitive conditioning. *Learning and Memory, 15,* 909–920.

Woodson, J. C. (2002). Including "learned sexuality" in the organization of sexual behavior. *Neuroscience & Biobehavioral Reviews, 26,* 69–80.

Wright, A. A., & Delius, J. D. (1994). Scratch and match: Pigeons learn matching and oddity with gravel stimuli. *Journal of Experimental Psychology: Animal Behavior Processes, 20,* 108–112.

Wright, A. A., & Katz, J. S. (2006). Mechanisms of same/different concept learning in primates and avians. *Behavioural Processes, 72,* 234–254.

Wright, A. A., & Katz, J. S. (2007). Generalization hypothesis of abstract-concept learning: Learning strategies and related issues in *Macaca mulatta, Cebus apella,* and *Columba livia. Journal of Comparative Psychology, 121,* 387–397.

Wright, A. A., & Lickteig, M. T. (2010). What is learned when concept learning fails?– A theory of restricted-domain relational learning. *Learning and Motivation, 41,* 273–286.

Wright, A. A., Cook, R. G., Rivera, J. J., Sands, S. F., & Delius, J. D. (1988). Concept learning by pigeons: Matching to sample with trial-unique video picture stimuli. *Animal Learning & Behavior, 16,* 436–444.

Wright, A. A., Katz, J. S., & Ma, W. J. (2012). How to be proactive about interference: Lessons from animal memory. *Psychological Science, 23,* 453–458.

Xe, Y. Q., Steketee, J. D., & Sun, W. L. (2012). Inactivation of the central nucleus of the amygdala reduces the effect of punishment on cocaine self-administration in rats. *European Journal of Neuroscience, 35,* 775–783.

Yerkes, R. M., & Morgulis, S. (1909). The method of Pavlov in animal psychology. *Psychological Bulletin, 6,* 257–273.

Yi, R., Mitchell, S. H., & Bickel, W. K. (2010). Delay discounting and substance abuse-dependence. In G. J. Madden & W. K. (Eds.), *Impulsivity: The behavioral and neurological science of discounting* (pp. 191–211). Washington, DC: American Psychological Association.

Yin, H., Barnet, R. C., & Miller, R. R. (1994). Second-order conditioning and Pavlovian conditioned inhibition: Operational similarities and differences. *Journal of Experimental Psychology: Animal Behavior Processes, 20,* 419–428.

Zapata, A., Minney, V. L., & Shippenberg, T. S. (2010). Shift from goal-directed to habitual cocaine seeking after prolonged experience in rats. *Journal of Neuroscience, 30,* 15457–15463.

Zelikowsky, M., & Fanselow, M. S. (2011). Conditioned analgesia, negative feedback, and error correction. In T. R. Schachtman & S. Reilly (Eds.), *Associative learning and conditioning theory: Human and non-human applications* (pp. 305–320). New York: Oxford University Press.

Zentall, T. R. (2001). The case for a cognitive approach to animal learning and behavior. *Behavioural Processes, 54,* 65–78.

Zentall, T. R. (2005). Animals may not be stuck in time. *Learning and Motivation, 36,* 208–225.

Zentall, T. R. (2010). Coding of stimuli by animals: Retrospection, prospection, episodic memory and future planning. *Learning and Motivation, 41,* 225–240.

Zentall, T. R., & Smeets, P. M. (Eds.). (1996). *Stimulus class formation in humans and animals. Advances in Psychology* (Vol. 117). New York: North-Holland (Elsevier Science).

Zentall, T. R., & Wasserman, E. A. (Eds.). (2012). *Oxford handbook of comparative cognition.* New York: Oxford University Press.

Zentall, T. R., Singer, R. A., & Stagner, J. P. (2008). Episodic-like memory: Pigeons can report location pecked when unexpectedly asked. *Behavioural Processes, 79,* 93–98.

Zhou, Y., & Riccio, D. C. (1995). Concussion-induced retrograde amnesia in rats. *Physiology & Behavior, 57,* 1107–1115.

Zimmer-Hart, C. L., & Rescorla, R. A. (1974). Extinction of Pavlovian conditioned inhibition. *Journal of Comparative and Physiological Psychology, 86,* 837–845.

Zoladek, L., & Roberts, W. A. (1978). The sensory basis of spatial memory in the rat. *Animal Learning & Behavior, 6,* 77–81.

Zolotor, A. J., & Puzia, M. E. (2010). Bans against corporal punishment: A systematic review of the laws, changes in attitudes and behaviours. *Child Abuse Review, 19,* 229–247.

Name Index

Subject Index

The Limbic System

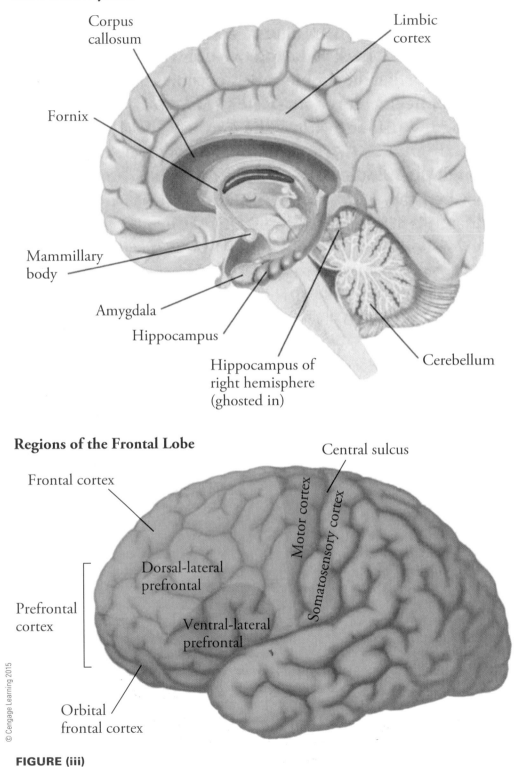

Corpus callosum

Fornix

Mammillary body

Amygdala

Hippocampus

Hippocampus of right hemisphere (ghosted in)

Limbic cortex

Cerebellum

Regions of the Frontal Lobe

Central sulcus

Frontal cortex

Dorsal-lateral prefrontal

Prefrontal cortex

Ventral-lateral prefrontal

Motor cortex

Somatosensory cortex

Orbital frontal cortex

© Cengage Learning 2015

FIGURE (iii)